PHYSICAL ANTHROPOLOGY
94/95

Third Edition

A Library of Information from the Public Press

Editor

Elvio Angeloni
Pasadena City College

Elvio Angeloni received his B.A. from UCLA in 1963, his
M.A. in anthropology from UCLA in 1965, and his M.A. in
communication arts from Loyola Marymount University in
1976. He has produced several films, including "Little
Warrior," winner of the Cinemedia VI Best Bicentennial
Theme, and "Broken Bottles," shown on PBS. He most
recently served as an academic advisor on the instructional
television series, "Faces of Culture."

Cover illustration by Mike Eagle

The Dushkin Publishing Group, Inc.
Sluice Dock, Guilford, Connecticut 06437

The Annual Editions Series

Annual Editions is a series of over 60 volumes designed to provide the reader with convenient, low-cost access to a wide range of current, carefully selected articles from some of the most important magazines, newspapers, and journals published today. Annual Editions are updated on an annual basis through a continuous monitoring of over 300 periodical sources. All Annual Editions have a number of features designed to make them particularly useful, including topic guides, annotated tables of contents, unit overviews, and indexes. For the teacher using Annual Editions in the classroom, an Instructor's Resource Guide with test questions is available for each volume.

VOLUMES AVAILABLE

Africa
Aging
American Foreign Policy
American Government
American History, Pre-Civil War
American History, Post-Civil War
Anthropology
Biology
Business Ethics
Canadian Politics
Child Growth and Development
China
Comparative Politics
Computers in Education
Computers in Business
Computers in Society
Criminal Justice
Drugs, Society, and Behavior
Dying, Death, and Bereavement
Early Childhood Education
Economics
Educating Exceptional Children
Education
Educational Psychology
Environment
Geography
Global Issues
Health
Human Development
Human Resources
Human Sexuality
India and South Asia
International Business
Japan and the Pacific Rim

Latin America
Life Management
Macroeconomics
Management
Marketing
Marriage and Family
Mass Media
Microeconomics
Middle East and the Islamic World
Money and Banking
Multicultural Education
Nutrition
Personal Growth and Behavior
Physical Anthropology
Psychology
Public Administration
Race and Ethnic Relations
Russia, Eurasia, and Central/Eastern
   Europe
Social Problems
Sociology
State and Local Government
Third World
Urban Society
Violence and Terrorism
Western Civilization,
   Pre-Reformation
Western Civilization,
   Post-Reformation
Western Europe
World History, Pre-Modern
World History, Modern
World Politics

Library of Congress Cataloging in Publication Data
Main entry under title: Annual editions: Physical anthropology. 1994/95.
   1. Physical anthropology—Periodicals. I. Angeloni, Elvio, *comp.* II. Title: Physical anthropology.
ISBN 1–56134–285–8   573'.05

Third Edition

Manufactured in the United States of America

Printed on Recycled Paper

Editors/ Advisory Board

To the Reader

In publishing ANNUAL EDITIONS we recognize the enormous role played by the magazines, newspapers, and journals of the *public press* in providing current, first-rate educational information in a broad spectrum of interest areas. Within the articles, the best scientists, practitioners, researchers, and commentators draw issues into new perspective as accepted theories and viewpoints are called into account by new events, recent discoveries change old facts, and fresh debate breaks out over important controversies.

Many of the articles resulting from this enormous editorial effort are appropriate for students, researchers, and professionals seeking accurate, current material to help bridge the gap between principles and theories and the real world. These articles, however, become more useful for study when those of lasting value are carefully *collected, organized, indexed,* and *reproduced* in a *low-cost format,* which provides easy and permanent access when the material is needed. That is the role played by *Annual Editions.* Under the direction of each volume's *Editor,* who is an expert in the subject area, and with the guidance of an *Advisory Board,* we seek each year to provide in each ANNUAL EDITION a current, well-balanced, carefully selected collection of the best of the public press for your study and enjoyment. We think you'll find this volume useful, and we hope you'll take a moment to let us know what you think.

This third edition of *Annual Editions: Physical Anthropology 94/95* contains a variety of articles relating to human evolution. The articles were selected for their timeliness, relevance to issues not easily treated in the standard physical anthropology textbook, and clarity of presentation.

Whereas textbooks tend to reflect the consensus within the field, *Annual Editions: Physical Anthropology 94/95* provides a forum for the controversial. We do this in order to convey to the student the sense that the study of human development is in itself an evolving entity in which each discovery encourages further research, and each added piece of the puzzle raises new questions about the total picture.

Our final criterion for selecting articles has to do with their readability. All too often, the excitement of a new discovery or a fresh idea is deadened by the weight of a ponderous presentation. We seek to avoid that by incorporating essays written with enthusiasm and with the desire to communicate some very special ideas to the general public.

Included in this volume are a number of features designed to be useful for students, researchers, and professionals in the field of anthropology. While the articles are arranged along the lines of broadly unifying subject areas, the *topic guide* can be used to establish specific reading assignments tailored to the needs of a particular course of study. Other useful features include the *table of contents abstracts,* which summarize each article and present key concepts in bold italics, and a comprehensive *index.* In addition, each unit is preceded by an overview that provides a background for informed reading of the articles, emphasizes critical issues, and presents *challenge questions.*

In contrast to the usual textbook, which by its nature cannot be easily revised, this book will be continually updated in order to reflect the dynamic, changing character of its subject. Those involved in producing *Annual Editions: Physical Anthropology 94/95* wish to make the next one as useful and effective as possible. Your criticism and advice are welcomed. Please fill out the article rating form on the last page of the book and let us know your opinions. Any anthology can be improved, and this will continue to be.

Elvio Angeloni
Editor

Contents

Unit
1

Natural Selection

Six articles examine the link between genetics and the process of natural selection.

(3.) 95/2

Set 7/2/94

(1.) 95/2   Set 1/94

94/3 MD

94/3 MD

The concepts in bold italics are developed in the article. For further expansion please refer to the Topic Guide and the Index.

Unit 2

Primates

Seven selections examine some of the social relationships in the primate world and how they mirror human society.

The concepts in bold italics are developed in the article. For further expansion please refer to the Topic Guide and the Index.

Unit 3

Sex and Society

Four articles discuss the relationship between the sexes and the evolution of a social structure.

Unit 4

The Hominid Transition

Five articles examine the enigma of human evolution from the ape. A definitive link between apes and humans has yet to be made.

The concepts in bold italics are developed in the article. For further expansion please refer to the Topic Guide and the Index.

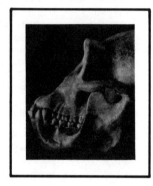

Unit 5

The Fossil Evidence

Five selections discuss the fossil evidence for hominid
evolution.

The concepts in bold italics are developed in the article. For further expansion please refer to the Topic Guide and the Index.

Unit 6

Late Hominid Evolution

Seven articles examine human evolution and some of the newest fossil discoveries that add further clues to humanity's development.

The concepts in bold italics are developed in the article. For further expansion please refer to the Topic Guide and the Index.

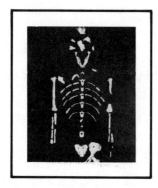

Unit 7

Living With the Past

Nine articles discuss evolutional theory and how our genetic heritage impacts on our present and future.

The concepts in bold italics are developed in the article. For further expansion please refer to the Topic Guide and the Index.

2.) 95/2

94/3
MD
Sek
1/94

NB! →

"Is there danger in being too smart?" (p. 235-8)
previous
edn (93/94)

94/3
FINAL

Topic Guide

This topic guide suggests how the selections in this book relate to topics of traditional concern to students and professionals involved with the study of physical anthropology. It is useful for locating articles that relate to each other for reading and research. The guide is arranged alphabetically according to topic. Articles may, of course, treat topics that do not appear in the topic guide. In turn, entries in the topic guide do not necessarily constitute a comprehensive listing of all the contents of each selection.

TOPIC AREA	TREATED IN:	TOPIC AREA	TREATED IN:
Aggression	7. Machiavellian Monkeys 8. What Are Friends For? 9. Leading Ladies 10. Young and the Reckless 11. "Science With a Capital S" 14. These Are Real Swinging Primates 16. "Everything *Else* You Always Wanted to Know About Sex . . ." 18. Dim Forest, Bright Chimps 29. Hard Times Among the Neanderthals 39. Farmers and Baboons in the Taita Hills	**Disease**	2. Pox Upon Our Genes 3. Curse and Blessing of the Ghetto 4. Arrow of Disease 5. Future of AIDS 6. Racial Odyssey 35. Value of Collections of Human Skeletons 38. Old Dog, Old Tricks 41. Reasonable Sleep 42. Saltshaker's Curse 43. What Good Is Feeling Bad?
Anatomy	15. Evolution of the Big O 17. What's Love Got to Do With It? 19. Flesh and Bone 21. Human Ancestors Walked Tall, Stayed Cool 24. Skull to Chew On 29. Hard Times Among the Neanderthals 35. Value of Collections of Human Skeletons 36. No Bone Unturned	**DNA (Deoxyribonucleic Acid)**	3. Curse and Blessing of the Ghetto 5. Future of AIDS 32. Search for Eve 33. Multiregional Model 37. DNA Wars
Archeology	28. Bamboo and Human Evolution 30. Old Masters 31. Dawn of Adornment 35. Value of Collections of Human Skeletons 36. No Bone Unturned	**Dominance Hierarchy**	8. What Are Friends For? 9. Leading Ladies 10. Young and the Reckless 14. These Are Real Swinging Primates 17. What's Love Got to Do With It?
Australopithecines	19. Flesh and Bone 23. Dawson's Dawn Man: The Hoax of Piltdown 24. Skull to Chew On 25. Pulse That Produced Us 26. Sizing Up Human Intelligence	**Fire**	28. Bamboo and Human Evolution
		Flourine Testing	23. Dawson's Dawn Man: The Hoax of Piltdown
Biorhythms	38. Old Dog, Old Tricks	**Forensic Anthropology**	35. Value of Collections of Human Skeletons 36. No Bone Unturned 37. DNA Wars
Biostratigraphy	25. Pulse That Produced Us 28. Bamboo and Human Evolution	**Genes**	2. Pox Upon Our Genes 3. Curse and Blessing of the Ghetto 5. Future of AIDS 37. DNA Wars 42. Saltshaker's Curse
Bipedalism	17. What's Love Got to Do With It? 19. Flesh and Bone 21. Human Ancestors Walked Tall, Stayed Cool 27. Scavenger Hunt	**Genetic Drift**	1. Growth of Evolutionary Science 3. Curse and Blessing of the Ghetto
Blood Groups	6. Racial Odyssey 37. DNA Wars	**Genetic Testing**	3. Curse and Blessing of the Ghetto 37. DNA Wars
Brain Size	25. Pulse That Produced Us 26. Sizing Up Human Intelligence	**Homo Erectus**	23. Dawson's Dawn Man: The Hoax of Piltdown 26. Sizing Up Human Intelligence 28. Bamboo and Human Evolution 32. Search for Eve 33. Multiregional Model
Catastrophism	1. Growth of Evolutionary Science		
Chain of Being	1. Growth of Evolutionary Science	**Homo Habilis**	25. Pulse That Produced Us 26. Sizing Up Human Intelligence
Creationism	1. Growth of Evolutionary Science	**Homo Sapiens**	26. Sizing Up Human Intelligence 32. Search for Eve 33. Multiregional Model
Cro-Magnons	23. Dawson's Dawn Man: The Hoax of Piltdown 30. Old Masters 31. Dawn of Adornment		

Natural Selection

As the twentieth century draws to a close and we reflect upon where science has taken us over the past 100 years, it should come as no surprise that the field of genetics has swept us along a path of profound insight into the human condition as well as heightened controversy as to how to handle this potentially dangerous knowledge of ourselves.

Certainly, Gregor Mendel in the late nineteenth century could not have anticipated that his study of pea plants would ultimately lead to the better understanding of over 3,000 genetically caused diseases, such as sickle-cell anemia, Huntington's chorea, and Tay-Sachs. Nor could he have foreseen the present-day controversies over such matters as surrogate motherhood, cloning, and genetic engineering.

The significance of Mendel's work, of course, was his discovery that hereditary traits are conferred by particular units that we now call "genes," a then-revolutionary notion that has been followed by a better understanding of how and why such units change. It is the knowledge of the process of "mutation," or the alteration of the chemical structure of the gene, which is now providing us with the potential to control the genetic fate of individuals.

The other side of the evolutionary coin, as discussed in "The Growth of Evolutionary Science," is natural selection, a concept provided by Charles Darwin and Alfred Wallace. This refers to the "weeding out" of unfavorable mutations and the perpetuation of favorable ones. Although the pace and manner in which such forces become evident in the fossil record has been the subject of a great deal of recent hypothesizing, they nevertheless do account for the peculiarly human characteristics described by Boyce Rensberger in "Racial Odyssey."

It seems that as we gain a better understanding of both

of these processes, mutation and natural selection, we draw nearer to that time when we may even control the evolutionary direction of our species. Knowledge itself, of course, is neutral—its potential for good or ill being determined by those who happen to be in the position to use it. Consider the possibility of eliminating some of the harmful hereditary traits discussed in "Curse and Blessing of the Ghetto," by Jared Diamond. While it is true that many deleterious genes do get weeded out of the population by means of natural selection, there are other harmful ones, Diamond points out, that may actually have a good side to them and will therefore be perpetuated. It may be, for example, that some men are dying from a genetically caused overabundance of iron in their blood systems in a trade-off that allows some women to absorb sufficient amounts of the element to guarantee their own survival. The question of whether or not we should eliminate such a gene would seem to depend upon which sex we decide should reap the benefit.

The issue of just what is a beneficial application of scientific knowledge is a matter for debate. Who will have the final word as to how these technological breakthroughs will be employed in the future? Even with the best of intentions, how can we be certain of the long-range consequences of our actions in such a complicated field? Note, for example, the sweeping effects of ecological change upon the viruses of the world, which in turn seem to be paving the way for new waves of human epidemics. Generally speaking, there is an element of purpose and design in our machinations. Yet, even with this clearly in mind, the whole process seems to be escalating out of human control. As Jared Diamond ("The Arrow of Disease") and Geoffrey Cowley ("The Future of

AIDS") point out, it seems that the whole world has become an experimental laboratory in which we know not what we do until we have already done it.

As we read the articles in this section and contemplate the significance of genetic diseases for human evolution, we can hope that a better understanding of congenital diseases will lead to a reduction of human suffering. At the same time, we must remain aware that, rather than reduce the misery that exists in the world, someone, at some time, may actually use the same knowledge to increase it.

Looking Ahead: Challenge Questions

In nature, how is it that design can occur without a designer, orderliness without a purpose?

Why is it difficult to study natural selection in humans?

Why are epidemic diseases more common today than in our hunting and gathering past?

How and why might the ABO blood group be related to epidemic diseases?

Should people be told they are going to die of a disease from which they are presently suffering and for which there is no cure?

How is it possible to test for deleterious genes?

Why is Tay-Sachs disease so common among Eastern European Jews?

How do ecological changes cause new viruses to emerge?

Why was post-Columbian disease transmission between Europe and the Americas so unidirectional?

What do you predict for the future of the AIDS epidemic?

Can the human species be subdivided into racial categories?

Charles R. Darwin.

The Growth
of
Evolutionary Science

Douglas J. Futuyma

Today, the theory of evolution is an accepted fact for everyone but a fundamentalist minority, whose objections are based not on reasoning but on doctrinaire adherence to religious principles.

—James D. Watson, 1965*

In 1615, Galileo was summoned before the Inquisition in Rome. The guardians of the faith had found that his "proposition that the sun is the center [of the solar system] and does not revolve about the earth is foolish, absurd, false in theology, and heretical, because expressly contrary to Holy Scripture." In the next century, John

Wesley declared that "before the sin of Adam there were no agitations within the bowels of the earth, no violent convulsions, no concussions of the earth, no earthquakes, but all was unmoved as the pillars of heaven." Until the seventeenth century, fossils were interpreted as "stones of a peculiar sort, hidden by the Author of Nature for his own pleasure." Later they were seen as remnants of the Biblical deluge. In the middle of the eighteenth century, the great French naturalist Buffon speculated on the possibility of cosmic and organic evolution and was forced by the clergy to recant: "I abandon everything in my book respecting the formation of the earth, and generally all of which may be contrary to the narrative of Moses." For had not St. Augustine written, "Nothing is to be accepted save on the authority of Scrip-

ture, since greater is that authority than all the powers of the human mind"?

When Darwin published *The Origin of Species,* it was predictably met by a chorus of theological protest. Darwin's theory, said Bishop Wilberforce, "contradicts the revealed relations of creation to its Creator." "If the Darwinian theory is true," wrote another clergyman, "Genesis is a lie, the whole framework of the book of life falls to pieces, and the revelation of God to man, as we Christians know it, is a delusion and a snare." When *The Descent of Man* appeared, Pope Pius IX was moved to write that Darwinism is "a system which is so repugnant at once to history, to the tradition of all peoples, to exact science, to observed facts, and even to Reason herself, [that it] would seem to need no refutation, did not alienation from God and the

*James D. Watson, a molecular biologist, shared the Nobel Prize for his work in discovering the structure of DNA.

leaning toward materialism, due to depravity, eagerly seek a support in all this tissue of fables."[1] Twentieth-century creationism continues this battle of medieval theology against science.

One of the most pervasive concepts in medieval and post-medieval thought was the "great chain of being," or *scala naturae*.[2] Minerals, plants, and animals, according to his concept, formed a gradation, from the lowliest and most material to the most complex and spiritual, ending in man, who links the animal series to the world of intelligence and spirit. This "scale of nature" was the manifestation of God's infinite benevolence. In his goodness, he had conferred existence on all beings of which he could conceive, and so created a complete chain of being, in which there were no gaps. All his creatures must have been created at once, and none could ever cease to exist, for then the perfection of his divine plan would have been violated. Alexander Pope expressed the concept best:

Vast chain of being! which from God began,
Natures aethereal, human, angel, man,
Beast, bird, fish, insect, what no eye can see,
No glass can reach; from Infinite to thee,
From thee to nothing.—On superior pow'rs
Were we to press, inferior might on ours;
Or in the full creation leave a void,
Where, one step broken, the great scale's destroy'd;
From Nature's chain whatever link you strike,
Tenth, or ten thousandth, breaks the chain alike.

Coexisting with this notion that all of which God could conceive existed so as to complete his creation was the idea that all things existed for man. As the philosopher Francis Bacon put it, "Man, if we look to final causes, may be regarded as the centre of the world . . . for the whole world works together in the service of man . . . all things seem to be going about man's business and not their own."

"Final causes" was another fundamental concept of medieval and post-medieval thought. Aristotle had distinguished final causes from efficient causes, and the Western world saw no reason to doubt the reality of both. The "efficient cause" of an event is the mechanism responsible for its occurrence: the cause of a ball's movement on a pool table, for example, is the impact of the cue or another ball. The "final cause," however, is the goal, or purpose for its occurrence: the pool ball moves because I wish it to go into the corner pocket. In post-medieval thought there was a final cause—a purpose—for everything; but purpose implies intention, or foreknowledge, by an intellect. Thus the existence of the world, and of all the creatures in it, had a purpose; and that purpose was God's design. This was self-evident, since it was possible to look about the world and see the palpable evidence of God's design everywhere. The heavenly bodies moved in harmonious orbits, evincing the intelligence and harmony of the divine mind; the adaptations of animals and plants to their habitats likewise reflected the divine intelligence, which had fitted all creatures perfectly for their roles in the harmonious economy of nature.

Before the rise of science, then, the causes of events were sought not in natural mechanisms but in the purposes they were meant to serve, and order in nature was evidence of divine intelligence. Since St. Ambrose had declared that "Moses opened his mouth and poured forth what God had said to him," the Bible was seen as the literal word of God, and according to St. Thomas Aquinas, "Nothing was made by God, after the six days of creation, absolutely new." Taking Genesis literally, Archbishop Ussher was able to calculate that the earth was created in 4004 B.C. The earth and the heavens were immutable, changeless. As John Ray put it in 1701 in *The Wisdom of God Manifested in the Works of the Creation,* all living and nonliving things were "created by God at first, and by Him conserved to this Day in the same State and Condition in which they were first made."[3]

The evolutionary challenge to this view began in astronomy. Tycho Brahe found that the heavens were not immutable when a new star appeared in the constellation Cassiopeia in 1572. Copernicus displaced the earth from the center of the universe, and Galileo found that the perfect heavenly bodies weren't so perfect: the sun had spots that changed from time to time, and the moon had craters that strongly implied alterations of its surface. Galileo, and after him Buffon, Kant, and many others, concluded that change was natural to all things.

A flood of mechanistic thinking ensued. Descartes, Kant, and Buffon concluded that the causes of natural phenomena should be sought in natural laws. By 1755, Kant was arguing that the laws of matter in motion discovered by Newton and other physicists were sufficient to explain natural order. Gravitation, for example, could aggregate chaotically dispersed matter into stars and planets. These would join with one another until the only ones left were those that cycled in orbits far enough from each other to resist gravitational collapse. Thus order might arise from natural processes rather than from the direct intervention of a supernatural mind. The "argument from design"—the claim that natural order is evidence of a designer—had been directly challenged. So had the universal belief in final causes. If the arrangement of the planets could arise merely by the laws of Newtonian physics, if the planets could be born, as Buffon suggested, by a collision between a comet and the sun, then they did not exist for any purpose. They merely came into being through impersonal physical forces.

From the mutability of the heavens, it was a short step to the mutability of the earth, for which the evidence was far more direct. Earthquakes and volcanoes showed how unstable terra firma really is. Sedimentary rocks showed that materials eroded from mountains could be compacted over the ages. Fossils of marine shells on mountaintops proved that the land must once have been under the sea. As early as 1718, the Abbé Moro and the French academician Bernard de Fontenelle had concluded that the Biblical deluge could not explain the fossilized oyster beds and tropical plants that were found in France. And what of the great, unbroken chain of being if the rocks were full of extinct species?

To explain the facts of geology, some authors—the "catastrophists"—supposed that the earth had gone through a series of great floods and other catastrophes that successively extinguished different groups of animals. Only this, they felt, could account for the discovery that higher and lower geological strata had different fossils. Buffon, however, held that to explain nature we should look to the natural causes we see operating around us: the gradual action of erosion and the slow buildup of land during volcanic eruptions. Buffon thus proposed what came to be the foundation of geology, and indeed of all science, the principle of uniformitarianism, which holds that the same causes that operate now have always operated. By 1795, the Scottish geologist James Hutton had suggested that "in examining things present we have data from which to reason with regard to what has been." His conclusion was that since "rest exists not anywhere," and the forces that change the face of the earth move with ponderous slowness, the mountains and canyons of the world must have come into existence over countless aeons.

If the entire nonliving world was in constant turmoil, could it not be that living things themselves changed? Buffon came close to saying so. He realized that the earth had seen the extinction of countless species, and supposed that those that perished had been the weaker ones. He recognized that domestication and the forces of the environment could modify the variability of many species. And he even mused, in 1766, that species might have developed from common ancestors:

If it were admitted that the ass is of the family of the horse, and different from the horse only because it has varied from the original form, one could equally well say that the ape is of the family of man, that he is a degenerate man, that man and ape have a common origin; that, in fact, all the families among plants as well as animals have come from a single stock, and that all animals are descended from a single animal, from which have sprung in the course of time, as a result of process

or of degeneration, all the other races of animals. For if it were once shown that we are justified in establishing these families; if it were granted among animals and plants there has been (I do not say several species) but even a single one, which has been produced in the course of direct descent from another species . . . then there would no longer be any limit to the power of nature, and we should not be wrong in supposing that, with sufficient time, she has been able from a single being to derive all the other organized beings.[4]

This, however, was too heretical a thought; and in any case, Buffon thought the weight of evidence was against common descent. No new species had been observed to arise within recorded history, Buffon wrote; the sterility of hybrids between species appeared an impossible barrier to such a conclusion; and if species had emerged gradually, there should have been innumerable intermediate variations between the horse and ass, or any other species. So Buffon concluded: "But this [idea of a common ancestor] is by no means a proper representation of nature. We are assured by the authority of revelation that all animals have participated equally in the grace of direct Creation and that the first pair of every species issued fully formed from the hands of the Creator."

Buffon's friend and protégé, Jean Baptiste de Monet, the Chevalier de Lamarck, was the first scientist to take the big step. It is not clear what led Lamarck to his uncompromising belief in evolution; perhaps it was his studies of fossil molluscs, which he came to believe were the ancestors of similar species living today. Whatever the explanation, from 1800 on he developed the notion that fossils were not evidence of extinct species but of ones that had gradually been transformed into living species. To be sure, he wrote, "an enormous time and wide variation in successive conditions must doubtless have been required to enable nature to bring the organization of animals to that degree of complexity and development in which we see it at its perfection"; but "time has no limits and can be drawn upon to any extent."

Lamarck believed that various lineages of animals and plants arose by a

continual process of spontaneous generation from inanimate matter, and were transformed from very simple to more complex forms by an innate natural tendency toward complexity caused by "powers conferred by the supreme author of all things." Various specialized adaptations of species are consequences of the fact that animals must always change in response to the needs imposed on them by a continually changing environment. When the needs of a species change, so does its behavior. The animal then uses certain organs more frequently than before, and these organs, in turn, become more highly developed by such use, or else "by virtue of the operations of their own inner senses." The classic example of Lamarckism is the giraffe: by straining upward for foliage, it was thought, the animal had acquired a longer neck, which was then inherited by its offspring.

In the nineteenth century it was widely believed that "acquired" characteristics—alterations brought about by use or disuse, or by the direct influence of the environment—could be inherited. Thus it was perfectly reasonable for Lamarck to base his theory of evolutionary change partly on this idea. Indeed, Darwin also allowed for this possibility, and the inheritance of acquired characteristics was not finally prove impossible until the 1890s.

Lamarck's ideas had a wide influence; but in the end did not convince many scientists of the reality of evolution. In France, Georges Cuvier, the foremost paleontologist and anatomist of his time, was an influential opponent of evolution. He rejected Lamarck's notion of the spontaneous generation of life, found it inconceivable that changes in behavior could produce the exquisite adaptations that almost every species shows, and emphasized that in both the fossil record and among living animals there were numerous "gaps" rather than intermediate forms between species. In England, the philosophy of "natural theology" held sway in science, and the best-known naturalists continued to believe firmly that the features of animals and plants were evidence of God's design. These devout Christians included the foremost geologist of the day, Charles Lyell, whose *Principles of Geology* established uniformitarianism once and for all as a guiding principle. But Lyell was such a thorough uniformitarian that he believed in a steady-state world, a world that was always in balance between forces such as erosion and mountain building, and so was forever the same. There was no room for evolution, with its concept of steady change, in Lyell's world view, though he nonetheless had an enormous impact on evolutionary thought, through his influence on Charles Darwin.

Darwin (1809–1882) himself, unquestionably one of the greatest scientists of all time, came only slowly to an evolutionary position. The son of a successful physician, he showed little interest in the life of the mind in his early years. After unsuccessfully studying medicine at Edinburgh, he was sent to Cambridge to prepare for the ministry, but he had only a half-hearted interest in his studies and spent most of his time hunting, collecting beetles, and becoming an accomplished amateur naturalist. Though he received his B.A. in 1831, his future was quite uncertain until, in December of that year, he was enlisted as a naturalist aboard *H.M.S. Beagle,* with his father's very reluctant agreement. For five years (from December 27, 1831, to October 2, 1836) the *Beagle* carried him about the world, chiefly along the coast of South America, which it was the *Beagle*'s mission to survey. For five years Darwin collected geological and biological specimens, made geological observations, absorbed Lyell's *Principles of Geology,* took voluminous notes, and speculated about everything from geology to anthropology. He sent such massive collections of specimens back to England that by the time he returned he had already gained a substantial reputation as a naturalist.

Shortly after his return, Darwin married and settled into an estate at Down where he remained, hardly traveling even to London, for the rest of his life. Despite continual ill health, he

pursued an extraordinary range of biological studies: classifying barnacles, breeding pigeons, experimenting with plant growth, and much more. He wrote no fewer than sixteen books and many papers, read voraciously, corresponded extensively with everyone, from pigeon breeders to the most eminent scientists, whose ideas or information might bear on his theories, and kept detailed notes on an amazing variety of subjects. Few people have written authoritatively on so many different topics: his books include not only *The Voyage of the Beagle, The Origin of Species,* and *The Descent of Man,* but also *The Structure and Distribution of Coral Reefs* (containing a novel theory of the formation of coral atolls which is still regarded as correct), *A Monograph on the Sub-class Cirripedia* (the definitive study of barnacle classification), *The Various Contrivances by Which Orchids are Fertilised by Insects, The Variation of Animals and Plants Under Domestication* (an exhaustive summary of information on variation, so crucial to his evolutionary theory), *The Effects of Cross and Self Fertilisation in the Vegetable Kingdom* (an analysis of sexual reproduction and the sterility of hybrids between species), *The Expression of the Emotions in Man and Animals* (on the evolution of human behavior from animal behavior), and *The Formation of Vegetable Mould Through the Action of Worms.* There is every reason to believe that almost all these books bear, in one way or another, on the principles and ideas that were inherent in Darwin's theory of evolution. The worm book, for example, is devoted to showing how great the impact of a seemingly trivial process like worm burrowing may be on ecology and geology if it persists for a long time. The idea of such cumulative slight effects is, of course, inherent in Darwin's view of evolution: successive slight modifications of a species, if continued long enough, can transform it radically.

When Darwin embarked on his voyage, he was a devout Christian who did not doubt the literal truth of the Bible, and did not believe in evolution any

more than did Lyell and the other English scientists he had met or whose books he had read. By the time he returned to England in 1836 he had made numerous observations that would later convince him of evolution. It seems likely, however, that the idea itself did not occur to him until the spring of 1837, when the ornithologist John Gould, who was working on some of Darwin's collections, pointed out to him that each of the Galápagos Islands, off the coast of Ecuador, had a different kind of mockingbird. It was quite unclear whether they were different varieties of the same species, or different species. From this, Darwin quickly realized that species are not the discrete, clear-cut entities everyone seemed to imagine. The possibility of transformation entered his mind, and it applied to more than the mockingbirds: "When comparing . . . the birds from the separate islands of the Galápagos archipelago, both with one another and with those from the American mainland, I was much struck how entirely vague and arbitrary is the distinction between species and varieties."

In July 1837 he began his first notebook on the "Transmutation of Species." He later said that the Galápagos species and the similarity between South American fossils and living species were at the origin of all his views.

During the voyage of the *Beagle* I had been deeply impressed by discovering in the Pampean formation great fossil animals covered with armour like that on the existing armadillos; secondly, by the manner in which closely allied animals replace one another in proceeding southward over the continent; and thirdly, by the South American character of most of the productions of the Galápagos archipelago, and more especially by the manner in which they differ slightly on each island of the group; none of these islands appearing to be very ancient in a geological sense. It was evident that such facts as these, as well as many others, could be explained on the supposition that species gradually become modified; and the subject has haunted me.

The first great step in Darwin's thought was the realization that evolution had occurred. The second was his brilliant insight into the possible cause of evolutionary change. Lamarck's

1. NATURAL SELECTION

Figure 1. *Some species of Galápagos finches. Several of the most different species are represented here; intermediate species also exist. Clockwise from lower left are a male ground-finch (the plumage of the female resembles that of the tree-finches); the vegetarian tree-finch; the insectivorous tree-finch; the warbler-finch; and the woodpecker-finch, which uses a cactus spine to extricate insects from crevices. The slight differences among these species, and among species in other groups of Galápagos animals such as giant tortoises, were one of the observations that led Darwin to formulate his hypothesis of evolution. (From D. Lack, Darwin's Finches [Oxford: Oxford University Press, 1944].)*

characteristics, the struggle to survive must favor some variant individuals over others. These survivors would then pass on their characteristics to future generations. Repetition of this process generation after generation would gradually transform the species.

Darwin clearly knew that he could not afford to publish a rash speculation on so important a subject without developing the best possible case. The world of science was not hospitable to speculation, and besides, Darwin was dealing with a highly volatile issue. Not only was he affirming that evolution had occurred, he was proposing a purely material explanation for it, one that demolished the argument from design in a single thrust. Instead of publishing his theory, he patiently amassed a mountain of evidence, and finally, in 1844, collected his thoughts in an essay on natural selection. But he still didn't publish. Not until 1856, almost twenty years after he became an evolutionist, did he begin what he planned to be a massive work on the subject, tentatively titled *Natural Selection.*

Then, in June 1858, the unthinkable happened. Alfred Russel Wallace (1823–1913), a young naturalist who had traveled in the Amazon Basin and in the Malay Archipelago, had also become interested in evolution. Like Darwin, he was struck by the fact that "the most closely allied species are found in the same locality or in closely adjoining localities and . . . therefore the natural sequence of the species by affinity is also geographical." In the throes of a malarial fever in Malaya, Wallace conceived of the same idea of natural selection as Darwin had, and sent Darwin a manuscript "On the Tendency of Varieties to Depart Indefinitely from the Original Type." Darwin's friends Charles Lyell and Joseph Hooker, a botanist, rushed in to help Darwin establish the priority of his ideas, and on July 1, 1858, they presented to the Linnean Society of London both Wallace's paper and extracts from Darwin's 1844 essay. Darwin abandoned his big book on natural selection and condensed the argument into a 490-page "abstract" that was published on November 24, 1859, under the title

theory of "felt needs" had not been convincing. A better one was required. It came on September 18, 1838, when after grappling with the problem for fifteen months, "I happened to read for amusement Malthus on Population, and being well prepared to appreciate the struggle for existence which everywhere goes on from long-continued observation of the habits of animals and plants, it at once struck me that under these circumstances favorable variations would tend to be preserved, and unfavorable ones to be destroyed. The result of this would be the forma-

tion of new species. Here, then, I had at last got a theory by which to work."

Malthus, an economist, had developed the pessimistic thesis that the exponential growth of human populations must inevitably lead to famine, unless it were checked by war, disease, or "moral restraint." This emphasis on exponential population growth was apparently the catalyst for Darwin, who then realized that since most natural populations of animals and plants remain fairly stable in numbers, many more individuals are born than survive. Because individuals vary in their

The Origin of Species by Means of Natural Selection; or, the Preservation of Favored Races in the Struggle for Life. Because it was an abstract, he had to leave out many of the detailed observations and references to the literature that he had amassed, but these were later provided in his other books, many of which are voluminous expansions on the contents of *The Origin of Species.*

The first five chapters of the *Origin* lay out the theory that Darwin had conceived. He shows that both domesticated and wild species are variable, that much of that variation is hereditary, and that breeders, by conscious selection of desirable varieties, can develop breeds of pigeons, dogs, and other forms that are more different from each other than species or even families of wild animals and plants are from each other. The differences between related species then are no more than an exaggerated form of the kinds of variations one can find in a single species; indeed, it is often extremely difficult to tell if natural populations are distinct species or merely well-marked varieties.

Darwin then shows that in nature there is competition, predation, and a struggle for life.

Owing to this struggle, variations, however slight and from whatever cause proceeding, if they be in any degree profitable to the individuals of a species, in their infinitely complex relations to other organic beings and to their physical conditions of life, will tend to the preservation of such individuals, and will generally be inherited by the offspring. The offspring, also, will thus have a better chance of surviving, for, of the many individuals of any species which are periodically born, but a small number can survive. I have called this principle, by which each slight variation, if useful, is preserved, by the term natural selection, in order to mark its relation to man's power of selection.

Darwin goes on to give examples of how even slight variations promote survival, and argues that when populations are exposed to different conditions, different variations will be favored, so that the descendants of a species become diversified in structure, and each ancestral species can give rise to several new ones. Although "it is probable that each form remains for long

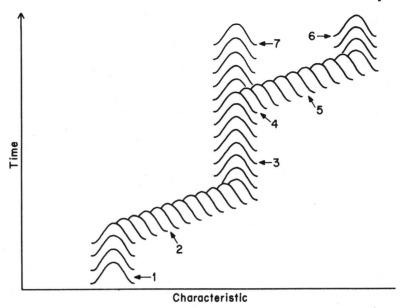

Figure 2. *Processes of evolutionary change. A characteristic that is variable (1) often shows a bell-shaped distribution—individuals vary on either side of the average. Evolutionary change (2) consists of a shift in successive generations, after which the characteristic may reach a new equilibrium (3). When the species splits into two different species (4), one of the species may undergo further evolutionary change (5) and reach a new equilibrium (6). The other may remain unchanged (7) or not. Each population usually remains variable throughout this process, but the average is shifted, ordinarily by natural selection.*

periods unaltered," successive evolutionary modifications will ultimately alter the different species so greatly that they will be classified as different genera, families, or orders.

Competition between species will impel them to become more different, for "the more diversified the descendants from any one species become in structure, constitution and habits, by so much will they be better enabled to seize on many and widely diversified places in the polity of nature, and so be enabled to increase in numbers." Thus different adaptations arise, and "the ultimate result is that each creature tends to become more and more improved in relation to its conditions. This improvement inevitably leads to the greater advancement of the organization of the greater number of living beings throughout the world." But lowly organisms continue to persist, for "natural selection, or the survival of the fittest, does not necessarily include progressive development—it only takes advantage of such variations as arise and are beneficial to each creature under its complex relations of life." Probably no organism has reached

a peak of perfection, and many lowly forms of life continue to exist, for "in some cases variations or individual differences of a favorable nature may never have arisen for natural selection to act on or accumulate. In no case, probably, has time sufficed for the utmost possible amount of development. In some few cases there has been what we must call retrogression of organization. But the main cause lies in the fact that under very simple conditions of life a high organization would be of no service. . . ."

In the rest of *The Origin of Species,* Darwin considers all the objections that might be raised against his theory; discusses the evolution of a great array of phenomena—hybrid sterility, the slave-making instinct of ants, the similarity of vertebrate embryos; and presents an enormous body of evidence for evolution. He draws his evidence from comparative anatomy, embryology, behavior, geographic variation, the geographic distribution of species, the study of rudimentary organs, atavistic variations ("throwbacks"), and the geological record to show how all of biology provides testimony that species have descended with modification from common ancestors.

Darwin's triumph was in synthesizing ideas and information in ways that no one had quite imagined before. From Lyell and the geologists he learned uniformitarianism: the cause of past events must be found in natural forces that operate today; and these, in the vastness of time, can accomplish great change. From Malthus and the nineteenth-century economists he learned of competition and the struggle for existence. From his work on barnacles, his travels, and his knowledge of domesticated varieties he learned that species do not have immutable essences but are variable in all their properties and blend into one another gradually. From his familiarity with the works of Whewell, Herschel, and other philosophers of science he developed a powerful method of pursuing science, the "hypothetico-deductive" method, which consists of formulating a hypothesis or speculation, deducing the logical predictions that must follow from the hypothesis, and then testing the hypothesis by seeing whether or not the predictions are verified. This was by no means the prevalent philosophy of science in Darwin's time.[5]

Darwin brought biology out of the Middle Ages. For divine design and unknowable supernatural forces he substituted natural material causes that could be studied by the methods of science. Instead of catastrophes unknown to physical science he invoked forces that could be studied in anyone's laboratory or garden. He replaced a young, static world by one in which there had been constant change for countless aeons. He established that life had a history, and this proved the essential view that differentiated evolutionary thought from all that had gone before.

For the British naturalist John Ray, writing in 1701, organisms had no history—they were the same at that moment, and lived in the same places, doing the same things, as when they were first created. For Darwin, organisms spoke of historical change. If there has indeed been such a history, then fossils in the oldest rocks must differ from those in younger rocks: trilobites, dinosaurs, and mammoths will not be mixed together but will appear in some temporal sequence. If species come from common ancestors, they will have the same characteristics, modified for different functions: the same bones used by bats for flying will be used by horses for running. If species come from ancestors that lived in different environments, they will carry the evidence of their history with them in the form of similar patterns of embryonic development and in vestigial, rudimentary organs that no longer serve any function. If species have a history, their geographical distribution will reflect it: oceanic islands won't have elephants because they wouldn't have been able to get there.

Once the earth and its living inhabitants are seen as the products of historical change, the theological philosophy embodied in the great chain of being ceases to make sense; the plenitude, or fullness, of the world becomes not an eternal manifestation of God's bountiful creativity but an illusion. For most of earth's history, most of the present species have not existed; and many of those that did exist do so no longer. But the scientific challenge to medieval philosophy goes even deeper. If evolution has occurred, and if it has proceeded from the natural causes that Darwin envisioned, then the adaptations of organisms to their environment, the intricate construction of the bird's wing and the orchid's flower, are evidence not of divine design but of the struggle for existence. Moreover, and this may be the deepest implication of all, Darwin brought to biology, as his predecessors had brought to astronomy and geology, the sufficiency of efficient causes. No longer was there any reason to look for final causes or goals. To the questions "What purpose does this species serve? Why did God make tapeworms?" the answer is "To no purpose." Tapeworms were not put here to serve a purpose, nor were planets, nor plants, nor people. They came into existence not by design but by the action of impersonal natural laws.

By providing materialistic, mecha-nistic explanations, instead of miraculous ones, for the characteristics of plants and animals, Darwin brought biology out of the realm of theology and into the realm of science. For miraculous spiritual forces fall outside the province of science; all of science is the study of material causation.

Of course, *The Origin of Species* didn't convince everyone immediately. Evolution and its material cause, natural selection, evoked strong protests from ecclesiastical circles, and even from scientists.[6] The eminent geologist Adam Sedgwick, for example, wrote in 1860 that species must come into existence by creation,

a power I cannot imitate or comprehend; but in which I can believe, by a legitimate conclusion of sound reason drawn from the laws and harmonies of Nature. For I can see in all around me a design and purpose, and a mutual adaptation of parts which I *can* comprehend, and which prove that there is exterior to, and above, the mere phenomena of Nature a great prescient and designing cause. . . . The pretended physical philosophy of modern days strips man of all his moral attributes, or holds them of no account in the estimate of his origin and place in the created world. A cold atheistical materialism is the tendency of the so-called material philosophy of the present day.

Among the more scientific objections were those posed by the French paleontologist François Pictet, and they were echoed by many others. Since Darwin supposes that species change gradually over the course of thousands of generations, then, asked Pictet, "Why don't we find these gradations in the fossil record . . . and why, instead of collecting thousands of identical individuals, do we not find more intermediary forms? . . . How is it that the most ancient fossil beds are rich in a variety of diverse forms of life, instead of the few early types Darwin's theory leads us to expect? How is it that no species has been seen to evolve during human history, and that the 4000 years which separates us from the mummies of Egypt have been insufficient to modify the crocodile and the ibis?" Pictet protested that, although slight variations might in time alter a species slightly, "all known facts demonstrate . . . that the prolonged influence of modifying causes has an action which is constantly restrained within sufficiently confined limits."

The anatomist Richard Owen likewise denied "that . . . variability is progressive and unlimited, so as, in the course of generations, to change the species, the genus, the order, or the class." The paleontologist Louis Agassiz insisted that organisms fall into discrete groups, based on uniquely different created plans, between which no intermediates could exist. He chose the birds as a group that showed the sharpest of boundaries. Only a few years later, in 1868, the fossil *Archaeopteryx,* an exquisite intermediate between birds and reptiles, demolished Agassiz's argument, and he had no more to say on the unique character of the birds.

Within twelve years of *The Origin of Species,* the evidence for evolution had been so thoroughly accepted that the philosopher and mathematician Chauncey Wright could point out that among the students of science, "orthodoxy has been won over to the doctrine of evolution." However, Wright continued, "While the general doctrine of evolution has thus been successfully redeemed from theological condemnation, this is not yet true of the subordinate hypothesis of Natural Selection."

Natural selection turned out to be an extraordinarily difficult concept for people to grasp. St. George Mivart, a Catholic scholar and scientist, was not unusual in equating natural selection with chance. "The theory of Natural Selection may (though it need not) be taken in such a way as to lead man to regard the present organic world as formed, so to speak, *accidentally,* beautiful and wonderful as is the confessedly haphazard result." Many like him simply refused to understand that natural selection is the antithesis of chance and consequently could not see how selection might cause adaptation or any kind of progressive evolutionary change. Even in the 1940s there were those, especially among paleontologists, who felt that the progressive evolution of groups like the horses, as revealed by the fossil record, must

have had some unknown cause other than natural selection. Paradoxically, then, Darwin had convinced the scientific world of evolution where his predecessors had failed; but he had not convinced all biologists of his truly original theory, the theory of natural selection.

Natural selection fell into particular disrepute in the early part of the twentieth century because of the rise of genetics—which, as it happened, eventually became the foundation of the modern theory of evolution. Darwin's supposition that variation was unlimited, and so in time could give rise to strikingly different organisms, was not entirely convincing because he had no good idea of where variation came from. In 1865, the Austrian monk Gregor Mendel discovered, from his crosses of pea plants, that discretely different characteristics such as wrinkled versus smooth seeds were inherited from generation to generation without being altered, as if they were caused by particles that passed from parent to offspring. Mendel's work was ignored for thirty-five years, until, in 1900, three biologists discovered his paper and realized that it held the key to the mystery of heredity. One of the three, Hugo de Vries, set about to explore the problem as Mendel had, and in the course of his studies of evening primroses observed strikingly different variations arise, *de novo.* The new forms were so different that de Vries believed they represented new species, which had arisen in a single step by alteration or, as he called it, mutation, of the hereditary material.

In the next few decades, geneticists working with a great variety of organisms observed many other drastic changes arise by mutation: fruit flies (*Drosophila*), for example, with white instead of red eyes or curled instead of straight wings. These laboratory geneticists, especially Thomas Hunt Morgan, an outstanding geneticist at Columbia University, asserted that evolution must proceed by major mutational steps, and that mutation, not natural selection, was the cause of evolution. In their eyes, Darwin's theory was dead on two counts: evolution was not

gradual, and it was not caused by natural selection. Meanwhile, naturalists, taxonomists, and breeders of domesticated plants and animals continued to believe in Darwinism, because they saw that populations and species differed quantitatively and gradually rather than in big jumps, that most variation was continuous (like height in humans) rather than discrete, and that domesticated species could be altered by artificial selection from continuous variation.

The bitter conflict between the Mendelian geneticists and the Darwinians was resolved in the 1930s in a "New Synthesis" that brought the opposing views into a "neo-Darwinian" theory of evolution.[7] Slight variations in height, wing length, and other characteristics proved, under careful genetic analysis, to be inherited as particles, in the same way as the discrete variations studied by the Mendelians. Thus a large animal simply has inherited more particles, or genes, for large size than a smaller member of the species has. The Mendelians were simply studying particularly well marked variations, while the naturalists were studying more subtle ones. Variations could be very slight, or fairly pronounced, or very substantial, but all were inherited in the same manner. All these variations, it was shown, arose by a process of mutation of the genes.

Three mathematical theoreticians, Ronald Fisher and J. B. S. Haldane in England and Sewall Wright in the United States, proved that a newly mutated gene would not automatically form a new species. Nor would it automatically replace the preexisting form of the gene, and so transform the species. Replacement of one gene by a mutant form of the gene, they said, could happen in two ways. The mutation could enable its possessors to survive or reproduce more effectively than the old form; if so, it would increase by natural selection, just as Darwin had said. The new characteristic that evolved in this way would ordinarily be considered an improved adaptation.

Sewall Wright pointed out, however, that not all genetic changes in species need be adaptive. A new mutation might be no better or worse than the preexisting gene—it might simply be "neutral." In small populations such a mutation could replace the previous gene purely by chance—a process he called random genetic drift. The idea, put crudely, is this. Suppose there is a small population of land snails in a cow pasture, and that 5 percent of them are brown and the rest are yellow. Purely by chance, a greater percentage of yellow snails than of brown ones get crushed by cows' hooves in one generation. The snails breed, and there will now be a slightly greater percentage of yellow snails in the next generation than there had been. But in the next generation, the yellow ones may suffer more trampling, purely by chance. The proportion of yellow offspring will then be lower again. These random events cause fluctuations in the percentage of the two types. Wright proved mathematically that eventually, if no other factors intervene, these fluctuations will bring the population either to 100 percent yellow or 100 percent brown, purely by chance. The population will have evolved, then, but not by natural selection; and there is no improvement of adaptation.

During the period of the New Synthesis, though, genetic drift was emphasized less than natural selection, for which abundant evidence was discovered. Sergei Chetverikov in Russia, and later Theodosius Dobzhansky working in the United States, showed that wild populations of fruit flies contained an immense amount of genetic variation, including the same kinds of mutations that the geneticists had found arising in their laboratories. Dobzhansky and other workers went on to show that these variations affected survival and reproduction: that natural selection was a reality. They showed, moreover, that the genetic differences among related species were indeed compounded of the same kinds of slight genetic variations that they found within species. Thus the taxonomists and the geneticists converged onto a neo-Darwinian theory of evolution: evolution is due not to mutation *or* natural selection, but to both. Random mutations provide abundant genetic variation; natural selection, the antithesis of randomness, sorts out the useful from the deleterious, and transforms the species.

In the following two decades, the paleontologist George Gaylord Simpson showed that this theory was completely adequate to explain the fossil record, and the ornithologists Bernhard Rensch and Ernst Mayr, the botanist G. Ledyard Stebbins, and many other taxonomists showed that the similarities and differences among living species could be fully explained by neo-Darwinism. They also clarified the meaning of "species." Organisms belong to different species if they do not interbreed when the opportunity presents itself, thus remaining genetically distinct. An ancestral species splits into two descendant species when different populations of the ancestor, living in different geographic regions, become so genetically different from each other that they will not or cannot interbreed when they have the chance to do so. As a result, evolution can happen without the formation of new species: a single species can be genetically transformed without splitting into several descendants. Conversely, new species can be formed without much genetic change. If one population becomes different from the rest of its species in, for example, its mating behavior, it will not interbreed with the other populations. Thus it has become a new species, even though it may be identical to its "sister species" in every respect except its behavior. Such a new species is free to follow a new path of genetic change, since it does not become homogenized with its sister species by interbreeding. With time, therefore, it can diverge and develop different adaptations.

The conflict between the geneticists and the Darwinians that was resolved in the New Synthesis was the last major conflict in evolutionary science. Since that time, an enormous amount of research has confirmed most of the major conclusions of neo-Darwinism. We now know that populations contain very extensive genetic variation that continually arises by mutation of preexisting genes. We also know what genes are and how they become mutated. Many instances of the reality of natural selection in wild populations have been documented, and there is extensive evidence that many species form by the divergence of different populations of an ancestral species.

The major questions in evolutionary biology now tend to be of the form, "All right, factors x and y both operate in evolution, but how important is x compared to y?" For example, studies of biochemical genetic variation have raised the possibility that nonadaptive, random change (genetic drift) may be the major reason for many biochemical differences among species. How important, then, is genetic drift compared to natural selection? Another major question has to do with rates of evolution: Do species usually diverge very slowly, as Darwin thought, or does evolution consist mostly of rapid spurts, interspersed with long periods of constancy? Still another question is raised by mutations, which range all the way from gross changes of the kind Morgan studied to very slight alterations. Does evolution consist entirely of the substitution of mutations that have very slight effects, or are major mutations sometimes important too? Partisans on each side of all these questions argue vigorously for their interpretation of the evidence, but they don't doubt that the major factors of evolution are known. They simply emphasize one factor or another. Minor battles of precisely this kind go on continually in every field of science; without them there would be very little advancement in our knowledge.

Within a decade or two of *The Origin of Species,* the belief that living organisms had evolved over the ages was firmly entrenched in biology. As of 1982, the historical existence of evolution is viewed as fact by almost all biologists. To explain how the fact of evolution has been brought about, a theory of evolutionary mechanisms—mutation, natural selection, genetic drift, and isolation—has been developed.[8] But exactly what is the evidence for the fact of evolution?

NOTES

1. Andrew Dickson White, *A History of the Warfare of Science with Theology in Christendom* vol. I (London: Macmillan, 1896; reprint ed., New York: Dover, 1960).

2. A. O. Lovejoy, *The Great Chain of Being* (Cambridge, Mass.: Harvard University Press, 1936).

3. Much of this history is provided by J. C. Greene, *The Death of Adam: Evolution and its Impact on Western Thought* (Ames: Iowa State University Press, 1959).

4. A detailed history of this and other developments in evolutionary biology is given by Ernst Mayr, *The Growth of Biological Thought: Diversity, Evolution, Inheritance* (Cambridge, Mass.: Harvard University Press, 1982).

5. See D. L. Hull, *Darwin and His Critics* (Cambridge, Mass.: Harvard University Press, 1973).

6. *Ibid.*

7. E. Mayr and W. B. Provine, *The Evolutionary Synthesis* (Cambridge, Mass.: Harvard University Press, 1980).

8. Our modern understanding of the mechanisms of evolution is described in many books. Elementary textbooks include G. L. Stebbins, *Processes of Organic Evolution,* (Englewood Cliffs, N.J.: Prentice-Hall, 1971), and J. Maynard Smith, *The Theory of Evolution* (New York: Penguin Books, 1975). More advanced textbooks include Th. Dobzhansky, F. J. Ayala, G. L. Stebbins, and J. W. Valentine, *Evolution* (San Francisco: Freeman, 1977), and D. J. Futuyma, *Evolutionary Biology* (Sunderland, Mass.: Sinauer, 1979). Unreferenced facts and theories described in the text are familiar enough to most evolutionary biologists that they will be found in most or all of the references cited above.

A Pox Upon Our Genes

Smallpox vanished twelve years ago, but its genetic legacy may still linger within us

Jared Diamond

Jared Diamond teaches physiology at UCLA and studies the evolution of New Guinea birds.

Human evolution holds a special fascination for us. Granted, it's much easier to study natural selection in creatures like bacteria and fruit flies, which we manipulate experimentally without compunction. Granted, the general principles thereby uncovered may also apply to humans. But let's face it: bacteria and general principles aren't what we're most curious about. What we really want to know are the particulars of how we came to be who we are.

Unfortunately, attempts to study natural selection in humans face daunting obstacles. You can't take any woman you choose and mate her to any man you choose in order to observe the resultant progeny. You can't irradiate, heat shock, or dissect humans. You can't inoculate them with lethal diseases, although that experiment would be especially interesting because diseases were a major selective force on us until the advent of modern medicine.

This piece is about an ingenious attempt to study natural selection in humans without resorting to morally unacceptable manipulations. Twenty-five years ago, nature visited a tragic experiment on rural areas of India in the form of a virulent outbreak of smallpox. Nature used abominably ex-

cellent experimental design, matching children who died against brothers or sisters who survived. Analysis of the results by two scientists yielded insights into the scars that smallpox, one of the great modern killers of humans, has left on our genes.

The study that resulted was unique in the annals of medicine. It will never be repeated because smallpox itself has been eliminated. Thus, it will be remembered as our last, and best, chance to understand what may have been an important determinant of our blood groups.

Despite the virtual halt in human skeletal evolution since the end of the Ice Age, the genes for our soft tissues (including blood cells) continue to undergo changes in response to natural selection. However, the important selective agents are no longer large, visible enemies, like lions, but tiny, invisible ones: microbes. With the beginnings of agriculture about 10,000 years ago, infectious diseases probably began to claim an increasing toll of human life, eventually becoming the leading cause of our mortality. As human numbers soared, we became susceptible to diseases that tend to die out in small populations but that can maintain themselves in large ones, which offer continuing supplies of not-yet-infected victims. Agriculture also made us sedentary, and we began to live in the midst of our own effluents and hence to infect one another more easily with pathogens in our feces, urine, and

exhaled air. As we domesticated animals and came to live amidst them, we caught still other diseases.

It's true of some infectious diseases, as of some other causes of death, that certain people are genetically more susceptible than others. Since more resistant individuals are more likely to survive and to leave more offspring, selection operating over the last 10,000 years must have caused a genetic revolution in our soft tissues. In a previous [article] ("Blood, Genes, and Malaria," *Natural History,* February 1989), I discussed genetic resistance to malaria, the leading infectious disease of the Old World tropics. But a disease much more familiar to Americans and Europeans is smallpox. Until the recent eradication of smallpox, American citizens traveling abroad required two pieces of paper in order to reenter the United States: a valid passport and proof of recent smallpox vaccination.

Smallpox is caused by one of a group of microbes called pox viruses. While the virus (and hence the disease) is confined to humans, it is closely related to viruses that cause similar diseases in various domestic animals, including cows (cowpox), sheep, goats, horses, and pigs. The smallpox virus probably developed by mutations from one of these animal viruses after we began living in close association with animals.

Imagine smallpox suddenly being introduced into a small and isolated population without any previous exposure to smallpox or related viruses. If all the people have plenty of contact with one another, then smallpox will quickly spread, infecting everybody. Many people will die, but those who survive will develop antibodies to smallpox and will thereby become resistant. As a result, smallpox will have killed or immunized the whole population and will die out, because the virus doesn't infect animals.

Although the disease thus can't persist for long in a small, isolated population, it can last indefinitely as it spreads through a large population in contact with other large populations. Going from one area to another, it can return to an area after a new crop of previously unexposed babies has become available for infection. This need for large numbers of hosts, plus the close similarity of the smallpox virus to domestic animal viruses, is the reason for believing that smallpox probably appeared only after the rise of agriculture.

Just where and when did smallpox first infect us? It must have evolved somewhere in the Old World, since the New World was free of smallpox until it arrived with Spanish conquistadors about 1507. Our oldest certain evidence consists of three Egyptian mummies, dating from the period 1570–1085 B.C., with well-preserved skins that show the characteristic rash caused by smallpox. One of the mummies was Pharaoh Ramses V, whose titles of Mighty Bull, Repulser of Millions, Golden God of the Sun, and Lord of the Two Lands were powerless to protect him against this virus. Smallpox is also known to have existed in India and China before the time of Christ. But it remains unclear how much earlier than 1570 B.C., and exactly where within the Old World, the fatal mutation that transformed some animal virus into smallpox first occurred.

Many devastating smallpox epidemics are known to have killed one-quarter to one-half of the affected populations. Thus, smallpox has often changed the course of human history. It may have caused the famous plague that decimated Athens in 430 B.C. and helped seal her doom in her war against Sparta. Epidemics beginning

about A.D. 165 may have contributed to the decline of the Roman Empire. Titled victims besides Ramses V include Marcus Aurelius of Rome, Peter II of Russia, and Louis XV of France.

But the most far-reaching effects of smallpox were in the New World, where Spanish explorers carrying the disease encountered Indian populations large enough to sustain smallpox but with no previous exposure and no antibodies. Hence the disease played a decisive role in the astonishing conquests of the Aztec and Inca empires, each with millions of inhabitants, by groups of just a few hundred Spaniards. In Mexico, after Cortés had lost two-thirds of his tiny force and retreated to the coast from the Aztec capital of Tenochtitlán (modern Mexico City), a smallpox epidemic killed half of the Aztecs, including Montezuma's successor, Cuitláhuac. In Peru an epidemic that spread southward from Central America, before Pizarro and other Spaniards reached the area, killed the Inca emperor Huayna Capac, killed his designated heir, Ninan Cuyoche, and plunged the empire into civil war between the rival would-be emperors Huáscar and Atahualpa. Cortés and Pizarro triumphed not only because smallpox had killed so many Indian soldiers, including their commanders, but also because a disease that killed Indians, and spared the already resistant Spaniards, demoralized those Indians who survived the epidemic.

As is true of other diseases, individuals must vary in their genetic resistance to smallpox, and the more resistant individuals are more likely to survive epidemics. In populations exposed to the virus for many generations, the frequencies of genes associated with resistance must have risen. Today, only twelve years since smallpox claimed its last victim, those resistant genes should still be common. What might those genes be? For reasons that I shall mention, the genes responsible for our so-called ABO blood types are likely candidates. I must now digress for a simplified crash course in hematology.

Blood is typed according to various protein-and-sugar compounds occupying the surfaces of our red blood cells (hence the name "blood group substances"). While most such substances are found only on our red cells, the ABO substances, which are the best known, are also present on other cells of our body. Each of us has either substance A alone, B alone, both A and B, or neither, and is correspondingly classified as having blood type A, B, AB, or O, respectively. (Strictly speaking, we have two copies of each gene, one inherited from our father and one from our mother, and each copy may be either the A, B, or O form, or allele. Thus, a type-A person has either two As or else one A and one O allele, while a type-O person must have two O alleles.)

In addition, each of us in infancy develops antibodies to the substances he or she lacks. People of type O develop antibodies to both the A and B substances; those of type A develop antibodies only to the B substance, and vice versa; and those of type AB develop neither antibody.

We pay attention to our blood types mainly when they cause us trouble. For example, if a patient of type B receives a transfusion of type-A blood, the transfused cells with the A substance are destroyed by the patient's anti-A antibody, with possibly lethal consequences to the patient. This problem appeared only with the rise of modern medicine and blood transfusions, but a similar problem can arise naturally when a woman is pregnant with a fetus bearing a blood group substance against which she has antibodies. For instance, if a type-O mother carries a fetus that inherited group A from the father, the mother's anti-A antibodies may cause the fetus to abort or may leave it damaged at birth. That doesn't mean, though, that all you type-O women should reject a type-A or type-B suitor, or that you should fret through your pregnancy if you marry that suitor. Only a small fraction of pregnancies in ABO-incompatible marriages actually result in medical complications.

Why, since almost all known effects of blood group substances are thus harmful, do we have differing blood types at all? The reason remains unclear. Perhaps they function as chemical passwords to help us distinguish our own cells from invading microbes or cancer cells that we ought to destroy.

In almost all human populations the O allele is more frequent than the A and B alleles combined. The occasional loss of type-A or type-B fetuses because of incompatibility with their mothers would therefore tend to eliminate the A and B alleles if there were no other important selective factors acting on ABO genes. In fact, as predicted by this reasoning, the O allele tends to be especially common in isolated human populations on islands or mountains out of the mainstream of migration and, therefore, out of the path of infection. But A and B are common in mainstream populations of the Old World, with A being especially frequent in Europe, B in Asia. What compensating advantage peculiar to group A in Europe accounts for its higher frequency there, and similarly for group B in Asia?

One possibility is that certain of the ABO blood groups might confer resistance against fatal diseases common (or formerly common) on certain continents but not on others. Beginning in 1953, convincing associations between ABO blood type and susceptibility to cancer began to be discovered. For example, the risk of stomach cancer is 20 percent higher for Europeans of type A than those of type O. But cancers are not major causes of death in children and young adults and therefore should not be the major determinants of blood type.

A much more plausible explanation for ABO gene frequencies is that they were influenced by the infectious diseases that were major killers of humans. A potential mechanism for such an influence is that the surfaces of some microbes prove to bear substances similar to the ABO blood groups. This suggests a clever evolutionary trick by the microbes to deceive their hosts. For instance, if a microbe's surface is coated with the microbe's own peculiar substances, the host is likely to recognize the microbe

as foreign, develop antibodies against it, and destroy it. But a microbe coated with the A substance would slip past the defenses of a type-A person, since we do not normally develop antibodies against our own proteins.

In the 1960s two kinds of evidence were advanced for a susceptibility of type-A people to smallpox. The first was a still-unresolved claim that a virus closely related to the smallpox virus does have substances like group A on its surface. The second consisted of two statistical studies that compared how frequencies of blood group A and of smallpox varied among different areas of India and Africa. Areas with high frequencies of smallpox proved to have low frequencies of group A, suggesting that smallpox had killed off people with group A.

As recently as the 1960s, in rural areas of India, lack of resources for vaccination, limited access to modern medical care, and lack of understanding of hygiene and disease transmission combined to make smallpox epidemics virtually annual occurrences. Children sick with smallpox shared the same room, and often the same bed, with their brothers and sisters, thereby insuring widespread exposure to the disease. As many as half of the smallpox patients died.

In 1965 and 1966 two scientists, Dr. F. Vogel and Dr. M. R. Chakravartti, realizing that a comparative study of survivors and victims might yield clues about genetic resistance to the disease, attempted to locate all cases of smallpox during severe epidemics in some villages and small towns. They found a total of 415 unvaccinated smallpox patients. For all but eight of these patients, they were also able to find a healthy brother or sister to consider as a "control subject"—that is, someone as similar as possible genetically to the patient and living in the same house, but differing in not having contracted smallpox despite close exposure. Drops of blood drawn from the fingertips sufficed to identify the ABO blood types of the patients and their siblings. Although 52 percent of the patients—217 out of 415—died in this severe

epidemic, risk of death varied greatly with ABO blood type.

Among the 415 patients, 261 carried blood group A (that is, their blood type was A or AB), while 154 lacked A (their blood type was B or O). Among the 407 healthy subjects, only 80 carried group A, while 327 lacked it—which strongly suggests that the As were susceptible and the non-As resistant. The ratio of A to non-A among the patients (261:154), divided by the ratio of A to non-A among the controls (80:327), was 7—meaning that a person with group A had a seven times greater risk of contracting smallpox than someone without group A.

The 415 patients were then classified according to the severity or the mildness of their symptoms. Among the 283 severe cases, most (201) had blood group A, and only 82 lacked it. Among the mild cases, only 60 had group A, while 72 lacked it. Hence, once they had contracted smallpox, patients with group A were three times more likely to develop a severe case.

When the 415 patients were classified as to whether they died or survived, most (155) of the 217 who died had group A, and only 62 lacked it. The proportions were more nearly equal among those who survived: 106 had group A, and 92 lacked it. Hence, once a person had contracted smallpox, patients with group A had a doubled risk of dying.

Since people with group A are much more likely to contract smallpox, to develop a severe case of it, and to die of it, why hasn't the gene for group A been virtually eliminated in India, Europe, and other areas where smallpox has been a major killer for a long time, leaving all the survivors with group O or B?

Perhaps the answer is that other, equally widespread infectious diseases spared people with group A and penalized those with other blood groups. There is suggestive evidence that the Black Death (bubonic plague), which killed about one-third of medieval Europe's population, preferentially attacked the bearers of group O, as does cholera, whose death toll in India rivaled that of smallpox. These two diseases may have favored A at the expense of O in India and Europe. Conversely, those with blood type O may be relatively resistant to syphilis, which may have originated in the New World and thus contributed to the very high frequencies (approaching 100 percent) of group O among Central and South American Indians. Thus, ABO blood group frequencies may represent a compromise among the selective effects of numerous diseases. If so, why do geneticists consider the evidence little more than speculative?

In the case of smallpox, although the study by Vogel and Chakravartti yielded a clear picture, three other studies in India and one in Brazil failed to detect differences in ABO frequencies between smallpox patients and controls. Vogel and Chakravartti noted many reasons why the considered their 1965–66 study much more convincing. Most of their patients were unvaccinated children without medical care, exposed to an especially virulent epidemic, while many patients in the other studies were apparently vaccinated adults receiving medical care in large urban hospitals and possibly exposed to a less virulent epidemic. As a result, mortality in the other studies was only 0–16 percent, compared to 52 percent in the 1965–66 study. Vogel and Chakravartti studied all patients that

they could locate in a small area and compared the patients with siblings living in the same house. The other studies used the biased sample of patients presenting themselves as an urban hospital and compared their blood groups with those of "control subjects" from other areas. However, blood group frequencies vary greatly with caste, religion, ethnic affiliation, and locality within India. Thus, Vogel and Chakravartti appear to me correct in claiming that their study involved a much less biased set of "experimental" subjects, a set of control subjects much better matched to the experimental subjects, and a much greater selective effect of the smallpox epidemic, which in this case was severe.

If the study had involved mice, these claims, counterclaims, and discrepancies would have been resolved by further studies. Larger blood samples would have been drawn to permit measurement of other possible genetic resistance factors besides ABO blood groups. But—thank God—the opportunity to continue studies of smallpox in humans has vanished. As a result of a major effort that began in 1966 to eliminate smallpox throughout the world, no natural cases have been recorded since Ali Maow Maalin developed the telltale rash in Merka Town, Somalia, on October 26, 1977. Hence,

the study by Vogel and Chakravartti will remain unique. Similarly, our prospects for learning more about the genetic influences of bubonic plague and syphilis are slim, since plague has virtually vanished except in remote areas, while syphilis can now be treated as soon as it is detected.

Does this mean that these killers of the past are now of purely academic interest? Not al all. First, the slow-healing scars that they left on our genes, possibly in the form of altered ABO frequencies, will linger in us for many generations. But—perhaps more important—what they did to us in the past serves as a model for what AIDS is doing to us today.

It's well known that individuals exposed to AIDS vary in their risk of becoming infected, and that infected individuals vary in the rate at which their disease progresses. These facts suggest the possibility of genetic differences in susceptibility to AIDS, as is true of many other diseases. In some areas of the world the eventual AIDS-related mortality rate may come to rival that of the great past epidemics of smallpox and plague. If so, AIDS too may be in the process of causing big shifts in human gene frequencies, although we can't yet specify which genes are involved. Natural selection is not a theoretical postulate, but a grimly continuing reality.

Curse and Blessing of the Ghetto

Tay-Sachs disease is a choosy killer, one that for centuries targeted Eastern European Jews above all others. By decoding its lethal logic, we can learn a lot about how genetic diseases evolve—and how they can be conquered.

Jared Diamond

Contributing editor Jared Diamond is a professor of physiology at the UCLA School of Medicine.

Marie and I hated her at first sight, even though she was trying hard to be helpful. As our obstetrician's genetics counselor, she was just doing her job, explaining to us the unpleasant results that might come out of the genetic tests we were about to have performed. As a scientist, though, I already knew all I wanted to know about Tay-Sachs disease, and I didn't need to be reminded that the baby sentenced to death by it could be my own.

Fortunately, the tests would reveal that my wife and I were not carriers of the Tay-Sachs gene, and our preparenthood fears on that matter at least could be put to rest. But at the time I didn't yet know that. As I glared angrily at that poor genetics counselor, so strong was my anxiety that now, four years later, I can still clearly remember what was going through my mind: If I were an evil deity, I thought, trying to devise exquisite tortures for babies and their parents, I would be proud to have designed Tay-Sachs disease.

Tay-Sachs is completely incurable, unpreventable, and preprogrammed in the genes. A Tay-Sachs infant usually appears normal for the first few months after birth, just long enough for the parents to grow to love him. An exaggerated "startle reaction" to sounds

is the first ominous sign. At about six months the baby starts to lose control of his head and can't roll over or sit without support. Later he begins to drool, breaks out into unmotivated bouts of laughter, and suffers convulsions. Then his head grows abnormally large, and he becomes blind. Perhaps what's most frightening for the parents is that their baby loses all contact with his environment and becomes virtually a vegetable. By the child's third birthday, if he's still alive, his skin will turn yellow and his hands pudgy. Most likely he will die before he's four years old.

My wife and I were tested for the Tay-Sachs gene because at the time we rated as high-risk candidates, for two reasons. First, Marie was carrying twins, so we had double the usual chance to bear a Tay-Sachs baby. Second, both she and I are of Eastern European Jewish ancestry, the population with by far the world's highest Tay-Sachs frequency.

In peoples around the world Tay-Sachs appears once in every 400,000 births. But it appears a hundred times more frequently—about once in 3,600 births—among descendants of Eastern European Jews, people known as Ashkenazim. For descendants of most other groups of Jews—Oriental Jews, chiefly from the Middle East, or Sephardic Jews, from Spain and other Mediterranean countries—the frequency of Tay-Sachs disease is no higher than in non-Jews. Faced with such a clear

correlation, one cannot help but wonder: What is it about this one group of people that produces such an extraordinarily high risk of this disease?

Finding the answer to this question concerns all of us, regardless of our ancestry. Every human population is especially susceptible to certain diseases, not only because of its life-style but also because of its genetic inheritance. For example, genes put European whites at high risk for cystic fibrosis, African blacks for sickle-cell disease, Pacific Islanders for diabetes—and Eastern European Jews for ten different diseases, including Tay-Sachs. It's not that Jews are notably susceptible to genetic diseases in general; but a combination of historical factors has led to Jews' being intensively studied, and so their susceptibilities are far better known than those of, say, Pacific Islanders.

Tay-Sachs exemplifies how we can deal with such diseases; it has been the object of the most successful screening program to date. Moreover, Tay-Sachs is helping us understand how ethnic diseases evolve. Within the past couple of years discoveries by molecular biologists have provided tantalizing clues to precisely how a deadly gene can persist and spread over the centuries. Tay-Sachs may be primarily a disease of Eastern European Jews, but through this affliction of one group of people, we gain a window on how our genes simultaneously curse and bless us all.

The disease's hyphenated name comes from the two physicians—British ophthalmologist W. Tay and New York neurologist B. Sachs—who independently first recognized the disease, in 1881 and 1887, respectively. By 1896 Sachs had seen enough cases to realize that the disease was most common among Jewish children.

Not until 1962, however, were researchers able to trace the cause of the affliction to a single biochemical abnormality: the excessive accumulation in nerve cells of a fatty substance called G_{M2} ganglioside. Normally G_{M2} ganglioside is present at only modest levels in cell membranes, because it is constantly being broken down as well as synthesized. The breakdown depends on the enzyme hexosaminidase A, which is found in the tiny structures within our cells known as lysosomes. In the unfortunate Tay-Sachs victims this enzyme is lacking, and without it the ganglioside piles up and produces all the symptoms of the disease.

We have two copies of the gene that programs our supply of hexosaminidase A, one inherited from our father, the other from our mother; each of our parents, in turn, has two copies derived from their own parents. As long as we have one good copy of the gene, we can produce enough hexosaminidase A to prevent a buildup of G_{M2} ganglioside and we won't get Tay-Sachs. This genetic disease is of the sort termed recessive rather than dominant—meaning that to get it, a child must inherit a defective gene not just from one parent but from both of them. Clearly, each parent must have had one good copy of the gene along with the defective copy—if either had had two defective genes, he or she would have died of the disease long before reaching the age of reproduction. In genetic terms the diseased child is homozygous for the defective gene and both parents are heterozygous for it.

None of this yet gives any hint as to why the Tay-Sachs gene should be most common among Eastern European Jews. To come to grips with that question, we must take a short detour into history.

From their biblical home of ancient Israel, Jews spread peacefully to other Mediterranean lands, Yemen, and India. They were also dispersed violently through conquest by Assyrians, Babylonians, and Romans. Under the Carolingian kings of the eighth and ninth centuries Jews were invited to settle in France and Germany as traders and financiers. In subsequent centuries, however, persecutions triggered by the Crusades gradually drove Jews out of Western Europe; the process culminated in their total expulsion from Spain in 1492. Those Spanish Jews—called Sephardim—fled to other lands around the Mediterranean. Jews of France and Germany—the Ashkenazim—fled east to Poland and from there to Lithuania and western Russia, where they settled mostly in towns, as businessmen engaged in whatever pursuit they were allowed.

It seems unlikely that genetic accidents would have pumped up the frequency of the same gene not once but twice in the same population.

There the Jews stayed for centuries, through periods of both tolerance and oppression. But toward the end of the nineteenth century and the beginning of the twentieth, waves of murderous anti-Semitic attacks drove millions of Jews out of Eastern Europe, with most of them heading for the United States. My mother's parents, for example, fled to New York from the Lithuanian pogroms of the 1880s, while my father's parents fled from the Ukrainian pogroms of 1903-6. The more modern history of Jewish migration is probably well known to you all: most Jews who remained in Eastern Europe were exterminated during World War II, while most the survivors immigrated to the United States and Israel. Of the 13 million Jews alive today, more than three-quarters are Ashkenazim, the descendants of the Eastern European

Jews and the people most at risk for Tay-Sachs.

Have these Jews maintained their genetic distinctness through the thousands of years of wandering? Some scholars claim that there has been so much intermarriage and conversion that Ashkenazic Jews are now just Eastern Europeans who adopted Jewish culture. However, modern genetic studies refute that speculation.

First of all, there are those ten genetic diseases that the Ashkenazim have somehow acquired, by which they differ both from other Jews and from Eastern European non-Jews. In addition, many Ashkenazic genes turn out to be ones typical of Palestinian Arabs and other peoples of the Eastern Mediterranean areas where Jews originated. (In fact, by genetic standards the current Arab-Israeli conflict is an internecine civil war.) Other Ashkenazic genes have indeed diverged from Mediterranean ones (including genes of Sephardic and Oriental Jews) and have evolved to converge on genes of Eastern European non-Jews subject to the same local forces of natural selection. But the degree to which Ashkenazim prove to differ genetically from Eastern European non-Jews implies an intermarriage rate of only about 15 percent.

Can history help explain why the Tay-Sachs gene in particular is so much more common in Ashkenazim than in their non-Jewish neighbors or in other Jews? At the risk of spoiling a mystery, I'll tell you now that the answer is yes, but to appreciate it, you'll have to understand the four possible explanations for the persistence of the Tay-Sachs gene.

First, new copies of the gene might be arising by mutation as fast as existing copies disappear with the death of Tay-Sachs children. That's the most likely explanation for the gene's persistence in most of the world, where the disease frequency is only one in 400,000 births—that frequency reflects a typical human mutation rate. But for this explanation to apply to the Ashkenazim would require a mutation rate of at least one per 3,600 births—far above the frequency observed for any human gene. Furthermore, there would be no precedent for one particular gene mutating so much more often in one human population than in others.

As a second possibility, the Ashkenazim might have acquired the Tay-Sachs gene from some other people who already had the gene at high frequency. Arthur Koestler's controversial book *The Thirteenth Tribe,* for example, popularized the view that the Ashkenazim are really not a Semitic people but are instead descended from the Khazar, a Turkic tribe whose rulers converted to Judaism in the eighth century. Could the Khazar have brought the Tay-Sachs gene to Eastern Europe? This speculation makes good romantic reading, but there is no good evidence to support it. Moreover, it fails to explain why deaths of Tay-Sachs children didn't eliminate the gene by natural selection in the past 1,200 years, nor how the Khazar acquired high frequencies of the gene in the first place.

The third hypothesis was the one preferred by a good many geneticists until recently. It invokes two genetic processes, termed the founder effect and genetic drift, that may operate in small populations. To understand these concepts, imagine that 100 couples settle in a new land and found a population that then increases. Imagine further that one parent among those original 100 couples happens to have some rare gene, one, say, that normally occurs at a frequency of one in a million. The gene's frequency in the new population will now be one in 200 as a result of the accidental presence of that rare founder.

Or suppose again that 100 couples found a population, but that one of the 100 men happens to have lots of kids by his wife or that he is exceptionally popular with other women, while the other 99 men are childless or have few kids or are simply less popular. That one man may thereby father 10 percent rather than a more representative one percent of the next generation's babies, and their genes will disproportionately reflect that man's genes. In other words, gene frequencies will have drifted between the first and second generation.

Through these two types of genetic accidents a rare gene may occur with an unusually high frequency in a small expanding population. Eventually, if the gene is harmful, natural selection will bring its frequency back to normal by killing off gene bearers. But if the resultant disease is recessive—if heterozygous individuals don't get the disease and only the rare, homozygous individuals die of it—the gene's high frequency may persist for many generations.

These accidents do in fact account for the astonishingly high Tay-Sachs gene frequency found in one group of Pennsylvania Dutch: out of the 333 people in this group, 98 proved to carry the Tay-Sachs gene. Those 333 are all descended from one couple who settled in the United States in the eighteenth century and had 13 children. Clearly, one of that founding couple must have carried the gene. A similar accident may explain why Tay-Sachs is also relatively common among French Canadians, who number 5 million today but are descended from fewer than 6,000 French immigrants who arrived in the New World between 1638 and 1759. In the two or three centuries since both these founding events, the high Tay-Sachs gene frequency among Pennsylvania Dutch and French Canadians has not yet had enough time to decline to normal levels.

The same mechanisms were once proposed to explain the high rate of Tay-Sachs disease among the Ashkenazim. Perhaps, the reasoning went, the gene just happened to be overrepresented in the founding Jewish population that settled in Germany or Eastern Europe. Perhaps the gene just happened to drift up in frequency in the Jewish populations scattered among the isolated towns of Eastern Europe.

But geneticists have long questioned whether the Ashkenazim population's history was really suitable for these genetic accidents to have been significant. Remember, the founder effect and genetic drift become significant only in small populations, and the founding populations of Ashkenazim may have been quite large. Moreover, Ashkenazic communities were consid-

erably widespread; drift would have sent gene frequencies up in some towns but down in others. And, finally, natural selection has by now had a thousand years to restore gene frequencies to normal.

Granted, those doubts are based on historical data, which are not always as precise or reliable as one might want. But within the past several years the case against those accidental explanations for Tay-Sachs disease in the Ashkenazim has been bolstered by discoveries by molecular biologists.

Like all proteins, the enzyme absent in Tay-Sachs children is coded for by a piece of our DNA. Along that particular stretch of DNA there are thousands of different sites where a mutation could occur that would result in no enzyme and hence in the same set of symptoms. If molecular biologists had discovered that all cases of Tay-Sachs in Ashkenazim involved damage to DNA at the same site, that would have been strong evidence that in Ashkenazim the disease stems from a single mutation that has been multiplied by the founder effect or genetic drift— in other words, the high incidence of Tay-Sachs among Eastern European Jews is accidental.

In reality, though, several different mutations along this stretch of DNA have been identified in Ashkenazim, and two of them occur much more frequently than in non-Ashkenazim populations. It seems unlikely that genetic accidents would have pumped up the frequency of the same gene not once but twice in the same population.

And that's not the sole unlikely coincidence arguing against accidental explanations. Recall that Tay-Sachs is caused by the excessive accumulation of one fatty substance, G_{M2} ganglioside, from a defect in one enzyme, hexosaminidase A. But Tay-Sachs is one of ten genetic diseases characteristic of Ashkenazim. Among those other nine, two—Gaucher's disease and Niemann-Pick disease—result from the accumulation of two other fatty substances similar to G_{M2} ganglioside, as a result of defects in two other enzymes similar to hexosaminidase A. Yet our bodies contain thousands of different enzymes. It would have been an incredible roll of the genetic dice if, by nothing more than chance, Ashkenazim had independently acquired mutations in three closely related enzymes—and had acquired mutations in one of those enzymes twice.

All these facts bring us to the fourth possible explanation of why the Tay-Sachs gene is so prevalent among Ashkenazim: namely, that something about them favored accumulation of G_{M2} ganglioside and related fats.

For comparison, suppose that a friend doubles her money on one stock while you are getting wiped out with your investments. Taken alone, that could just mean she was lucky on that one occasion. But suppose that she doubles her money on each of two different stocks and at the same time rings up big profits in real estate while also making a killing in bonds. That implies more than lady luck; it suggests that something about your friend—like shrewd judgment—favors financial success.

What could be the blessings of fat accumulation in Eastern European Jews? At first this question sounds weird. After all, that fat accumulation

was noticed only because of the curses it bestows: Tay-Sachs, Gaucher's, or Niemann-Pick disease. But many of our common genetic diseases may persist because they bring both blessings and curses (see "The Cruel Logic of Our Genes," *Discover,* November 1989). They kill or impair individuals who inherit two copies of the faulty gene, but they help those who receive only one defective gene by protecting them against other diseases. The best understood example is the sickle-cell gene of African blacks, which often kills homozygotes but protects heterozygotes against malaria. Natural selection sustains such genes because more heterozygotes than normal individuals survive to pass on their genes, and those extra gene copies offset the copies lost through the deaths of homozygotes.

So let us refine our question and ask, What blessing could the Tay-Sachs gene bring to those individuals who are heterozygous for it? A clue first emerged back in 1972, with the publication of the results of a questionnaire that had asked U.S. Ashkenzaic parents of Tay-Sachs children what their own Eastern European-born parents had

We're not a melting pot, and we won't be for a long time. Each ethnic group has some characteristic genes of its own, a legacy of its distinct history.

died of. Keep in mind that since these unfortunate children had to be homozygotes, with two copies of the Tay-Sachs gene, all their parents had to be heterozygotes, with one copy, and half of the parents' parents also had to be heterozygotes.

As it turned out, most of those Tay-Sachs grandparents had died of the usual causes: heart disease, stroke, cancer, and diabetes. But strikingly, only one of the 306 grandparents had died of tuberculosis, even though TB was generally one of the big killers in these grandparents' time. Indeed, among the general population of large Eastern European cities in the early twentieth century, TB caused up to 20 percent of all deaths.

This big discrepancy suggested that

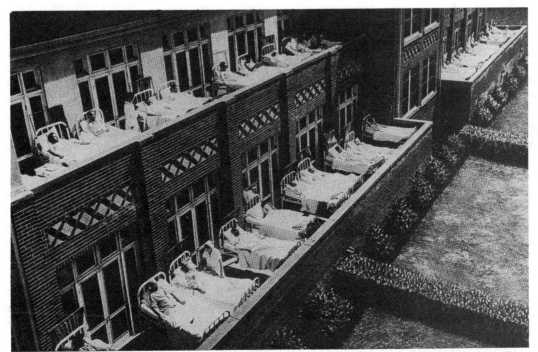

Records at a Jewish TB sanatorium in Denver indicated that among patients born in Europe between 1860 and 1910, Jews from Austria and Hungary were overrepresented. (Photo credit: AMC Cancer Research Center, Denver)

Tay-Sachs heterozygotes might somehow have been protected against TB. Interestingly, it was already well known that Ashkenazim in general had some such protection: even when Jews and non-Jews were compared within the same European city, class, and occupational group (for example, Warsaw garment workers), Jews had only half the TB death rate on non-Jews, despite their being equally susceptible to infection. Perhaps, one could reason, the Tay-Sachs gene furnished part of that well-established Jewish resistance.

A second clue to a heterozygote advantage conveyed by the Tay-Sachs gene emerged in 1983, with a fresh look at the data concerning the distributions of TB and the Tay-Sachs gene within Europe. The statistics showed that the Tay-Sachs gene was nearly three times more frequent among Jews originating from Austria, Hungary, and Czechoslovakia—areas where an amazing 9 to 10 percent of the population were heterozygotes—than among Jews from Poland, Russia, and Germany. At the same time records from an old Jewish TB sanatorium in Denver in 1904 showed that among patients born in Europe between 1860 and 1910, Jews from Austria and Hungary were overrepresented.

Initially, in putting together these two pieces of information, you might be tempted to conclude that because the highest frequency of the Tay-Sachs gene appeared in the same geographic region that produced the most cases of TB, the gene in fact offers no protection whatsoever. Indeed, this was precisely the mistaken conclusion of many researchers who had looked at these data before. But you have to pay careful attention to the numbers here: even at its highest frequency the Tay-Sachs gene was carried by far fewer people than would be infected by TB. What the statistics really indicate is that where TB is the biggest threat, natural selection produces the biggest response.

Think of it this way: You arrive at an island where you find that all the inhabitants of the north end wear suits of armor, while all the inhabitants of the south end wear only cloth shirts. You'd be pretty safe in assuming that warfare is more prevalent in the north—and that war-related injuries account for far more deaths there than in the south. Thus, if the Tay-Sachs gene does indeed lend heterozygotes some protection against TB, you would expect to find the gene most often precisely where you find TB most often. Similarly, the sickle-cell gene reaches its highest frequencies in those parts of Africa where malaria is the biggest risk.

But you may believe there's still a hole in the argument: If Tay-Sachs heterozygotes are protected against TB, you may be asking, why is the gene common just in the Ashkenazim? Why did it not become common in the non-Jewish populations also exposed to TB in Austria, Hungary, and Czechoslovakia?

At this point we must recall the peculiar circumstances in which the Jews of Eastern Europe were forced to live. They were unique among the world's ethnic groups in having been virtually confined to towns for most of the past 2,000 years. Being forbidden to own land, Eastern European Jews were not peasant farmers living in the countryside, but businesspeople forced to live in crowded ghettos, in an environment where tuberculosis thrived.

Of course, until recent improvements in sanitation, these towns were not very healthy places for non-Jews either. Indeed, their populations couldn't sustain themselves: deaths exceeded births, and the number of dead had to be balanced by continued emigration from the countryside. For non-Jews, therefore, there was no genetically distinct urban population. For ghetto-bound Jews, however, there could be no emigration from the countryside; thus the Jewish population was under the strongest selection to evolve genetic resistance to TB.

Those are the conditions that probably led to Jewish TB resistance, whatever particular genetic factors prove to underlie it. I'd speculate that G_{M2} and related fats accumulate at slightly higher-than-normal levels in heterozygotes, although not at the lethal levels seen in homozygotes. (The fat accumulation in heterozygotes probably takes place in the cell membrane, the cell's "armor.") I'd also speculate that the accumulation provides heterozygotes with some protection against TB, and that's why the genes for Tay-Sachs, Gaucher's, and Niemann-Pick disease reached high frequencies in the Ashkenazim.

Having thus stated the case, let me make clear that I don't want to overstate it. The evidence is still speculative. Depending on how you do the calculation, the low frequency of TB deaths in Tay-Sachs grandparents either barely reaches or doesn't quite reach the level of proof that statisticians require to accept an effect as real rather than as one that's arisen by chance. Moreover, we have no idea of the biochemical mechanism by which fat accumulation might confer resistance against TB. For the moment, I'd say that the evidence points to some selective advantage of Tay-Sachs heterozygotes among the Ashkenazim, and that TB resistance is the only plausible hypothesis yet proposed.

For now Tay-Sachs remains a speculative model for the evolution of ethnic diseases. But it's already a proven model of what to do about them. Twenty years ago a test was developed to identify Tay-Sachs heterozygotes, based on their lower-than-normal levels of hexosaminidase A. The test is simple, cheap, and accurate: all I did was to donate a small sample of my blood, pay $35, and wait a few days to receive the results.

If that test shows that at least one member of a couple is not a Tay-Sachs heterozygotre, then any child of theirs can't be a Tay-Sachs homozygote. If both parents prove to be heterozygotes, there's a one-in-four chance of their child being a homozygote; that can then be determined by other tests performed on the mother early in pregnancy. If the results are positive, it's early enough for her to abort, should she choose to. That critical bit of knowledge has enabled parents who had gone through the agony of bearing a Tay-Sachs baby and watching him die to find the courage to try again.

The Tay-Sachs screening program launched in the United States in 1971 was targeted at the high-risk population: Ashkenazic Jewish couples of childbearing age. So successful has this approach been that the number of Tay-Sachs babies born each year in this country has declined tenfold. Today, in fact, more Tay-Sachs cases appear here in non-Jews than in Jews, because only the latter couples are routinely tested. Thus, what used to be the classic genetic disease of Jews is so no longer.

There's also a broader message to the Tay-Sachs story. We commonly refer to the United States as a melting pot, and in many ways that metaphor is apt. But in other ways we're not a melting pot, and we won't be for a long time. Each ethnic group has some characteristic genes of its own, a legacy of its distinct history. Tuberculosis and malaria are not major causes of death in the United States, but the genes that some of us evolved to protect ourselves against them are still frequent. Those genes are frequent only in certain ethnic groups, though, and they'll be slow to melt through the population.

With modern advances in molecular genetics, we can expect to see more, not less, ethnically targeted practice of medicine. Genetic screening for cystic fibrosis in European whites, for example, is one program that has been much discussed recently; when it comes, it will surely be based on the Tay-Sachs experience. Of course, what that may mean someday is more anxiety-ridden parents-to-be glowering at more dedicated genetics counselors. It will also mean fewer babies doomed to the agonies of diseases we may understand but that we'll never be able to accept.

The Arrow of Disease

When Columbus and his successors invaded the Americas, the most potent weapon they carried was their germs. But why didn't deadly disease flow in the other direction, from the New World to the Old?

Jared Diamond

Jared Diamond is a contributing editor of Discover, *a professor of physiology at the UCLA School of Medicine, a recipient of a MacArthur genius award, and a research associate in ornithology at the American Museum of Natural History. Expanded versions of many of his* Discover *articles appear in his book* The Third Chimpanzee: The Evolution and Future of the Human Animal, *which won Britain's 1992* copus *prize for best science book. Not least among his many accomplishments was his rediscovery in 1981 of the long-lost bowerbird of New Guinea. Diamond wrote about pseudohermaphrodites for* Discover*'s special June issue on the science of sex.*

The three people talking in the hospital room were already stressed out from having to cope with a mysterious illness, and it didn't help at all that they were having trouble communicating. One of them was the patient, a small, timid man, sick with pneumonia caused by an unidentified microbe and with only a limited command of the English language. The second, acting as translator, was his wife, worried about her husband's condition and frightened by the hospital environment. The third person in the trio was an inexperienced young doctor, trying to figure out what might have brought on the strange illness. Under the stress, the doctor was forgetting everything he had been taught about patient confidentiality. He com-

mitted the awful blunder of requesting the woman to ask her husband whether he'd had any sexual experiences that might have caused the infection.

As the young doctor watched, the husband turned red, pulled himself together so that he seemed even smaller, tried to disappear under his bed sheets, and stammered in a barely audible voice. His wife suddenly screamed in rage and drew herself up to tower over him. Before the doctor could stop her, she grabbed a heavy metal bottle, slammed it onto her husband's head, and stormed out of the room. It took a while for the doctor to elicit, through the man's broken English, what he had said to so enrage his wife. The answer slowly emerged: he had admitted to repeated intercourse with sheep on a recent visit to the family farm; perhaps that was how he had contracted the mysterious microbe.

This episode, related to me by a physician friend involved in the case, sounds so bizarrely one of a kind as to be of no possible broader significance. But in fact it illustrates a subject of great importance: human diseases of animal origins. Very few of us may love sheep in the carnal sense. But most of us platonically love our pet animals, like our dogs and cats; and as a society; we certainly appear to have an inordinate fondness for sheep and other livestock, to judge from the vast numbers of them that we keep.

Some of us—most often our children—pick up infectious diseases from our pets. Usually these illnesses remain

no more than a nuisance, but a few have evolved into far more. The major killers of humanity throughout our recent history—smallpox, flu, tuberculosis, malaria, plague, measles, and cholera—are all infectious diseases that arose from diseases of animals. Until World War II more victims of war died of microbes than of gunshot or sword wounds. All those military histories glorifying Alexander the Great and Napoleon ignore the ego-deflating truth: the winners of past wars were not necessarily those armies with the best generals and weapons, but those bearing the worst germs with which to smite their enemies.

The grimmest example of the role of germs in history is much on our minds this month, as we recall the European conquest of the Americas that began with Columbus's voyage of 1492. Numerous as the Indian victims of the murderous Spanish conquistadores were, they were dwarfed in number by the victims of murderous Spanish microbes. These formidable conquerors killed an estimated 95 percent of the New World's pre-Columbian Indian population.

Why was the exchange of nasty germs between the Americas and Europe so unequal? Why didn't the reverse happen instead, with Indian diseases decimating the Spanish invaders, spreading back across the Atlantic, and causing a 95 percent decline in *Europe's* human population?

Similar questions arise regarding the decimation of many other native peoples by European germs, and regarding the decimation of would-be European conquistadores in the tropics of Africa and Asia.

Naturally, we're disposed to think about diseases from our own point of view: What can we do to save ourselves and to kill the microbes? Let's stamp out the scoundrels, and never mind what *their* motives are!

In life, though, one has to understand the enemy to beat him. So for a moment, let's consider disease from the microbes' point of view. Let's look beyond our anger at their making us sick in bizarre ways, like giving us genital sores or diarrhea, and ask why it is that they do such things. After all, microbes are as much a product of natural selection as we are, and so their actions must have come about because they confer some evolutionary benefit.

Basically, of course, evolution selects those individuals that are most effective at producing babies and at helping those babies find suitable places to live. Microbes are marvels at this latter requirement. They have evolved diverse ways of spreading from one person to another, and from animals to people. Many of our symptoms of disease actually represent ways in which some clever bug modifies our bodies or our behavior such that we become enlisted to spread bugs.

The most effortless way a bug can spread is by just waiting to be transmitted passively to the next victim. That's the strategy practiced by microbes that wait for one host to be eaten by the next—salmonella bacteria, for example, which we contract by eating already-infected eggs or meat; or the worm responsible for trichinosis, which waits for us to kill a pig and eat it without properly cooking it.

As a slight modification of this strategy; some microbes don't wait for the old host to die but instead hitchhike in the saliva of an insect that bites the old host and then flies to a new one. The free ride may be provided by mosquitoes, fleas, lice, or tsetse flies, which spread malaria, plague, typhus, and sleeping sickness, respectively. The

dirtiest of all passive-carriage tricks is perpetrated by microbes that pass from a woman to her fetus—microbes such as the ones responsible for syphilis, rubella (German measles), and AIDS. By their cunning these microbes can already be infecting an infant before the moment of its birth.

Other bugs take matters into their own hands, figuratively speaking. They actively modify the anatomy or habits of their host to accelerate their transmission. From our perspective, the open genital sores caused by venereal diseases such as syphilis are a vile indignity. From the microbes' point of view, however, they're just a useful device to enlist a host's help in inoculating the body cavity of another host with microbes. The skin lesions caused by smallpox similarly spread microbes by direct or indirect body contact (occasionally very indirect, as when U.S. and Australian whites bent on wiping out "belligerent" native peoples sent them gifts of blankets previously used by smallpox patients).

From our viewpoint, diarrhea and coughing are "symptoms" of disease. From a bug's viewpoint, they're clever evolutionary strategies to broadcast the bug. That's why it's in the bug's interests to make us "sick."

More vigorous yet is the strategy practiced by the influenza, common cold, and pertussis (whooping cough) microbes, which induce the victim to cough or sneeze, thereby broadcasting the bugs toward prospective new hosts. Similarly the cholera bacterium induces a massive diarrhea that spreads bacteria into the water supplies of potential new victims. For modification of a host's behavior, though, nothing matches the rabies virus, which not only gets into the saliva of an infected dog but drives the dog into a frenzy of

biting and thereby infects many new victims.

Thus, from our viewpoint, genital sores, diarrhea, and coughing are "symptoms" of disease. From a bug's viewpoint, they're clever evolutionary strategies to broadcast the bug. That's why it's in the bug's interests to make us "sick." But what does it gain by killing us? That seems self-defeating, since a microbe that kills its host kills itself.

Though you may well think it's of little consolation, our death is really just an unintended by-product of host symptoms that promote the efficient transmission of microbes. Yes, an untreated cholera patient may eventually die from producing diarrheal fluid at a rate of several gallons a day. While the patient lasts, though, the cholera bacterium profits from being massively disseminated into the water supplies of its next victims. As long as each victim thereby infects, on average, more than one new victim, the bacteria will spread, even though the first host happens to die.

So much for the dispassionate examination of the bug's interests. Now let's get back to considering our own selfish interests: to stay alive and healthy, best done by killing the damned bugs. One common response to infection is to develop a fever. Again, we consider fever a "symptom" of disease, as if it developed inevitably without serving any function. But regulation of body temperature is under our genetic control, and a fever doesn't just happen by accident. Because some microbes are more sensitive to heat than our own bodies are, by raising our body temperature we in effect try to bake the bugs to death before we get baked ourselves.

Another common response is to mobilize our immune system. White blood cells and other cells actively seek out and kill foreign microbes. The specific antibodies we gradually build up against a particular microbe make us less likely to get reinfected once we are cured. As we all know there are some illnesses, such as flu and the common cold, to which our resistance is only temporary; we can eventually contract the illness again. Against other illnesses, though—including measles, mumps, rubella, pertussis, and the now-defeated menace of smallpox—antibodies stimulated by one infection confer lifelong immunity. That's the principle behind vaccination—to stimulate our antibody production without our having to go through the actual experience of the disease.

Alas, some clever bugs don't just cave in to our immune defenses. Some have learned to trick us by changing their antigens, those molecular pieces of the microbe that our antibodies recognize. The constant evolution or recycling of new strains of flu, with differing antigens, explains why the flu you got two years ago didn't protect you against the different strain that arrived this year. Sleeping sickness is an even more slippery customer in its ability to change its antigens rapidly.

We and our pathogens are now locked in an escalating evolutionary contest, with the death of one contestant the price of defeat, and with natural selection playing the role of umpire.

Among the slipperiest of all is the virus that causes AIDS, which evolves new antigens even as it sits within an individual patient, until it eventually overwhelms the immune system.

Our slowest defensive response is through natural selection, which changes the relative frequency with which a gene appears from generation to generation. For almost any disease some people prove to be genetically more resistant than others. In an epidemic, those people with genes for resistance to that particular microbe are more likely to survive than are people lacking such genes. As a result, over the course of history human populations repeatedly exposed to a particular pathogen tend to be made up of individuals with genes that resist the

appropriate microbe just because unfortunate individuals without those genes were less likely to survive to pass their genes on to their children.

Fat consolation, you may be thinking. This evolutionary response is not one that does the genetically susceptible dying individual any good. It does mean, though, that a human population as a whole becomes better protected.

In short, many bugs have had to evolve tricks to let them spread among potential victims. We've evolved counter-tricks, to which the bugs have responded by evolving counter-counter-tricks. We and our pathogens are now locked in an escalating evolutionary contest, with the death of one contestant the price of defeat, and with natural selection playing the role of umpire.

The form that this deadly contest takes varies with the pathogens: for some it is like a guerrilla war, while for others it is a blitzkrieg. With certain diseases, like malaria or hook-worm, there's a more or less steady trickle of new cases in an affected area, and they will appear in any month of any year. Epidemic diseases, though, are different: they produce no cases for a long time, then a whole wave of cases, then no more cases again for a while.

Among such epidemic diseases, influenza is the most familiar to Americans, this year having been a particularly bad one for us (but a great year for the influenza virus). Cholera epidemics come at longer intervals, the 1991 Peruvian epidemic being the first one to reach the New World during the twentieth century. Frightening as today's influenza and cholera epidemics are, though, they pale beside the far more terrifying epidemics of the past, before the rise of modern medicine. The greatest single epidemic in human history was the influenza wave that killed 21 million people at the end of the First World War. The black death, or bubonic plague, killed one-quarter of Europe's population between 1346 and 1352, with death tolls up to 70 percent in some cities.

The infectious diseases that visit us as epidemics share several characteristics. First, they spread quickly and efficiently from an infected person to nearby healthy people, with the result that the whole population gets exposed within a short time. Second, they're "acute" illnesses: within a short time, you either die or recover completely. Third, the fortunate ones of us who do recover develop antibodies that leave us immune against a recurrence of the disease for a long time, possibly our entire lives. Finally, these diseases tend to be restricted to humans; the bugs causing them tend not to live in the soil or in other animals. All four of these characteristics apply to what Americans think of as the once more-familiar acute epidemic diseases of childhood, including measles, rubella, mumps, pertussis, and smallpox.

It is easy to understand why the combination of those four characteristics tends to make a disease run in epidemics. The rapid spread of microbes and the rapid course of symptoms mean that everybody in a local human population is soon infected, and thereafter either dead or else recovered and immune. No one is left alive who could still be infected. But since the microbe can't survive except in the bodies of living people, the disease dies out until a new crop of babies reaches the susceptible age—and until an infectious person arrives from the outside to start a new epidemic.

A classic illustration of the process is given by the history of measles on the isolated Faeroe Islands in the North Atlantic. A severe epidemic of the disease reached the Faeroes in 1781, then died out, leaving the islands measles-free until an infected carpenter arrived on a ship from Denmark in 1846. Within three months almost the whole Faeroes population—7,782 people—had gotten measles and then either died or recovered, leaving the measles virus to disappear once again until the next epidemic. Studies show that measles is likely to die out in any human population numbering less than half a million people. Only in larger populations can measles shift from one local area to another, thereby persisting until enough babies have been born in the originally infected area to permit the disease's return.

Rubella in Australia provides a similar example, on a much larger scale. As of 1917 Australia's population was still only 5 million, with most people living in scattered rural areas. The sea voyage to Britain took two months, and land transport within Australia itself was slow. In effect, Australia didn't even consist of a population of 5 million, but of hundreds of much smaller populations. As a result, rubella hit Australia only as occasional epidemics, when an infected person happened to arrive from overseas and stayed in a densely populated area. By 1938, though, the city of Sydney alone had a population of over one million, and people moved frequently and quickly by air between London, Sydney, and other Australian cities. Around then, rubella for the first time was able to establish itself permanently in Australia.

What's true for rubella in Australia is true for most familiar acute infectious diseases throughout the world. To sustain themselves, they need a human population that is sufficiently numerous and densely packed that a new crop of susceptible children is available for infection by the time the disease would otherwise be waning. Hence measles and other such diseases are also known as "crowd diseases."

Crowd diseases could not sustain themselves in small bands of hunter-gatherers and slash-and-burn farmers. As tragic recent experience with Amazonian Indians and Pacific Islanders confirms, almost an entire tribelet may be wiped out by an epidemic brought by an outside visitor, because no one in the tribelet has any antibodies against the microbe. In addition, measles and some other "childhood" diseases are more likely to kill infected adults than children, and all adults in the tribelet are susceptible. Having killed most of the tribelet, the epidemic then disappears. The small population size explains why tribelets can't sustain epidemics introduced from the outside; at the same time it explains why they could never evolve epidemic diseases of their own to give back to the visitors.

That's not to say that small human populations are free from all infectious diseases. Some of their infections are caused by microbes capable of maintaining themselves in animals or in soil, so the disease remains constantly available to infect people. For example, the yellow fever virus is carried by African wild monkeys and is constantly available to infect rural human populations of Africa. It was also available to be carried to New World monkeys and people by the transatlantic slave trade.

Other infections of small human populations are chronic diseases, such as leprosy and yaws, that may take a very long time to kill a victim. The victim thus remains alive as a reservoir of microbes to infect other members of the tribelet. Finally, small human populations are susceptible to nonfatal infections against which we don't develop immunity, with the result that the same person can become reinfected after recovering. That's the case with hookworm and many other parasites.

All these types of diseases, characteristic of small, isolated populations, must be the oldest diseases of humanity. They were the ones that we could evolve and sustain through the early millions of years of our evolutionary history, when the total human population was tiny and fragmented. They are also shared with, or are similar to the diseases of, our closest wild relatives, the African great apes. In contrast, the evolution of our crowd diseases could only have occurred with the buildup of large, dense human populations, first made possible by the rise of agriculture about 10,000 years ago, then by the rise of cities several thousand years ago. Indeed, the first attested dates for many familiar infectious diseases are surprisingly recent: around 1600 B.C. for smallpox (as deduced from pockmarks on an Egyptian mummy), 400 B.C. for mumps, 1840 for polio, and 1959 for AIDS.

Agriculture sustains much higher human population densities than does hunting and gathering—on average, 10 to 100 times higher. In addition, hunter-gatherers frequently shift camp,

leaving behind their piles of feces with their accumulated microbes and worm larvae. But farmers are sedentary and live amid their own sewage, providing microbes with a quick path from one person's body into another person's drinking water. Farmers also become surrounded by disease-transmitting rodents attracted by stored food.

Some human populations make it even easier for their own bacteria and worms to infect new victims, by intentionally gathering their feces and urine and spreading it as fertilizer on the fields where people work. Irrigation agriculture and fish farming provide ideal living conditions for the snails carrying schistosomes, and for other flukes that burrow through our skin as we wade through the feces-laden water.

If the rise of farming was a boon for our microbes, the rise of cities was a veritable bonanza, as still more densely packed human populations festered under even worse sanitation conditions. (Not until the beginning of the twentieth century did urban populations finally become self-sustaining; until then, constant immigration of healthy peasants from the countryside was necessary to make good the constant deaths of city dwellers from crowd diseases.) Another bonanza was the development of world trade routes, which by late Roman times effectively joined the populations of Europe, Asia, and North Africa into one giant breeding ground for microbes. That's when smallpox finally reached Rome as the "plague of Antonius," which killed millions of Roman citizens between A.D. 165 and 180.

Similarly, bubonic plague first appeared in Europe as the plague of Justinian (A.D. 542–543). But plague didn't begin to hit Europe with full force, as the black death epidemics, until 1346, when new overland trading with China provided rapid transit for flea-infested furs from plague-ridden areas of Central Asia. Today our jet planes have made even the longest intercontinental flights briefer than the duration of any human infectious disease. That's how an Aerolíneas Argentinas airplane, stopping in Lima, Peru, earlier this year, managed to deliver dozens of cholera-infected people the same day to my city of Los Angeles, over 3,000 miles away. The explosive increase in world travel by Americans, and in immigration to the United States, is turning us into another melting pot—this time of microbes that we previously dismissed as just causing exotic diseases in far-off countries.

The explosive increase in world travel by Americans, and in immigration to the United States, is turning us into another melting pot— this time of microbes that we'd dismissed as causing disease in far-off countries.

When the human population became sufficiently large and concentrated, we reached the stage in our history when we could at last sustain crowd diseases confined to our species. But that presents a paradox: such diseases could never have existed before. Instead they had to evolve as new diseases. Where did those new diseases come from?

Evidence emerges from studies of the disease-causing microbes themselves. In many cases molecular biologists have identified the microbe's closest relative. Those relatives also prove to be agents of infectious crowd diseases—but ones confined to various species of domestic animals and pets! Among animals too, epidemic diseases require dense populations, and they're mainly confined to social animals that provide the necessary large populations. Hence when we domesticated social animals such as cows and pigs, they were already afflicted by epidemic diseases just waiting to be transferred to us.

For example, the measles virus is most closely related to the virus causing rinderpest, a nasty epidemic disease of cattle and many wild cud-chewing mammals. Rinderpest doesn't affect humans. Measles, in turn, doesn't affect cattle. The close similarity of the measles and rinderpest viruses suggests that the rinderpest virus transferred from cattle to humans, then became the measles virus by changing its properties to adapt to us. That transfer isn't surprising, considering how closely many peasant farmers live and sleep next to cows and their accompanying feces, urine, breath, sores, and blood. Our intimacy with cattle has been going on for the 8,000 years since we domesticated them—ample time for the rinderpest virus to discover us nearby. Other familiar infectious diseases can similarly be traced back to diseases of our animal friends.

Given our proximity to the animals we love, we must constantly be getting bombarded by animal microbes. Those invaders get winnowed by natural selection, and only a few succeed in establishing themselves as human diseases. A quick survey of current diseases lets us trace four stages in the evolution of a specialized human disease from an animal precursor.

In the first stage, we pick up animal-borne microbes that are still at an early stage in their evolution into specialized human pathogens. They don't get transmitted directly from one person to another, and even their transfer from animals to us remains uncommon. There are dozens of diseases like this that we get directly from pets and domestic animals. They include cat scratch fever from cats, leptospirosis from dogs, psittacosis from chickens and parrots, and brucellosis from cattle. We're similarly susceptible to picking up diseases from wild animals, such as the tularemia that hunters occasionally get from skinning wild rabbits.

In the second stage, a former animal pathogen evolves to the point where it does get transmitted directly between people and causes epidemics. However, the epidemic dies out for several reasons—being cured by modern medicine, stopping when everybody has been infected and died, or stopping when everybody has been infected and become immune. For example, a previously unknown disease termed *o'nyong-nyong* fever appeared in East Africa in 1959 and infected several million Africans. It probably arose from a virus of monkeys and was transmitted to humans by mosquitoes. The fact that patients recovered quickly and became immune to further attack helped cause the new disease to die out quickly.

The annals of medicine are full of diseases that sound like no known disease today but that once caused terrifying epidemics before disappearing as mysteriously as they had come. Who alive today remembers the "English sweating sickness" that swept and terrified Europe between 1485 and 1578, or the "Picardy sweats" of eighteenth- and nineteenth-century France?

A third stage in the evolution of our major diseases is represented by former animal pathogens that establish themselves in humans and that do not die out; until they do, the question of whether they will become major killers of humanity remains up for grabs. The future is still very uncertain for Lassa fever, first observed in 1969 in Nigeria and caused by a virus probably derived from rodents. Better established is Lyme disease, caused by a spirochete that we get from the bite of a tick. Although the first known human cases in the United States appeared only as recently as 1962, Lyme disease is already reaching epidemic proportions in the Northeast, on the West Coast, and in the upper Midwest. The future of AIDS, derived from monkey viruses, is even more secure, from the virus's perspective.

The final stage of this evolution is represented by the major, long-established epidemic diseases confined to humans. These diseases must have been the evolutionary survivors of far more pathogens that tried to make the jump to us from animals—and mostly failed.

Diseases represent evolution in progress, as microbes adapt by natural selection to new hosts. Compared with cows' bodies, though, our bodies offer different immune defenses and different chemistry. In that new environment, a microbe must evolve new ways to live and propagate itself.

The best-studied example of microbes evolving these new ways involves myxomatosis, which hit Australian rabbits in 1950. The myxoma virus, native to a wild species of Brazilian rabbit, was known to cause a lethal epidemic in European domestic rabbits, which are a different species. The virus was intentionally introduced to Australia in the hopes of ridding the continent of its plague of European rabbits, foolishly introduced in the nineteenth century. In the first year, myxoma produced a gratifying (to Australian farmers) 99.8 percent mortality in infected rabbits. Fortunately for the rabbits and unfortunately for the farmers, the death rate then dropped in the second year to 90 percent and eventually to 25 percent, frustrating hopes of eradicating rabbits completely from Australia. The problem was that the myxoma virus evolved to serve its own interests, which differed from the farmers' interests and those of the rabbits. The virus changed to kill fewer rabbits and to permit lethally infected ones to live longer before dying. The result was bad for Australian farmers but good for the virus: a less lethal myxoma virus spreads baby viruses to more rabbits than did the original, highly virulent myxoma.

For a similar example in humans, consider the surprising evolution of syphilis. Today we associate syphilis with genital sores and a very slowly developing disease, leading to the death of untreated victims only after many years. However, when syphilis was first definitely recorded in Europe in 1495, its pustules often covered the body from the head to the knees, caused flesh to fall off people's faces, and led to death within a few months. By 1546 syphilis had evolved into the disease with the symptoms known to us today. Apparently, just as with myxomatosis, those syphilis spirochetes evolved to keep their victims alive longer in order to transmit their spirochete offspring into more victims.

How, then, does all this explain the outcome of 1492—that Europeans conquered and depopulated the New World, instead of Native Americans conquering and depopulating Europe?

Part of the answer, of course, goes back to the invaders' technological advantages. European guns and steel swords were more effective weapons than Native American stone axes and wooden clubs. Only Europeans had ships capable of crossing the ocean and horses that could provide a decisive advantage in battle. But that's not the whole answer. Far more Native Americans died in bed than on the battlefield—the victims of germs, not of guns and swords. Those germs undermined Indian resistance by killing most Indians and their leaders and by demoralizing the survivors.

The role of disease in the Spanish conquests of the Aztec and Inca empires is especially well documented. In 1519 Cortés landed on the coast of Mexico with 600 Spaniards to conquer the fiercely militaristic Aztec Empire, which at the time had a population of many millions. That Cortés reached the Aztec capital of Tenochtitlán, escaped with the loss of "only" two-thirds of his force, and managed to fight his way back to the coast demonstrates both Spanish military advantages and the initial naïveté of the Aztecs. But when Cortés's next onslaught came, in 1521, the Aztecs were no longer naive; they fought street by street with the utmost tenacity.

What gave the Spaniards a decisive advantage this time was smallpox, which reached Mexico in 1520 with the arrival of one infected slave from Spanish Cuba. The resulting epidemic proceeded to kill nearly half the Aztecs. The survivors were demoralized by the mysterious illness that killed Indians and spared Spaniards, as if advertising the Spaniards' invincibility. By 1618 Mexico's initial population of 20 million had plummeted to about 1.6 million.

Pizarro had similarly grim luck when he landed on the coast of Peru in 1531 with about 200 men to conquer the Inca Empire. Fortunately for Pizarro, and unfortunately for the Incas, smallpox had arrived overland around 1524, killing much of the Inca population, including both Emperor Huayna Capac and his son and designated successor, Ninan Cuyoche. Because of the vacant throne, two other sons of Huayna Capac, Atahuallpa and Huáscar, became embroiled in a civil war that Pizarro exploited to conquer the divided Incas.

In the century or two following Columbus's arrival in the New World, the Indian population declined by about 95 percent. The main killers were European germs, to which the Indians had never been exposed.

When we in the United States think of the most populous New World societies existing in 1492, only the Aztecs and Incas come to mind. We forget that North America also supported populous Indian societies in the Mississippi Valley. Sadly, these societies too would disappear. But in this case conquistadores contributed nothing directly to the societies' destruction; the conquistadores' germs, spreading in advance, did everything. When De Soto marched through the Southeast in 1540, he came across Indian towns abandoned two years previously because nearly all the inhabitants had died in epidemics. However, he was still able to see some of the densely populated towns lining the lower Mississippi. By a century and a half later, though, when French settlers returned to the lower Mississippi, almost all those towns had vanished. Their relics are the great mound sites of the Mississippi Valley. Only recently have we come to realize that the mound-building societies were still largely intact when Columbus arrived, and that they collapsed between 1492 and the systematic European exploration of the Mississippi.

When I was a child in school, we were taught that North America had originally been occupied by about one million Indians. That low number helped justify the white conquest of what could then be viewed as an almost empty continent.

1. NATURAL SELECTION

However, archeological excavations and descriptions left by the first European explorers on our coasts now suggest an initial number of around 20 million. In the century or two following Columbus's arrival in the New World, the Indian population is estimated to have declined by about 95 percent.

The main killers were European germs, to which the Indians had never been exposed and against which they therefore had neither immunologic nor genetic resistance. Smallpox, measles, influenza, and typhus competed for top rank among the killers. As if those were not enough, pertussis, plague, tuberculosis, diphtheria, mumps, malaria, and yellow fever came close behind. In countless cases Europeans were actually there to witness the decimation that occurred when the germs arrived. For example, in 1837 the Mandan Indian tribe, with one of the most elaborate cultures in the Great Plains, contracted smallpox thanks to a steamboat traveling up the Missouri River from St. Louis. The population of one Mandan village crashed from 2,000 to less than 40 within a few weeks.

The one-sided exchange of lethal germs between the Old and New worlds is among the most striking and consequence-laden facts of recent history. Whereas over a dozen major infectious diseases of Old World origins became established in the New World, not a single major killer reached Europe from the Americas. The sole possible exception is syphilis, whose area of origin still remains controversial.

That one-sidedness is more striking with the knowledge that large, dense human populations are a prerequisite for the evolution of crowd diseases. If recent reappraisals of the pre-Columbian New World population are correct, that population was not far below the contemporaneous population of Eurasia. Some New World cities, like Tenochtitlán, were among the world's most populous cities at the time. Yet Tenochtitlán didn't have awful germs waiting in store for the Spaniards. Why not?

One possible factor is that the rise of dense human populations began somewhat later in the New World than in the Old. Another is that the three most populous American centers—the Andes, Mexico, and the Mississippi Valley—were never connected by regular fast trade into one gigantic breeding ground for microbes, in the way that Europe, North Africa, India, and China became connected in late Roman times.

The main reason becomes clear, however, if we ask a simple question: From what microbes could any crowd diseases of the Americas have evolved? We've seen that Eurasian crowd diseases evolved from diseases of domesticated herd animals. Significantly, there were many such animals in Eurasia. But there were only five animals that became domesticated in the Americas: the turkey in Mexico and parts of North America, the guinea pig and llama/alpaca (probably derived from the same original wild species) in the Andes, the Muscovy duck in tropical South America, and the dog throughout the Americas.

That extreme paucity of New World domestic animals reflects the paucity of wild starting material. About 80 percent of the big wild mammals of the Americas became extinct at the end of the last ice age, around 11,000 years ago, at approximately the same time that the first well-attested wave of Indian hunters spread over the Americas. Among the species that disappeared were ones that would have yielded useful domesticates, such as American horses and camels. Debate still rages as to whether those extinctions were due to climate changes or to the impact of Indian hunters on prey that had never seen humans. Whatever the reason, the extinctions removed most of the basis for Native American animal domestication—and for crowd diseases.

The few domesticates that remained were not likely sources of such diseases. Muscovy ducks and turkeys don't live in enormous flocks, and they're not naturally endearing species (like young lambs) with which we have much physical contact. Guinea pigs may have contributed a trypanosome infection like Chagas' disease or leishmaniasis to our catalog of woes, but

that's uncertain. Initially the most surprising absence is of any human disease derived from llamas (or alpacas), which are tempting to consider as the Andean equivalent of Eurasian livestock. However, llamas had three strikes against them as a source of human pathogens: their wild relatives don't occur in big herds as do wild sheep, goats, and pigs; their total numbers were never remotely as large as the Eurasian populations of domestic livestock, since llamas never spread beyond the Andes; and llamas aren't as cuddly as piglets and lambs and aren't kept in such close association with people. (You may not think of piglets as cuddly, but human mothers in the New Guinea highlands often nurse them, and they frequently live right in the huts of peasant farmers.)

The importance of animal-derived diseases for human history extends far beyond the Americas. Eurasian germs played a key role in decimating native peoples in many other parts of the world as well, including the Pacific islands, Australia, and southern Africa. Racist Europeans used to attribute those conquests to their supposedly better brains. But no evidence for such better brains has been forthcoming. Instead, the conquests were made possible by Europeans nastier germs, and by the technological advances and denser populations that Europeans ultimately acquired by means of their domesticated plants and animals.

So on this 500th anniversary of Columbus's discovery, let's try to regain our sense of perspective about his hotly debated achievements. There's no doubt that Columbus was a great visionary, seaman, and leader. There's also no doubt that he and his successors often behaved as bestial murderers. But those facts alone don't fully explain why it took so few European immigrants to initially conquer and ultimately supplant so much of the native population of the Americas. Without the germs Europeans brought with them—germs that were derived from their animals—such conquests might have been impossible.

The Future of AIDS

*New research suggests HIV is not a new virus but an old one that grew deadly.
Can we turn the process around?*

Geoffrey Cowley

Ten years ago, Benjamin B. got what might have been a death sentence. Hospitalized for colon surgery, the Australian retiree received a blood transfusion tainted with the AIDS virus. That he's alive at all is remarkable, but that's only half of the story. Unlike most long-term HIV survivors, he has suffered no symptoms and no loss of immune function. He's as healthy today as he was in 1983—and celebrating his 81st birthday. Benjamin B. is just one of five patients who came to the attention of Dr. Brett Tindall, an AIDS researcher at the University of New South Wales, as he was preparing a routine update on transfusion-related HIV infections last year. All five were infected by the same donor. And seven to 10 years later, none has suffered any effects.

The donor turned out to be a gay man who had contracted the virus during the late 1970s or early '80s, then given blood at least 26 times before learning he was infected. After tracking him down, Tindall learned, to his amazement, that the man was just as healthy as the people who got his blood. "We know that HIV causes AIDS," Tindall says. "We also know that a few patients remain well for long periods, but we've never known why. Is it the vitamins they take? Is it some gene they have in common? This work suggests it has more to do with the virus. I think we've found a harmless strain."

He may also have found the viral equivalent of a fossil, a clue to the origin, evolution and future of the AIDS epidemic. HIV may not be a new and inherently deadly virus, as is commonly assumed, but an old one that has recently acquired deadly tendencies. In a forthcoming book, Paul Ewald, an evolutionary biologist at Amherst College, argues that HIV may have infected people benignly for decades, even centuries, before it started causing AIDS. He traces its virulence to the social upheavals of the 1960s and '70s, which not only sped its movement through populations but rewarded it for reproducing more aggressively within the body.

The idea may sound radical, but it's not just flashy speculation. It reflects a growing awareness that parasites, like everything else in nature, evolve by natural selection, changing their character to adapt to their environments. Besides transforming our understanding of AIDS, the new view could yield bold strategies for fighting it. Viruses can evolve tens of thousands of times faster than plants or animals, and few evolve as fast as HIV. Confronted by a drug or an immune reaction, the virus readily mutates out of its range. A few researchers are now trying to exploit that very talent, using drugs to force HIV to mutate until it can no longer function. A Boston team, led by medical student Yung-Kang Chow, made headlines last month by showing that the technique works perfectly in a test tube. Human trials are now in the works, but better drug treatment isn't the only hope rising from an evolutionary outlook. If rapid spread is what turned HIV into a killer, then condoms and clean needles may ultimately do more than prevent new infections. Used widely enough, they might drive the AIDS virus toward the benign form sighted in Australia.

I. WHERE DID HIV COME FROM?

Viruses are the ultimate parasites. Unlike bacteria, which absorb nutrients, excrete waste and reproduce by dividing, they have no life of their own. They're mere shreds of genetic information, encoded in DNA or RNA, that can integrate themselves into a living cell and use its machinery to run off copies of themselves. Where the first one came from is anyone's guess, but today's viruses are, like any plant or animal, simply descendants of earlier forms.

Most scientists agree that the human immunodeficiency viruses—HIV-1 and HIV-2—are basically ape or monkey viruses. Both HIVs are genetically similar to viruses found in African primates, the so called SIVs. In fact, as the accompanying tree illustrates, the HIVs have more in common with simian viruses than they do with each other. HIV-2, found mainly in West Africa, is so similar to the SIV that infects the sooty mangabey—an ash-colored monkey from the same region—that it doesn't really qualify as a separate viral species. "When you see HIV-2," says Gerald Myers, head of the HIV database project at the Los

1. NATURAL SELECTION

Alamos National Laboratory, "you may not be looking at a human virus but at a mangabey virus in a human." HIV-1, the virus responsible for the vast majority of the world's AIDS cases, bears no great resemblance to HIV-2 or the monkey SIVs, but it's very similar to SIV cpz, a virus recovered in 1990 from a wild chimpanzee in the West African nation of Gabon.

The prevailing theory holds that humans were first infected through direct contact with primates, and that the SIVs they contracted have since diverged by varying degrees from their ancestors. It's possible, of course, that the HIVs and SIVs evolved separately, or even that humans were the original carriers. But the primates-to-people scenario has a couple of points in its favor. First, the SIVs are more varied than the HIVs, which suggests they've been evolving longer. Second, it's easier to imagine people being infected by chimps or monkeys than vice versa. Humans have hunted and handled other primates for thousands of years. Anyone who was bitten or scratched, or who cut himself butchering an animal, could have gotten infected.

Until recently, it was unclear whether people could contract SIV directly from primates, but a couple of recent accidents have settled that issue. In one case, reported last summer by the Centers for Disease Control, a lab technician at a primate-research center jabbed herself with a needle containing blood from an infected macaque. The infection didn't take—she produced antibodies to SIV only for a few months—but she was just lucky. Another lab worker, who handled monkey tissues while suffering from skin lesions, has remained SIV-positive for two years. In a recent survey of 472 blood samples drawn from primate handlers, health officials found that three of those tested positive as well. No one knows whether the people with SIV eventually develop AIDS, but the potential for cross-species transmission is now clear.

Far less clear is when the first such transmission took place. The most common view holds that since AIDS is a new epidemic, the responsible vi-

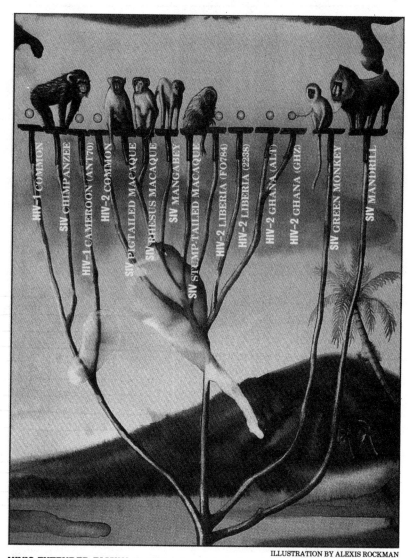

ILLUSTRATION BY ALEXIS ROCKMAN

HIV'S EXTENDED FAMILY: Today's viruses are descendants of earlier forms. This family tree shows that the human AIDS viruses, HIV–1 and HIV–2, are more closely related to viruses found in primates (the SIVs) than to each other.

ruses must have entered humans within the past few decades. That's a reasonable suspicion, but it raises a sticky question. Why, if people have been handling primates in Africa for thousands of years, did SIV take until now to jump species?

One possibility is that humans recently opened some avenue that hasn't existed in the past. Some theorists argue, for example, that AIDS was spawned by a polio-vaccination program carried out in Africa during the late 1950s. During that four-year effort, 325,000 Africans received an oral polio vaccine produced in kidney cells from African green monkeys. Even if the vaccine was contaminated with SIV—which hasn't been estab-

lished—blaming it for AIDS would be hasty. For the SIVs found in African green monkeys bear too little resemblance to HIV-1, the primary human AIDS virus, to be its likely progenitor. In order to link HIV-1 to those early lots of polio vaccine, someone would have to show that they contained a monkey virus never yet found in actual monkeys.

The alternative view—that the HIVs are old viruses—is just as hard to prove, but it requires fewer tortured assumptions. Dr. Jay Levy, an AIDS researcher at the University of California, San Francisco, puts it this way: "We know that all these other primates harbor lentiviruses [the class that includes the SIVs and HIVs]. Why should humans be any exception?" If the HIVs were on hand before the AIDS epidemic began, the key question is not where they came from but whether they always caused the disease.

II. WAS HIV ONCE LESS DEADLY?

If HIV had always caused AIDS, one would expect virus and illness to emerge together in the historical record. Antibodies to HIV have been detected in rare blood samples dating back to 1959, yet the first African AIDS cases were described in the early 1980s, when the disease started decimating the cities of Rwanda, Zaire, Zambia and Uganda. When Dr. Robert Biggar, an epidemiologist at the National Cancer Institute, pored over African hospital records looking for earlier descriptions of AIDS-like illness he didn't find any. It's possible, of course, that the disease was there all along, just too rare to be recognized as a distinct condition. But the alternative view is worth considering. There are intriguing hints that HIV hasn't always been so deadly.

Any population of living things, from fungi to rhinoceri, includes genetically varied individuals, which pass essential traits along to their progeny. As Charles Darwin discerned more than a century ago, the individuals best designed to exploit a particular environment tend to produce the greatest number of viable offspring. As generations pass, beneficial traits become more and more pervasive in the population. There's no universal recipe for reproductive success; different environments favor different traits. But by preserving some and discarding others, every environment molds the species it supports.

Viruses aren't exempt from the process. Their purpose, from a Darwinian perspective, is simply to make as many copies of themselves as they can. Other things being equal, those that replicate fastest will become the most plentiful within the host, and so stand the best chance of infecting other hosts on contact. But there's a catch. If a microbe reproduces too aggressively inside its host, or invades too many different tissues, it may kill the host—and itself—without getting passed along at all. The most successful virus, then, is not necessarily the most or the least virulent. It's one that exploits its host most effectively.

As Ewald and others have shown, that mandate can drive different microbes to very different levels of nastiness. Because they travel via social contact between people, cold and flu viruses can't normally afford to immobilize us. To stay in business, they need hosts who are out coughing, sneezing, shaking hands and sharing pencils. But the incentives change when a parasite has other ways of getting around. Consider tuberculosis or diphtheria. Both deadly diseases are caused by bacteria that can survive for weeks or months outside the body. They can reproduce aggressively in the host, ride a cough into the external environment, then wait patiently for another host to come along. By the same token, a parasite that can travel from person to person via mosquito or some other vector has little reason to be gentle. As long as malaria sufferers can still feed hungry mosquitoes, their misery is of little consequence to the microbe. Indeed, a

host who can't wield a fly swatter may be preferable to one who can.

These patterns aren't set in stone. A shift in circumstances may push a normally mild-mannered parasite toward virulence, or vice versa. One of the most devastating plagues in human history was caused by a mere influenza virus, which swept the globe in 1918, leaving 20 million corpses in its wake. Many experts still regard the disaster as an accident, triggered by the random reshuffling of viral genes. But from an evolutionary perspective, it's no coincidence that the flu grew so deadly when it did. World War I was

HIV Today and Tomorrow

Worldwide, more than 12 million people are infected with HIV. The great majority live in Africa, south of the Sahara. But as the inset shows, Asia is poised to become the plague's next epicenter.

Estimated/projected new adult HIV infections per year

ROHR—NEWSWEEK
SOURCE: WORLD HEALTH ORGANIZATION

raging in 1918. Great numbers of soldiers were huddled in the European trenches, where even the most ravaged host stood an excellent chance of infecting many others. For a flu virus, the incentives favoring restraint would have vanished in those circumstances. Rather than rendering the host useless, extreme virulence would simply make him more infectious.

Ewald suspects that HIV has recently undergone a similar transformation. Unlike influenza viruses, which infect cells in the respiratory tract and spread through coughs and sneezes, the HIVs insinuate themselves into white blood cells. Infected cells (or the new viruses they produce) can pass between people, but only during sex or other exchanges of body fluid. Confined to an isolated population where no carrier had numerous sex partners, a virus like HIV would gain nothing from replicating aggressively within the body; it would do best to lie low, leaving the host alive and mildly infectious for many years. But if people's sexual networks suddenly expanded, fresh hosts would become more plentiful, and infected hosts more dispensable. An HIV strain that replicated wildly might kill people in three years instead of 30, but by making them more infectious while they lasted, it would still come out ahead.

Is that what actually happened? There's no question that social changes have hastened the spread of HIV. Starting in the 1960s, war, tourism and commercial trucking forced the outside world on Africa's once isolated villages. At the same time, drought and industrialization prompted mass migrations from the countryside into newly teeming cities. Western monogamy had never been common in Africa, but as the French medical historian Mirko Grmek notes in his book "History of AIDS," urbanization shattered social structures that had long constrained sexual behavior. Prostitution exploded, and venereal disease flourished. Hypodermic needles came into wide use during the same period, creating yet another mode of infection. Did these trends actually turn a chronic but relatively benign infection into a killer? The evidence is circumstantial, but it's hard to discount.

If Ewald is right, and HIV's deadliness is a consequence of its rapid spread, then the nastiest strains should show up in the populations where it's moving the fastest. To a surprising degree, they do. It's well known, for example, that HIV-2 is far less virulent than HIV-1. "Going on what we've seen so far, we'd have to say that HIV-1 causes AIDS in 90 percent of those infected, while HIV-2 causes AIDS in 10 percent or less," says Harvard AIDS specialist Max Essex. "Maybe everyone infected with HIV-2 will progress to AIDS after 40 or 50 years, but that's still in the realm of reduced virulence." From Ewald's perspective, it's no surprise that HIV-2, the strain found in West Africa, is the gentle one. West Africa has escaped much of the war, drought and urbanization that fueled the spread of HIV-1 in the central and eastern parts of the continent. "HIV-2 appears to be adapted for slow transmission in areas with lower sexual contact," he concludes, "and HIV-1 for more rapid transmission in areas with higher sexual contact."

The same pattern shows up in the way each virus affects different populations. HIV-2 appears particularly mild in the stable and isolated West African nation of Senegal. After following a group of Senegalese prostitutes for six years, Harvard researchers found that those testing positive for HIV-2 showed virtually no sign of illness. In laboratory tests, researchers at the University of Alabama found that Senegalese HIV-2 didn't even kill white blood cells when allowed to infect them in a test tube. Yet HIV-2 is a killer in the more urban and less tradition-bound Ivory Coast. In a survey of hospital patients in the city of Abidjan, researchers from the U.S. Centers for Disease Control found that HIV-2 was associated with AIDS nearly as often as HIV-1.

The variations within HIV-1 are less clear-cut, but they, too, lend support to Ewald's idea. Though the evidence is mixed, there are hints that IV drug users (whose transmission rates have remained high for the past decade) may be contracting deadlier strains of HIV-1 than gay men (whose transmission rates have plummeted). In a 1990 study of infected gay men, fewer than 8 percent of those not receiving early treatment developed AIDS each year. In a more recent study of IV drug users, the proportion of untreated carriers developing AIDS each year was more than 17 percent.

Together, these disparities suggest that HIV assumes different personalities in different settings, becoming more aggressive when it's traveling rapidly through a population. But because so many factors affect the health of infected people, the strength of the connection is unclear. "This is exactly the right way to think about virulence," says virologist Stephen Morse of New York's Rockefeller University. "Virulence should be dynamic, not static. The question is, how dynamic?

A Hypothetical History of AIDS

Why did HIV suddenly emerge as a global killer? According to one theory, the virus has infected people for centuries, but recent social changes have altered its character.

BEFORE 1960
Rural Africans contracted benign ancestral forms of HIV from primates. Because the viruses spread so slowly among people, they couldn't afford to become virulent.

1960 TO 1975
War, drought, commerce and urbanization shattered African social institutions. HIV spread rapidly, becoming more virulent as transmission accelerated.

1975 TO PRESENT
Global travel placed HIV in broader circulation. Shifting sexual mores and modern medical practices, such as blood transfusion, made many populations susceptible.

THE FUTURE
If social changes can turn a benign virus deadly, the process should be reversible. Simply slowing transmission may help drive fast-killing strains out of circulation.

We know that a pathogen like HIV has a wide range of potentials, but we can't yet say just what pressures are needed to generate a particular outcome."

The best answers to Morse's question may come from laboratory studies. A handful of biologists are now devising test-tube experiments to see more precisely how transmission rates shape a parasite's character. Zoologist James Bull of the University of Texas at Austin has shown, for example, that a bacteriophage (a virus that infects bacteria) kills bacterial cells with great abandon when placed in a test tube and given plenty of new cells to infect. Like HIV in a large, active sexual network, it can afford to kill individual hosts without wiping itself out in the process. Yet the same virus becomes benign when confined to individual cells and their offspring (a situation perhaps akin to pre-epidemic HIV's). With a good animal model, researchers might someday manage to test Ewald's hypotheses about HIV with the same kind of precision.

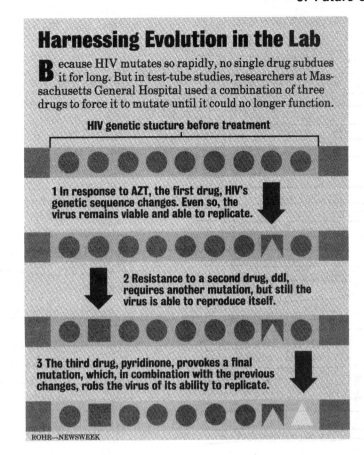

Harnessing Evolution in the Lab

Because HIV mutates so rapidly, no single drug subdues it for long. But in test-tube studies, researchers at Massachusetts General Hospital used a combination of three drugs to force it to mutate until it could no longer function.

HIV genetic stucture before treatment

1 In response to AZT, the first drug, HIV's genetic sequence changes. Even so, the virus remains viable and able to replicate.

2 Resistance to a second drug, ddI, requires another mutation, but still the virus is able to reproduce itself.

3 The third drug, pyridinone, provokes a final mutation, which, in combination with the previous changes, robs the virus of its ability to replicate.

ROHR—NEWSWEEK

III. CAN HIV BE TAMED?

Until recently, medical science seemed well on its way to controlling the microbial world. Yet after 10 years and billions of dollars in research, HIV still has scientists over a barrel. The secret of its success can be summed up in one word: mutability. Because HIV's method of replication is so error prone (its genes mutate at a million times the rate of our own), it produces extremely varied offspring, even within an individual host. Whenever a drug or immune response successfully attacks one variant, another arises to flourish in its place. Even when an AIDS drug works broadly enough to check HIV's growth, it rarely works for long. AZT, for example, can help prevent symptoms for a couple of years. But people on AZT still get AIDS, as the viral populations in their bodies evolve toward resistant forms.

There may not be a drug or vaccine on earth that could subdue such a protean parasite. But from a Darwinian perspective, killing HIV is not the only way to combat AIDS. We know the virus changes rapidly in response to outside pressures. Logic suggests that if we simply applied the right pressures—within a community, or even within a patient's body—we might begin to tame it.

It's well known that condoms and clean needles can save lives by preventing HIV infection. From an evolutionary perspective, there is every reason to think they could do more. Used widely enough, those same humble implements might push the virus toward more benevolent forms, simply by depriving virulent strains of the high transmission rates they need to survive. Gay men are already engaged in that exercise. Studies suggest that, thanks to safer sex, the rate of new infections among gays declined five to tenfold during the 1980s. There are tantalizing hints that HIV has grown less noxious in the same population over the same period. In a 1991 study, researchers at the National Institutes of Health (NIH) calculated the rates at which infected people from different risk groups were developing AIDS each year. They found that as of 1987, the rate declined sharply among gay men, suggesting the virus was taking longer to cause illness. Part of the change was due to AZT, which can delay the onset of symptoms. But when the NIH researchers corrected for AZT use, there was still a mysterious shortage of AIDS cases. From Ewald's viewpoint, the shortfall was not only unsurprising but predictable.

How far could such a trend be pushed? Would broader, better prevention efforts eventually turn today's deadliest HIV-1 into something as benign as Senegal's HIV-2? No one knows. But the prospect of domesticating the AIDS virus, even partially, should excite public-health officials. Condoms and clean needles are exceedingly cheap medicine. They can save lives even if they fail to change the course of evolution—and judging from the available evidence, they might well succeed.

In the meantime, more than 12 million people are carrying today's HIV, and those who get AIDS are still dying. Fortunately, as Yung-Kang Chow and his colleagues at Massachusetts General Hospital showed last month, there's more than one way to manipulate viral evolution. The researchers managed, in a test-tube experiment, to outsmart HIV at its own game. Their trick was to combine three drugs—AZT, ddI and pyridinone—that disarm the same part of the virus (an enzyme called reverse transcriptase).

Any of those drugs can foil HIV's efforts to colonize host cells. When HIV encounters them individually, or even in pairs, it gradually mutates into resistant forms and goes on about its business. But each mutation makes the virus slightly less efficient—and as Chow's group demonstrated, there comes a point where mutation itself hobbles the virus (see chart on previous page). By engineering an HIV mutant that contained three different mutations (one in response to each of the three drugs), the researchers ended up with a virus that was too deformed to function at all. If virgin HIV can't function in the presence of the three drugs—and if triply mutated HIV can't function at all—then the three-drug regimen should, theoretically, do wonders for patients.

It's a long way from the test tube to the clinic; many treatments have shown great promise in lab experiments, only to prove ineffective or highly toxic in people. Upcoming clinical trials will determine whether patients actually benefit from Chow's combination of drugs. The beauty of the new approach, however, is that it's not limited to any particular combination. While the Boston team experiments with drugs directed against reverse transcriptase, researchers at New York's Aaron Diamond AIDS Research Center are trying the same tack against another viral target (an enzyme called protease). "This virus has impressed us again and again with its ability to change," says Dr. David Ho, director of the Aaron Diamond Center. "It always has a new strategy to counter our efforts. Now we're asking it to make a tradeoff. We're saying, 'Go ahead and mutate, because we think that if you mutate in the right place, you'll do less damage to the patient'."

IV. CAN THE NEXT AIDS BE AVOIDED?

The forces that brought us this plague can surely bring us others. By encroaching on rain forests and wilderness areas, humanity is placing itself in ever-closer contact with other animal species and their obscure, deadly parasites. Other activities, from irrigation to the construction of dams and cities, can create new diseases by expanding the range of the rodents or insects that carry them. Stephen Morse, the Rockefeller virologist, studies the movement of microbes among populations and species, and he worries that human activities are speeding the flow of viral traffic. More than a dozen new diseases have shown up in humans since the 1960s, nearly all of them the result of once exotic parasites exploiting new opportunities. "The primary problem," Morse concludes, "is no longer virological but social."

The Ebola virus is often cited as an example of the spooky pathogens in our future. The virus first struck in August 1976, when a trader arrived at a mission hospital in northern Zaire, fever raging and blood oozing from every orifice. Within days the man died, and nearly half of the nurses at the hospital were stricken. Thirty-nine died, and as hospital patients contracted the virus, it spread to 58 neighboring villages. Ebola fever ended up striking 1,000 people in Zaire and nearby Sudan, killing 500. Epidemiologists feared it would spread more widely, but the outbreaks subsided as quickly as they had begun. From a

As Human Habits Change, New Viruses Emerge

VIRUS, DISEASE	SYMPTOMS	ORIGIN	STATUS
JUNIN Argentine Hemorrhagic Fever	Fever, muscle pain, rash, internal bleeding and, sometimes, tremors or convulsions. Mortality rate: 10 to 20 percent.	First recognized in 1953, Junin has emerged as a result of an increase in corn cultivation in northern Argentina. Carried by mice.	A rodent-control program brought the virus's Bolivian cousin, Machupo, under control, but Junin has expanded its reach in recent decades. It strikes 400 to 600 people annually.
EBOLA African Hemorrhagic Fever	Fever, vomiting, rash, muscle pain, gastrointestinal bleeding, shock. A deadly virus, Ebola kills at least half its victims.	Virtually identical to Marburg, a virus found in Germany in 1967, Ebola was first reported in 1976. Its origin is unknown.	An outbreak in Africa killed 500 in 1976. Philippine monkeys sent to a Reston, Va., research lab brought a related—but not lethal—virus here in 1989, leading to curbs on monkey imports.
DENGUE Dengue Fever	Headache, fever, muscle pain, chills. More severe dengue hemorrhagic fever can cause internal bleeding and death.	Dengue has long plagued tropical Asia, South America and the Caribbean, favoring densely populated, mosquito-infested areas.	Infects more than 30 million people annually. Rare in U.S. but could spread more widely since a shipment of used tires brought virus-transmitting Asian tiger mosquitoes ashore in 1985.
HTLVs Leukemia, TSP	Leukemia is a cancer of white blood cells which can spread to other organs. TSP is a degenerative neurological disorder.	HTLV-1 was first reported in 1980, but studies suggest that it and the related virus HTLV-2 have attacked humans for millenniums.	HTLVs are transmitted in the same manner as HIV but, so far, appear less deadly. One recent study found that up to 20 percent of IV drug users in Los Angeles are infected.

SOURCE: STEPHEN S. MORSE—THE ROCKEFELLER UNIVERSITY, PAUL EWALD—AMHERST COLLEGE

Darwinian perspective, that's no great surprise. A parasite that kills that rapidly has little chance of sustaining a chain of infection unless it can survive independently of its host.

More worrisome is a virus like HTLV, a relative of HIV that infects the same class of blood cells and is riding the same waves through new populations. Though recognized only since the 1970s, the HTLVs (HTLV-1 and HTLV-2) appear to be ancient. About one in 20 HTLV-1 infections leads eventually to leukemia, lymphoma or a paralyzing neurologic disorder called TSP. The virus is less aggressive than HIV-1—it typically takes several decades to cause any illness—but its virulence seems to vary markedly from one setting to the next. In Japan, the HTLV-related cancers typically show up in 60-year-olds who were infected by their mothers in the womb. In the Caribbean, where the virus is more often transmitted through sex, the average latency is much shorter. It's not unusual for people to develop symptoms in their 40s.

HTLV may not mutate as readily as HIV, but it is subject to the same natural forces. If human activities can turn one virus into a global killer, it's only prudent to suspect they could do the same to another. "HTLV is a threat," says Ewald, "not because it has escaped from some secluded source, but because it may evolve increased virulence." HTLV-1 is only one tenth as prevalent as HIV in the United States, but it has gained a strong foothold among IV drug users, whose shared needles are a perfect breeding ground for virulent strains.

No one knows whether HTLV could cause an epidemic like AIDS. Fortunately, we don't have to wait passively to find out. We're beginning to see how our actions mold the character of our parasites. No one saw the last epidemic coming. This time, that's not an excuse.

Racial Odyssey

Boyce Rensberger

The human species comes in an artist's palette of colors: sandy yellows, reddish tans, deep browns, light tans, creamy whites, pale pinks. It is a rare person who is not curious about the skin colors, hair textures, bodily structures and facial features associated with racial background. Why do some Africans have dark brown skin, while that of most Europeans is pale pink? Why do the eyes of most "white" people and "black" people look pretty much alike but differ so from the eyes of Orientals? Did one race evolve before the others? If so, is it more primitive or more advanced as a result? Can it be possible, as modern research suggests, that there is no such thing as a pure race? These are all honest, scientifically worthy questions. And they are central to current research on the evolution of our species on the planet Earth.

Broadly speaking, research on racial differences has led most scientists to three major conclusions. The first is that there are many more differences among people than skin color, hair texture and facial features. Dozens of other variations have been found, ranging from the shapes of bones to the consistency of ear wax to subtle variations in body chemistry.

The second conclusions is that the overwhelming evolutionary success of the human species is largely due to its great genetic variability. When migrating bands of our early ancestors

reached a new environment, at least a few already had physical traits that gave them an edge in surviving there. If the coming centuries bring significant environmental changes, as many believe they will, our chances of surviving them will be immeasurably enhanced by our diversity as a species.

There is a third conclusion about race that is often misunderstood. Despite our wealth of variation and despite our constant, everyday references to race, no one has ever discovered a reliable way of distinguishing one race from another. While it is possible to classify a great many people on the basis of certain physical features, there are no known feature or groups of features that will do the job in all cases.

Skin color won't work. Yes, most Africans from south of the Sahara and their descendants around the world have skin that is darker than that of most Europeans. But there are millions of people in India, classified by some anthropologists as members of the Caucasoid, or "white," race who have darker skins than most Americans who call themselves black. And there are many Africans living in sub-Sahara Africa today whose skins are no darker than the skins of many Spaniards, Italians, Greeks or Lebanese.

What about stature as a racial trait? Because they are quite short, on the average, African Pygmies have been considered racially distinct from other dark-skinned Africans. If stature, then, is a racial criterion, would one include

in the same race the tall African Watusi and the Scandinavians of similar stature?

The little web of skin that distinguishes Oriental eyes is said to be a particular feature of the Mongoloid race. How, then, can it be argued that the American Indian, who lacks this epicanthic fold, is Mongoloid?

Even more hopeless as racial markers are hair color, eye color, hair form, the shapes of noses and lips or any of the other traits put forth as typical of one race or another.

NO NORMS

Among the tall people of the world there are many black, many white and many in between. Among black people of the world there are many with kinky hair, many with straight or wavy hair, and many in between. Among the broad-nosed, full-lipped people of the world there are many with dark skins, many with light skins and many in between.

How did our modern perceptions of race arise? One of the first to attempt a scientific classification of peoples was Carl von Linné, better known as Linnaeus. In 1735, he published a classification that remains the standard today. As Linnaeus saw it there were four races, classifiable geographically and by skin color. The names Linnaeus gave them were *Homo sapiens Africanus nigrus* (black African human being), *H. sapiens Americanus rube-*

scens (red American human being), *H. sapiens Asiaticus fuscusens* (brownish Asian human being), and *H. sapiens Europaeus albescens* (white European human being). All, Linnaeus recognized, were members of a single human species.

A species includes all individuals that are biologically capable of interbreeding and producing fertile offspring. Most matings between species are fruitless, and even when they succeed, as when a horse and a donkey interbreed and produce a mule, the progeny are sterile. When a poodle mates with a collie, however, the offspring are fertile, showing that both dogs are members of the same species.

Even though Linnaeus's system of nomenclature survives, his classifications were discarded, especially after voyages of discovery revealed that there were many more kinds of people than could be pigeonholed into four categories. All over the world there are small populations that don't fit. Among the better known are:

- The so-called Bushmen of southern Africa, who look as much Mongoloid as Negroid.
- The Negritos of the South Pacific, who do look Negroid but are very far from Africa and have no known links to that continent.
- The Ainu of Japan, a hairy aboriginal people who look more Caucasoid than anything else.
- The Lapps of Scandinavia, who look as much like Eskimos as like Europeans.
- The aborigines of Australia, who often look Negroid but many of whom have straight or wavy hair and are often blond as children.
- The Polynesians, who seem to be a blend of many races, the proportions differing from island to island.

To accommodate such diversity, many different systems of classification have been proposed. Some set up two or three dozen races. None has ever satisfied all experts.

CLASSIFICATION SYSTEM

Perhaps the most sweeping effort to impose a classification upon all the peoples of the world was made by the American anthropologist Carleton Coon. He concluded there are five basic races, two of which have major subdivisions: Caucasoids; Mongloids; full-size Australoids (Australian aborigines); dwarf Australoids (Negritos—Andaman Islanders and similar peoples); full-size Congoids (African Negroids); dwarf Congoids (African Pygmies); and Capoids (the so-called Bushmen and Hottentots).

In his 1965 classic, *The Living Races of Man,* Coon hypothesized that before A.D. 1500 there were five pure races—five centers of human population that were so isolated that there was almost no mixing.

Each of these races evolved independently, Coon believed, diverging from a pre-*Homo sapiens* stock that was essentially the same everywhere. He speculated that the common ancestor evolved into *Homo sapiens* in five separate regions at five different times, beginning about 35,000 years ago. The populations that have been *Homo sapiens* for the shortest periods of time, Coon said, are the world's "less civilized" races.

The five pure races remained distinct until A.D. 1500; then Europeans started sailing the world, leaving their genes—as sailors always have—in every port and planting distant colonies. At about the same time, thousands of Africans were captured and forcibly settled in many parts of the New World.

That meant the end of the five pure races. But Coon and other experts held that this did not necessarily rule out the idea of distinct races. In this view, there *are* such things as races; people just don't fit into them very well anymore.

The truth is that there is really no hard evidence to suggest that five or any particular number of races evolved independently. The preponderance of evidence today suggests that as traits typical of fully modern people arose in any one place, they spread quickly to all human populations. Advances in intelligence were almost certainly the fastest to spread. Most anthropologists and geneticists now believe that human

beings have always been subject to migrating and mixing. In other words, there probably never were any such things as pure races.

Race mixing has not only been a fact of human history but is, in this day of unprecedented global mobility, taking place at a more rapid rate than ever. It is not farfetched to envision the day when, generations hence, the entire "complexion" of major population centers will be different. Meanwhile, we can see such changes taking place before our eyes, for they are a part of everyday reality.

HYBRID VIGOR

Oddly, those who assert scientific validity for their notions of pure and distinct races seem oblivious of a basic genetic principle that plant and animal breeders know well: too much inbreeding can lead to proliferation of inferior traits. Crossbreeding with different strains often produces superior combinations and "hybrid vigor."

The striking differences among people may very well be a result of constant genetic mixing. And as geneticists and ecologists know, in diversity lies strength and resilience.

To understand the origin and proliferation of human differences, one must first know how Darwinian evolution works.

Evolution is a two-step process. Step one is mutation: somehow a gene in the ovary or testes of an individual is altered, changing the molecular configuration that stores instructions for forming a new individual. The children who inherit that gene will be different in some way from their ancestors.

Step two is selection: for a racial difference, or any other evolutionary change to arise, it must survive and be passed through several generations. If the mutation confers some disadvantage, the individual dies, often during embryonic development. But if the change is beneficial in some way, the individual should have a better chance of thriving than relatives lacking the advantage.

DISEASE ORIGINS

The gene for sickle cell anemia, a disease found primarily among black people, appears to have evolved because its presence can render its bearer resistant to malaria. Such a trait would have obvious value in tropical Africa.

A person who has sickle cell anemia must have inherited genes for the disease from both parents. If a child inherits only one sickle cell gene, he or she will be resistant to malaria but will not have the anemia. Paradoxically, inheriting genes from both parents does not seem to affect resistance to malaria.

In the United States, where malaria is practically nonexistent, the sickle cell gene confers no survival advantage and is disappearing. Today only about 1 out of every 10 American blacks carries the gene.

Many other inherited diseases are found only in people from a particular area. Tay-Sachs disease, which often kills before the age of two, is almost entirely confined to Jews from parts of Eastern Europe and their descendants elsewhere. Paget's disease, a bone disorder, is found most often among those of English descent. Impacted wisdom teeth are a common problem among Asians and Europeans but not among Africans. Children of all races are able to digest milk because their bodies make lactase, the enzyme that breaks down lactose, or milk sugar. But the ability to digest lactose in adulthood is a racially distributed trait.

About 90 percent of Orientals and blacks lose this ability by the time they reach adulthood and become quite sick when they drink milk.

Even African and Asian herders who keep cattle or goats rarely drink fresh milk. Instead, they first treat the milk with fermentation bacteria that break down lactose, in a sense predigesting it. They can then ingest the milk in the form of yogurt or cheese without any problem.

About 90 percent of Europeans and their American descendants, on the other hand, continue to produce the enzyme throughout their lives and can drink milk with no ill effects.

NATURAL SELECTION

If a new trait is beneficial, it will bring reproductive success to its bearer. After several generations of multiplication, bearers of the new trait may begin to outnumber nonbearers. Darwin called this natural selection to distinguish it from the artificial selection exercised by animal breeders.

Skin color is the human racial trait most generally thought to confer an evolutionary advantage of this sort. It has long been obvious in the Old World that the farther south one goes, the darker the skin color. Southern Europeans are usually somewhat darker than northern Europeans. In North Africa, skin colors are darker still, and, as one travels south, coloration reaches its maximum at the Equator. The same progressions holds in Asia, with the lightest skins to the north. Again, as one moves south, skin color darkens, reaching in southern India a "blackness" equal to that of equatorial Africans.

This north-south spectrum of skin color derives from varying intensities of the same dark brown pigment called melanin. Skin cells simply have more or less melanin granules to be seen against a background that is pinkish because of the underlying blood vessels. All races can increase their melanin concentration by exposure to the sun.

What is it about northerly latitudes in the Northern Hemisphere that favors less pigmentation and about southerly latitudes that favors more? Exposure to intense sunlight is not the only reason why people living in southerly latitudes are dark. A person's susceptibility to rickets and skin cancer, his ability to withstand cold and to see in the dark may also be related to skin color.

The best-known explanation says the body can tolerate only a narrow range of intensities of sunlight. Too much causes sunburn and cancer, while too little deprives the body of vitamin D, which is synthesized in the skin under the influence of sunlight. A dark complexion protects the skin from the harmful effects of intense sunlight. Thus, albinos born in equatorial regions have a high rate of skin cancer. On the other hand, dark skin in northerly latitudes screens out sunlight needed for the synthesis of vitamin D. Thus, dark-skinned children living in northern latitudes had high rates of rickets—a bone-deforming disease caused by a lack of vitamin D—before their milk was routinely fortified. In the sunny tropics, dark skin admits enough light to produce the vitamin.

Recently, there has been some evidence that skin colors are linked to differences in the ability to avoid injury from the cold. Army researchers found that during the Korean War blacks were more susceptible to frostbite than were whites. Even among Norwegian soldiers in World War II, brunettes had a slightly higher incidence of frostbite than did blonds.

EYE PIGMENTATION

A third link between color and latitude involves the sensitivity of the eye to various wavelengths of light. It is known that dark-skinned people have more pigmentation in the iris of the eye and at the back of the eye where the image falls. It has been found that the less pigmented the eye, the more sensitive it is to colors at the red end of the spectrum. In situations illuminated with reddish light, the northern European can see more than a dark African sees.

It has been suggested that Europeans developed lighter eyes to adapt to the longer twilights of the North and their greater reliance on firelight to illuminate caves.

Although the skin cancer-vitamin D hypothesis enjoys wide acceptance, it may well be that resistance to cold, possession of good night vision and other yet unknown factors all played roles in the evolution of skin colors.

Most anthropologists agree that the original human skin color was dark brown, since it is fairly well established that human beings evolved in the tropics of Africa. This does not, however, mean that the first people were Negroids, whose descendants, as they moved north, evolved into light-skinned Caucasoids. It is more likely that the skin color of various populations changed several times from dark to light and back as people moved from one region to another.

Consider, for example, that long before modern people evolved, *Homo erectus* had spread throughout Africa, Europe and Asia. The immediate ancestor of *Homo sapiens, Homo erectus,* was living in Africa 1.5 million years ago and in Eurasia 750,000 years ago. The earliest known forms of *Homo sapiens* do not make their appearance until somewhere between 250,000 and 500,000 years ago. Although there is no evidence of the skin color of any hominid fossil, it is probable that the *Homo erectus* population in Africa had dark skin. As subgroups spread into northern latitudes, mutations that reduced pigmentation conferred survival advantages on them and lighter skins came to predominate. In other words, there were probably black *Homo erectus* peoples in Africa and white ones in Europe and Asia.

Did the black *Homo erectus* populations evolve into today's Negroids and the white ones in Europe into today's Caucasoids? By all the best evidence, nothing like this happened. More likely, wherever *Homo sapiens* arose it proved so superior to the *Homo erectus* populations that it eventually replaced them everywhere.

If the first *Homo sapiens* evolved in Africa, they were probably dark-skinned; those who migrated northward into Eurasia lost their pigmentation. But it is just as possible that the first *Homo sapiens* appeared in northern climes, descendants of white-skinned *Homo erectus*. These could have migrated southward toward Africa, evolving darker skins. All modern races, incidentally, arose long after the brain had reached its present size in all parts of the world.

North-south variations in pigmentation are quite common among mammals and birds. The tropical races tend to be darker in fur and feather, the desert races tend to be brown, and those near the Arctic Circle are lighter colored.

There are exceptions among humans. The Indians of the Americas, from the Arctic to the southern regions of South America, do not conform to the north-south scheme of coloration. Though most think of Indians as being reddish-brown, most Indians tend to be relatively light skinned, much like their presumed Mongoloid ancestors in Asia. The ruddy complexion that lives in so many stereotypes of Indians is merely what years of heavy tanning can produce in almost any light-skinned person. Anthropologists explain the color consistency as a consequence of the relatively recent entry of people into the Americas—probably between 12,000 and 35,000 years ago. Perhaps they have not yet had time to change.

Only a few external physical differences other than color appear to have adaptive significance. The strongest cases can be made for nose shape and stature.

WHAT'S IN A NOSE

People native to colder or drier climates tend to have longer, more beak-shaped noses than those living in hot and humid regions. The nose's job is to warm and humidify air before it reaches sensitive lung tissues. The colder or drier the air is, the more surface area is needed inside the nose to get it to the right temperature or humidity. Whites tend to have longer and beakier noses than blacks or Orientals. Nevertheless, there is great variation within races. Africans in the highlands of East Africa have longer noses than Africans from the hot, humid lowlands, for example.

Stature differences are reflected in the tendency for most northern peoples to have shorter arms, legs and torsos and to be stockier than people from the tropics. Again, this is an adaptation to heat or cold. One way of reducing heat loss is to have less body surface, in relation to weight or volume, from which heat can escape. To avoid overheating, the most desirable body is long limbed and lean. As a result, most Africans tend to be lankier than northern Europeans. Arctic peoples are the shortest limbed of all.

Hair forms may also have a practical role to play, but the evidence is weak. It has been suggested that the more tightly curled hair of Africans insulates the top of the head better than does straight or wavy hair. Contrary to expectation, black hair serves better in this role than white hair. Sunlight is absorbed and converted to heat at the outer surface of the hair blanket; it radiates directly into the air. White fur, common on Arctic animals that need to absorb solar heat, is actually transparent and transmits light into the hair blanket, allowing the heat to form within the insulating layer, where it is retained for warmth.

Aside from these examples, there is little evidence that any of the other visible differences among the world's people provide any advantage. Nobody knows, for example, why Orientals have epicanthic eye folds or flatter facial profiles. The thin lips of Caucasoids and most Mongoloids have no known advantages over the Negroid's full lips. Why should middle-aged and older Caucasoid men go bald so much more frequently than the men of other races? Why does the skin of Bushmen wrinkle so heavily in the middle and later years? Or why does the skin of Negroids resist wrinkling so well? Why do the Indian men in one part of South America have blue penises? Why do Hottentot women have such unusually large buttocks?

1. NATURAL SELECTION

There are possible evolutionary explanations for why such apparently useless differences arise.

One is a phenomenon known as sexual selection. Environmentally adaptive traits arise, Darwin thought, through natural selection—the environment itself chooses who will thrive or decline. In sexual selection, which Darwin also suggested, the choice belongs to the prospective mate.

In simple terms, ugly individuals will be less likely to find mates and reproduce their genes than beautiful specimens will. Take the blue penis as an example. Women might find it unusually attractive or perhaps believe it to be endowed with special powers. If so, a man born with a blue penis will find many more opportunities to reproduce his genes than his ordinary brothers.

Sexual selection can also operate when males compete for females. The moose with the larger antlers or the lion with the more imposing mane will stand a better chance of discouraging less well-endowed males and gaining access to females. It is possible that such a process operated among Caucasoid males, causing them to become markedly hairy, especially around the face.

ATTRACTIVE TRAITS

Anthropologists consider it probable that traits such as the epicanthic fold or the many regional differences in facial features were selected this way.

Yet another method by which a trait can establish itself involves accidental selection. It results from what biologists call genetic drift.

Suppose that in a small nomadic band a person is born with perfectly parallel fingerprints instead of the usual loops, whorls or arches. That person's children would inherit parallel fingerprints, but they would confer no survival advantages. But if our family decides to strike out on its own, it will become the founder of a new band consisting of its own descendants, all with parallel fingerprints.

Events such as this, geneticists and anthropologists believe, must have oc-

curred many times in the past to produce the great variety within the human species. Among the apparently neutral traits that differ among populations are:

Ear Wax

There are two types of ear wax. One is dry and crumbly and the other is wet and sticky. Both types can be found in every major population, but the frequencies differ. Among northern Chinese, for example, 98 percent have dry ear wax. Among American whites, only 16 percent have dry ear wax. Among American blacks the figure is 7 percent.

Scent Glands

As any bloodhound knows, every person has his or her own distinctive scent. People vary in the mixture of odoriferous compounds exuded through the skin—most of it coming from specialized glands called apocrine glands. Among whites, these are concentrated in the armpits and near the genitals and anus. Among blacks, they may also be found on the chest and abdomen. Orientals have hardly any apocrine glands at all. In the words of the Oxford biologist John R. Baker, "The Europids and Negrids are smelly, the Mongoloids scarcely or not at all." Smelliest of all are northern European, or so-called Nordic, whites. Body odor is rare in Japan. It was once thought to indicate a European in the ancestry and to be a disease requiring hospitalization.

Blood Groups

Some populations have a high percentage of members with a particular blood group. American Indians are overwhelmingly group O—100 percent in some regions. Group A is most common among Australian aborigines and the Indians in western Canada. Group B is frequent in northern India, other parts of Asia and western Africa.

Advocates of the pure-race theory once seized upon blood groups as possibly unique to the original pure races. The proportions of groups found today,

they thought, would indicate the degree of mixing. It was subsequently found that chimpanzees, our closest living relatives, have the same blood groups as humans.

Taste

PTC (phenylthiocarbamide) is a synthetic compound that some people can taste and other cannot. The ability to taste it has no known survival value, but it is clearly an inherited trait. The proportion of persons who can taste PTC varies in different populations: 50 to 70 percent of Australian aborigines can taste it, as can 60 to 80 percent of all Europeans. Among East Asians, the percentage is 83 to 100 percent, and among Africans, 90 to 97 percent.

Urine

Another indicator of differences in body chemistry is the excretion of a compound known as BAIB (beta-amino-isobutyric acid) in urine. Europeans seldom excrete large quantities, but high levels of excretion are common among Asians and American Indians. It had been shown that the differences are not due to diet.

No major population has remained isolated long enough to prevent any unique genes from eventually mixing with those of neighboring groups. Indeed, a map showing the distribution of so-called traits would have no sharp boundaries, except for coastlines. The intensity of a trait such as skin color, which is controlled by six pairs of genes and can therefore exist in many shades, varies gradually from one population to another. With only a few exceptions, every known genetic possibility possessed by the species can be found to some degree in every sizable population.

EVER-CHANGING SPECIES

One can establish a system of racial classification simply by listing the features of populations at any given moment. Such a concept of race is, however, inappropriate to a highly mobile and ever-changing species such as *Homo sapiens.* In the short view, races may seem distinguishable, but in biology's long haul, races come and go. New ones arise and blend into neighboring groups to create new and racially stable populations. In time, genes from these groups flow into other neighbors, continuing the production of new permutations.

Some anthropologists contend that at the moment American blacks should be considered a race distinct from African blacks. They argue that American blacks are a hybrid of African blacks and European whites. Indeed, the degree of mixture can be calculated on the basis of a blood component known as the Duffy factor.

In West Africa, where most of the New World's slaves came from, the Duffy factor is virtually absent. It is present in 43 percent of American whites. From the number of American blacks who are now "Duffy positive" it can be calculated that whites contributed 21 percent of the genes in the American black population. The figure is higher for blacks in northern and western states and lower in the South. By the same token, there are whites who have black ancestors. The number is smaller because of the tendency to identify a person as black even if only a minor fraction of his ancestors were originally from Africa.

The unwieldiness of race designations is also evident in places such as Mexico where most of the people are, in effect, hybrids of Indians (Mongoloid by some classifications) and Spaniards (Caucasoid). Many South American populations are tri-hybrids—mixtures of Mongoloid, Caucasoid and Negroid. Brazil is a country where the mixture has been around long enough to constitute a racially stable population. Thus, in one sense, new races have been created in the United States, Mexico and Brazil. But in the long run, those races will again change.

Sherwood Washburn, a noted anthropologist, questions the usefulness of racial classification: "Since races are open systems which are intergrading, the number of races will depend on the purpose of the classification. I think we should require people who propose a classification of races to state in the first place why they wish to divide the human species."

The very notion of a pure race, then, makes no sense. But, as evolutionists know full well, a rich genetic diversity within the human species most assuredly *does.*

Primates

Primates are fun. They are active, intelligent, colorful, emotionally expressive, and unpredictable. In other words, observing them is like holding up an opaque mirror to ourselves. The image may not be crystal clear or, indeed, what some would consider flattering, but it is certainly familiar enough to be illuminating.

Primates are, of course, but one of many orders of mammals that adaptively radiated into the variety of ecological niches vacated at the end of the Age of Reptiles about 65 million years ago. Whereas some mammals took to the sea (cetaceans), and some took to the air (chiroptera, or bats), primates are characterized by an arboreal or forested adaptation. Whereas some mammals can be identified by their food-getting habits, such as the meat-eating carnivores, primates have a penchant for eating almost anything and are best described as omnivorous. In taking to the trees, however, primates did not simply develop a full-blown set of distinguishing characteristics that set them off easily from other orders of mammals, the way the rodent order can be readily identified by its gnawing set of front teeth. Rather, each primate seems to represent degrees of anatomical, biological, and behavioral characteristics on a continuum of progress with respect to the particular traits we humans happen to be interested in.

None of this is meant to imply, of course, that the living primates are our ancestors. Since the prosimians, monkeys, and apes are our contemporaries, they are no more our ancestors than we are theirs and, as living end-products of evolution, we have all descended from a common stock in the distant past.

So, if we are interested primarily in our own evolutionary past, why study primates at all? Because, by the criteria we have set up as significant milestones in the evolution of humanity, an inherent reflection of our own bias, they have not evolved as far as we have. They and their environments, therefore, may represent glimmerings of the evolutionary stages and ecological circumstances through which our own ancestors may have gone. What we stand to gain, for instance, is an educated guess as to how our own ancestors might have appeared and behaved as semierect creatures before becoming bipedal. It is in the spirit of this type of inquiry that Robert Sapolsky ("The Young and the Reckless") asks why, in the case of "adolescent transfer," young primate males will risk life and limb to move from one troop to another. Aside from being a pleasure to observe, then, living primates can teach us something about our past.

Another reason for studying primates is that they allow us to test certain notions too often taken for granted. For instance, Barbara Smuts, in "What Are Friends For?" reveals that friendship bonds, as illustrated by the olive baboons of East Africa, have little if anything to do with a sexual division of labor or even sexual exclusivity between a pair-bonded male and female. In still another baboon study, Jeanne Altmann ("Leading Ladies") found that elderly females, regardless of rank or sex, play a leadership role at critical times in group movements. In both articles, authored by women whose research is impeccable, there is the challenge to the traditional male-oriented idea that primate societies are dominated solely by males and for males.

If nothing else, these articles show that relationships between the sexes are subject to wide variation, that the kinds of answers obtained depend upon the kinds of questions asked, and that we have to be very careful in making inferences about human beings from any one particular primate study. We may, if we are not careful, draw conclusions that say more about our own skewed perspectives than about what we claim to understand. For a more explicit exposition of these points see "Science With a Capital S" by Sy Montgomery.

Still another benefit of primate field research is that it provides us with perspectives that the bones and stones of the fossil hunters will never reveal: a sense of the richness and variety of social patterns that must have existed in the primate order for so many tens of millions of years. (See James Shreeve's article, "Machiavellian Monkeys," Sy Montgomery's article, "Dian Fossey and Digit," and Don Lessem's article, "Biruté Galdikas.")

Finally, there is a sense of urgency in the study of primates as we contemplate the dreaded possibility of their imminent extinction. We have already lost 14 species of lemurs in the past thousand years (most of which were larger than the contemporary forms), and the fate of most other free-ranging primates is in the balance. It is with considerable irony that future generations may come to envy us as having been among the first and last people to be able to observe our closest relatives in their natural habitats. If for no other reason, we need to collect as much information as we can about primates while they are still with us.

Looking Ahead: Challenge Questions

What is the role of deception among primates and how might it have led to greater intelligence?

Why is friendship important to olive baboons, and what implications does this have for the origins of pair-bonding in hominid evolution?

Under what circumstances do female baboons become "leading ladies"?

What are the advantages of a primate species of "adolescent transfer"?

What is the "new ethology" and how does it differ from previous primate field studies?

Why is the mountain gorilla in danger of extinction?

If orangutans are so intelligent, why are they of such a "different mind" than chimpanzees and gorillas?

Machiavellian Monkeys

The sneaky skills of our primate cousins suggest that we may owe our great intelligence to an inherited need to deceive.

James Shreeve

This is a story about frauds, cheats, liars, faithless lovers, incorrigible con artists, and downright thieves. You're gonna love 'em.

Let's start with a young rascal named Paul. You'll remember his type from your days back in the playground. You're minding your own business, playing on the new swing set, when along comes Paul, such a little runt that you hardly notice him sidle up to you. All of a sudden he lets out a scream like you've run him through with a white-hot barbed harpoon or something. Of course the teacher comes running, and the next thing you know you're being whisked inside with an angry finger shaking in our face. That's the end of recess for you. But look out the window: there's Paul, having a great time on *your* swing. Cute kid.

Okay, you're a little older now and a little smarter. You've got a bag of chips stashed away in your closet, where for once your older brother won't be able to find them. You're about to open the closet door when he pokes his head in the room. Quickly you pretend to be fetching your high tops; he gives you a look but he leaves. You wait a couple of minutes, lacing up the sneakers in case he walks back in, then you dive for the chips. Before you can get the bag open, he's over your shoulder, snatching it out of your hands. "Nice try, punk," he says through a mouthful,

"but I was hiding outside your room the whole time."

This sort of trickery is such a common part of human interaction that we hardly notice how much time we spend defending ourselves against it or perpetrating it ourselves. What's so special about the fakes and cheaters here, however, is that they're not human. Paul is a young baboon, and your big brother is, well, a chimpanzee. With some admittedly deceptive alterations of scenery and props, the situations have been lifted from a recent issue of *Primate Report*. The journal is the work of Richard Byrne and Andrew Whiten, two psychologists at the University of St. Andrews in Scotland, and it is devoted to cataloging the petty betrayals of monkeys and apes as witnessed by primatologists around the world. It is a testament to the evolutionary importance of what Byrne and Whiten call Machiavellian intelligence— a facility named for the famed sixteenth-century author of *The Prince,* the ultimate how-to guide to prevailing in a complex society through the judicious application of cleverness, deceit, and political acumen.

Deception is rife in the natural world. Stick bugs mimic sticks. Harmless snakes resemble deadly poisonous ones. When threatened, blowfish puff themselves up and cats arch their backs and bristle their hair to seem bigger than they really are. All these animals could be said to practice deception because they fool other animals—usu-

ally members of other species—into thinking they are something that they patently are not. Even so, it would be overreading the situation to attribute Machiavellian cunning to a blowfish, or to accuse a stick bug of being a lying scoundrel. Their deceptions, whether in their looks or in their actions, are programmed genetic responses. Biology leaves them no choice but to dissemble: they are just being true to themselves.

The kind of deception that interests Byrne and Whiten—what they call tactical deception—is a different kettle of blowfish altogether. Here an animal has the mental flexibility to take an "honest" behavior and use it in such a way that another animal—usually a member of the deceiver's own social group—is misled, thinking that a normal, familiar state of affairs is under way, while, in fact, something quite different is happening.

Take Paul, for example. The real Paul is a young chacma baboon that caught Whiten's attention in 1983, while he and Byrne were studying foraging among the chacma in the Drakensberg Mountains of southern Africa. Whiten saw a member of Paul's group, an adult female named Mel, digging in the ground, trying to extract a nutritious plant bulb. Paul approached and looked around. There were no other baboons within sight. Suddenly he let out a yell, and within seconds his mother came running, chasing the startled Mel over a small cliff. Paul then took the bulb for himself.

In this case the deceived party was Paul's mother, who was misled by his scream into believing that Paul was being attacked, when actually no such attack was taking place. As a result of her apparent misinterpretation Paul was left alone to eat the bulb that Mel had carefully extracted—a morsel, by the way, that he would not have had the strength to dig out on his own.

If Paul's ruse had been an isolated case, Whiten might have gone on with his foraging studies and never given it a second thought. But when he compared his field notes with Byrne's, he noticed that both their notebooks were sprinkled with similar incidents and had been so all summer long. After they returned home to Scotland, they boasted about their "dead smart" baboons to their colleagues in pubs after conferences, expecting them to be suitably impressed. Instead the other researchers countered with tales about their own shrewd vervets or Machiavellian macaques.

"That's when we realized that a whole phenomenon might be slipping through a sieve," says Whiten. Researchers had assumed that this sort of complex trickery was a product of the sophisticated human brain. After all, deceitful behavior seemed unique to humans, and the human brain is unusually large, even for primates—"three times as big as you would expect for a primate of our size," notes Whiten, if you're plotting brain size against body weight.

But if primates other than humans deceived one another on a regular basis, the two psychologists reasoned, then it raised the extremely provocative possibility that the primate brain, and ultimately the human brain, is an instrument crafted for social manipulation. Humans evolved from the same evolutionary stock as apes, and if tactical deception was an important part of the lives of our evolutionary ancestors, then the sneakiness and subterfuge that human beings are so manifestly capable of might not be simply a result of our great intelligence and oversize

brain, but a driving force behind their development.

To Byrne and Whiten these were ideas worth pursuing. They fit in with a theory put forth some years earlier

---

Suddenly Paul let out a yell, and his mother came running, chasing Mel over a small cliff.

---

by English psychologist Nicholas Humphrey. In 1976 Humphrey had eloquently suggested that the evolution of primate intelligence might have been spurred not by the challenges of environment, as was generally thought, but rather by the complex cognitive demands of living with one's own companions. Since then a number of primatologists had begun to flesh out his theory with field observations of politically astute monkeys and apes.

Deception, however, had rarely been reported. And no wonder: If chimps, baboons, and higher primates generally are skilled deceivers, how could one ever know it? The best deceptions would by their very nature go undetected by the other members of the primate group, not to mention by a human stranger. Even those ruses that an observer could see through would have to be rare, for if used too often, they would lose their effectiveness. If Paul always cried wolf, for example, his mother would soon learn to ignore his ersatz distress. So while the monkey stories swapped over beers certainly suggested that deception was widespread among higher primates, it seemed unlikely that one or even a few researchers could observe enough instances of it to scientifically quantify how much, by whom, when, and to what effect.

Byrne and Whiten's solution was to extend their pub-derived data base with a more formal survey. In 1985 they sent a questionnaire to more than 100 primatologists working both in the field and in labs, asking them to report back any incidents in which they felt their subjects had perpetrated decep-

tion on one another. The questionnaire netted a promising assortment of deceptive tactics used by a variety of monkeys and all the great apes. Only the relatively small-brained and socially simple lemur family, which includes bush babies and lorises, failed to elicit a single instance. This supported the notion that society, sneakiness, brain size, and intelligence are intimately bound up with one another. The sneakier the primate, it seemed, the bigger the brain.

Byrne and Whiten drew up a second, much more comprehensive questionnaire in 1989 and sent it to hundreds more primatologists and animal behaviorists, greatly increasing the data base. Once again, when the results were tallied, only the lemur family failed to register a single case of deception.

All the other species, however, represented a simian rogues' gallery of liars and frauds. Often deception was used to distract another animal's attention. In one cartoonish example, a young baboon, chased by some angry elders, suddenly stopped, stood on his hind legs, and stared at a spot on the horizon, as if he noticed the presence of a predator or a foreign troop of baboons. His pursuers braked to a halt and looked in the same direction, giving up the chase. Powerful field binoculars revealed that no predator or baboon troop was anywhere in sight.

Sometimes the deception was simply a matter of one animal hiding a choice bit of food from the awareness of those strong enough to take it away. One of Jane Goodall's chimps, for example, named Figan, was once given some bananas after the more dominant members of the troop had wandered off. In the excitement, he uttered some loud "food barks"; the others quickly returned and took the bananas away. The next day Figan again waited behind the others and got some bananas. This time, however, he kept silent, even though the human observers, Goodall reported, "could hear faint choking sounds in his throat."

Concealment was a common ruse in sexual situations as well. Male monkeys and chimpanzees in groups have fairly strict hierarchies that control their access to females. Animals at the top of the order intimidate those lower down, forcing them away from females. Yet one researcher reported seeing a male stump-tailed macaque of a middle rank leading a female out of sight of the more dominant males and then mating with her silently, his climax unaccompanied by the harsh, low-pitched grunts that the male stump-tailed normally makes. At one point during the tryst the female turned and stared into his face, then covered his mouth with her hand. In another case a subordinate chimpanzee, aroused by the presence of a female in estrus, covered his erect penis with his hand when a dominant male approached, thus avoiding a likely attack.

In one particularly provocative instance a female hamadryas baboon slowly shuffled toward a large rock, appearing to forage, all the time keeping an eye on the most dominant male in the group. After 20 minutes she ended up with her head and shoulders visible to the big, watchful male, but with her hands happily engaged in the elicit activity of grooming a favorite subordinate male, who was hidden from view behind the rock.

Baboons proved singularly adept at a form of deception that Byrne and Whiten call "using a social tool." Paul's scam is a perfect example: he fools his mother into acting as a lever to pry the plant bulb away from the adult female, Mel. But can it be said unequivocally that he intended to deceive her? Perhaps Paul had simply learned through trial and error that letting out a yell brought his mother running and left him with food, in which case there is no reason to endow his young baboon intellect with Machiavellian intent. How do we know that Mel didn't actually threaten Paul in some way that Byrne and Whiten, watching, could not comprehend? While we're at it, how do we know that any of the primate deceptions reported here were really deliberate, conscious acts?

"It has to be said that there is a whole school of psychology that would deny such behavior even to humans," says Byrne. The school in question—strict behaviorism—would seek an explanation for the baboons' behavior not by trying to crawl inside their head but by carefully analyzing observable behaviors and the stimuli that might be triggering them. Byrne and Whiten's strategy against such skepticism was to be hyperskeptical themselves. They accepted that trial-and-error learning or simple conditioning, in which an animal's actions are reinforced by a reward, might account for a majority of the incidents reported to them—even when they believed that tactical deception was really taking place. But when explaining things "simply" led to a maze of extraordinary coincidences and tortuous logic, the evidence for deliberate deception seemed hard to dismiss.

Society, sneakiness, brain size, and intelligence are intimately bound up with one another.

Paul, for instance, *might* have simply learned that screaming elicits the reward of food, via his mother's intervention. But Byrne witnessed him using the same tactic several times, and in each case his mother was out of sight, able to hear his yell but not able to see what was really going on. If Paul was simply conditioned to scream, why would he do so only when his mother could not see who was—or was not—attacking her son?

Still, it is possible that she was not intentionally deceived. But in at least one other, similar case there is virtually no doubt that the mother was responding to a bogus attack, because the alleged attacker was quite able to verbalize his innocence. A five-year-old male chimp named Katabi, in the process of weaning, had discovered that the best way to get his reluctant mother to suckle him was to convince her he needed reassurance. One day Katabi approached a human observer—Japanese primatologist Toshisada Nish-

ida—and began to screech, circling around the researcher and waving an accusing hand at him. The chimp's mother and her escort immediately glared at Nishida, their hair erect. Only by slowly backing away from the screaming youngster did Nishida avoid a possible attack from the two adult chimps.

"In fact I did nothing to him," Nishida protested. It follows that the adults were indeed misled by Katabi's hysterics—unless there was some threat in Nishida unknown even to himself.

"If you try hard enough," says Byrne, "you can explain every single case without endowing the animal with the ability to deceive. But if you look at the whole body of work, there comes a point where you have to strive officiously to deny it."

The cases most resistant to such officious denials are the rarest—and the most compelling. In these interactions the primate involved not only employed tactical deception but clearly understood the concept. Such comprehension would depend upon one animal's ability to "read the mind" of another: to attribute desires, intentions, or even beliefs to the other creature that do not necessarily correspond to its own view of the world. Such mind reading was clearly evident in only 16 out of 253 cases in the 1989 survey, all of them involving great apes.

For example, consider Figan again, the young chimp who suppressed his food barks in order to keep the bananas for himself. In his case, mind reading is not evident: he might simply have learned from experience that food barks in certain contexts result in a loss of food, and thus he might not understand the nature of his own ruse, even if the other chimps are in fact deceived.

But contrast Figan with some chimps observed by Dutch primatologist Frans Plooij. One of these chimps was alone in a feeding area when a metal box containing food was opened electronically. At the same moment another chimp happened to approach. (Sound familiar? It's your older brother again.) The first chimp quickly closed the metal box (that's you hiding your chips), walked away, and sat down, looking around as if nothing had happened. The second chimp departed, but after going some distance away he hid behind a tree and peeked back at the first chimp. When the first chimp thought the coast was clear, he opened the box. The second chimp ran out, pushed the other aside, and ate the bananas.

Chimp One might be a clever rogue, but Chimp Two, who counters his deception with a ruse of his own, is the true mind reader. The success of his ploy is based on his insight that Chimp One was trying to deceive *him* and on his ability to adjust his behavior accordingly. He has in fact performed a prodigious cognitive leap—proving himself capable of projecting himself into another's mental space, and becoming what Humphrey would call a natural psychologist.

Niccolò Machiavelli might have called him good raw material. It is certainly suggestive that only the great apes—our closest relatives—seem capable of deceits based on such mind reading, and chimpanzees most of all. This does not necessarily mean that chimps are inherently more intelligent: the difference may be a matter of social organization. Orangutans live most of their lives alone, and thus they would not have much reason to develop such a complex social skill. And gorillas live in close family groups, whose members would be more familiar, harder to fool, and more likely to punish an attempted swindle. Chimpanzees, on the other hand, spend their lives in a shifting swirl of friends and relations, where small groups constantly form and break apart and reform with new members.

"What an opportunity for lying and cheating!" muses Byrne. Many anthropologists now believe that the social life of early hominids—our first non-ape ancestors—was much like that of chimps today, with similar opportunities to hone their cognitive skills on one another. Byrne and Whiten stop just short of saying that mind reading is the key to understanding the growth of human intelligence. But it would be disingenuous to ignore the possibility. If you were an early hominid who could comprehend the subjective impressions of others and manipulate them to your own ends, you might well have a competitive advantage over those less psychosocially nimble, perhaps enjoying slightly easier access to food and to the mating opportunities that would ensure your genetic survival.

Consider too how much more important your social wits would be in a world where the targets of your deceptions were constantly trying to outsmart *you*. After millennia of intrigue and counterintrigue, a hominid species might well evolve a brain three times bigger than it "should" be—and capable of far more than deceiving other hominids. "The ability to attribute other intentions to other people could have been an enormous building block for many human achievements, including language," says Whiten. "That this leap seems to have been taken by chimps and possibly the other great apes puts that development in human mentality quite early."

So did our intellect rise to its present height on a tide of manipulation and deceit? Some psychologists, even those who support the notion that the evolution of intelligence was socially driven, think that Byrne and Whiten's choice of the loaded adjective *Machiavellian* might be unnecessarily harsh.

"In my opinion," says Humphrey, "the word gives too much weight to the hostile use of intelligence. One of the functions of intellect in higher primates and humans is to keep the social unit together and make it able to successfully exploit the environment. A lot of intelligence could better be seen as driven by the need for cooperation and compassion." To that, Byrne and Whiten only point out that cooperation is itself an excellent Machiavellian strategy—sometimes.

The Scottish researchers are not, of course, the first to have noticed this. "It is good to appear clement, trustworthy, humane, religious, and honest, and also to be so," Machiavelli advised his aspiring Borgia prince in 1513. "But always with the mind so disposed that, when the occasion arises not to be so, you can become the opposite."

What Are Friends For?

*Among East African baboons, friendship means companions, health, safety . . .
and, sometimes, sex*

Barbara Smuts

Virgil, a burly adult male olive baboon, closely followed Zizi, a middle-aged female easily distinguished by her grizzled coat and square muzzle. On her rump Zizi sported a bright pink swelling, indicating that she was sexually receptive and probably fertile. Virgil's extreme attentiveness to Zizi suggested to me—and all rival males in the troop—that he was her current and exclusive mate.

Zizi, however, apparently had something else in mind. She broke away from Virgil, moved rapidly through the troop, and presented her alluring sexual swelling to one male after another. Before Virgil caught up with her, she had managed to announce her receptive condition to several of his rivals. When Virgil tried to grab her, Zizi screamed and dashed into the bushes with Virgil in hot pursuit. I heard sounds of chasing and fighting coming from the thicket. Moments later Zizi emerged from the bushes with an older male named Cyclops. They remained together for several days, copulating

often. In Cyclops's presence, Zizi no longer approached or even glanced at other males.

Primatologists describe Zizi and other olive baboons (*Papio cynocephalus anubis*) as promiscuous, meaning that both males and females usually mate with several members of the opposite sex within a short period of time. Promiscuous mating behavior characterizes many of the larger, more familiar primates, including chimpanzees, rhesus macaques, and gray langurs, as well as olive, yellow, and chacma baboons, the three subspecies of savanna baboon. In colloquial usage, promiscuity often connotes wanton and random sex, and several early studies of primates supported this stereotype. However, after years of laboriously recording thousands of copulations under natural conditions, the Peeping Toms of primate fieldwork have shown that, even in promiscuous species, sexual pairings are far from random.

Some adult males, for example, typically copulate much more often than

others. Primatologists have explained these differences in terms of competition: the most dominant males monopolize females and prevent lower-ranking rivals from mating. But exceptions are frequent. Among baboons, the exceptions often involve scruffy, older males who mate in full view of younger, more dominant rivals.

A clue to the reason for these puzzling exceptions emerged when primatologists began to question an implicit assumption of the dominance hypothesis—that females were merely passive objects of male competition. But what if females were active arbiters in this system? If females preferred some males over others and were able to express these preferences, then models of mating activity based on male dominance alone would be far too simple.

Once researchers recognized the possibility of female choice, evidence for it turned up in species after species. The story of Zizi, Virgil, and Cyclops is one of hundreds of examples of female primates rejecting the sexual advances of particular males and enthusiastically cooperating with others. But what is the basis for female choice? Why might they prefer some males over others?

This question guided my research on the Eburru Cliffs troop of olive baboons, named after one of their favorite sleeping sites, a sheer rocky outcrop rising several hundred feet above the floor of the Great Rift Valley, about 100 miles northwest of Nairobi, Kenya. The 120 members of Eburru Cliffs spent their days wandering through open grassland studded with occasional acacia thorn trees. Each night they retired to one of a dozen sets of cliffs that provided protection from nocturnal predators such as leopards.

Most previous studies of baboon sexuality had focused on females who, like Zizi, were at the peak of sexual receptivity. A female baboon does not mate when she is pregnant or lactating, a period of abstinence lasting about eighteen months. The female then goes into estrus, and for about two weeks out of every thirty-five-day cycle, she mates. Toward the end of this two week period she may ovulate, but usually the female undergoes four or five estrous cycles before she conceives. During pregnancy, she once again resumes a chaste existence. As a result, the typical female baboon is sexually active for less than 10 percent of her adult life. I thought that by focusing on the other 90 percent, I might learn something new. In particular, I suspected that routine, day-to-day relationships between males and pregnant or lactating (nonestrous) females might provide clues to female mating preferences.

Nearly every day for sixteen months, I joined the Eburru Cliffs baboons at their sleeping cliffs at dawn and traveled several miles with them while they foraged for roots, seeds, grass, and occasionally, small prey items, such as baby gazelles or hares (see "Predatory Baboons of Kekopey," *Natural History,* March 1976). Like all savanna baboon troops, Eburru Cliffs functioned as a cohesive unit organized around a core of related females, all of whom were born in the troop. Unlike the females, male savanna baboons

leave their natal troop to join another where they may remain for many years, so most of the Eburru Cliffs adult males were immigrants. Since membership in the troop remained relatively constant during the period of my study, I learned to identify each individual. I relied on differences in size, posture, gait, and especially, facial features. To the practiced observer, baboons look as different from one another as human beings do.

As soon as I could recognize individuals, I noticed that particular females tended to turn up near particular males again and again. I came to think of these pairs as friends. Friendship among animals is not a well-documented phenomenon, so to convince skeptical colleagues that baboon friendship was real, I needed to develop objective criteria for distinguishing friendly pairs.

I began by investigating grooming, the amiable simian habit of picking through a companion's fur to remove dead skin and ectoparasites (see "Little Things That Tick Off Baboons," *Natural History,* February 1984). Baboons spend much more time grooming than is necessary for hygiene, and previous research had indicated that it is a good measure of social bonds.

Although eighteen adult males lived in the troop, each nonestrous female performed most of her grooming with just one, two, or occasionally, three males. For example, of Zizi's twenty-four grooming bouts with males, Cyclops accounted for thirteen, and a second male, Sherlock, accounted for all the rest. Different females tended to favor different males as grooming partners.

Another measure of social bonds was simply who was observed near whom. When foraging, traveling, or resting, each pregnant or lactating female spent a lot of time near a few males and associated with the others no more often than expected by chance. When I compared the identities of favorite grooming partners and frequent companions, they overlapped almost completely. This enabled me to develop a formal definition of friendship: any male that scored high on both

grooming and proximity measures was considered a friend.

Virtually all baboons made friends; only one female and the three males who had most recently joined the troop lacked such companions. Out of more than 600 possible adult female-adult male pairs in the troop, however, only about one in ten qualified as friends; these really were special relationships.

Several factors seemed to influence which baboons paired up. In most cases, friends were unrelated to each other, since the male had immigrated from another troop. (Four friendships, however, involved a female and an adolescent son who had not yet emigrated. Unlike other friends, these related pairs never mated.) Older females tended to be friends with older males; younger females with younger males. I witnessed occasional May-December romances, usually involving older females and young adult males. Adolescent males and females were strongly rule-bound, and with the exception of mother-son pairs, they formed friendships only with one another.

Regardless of age or dominance rank, most females had just one or two male friends. But among males, the number of female friends varied greatly from none to eight. Although high-ranking males enjoyed priority of access to food and sometimes mates, dominant males did not have more female friends than low-ranking males. Instead it was the older males who had lived in the troop for many years who had the most friends. When a male had several female friends, the females were often closely related to one another. Since female baboons spend a lot of time near their kin, it is probably easier for a male to maintain bonds with several related females at once.

When collecting data, I focused on one nonestrous female at a time and kept track of her every movement toward or away from any male; similarly, I noted every male who moved toward or away from her. Whenever the female and a male moved close enough to exchange intimacies, I wrote down exactly what happened. When foraging together, friends tended to remain a few yards apart. Males more often wandered away from females than the reverse, and females, more often than males, closed the gap. The female behaved as if she wanted to keep the male within calling distance, in case she needed his protection. The male, however, was more likely to make approaches that brought them within actual touching distance. Often, he would plunk himself down right next to his friend and ask her to groom him by holding a pose with exaggerated stillness. The female sometimes responded by grooming, but more often, she exhibited the most reliable sign of true intimacy: she ignored her friend and simply continued whatever she was doing.

In sharp contrast, when a male who was not a friend moved close to a female, she dared not ignore him. She stopped whatever she was doing and held still, often glancing surreptitiously at the intruder. If he did not move away, she sometimes lifted her tail and presented her rump. When a female is not in estrus, this is a gesture of appeasement, not sexual enticement. Immediately after this respectful acknowledgement of his presence, the female would slip away. But such tense interactions with nonfriend males were rare, because females usually moved away before the males came too close.

These observations suggest that females were afraid of most of the males in their troop, which is not surprising: male baboons are twice the size of females, and their canines are longer and sharper than those of a lion. All Eburru Cliffs males directed both mild and severe aggression toward females. Mild aggression, which usually involved threats and chases but no body contact, occurred most often during feeding competition or when the male redirected aggression toward a female after losing a fight with another male. Females and juveniles showed aggression toward other females and juveniles in similar circumstances and occasionally inflicted superficial wounds. Severe aggression by males, which involved body contact and sometimes biting, was less common and also more puzzling, since there was no apparent cause.

An explanation for at least some of these attacks emerged one day when I was watching Pegasus, a young adult male, and his friend Cicily, sitting together in the middle of a small clearing. Cicily moved to the edge of the clearing to feed, and a higher-ranking female, Zora, suddenly attacked her. Pegasus stood up and looked as if he were about to intervene when both females disappeared into the bushes. He sat back down, and I remained with him. A full ten minutes later, Zora appeared at the edge of the clearing; this was the first time she had come into view since her attack on Cicily. Pegasus instantly pounced on Zora, repeatedly grabbed her neck in his mouth and lifted her off the ground, shook her whole body, and then dropped her. Zora screamed continuously and tried to escape. Each time, Pegasus caught her and continued his brutal attack. When he finally released her five minutes later she had a deep canine gash on the palm of her hand that made her limp for several days.

This attack was similar in form and intensity to those I had seen before and labeled "unprovoked." Certainly, had I come upon the scene after Zora's aggression toward Cicily, I would not have understood why Pegasus attacked Zora. This suggested that some, perhaps many, severe attacks by males actually represented punishment for actions that had occurred some time before.

Whatever the reasons for male attacks on females, they represent a serious threat. Records of fresh injuries indicated that Eburru Cliffs adult females received canine slash wounds from males at the rate of one for every female each year, and during my study, one female died of her injuries. Males probably pose an even greater threat to infants. Although only one infant was killed during my study, observers in Botswana and Tanzania have seen recent male immigrants kill several young infants.

Protection from male aggression, and from the less injurious but more frequent aggression of other females and juveniles, seems to be one of the main advantages of friendship for a female baboon. Seventy times I observed an adult male defend a female or her offspring against aggression by another troop member, not infrequently a high-ranking male. In all but six of these cases, the defender was a friend. Very few of these confrontations involved actual fighting; no male baboon, subordinate or dominant, is anxious to risk injury by the sharp canines of another.

Males are particularly solicitous guardians of their friends' youngest infants. If another male gets too close to an infant or if a juvenile female plays with it too roughly, the friend may intervene. Other troop members soon learn to be cautious when the mother's friend is nearby, and his presence provides the mother with a welcome respite from the annoying pokes and prods of curious females and juveniles obsessed with the new baby. Male baboons at Gombe Park in Tanzania and Amboseli Park in Kenya have also been seen rescuing infants from chimpanzees and lions. These several forms of male protection help to explain why females in Eburru Cliffs stuck closer to their friends in the first few months after giving birth than at any other time.

The male-infant relationship develops out of the male's friendship with the mother, but as the infant matures, this new bond takes on a life of its own. My co-worker Nancy Nicolson found that by about nine months of age, infants actively sought out their male friends when the mother was a few yards away, suggesting that the male may function as an alternative caregiver. This seemed to be especially true for infants undergoing unusually early or severe weaning. (Weaning is generally a gradual, prolonged process, but there is tremendous variation among mothers in the timing and intensity of weaning. See "Mother Baboons," *Natural History,* September 1980). After being rejected by the mother, the crying infant often approached the male friend and sat huddled against him until its whimpers subsided. Two of the infants in Eburru Cliffs lost their mothers when they were still quite young. In each case, their bond with the mother's friend subsequently intensified, and—perhaps as a result—both infants survived.

A close bond with a male may also improve the infant's nutrition. Larger than all other troop members, adult males monopolize the best feeding sites. In general, the personal space surrounding a feeding male is inviolate, but he usually tolerates intrusions by the infants of his female friends, giving them access to choice feeding spots.

Although infants follow their male friends around rather than the reverse, the males seem genuinely attached to their tiny companions. During feeding, the male and infant express their pleasure in each other's company by sharing spirited, antiphonal grunting duets. If the infant whimpers in distress, the male friend is likely to cease feeding, look at the infant, and grunt softly, as if in sympathy, until the whimpers cease. When the male rests, the infants of his female friends may huddle behind him, one after the other, forming a "train," or, if feeling energetic, they may use his body as a trampoline.

When I returned to Eburru Cliffs four years after my initial study ended, several of the bonds formed between males and the infants of their female friends were still intact (in other cases, either the male or the infant or both had disappeared). When these bonds involved recently matured females, their long-time male associates showed no sexual interest in them, even though the females mated with other adult males. Mothers and sons, and usually maternal siblings, show similar sexual inhibitions in baboons and many other primate species.

The development of an intimate relationship between a male and the infant of his female friend raises an obvious question: Is the male the infant's father? To answer this question definitely we would need to conduct genetic analysis, which was not possible for these baboons. Instead, I estimated paternity probabilities from observations of the temporary (a few hours or days) exclusive mating relationships, or consortships, that estrous females form with a series of different males. These estimates were apt to be fairly accurate, since changes in the female's sexual swelling allow one to pinpoint the timing of conception to within a few days. Most females consorted with only two or three males during this period, and these males were termed likely fathers.

In about half the friendships, the male was indeed likely to be the father of his friend's most recent infant, but in the other half he was not—in fact, he had never been seen mating with the female. Interestingly, males who were friends with the mother but not likely fathers nearly always developed a relationship with her infant, while males who had mated with the female but were not her friend usually did not. Thus friendship with the mother, rather than paternity, seems to mediate the development of male-infant bonds. Recently, a similar pattern was documented for South American capuchin monkeys in a laboratory study in which paternity was determined genetically.

These results fly in the face of a prominent theory that claims males will invest in infants only when they are closely related. If males are not fostering the survival of their own genes by caring for the infant, then why do they do so? I suspected that the key was female choice. If females preferred to mate with males who had already demonstrated friendly behavior, then friendships with mothers and their infants might pay off in the future when the mothers were ready to mate again.

To find out if this was the case, I examined each male's sexual behavior with females he had befriended before they resumed estrus. In most cases, males consorted considerably more often with their friends than with other females. Baboon females typically mate with several different males, including both friends and nonfriends, but prior friendship increased a male's probability of mating with a female above what it would have been otherwise.

This increased probability seemed to reflect female preferences. Females occasionally overtly advertised their disdain for certain males and their desire for others. Zizi's behavior, described above, is a good example. Virgil was not one of her friends, but Cyclops was. Usually, however, females expressed preferences and aversions more subtly. For example, Delphi, a petite adolescent female, found herself pursued by Hector, a middle-aged adult male. She did not run away or refuse to mate with him, but whenever he wasn't watching, she looked around for her friend Homer, an adolescent male. When she succeeded in catching Homer's eye, she narrowed her eyes and flattened her ears against her skull, the friendliest face one baboon can send another. This told Homer she would rather be with him. Females expressed satisfaction with a current consort partner by staying close to him, initiating copulations, and not making advances toward other males. Baboons are very sensitive to such cues, as indicated by an experimental study in which rival hamadryas baboons rarely challenged a male-female pair if the female strongly preferred her current partner. Similarly, in Eburru Cliffs, males were less apt to challenge consorts involving a pair that shared a long-term friendship.

Even though females usually consorted with their friends, they also mated with other males, so it is not surprising that friendships were most vulnerable during periods of sexual activity. In a few cases, the female consorted with another male more often than with her friend, but the friendship survived nevertheless. One female, however, formed a strong sexual bond with a new male. This bond persisted after conception, replacing her previous friendship. My observations suggest that adolescent and young adult females tend to have shorter, less stable friendships than do older females. Some friendships, however, last a very long time. When I returned to Eburru Cliffs six years after my study began, five couples were still together. It is possible that friendships occasionally last for life (baboons probably live twenty to thirty years in the wild), but it will require longer studies, and some very patient scientists, to find out.

By increasing both the male's chances of mating in the future and the likelihood that a female's infant will survive, friendship contributes to the reproductive success of both partners. This clarifies the evolutionary basis of friendship-forming tendencies in baboons, but what does friendship mean to a baboon? To answer this question we need to view baboons as sentient beings with feelings and goals not unlike our own in similar circumstances. Consider, for example, the friendship between Thalia and Alexander.

The affair began one evening as Alex and Thalia sat about fifteen feet apart on the sleeping cliffs. It was like watching two novices in a singles bar. Alex stared at Thalia until she turned and almost caught him looking at her. He glanced away immediately, and then she stared at him until his head began to turn toward her. She suddenly became engrossed in grooming her toes. But as soon as Alex looked away, her gaze returned to him. They went on like this for more than fifteen minutes, always with split-second timing. Finally, Alex managed to catch Thalia looking at him. He made the friendly eyes-narrowed, ears-back face and smacked his lips together rhythmically. Thalia froze, and for a second she looked into his eyes. Alex approached, and Thalia, still nervous, groomed him. Soon she calmed down, and I found them still together on the cliffs the next morning. Looking back on this event months later, I realized that it marked the beginning of their friendship. Six years later, when I returned to Eburru Cliffs, they were still friends.

If flirtation forms an integral part of baboon friendship, so does jealously. Overt displays of jealousy, such as chasing a friend away from a potential rival, occur occasionally, but like humans, baboons often express their emotions in more subtle ways. One evening a colleague and I climbed the cliffs and settled down near Sherlock, who was friends with Cybelle, a middle-aged female still foraging on the ground below the cliffs. I observed Cybelle while my colleague watched Sherlock, and we kept up a running commentary. As long as Cybelle was feeding or interacting with females, Sherlock was relaxed, but each time she approached another male, his body would stiffen, and he would stare intently at the scene below. When Cybelle presented politely to a male who had recently tried to befriend her, Sherlock even made threatening sounds under his breath. Cybelle was not in estrus at the time, indicating that male baboon jealousy extends beyond the sexual arena to include affiliative interactions between a female friend and other males.

Because baboon friendships are embedded in a network of friendly and antagonistic relationships, they inevitably lead to repercussions extending beyond the pair. For example, Virgil once provoked his weaker rival Cyclops into a fight by first attacking Cyclops's friend Phoebe. On another occasion, Sherlock chased Circe, Hector's best friend, just after Hector had chased Antigone, Sherlock's friend.

In another incident, the prime adult male Triton challenged Cyclops's possession of meat. Cyclops grew increasingly tense and seemed about to abandon the prey to the younger male. Then Cyclops's friend Phoebe appeared with her infant Phyllis. Phyllis wandered over to Cyclops. He immediately grabbed her, held her close, and threatened Triton away from the prey. Because any challenge to Cyclops now involved a threat to Phyllis as well, Triton risked being mobbed by Phoebe and her relatives and friends. For this reason, he backed down. Males frequently use the infants of their female friends as buffers in this way. Thus, friendship involves costs as well as benefits because it makes the participants vulnerable to social manipulation or redirected aggression by others.

Finally, as with humans, friendship seems to mean something different to each baboon. Several females in Eburru Cliffs had only one friend. They were devoted companions. Louise and Pandora, for example, groomed their friend Virgil and no other male. Then there was Leda, who, with five friends, spread herself more thinly than any other female. These contrasting patterns of friendship were associated with striking personality differences. Louise and Pandora were unobtrusive females who hung around quietly with Virgil and their close relatives. Leda seemed to be everywhere at once, playing with infants, fighting with juveniles, and making friends with males. Similar differences were apparent among the males. Some devoted a great deal of time and energy to cultivating friendships with females, while others focused more on challenging other males. Although we probably will never fully understand the basis of these individual differences, they contribute immeasurably to the richness and complexity of baboon society.

Male-female friendships may be widespread among primates. They have been reported for many other groups of savanna baboons, and they also occur in rhesus and Japanese Macaques, capuchin monkeys, and perhaps in bonobos (pygmy chimpanzees). These relationships should give us pause when considering popular scenarios for the evolution of male-female relationships in humans. Most of these scenarios assume that, except for mating, males and females had little to do with one another until the development of a sexual division of labor, when, the story goes, females began to rely on males to provide meat in exchange for gathered food. This, it has been argued, set up new selection pressures favoring the development of long-term bonds between individual males and females, female sexual fidelity, and as paternity certainty increased, greater male investment in the offspring of these unions. In other words, once women began to gather and men to hunt, presto—we had the nuclear family.

This scenario may have more to do with cultural biases about women's economic dependence on men and idealized views of the nuclear family than with the actual behavior of our hominid ancestors. The nonhuman primate evidence challenges this story in at least three ways.

First, long-term bonds between the sexes can evolve in the absence of a sexual division of labor of food sharing. In our primate relatives, such relationships rest on exchanges of social, not economic, benefits.

Second, primate research shows that highly differentiated, emotionally intense male-female relationships can occur without sexual exclusivity. Ancestral men and women may have experienced intimate friendships long before they invented marriage and norms of sexual fidelity.

Third, among our closest primate relatives, males clearly provide mothers and infants with social benefits even when they are unlikely to be the fathers of those infants. In return, females provide a variety of benefits to the friendly males, including acceptance into the group and, at least in baboons, increased mating opportunities in the future. This suggests that efforts to reconstruct the evolution of hominid societies may have overemphasized what the female must supposedly do

(restrict her mating to just one male) in order to obtain male parental investment.

Maybe it is time to pay more attention to what the male must do (provide benefits to females and young) in order to obtain female cooperation. Perhaps among our ancestors, as in baboons today, sex and friendship went hand in hand. As for marriage—well, that's another story.

Leading Ladies

In baboon society, elderly females often call the shots

Jeanne Altmann

As her young infant alternately suckled and dozed in the shelter of her lap, the elderly baboon, known to us as Handle, stared intently toward the distant grove of trees. The five dozen members of her group sat intensely in clusters nearby. Indecision was in the air, and even the playful juveniles seemed to sense it, staying closer to their older relatives than they had all day. A short while before, as they were heading southward toward a grove of trees in which to spend the night, the group had spotted a leopard—the baboons' major predator. Although the leopard was no longer visible, the chatter of vervet monkeys in the distance, near the intended sleeping trees, confirmed that danger would await the baboons if they continued as planned. The sun was dropping rapidly now, and the short equatorial dusk would give the baboons little time to make a decision: stick to the original plan or strike out for one of the other groves—all farther away—scattered across their East African savanna home. If they didn't act fast, darkness would overtake them far from the safety of tall trees.

Occasionally, one young adult or another gave rapid, soft vocalizations and started moving tentatively toward the original grove or in another direction, but the other baboons remained in place and the initiator soon sat again. After ten long minutes, in a single, smooth motion, Handle stood, her infant still clutching her sides but now riding under her, and began to move decisively westward toward a grove still hidden in the dusty, dry-season haze. Barely a few seconds later, her

daughter Heko followed with her own infant on her back. Handle paused as she looked back; throughout the group, baboons responded with soft grunts and moved to follow her. The rippling motion rapidly grew into a wave, and soon, all the baboons followed, silent except for the protests of tired youngsters for whom first the tension and now the sudden rapid pace were too much. By the time the baboons reached the grove, the light was nearly gone, and the animals were little more than silhouettes as they ascended the trees. I just barely made out Handle as, hunched stiffly over her sleeping infant, she settled onto a comfortable branch for the night.

During more than twenty years observing baboons in Amboseli National Park in southern Kenya, my colleagues and I have seen one elderly female after another serve as leaders at critical times in group movements. Actual fights with predators or other baboon groups usually involve many troop members; then, adult males are often in the fore, but each animal seems to know or decide for itself whether to flee, hang back, or threaten the intruders. In contrast, the decisive role of elderly females more often is seen at "controversial" moments in group movements, when all will take the same route, but just which route is not clear or agreed upon. At those times, elderly females (those over about fifteen years of age) seem to make the choices that are followed. We don't know for sure why the "opinions" of these females carry so much weight. Social rank is not the answer, for we have seen high-, low-, and mid-ranking individuals (such as Handle) lead the group. The permanent mem-

bers of baboon society are the females, and many older females tend to have several daughters and other descendants in the group. Could the most influential females simply have the most descendants? Certain evidence seems to support this. Like Handle, elderly Alto had many offspring and she, too, was a leader at times. In contrast, we have never observed eighteen-year-old Dotty, who has few offspring, or Dotty's age-mate Janet, who has none, assume leadership roles.

The equation cannot be a simple one, however, for another elderly female, low-ranking Este, had few offspring and yet was often a leader at critical junctures in the troop's life. Perhaps the explanation lies in the extent to which the leaders are enmeshed in a longstanding, complex network of social relationships. Unlike males, who change group membership when they mature, females spend their whole lives in the group in which they are born. Certainly, twenty-three year-old Handle has had a long time to build up a social network. Although none of her elders and few of her peers are still alive, all of the group's youngsters have grown up knowing her.

Few baboons live long enough to develop the kind of rich social network Handle enjoys. Less than half the baboons in the population survive infancy, and once they reach adulthood (at age six for females and eight for males) the annual death rate is about 10 percent. The rare elderly survivors like Handle usually seem somewhat slow and stiff. They sometimes drop to the rear of the group, especially in the morning cold, as the baboons set off for the day's six-mile foraging trek, and in the late afternoon, when the fatigued animals move to a sleeping grove. Although Handle actually still seems fairly spry, her teeth are very worn, and her weight seems to have declined in recent years, suggesting that she may need to spend more time feeding to obtain enough digestible food.

Not surprisingly, perhaps, Handle, like other elderly females, often seems to be somewhat separate from younger members of the group and to have less time to interact with them. And yet she is undeniably an active group member. Several factors of baboon life help keep it that way. Baboon females continue to bear young throughout their lives (although slightly less frequently), and when infants are born, relatives, friends, and just plain curious acquaintances cluster about the infant and its mother. Motherhood is a way of renewing and reinforcing social ties. These ties are further cemented by grooming, the baboons' way of keeping in close touch—calming one another down, sharing messages. Females groom their grown daughters, special unrelated male friends, and others in the troop. We think it significant that Handle has long been one of the group's most frequent, and most thorough, groomers.

The life of male baboons follows quite a different path. Even as two- or three-year-olds, they begin to move away from their mothers' world. Young females increasingly reciprocate their mothers' grooming; young males do not, and their mothers soon discontinue grooming them. In addition, the young males' social interactions involve more partners outside their maternal lineage, so that by the time males leave their birth group, at eight or nine years of age, they have experienced a broader range of social relationships than have their female peers. This is probably of great value, considering the tasks they face: those males that survive to immigrate into another group must deal with a hostile reception by the resident males. They must also develop all new relationships with both males and females, including potential sexual partners. And unlike females (who inherit their mother's social rank and retain it throughout adulthood), males must compete for the rank they attain and cannot expect to keep it: for males, status peaks in young adulthood and declines more or less rapidly soon thereafter. Social relationships may change even more for those males who, like Handle's first-

born son, Hans, switch groups several times. Moreover, males do much less grooming than females and, at least as young adults, do so primarily with potential sexual partners.

For all these reasons, we might expect to find that aging males are less socially integrated and have fewer social resources. However, studies increasingly document long-term friendships, involving grooming and some infant care, between mature males and females. Sometimes older males in these relationships have even greater success sexually than do dominant, younger males. Newly weaned youngsters may also benefit from the protective friendship of older males, who occasionally perform acts of heroism—defending the youngsters from injury by other adult males or rescuing and carrying them to safety when they cannot keep up with the group's rapid flight from predators.

Reaching old age may be rare in savanna baboon society, but those individuals that do survive are much more than decrepit hangers-on. As fellow primates, they suggest some of the many ways of growing old and contributing to a complex social world.

The Young and the Reckless

*Every day young primates leave the comfort of home to live through weeks
and months of abuse at the hands of beastly strangers.
Why in the world do they—and we—do it?*

Robert Sapolsky

I remember going off to college. I was
so nervous and excited that I had the
runs for a week beforehand. What if
they had made a mistake by admitting
me? Suppose I never made any
friends? Would these really turn out to
be the best years of my life? Queasy
and vertiginous, I packed my bags onto
a Greyhound bus, squirreling a bottle
of Kaopectate into my knapsack.

Actually, getting my bowels into
such an uproar proved to be quite
justified, given the momentous fresh-
man-year events that awaited me: the
epiphany when I knew I was never
going to understand photosynthesis and
should give up on being a biology
major (I switched to bioanthropology);
the realization, as I contemplated four
years of purple yogurt and Polynesian
meatless meatballs in the cafeteria, that
my mother was a fabulous cook; my
first lesson in political correctness—I
learned that I was now surrounded by
women and not by girls; the infinitely
pleasant discovery that some of those
women were willing to talk to me now
and then; the wonder of watching older
guys suavely work references to
Claude Lévi-Strauss and Buckminster
Fuller into casual conversation; the
giddy pleasure at finding that a joke
that worked in high school worked
equally well here too; the calming ritual of fighting with my roommate every evening over whether to open or
close the window.

Growing up, and growing away. Off
to college, off to war, off to work in the
city, off to settle in a new world—home
is never the same again, and sometimes
home is never even seen again. What is
striking about this maturational event
is that it is central not only to us
humans but to many of our primate
relatives as well. The process of growing up and growing away has a remarkably familiar look of excitement
and discovery and challenge.

Some primates, such as orangutans,
lead solitary lives, meeting only for the
occasional mating. But the average
group of primates is supremely social,
whether it is a family of a dozen gorillas living in a mountain rain forest, a
band of 20 langur monkeys on the
outskirts of an Indian village, or a
troop of 100 baboons in the African
grasslands. In such groups an infant is
born into a world filled with relatives,
friends, and adversaries, surrounded
by intrigue, double-dealing, trysts, and
heroics—the staples of great small-
town gossip. Pretty heady stuff for the
kid that's learning who it can trust and
what the rules are, along with its species' equivalent of table manners.

Most young primates get socialized
in this way quite effectively, and home
must seem homier all the time. Then,
inevitably, a lot of the young must leave
the group and set out on their own. It is
a simple fact driven by genetics and
evolution: if everyone stayed on, matured, and reproduced there, and if
their kids stayed on, and their kids'

kids too, then ultimately everyone
would be pretty closely related. You
would have the classic problems of
inbreeding—lots of funny-looking kids
with six fingers and two tails (as well
as more serious genetic problems).

Thus essentially all social primates
have evolved mechanisms for adolescent emigration from one group to
another. Not all adolescents have to
leave. The problem of inbreeding is
typically solved so long as all the adolescents of one sex go and make their
fortune elsewhere; the members of the
other sex can remain at home and mate
with the newcomers immigrating to the
group. In chimpanzees and gorillas, it
is typically the females who leave for
new groups, while the males stay home
with their mothers. But among most
Old World monkeys—baboons, macaques, langurs—it is the males who
make the transfer. Why one sex transfers in one species but not in another is
a complete mystery, the sort that keeps
primatologists arguing with each other
ad nauseam.

This pattern of adolescent transfer
solves the specter of inbreeding. But to
look at it just as a solution to an
evolutionary problem is absurdly mechanistic. You can't lose sight of the fact
that those are real animals going
through the harrowing process. It is a
remarkable thing to observe: every
day, in the world of primates, someone
young and frightened picks up, leaves
Mommy and everyone it knows, and
heads off into the unknown.

The transfer pattern I know best is the one among the baboons I study in the grasslands of East Africa. Two troops encounter each other at midday at some sort of natural boundary—a river, for example. As is the baboon propensity in such settings, the males of the two troops carry on with a variety of aggressive displays, hooting and hollering with what they no doubt hope is a great air of menace. Eventually everyone gets bored and goes back to eating and lounging, ignoring the interlopers on the other side of the river. Suddenly you spot the kid—some adolescent in your troop. He stands there at the river's edge, absolutely riveted. New baboons, a whole bunch of 'em! He runs five steps toward them, runs four back, searches among the other members of his troop to see why no one else seems mesmerized by the strangers. After endless contemplation, he gingerly crosses the river and sits on the very edge of the other bank, scampering back down in a panic should any new baboon so much as glance at him.

A week later, when the troops run into each other again, the kid repeats the pattern. Except this time he spends the afternoon sitting at the edge of the new troop. At the next encounter he follows them for a short distance before the anxiety becomes too much and he turns back. Finally, one brave night, he stays with them. He may vacillate awhile longer, perhaps even ultimately settling on a third troop, but he has begun his transfer into adulthood.

And what an awful experience it is—a painfully lonely, peripheralized stage of life. There are no freshman orientation weeks, no cohorts of newcomers banding together and covering their nervousness with bravado. There is just a baboon kid, all alone on the edge of a new group, and no one there could care less about him. Actually, that is not true—there are often members of the new troop who pay quite a lot of attention, displaying some of the least charming behavior seen among social primates, and most reminiscent of that of their human cousins. Suppose you are a low-ranking member of that troop: perhaps a puny kid a year or so after your own transfer, or an aging male in decline. You spend most of your time losing fights, being pushed around, having food taken from you by someone of higher rank. You have a list of grievances a mile long and there's little you can do about it. Sure there are youngsters in the troop that you could harass pretty successfully, but if they are pretransfer age, their mothers—and maybe their fathers and their whole extended family—will descend on you like a ton of bricks. Then suddenly, like a gift from heaven, a new even punier kid shows up: someone to take it out on. (Among chimps, where females do the transferring, the same thing occurs; resident females are brutally aggressive toward the new female living on the group's edge.)

Yet that's only the beginning of a transfer animal's problems. When, as part of my studies of disease patterns among baboons, I anesthetize and examine transfer males, I find that these young animals are just teeming with parasites. There is no longer anyone to groom them, to sit with them and methodically clean their fur, half for hygiene, half for friendship. And if no one is interested in grooming a recent transfer animal, certainly no one is interested in anything more intimate than that—in short, it is a time of life filled with masturbation. The young males suffer all the indignities of being certified primate geeks. *Just like college*

They are also highly vulnerable. If a predator attacks, the transfer animal—who is typically peripheral and exposed to begin with—is not likely to recognize the group's signals and has no one to count on for his defense. I witnessed an incident like this during one of my first research stints in Africa. The unfortunate animal was so new to my group that he rated only a number, 273, instead of a name. The troop was meandering in the midday heat and descended down the bank of a dry streambed into some bad luck: a half-asleep lioness. Panic ensued, with animals running every which way as the lioness stirred—while Male 273 stood bewildered and terribly visible.

He was badly mauled and, in a poignant act, crawled for miles to return to his former home troop and die near his mother.

In short, the transfer period is one of the most dangerous and miserable times in a primate's life. Yet, almost inconceivably, life gets better. One day an adolescent female will sit beside our transfer male and briefly groom him. Some afternoon everyone hungrily descends on a tree in fruit and the older adolescent males forget to chase the newcomer away. One morning the adolescent and an adult male exchange greetings (which, among male baboons, consists of yanking on each other's penises, a social gesture predicated on trust if ever I saw one). And someday, inevitably, a terrified new transfer male appears on the scene, and our hero, to his perpetual shame perhaps, indulges in the aggressive pleasures of finding someone lower on the ladder to bully.

In a gradual process of assimilation, the transfer animal makes a friend, finds an ally, mates, and rises in the hierarchy of the troop. It can take years. Which is why Hobbes was such an extraordinary beast.

Three years ago my wife and I were spending the summer working with a baboon troop at Amboseli National Park in Kenya, a research site run by the behavioral biologists Jeanne and Stuart Altmann from the University of Chicago. I study the relationships between a baboon's rank and personality, how its body responds to stress, and what sorts of stress-related diseases it gets. In order to get the physiological data—blood samples to gauge an animal's stress hormone levels, immune system function, and so on—you have to anesthetize the baboon for a few hours with the aid of a small aluminum blow-gun and drug-filled darts. Fill the dart with the right amount of anesthetic, walk up to a baboon, aim, and blow, and he is snoozing five minutes later. Naturally it's not quite that simple—you can dart only in the mornings (to control for the effect of circadian rhythms on the animal's hormones). You must ensure there are no predators around to shred the guy, and you must make certain he doesn't climb a tree before passing out. And most of all, you have to dart and remove him from the troop when none of the other baboons are looking so that you don't alarm them and disrupt their habituation to the scientists. So essentially, what I do with my college education is creep around in the bushes after a bunch of baboons, waiting for the instant when they are all looking the other way so that I can zip a dart into someone's tush.

It was about halfway through the season. We were just beginning to get to know the baboons in our troop (named Hook's troop, for a long-deceased matriarch) and were becoming familiar with their daily routine. Each night they slept in their favorite grove of trees; each morning they rolled out of bed to forage for food in an open savanna strewn with volcanic rocks tossed up eons ago by nearby Mount Kilimanjaro. It was the dry season, which meant the baboons had to do a bit more walking than usual to find food and water, but there was still plenty of both, and the troop had time to lounge around in the shade during the afternoon heat. Dominating the social hierarchy among the males was an imposing character named Ruto, who had joined the troop a few years before and had risen relatively quickly in the ranks. Number two was a male named Fatso, who had had the misfortune of being a rotund adolescent when he'd transferred into the troop years before and was named by a callous researcher. Fat he was no longer. Now a muscular prime-age male, he was Ruto's most obvious competitor, though still clearly subordinate. It was a fairly peaceful period for the troop; mail was delivered regularly and the trains ran on time.

Then one morning we arrived to find the baboons in complete turmoil. It is not an anthropomorphism to say that everyone was mightily frazzled. There was a new transfer male, and not someone meekly scurrying about the periphery. He was in the middle of the troop, raising hell—threatening, chasing, and whacking everyone in sight. This nasty, brutish animal was soon named Hobbes (in deference to the seventeenth-century English philosopher who described the life of man as solitary, poor, nasty, brutish, and short).

This is an extremely rare, though not unheard of, event among baboons. The transfer male in such cases is usually a big, muscular, intimidating kid. Maybe he is older than the average seven-year-old transfer male, or perhaps this is his second transfer and he picked up confidence from his first emigration. Maybe he is the son of a high-ranking female in his old troop, raised to feel cocky. In any case, the rare animal with these traits comes on like a truck. And he often gets away with it for a time. As long as he keeps pushing, it will be a while before any of the resident males works up the nerve to confront him. Nobody knows him yet; thus no one knows if he is asking for a fatal injury by being the first fool to challenge this aggressive maniac.

And this was Hobbes's style. The intimidated males stood around helplessly. Fatso discovered all sorts of errands he had to run elsewhere. Ruto hid behind females. No one else was going to take a stand. Hobbes rose to the number one rank in the troop within a week.

Despite his sudden ascendancy Hobbes's success wasn't going to last forever. He was still a relatively inexperienced kid, and eventually one of the bigger males was bound to cut him down to size. Hobbes had about a month's free ride. At this point he did something brutally violent but which made a certain grim evolutionary sense. He began to selectively attack pregnant females. He beat and mauled them, causing three out of four to abort within a few days.

One of the great clichés of animal behavior in the context of evolution is that animals act for the good of the species. This idea was discredited in the 1960s but continues to permeate *Wild Kingdom*-like versions of animal behavior. The more accurate view is that animals usually behave in ways that maximize their own reproduction and the reproduction of their close relatives. This helps explain extraordinary acts of altruism and self-sacrifice in some circumstances, and sickening aggression in others. It's in this context that Hobbes's attacks make sense. Were those females to carry through their pregnancies and raise their offspring, they would not be likely to mate again for two years—and who knows where Hobbes would be at that point. Instead he harassed the females into aborting, and they were ovulating again a few weeks later. Although female baboons have a say in whom they mate with, in the case of someone as forceful as Hobbes they have little choice: within weeks Hobbes, still the dominant male in the troop, was mating with two of those three females. (This is not to imply that Hobbes had read his textbooks on evolution, animal behavior, and primate obstetrics and had thought through this strategy. The wording here is a convenient shorthand for the more correct way of stating that his pattern of behavior was almost certainly an unconscious, evolved one.)

As it happened, Hobbes's arrival on the scene—just as we had darted and tested about half the animals for our studies—afforded us a rare opportunity. We could compare the physiology of the troop before and after his tumultuous transfer. And in a study recently published with Jeanne Altmann and Susan Alberts, I documented the not very surprising fact that Hobbes was stressing the bejesus out of these animals. Their blood levels of cortisol (also known as hydrocortisone), one of the hormones most reliably secreted during stress, rose significantly. At the same time, their numbers of white blood cells, or lymphocytes, the sentinel cells of the immune system that defend the body against infections, declined markedly—another highly reliable index of stress. These stress-response markers were most pronounced in the animals getting the most grief from Hobbes. Unmolested females had three times as many circulating lymphocytes as one poor female who was attacked five times during those first two weeks.

An obvious question: Why doesn't every new transfer male try something as audaciously successful as Hobbes? For one thing, most transfer males are too small at the typical transfer age of seven years to intimidate a gazelle, let alone an 80-pound adult male baboon. (Hobbes, unusually, weighed a good 70 pounds.) Most don't have the personality needed for this sort of unpleasantry. Moreover, it's a risky strategy, as someone like Hobbes stands a good chance of sustaining a crippling injury early in life.

But there was another reason as well, which didn't become apparent until later. One morning, when Hobbes was concentrating on who to hassle next and paying no attention to us, I managed to put a dart into his haunches. Months later, when examining his blood sample in the laboratory, we found that Hobbes had among the highest levels of cortisol in the troop and extremely low lymphocyte counts, less than one-quarter the troop average. (Ruto and Fatso, sitting on the sidelines now, had three and six times as many lymphocytes as Hobbes had.) The young baboon was experiencing a massive stress response himself, larger even than those of the females he was harassing, and certainly larger than is typical of the other, meek transfer males I've studied. In other words, it doesn't come cheap to be a bastard 12 hours a day—a couple of months of this sort of thing is likely to exert a physiological toll.

As a postscript, Hobbes did not hold on to his position. Within five months he was toppled, dropping down to number three in the hierarchy. After three years in the troop, he disappeared into the sunset, transferring out to parts unknown to try his luck in some other troop.

All this only reaffirms that transferring is awful for adolescents—whether they're average geeks opting for the route of slow acceptance or rare animals like Hobbes who try to take a troop by storm. Either way it's an ordeal, and the young animals pay a heavy price. The marvel is that they keep on doing it. Transferring may solve the inbreeding problem for a population; but what's in it for the individual?

Adolescent transfer is a feature of many social mammals, not just primates, and the mechanisms can differ. Sometimes transfer can arise from intrasexual competition—a fancy way of saying that the adolescents are driven from the group by a more powerful same-sex competitor. You see this in species like gazelles and impalas, for example. The core social group consists of a single breeding male, a large collection of females, and their offspring. At any given point some of those male off-spring are likely to be entering puberty. But since the breeding male typically doesn't hold on to his precarious position for long, he is probably not the father of these adolescent males. He doesn't view them as sons coming of age but as unrelated males becoming reproductive competitors. At their first signs of puberty he violently drives them out of the group.

In primates, however, forced dispersion almost never happens. Critically, these adolescents choose to go—even though the move seems crazy. After all, they live in a troop surrounded by family and friends. They know their home turf—which trees are fruiting at what time of year, where the local predators tend to lurk. Yet they leave these home comforts to endure parasites, predators, and loneliness. And why? To dwell among strangers who treat them terribly. It makes no sense, from the standpoint of the individual animal. Behaviorist theories state this more formally: animals, including humans, tend to do things for which they are rewarded and tend not to do things for which they get punished. Yet here they are, leaving their comfortable, rewarding world in order to be amply dumped on far away. Furthermore, animals tend to hate novelty. Put a rat in a new cage, give it a new feeding pattern, and it exhibits a stress response. Yet here young primates are risking life and limb for novelty. Old World monkeys have been known to transfer up to five times over their lifetime, or travel nearly 40 miles to a new troop. Why should any individual in its right mind want to do this?

I do not know why transfer occurs, but it is clearly very deeply rooted. Humans, in part because their diets are adaptable, are the most widely distributed mammal on Earth, inhabiting nearly every godforsaken corner of this planet. Among our primate relatives, those with the least finicky of diets, such as baboons, are also among the most widely distributed beasts on Earth (African baboons range from desert to rain forest, from mountain to savanna). Inevitably, someone had to be the first to set foot in each of those new worlds, an individual who transferred in a big way. And it is overwhelmingly likely a young individual who did that.

This love affair with risk and novelty seems to be why the young of all our primate species are the most likely to die of accidents, doing foolhardy things while their elders cluck over how they told them so. And it is also the reason that the young are most likely to discover something really new and extraordinary, whether in the physical or the intellectual realm. When the novel practice of washing food in seawater was discovered by snow monkeys in Japan, it was a youngster who did so, and it was her playmates who picked up the adaptation; hardly any of the older animals did. And when Darwin's ideas about evolution swept through academic primates in the mid-nineteenth century, it was the new, up-and-coming generation of scientists that embraced his ideas with the greatest enthusiasm.

You don't have to search far for other examples. Think of the tradition of near-adolescent mathematicians revolutionizing their fields, or of the young Picasso and Stravinsky galvanizing twentieth-century culture. Think about teenagers inevitably, irresistibly wanting to drive too fast, or trying out some new improvisatory sport guaranteed to break their necks, or marching off in an excited frenzy to whatever stupid war their elders have invented. Think of the endless young people leaving their homes, homes perhaps rife with poverty or oppression, but still their homes, to go off to find new worlds.

Part of the reason for the evolutionary success of primates, human or otherwise, is that we are a pretty smart collection of animals. What's more, our thumbs work in particularly fancy and advantageous ways, and we're more flexible about food than most. But our primate essence is more than just abstract reasoning, dexterous thumbs, and omnivorous diets. Another key to our success must have something to do with this voluntary transfer process, this primate legacy of getting an itch around adolescence. How did voluntary dispersal evolve? What is going on with that individual's genes, hormones, and neurotransmitters to make it hit the road? We don't know, but we do know that following this urge is one of the most resonantly primate of acts. A young male baboon stands riveted at the river's edge; an adolescent female chimp cranes to catch a glimpse of the chimps from the next valley. New animals, a whole bunch of 'em! To hell with logic and sensible behavior, to hell with tradition and respecting your elders, to hell with this drab little town, and to hell with that knot of fear in your stomach. Curiosity, excitement, adventure—the hunger for novelty is something fundamentally daft, rash, and enriching that we share with our whole taxonomic order.

"Science with a Capital S"

Sy Montgomery

Situated to the west of the eastern fork of the Rift Valley of Tanzania, Olduvai Gorge is a thirty-mile-long moonscape, flooded with white-hot light. There is little soil here: in places, all the eye can see is a vast expanse of cracked and bouldered white and gray calcrete, a type of limestone. The summer sun sears your skin, burning right through cotton clothing. Grass dries to straw; the tops of the few acacias seem flattened by the brittle heat. It is so dusty that if you blow your nose at the end of the day, mud comes out. Everything your senses tell you is sharp-edged, metallic, stark. It seems as if bones are the only thing this soil will grow.

But as Louis Leakey searched for those bones, in his imagination this land was ripe and lush. When Jane Goodall first came to Olduvai in 1957, accompanying Louis and Mary on a dig, he told Jane of the paradise early man would have found here. The gorge exposes the graveyards of vanished lakes and streams, whose waters would have drawn plentiful game, easy hunting. Nearby forests would have offered cool shade, shelter, nuts, and fruits. When Jane first came to Olduvai, *Zinjanthropus* and *Homo habilis* were yet to be unearthed, but Louis was sure such finds awaited him. Man's ancestors, he knew, would have flourished by Olduvai's lakeshores.

On that dig Jane remembers holding in her hands the fossilized bone of a prehistoric animal that early man might have hunted by the vanished lake. It was then she realized the full extent of Louis's quest: here was the fossil, but what had this being really looked like? How did it communicate with others of its kind? How was its family organized? How did it move? What was the scent of its skin?

These were the questions Louis pondered about the ancestors of mankind. For clues Louis looked to another lakeshore, several hundred miles to the west. There, roaming a thirty-square-mile park, still lived large-brained, agile-handed primates, animals so like man that early explorers had described them as human. And though others of their kind lived mostly in dense tropical rain forests, here, by the shores of Lake Tanganyika, they shared the environment that primitive man had enjoyed at Olduvai two million years ago. It was at Olduvai that Louis first told Jane about them: they were the chimpanzees of Gombe.

To travel to Gombe from Kigoma, the largest town in the region, you wait for the water taxi to make its wet landing on the shore of Lake Tanganyika. You may have to wait under a hot sun for many hours because the boat doesn't adhere to a schedule; meanwhile dozens of children crowd around, whispering "Muzungu!" (white person) while eyeing and interpreting your every movement with murmurs of KiSwahili or KiHa. The water taxi is a long, low, rough-hewn wooden boat, crowded with perhaps eighty people and their gear: live chickens, baskets of fruit, furniture, logs, neatly tied bundles of clothes. There aren't any seats; people sit on the rim of the boat or on fat burlap sacks stuffed with the odoriferous sardinelike fish called *dagaa*. Mud-and-thatch fisherman's huts dot the shore. On moonless nights the fishermen hoist their red nets, heavy with *dagaa*, by lamplight; at every fishing village you approach along the trip, you'll see *dagaa* on the beach, drying in the sun, glittering like tinsel. As the boat ap-proaches the shore to take on passengers and cargo, the shallows sparkle with the silver-blue, iridescent scales.

The twelve-mile journey takes two or three hours, depending on how frequently the motor cuts out. When it breaks down, passengers discuss the problem animatedly, and finally the men search their pockets for a penknife with which to attempt repairs. Women wrapped in bright-patterned cloth, on their way to visit other villages, pass their babies back and forth among the other passengers, trying to shelter them from the sun with their *kangas*.

As the boat nears the shore of the park, Gombe looks much as Jane Goodall found it when she landed here, in a government-owned aluminum dinghy, with Vanne, a game ranger, and an African cook on July 16, 1960. The beach is narrow, only a dozen yards of brown sand and pastel pebbles. The mountains rise sharply from the beach to tower 2,500 feet above the lake. They are fissured with gorges and streams, their valleys thick with tropical trees. Vanne was secretly horrified at the steepness of the slopes, the density of the forests; but to Jane, Gombe was a storybook dream fulfilled.

The forest looks like a *Tarzan* movie set: palms and ferns on the lower slopes and, higher up, buttressed trees soaring to 100 feet, vines tangling in the canopy. The light is diffused by the tracery of leaves above, dappling the ground like a fawn's back. The tops of the mountains are covered with golden, grassy slopes, inviting one to climb.

Despite the steep slopes, Gombe is a comfortable place. The temperature here by day is seldom hotter than 85 degrees Fahrenheit, seldom cooler than 60. The dry season, which lasts from June to October, is idyllic. On the beach the sun's bright heat is cooled by the breeze off the lake. You can swim in the clear blue water; it harbors none of the snails that infect so many other African lakes with deadly bilharzia. Cold streams bubble through every valley; the water is safe to drink. Biting insects, poisonous snakes, and toxic plants are few. In the glorious dry season, this is a place that invites walking in sandals and shorts.

Once the boat leaves, you hear only the sound of the waves lapping, as peaceful as breathing. A few dozen yards takes you to the edge of the forest, and you can hear the bubbling of Kakombe Stream, the rattling of dry palm fronds ready to fall, the cackling trills and high-pitched chirps of birds, the barks of the beetle-browed baboons. Little lizards trickle down tree trunks like raindrops. Within an hour of your arrival, you may glimpse coppery red-tailed monkeys cascading through the canopy or the chestnut flash of a bush-buck, a goat-sized antelope with spiral horns. Entering this jungle paradise of clear water, cool shade, and bright sun feels like a homecoming, familiar as a half-remembered dream.

When Jane embarked on her great adventure, she thought it might occupy at most two years of her life. She and her mother unpacked their gear: tents and tins and bedding, old binoculars borrowed from Louis, and tableware consisting of two tin plates, a cup without a handle and a thermos top. Jane remembers feeling a curious sense of awed detachment that first day. "What had I, the girl standing on the government launch in her jeans, to do with the girl who in a few days would be searching those very mountains for wild chimpanzees?" she recalls in her book *In the Shadow of Man.* "Yet by the time I went to sleep that night the transformation had already taken place." That night she pulled her cot from the tent to sleep out under the open sky.

Studying primates as a route to understanding man is an idea whose roots go back to the 1920s. Robert Yerkes, the American psychologist who founded and ran the Yale Laboratory of Primate Biology

from 1924 to 1943, considered chimpanzees "psychobiological gold mines." The chimp, in his view, was to be "a servant of science." To accomplish this goal, men were to "shape it intelligently to specification, instead of trying to preserve its natural characteristics." Using chimps as surrogate humans, scientists could, it was hoped, experiment in the laboratory to pioneer new ways to remodel humans psychologically, to make people happier and more productive.

The purpose of investigating the natural lives of primates was primarily to learn the "substrate" upon which man's "artificial" culture and language was imposed. Yet even in these so-called naturalistic studies, man's controlling hand often willfully manipulated the "natural" lives he had come to observe. Clarence Ray Carpenter's studies of "free-ranging" monkeys on Cayo Santiago in the late 1930s are considered one of the more important naturalistic studies of the era. But the 450 rhesus monkeys in his study colony had been captured in India and transported to Cayo Santiago in 1938. Attempting to investigate issues of sex and dominance in the group, he experimentally manipulated the social structure. In one experiment he removed the leader, then the emerging new leader, and so on down the line. "Naturalistic" studies included experimentally implanting electrodes in the brains of free-ranging monkeys and castrating and releasing males.

But Jane Goodall, sleeping out under the open sky, envisioned no experiments, no manipulation. Her vision was one of approach, of trust: she asked only that the chimpanzees admit her silent presence into their lives.

We soon realized it would be impossible to habituate them to our presence," wrote the primatologist Vernon Reynolds in 1960 after a nine-month study of wild chimpanzees in Uganda. He and his wife, Frances, had hoped the chimps would become used to their presence; they never did. The chimps fled as soon as they saw the two researchers.

This had also happened to Henry Nissen. In his forty-nine days of observation in French Guinea, he was unable to study them at close range. He was forced to hide from the chimps in order to see them, and the foliage that hid him from view often obscured his view of the animals.

Before leaving for Gombe, Jane had spoken with wildlife researchers in both Nairobi and London, and they all said she should not get her hopes up. The chimps would never get used to human observers.

When Jane began her study, her two Tanzanian scouts located chimps for her daily. Crawling through the clotted undergrowth of the lower valley forests, crisscrossing streams, hiking up the mountain slopes, they would follow the chimpanzees' hooting calls. But once the animals were located, Jane could watch them only from far away. Through her binoculars she saw mostly groups of chimpanzees climbing up tree trunks and then, many hours later, climbing back down. The chimpanzees' movements were obscured by the leaves of the *msulula* trees in which they were feeding. Jane and her scouts tried to approach closer for a better view, but even at 500 yards the chimps would flee from the three approaching humans.

From the beginning Jane had wanted to pursue her study alone. Her mother had come with her because the local government officials—Tanzania was then Tanganyika, under British rule—would not hear of a young English girl working in the jungle without a proper British chaperone. The two scouts accompanying her daily were there by order of the game warden, for Jane's safety. There were buffalo in the forests, and Jane remembered the gashes left on a tree by a bull that had charged in fury at a fisherman, who climbed the tree to escape. She occasionally saw leopards at close range; one left a neat pile of dung at a spot where she often sat. And the chimpanzees themselves could be dangerous. Waha tribesmen told her that once a man had climbed a palm to pick the fruits and failed to notice an adult male chimp was there. The animal charged down the tree, swiped at the man, and knocked out his eye.

Yet Jane longed to be alone in the forest. She reasoned that it would be easier for the chimps to accept a single human. The first few months of study were frustrating, and she felt pressured. Louis had secured only enough funds to cover six months, no more money would be forthcoming if she could report only a few glimpses of black hairy arms reaching down from the foliage to pull fruits out of sight. At one point Jane wrote her "Fairy Foster Father": "Life is depressing—wet, chimpless, and it seems impecunious. Fruit not fruiting. Chimps vanishing. Me being ill. Oh, just —— everything." She signed off, "A despondent and sad FC."

By the third month both Jane and Vanne were ill with malaria. The doctor in Kigoma had assured them, for reasons Jane still cannot fathom, that there was no malaria in Gombe, so they had brought no malaria pills. Vanne's fever soared to 105 each night. When Jane's fever finally broke, nearly two weeks later, she stole out of the tent at dawn. She headed, alone, for the mountain that rose directly above her two-tent camp.

A twenty-minute climb brought her to an open overlook about a thousand feet above the lake. A large flat rock offered a seat for an excellent view of the forested valleys below. It is not a hidden vantage point; any animal with reasonable eyesight can see a person up here from a quarter of a mile away. Heart hammering from the climb, Jane sat quietly, her legs folded beneath her.

She had been there scarcely fifteen minutes when three chimps appeared in a ravine below, only eighty yards away. They stood and stared at her boldly, considering, then calmly moved on. At that point Jane knew: the peak was the altar on which she could offer them her presence, like a promise: I am here. I am harmless. I wait.

Jane now says that day marked the turning point in her study. Later that morning she watched a group of chimps, screaming and hooting, careen down the opposite mountain slope and begin feeding on figs in the valley

below. Another group appeared about twenty minutes later in the bare ravine where she had earlier seen the three. They stopped also to stare at her and then moved on without alarm.

Thereafter, nearly every day she would make the predawn pilgrimage to the Peak (when Jane writes about the Peak it is sanctified with a capital letter). No longer did the scouts need to accompany her; they knew Jane was safe up there. They knew where to reach her. Carrying her clothing and a thermos, she would often climb the mountain naked in the glimmering dawn. Though she carried her clothes so they would not become wet and cold in the dew, she came to enjoy the feel of the wet grass against her legs, the cool darkness wrapping her body. It was like a purification ritual before going to a sacred place. Though the spot is still used today by Gombe research workers, it is considered to belong in some way to her alone; they call it Jane's Peak.

At the Peak Jane always donned the same dull-colored clothing, and once seated, she remained utterly still. Clearly visible, with her presence Jane reiterated her promise to the chimps, an incantation, an offering: I am here. I am harmless. I wait. To you, said her silent form, I give the choice: to flee or approach or ignore.

The chimps passed by her nearly every day to get to the figs fruiting in the valley. She came to recognize the individuals. And like Adam in the Garden of Eden, one of her first acts was to name the animals. Mr. McGregor was an old, balding male who reminded her of the gardener in *The Tale of Peter Rabbit*. She named Olly after her own aunt. Goliath was a powerful male in his prime; his gentle, handsome friend she called David Graybeard. Often, she noticed, when Goliath's body would grow with excitement, his hair erect, David would wrap an arm around his friend or gently touch his groin. Goliath's hair would go flat and smooth again.

Earlier naturalists and explorers had portrayed chimps as violent brutes. Their journals emphasized the chimps' "maniacal screams," their "murderous

rages," their sudden, powerful movements.

"They goe many together, and kill many negroe that travaile in the woods," claimed the African traveler Andrew Battel in the 1613 volume *His Pilgrims*. He claimed that chimpanzees were strong and vicious enough to kill elephants, "which come to feed where they be, and so beat them with their clubbed fists and pieces of wood that they will runne roaring away from them."

"These monkeys have an ugly face," quotes another seventeenth-century text. "They are very wicked and bold . . . so bold that they attack man."

But watching these animals that men had seen as violent, maniacal, and murderous, Jane was most impressed by the chimps' gestures of gentle affection, their quest for comfort. The difference in perception recalls the results of a study conducted by psychologists Susan Pollak and Carol Gilligan. They showed men and women a picture of acrobats performing on a trapeze and asked the respondents to write stories about the image. The men wrote stories of violence and betrayal. One imagined a scene in which one of the acrobats purposely drops another, who then plunges to her death. The women wrote stories about the two acrobats working together carefully and gently. Many women included in their stories a safety net that was not shown in the picture.

From her perch on the Peak, Jane watched the chimps greet each other with embraces and open-mouthed kisses. Sometimes a chimp would offer a hand to be kissed in greeting, like a Victorian lady. She often saw them hold hands with each other, as people do walking down the street. She watched them build their sumptuous leafy nests at dusk, high in the trees. When she could reach them, Jane would climb into the nests after the chimps had left for the day. She could feel the springy softness of the carefully woven branches and leaves. Often, she found, the chimps would construct pillows for their heads. Each individual slept in its treetop nest alone, except for infants, who slept in their mother's nest, curled in her arms.

Jane learned that the chimps' "maniacal screams" were often hoots of pleasure, heralding the discovery of a tree laden with fruit. Sometimes in their excitement they would hug one another, as if in joyful congratulation. Before picking a fruit, a chimp would often test it for ripeness, squeezing it gently with thumb and fingers, like a canny old lady at the grocery store.

Jane would taste the fruits the chimps ate: often they were bitingly acidic. She even tried eating termites, which she found rather tasteless. She began to share the chimps' sensory world, their perceptions: she will speak of a tree "laden with luscious fruit," even though to human tastes the fruits are too tart. She could almost feel the calm spreading through the bodies of the chimpanzees as they sat grooming one another, lavishing intense concentration on bringing pleasure to another.

Jane would watch and write down what she saw in her notebook. At night she would return to camp to exchange news with her mother over a dinner prepared by Dominic, the cook: he baked bread in a pit oven and made stews from tinned meat and fresh vegetables bought in Kigoma. A houseman washed her clothes, laying them out to dry on the *dagaa*-scented beach, and then pressed them with a hand iron filled with hot coals.

While Jane observed the chimps, her mother began a sort of clinic at the base camp, dispensing aspirin and bandages to the local fishermen. After dinner Jane would transcribe her notes into narrative, typing by the light of the kerosene lamp. Sometimes she would spend the night at the Peak to be nearer the chimps.

When Vanne left after five months at Gombe, Jane was lonely at first, but within a few weeks she came to cherish her solitude, especially her nights at the Peak. She had her scouts carry a trunk up there, with some tinned beans, a mug and some coffee, a blanket, and a sweater; these were her luxuries. "There's a special fascination about the sudden nightfall in the forest, when the sounds of the day give place to the more mysterious sounds of the night," she later said of her nights at the Peak. "I felt part of the mountain world around me, completely alone, completely at peace."

In the fifth month of her study, Jane made two discoveries that caused worldwide excitement. "For both of them," she wrote, "I had David Graybeard to thank."

One day Jane saw David sitting in the branches of a tree with a female and a youngster, who were reaching toward his mouth with outstretched hands, as if begging. In David's mouth was a pink object. Jane realized that it was meat.

David, after chewing the meat with bits of leaves, often spat out the wad into the hands of the female. Once he dropped a piece of flesh, and when it fell to the ground the youngster followed it. An adult bushpig ran from the undergrowth, charging at the young chimp. Jane saw three striped piglets with the adult and realized that the chimps were eating a piglet.

Until that time scientists had thought that chimps were vegetarians. Though it was believed they might supplement their diet with insects and perhaps small rodents, no one had imagined that chimps might hunt, kill, and eat mammals this large.

Within two weeks of that discovery, when Jane was on her way up to the Peak, she saw David Graybeard again in the grass sixty yards away. Focusing her binoculars, she saw that he was sitting by the red, drip-sand castle of a termite mound, pushing a long grass stem inside. After a few minutes he withdrew the stem and plucked something from the end with his lips.

For more than a week Jane watched and waited near the termite mound. David reappeared on the eighth day, along with Goliath. She saw them bite off the ends of their fishing stems when they became bent. She saw them carefully select new stems, twigs, and vines, often collecting "spares" from far away. She saw them carefully peel the leaves from twigs to fashion the tool.

She cabled Louis with her discoveries: like man, chimps hunt and eat large mammals and share the meat. Like man, chimps both use and make tools.

Ironically, the agency that had funded her first months of study, the Wilkie Brothers Foundation, was begun by Leighton and Robert Wilkie, inventors of cutting tools, machines, and processes. The brothers firmly believed that making and using tools was what had made man human; it was Louis's finds of primitive tools that had drawn their attention to him and his projects. "Man is a tool-using animal. . . . Without tools he is nothing, with tools he is all," read the brochure for their foundation. Indeed, tool use was part of the definition of man at the time. After receiving Jane's cable, Louis wrote to her: "I feel that scientists holding to this definition are faced with three choices: they must accept chimpanzees as man, by definition; they must redefine man; or they must redefine tools."

Louis wrote to the National Geographic Society about his protégée's findings. In her first eighteen months of research she had made "completely outstanding discoveries . . . of the very highest scientific importance." Louis's perennial funder soon offered £500, the equivalent at that time of $1,500, to continue the study.

Louis decided that Jane would need proper credentials in order for her findings to be taken seriously; she had only a diploma from a secretarial school in London. Louis negotiated an unprecedented agreement with Cambridge University: Jane would bypass the usual bachelor's degree and, after several semesters of courses at Cambridge, would submit the writeup of her study as a thesis for her Ph.D. in ethology, the study of animal behavior. To Jane this was a huge nuisance. "I didn't want a Ph.D.," she recalls. "I spent as little time there [Cambridge] as possible." From the beginning of 1961 until her thesis was accepted in 1965, her observations at Gombe were broken up each year by a dreary Cambridge semester. She remembers cold gray days, frozen water pipes, and longing to be with the chimps. And she remembers being told politely, again and again, that she was doing it all wrong.

In her first eighteen months of study, Jane had taken few measurements; she described in words, not numbers. She did not begin with a theory; instead she wrote down what she saw and what she felt, receptive to the dramas unfolding. Her focus was on the individual, not the archetype. Her subjects were not numbered but named. Her approach was intuitive, personal, receptive and narrative at a time when ethology was becoming increasingly theoretical, impersonal, experimental, and statistical.

Hers was the approach that women typically take in configuring the world: emphasizing relationships rather than rules, individuals rather than generalities, receptivity rather than control. Jane's approach was maverick for the very reason it was rejected: she was applying a feminine approach to a field that was dominated and defined by male views and values.

Women had seldom worked in field primatology; when they did, it was usually in the company of a Ph.D. husband. Her name would appear in the acknowledgments of scientific papers that came out of the field work or, less frequently, she would be listed as coauthor. An extensive search of the scientific literature by biologist Donna Harraway, author of *Primate Visions,* revealed not a single book written by a woman Ph.D. primatologist before 1960.

Jane's Cambridge adviser, Robert Hinde, was dismayed with her methods. He pushed measurement and numerical analysis. Jane remembers, "He would suggest things like, 'When you get back to Gombe,'—and this was after I had spent only eighteen months there—'you should measure the distances between where the chimps are feeding and the level they are in the canopy.' " Numbers, not narrative, would tell the scientific truth, he insisted; statistics, not intuitions, would reveal empirical reality.

A highly respected English ethologist, Hinde stood at the forefront of a field whose practitioners were at that time struggling to transform them-

selves from naturalists to scientists. Naturalists, typified by the self-taught nineteenth- and early twentieth-century explorers, merely scribbled their descriptions in their notebooks. In the 1960s scientists, those bright young men in white coats, were supposed to be the saviors of the world. Guided by logic, propelled by measurement and experiment, scientists promised the breakthroughs leading to the Great Big Beautiful Tomorrow lauded at every World's Fair, when, thanks to man's increasing control over the universe, life would be easier, more comfortable, more productive, more affluent.

Robert Hinde was one of the young Turks taking ethology in a direction new and different from that envisioned by Konrad Lorenz, its founder. Lorenz, a Bavarian naturalist, is best known for his discovery of the phenomenon known as imprinting; newly hatched ducklings and goslings will follow the first moving object they see and respond to it as to a mother. In a front-page photo in the *New York Times* tagged to his February 1989 obituary, Lorenz is pictured as he is best remembered: a white-bearded old man followed by a parade of greylag goslings that have imprinted on him.

Lorenz discovered and named many of the basic principles of animal behavior, especially many of the stereotyped inborn behaviors of birds. But he firmly believed that animals had thoughts, feelings, and motives. He made most of his discoveries without performing a single experiment. He did not intend to interfere with the behavior of any animal in the wild; a keen observer, he relied on his senses, intuition, and many thousands of hours of observation to reveal the *gestalt* of an animal's natural behavior.

But by the late 1950s Lorenz's influence was waning. The new ethology was largely an experimental science, as characterized by the work of Niko Tinbergen, Lorenz's friend and colleague, best known for his work on wasps and other insects. No longer was it enough to present narratives of field notes, as the naturalist-explorers had. The new ethology was problem-oriented, quantitative, experimental. The

old naturalists were now dismissed as mere "butterfly collectors." "In science, butterfly collecting isn't good enough anymore," said Nancy De Vore who, with her husband, Irven De Vore, was studying baboons in Kenya at the time. "If you don't have a theory informing what you're doing, and the numbers to back it up, it doesn't do to just write down everything you see."

The 850 pages of meticulously typed, carefully observed notes Jane had amassed over her first eighteen months at Gombe amounted to little more than a huge and immensely colorful butterfly collection. Hers was a collection of portraits of individual animals: Flo playing with her youngsters; David soothing the irritable Goliath with a touch of his hand; timid Olly, crouching and uttering soft grunts in front of more dominant individuals.

From the start Jane focused on the differences between individuals. And this, too, Carol Gilligan tells us, is a feminine characteristic: women tend to "insist on the particular . . . resisting a categorical formation." Men see things clearly ordered by theories, laws and rules; but when a woman makes a decision, it is "a contextual judgment, bound to the particulars of time and place," Gilligan explains in her book on psychological theory and women's development, *In a Different Voice.*

But exploring individual differences was precisely the opposite of the goal ethology set for itself in the 1960s. "Today you wouldn't dream of not recognizing individuality," says primatologist Alison Jolly, well known for her research on lemurs. But when Jolly was a graduate student, about the same time Jane was studying at Cambridge, she remembers that "there was constant pressure for scientists to talk about *the* adult male, *the* adult female-archetypes." Ethology was mainly concerned with discovering the "mechanisms" underlying universal behaviors, not individual motives sculpting differing responses.

Because animals were considered "models" rather than thinking, feeling individuals, animals under study were typically numbered, not named. Jane was not the first to name her study animals—Irven De Vore had named his baboon subjects in 1958—but she was still frowned upon for doing so. The first journal to which she submitted a scientific paper, *Annals of the New York Academy of Science,* sent it back, insisting she number the chimps instead of naming them. The editors crossed out Jane's references to chimps as "he" or "she" and replaced each one with "it"; they changed each "who" to "which." Jane refused to make the changes, and the paper was published anyway.

Regardless of her methods, Jane's discoveries at Gombe were too spectacular to ignore. As her renown grew, thanks to articles in *National Geographic* her fame bruised academic egos. What right had this young female amateur to steal the spotlight from those to whom it rightfully belonged, those who had devoted years of study and meticulously calculated methodology to their theories? Whispered attacks on Jane swelled, focusing on the aspects that set her apart from the male Ph.D.s whose turf she had invaded: many scientists dismissed her as a "blond bimbo" recalls Mary Smith, Jane's editor at *National Geographic.* "It was easy to make jokes about 'Me Jane, you Tarzan and the apes,' " she said.

Biruté Galdikas remembers that when she was an undergraduate at UCLA, one of her female professors offered this assessment of Jane's career: "The only reason she's so famous is because of her great legs in those short shorts in the films." Many years later Biruté told Jane about that comment. "I don't let that sort of thing bother me," Jane told her. "I just don't listen to it anymore."

Nor did Jane heed all her adviser's suggestions. She continued to record her observations mostly as a narrator, writing in her notebook, later speaking into a tape recorder. She continued to focus on individual differences. She continued to name her study subjects. Jane doesn't like to talk about her early disagreements with her Cambridge colleagues; neither does Robert Hinde. "He's totally different now, anyway," she says, dismissing the past; Hinde is

now a close friend and an adviser to the institute that bears Jane's name.

In spite of their early disagreements, Jane's thesis was accepted and her degree awarded in 1965. Not awarding it would have caused much embarrassment at Cambridge; by that time her work had been heavily publicized in *National Geographic,* and in both 1963 and 1964 she had been awarded the society's Franklin Burr Award for Contribution to Science. But her thesis was not widely respected by her colleagues. When Dian Fossey was sent off to Cambridge to get her Ph.D., she wrote to her friends the Schwartzels that Jane's thesis "is now considered in the University School the perfect example of what not to do."

When you mention these criticisms today, Jane replies in a voice a shade sharper and louder than her normal speaking voice: "I didn't give two hoots for what they thought. They were wrong, and I was right. That's why I was lucky that I never was going into any of these things for science. And as I didn't care about the Ph.D., it didn't matter. I would listen, I just wouldn't do what they said. Then I could go back to what I was doing at Gombe."

During the rainy season of Jane's first year at Gombe, after Christmas, the chimpanzees became bold in her presence. Sometimes she would find herself surrounded by screaming, thrashing chimpanzees: black shapes, yellow teeth, hurling at her an angry wall of sound. With hair erect, they would shake branches, scream threats, and then vanish, their voices hanging in the air. Once as Jane was lying flat on the wet ground, sheltered under a plastic sheet from the rain, a large male hit her hard on the head with his hand. When she sat up, he moved away. And Jane felt a sense of triumph along with relief: this was contact of a sort.

After she returned from her first semester at Cambridge, she found the chimps more accustomed to her. Now she could follow them through the forest. David Graybeard was particularly patient and tolerant of her follows;

sometimes he even seemed to welcome her company. He would wait for her to catch up to him, pausing to look back in her direction as she stumbled over vines or belly-crawled along overgrown pig trails, just as he would wait for his friends Goliath and William.

Jane spent many hours alone with David Graybeard. One day as she sat with him near a stream, she saw a red palm nut on the ground nearby; she picked it up and offered it to him on her open palm. At first he turned his head away. But when she moved her hand closer, she recalls in *Shadow,* "he looked at it, and then at me, and then he took the fruit, and at the same time held my hand firmly and gently with his own. As I sat motionless he released my hand, looked down at the nut, and dropped it to the ground."

David had not accepted her gift, but he had given her one far more profound:

At that moment there was no need of any scientific knowledge to understand his communication of reassurance. The soft pressure of his fingers spoke to me not through my intellect but through a more primitive emotional channel: the barrier of untold centuries which has grown up during the separate evolution of man and chimpanzee was, for those few seconds, broken down.

On another evening Jane returned to camp to find Dominic very excited: a large male chimpanzee had walked into her camp and spent an hour feeding in the fruiting palm tree near her tent.

The next day Jane stayed in camp. About ten in the morning David Graybeard walked past her tent to climb the palm tree. He returned daily, as long as the tree continued to fruit. And although "there was a limit to the amount of information one could gain from watching a lone male guzzling palm nuts," she wrote in *Shadow,* she would sometimes stay in camp and wait for him, "just for the intense pleasure of seeing him so close and so unafraid."

A few weeks later Jane suffered another bout of malaria. A different palm in camp was fruiting, and David resumed his visits. One day when she left a banana on a table, David, hair suddenly erect with boldness, snatched it. Thereafter Jane told Dominic to leave bananas out when he saw David around. The chimp began to visit regularly and occasionally would bring his high-ranking friend Goliath and, later, timid William.

At about this time Hugo van Lawick came to Gombe. The bananas proved to be a filmmaker's bonanza. Judy Goodall's efforts to photograph the chimps at Gombe had been ruined by constant rain and fleeing subjects. Hugo's skill and luck were greater. Drawn to the pile of bananas, the chimpanzees came to camp regularly. Before Hugo's whirring camera they shared and squabbled over the fruits, occasionally arguing with baboons over the provisions. They also discovered the salty taste of sweaty garments left out to dry, and chewed and sucked on them. Hugo filmed David accepting a banana from Jane's hand: first he swaggered from side to side, hair erect, and then very gently grasped the offering.

Jane's provisioning the chimps with bananas was later strongly criticized, even by Louis, who vehemently objected. "I feel it is creating a most dangerous and impossible situation," Louis wrote her in 1964, "which might lead to these chimpanzees being shot." Provisioning could make the chimpanzees dangerously bold and greedy, he warned; having lost their fear of humans, they might begin to raid villagers' houses, and if this happened, the Africans would probably retaliate: "It is not right and I cannot be a party to it."

But in 1962 the bananas provided a bridge to a new level of intimacy. It was while David Graybeard was eating a banana that Jane first ventured to touch him. Squatting close beside him, Jane slowly moved her hand toward his shoulder and parted his fur with her fingers. David brushed her hand away as casually as if it were a fly. When she reached for him again, he let her groom him for a full minute. It was Christmas Day.

The photos and films that Hugo took of Jane among the chimps deeply moved Western audiences. Jane, girlish in her ponytail, shorts, and sandals, rounds a bend, stepping from the bushes into a clearing, as a young chimp raises a hand to her as in greeting. Jane reaches out, her pale arm balletic, to touch the outreached hand of Flo's infant son Flint—the image of the reaching hands of God and Adam in the Sistine chapel.

Never had National Geographic found such a treasure trove for its films and magazine. Jane's first article on her work, "My Life among Wild Chimpanzees," which appeared in 1963, was so popular that the issue sold out and the society had to reprint it. Between 1962 and 1989 National Geographic made five films about her, more footage than they devoted to any other investigator, including Louis Leakey.

Edwin Snider, the society's vice president, had been skeptical when he first met Jane. Shy and slim, so proper and English that even her smile seemed restrained, her lips covering her teeth, she didn't seem tough enough to do the job. "She looked like someone who would seem more at home at an English garden party than in the jungle," he recalls. But it was Jane's fragility, her vulnerability before the chimpanzees' great strength, that made her story so compelling: the beauty among the beasts, at once myth, fable, and adventure story.

Introducing Jane to an audience gathered at National Geographic's Washington headquarters in 1964, Melvin Payne invoked Edgar Rice Burrough's tales of Tarzan and his English bride, Jane: "Truth is stranger than fiction, and fiction can be transformed into prophecy," he said. "Here we have a perfect example of that evolution, for this lovely English lady called Jane has likewise traded her comfortable home in England for the primitive life of the African wilderness among the great apes."

Jane's work and life had a storybook quality, echoing the themes of the childhood books she had cherished growing up. In her *National Geographic* articles and her books, Jane's own story was entwined with that of the chimps, and it read even more like a fairy tale: in 1964 the brave young adventuress's bylines include the title "Baroness." In 1967 she gave birth to a golden-haired son, and *Grub the Bush Baby,* as she titled a 1971 book, gave occasion for more films and articles.

Many of Jane's early lectures were given titles befitting children's books: "Family Life in Chimpland"; "My Life among the Wild Chimpanzees." In an English-accented voice as low and steady as a lullaby, Jane was constantly pointing out the ways in which chimps were "just like people": "Every chimpanzee, just like every human being, has his own character and personality," begins her narration to Hugo's 1963 film shown at National Geographic, which introduces David Graybeard and Goliath, Flo and Fifi, Olly and her daughter Gilka. Often her words seem to have been borrowed from Doctor Dolittle, who talked with the animals. Chimps call as they wake in the morning in their treetop nests: "Here David is telling Goliath it is time to get up." A family of chimps forms a grooming chain: "Here you see a sort of forest beauty parlor." At a time when scientists regarded animals as "stimulus-response machines" with no conscious purpose, Jane freely spoke of the chimps' emotions, moods, and motives. As Olly's one-and-a-half-year-old daughter clutches herself with crossed arms, Jane narrates: "Gilka still feels far more confident if she can hang onto something, even if it's only herself."

As Louis had wooed audiences with his showmanship and bravura, Jane enchanted her listeners with her storytelling. Her slight shyness before the microphone—she still sometimes looks at a mike as if she's never seen such an object before—only set off her poise, a large jewel in a slender setting. Her story is the drama of contact, of touch, of equality between species. "This is not the story of man's stewardship," writes Donna Harraway in *Primate Visions,* "but of his homecoming, not just in peace but in equality . . . a narrative not of civil rights, but of natural rights."

But this is not the story that Science was constructing for man. The year National Geographic published Jane's first book, *My Friends the Wild Chim-*

panzees, 1967, an American named Harry Harlow received the National Science Medal for his work with rhesus monkeys. He did not work in a jungle; he did not need binoculars to make his observations. He did not wait, as Jane did, for the dramas of his subjects' lives to unfold. Harlow created the dramas he was to witness; in his laboratory at the University of Wisconsin in Madison, he exercised absolute control over both the actors and the stage.

Harlow used monkeys as psychological stand-ins for man. He is best known for his invention of the "surrogate mother": this was a model to which baby monkeys, raised in isolation, would pitifully cling when confronted with a frightening stimulus. The baby monkeys would rush to the surrogate mother, frantic for comfort and solace, even if the model was equipped with a catapult to toss the infant away, even if it blasted compressed air into the infant's face. He powerfully demonstrated the psychological need for contact, a need deeper even than that of relief from physical pain.

While Jane was quietly, patiently watching and waiting, it was Harlow's genius that was honored in Western science: the genius of manipulation, of experiment. "The taproot of science is the aim to control," Donna Harraway comments in *Primate Visions*; the laboratory, not the wild, yields the kind of knowledge that enhances control.

Harlow's experiments brought control of primate minds and emotions to undreamed-of-levels of sophistication. His laboratory inventions read like a Christmas shopping list for the Marquis de Sade: the "well of despair" was an isolation chamber designed to produce, for study, profound depression in baby monkeys. He created the "iron maiden," a surrogate mother covered with hidden brass spikes that would emerge at a touch of the experimenter's button. This device, like the other "evil mothers" he created, was supposed to demonstrate the infant's deep need for maternal comfort, even when the mother was inherently punishing and evil. He developed the

"rape rack," a device to immobilize the female monkey while artificially inseminating her. Using artificial means, Harlow produced far more baby monkeys with which to stock other labs than healthy wild animals could produce.

Honored with some of the most prestigious awards in his field, founder of two major research laboratories, Harry Harlow epitomized the role of the scientist as male manipulator, inventor, experimenter. Godlike in his power over his research subjects, the scientist was equally Godlike in promising a future in which man's increasing control over the universe would exalt his power.

In universities, Jane says, these messages still persist: "First of all, it's wonderful to be a scientist. Secondly, if you become a scientist, you become one of the elite, you wear a white coat, you're ranked with God, and what you say will be believed. Thirdly, if you're going to be a scientist you've got to be very objective; you mustn't get emotionally involved about those things.

"So what the message is that's coming out, you must be a scientist first and human being second. And I think that's what's gone wrong. I mean it's appalling to me to see science with a big capital S: it's turning people into machines."

Jane's science is lowercase, a woman crouching humbly in the grass, receptive, allowing approach. When Geza Teleki arrived at Gombe in 1968—never having worked in Africa, never having worked with primates—he asked Jane to explain her approach to him, how she expected him to work with the chimps. "And she couldn't do it," he remembers. "She got really exasperated. She ended up saying to me, 'Look, I can't explain it to you, you'll find out when you get there. There's only one thing to keep in mind: if you're going down the trail, and you see a chimp coming the other way, you are the one to get off the trail, not the chimp. You don't belong here. The chimp belongs here.'

"And that, to me, summarizes Jane Goodall," Geza continues. "Everything else is less important. Career is

less important. Science is less important. Fame is less important than doing the right thing when you're dealing with the natural environment. I didn't understand it at the time. I thought she was a little weird. It's not the kind of thing you want to deal with when your only interest is starting a career as a professional. But that message has directed my life for the past twenty years."

Doing the right thing when you're dealing with the natural environment." At no time was this credo thrown into sharper, more revealing relief than during the Gombe polio epidemic of 1966. "Nothing that happened at Gombe before or since that has been as horrible—nothing," Jane says. "They were among the darkest days of my life—a living nightmare."

In the dry season of that year, Olly's four-week-old baby became ill. At first it seemed that the infant was having trouble gripping its mother's belly as they traveled; the next day his four limbs hung limply. The following day Olly appeared in camp, with Gilka, her adolescent daughter. The infant's corpse was slung over Olly's shoulder.

At the time Jane and Hugo did not know that Olly's infant was the first victim of an epidemic that would eventually claim the lives of six of the Gombe chimps. Jane was then pregnant with Grub; neither she nor Hugo had had the full course of polio vaccine. But when the couple linked the chimps' paralyzing disease to an outbreak of polio among Africans in a nearby village, they panicked.

Reaching Louis by radio telephone, they engineered an arrangement with Pfizer Laboratories in Nairobi. The firm would donate oral polio vaccine and fly it in to Gombe for Jane, Hugo, their staff, and the chimps. The vaccine would be administered to the chimps hidden in bananas. But for some of the chimps, help came too late. The nightmarish agony of Mr. McGregor haunts Jane to this day.

In November 1966, Hugo saw Flo and Fifi and Flint staring into a low bush and giving soft, *hoo* calls; he could not see what they were looking at. At dusk, when Jane and Hugo went to investigate, they first saw swarms of flies. "We were expecting to see some dead animal as we cautiously moved closer," Jane wrote in an article for *National Geographic.* But instead they found Mr. McGregor. Sitting on the ground, the old chimp was reaching for some purple berries on a bush over his head. "It was not until he wanted to reach another cluster of the fruit that we realized the horror of what had happened, for to move he had to seize hold of a low branch, both his legs trailing uselessly behind him," she wrote. They realized later he must have traveled a long way in this manner; even the tough callosities on his buttocks were raw and bleeding from dragging along the ground. Polio had robbed him of control of the sphincter muscles; his feces, urine, and blood had drawn the flies.

That night they watched in amazement as McGregor, using only his arms, pulled himself into a low-branched tree and built himself a nest. The next morning they followed his trail and were staggered at the distance he had dragged himself: more than 150 yards. "For the next ten days—and it seemed ten years—we followed, hoping in vain we might see some flicker of life return [to his legs]," Jane wrote.

"We did all that we could to help," she wrote. At first, nervous when they approached him too closely, he threatened them by raising an arm and barking. But after two days "he seemed to sense that we were only trying to help," Jane wrote. He would lie still while she squeezed water from a sponge into his open mouth. Hugo and Jane prepared a basket of bananas, palm nuts, leaves, and berries and with a long stick pushed it up to him in his nest. To kill the flies that were torturing him, they sprayed him with insecticide.

One evening when they went out with his supper, they found McGregor on the ground. From the angle of his shoulder, they saw he had dislocated an arm. "We knew that in the morning we would have to shoot our old friend," Jane wrote. She spent much of that last night with him. As dusk fell he looked up frequently into the tree above him;

Jane realized he wanted to make a nest. She cut some vegetation and took it to him in a large pile; without hesitation, he took the leafy twigs and branches and with his good hand and his chin tucked them beneath himself to make a comfortable pillow. She returned to see him later that night. "It says very much for the extent to which we had won his trust and confidence, that, having heard my voice, he closed his eyes and went back to sleep, three feet away, and with his back to me and my bright pressure lamp."

The next morning, while he was grunting with pleasure over two eggs they had brought him—his favorite food—Hugo and Jane shot their old friend.

Decades later Jane is still defending the choices she made during the polio epidemic: to act instead of watch, choosing empathy over objectivity. Anthropologists, working with groups of "primitive" peoples, are often faced with similar dilemmas. When sickness or famine strikes a village, the anthropologist must choose either to act—providing Western medicines, nursing care and food, interfering in the lives she has come to observe—or to merely watch and chronicle, leaving the group "unpolluted" by Western "interference."

There were other times in her study when Jane chose to "interfere." When chimps were sick, she provisioned them with antibiotic-laden bananas. When Gilka developed a fungal growth on her face, Jane had the growth biopsied and later gave Gilka medication to control the disease. When old Flo was dying, Jane fed her eggs to make her last days more pleasant.

"There are some scientists who frown upon such practices, believing that nature should run its course," Jane wrote in an early chapter of *The Chimpanzees of Gombe,* a scholarly compilation of her first twenty-six years of work. "It seems to me, however, that humans have already interfered to such a major extent, usually in a very *negative* way . . . with so many animals in so many places that a certain amount of *positive* interference is desirable."

At many of her lectures, when the polio epidemic is mentioned, a mem-

ber of the audience asks: "Why did you interfere?" Usually the question comes from a man. For men, observes psychologist Carol Gilligan, "the moral imperative appears rather as an injunction to respect the rights of others and thus to *protect from interference* the rights to life and self-fulfillment" (italics mine). But for women, "The moral imperative that emerges repeatedly in interviews . . . is an injunction to care, a responsibility to discern and *alleviate* the 'real and recognizable trouble' of this world" (italics mine).

More recently Jane spoke about the polio epidemic to a group of physical therapists, most of whom were women. Their question, at first mention of the disease, was different: "Did you try to help?"

By the second decade of Jane's research, her tiny campsite had been transformed into the Gombe Stream Research Centre, an international collaborative research community. Her first three students arrived in 1966; by 1972 more than a hundred people—African staff and their families, American and British undergraduate and graduate students—were supporting a study of fifty-four chimpanzees and the troops of baboons who shared their land.

By this time most of the chimps were regularly visiting Jane's banana feeding station, which by now had a building of its own and was equipped with underground bins that the researchers could open or close as the situation demanded. They monitored attendance rates at the station daily and maintained charts on group structure and activities, vocalizations, and gestures. Increasing emphasis was placed on following individual chimps and groups in the forest. "There was so much to be found out, one person couldn't begin to answer all the millions of questions springing to mind," Jane remembers. "I needed the help badly."

After Grub's birth in 1967, Jane spent less time with the chimps. She and Grub often accompanied Hugo to his camp in the Serengeti while he worked on a documentary and a book on wild African dogs. Students took over the day-to-day collection of data from 1967 to 1969, when the Serengeti project ended. From 1971 to 1975 Jane spent a semester each year as a visiting professor at Stanford University in California.

Many of Jane's students were recruited from this institution and from Cambridge. By this time conditions at camp were more comfortable, though still Spartan. The students lived in prefab metal cabins, the windows covered with wire mesh to prevent the chimps from climbing in, the tin roofs covered with thatch (Jane hated the appearance of gleaming metal). In 1972 a brick dining hall was built near the beach, and the students dined there at night with Jane and Hugo when they were in residence. Emelie Bergman (who later married Gombe researcher David Riss) recalls dinners as decorous and pleasant, a "familylike atmosphere." After a bath in the lake, the students would dress neatly for dinner—a nod to Jane's proper English upbringing. They'd wait politely for everyone to arrive before eating the meal of rice, cabbage, and fish, or sometimes fresh meat and fruit from the market in Kigoma. After the meal a student would often give an informal talk about her work, or, if the generator was working, they might all listen to music on a cassette player.

But of course the chimps dominate students' memories of Gombe. "Everyone who worked at Gombe had chimps that they especially identified with," remembers Geza Teleki. Typically, male chimps got on best with male workers, and females with females. Geza had a special relationship with Leakey. Easily recognized because of a scar under one eyelid, which revealed a white patch around that iris, Leakey had, of course, been named in honor of Jane's mentor. He was also the first male chimp Jane knew who would try to take away two females to mate with at the same time. By the time Geza met him, Leakey was old and, as he puts it, "semi-retired." The wonder of that relationship stays with him now, two decades later.

"I never gave Leakey anything, never coerced him with anything, never rewarded him, never willingly touched him," Geza remembers. The relationship "was not based on interaction, favors, or any of the usual things whereby we forge links with animals around us. Yet there was a sort of mutual attraction, for reasons I can't explain. There were times I would sit down some distance from him, and like as not he'd come and sit next to me, and then lie down and put his head on my tennis shoe. I did a lot of follows of Leakey simply because he seemed to like to have me around. If I got left behind or lost, he'd come back and find me."

Geza had not dreamed that such a relationship was possible between himself and a wild animal. He had read, of course, of Jane's relationships with David Graybeard, Flo, Mr. McGregor, and the others; he knew that she had bridged the gap between human and animal. But until he experienced this himself, he did not realize that Jane had built a bridge strong enough for others to cross.

That the chimps were far from harmless only augmented the human observers' awe at their normally gentle behavior. When the chimpanzees did become aggressive, they usually directed their actions toward male observers. Richard Wrangham was once used as a "display tool" by a seventeen-year-old male named Charlie. Hair erect, Charlie rushed down a bank at the student, grabbed his ankle, and dragged him several dozen yards through the foliage in an attempt to impress some other chimps watching nearby. "While I squawked and thrashed, I added a lot to his display," Richard recalls thoughtfully. "I was much better than if he had used relatively silent and immobile branches."

Although there were several other such incidents, during the first decade of research no chimpanzee ever seriously injured a human observer at Gombe; this seemed a powerful testament to the animals' inherent gentleness. It bore out the portrait Jane had been painting of them: excitable at times, but intrinsically peaceful beings,

an attractive ancestor of the potentially peaceful human species.

But with other eyes watching them, during the second decade of Gombe research, "My Friends the Wild Chimpanzees" turned out to be cannibals, infant killers, and warmongers.

The picture painted of these animals today is very different from what Jane initially saw alone," says John Mitani, a primatologist who has studied all three species of great apes. "Goodall, like Fossey, went into the field thinking these were cute, cuddly creatures. They were prone not to see things happening," John's suggestion recalls the stories women wrote about the pictures of trapeze artists in Pollak and Gilligan's psychological study: they imagined safety nets when none were present in the picture. "The single most important reason they didn't see these things [cannibalism and warfare]" John quickly adds, "is the fact that they're tough animals to study, and these are rare events; but these women also had ingrained biases. And this isn't a criticism," he emphasizes. "It points to the need for perseverance."

At first, said Jane, "I couldn't believe it." Jane had heard reports, from the Japanese researchers working south of Gombe in the Mahale Mountains, of cannibalism and warfare among chimps. "We were all scornful," she remembers. "We all said, 'They must have made a mistake.' " But soon the evidence was too obvious to ignore.

In 1972 the researchers recognized the existence of a new group at Gombe. The Kahama community, as it was called, comprised six mature males, including the powerful Goliath, and three females. They had broken off from the study community, known as the Kasakela group, and had set up new territory to the south. Males from the Kasakela community set out on regular raids with one objective in mind: to murder the members of the Kahama group.

Emelie Bergman recorded one such raid in February 1975:

Faben, Flo's eldest son, led the Kasakela party of five adult males and one adolescent. They traveled slowly, cautiously south until they reached a tree, which they climbed. For forty-five minutes they stared toward the Kahama group's range.

It was then that the group spotted Goliath, who was now quite old. His head and back were partially bald; his teeth were worn to the gums. Faben gave pant-hoots and raced toward the old male, pushing him to the ground. Then all the chimps attacked. For twenty minutes they savaged Goliath, twisting his limbs, dragging him along the ground, pounding his shoulder blades, biting his thigh. At first Goliath tried to protect his head with his arms, but then he gave up and lay still. Roaring pant-hoots, drumming on trees with feet and hands, the war party dispersed to the forest, victorious.

When they had gone, Emelie saw Goliath try to sit up; he couldn't. She left him shivering and bleeding; she wanted to help but, without any medical supplies, she was unable to do so. The students and staff searched intensively for Goliath for many days thereafter; but like all the other victims of these systematic brutal attacks, Goliath was never seen again.

That time, says Jane, was the most brutal in Gombe's history. Soon the humans, too, would be held hostage to a wave of brutality. It was as if evil had seized the community, both chimps and humans, in a fist of rage. It was during the early part of the chimpanzees' era of warfare, on May 19, 1975, that violence struck the humans of Gombe Wildlife Research Institute and changed its history forever.

That evening Jane retired early; she had a sore eye, and the brightness of her kerosene lamp further pained her, so she turned it out earlier than normal. Had it not been for that sore eye, surely, she says today, she would have been kidnaped.

A few minutes later Jane heard the motor of an approaching boat; she assumed it was the water taxi stopping at Gombe to see if they had petrol.

She did not realize until hours later, when Grub's tutor came running along the beach to her house, that Gombe was facing an emergency. At first she

learned only that Emelie Bergman's typewriter had been found lying upside down on a path and Emelie's house was empty.

Forty armed guerrillas, members of the Marxist Popular Revolutionary Party, had crossed the lake from Zaire. They had kidnaped Emelie, along with three Americans: Stanford graduate student Barbara Smuts, twenty-four, and undergraduates Kenneth Smith, twenty-two, and Jane Hunter, twenty-one. The terrorists had beaten a member of Jane's Tanzanian staff, but the man refused to reveal where the other American students were sleeping.

The student hostages later made a pact that they would never talk about the kidnaping. "There were so many terrorists, they might get ideas," Emelie explains today. She will only say that she and the others were held in a jungle hut forty miles across the lake in Zaire, and that the terrorists never knew their hostages were participants in the most famous field study in Western history. "All they knew about us was that we were white," Emelie said. That was bait enough. Emelie was released to carry the captor's demands to the Tanzanian government: $460,000 in cash, the release of party leaders from Tanzanian jails, and dozens of rifles. Otherwise the remaining three hostages would be killed.

Gombe was evacuated when negotiations began. "Tanzania will not be blackmailed," pledged President Julius Nyerere. Nonetheless a deal was negotiated with the help of the parents of the kidnaped students and Stanford University. The students were released safely and returned home to their parents. But from that time on, whites at Gombe were considered terrorist bait. Her African staff returned to the research station to take data on their own, but Jane was marooned at Dar es Salaam, where her new husband, Derek Bryceson, lived. Derek and Jane had married a year after her divorce from Hugo, when Grub was seven years old.

In August Jane's staff reached her in Dar by radio with fresh horror: Passion, with the aid of her adolescent daughter, Pom, had seized Olly's three-

week-old granddaughter. The mother-daughter team had then spent five hours eating the body of the infant.

To Jane the news was a stunning blow. "This was the hardest thing to understand and accept that's ever happened at Gombe," she says today. Though the news of the Kasakela warriors shocked her, essentially their actions made sense: brutal, warring males staging a takeover of territory closely mirrored the behavior of modern man; here, in the chimps, lurked the "dawn warrior"; the roots of our violence ran deep. The terrorist raid on Gombe horrified and angered Jane: but it was part of an understandable pattern of human violence—a pattern to which her Gombe chimps had provided such an Edenic and peaceful alternative. But females preying on babies—that was different. The mother-daughter bond had been contorted into a grotesque cannibalistic partnership.

Jane still does not understand what drove Passion and Pom to their attacks. But she vividly remembers that Passion, when Pom was born in 1965, had proved "extraordinarily inefficient and indifferent" as a mother. Unlike solicitous Flo, who responded with comfort to her offspring's every whimper, when Pom would cry with hunger, Passion would not guide the infant's mouth to her nipple; Pom had to find it for herself. As Pom became older, Passion did not always gather her baby in her arms and tuck her under her belly before moving off; instead she would simply walk away, and Pom would run, whimpering, to catch up.

Jane had known Passion since her early days at Gombe; she appears along with David Graybeard in many of Hugo's early photographs. When Jane named this chimp, she was not thinking of passion in the sense of suffering.

Over the next two years Jane's African staff saw Passion and Pom kill and eat three infants of the Kasakela community. Between 1974 and 1977 two other infants vanished during their first month of life, and three mothers, known or thought to be pregnant, miscarried. During the period of Passion and Pom's cannibalistic attacks, only one Kasakela mother—Flo's daughter, Fifi—successfully raised an infant.

Jane herself observed none of the incidents of cannibalism. After the hostage crisis she was prohibited from returning to Gombe for a time; when she finally was allowed to go back, it was only for a few days a month. She did, however, witness Passions' unsuccessful solo attack on a female with her baby, which occurred in the top of a tree. Jane realized that without Pom's help Passion was unable to kill other mothers' babies.

In November 1976, two African staff members recorded an attack by Passion and Pom on the three-week-old daughter of the gentle female named Melissa. Melissa's other daughter, six-year-old Gremlin, ran to the field assistants, stood upright and looked into their eyes, then at the scene before her, as if she were begging for help. The two assistants threw rocks at Passion and Pom, and some of the rocks hit them, but the pair didn't seem to notice. Passion held Melissa to the ground as Pom bit the baby's head. Using one foot, Passion pushed at Melissa's chest while Pom pulled at her hands; finally Pom ran off with the infant, who was already dead.

Fifteen minutes later Melissa approached Passion. The two mothers stared at each other, then Passion reached out and touched Melissa's bleeding hand and embraced her. As Jane interprets it, "It was as if to say, 'I have no quarrel with you, I only want your baby.'"

Jane and her staff debated what to do to stop the killing. At one point they discussed tranquilizing Passion and disabling a nerve in her arm. The operation would have to be extraordinarily delicate, for Jane could not in conscience permanently cripple any chimp, no matter how much she personally disliked the animal. The disability would have to be reversible. But in 1977 Passion bore another baby, and motherhood was the functional equivalent of a disabled arm, said Jane: for the first few months one arm was always holding the baby. The killings and cannibalism stopped. Jane named the baby Pax—peace.

Jane doesn't relish talking about that violent era. In 1980 she reluctantly delivered a lecture titled "Cannibalism and Warfare in Chimp Society" at an L. S. B. Leakey Foundation fundraiser.

"The title of the lecture was chosen for me," she told the audience, as if in apology. "This isn't a subject that I prefer to emphasize above other aspects of chimpanzee behavior."

Yet for all its horror, the violence at Gombe proved beyond doubt the centerpiece of Jane's thesis: that the animal's individual temperaments, family backgrounds, and decisions were the basis of their history. "An individual chimp can have as much influence on the history of his or her community as an individual human can have on his or her tribe or country," Jane said. Passion and Pom's cannibalism affected a whole generation of chimpanzees: for three years they prevented all but one of the Kasakela mothers from raising an infant. And that the chimpanzee's era of warfare, cannibalism, and infanticide occurred against the backdrop of the terrorist raid on Gombe underscored Jane's point: "Chimpanzees are far more like humans than even we ever thought."

For Jane this era of violence was followed by a time of unparalleled fame and unparalleled sorrow. Between 1974 and 1984 she was honored with five internationally respected awards, including the J. Paul Getty Wildlife Conservation Prize of $50,000. Journalists seized upon the lurid behavior of the chimpanzees to produce a flood of publicity; National Geographic filmed another TV special.

What these stories and the film didn't mention was that Jane was by now spending very little time at Gombe. After the kidnaping, the Tanzanian government forbade her to have white students stay there for any long-term study, and her own visits to Gombe were short, secretive, and restricted to a few weeks at a time.

When she was not lecturing abroad to wildly enthusiastic audiences, Jane spent much of her time with her new husband. Friends describe Derek as "the love of her life" and their marriage as "blissful." Jane had loved Hugo, remembers Emelie Bergman-Riss, but their relationship, like the chain-smoking baron himself, was always "high-pressure." The couple had once had to make a rule that they would take one evening off a week, forcing themselves to simply enjoy each other's company. Their separation and divorce in 1974 occurred after Hugo had complained to friends that he was "tired of being Mr. Goodall." He was no longer willing to set aside his photography to be administrator of his wife's camp.

But with the easygoing "Mr. B.," as Jane's students called Derek, life became more relaxed. In the days before the kidnaping he visited Jane at Gombe often, and when they were apart they talked daily on the radio-telephone. Often they took vacations together, flying in the plane he piloted or boating and fishing with Grub near Derek's home in Dar es Salaam. An RAF pilot during World War II, Derek was a close friend and next-door neighbor of Tanzania's first president, Julius Nyerere. Derek had served as the only white member of parliament after Tanzania won independence in 1961. His political power allowed him to protect his new wife's project; his clout as director of Tanzania's national parks was crucial to resolving the kidnaping dilemma; and during his years in that position he took over many administrative chores. He also embargoed tourism at Gombe.

But after only five years of blissful marriage, Derek became ill with cancer. By the time it was diagnosed, the doctors said it was too late to intervene. In desperation he sought treatment at an alternative medical clinic in Hannover, West Germany. Jane stayed in a pensione while Derek was receiving treatments; she often picked wildflowers for her husband on her walk across the field that separated her flat from the hospital. Jane was devastated when Derek died in October 1980. She still wears his gold wedding band.

The prohibition on tourists to Gombe was lifted after Derek's death. Today the students' dining hall has been transformed, with flimsy particle-board partitions, into guest rooms for tourists. Tanzanian park officials have moved into the tin-roofed quarters Jane had built for her African research staff and their families; her thirty workers have had to double up under the new arrangement to accommodate the park officials and rangers. Though a dozen or so tour operators now bring white visitors to Gombe, white researchers are still prohibited from working at the site except under special conditions. Jane now gets out to Gombe only a few times a year for only a few weeks at a time.

Today, a recent poll reveals, Jane Goodall is the most easily recognizable living scientist in the Western world. Her studies at Gombe "will rank forever as one of the great achievements of scientific dedication combined with stunning results," wrote the eminent Harvard biologist and historian of science Stephen Jay Gould in a 1989 column in the magazine *Natural History*.

"Her work is almost comparable with Einstein's," says Roger Fouts, whose work with the sign-language-using chimpanzee Washoe has challenged man's claim to uniqueness as a language user, just as did Jane's findings of hunting, warfare, and the use of tools by chimps.

Jane's approach, once ridiculed as amateurish, is now often held up as a standard to which other field ethologists should aspire. Now some respected scientists are beginning to argue that it is the lens of theory and methodology that clouds vision, not the focus of

empathy. "Most scientists come supplied with theories and force the animals to fit the theory," continues Roger Fouts. "Jane's is a humble science. She asks the animals to tell her about themselves."

Says John Mitani: "One of the maladies of the field today is the studies are too methodologically rigorous. People don't watch the animals anymore. You have an idea and go out to test your idea—and you have blinders on."

He echoes the lament of Konrad Lorenz; in his 1981 book, *The Foundations of Ethology,* Lorenz wrote that many modern researchers "do not accept perception as a source of knowledge. . . . I regret that a very large proportion of the younger researchers who consider themselves ethologists show a deplorable lack of knowledge of animals." Lorenz called for a resurgence of "amateurism," of long-term endeavors sustained by the observer's sheer love of his subject: this, he wrote, "can only be accomplished by those men whose gaze, through a wholly irrational delight in the beauty of the object, stays riveted to it."

Jane's work has ushered in the glimmerings of a new way of doing science, a scientific outlook that draws upon the feminine emphasis upon individuality, relationships, and empathy. Stephen Jay Gould wrote in the introduction to the 1988 revised edition of Jane's *In the Shadow of Man:* "We think of science as manipulation, experiment, and quantification. . . . The laboratory technique of stripping away uniqueness and finding quantifiable least common denominators cannot capture the richness of real history."

Jane's strength is that she relinquished control. Today this strength is honored, not as a passive act, as the men before her might have seen it, but as an achievement—one that allowed her to see and inspired her to stay. In *The Chimpanzees of Gombe* Jane wrote: "I readily admit to a high level of emotional involvement with individual chimpanzees—without which, I suspect, the research would have come to an end many years ago."

Many women ethologists have followed Jane's path, bringing an emotional and empathetic involvement to their long-term relationships with the animals they study. Many of them, like Jane, are storytellers, whose tales are of approach, of equality, of homecoming. Alison Jolly has written numerous popular books about the troops of lemurs in Madagascar that she has studied for more than twenty years; one of her books is titled *A World Like Our Own.* Barbara Smuts, once a student of Jane's, is well known for her long-term studies of baboon troops; and primatologist Shirley Strum concentrates on the role of friendship in baboon society in her recent book *Almost Human.* Cynthia Moss, who entered the field with no scientific training, describes her fourteen years among elephant herds at Amboseli National Park in Kenya in her emotional book *Elephant Memories.*

The most famous and most direct descendants of Jane's approach are Dian Fossey and Biruté Galdikas, who completed Louis Leakey's trio of "primates" and built directly upon Jane's pioneering work. In many ways the paths they took were even rougher than Jane's.

Dian Fossey and Digit

Sy Montgomery

Every breath was a battle to draw the ghost of her life back into her body. At age forty-two it hurt her even to breathe.

Dian Fossey had been asthmatic as a child and a heavy smoker since her teens; X-rays of her lungs taken when she graduated from college, she remembered, looked like "a road map of Los Angeles superimposed over a road map of New York." And now, after eight years of living in the oxygen-poor heights of Central Africa's Virunga Volcanoes, breathing the cold, sodden night air, her lungs were crippled. The hike to her research camp, Karisoke, at 10,000 feet, took her graduate students less than an hour; for Dian it was a gasping two-and-a-half-hour climb. She had suffered several bouts of pneumonia. Now she thought she was coming down with it again.

Earlier in the week she had broken her ankle. She heard the bone snap when she fell into a drainage ditch near her corrugated tin cabin. She had been avoiding a charging buffalo. Two days later she was bitten by a venomous spider on the other leg. Her right knee was swollen huge and red; her left ankle was black. But she would not leave the mountain for medical treatment in the small hospital down in Ruhengeri. She had been in worse shape before. Once, broken ribs punctured a lung; another time she was bitten by a dog thought to be rabid. Only when her temperature reached 105 and her symptoms clearly matched those described in her medical book for rabies had she allowed her African staff to carry her down on a litter.

Dian was loath to leave the camp in charge of her graduate students, two of whom she had been fighting with bit-terly. Kelly Steward and Sandy Harcourt, once her closest camp colleagues and confidantes, had committed the unforgivable error of falling in love with each other. Dian considered this a breach of loyalty. She yelled at them. Kelly cried and Sandy sulked.

But on this May day of 1974 Sandy felt sorry for Dian. As a gesture of conciliation, he offered to help her hobble out to visit Group 4. Splinted and steadied by a walking stick, she quickly accepted.

Group 4 was the first family of mountain gorillas Dian had contacted when she established her camp in Rwanda in September 1967. A political uprising had forced her to flee her earlier research station in Zaire. On the day she founded Karisoke—a name she coined by combining the names of the two volcanoes between which her camp nestled, Karisimbi and Visoke—poachers had led her to the group. The two Batwa tribesmen had been hunting antelope in the park—an illegal practice that had been tolerated for decades—and they offered to show her the gorillas they had encountered.

At that first contact, Dian watched the gorillas through binoculars for forty-five minutes. Across a ravine, ninety feet away, she could pick out three distinctive individuals in the fourteen-member group. There was a majestic old male, his black form silvered from shoulder to hip. This 350-pound silverback was obviously the sultan of the harem of females, the leader of the family. One old female stood out, a glare in her eyes, her lips compressed as if she had swallowed vinegar. And one youngster was "a playful little ball of disorganized black fluff . . . full of mischief and curiosity," as Dian would later describe

him in *Gorillas in the Mist*. She guessed then that he was about five years old. He tumbled about in the foliage like an animated black dustball. When the lead silverback spotted Dian behind a tree, the youngster obediently fled at his call, but Dian had the impression that the little male would rather have stayed for a longer look at the stranger. In a later contact she noticed the juvenile's swollen, extended middle finger. After many attempts at naming him, she finally called him Digit.

It was Digit, now twelve, who came over to Dian as she sat crumpled and coughing among the foliage with Sandy. Digit, a gaunt young silverback, served his family as sentry. He left the periphery of his group to knuckle over to her side. She inhaled his smell. A good smell, she noted with relief: for two years a draining wound in his neck had hunched his posture and sapped his spirit. Systemic infection had given his whole body a sour odor, not the normal, clean smell of fresh sweat. During that time Digit had become listless. Little would arouse his interest: not the sex play between the group's lead silverback and receptive females, not even visits from Dian. Digit would sit at the edge of the group for hours, probing the wound with his fingers, his eyes fixed on some distant spot as if dwelling on a sad memory.

But today Digit looked directly into Dian's eyes. He chose to remain beside her throughout the afternoon, like a quiet visitor to a shut-in, old friends with no need to talk. He turned his great domed head to her, looking at her solemnly with a brown, cognizant gaze. Normally a prolonged stare from a gorilla is a threat. But Digit's gaze bore no aggression. He seemed to say: I know. Dian would later write that she believed Digit understood she was sick. And she returned to camp that afternoon, still limping, still sick, still troubled, but whole.

"We all felt we shared something with the gorillas," one of her students would later recall of his months at Karisoke. And it is easy to feel that way after even a brief contact with these huge, solemn beings. "The face of a gorilla," wrote nature writer David Quammen after just looking at a picture of one, "offers a shock of what feels like total recognition." To be in the presence of a mountain gorilla for even one hour simply rips your soul open with awe. They are the largest of the great apes, the most hugely majestic and powerful; but it is the gaze of a gorilla that transfixes, when its eyes meet yours. The naturalist George Schaller, whose year-long study preceded Dian's, wrote that this is a look found in the eye of no other animal except, perhaps, a whale. It is not so much intelligence that strikes you, but understanding. You feel there has been an exchange.

The exchange between Digit and Dian that day was deep and long. By then Digit had known Dian for seven years. She had been a constant in his growing up from a juvenile to a young blackback and now to a silverback sentry. He had known her longer than he had known his own mother, who had died or left his group before he was five; he had known Dian longer than he had known his father, the old silverback who died of natural causes less than a year after she first observed him. When Digit was nine, his three age-mates in Group 4 departed: his half sisters were "kidnaped" by rival silverbacks, as often happens with young females. Digit then adopted Dian as his playmate, and he would often leave the rest of the group to amble to her side, eager to examine her gear, sniff her gloves and jeans, tug gently at her long brown braid.

As for Dian, her relationship with Digit was stronger than her bonds with her mother, father, or stepfather. Though she longed for a husband and babies, she never married or bore children. Her relationship with Digit endured

longer than that with any of her lovers and outlasted many of her human friendships.

In her slide lectures in the United States, Dian would refer to him as "my friend, Digit." "Friend," she admitted, was too weak a word, too casual; but she could find no other. Our words are something we share with other humans; but what Dian had with Digit was something she guarded as uniquely hers.

A mountain gorilla group is one of the most cohesive family units found among primates, a fact that impressed George Schaller. Adult orangutans live mostly alone, males and females meeting to mate. Chimpanzees' social groupings are so loosely organized, changing constantly in number and composition, that Jane Goodall couldn't make sense of them for nearly a decade. But gorillas live in tight-knit, clearly defined families. Typically a group contains a lead silverback, perhaps his adult brother, half brother, or nephew, and several adult females and their offspring.

A gorilla group travels, feeds, plays, and rests together. Seldom is an individual more than a hundred feet away from the others. The lead silverback slows his pace to that of the group's slowest, weakest member. All adults tolerate the babies and youngsters in the group, often with great tenderness. A wide-eyed baby, its fur still curly as black wool, may crawl over the great black bulk of any adult with impunity; a toddler may even step on the flat, leathery nose of a silverback. Usually the powerful male will gently set the baby aside or even dangle it playfully from one of his immense fingers.

When Dian first discovered Group 4, she would watch them through binoculars from a hidden position, for if they saw her they would flee. She loved to observe the group's three infants toddle and tumble together. If one baby found the play too rough, it would make a coughing sound, and its mother would lumber over and cradle it tenderly to her breast. Dian watched Digit and his juvenile sisters play:

wrestling, rolling, and chasing games often took them as far as fifty feet from the hulking adults. Sometimes a silverback led the youngsters in a sort of square dance. Loping from one palmlike *Senecio* tree to another, each gorilla would grab a trunk for a twirl, then spin off to embrace another trunk down the slope, until all the gorillas lay in a bouncing pileup of furry black bodies. And then the silverback would lead the youngsters up the slope again for another game.

Within a year, this cheerful silverback eventually took over leadership of the group, after the old leader died. Dian named him Uncle Bert, after her uncle Albert Chapin. With Dian's maternal aunt, Flossie (Dian named a Group 4 female after her as well), Uncle Bert had helped care for Dian after her father left the family when she was three. While Dian was in college Bert and Flossie gave her money to help with costs that her holiday, weekend, and summer jobs wouldn't cover. Naming the silverback after her uncle was the most tender tribute Dian could have offered Bert Chapin: his was the name given to the group's male magnet, its leader, protector—and the centerpiece of a family life whose tenderness and cohesion Dian, as a child, could not have imagined.

Dian was a lonely only child. Her father's drinking caused the divorce that took him out of her life; when her mother, Kitty, remarried when Dian was five, even the mention of George Fossey's name became taboo in the house. Richard Price never adopted Dian. Each night she ate supper in the kitchen with the housekeeper. Her stepfather did not allow her at the dinner table with him and her mother until she was ten. Though Dian's stepfather, a building contractor, seemed wealthy, she largely paid her own way through school. Once she worked as a machine operator in a factory.

Dian seldom spoke of her family to friends, and she carried a loathing for her childhood into her adult life. Long after Dian left the family home in California, she referred to her parents as "the Prices." She would spit on the ground whenever her stepfather's name was mentioned. When her Uncle Bert died, leaving Dian $50,000, Richard Price badgered her with cables to Rwanda, pressing her to contest the will for more money; after Dian's death he had her will overturned by a California court, claiming all her money for himself and his wife.

Her mother and stepfather tried desperately to thwart Dian's plans to go to Africa. They would not help her finance her lifelong dream to go on safari when she was twenty-eight. She borrowed against three years of her salary as an occupational therapist to go. And when she left the States three years later to begin her study of the mountain gorillas, her mother begged her not to go, and her stepfather threatened to stop her.

She chose to remain in the alpine rain forest, as alone as she had ever been. She chose to remain among the King Kong beasts whom the outside world still considered a symbol of savagery, watching their gentle, peaceful lives unfold.

Once Dian, watching Uncle Bert with his family, saw the gigantic male pluck a handful of white flowers with his huge black hands. As the young Digit ambled toward him, the silverback whisked the bouquet back and forth across the youngster's face. Digit chuckled and tumbled into Uncle Bert's lap, "much like a puppy wanting attention," Dian wrote. Digit rolled against the silverback, clutching himself in ecstasy as the big male tickled him with petals.

By the end of her first three months in Rwanda, Dian was following two gorilla groups regularly and observing another sporadically. She divided most of her time between Group 5's fifteen members, ranging on Visoke's southeastern slopes, and Group 4. Group 8, a family of nine, all adult, shared Visoke's western slopes with Group 4.

Dian still could not approach them. Gorilla families guard carefully against intrusion. Each family has at least one member who serves as sentry, typically posted at the periphery of the group to watch for danger—a rival silverback or

a human hunter. Gorilla groups seldom interact with other families, except when females transfer voluntarily out of their natal group to join the families of unrelated silverbacks or when rival silverbacks "raid" a neighboring family for females.

Adult gorillas will fight to the death defending their families. This is why poachers who may be seeking only one infant for the zoo trade must often kill all the adults in the family to capture the baby. Once Dian tracked one such poacher to his village; the man and his wives fled before her, leaving their small child behind.

At first Dian observed the animals from a distance, silently, hidden. Then slowly, over many months, she began to announce her presence. She imitated their contentment vocalizations, most often the *naoom, naoom, naoom,* a sound like belching or deeply clearing the throat. She crunched wild celery stalks. She crouched, eyes averted, scratching herself loud and long, as gorillas do. Eventually she could come close enough to them to smell the scent of their bodies and see the ridges inside the roofs of their mouths when they yawned; at times she came close enough to distinguish, without binoculars, the cuticles of their black, humanlike fingernails.

She visited them daily; she learned to tell by the contour pressed into the leaves which animal had slept in a particular night nest, made from leaves woven into a bathtub shape on the ground. She knew the sound of each individual voice belching contentment when they were feeding. But it was more than two years before she knew the touch of their skin.

Peanuts, a young adult male in Group 8, was the first mountain gorilla to touch his fingers to hers. Dian was lying on her back among the foliage, her right arm outstretched, palm up. Peanuts looked at her hand intently; then he stood, extended his hand, and touched her fingers for an instant. *National Geographic* photographer Bob Campbell snapped the shutter only a moment afterward: that the photo is blurry renders it dreamlike. The 250-pound gorilla's right hand still hangs in

midair. Dian's eyes are open but unseeing, her lips parted, her left hand brought to her mouth, as if feeling for the lingering warmth of a kiss.

Peanuts pounded his chest with excitement and ran off to rejoin his group. Dian lingered after he left; she named the spot where they touched Fasi Ya Mkoni, "the Place of the Hands." With his touch, Peanuts opened his family to her; she became a part of the families she had observed so intimately for the past two years. Soon the gorillas would come forward and welcome her into their midst.

Digit was almost always the first member of Group 4 to greet her. "I received the impression that Digit really looked forward to the daily contacts," she wrote in her book. "If I was alone, he often invited play by flopping over on his back, waving stumpy legs in the air, and looking at me smilingly as if to say, 'How can you resist me?' "

At times she would be literally blanketed with gorillas, when a family would pull close around her like a black furry quilt. In one wonderful photo, Puck, a young female of Group 5, is reclining in back of Dian and, with the back of her left hand, touching Dian's cheek—the gesture of a mother caressing the cheek of a child.

Mothers let Dian hold their infants; silverbacks would groom her, parting her long dark hair with fingers thick as bananas, yet deft as a seamstress's touch. "I can't tell you how rewarding it is to be with them," Dian told a New York crowd gathered for a slide lecture in 1982. "Their trust, the cohesiveness, the tranquility . . ." Words failed her, and her hoarse, breathy voice broke. "It is really something."

Other field workers who joined Dian at Karisoke remember similar moments. Photographer Bob Campbell recalls how Digit would try to groom his sleeves and pants and, finding nothing groomable, would pluck at the hairs of his wrist; most of the people who worked there have pictures of themselves with young gorillas on their heads or in their laps.

But with Dian it was different. Ian Redmond, who first came to Karisoke in 1976, remembers one of the first times he accompanied Dian to observe Group 4. It was a reunion: Dian hadn't been out to visit the group for a while. "The animals filed past us, and each one paused and briefly looked into my face, just briefly. And then each one looked into Dian's eyes, at very close quarters, for half a minute or so. It seemed like each one was queuing up to stare into her face and remind themselves of her place with them. It was obvious they had a much deeper and stronger relationship with Dian than with any of the other workers."

In the early days Dian had the gorillas mostly to herself. It was in 1972 that Bob Campbell filmed what is arguably one of the most moving contacts between two species on record: Digit, though still a youngster, is huge. His head is more than twice the size of Dian's, his hands big enough to cover a dinner plate. He comes to her and with those enormous black hands gently takes her notebook, then her pen, and brings them to his flat, leathery nose. He gently puts them aside in the foliage and rolls over to snooze at Dian's side.

Once Dian spotted Group 4 on the opposite side of a steep ravine but knew she was not strong enough to cross it. Uncle Bert, seeing her, led the entire group across the ravine to her. This time Digit was last in line. "Then," wrote Dian, "he finally came right to me and gently touched my hair. . . . I wish I could have given them all something in return."

At times like these, Dian wept with joy. Hers was the triumph of one who has been chosen: wild gorillas would come to her.

The great intimacy of love is onlyness, of being the loved One. It is the kind of love most valued in Western culture; people choose only one "best" friend, one husband, one wife, one God. Even our God is a jealous one, demanding "Thou shalt have no other gods before Me."

This was a love Dian sought over and over again—as the only child of parents who did not place her first, as the paramour of a succession of married lovers. The love she sought most

desperately was a jealous love, exclusive—not *agape,* the Godlike, spiritual love of all beings, not the uniform, brotherly love, *philia.* The love Dian sought was the love that singles out.

Digit singled Dian out. By the time he was nine he was more strongly attracted to her than were any of the other gorillas she knew. His only age-mates in his family, his half sisters, had left the group or been kidnaped. When Digit heard Dian belch-grunting a greeting, he would leave the company of his group to scamper to greet her. To Digit, Dian was the sibling playmate he lacked. And Dian recognized his longing as clearly as she knew her own image in a mirror.

Dian had had few playmates as a child. She had longed for a pet, but her stepfather wouldn't allow her to keep even a hamster a friend offered, because it was "dirty." He allowed her a single goldfish; she was devastated when it died and was never allowed another.

But Digit was no pet. "Dian's relationship with the gorillas is really the highest form of human-animal relationship," observed Ian Redmond. "With almost any other human-animal relationship, that involves feeding the animals or restraining the animals or putting them in an enclosure, or if you help an injured animal—you do something to the animal. Whereas Dian and the gorillas were on completely equal terms. It was nothing other than the desire to be together. And that's as pure as you can get."

When Digit was young, he and Dian played together like children. He would strut toward her, playfully whacking foliage; she would tickle him; he would chuckle and climb on her head. Digit was fascinated by any object Dian had with her: once she brought a chocolate bar to eat for lunch and accidentally dropped it into the hollow stump of a tree where she was sitting next to Digit. Half in jest, she asked him to get it back for her. "And according to script," she wrote her Louisville friend, Betty Schartzel, "Digit reached one long, hairy arm into the hole and retrieved the candy bar." But the chocolate didn't appeal to

him. "After one sniff he literally threw it back into the hole. The so-called 'wild gorillas' are really very discriminating in their tastes!"

Dian's thermoses, notebooks, gloves, and cameras were all worthy of investigation. Digit would handle these objects gently and with great concentration. Sometimes he handed them back to her. Once Dian brought Digit a hand mirror. He immediately approached it, propped up on his forearms, and sniffed the glass. Digit pursed his lips, cocked his head, and then uttered a long sigh. He reached behind the mirror in search of the body connected to the face. Finding nothing, he stared at his reflection for five minutes before moving away.

Dian took many photos of all the gorillas, but Digit was her favorite subject. When the Rwandan Office of Tourism asked Dian for a gorilla photo for a travel poster, the slide she selected was one of Digit. He is pictured holding a stick of wood he has been chewing, his shining eyes a mixture of innocence and inquiry. He looks directly into the camera, his lips parted and curved as if about to smile. "Come to meet him in Rwanda," exhorts the caption. When his poster began appearing in hotels, banks, and airports, "I could not help feeling that our privacy was on the verge of being invaded," Dian wrote.

Her relationship with Digit was one she did not intend to share. Hers was the loyalty and possessiveness of a silverback: what she felt for the gorillas, and especially Digit, was exclusive, passionate, and dangerous.

No animal, Dian believed, was truly safe in Africa. Africans see most animals as food, skins, money. "Dian had a compulsion to buy every animal she ever saw in Africa," remembers her friend Rosamond Carr, an American expatriate who lives in nearby Gisenyi, "to save it from torture." One day Dian, driving in her Combi van, saw some children on the roadside, swinging a rabbit by the ears. She took it from them, brought it back to camp, and built a spacious hutch for it. Another time it would be a chicken: visiting villagers sometimes brought one to camp, intending, of course, that it be eaten. Dian would keep it as a pet.

Dian felt compelled to protect the vulnerable, the innocent. Her first plan after high school had been to become a veterinarian; after failing chemistry and physics, she chose occupational therapy; with her degree, she worked for a decade with disabled children.

One day Dian came to the hotel in Gisenyi where Rosamond was working as a manager. Dian was holding a monkey. She had seen it at a market, packed in a carton. Rosamond remembers, "I look and see this rotten little face, this big ruff of hair, and I say, 'Dian. I'm sorry, you cannot have that monkey in this hotel!' But Dian spent the night with the animal in her room anyway.

"Luckily for me, she left the next day. I have never seen anything like the mess. There were banana peels on the ceiling, sweet potatoes on the floor; it had broken the water bottle, the glasses had been smashed and had gone down the drain of the washbasin. And with that adorable animal she starts up the mountain."

Kima, as Dian named the monkey, proved no less destructive in camp. Full grown when Dian brought her, Kima bit people, urinated on Dian's typewriter, bit the heads off all her matches, and terrorized students on their way to the latrine, leaping off the roof of Dian's cabin and biting them. Yet Dian loved her, built a hatchway allowing Kima free access to her cabin, bought her toys and dolls, and had her camp cook prepare special foods for her. Kima especially liked french fries, though she discarded the crunchy outsides and ate only the soft centers. "Everyone in camp absolutely hated that animal," Rosamond says. "But Dian loved her."

Another of Dian's rescue attempts occurred one day when she was driving down the main street of Gisenyi on a provisioning trip. Spotting a man walking a rack-ribbed dog on a leash, she slammed on the brakes. "I want to buy that dog," she announced. The Rwandan protested that it was not for

sale. She got out of her Combi, lifted up the sickly animal, and drove off with it.

Rosamond learned of the incident from a friend named Rita who worked at the American embassy. For it was to Rita's home that the Rwandan man returned that afternoon to explain why the dog, which he had been taking to the vet for worming, had never made it to its destination. "Madame, a crazy woman stopped and stole your dog, and she went off with it in a gray van."

"Rita got her dog back," Rosamond continues. Dian had taken it to the hotel where she was staying overnight; when Rita tracked her down, she was feeding the dog steak in her room. "And that was typical of Dian. She had to save every animal she saw. And they loved her—every animal I ever saw her with simply loved her."

When Dian first came to Karisoke, elephants frequently visited her camp. Rosamond used to camp with Dian in those early days before the cabin was built. The elephants came so close that she remembers hearing their stomachs rumble at night. Once she asked Dian if she undressed at night. "Of course not, are you crazy?" Dian replied. "I go to bed in my blue jeans. I have to get up six times at night to see what's happening outside."

One night an elephant selected Dian's tent pole as a scratching post. Another time a wild elephant accepted a banana from Dian's hand. The tiny antelopes called duiker often wandered through camp; one became so tame it would follow Dian's laying hens around. A family of seven bushbucks adopted Karisoke as home, as did an ancient bull buffalo she named Mzee.

Dian's camp provided refuge from the poacher-infested, cattle-filled forest. For centuries the pygmylike Batwa had used these volcanic slopes as a hunting ground. And as Rwanda's human population exploded, the Virungas were the only source of bush meat left, and poaching pressure increased. Today you will find no elephants in these forests; they have all been killed by poachers seeking ivory.

If you look at the Parc National des Volcans from the air, the five volca-

noes, their uppermost slopes puckered like the lips of an old woman, seem to be standing on tiptoe to withdraw from the flood of cultivation and people below. Rwanda is the most densely populated country in Africa, with more than 500 people per square mile. Almost every inch is cultivated, and more than 23,000 new families need new land each year. In rural Rwanda outside of the national parks, if you wander from a path you are more likely to step in human excrement than the scat of a wild animal. The Parc des Volcans is thoroughly ringed with *shambas*, little farm plots growing bananas, peanuts, beans, manioc, and with fields of pyrethrum, daisylike flowers cultivated as a natural insecticide for export. The red earth of the fields seems to bleed from all the human scraping.

The proud, tall Batutsi have few other areas to pasture their cattle, the pride of their existence; everywhere else are shambas. From the start Dian tried to evict the herders from the park, kidnaping their cows and sometimes even shooting them. On the Rwandan side of the mountain, cattle herds were so concentrated, she wrote, that "many areas were reduced to dustbowls." She felt guilty, but the cattle destroyed habitat for the gorillas and other wild animals the park was supposed to protect. Worse were the snares set by the Batwa. Many nights she stayed awake nursing a duiker or bushbuck whose leg had been mangled in a trap. Dian lived in fear that one of the gorillas would be next.

The Batwa do not eat gorillas; gorillas fall victim to their snares, set for antelope, by accident. But the Batwa have for centuries hunted gorillas, to use the fingers and genitals of silverbacks in magic rituals and potions. And now the hunters found a new reason to kill gorillas: they learned that Westerners would pay high prices for gorilla heads for trophies, gorilla hands for ashtrays, and gorilla youngsters for zoos.

In March 1969, only eighteen months into her study, a friend in Ruhengeri came to camp to tell Dian that a young gorilla had been captured from the southern slopes of Mount Karisimbi. All ten adults in the group had been killed so that the baby could be taken for display in the Cologne Zoo. The capture had been approved by the park conservator, who was paid handsomely for his cooperation. But something had gone wrong: the baby gorilla was dying.

Dian took the baby in, a three- to four-year-old female she named Coco. The gorilla's wrists and feet had been bound with wire to a pole when the hunters carried her away from the corpses of her family; she had spent two or three weeks in a coffinlike crate, fed only corn, bananas, and bread, before Dian came to her rescue. When Dian left the park conservator's office, she was sure the baby would die. She slept with Coco in her bed, awakening amid pools of the baby's watery feces.

A week later came another sick orphan, a four- to five-year-old female also intended for the zoo. Her family had shared Karisimbi's southern slope with Coco's; trying to defend the baby from capture, all eight members of her group had died. Dian named this baby Pucker for the huge sores that gave her face a puckered look.

It took Dian two months to nurse the babies back to health. She transformed half her cabin into a giant gorilla playpen filled with fresh foliage. She began to take them into the forest with her, encouraging them to climb trees and vines. She was making plans to release them into a wild group when the park conservator made the climb to camp. He and his porters descended with both gorillas in a box and shipped them to the zoo in West Germany. Coco and Pucker died there nine years later, within a month of one another, at an age when, in the wild, they would have been mothering youngsters the same age they had been when they were captured.

Thereafter Dian's antipoaching tactics became more elaborate. She learned from a friend in Ruhengeri that the trade in gorilla trophies was flourishing; he had counted twenty-three gorilla heads for sale in that town in one year. As loyal as a silverback, as wary as a sentry, Dian and her staff patrolled the forest for snares and destroyed the gear poachers left behind in their temporary shelters.

Yet each day dawned to the barking of poachers' dogs. A field report she submitted to the National Geographic Society in 1972 gave the results of the most recent gorilla census: though her study groups were still safe, the surrounding areas of the park's five volcanoes were literally under siege. On Mount Muhavura census workers saw convoys of smugglers leaving the park every forty-five minutes. Only thirteen gorillas were left on the slopes of Muhavura. On neighboring Mount Gahinga no gorillas were left. In the two previous years, census workers had found fresh remains of slain silverbacks. And even the slopes of Dian's beloved Karisimbi, she wrote, were covered with poachers' traps and scarred by heavily used cattle trails; "poachers and their dogs were heard throughout the region."

It was that same year, 1972, that a maturing Digit assumed the role of sentry of Group 4. In this role he usually stayed on the periphery of the group to watch for danger; he would be the first to defend his family if they were attacked. Once when Dian was walking behind her Rwandan tracker, the dark form of a gorilla burst from the bush. The male stood upright to his full height of five and a half feet; his jaw gaped open, exposing black gums and three-inch canines as he uttered two long, piercing screams at the terrified tracker. Dian stepped into view, shoving the tracker down behind her, and stared into the animal's face. They recognized each other immediately. Digit dropped to all fours and ran back to his group.

Dian wrote that Digit's new role made him more serious. No longer was he a youngster with the freedom to roll and wrestle with his playmate. But Dian was still special to him. Once when Dian went out to visit the group during a downpour, the young silverback emerged from the gloom and stood erect before his crouching human friend. He pulled up a stalk of wild celery—a favorite gorilla food that Digit had seen Dian munch on many times—peeled it with his great hands, and dropped the stalk at her feet like an offering. Then he turned and left.

As sentry, Digit sustained the wound that sapped his strength for the next two years. Dian did not observe the fight, but she concluded from tracking clues that Digit had warded off a raid by the silverback leader of Group 8, who had previously kidnaped females from Group 4. Dian cringed each time she heard him coughing and retching. Digit sat alone, hunched and indifferent. Dian worried that his growth would be retarded. In her field notes she described his mood as one of deep dejection.

This was a time when Dian was nursing wounds of her own. She had hoped that Bob Campbell, the photographer, would marry her, as Hugo van Lawick had married Jane; but Bob left Karisoke for the last time at the end of May 1972, to return to his wife in Nairobi. Then she had a long affair with a Belgian doctor, who left her to marry the woman he had been living with. Dian's health worsened. Her trips overseas for primatology conferences and lecture tours were usually paired with hospital visits to repair broken bones and heal her fragile lungs. She feared she had tuberculosis. She noted her pain in her diary telegraphically: "Very lung-sick." "Coughing up blood." "Scum in urine."

When she was in her twenties, despite her asthma, Dian seemed as strong as an Amazon. Her large-boned but lanky six-foot frame had a coltish grace; one of her suitors, another man who nearly married her, described her as "one hell of an attractive woman," with masses of long dark hair and "eyes like a Spanish dancer." But now Dian felt old and ugly and weak. She used henna on her hair to try to cover the gray. (Dian told a friend that her mother's only comment about her first appearance on a National Geographic TV special was, "Why did you dye your hair that awful orange color?") In letters to friends Dian began to sign off as "The Fossil." She referred to her house as "the Mausoleum." In a cardboard album she made for friends from construction paper and magazine cutouts, titled "The Saga of Karisoke," she pasted a picture of a mummified corpse sitting upright on a bed. She realized that many of her students disliked her. Under the picture Dian printed a caption: "Despite their protests, she stays on."

By 1976 Dian was spending less and less time in the field. Her lungs and legs had grown too weak for daily contacts; she had hairline fractures on her feet. And she was overwhelmed with paperwork. She became increasingly testy with her staff, and her students feared to knock on her door. Her students wouldn't even see her for weeks at a time, but they would hear her pounding on her battered Olivetti, a task from which she would pause only to take another drag on an Impala *filtrée* or to munch sunflower seeds. Her students were taking the field data on the gorillas by this time: when Dian went out to see the groups, she simply visited with them.

One day, she ventured out along a trail as slippery as fresh buffalo dung to find Group 4. By the time she found them, the rain was driving. They were huddled against the downpour. She saw Digit sitting about thirty feet apart from the group. She wanted to join him but resisted; she now feared that her early contact with him had made him too human-oriented, more vulnerable to poachers. So she settled among the soaking foliage several yards from the main group. She could barely make out the humped black forms in the heavy mist.

On sunny days there is no more beautiful place on earth than the Virungas; the sunlight makes the *Senecio* trees sparkle like fireworks in midexplosion; the gnarled old *Hagenias,* trailing lacy beards of gray-green lichen and epiphytic ferns, look like friendly wizards, and the leaves of palms seem like hands upraised in praise. But rain transforms the forest into a cold, gray hell. You stare out, tunnel-visioned, from the hood of a dripping raincape, at a wet landscape cloaked as if in evil enchantment. Each drop of rain sends a splintering chill into the flesh, and your muscles clench with cold; you can cut yourself badly on the razorlike cutty grass and not even feel it. Even the gorillas, with their thick black fur coats, look miserable and lonely in the rain.

Minutes after she arrived, Dian felt an arm around her shoulders. "I looked up into Digit's warm, gentle brown eyes," she wrote in *Gorillas in the Mist.* He gazed at her thoughtfully and patted her head, then sat by her side. As the rain faded to mist, she laid her head down in Digit's lap.

On January 1, 1978, Dian's head tracker returned to camp late in the day. He had not been able to find Group 4. But he had found blood along their trail.

Ian Redmond found Digit's body the next day. His head and hands had been hacked off. There were five spear wounds in his body.

Ian did not see Dian cry that day. She was almost supercontrolled, he remembers. No amount of keening, no incantation or prayer could release the pain of her loss. But years later she filled a page of her diary with a single word, written over and over: "Digit Digit Digit Digit . . ."

Interview
Biruté Galdikas

Relinquishing a family and civilization for the rain forests of Borneo, the youngest of "Leakey's Angels" tracks the mysterious animals that "never left the Garden of Eden"

Don Lessem

Orangutan. The word is Indonesian, and spoken in that tongue, it has a gentle lilt: *orong-oo-tahn.* That is just the way Biruté Galdikas says the word—with reverence; never with a finishing *g* or abbreviated to *orang.* Human beings' third closest relative and the world's largest tree-dwelling animal, the orangutan, say the primatologists, is the most elusive and enigmatic of the great apes. The word itself conveys that sense of mystery. It means "person of the forest."

Lithuanian by heritage, German by birth, Canadian by upbringing and citizenship, Galdikas has spent most of the last 15 years deep within the rain forests of Borneo, documenting the solitary life-style of the orangutan. She now lives with her second husband—a Dayak tribesman—and their two children in a cabin beside a river, six hours from the nearest settlement.

Galdikas's research has yielded startling new insights into orangutan behavior. Geographically isolated from press attention and too busy to publish many of her findings, Galdikas remains the least known of "Leakey's Angels." Like chimpanzee researcher Jane Goodall and the late gorilla observer Dian Fossey, Galdikas was selected by anthropologist *extraordinaire* Louis B. Leakey to perform pioneer-

ing long-term studies of great apes in the wild. Galdikas, now forty, was chosen almost 20 years ago, not only for her zeal but for her academic qualifications. While Goodall was a secretary with a high school education, and Fossey a physical therapist, Galdikas received her master's degree in primatology at UCLA in 1969. She returned there in 1978 to earn her doctorate in anthropology. Her findings have not been so widely disputed as those of Goodall and Fossey. "Galdikas's methodology is the best of the three," says Washington University primatologist Robert Sussman. His sentiments are echoed by former Brandeis University primatologist David Horr Agee, the only person to conduct long-term research on orangutans before Galdikas. Agee, who spent three years studying orangutans in Indonesia, says, "Galdikas has provided us with the most detailed description of the orang way of life we have."

Galdikas's interest in orangutans long predates her academic work in primatology. "I don't believe in predestiny," she says. "You make your own fate, yet I was born to study orangutans and their forest. I believe my affinity for forests comes from my Lithuanian heritage. We are a forest people." The Galdikases, however, were an urban and urbane family. Brought by her physicist father and

mother to Toronto as a child, she grew up knowing only the trees of Hyde Park as forest, and orangutans only from books. As a serious and scholarly UCLA undergraduate, Galdikas met and married Rod Brindamour, a Canadian country boy and summer lumberjack who was very much her opposite.

Galdikas, twenty-two, and Brindamour had only each other for company when they left Canada for a remote stretch of forest in southern Borneo that was then called Tanjung Puting Reserve, now an Indonesian national park. From their hut the two would go off on daylong treks through the waist-deep mud of the swampy forests, struggling to keep pace with the orangutans overhead. In 1971 the National Geographic Society joined the Wilkie and Leakey foundations as supporters of Galdikas's research. Camp facilities were expanded, and native Dayaks hired to track orangutans. Brindamour, however, wanted to be a helicopter pilot and computer expert, not a primatologist. After seven and a half years with Galdikas at Tanjung Puting, he left in 1979. Forced to choose between Rod and the orangutans, Galdikas remained in Borneo. A year later their young son, Binti, who had been raised with orangutans as playmates, followed Brindamour back to Canada.

Galdikas's life at Tanjung Puting has dramatically changed since her early years there. A compound of buildings, including a dormitory and eating hall, has transformed the dockside camp, which now swarms with up to 25 Dayak assistants, plus American helpers. Thirty ex-captive orangutans, which Indonesian authorities have confiscated from illegal pet trade and remanded to Galdikas, have free run of the camp, picking pockets for candy, doors and suitcase locks for soap and playthings. Galdikas treats the ex-captives for illness and for injury from mistreatment; and to date, 25 have been successfully reintroduced to life in the wild. At the same time she tends to her own children, Filomena Jane, two, and Frederick, four, by her Dayak husband, Pak Bohap.

'The silence is ominous in the rain forest. There is an expectant air, like in a movie when the soundtrack stops and you know something will happen imminently.'

For four months every year Galdikas returns to Canada to lecture at Simon Fraser University and visit her elder son. Even when in North America, however, she still spends considerable time with orangutans. Writer Don Lessem conducted part of this interview at the Rio Grande Zoo in Albuquerque, New Mexico, where Galdikas made daily visits to an adolescent female orangutan. "Memela is a subordinate female here, so she has never had much attention," Galdikas explained as she fed the young ape yogurt and after-dinner mints. Demonstrating that she would give the shirt off her back to help orangutans, Galdikas presented her new knit sweater to Memela, who promptly grabbed it and admired its bright threads.

Much like the animals she studies, notes Lessem, Galdikas was initially evasive, even hostile, responding to inquiries with "You are nosy, aren't you?" "Use your head when you ask a question," and to a query on how it was she came to Canada from Germany, "By plane." But she soon overcame her icy mistrust and revealed the warm, generous nature known to friends, family, co-workers, and orangutans. Her facial expressions remained masked by smoky glasses, but there was no hiding her excitement when she spoke of her impending return to Borneo. "My family and my life's work are there. I love the Indonesian people and think I am becoming, slowly, one of them. Above all, I feel this special kinship with orangutans."

Omni: How did you originally connect with Louis Leakey?

Galdikas: The professor of a course at UCLA on archaeological dating techniques asked Leakey to speak. During the question-and-answer session, he really caught fire when asked about the relevance of studying great apes for understanding evolution. Then, patting his pocket, he took out a telegram from Dian Fossey saying that she had finally habituated some wild mountain gorillas. He was really proud, like a doting daddy. After the lecture I told him I wanted to study orangutans. He said he was going back to Africa the next day but would keep in touch. I walked out of that hall convinced I was going to study orangutans. It took nearly two and a half years to get funding. Leakey didn't care about formal education. He wanted enthusiasm, belief in what you were doing. "Always support someone who knows what he or she wants to do," he said.

Omni: Was it coincidence he chose women for all his great ape projects?

Galdikas: No. He steadfastly believed women were more patient and saw details better. Scientists who have shown films to male and female undergraduates have found that the females remember the seemingly irrelevant details better. In science, initially irrelevant details can prove highly relevant later on. Leakey gave me some little tests to gauge my powers of observation. He turned over some cards and asked me which were the reds and

which were the blacks. I immediately noticed that half of them were slightly bent. He claimed men didn't notice. He also claimed men will excite aggressive behavior in male pongids, whereas women excite protective tendencies in them. Wild orangutans can't distinguish men from women, but generally, I think Leakey was right.

Omni: Why didn't Leakey's imprimatur guarantee you the money you needed to begin your study?

Galdikas: Leakey never had any money until the end of his life. Even famous field researchers have to struggle all their lives. That is not the image you get from the glossy pages of magazines. But Leakey did have good contacts: He wrote to the head of the nature protection agency in the Indonesian government, who decided Tanjung Puting Reserve was where we should go. Nobody had been there—no researchers, no tourists. It had been a preserve since Dutch colonial times. It is fifty kilometers by boat from the nearest town. Some illegal hand loggers had abandoned a bark-walled hut near the river. We lived there for three years. We brought only two large green knapsacks. Mine had a typewriter in it.

Omni: What did the Indonesians think of you there?

Galdikas: The only Indonesians we saw the first few years were Malayu—small, slender Moslems who were after the sweet latex that goes into chewing gum. These wild-rubber collectors probably thought we planned to do something other than study orangutans—like logging, searching for oil, or collecting antiquities. The only other Westerners they'd seen were missionaries; the idea that we were at the reserve to proselytize orangutans made no sense to them.

Omni: What was your strategy when you first began searching for orangutans?

Galdikas: I would go one way, and Rod the other. I'd search, and Rod would make trails. I'd just take a jar full of cold coffee and go from early morning to late in the afternoon, up to my armpits in water. At first we thought we had to stay in the swamp because that's where George Schaller, the noted naturalist and early orangutan researcher, had seen them. On our initial trip down the river with local foresters, we saw what I thought were two females. As soon as we got close, they took off. I wanted to get out and follow but was told it was no use in the swamp. Even so, I was jubilant. A week or two later I saw a subadult male in a tree eating bark. He hiss-squeaked his annoyance, then went right back to eating. I watched him for five hours and was thrilled. Later I learned it was quite anomalous for a subadult to do a double take, display and vocalize, and not just run away. Animals usually went berserk the first time we saw them.

Omni: Describe the Bornean rain forest.

Galdikas: Tanjung Puting is not the cathedral forest of [nineteenth-century naturalist] Alfred Russel Wallace's description. The canopy is more open, although it's still "twilight at noon," as the phrase goes. The understory is poor, and so lots of seedlings and saplings crowd the earth. Overhead the trees are tall but not giants. Lianas and other vines aren't so predominant either, but you walk with difficulty through the mass of saplings and barely see a few meters ahead. It is hot, muggy, and the silence is ominous. You think of the rain forest as a cacophony of sounds, but unless you come in the early morning, when the female gibbons and birds are calling, it is virtually silent. You attend to every sound, and the snapping of a twig is amplified in your mind. There is an expectant air, like in a movie when the soundtrack stops and you know something will happen imminently. You don't see the full life of the forest until you sit for an hour or two. Gradually you being to notice birds, rodents, the occasional big mammal leaping by, or an orangutan crashing in the branches.

Omni: How do you find them?

Galdikas: With difficulty, especially if you don't know where they've made their nests the night before. I get up at three-third A.M. You want to be there before the orangutans leave their nests at dawn. I used to go alone. Now I go with my husband, Pak Bohap. I've

become pretty good at reading the signs of new nests and recent orangutan activity. I see things Westerners can't, but my skills are nothing compared to my husband's. He's hunted for food in these forests all his life. He moves barefoot, soundlessly. I need sneakers for the nettles, spines, and leeches. I snap twigs, which annoys him. I walk slowly on my own, looking for signs of orangutans. He walks quickly, then stops when he sees something, even a bent twig. He'll point out wood owls, and I'll see none until I train my binoculars and see two birds perched twenty meters up in a clump of leaves. His hearing, too, is just as remarkable. There's lots of white noise in the forest when it's windy: branches crashing, leaves dropping. But he'll hear an orangutan's long call or a slight crunch and go right to the point where the branch snapped and stop, using an unconscious trigonometry.

'I once saw a male fall sixty feet from a breaking branch, and he hit the ground so hard he bounced. He sat there a moment and then climbed back up.'

After I've spotted an orangutan, I follow it from food source to food source. About sixty percent of their active hours are spent at a food source, and they consume an enormous range of foods. They cover five hundred meters to two kilometers a day. When you are waist-deep in the swamp trying to keep up, that seems like quite a lot. Usually they are about thirty meters up in the trees—a ball of orange hair to the naked eye.

Orangutans are quite agile, but I've seen them take terrible falls. Once I heard a crash and saw a female holding her infant fall about sixty feet through branches to the ground. Both were fine, and they moved back up into the

canopy. I also saw a male fall about sixty feet straight down from a breaking branch, and he hit the ground so hard he bounced! He sat there a moment, dazed, then climbed back up.

Omni: How do you record your observations in the forest?

Galdikas: I note what the individual is doing in one-minute intervals: foraging, moving, resting, vocalizing, mating, and so on; where the animal is, what tree, how high; whether there are gibbons or maroon leaf monkeys calling, and so on. If I can afford the time, I follow them until it is too dark to see them, then return to the nest site at dawn. I don't follow infants and juveniles. You can't do everything.

Omni: How do you tell the sex and age when they are high in the trees?

Galdikas: There is no mistaking the males. The females weigh seventy to eighty pounds, and the males one hundred and fifty to two hundred pounds. When mature they develop these enormous cheek pads. Males are built like sumo wrestlers, but it is all muscle. They are incredibly strong. Orangutans *are* hard to sex as infants. The clitoris is huge, and from thirty meters below, it looks like a penis. Zoos make the mistake of calling little females males all the time.

You can recognize individuals by the size and shape of the face, missing fingers, scars; but you never know when you are going to see him or her again. Females don't go far, but males often range over thirty-five square kilometers. Their appearance as adults is completely different from their appearance as juveniles. One ex-captive male walked right into camp, and I didn't recognize him—until I looked closely and saw that he had one white eye. I'd known him as an adolescent eleven years before and hadn't seen him since. It's possible to differentiate individual orangutans by smell, but I'm not that good. Wild ones have a powerful odor. There was one ex-captive female that had a very pungent smell. Rod Brindamour, my former spouse, has a nose like a bloodhound's. He'd come back to the cabin one half hour after this orangutan had left, and he'd know she'd been there.

2. PRIMATES

Omni: How do you acclimatize the wild orangutans to your presence?

Galdikas: By encountering them repeatedly; you walk a fine line between not bothering them and acclimatizing them to the human observer. Most females in the thirty-five-square-kilometer study area are habituated. But one female took twelve years to habituate. Some males take a year or two. Others will never be habituated. Once they are accustomed to you, they are oblivious. They have no more interest in you than in a bump on a log. But when you first encounter them, their displays can be aggressive—vocalizing, throwing branches. And even with females who have been habituated, if you don't see them for a year, they may become unhabituated. Think of it this way: You don't like it when someone follows you. It makes you nervous. You might get used to it, but after a year off, you'll get belligerent all over again.

Omni: Have you ever been physically threatened by an orangutan?

Galdikas: Yes. The closest I ever came to death was when I was trapped between two logs in a windfall and couldn't move. A female orangutan was throwing branches and trying to topple a snag, a branchless dead tree, onto me. Females don't normally manipulate snags, so she lacked experience and didn't get me. Had it been an adult male that was trying to push the snag, I'd have been killed.

'Dominance is usually mediated through the long call, so named because it lasts up to four minutes.'

An adult male, Ralph, was sexually pursuing an ex-captive female in camp. Males can be very dangerous then. He stood right in front of me on a bridge. I'd had experience in assessing adult male nerve, and like the orangutans, I am slow to react. Had I jumped or winced, he would have attacked me.

Male orangutans are like karate champions: They have staring bouts to assess will, with occasional grappling. Finally, he backed off. I tell all my assistants to sit still if an orangutan approaches. But once one of our local workers was surprised by a male orangutan and ran as the orangutan started to charge. After that the orangutan would attack humans whenever he saw them. Rod said, "We can't have that." He was made of stainless steel. He went after the orangutan and charged him back. After that, things were all right again.

It's mostly bluff with orangutans. Other animals in those forests are much more dangerous. The most frightening are the Malayan sun bears, very belligerent little honey eaters. I avoid going near wild pigs, but I am positively apprehensive in the presence of bears. You'll sit down under a tree, hoping you are not sitting on a poisonous snake, and a bear will come tearing straight down the tree. I was quite surprised when a bear came charging down like a cartoon character. They don't always run off, though. The local Malayu forest people say never turn your back on a bear—it will leap, do a backflip onto your front, and rip your chest open, Rod scared one, but after it came down from the tree, it circled and charged him. Rod hit it on the back with his machete, but these bears have such loose skin folds that it wasn't even cut. It just ran off.

Omni: Does combat establish a sort of dominance hierarchy among males?

Galdikas: Sometimes, but dominance is usually mediated through the long call, so named because it lasts up to four minutes. A distinctive vocalization of the adult male, it starts with a series of grumbles that function much like an opera singer clearing his or her throat. Then the adult male makes a sound like the trumpeting of an elephant. These bellows subside into sighs lasting a minute or two. The patterns are so individual, you can actually chart who it is.

Omni: Do the long calls serve only to establish dominance?

Galdikas: No, although individual calling rates correlate so clearly with dominance that at first I couldn't believe it. One male can easily find another by the call. The male cheek pads may act as an acoustic filtering device to enhance their sending and receiving responses. But it also is a way of telling females they are in the vicinity. It is very hard for one orangutan to find another in the forest—if the first one doesn't want to be found. The long call is a way the dominant males crash along saying, "Here I am, if you want me."

Omni: The females do the selecting?

Galdikas: Yes, they form consortships during receptivity that last three to ten days. Their mating is protracted, acrobatic, and vocal, lasting up to half an hour. Sometimes there are two, three, or four matings in the ventral-ventral position. The male may long-call before copulating. The female is rarely audible, unless it is a hiss-squeak directed at us if she is not used to humans. This low hiss sound, a mark of annoyance, is completely different from her response to "rape." Then, she screams or gives a loud grunt. This rape grunt is the female's loudest vocalization.

'Gorillas were all that mattered to Dian Fossey. She was like a gorilla in many ways: majestic, intelligent, sensitive, and gentle beneath a ferocious, blustering temper.'

Rape among orangutans is relatively infrequent, a reproductive tactic of subadult males. Most matings come during consortships with big adult males. The throat pouches or cheek pads don't fully develop on males until they are seventeen or eighteen, but they are already bigger than the females. Subadult males try to form consortships, but it is difficult for them. If a big male approaches, he'll drive them away. To overcome this problem, they copulate forcibly. Rape is a low-risk tactic. The orangutans struggle, but it is very focused. When he wins, she acquiesces, and the aggression is over. There isn't any coyness or teasing in these fights. In one resisted-mating sequence, the pair ended up on the ground with the female screaming before copulating. Subadults aren't about to confront the adult males, who play for keeps. When an adult male establishes a consort relationship, he invests a lot in guarding his mate. A subadult rapist could get badly hurt.

Omni: Aren't females much more sociable than males?

Galdikas: Yes, they form friendships, and although they do have enemies, they are mostly friendly or neutral toward other females. A female will nurse her offspring for eight years, so they are seldom alone then. By comparison, chimpanzees have six years on average, gorillas four to five, between successive live births. Because orangutans are solitary or semisolitary, they might need a longer time with their mothers to learn foraging techniques and, perhaps, to grow to maturity because of the low-protein content of their diet. Orangutans live at least into their fifties or sixties. I saw a fully mature female orangutan when I began my work and have seen her again fifteen years later—and she hasn't gotten much older looking. She must be at least thirty-five and still looks to be in the prime of her life.

'Orangutans . . . [have] a different mind from those of chimpanzees or gorillas, but it is certainly of equal intelligence. They aren't so excitable as chimps.'

Omni: Is there an orangutan personality?

Galdikas: There are many. They are incredibly gentle beneath their bluster and very easy to get along with. They aren't devious or deceitful like chimpanzees, which are so much like us in aggressiveness, tool use, and the beginnings of culture. You won't see much politics among orangutans, but you will find an incredible strength of character. Put a chimpanzee in a zoo, and it changes very quickly. But you can never take the orangutan out of an orangutan. That has to do with their semisolitary nature.

Omni: Are they as smart as chimpanzees and gorillas?

Galdikas: Wild orangutans don't use tools, say, in the way a chimp works a stick to get termites, but they have incredible cognitive abilities that they use in locomoting and in processing food, abilities that are equivalent to those required for tool use. They have astounding memories. Put a gorilla or a chimp in a cage; they will try to get out, get frustrated, and quit. One zoo-keeper told me she had an orangutan try to pick at a weak spot in its cage for a week. She brought the orangutan back to the same cage years later, and it immediately went back to picking at the same spot. They are great at picking locks. Theirs is a different mind from those of chimpanzees or gorillas, but it is certainly of equal intelligence. They aren't so excitable as chimps. There is a reserve, a detachment about them. They don't allow you too close to them. That serenity has always appealed to me.

Omni: Is that what first attracted you to studying orangutans?

Galdikas: Yes, and their eyes. Orangutans have such humanness. Perhaps it's because they have white around their eyes like we do. I was always drawn to their eyes. I told Rod Brindamour when we met that I wanted to go to Sumatra or Borneo to study orangutans. He didn't even know what color they were. He'd never seen one.

Omni: Were you ever so frustrated that you thought of quitting?

Galdikas: No, we had come prepared to slog through the swamps the rest of our lives. It was very rough the first year or two, before we set up the study-area trails. What we missed most were books, but we had each other. And Rod had all sorts of forest skills. He managed camp; bought supplies; did photography, mapping; recorded the long calls. He's an incredibly courageous, talented person. After three years I went to a conference in Austria and spent a few days in North America. He didn't leave camp for four years. It was his home as much as mine.

Omni: How was raising a child in such isolated conditions?

Galdikas: Very difficult. People see those *National Geographic* pictures of Binti as a baby playing with orangutans and think we just let him run around with the ex-captives. We were terribly afraid he might pick up some disease, so we'd grab the orangutans and give them a bath before we let any of them near him. We were constantly worried he might get eaten by Bornean bearded pigs.

Omni: What does Binti think of orangutans now that he's back in Canada?

Galdikas: He likes them, yet when he was a toddler he resented the attention they received. I took him to see the Clint Eastwood movie with the orangutan [*Every Which Way but Loose*] when he was four, and he said angrily, "Orangutan is not people." That pretty well summed up his attitude at the time. Now he thinks orangutans are interesting and enjoys them.

Omni: What did you think of the Eastwood movie at the time?

Galdikas: It was fun. I thought Clint Eastwood and the orangutan had a good relationship. I'm a lot happier with that situation than with the lack of attention orangutans get in many zoos.

Omni: How many ex-captive orangutans have you cared for?

Galdikas: About eighty. There are thirty in camp now, and another thirty have been returned to the wild. Many have died—they came to us very sick and died quickly. And several have been born to ex-captives. They all have free run of the camp, but we try and keep doors closed to keep them out. When we started working with them, I was the only woman in camp, so the infants would adopt me. I remember carrying one frail little infant all swaddled in blankets with me to a doctor, and people at the clinic glancing over at me, wondering to themselves, I'm sure, *Just where did this woman get such a hairy baby?*

Now that I have children of my own, I can't go through that all over again. But it is essential they form a relationship with another animal, preferably another orangutan. Many orangutans are very nurturing; we've even had males that allowed infants to suckle from their breasts. When an ex-captive is ready for release, we let it go on the other side of the river from camp so it won't interfere with our wild study population. We allowed one wild female to feed at our station because our camp is in the core area of her home range. But you can't let wild adult males in. They can be very dangerous. Ex-captives are safe to be around, and generally we've never had a serious injury in camp. We have had problems, however, depending upon how they've been treated before they came. They love to wrestle and don't know their own strength when they're young. One ex-captive would attack blonds. Once he attacked me when I was nine months pregnant. I was wrestling with another orangutan and fell over. He saw me down, vulnerable, and rushed in and took a big bite out of my arm.

Omni: Do you yourself feed the ex-captive orangutans?

Galdikas: No, I couldn't spend the necessary time twice a day. Years ago it was a problem because the ex-captive males are real sexists—they attack men. They didn't feel competitive with females, so for a short while we used women to feed them. But one woman was menstruating, and she was physically attacked. That stopped that. Until Pak Bohap came. He has a presence: The orangutans are scared of him.

One day Rod and I drove to a Dayak village. A man in his twenties—quite short, about five feet two inches, and big shouldered—came out to the jeep, opened the door, and threw his stuff in. He didn't say a word, but I knew from first sight that this Bohap was someone. He was so supremely self-confident. We eventually became friends, but it was years before we became engaged and married. That all happened after Rod left.

Omni: Why did your first husband leave?

Galdikas: Rod had been there a long time for someone who did not consider orangutans his lifework. He had wanted to be a helicopter pilot, but he had health problems. He still wanted to work with computers. When he finally left in 1979, he had such a huge tropical ulcer on his leg he could barely walk to the plane. Years of wounds festering in that dampness had made purple holes in his legs. He had been very healthy, and he resented his loss of health. The ulcers cleared up in two weeks, once he got back.

Omni: Has your own health been compromised by life there?

'Rod left saying I loved orangutans more than him. I still loved him, but he said his wife had to love him more than anything else on Earth. I've given up a lot for orangutans.'

Galdikas: I'm sure. The climate does sap your energy. I brought some of it on myself by not eating or resting sufficiently. I'm much more careful about my diet now, and Pak Bohap makes sure I eat. I used to smoke clove cigarettes, which are popular there. They are highly carcinogenic and can burn holes in your lungs. Many Westerners take up smoking in Indonesia. It sounds curious, as if you wanted to bring your own bit of pollution into this pristine world. It is slow when you are watching orangutans all day, and you can't read a book. So you smoke.

Omni: Describe your relationship with your husband, Pak Bohap.

Galdikas: He's not like Western men—Rod, for instance, who just let you go your own way, even if you were doing something he disagreed with. He doesn't agree with my devotion to orangutans, but he respects it. Dayaks are only superficially Westernized—

wearing jeans, digital watches, and T-shirts. They are literate, but they still live within traditions thousands of years old. My husband admires American technology but has no wish to go there or to be anywhere else. Dayaks look upon Westerners as somewhat less civilized, too confrontational, too aggressive.

Omni: Are you becoming "Dayakized"?

Galdikas: In some ways. I'm a very different person than I was fifteen years ago. I never smiled in those *National Geographic* pictures and films. Now I smile all day long. If I don't know what to do, I smile. I'm less rushed, more patient—I've acquired an Indonesian sense of time. They are happy because they are deeply rooted, and I think that has rubbed off on me and made me a better person.

Bohap and I don't necessarily agree on a lot of things: culture, priorities. He is Keharingen Hindu, and his worldview comes from that. Mine is that of a scientist with a Judeo-Christian background. I see the overwhelming importance of evolution in nature. For a long time he refused to acknowledge that humans could be descended from apes, though he jokes that Europeans could be related to proboscis monkeys because both have such big noses. In my twenties I couldn't have been married to someone who didn't share my worldview, my sense of the importance of orangutans in the universe. Now I'm more broad-minded. Orangutans don't occupy a big place in Bohap's mind, like trees or the forces of nature do. But he knows them very well, as all Dayaks do. They have about ten different words for *orangutan*—with cheek pads, small pads, large—like the Eskimos' thirty words for *snow*.

Omni: Was your husband a hunter before he came to work in camp?

Galdikas: Yes, and a slash-and-burn horticulturist. It is a system we don't understand very well. Agronomists used to think it was destructive to the rain forest, but slash-and-burn cultivation is the agricultural system most in equilibrium with nature of any human life-style in the tropical rain forest. Farmers don't use draft animals. They cut a field in the primary forest, just big enough for one or two families to work, never larger than seventy-five by forty meters. It mimics the kind of clearing that occurs naturally. Birds and animals disperse seed quickly in the fields, and the primary forest comes back quickly. Twenty years later a monkey can't tell a Dayak field was ever there. The normal secondary-growth succession is not deflected. The problems come only when the shifting cultivators get chain saws and stop leaving the fields fallow.

Omni: Do orangutans ever eat the Dayak-cultivated fruit?

Galdikas: Yes. One man was growing durian fruits, which are so highly prized in Indonesia, they bring one dollar or more for just one. An orangutan was eating up this farmer's durians, and he got so angry he climbed into the tree to scare the orangutan off. The Dayaks are expert tree climbers and fearless, but that is complete madness. It's like going into the water with a spear to fight a crocodile. Even Mark Spitz shouldn't try that!

So the orangutan knocked him out of the tree, and he died before his family got him to a doctor. The man's neighbors went after the orangutan and killed it with their machetes. After the police investigated, they gave me the bones. You can see the machete marks on the skull.

Omni: Do you use only Dayak assistants in your camp?

Galdikas: We do, for tracking and tree climbing, because they are much better than the Malayu, who are probably better than most Westerners. With so many assistants, we can gather an incredible volume of data on orangutans that I could not generate myself. But it is not an arithmetic progression because we need two assistants in camp for every one in the field. You have to keep the river open and the trails clean. Once, a decade ago, when we just had Rod, myself, a Malayu assistant, and two Indonesian students, we each followed an orangutan for five days. We didn't match that kind of productivity with twenty-plus people in camp until December 1985. In those days the motivation was so intense. We

lived, slept, and stayed in the forest constantly. I'm still trying to get the first ten years of data written up. So far I've published only the first four.

Omni: What are the basic directions of your ongoing research?

Galdikas: We're looking at birth intervals and at copulation, hoping to relate them to the individual orangutan's overall reproductive fitness. We look at mother-offspring relations: Are first- and second-generation, or male and female, offspring treated differently? We assess how efficiently orangutans are utilizing the forest. Orangutans, by what they eat, defecate, or discard, are seed-dispersal agents for seventy percent of the species they eat in Tanjung Puting. How much of the way the forest looks—what fruit trees there are and how many—has to do with orangutans' feeding patterns?

The answers to these difficult questions might well tell us something important about the development of early hominids. The forest is the only home for orangutans and ninety percent of all primate species. To measure the orangutans' foraging impact, we need an independent measurement of what's in the forest—how it is distributed in space and time. That's why we have set up eight botanical plots that we monitor monthly. The plots contain five thousand trees in five different micro-habitat zones. We check each tree to see if it is fruiting, flowering, or leafless. The patterns seem somewhat irregular. Flowering and fruiting seem to be triggered by microclimatic changes: We can't predict when individual species will flower, but generally we've discovered that many flower and fruit after the end of a dry season. You need a little rain for the fruits to develop.

Omni: How do you chart the movements of the orangutans in the preserve?

Galdikas: We have covered the whole study area with grids of transects [lines of measurement crossing at right angles, used for mapping] five hundred meters apart along the cardinal directions. The transects are staked every twenty-five meters so we can note the precise position of an orangutan as we follow it across a transect.

Omni: What is to be gained from all these days, months, years of observation?

'The prospects for the survival of any rain forest not in reserves beyond the end of the century, anywhere on Earth, are pretty dismal.'

Galdikas: In the end I hope to flesh out something about how orangutans live in the wild; how they adapt to their environment; how many offspring they have and at what intervals; at what age the female first gives birth and the male gets cheek pads; and how long they live. With such long-lived animals it takes a lifetime to document such basic facts. If you don't see them for a long time, you get just a window of insight and often a skewed impression. Once you understand orangutan reproductive and foraging strategies, you can compare them to our own and to those of other great apes to see what similarities exist. That is the beauty of sociobiology.

Omni: What do you think your major contribution to the understanding of orangutans has been?

Galdikas: It is hard to single out any one discovery as most important. I have observed orangutans for hours on end on the forest floor. My main contribution is staying in one place, following one population longer than anyone. Right now I can tell you pretty much what these orangutans are doing over the short term in this area. I have yet to follow individuals from birth to death. That will take most, if not all, of my lifetime. And I am happy to do it.

Omni: How much awareness of the need for orangutan and forest preservation in Indonesia is because of your efforts?

Galdikas: We have tried to counter illegal trade in orangutans. I'm not Indonesian, but I can set an example by the way I live in the forest. As a guest here, public criticism and activism is not my place. If I do express my opinions on conservation policy, it is done privately, in governmental offices. Tanjung Puting was a game preserve when Rod and I came, an artifact of Dutch law. Hunting wasn't permitted, but you could clear-cut all the trees. Our goal was to make it into an inviolate habitat. We worked hard to persuade agencies to upgrade it to national park status. This happened in 1982. Indonesians who come here say, "We know who started it all."

I feel good about the future of Tanjung Puting and our role in it. I am not so optimistic about the rest of Borneo and Sumatra. The prospects for the survival of any rain forest not in reserves beyond the end of the century, anywhere on Earth, are pretty dismal.

Omni: Are the forests being logged heavily in Indonesia?

Galdikas: There is logging, and I used to get all hot and bothered about it. Now I realize that it, per se, is not what destroys the forest. I've seen the logging, and there isn't clear-cutting. It is selective and doesn't totally destroy the forest. People do. Population pressure—people clearing it to farm, not the Dayak shifting cultivation tradition—is what threatens the forest. A botanist told me the soils of Tanjung Puting can grow pineapples. But what is the market for that? Hawaii is giving it up. Or you can keep an area as forest. Done right, logging may be the answer.

Omni: What are the consequences of rain forest destruction?

Galdikas: With the possible exception of certain coral reefs, the tropical rain forest is the most complex ecosystem ever to evolve on this planet. Only about ten percent of the land is covered by rain forest, but at least sixty percent of all species live there. It is our Garden of Eden, and a vast loss of genetic material will occur if it goes. Evolution could come to a stop. It is "awesome," as my ten-year-old says, to contemplate all we get from these forests.

Omni: Your late colleague Dian Fossey was much criticized, both for her disinterest in conservation and for not publishing much of her data. Yet you praise her work in memorial lectures.

Galdikas: She couldn't worry about long-term projects when the short-term prospects for the survival of the gorillas were so dire. People were killing the gorillas left and right in front of

---

'Their emotions and intelligence are so similar to ours that we know when they are upset or happy.'

---

her. If that happened to orangutans, my attitude would change. As for criticisms about her lack of published data, that's typical of the snotty attitude of academia. She was looked down upon and had tremendous trouble getting money. She wouldn't come down from that mountain in Rwanda because she didn't have the money for gas. She didn't have an academic background or a lot of publications; but don't overlook the tremendous contribution she did make to our understanding. Her book *Gorillas in the Mist* is just packed with information. She was also accused of anthropomorphizing the gorillas. How can you avoid it with animals like gorillas and orangutans? Their emotions and intelligence are so similar to ours that we know when they are upset or happy. The Indonesian forestry department gave me some bears to rehabilitate. I couldn't read them. I had no way of predicting what they'd do next. But orangutans are no problem. We share ninety-eight percent of the same genetic material. We only separated ten million to fifteen million years ago. For gorillas it is ninety-nine percent and five million years. It is not anthropomorphizing to read what goes on with them in our terms as long as it doesn't interfere with your observations as a scientist. It didn't with Dian. It doesn't with me.

Omni: Did you know Fossey well?

Galdikas: We were friends and saw each other from time to time. Jane [Goodall], Dian, and I gave three talks together in the United States in 1981. And I spent some days with Dian in England before I first went to Indonesia in 1971. She was never much interested in orangutans; gorillas were all that mattered to her, and I was glad to hear her talk about them. But she and Jane are the only people I know of who have devoted their lives to studying an animal with no notion of personal gain. They liked nothing better than to be left alone. Dian was like a gorilla in many ways: majestic, intelligent, sensitive, gentle beneath a ferocious, blustering temper.

Omni: Some critics claim she courted her own death with her confrontational manner toward those she saw as threats to gorillas.

Galdikas: I don't think she wanted to be a martyr, but she became one, like Joan of Arc or Benigno Aquino. No doubt she will accomplish in death what she wanted in life—the protection of the mountain gorillas. The Rwandans have already said they will strengthen patrols. Her Digit Fund [for the gorillas] has received many contributions, and a national memorial may be made of her cabin.

Omni: Would you be willing to give your life, as you say she did, for your apes?

Galdikas: I might. I have, almost. Rod left saying I loved orangutans more than him. That's not the same as giving up life, but I still loved him. But he said his wife had to love him more than anything else on this earth. I've given up a lot for orangutans: I'll never have a life with Rod, a house with a mortgage paid off, or tenure, or any of the trappings of success. But even better, I have Pak Bohap. And, like Jane and Dian, I don't care about the rest.

There is an important way that Dian and I are different. I think she was stuck in a place where she believed gorillas were better than humans. They're not: They do all sorts of horrible things, like kill each other, though perhaps they do it without malice, unlike us. Dian died believing the worst about people. Maybe in that sense she was committing suicide. If I was involved in that sort of confrontational life, I'd have an armed guard. If my health was failing, as hers was, I'd give up smoking; she smoked like a chimney. I'm married. I have children. I have a strong belief in the future of humankind.

Omni: Haven't you turned your back on Western society?

Galdikas: I never turn my back on anything! Irvin DeVore, the Harvard anthropologist, says people are always looking for a Garden of Eden outside of society, whether it be among primitive hunter-gatherers or primates. I have looked for the animal that never left the Garden of Eden, never came down from the trees. But I've never been disillusioned with humankind. Working with orangutans has made me much more aware of humankind's compassion. The higher in my estimation orangutans rise, the higher we do. They've gone off on a path divergent from ours and developed this incredible strength of character denied us because we are a gregarious species. I always prided myself on my ability to withstand solitude. I enjoyed it, craved it. But I've followed orangutans day in, day out for a month, and they'd never meet another of their kind. And if they did, they'd run away to avoid contact. It was just mind-boggling to me. I began to realize that I'm not built that way, and I began to accept my humanness more. It is like in literature, Pound or Eliot or whoever said it: In the end you come back to a different kind of innocence, an innocence born of experience. Fossey was stuck in the middle of that wheel. I've come full circle.

Sex and Society

Any account of hominid evolution would be remiss if it did not at least attempt to explain that most mystifying of all human experiences: our sexuality.

No other aspect of our humanity, whether it be upright posture, tool-making ability, or intelligence in general, seems to elude our intellectual grasp at least as much as it dominates our subjective consciousness. While we are a very long way from reaching a consensus as to why it arose and what it is all about, there is widespread agreement that our very preoccupation with sex is in itself one of the hallmarks of being human. Even as we experience it and analyze it, we exalt it and condemn it. Beyond seemingly irrational fixations, however, there is the further tendency to project our own values upon the observations we make and the data we collect.

There are many who argue quite reasonably that the human bias has been more male- than female-oriented and that the recent "feminization" of anthropology has resulted in new kinds of research and refreshingly new theoretical perspectives. (See "Everything *Else* You Always Wanted to Know About Sex . . . But That We Were Afraid You'd Never Ask" by Jared Diamond.) Not only should we consider the source when evaluating the old theories, so goes the reasoning, but we should also welcome the source when considering the new. To take one example, traditional theory would have predicted that the reproductive competitiveness of muriqui monkeys, as described in "These Are Real Swinging Primates" by Shannon Brownlee, would be associated with greater size and aggression among males. That this is not so, that making love can be more important than making war and that females do not necessarily have to live in fear of competitive males, just goes to show that, even among monkeys, nothing can be taken for granted.

Perhaps the most difficult facet of human sexual behavior, dealt with in "The Evolution of the Big O" by Karen Wright, has to do with the pleasure factor. Are the subjective feelings that are associated with climax adaptive? If so, how can we even prove they exist in other creatures, in order to support any particular theory as to why these feelings develop?

Finally, there is the question of the social significance of sexuality in humans. Meredith Small shows in "What's Love Got to Do With It?" that the chimp-like bonobos of Zaire use sex to reduce tensions and cement social relations and, in so doing, have achieved a high degree of equality between the sexes. Whether or not we see parallels in the human species, says Small, depends upon our willingness to interpret bonobo behavior as a "modern version of our own ancestors' sex play" and this, in turn, may revolve around one's prior theoretical commitments.

Looking Ahead: Challenge Questions

How does human sexuality differ from that of other creatures?

How and why do the reproductive strategies of male and female primates differ?

How is it possible for the muriqui monkeys to be sexually competitive and yet gregarious and cooperative?

Under what circumstances does divorce become common in the human species?

What implications does bonobo sexual behavior have for understanding human evolution?

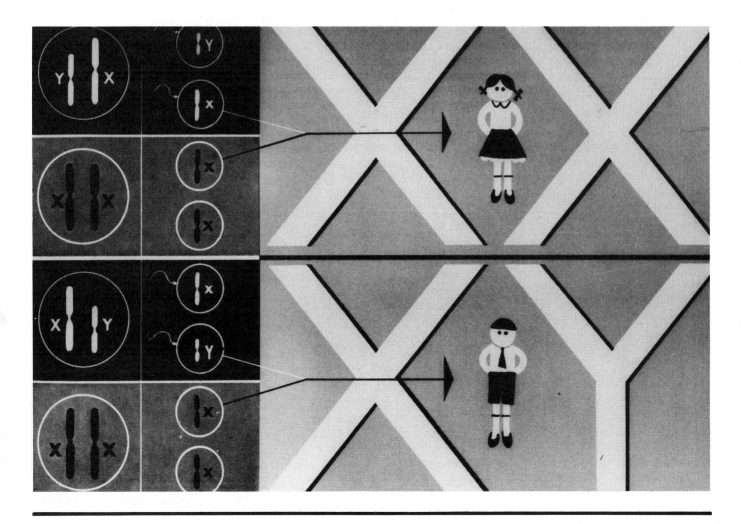

These Are Real Swinging Primates

There's a good evolutionary reason why the rare muriqui of Brazil should heed the dictum 'Make love, not war'

Shannon Brownlee

When I first heard of the muriqui four years ago, I knew right away that I had to see one. This is an unusual monkey, to say the least. To begin with, it's the largest primate in South America; beyond that, the males have very large testicles. We're talking gigantic, the size of billiard balls, which means that the 30-pound muriqui has *cojones* that would look more fitting on a 400-pound gorilla.

But it wasn't prurience that lured me to Brazil. My interest in the muriqui was intellectual, because more than this monkey's anatomy is extraordinary. Muriqui society is untroubled by conflict: troops have no obvious pecking order; males don't compete overtly for females; and, most un-monkeylike, these monkeys almost never fight.

The muriqui is also one of the rarest monkeys in the world. It lives in a single habitat, the Atlantic forest of southeastern Brazil. This mountainous region was once blanketed with forest from São Paulo to Salvador (*see map*), but several centuries of slash-and-burn agriculture have reduced it to fragments.

In 1969 Brazilian conservationist Alvaro Coutinho Aguirre surveyed the remaining pockets of forest and estimated that 2,000 to 3,000 muriquis survived. His data were all but ignored until Russell Mittermeier, a biologist, trained his sights on the muriquis ten years later. Known as Russel of the

Apes to his colleagues, Mittermeier, and American, directs the primate program for the World Wildlife Fund. He hopscotches from forest to forest around the world looking for monkeys in trouble and setting up conservation plans for them. In 1979 he and Brazilian zoologist Celio Valle retraced Aguirre's steps and found even fewer muriquis. Today only 350 to 500 are left, scattered among four state and national parks and six other privately held plots.

In 1981 Karen Strier, then a graduate student at Harvard, approached Mittermeier for help in getting permission to observe the muriqui. He took her to a coffee plantation called Montes Claros, near the town of Caratinga, 250 miles north of Rio de Janeiro. Over the next four years she studied the social behavior of the muriqui there—and came up with a provocative theory about how the monkey's unconventional behavior, as well as its colossal testicles, evolved. She reasoned that the evolution of both could be explained, at least in part, by the muriquis' need to avoid falling out of trees.

Last June I joined Strier, now a professor at Beloit (Wis.) College, on one of her periodic journeys to Montes Claros—clear mountains, in Portuguese. We arrived there after a disagreeable overnight bus trip over bad roads. As we neared the plantation, I found it difficult to believe there was a forest—much less a monkey—within miles. Through the grimy windows of the bus

I saw hillsides stripped down to russet dirt and dotted with spindly coffee plants and stucco farmhouses. There wasn't anything taller than a banana tree in sight. As the bus lurched around the last curve before our stop the forest finally appeared, an island of green amid thousands of acres of coffee trees and brown pastures.

Strier was eager to start looking for the muriquis—"There's a chance we won't see them the whole four days you're here," she said—so no sooner had we dropped our bags off at a cottage on the plantation than we set out along a dirt road into the forest. The trees closed around us—and above us, where they gracefully arched to form a vault of green filigree. Parrots screeched; leaves rustled; a large butterfly flew erratically by on transparent wings. By this time Strier had guided me onto a steep trail, along which she stopped from time to time to listen for the monkeys.

They appeared soon enough, but our first meeting was less than felicitous. After we had climbed half a mile, Strier motioned for me to stop. A muffled sound, like that of a small pig grunting contentedly, came from up ahead. We moved forward a hundred yards. Putting a finger to her lips, Strier sank to her haunches and looked up.

I did the same; twelve round black eyes stared back at me. A group of six muriquis squatted, silent, 15 feet above in the branches, watching us intently.

They began to grunt again. A sharp smell with undertones of cinnamon permeated the air. A light rain began to fall. I held out my palm to catch a drop. It was warm.

"Hey, this isn't rain!" I said.

Strier grinned and pointed to her head. "That's why I wear a hat," she said.

My enthusiasm for the muriquis waned slightly after that. We left them at dusk and retired to the cottage, where Strier described her arrival at Montes Claros four years earlier. Mittermeier acted as guide and interpreter during the first few days of her pilot study. He introduced her to the owner of the 5,000-acre plantation, Feliciano Miguel Abdala, then 73, who had preserved the 2,000-acre forest for more than 40 years. His is one of the only remaining tracts of Atlantic forest, and he agreed to let Strier use it as the site of her study. Then Mittermeier introduced her to the muriquis, assuring her they would be easy to see.

They weren't, and observing them closely is a little like stargazing on a rainy night: not only do you run the risk of getting wet, but you can also spend a lot of time looking up and never see a thing. Mittermeier was adept at spotting the monkeys in the forest, and helped Strier acquire this skill.

But brief glimpses of the monkeys weren't enough. "My strategy was to treat them like baboons, the only other species I'd ever studied," she says. "I thought I couldn't let them out of my sight." She tried to follow on the ground as they swung along in the trees. "They went berserk," she says. They threw branches, shrieked, urinated on her—or worse—and fled.

Even after the muriquis grew accustomed to her, keeping up with them wasn't easy. They travel as much as two miles a day, which is tough for someone picking her way through thick growth on the forest floor. As Strier and a Brazilian assistant learned the muriquis' habitual routes and daily patterns, they cleared trails. These helped, but the muriquis could still travel much faster than she could. "I've often thought the thing to have would be a jet

pack," Strier says. "It would revolutionize primatology. Your National Science Foundation grant would include binoculars, pencils, and a jet pack."

Observing muriquis is like stargazing on a rainy night. You may get wet, and you can spend hours looking and seeing nothing.

The monkeys move by brachiating, swinging hand over hand from branch to branch, much like a child on a jungle gym. Only one other group of monkeys brachiates; the rest clamber along branches on all fours. The muriquis' closest relatives are two other Latin American genera, the woolly monkeys and the spider monkeys— hence woolly spider monkey, its English name. But the muriqui is so unlike them that it has its own genus, *Brachyteles,* which refers to its diminutive thumb, an adaptation for swinging through the trees. Its species name is *arachnoides,* from the Greek for spider, which the muriqui resembles when its long arms, legs, and tail are outstretched.

Brachiating is a specialization that's thought to have evolved because it enables primates to range widely to feed on fruit. Curiously, though, muriquis have a stomach designed for digesting leaves. Strier found that their diet consists of a combination of the two foods. They eat mostly foliage, low-quality food for a monkey, but prefer flowers and fruits, like figs and the *caja manga,* which is similar to the mango. Year after year they return to certain trees when they bloom and bear fruit. The rest of the time the muriquis survive on leaves by passing huge quantities of them through their elongated guts, which contain special bacteria to help them digest the foliage. By the end of the day their bellies are so distended with greenery that even the males look pregnant.

We returned to the trail the next morning just after dawn. Condensation

trickled from leaves; howler monkeys roared and capuchins cooed and squeaked; a bird sang with the sweet, piercing voice of a piccolo. Then Strier had to mention snakes. "Watch out for snakes," she said blithely, scrambling on all fours up a steep bank. I followed her, treading cautiously.

The muriquis weren't where we had left them the day before. Strier led me along a ridge through a stand of bamboo, where a whisper of movement drifted up from the slope below. Maybe it was just the wind, but she thought it was the muriquis, so we sat down to wait. After a couple of hours, she confessed, "This part of research can get kind of boring."

By noon the faint noise became a distinct crashing. "That's definitely them," she said. "It's a good thing they're so noisy, or I'd never be able to find them." The monkeys, perhaps a dozen of them, swarmed uphill, breaking branches, chattering, uttering their porcine grunts as they swung along. At the crest of the ridge they paused, teetering in indecision while they peered back and forth before settling in some legume trees on the ridgetop. We crept down out of the bamboo to within a few feet of them, so close I noticed the cinnamon scent again—only this time I kept out of range.

Each monkey had its own feeding style. One hung upside down by its tail and drew the tip of a branch to its mouth; it delicately plucked the tenderest shoots with its rubbery lips. Another sat upright, grabbing leaves by the handful and stuffing its face. A female with twins—"Twins have never been seen in this species," Strier whispered as she excitedly scribbled notes—ate with one hand while hanging by the other and her tail. Her babies clung to the fur on her belly.

I had no trouble spotting the males. Their nether parts bulged unmistakably—blue-black or pink-freckled, absurd-looking monuments to monkey virility. I asked Strier what sort of obscene joke evolution was playing on the muriquis when it endowed them thus.

We were about to consider this question when a high-pitched whinnying began a few hundred yards away. Immediately a monkey just overhead pulled itself erect and let out an ear-splitting shriek, which set the entire troop to neighing like a herd of nervous horses. Then they took off down into the valley.

Strier and I had to plunge pell-mell into the underbrush or risk losing them for the rest of the day. "They're chasing the other troop," she said as we galloped downhill. A group of muriquis living on the opposite side of the forest had made a rare foray across the valley.

The monkeys we were observing swung effortlessly from tree to tree; we wrestled with thorny vines, and fell farther and farther behind. An impenetrable thicket forced us to backtrack in search of another route. By the time we caught up to the muriquis, they were lounging in a tree, chewing on unripe fruit and chuckling in a self-satisfied sort of way. The intruding troop was nowhere to be seen. "They must have scared the hell out of those other guys," said Strier, laughing.

Tolerance of another troop is odd behavior for monkeys, but not so odd as the fact that they never fight among themselves.

Such confrontations occur infrequently; muriquis ordinarily tolerate another troop's incursions. Strier thinks they challenge intruders only when there's a valuable resource to defend—like the fruit tree they were sitting in.

Tolerance of another troop is odd behavior for monkeys, but not as odd as the fact that members of a muriqui troop never fight among themselves. "They're remarkably placid," said Strier. "They wait in line to dip their hands into water collected in the bole of a tree. They have no apparent pecking order or dominance hierarchy. Males and females are equal in status, and males don't squabble over fe-

males." No other primate society is known to be so free of competition, not even that of gorillas, which have lately gained a reputation for being the gentle giants of the primate world.

Strier's portrayal of the muriqui brought to mind a bizarre episode that Katharine Milton, an anthropologist at the University of California at Berkeley, once described. While studying a troop of muriquis in another patch of the Atlantic forest, she observed a female mating with a half a dozen males in succession; that a female monkey would entertain so many suitors came as no surprise, but Milton was astonished at the sight of the males lining up behind the female "like a choo-choo train" and politely taking turns copulating. They continued in this manner for two days, stopping only to rest and eat, and never even so much as bared their teeth.

Primates aren't known for their graciousness in such matters, and I found Milton's report almost unbelievable. But Strier confirms it. She says that female muriquis come into heat about every two and a half years, after weaning their latest offspring, and repeatedly copulate during that five- to seven-day period with a number of males. Copulations, "cops" in animal-behavior lingo, last as long as 18 minutes, and average six, which for most primates (including the genus *Homo,* if Masters and Johnson are correct) would be a marathon. Yet no matter how long a male muriqui takes, he's never harassed by suitors-in-waiting.

Strier has a theory to explain the muriqui's benignity, based on a paper published in 1980 by Richard Wrangham, a primatologist at the University of Michigan. He proposed that the social behavior of primates could in large part be predicted by what the females eat.

This isn't a completely new idea. For years primatologists sought correlations between ecological conditions and social structure, but few patterns emerged—until Wrangham's ingenious insight that environment constrains the behavior of each sex differently. Specifically, food affects the sociability of females more than males.

Wrangham started with the generally accepted premise that both sexes in every species have a common aim: to leave as many offspring as possible. But each sex pursues this goal in its own way. The best strategy for a male primate is to impregnate as many females as he can. All he needs, as Wrangham points out, is plenty of sperm and plenty of females. As for the female, no matter how promiscuous she is, she can't match a male's fecundity. On average, she's able to give birth to only one offspring every two years, and her success in bearing and rearing it depends in part upon the quality of food she eats. Therefore, all other things being equal, male primates will spend their time cruising for babes, while females will look for something good to eat.

Wrangham's ingenious insight: the social behavior of primates can in large part be predicted by what the females eat.

Wrangham perceived that the distribution of food—that is, whether it's plentiful or scarce, clumped or evenly dispersed—will determine how gregarious the females of a particular species are. He looked at the behavior of 28 species and found that, in general, females forage together when food is plentiful and found in large clumps—conditions under which there's enough for all the members of the group and the clumps can be defended against outsiders. When clumps become temporarily depleted, the females supplement their diet with what Wrangham calls subsistence foods. He suggest that female savanna baboons, for example, live in groups because their favorite foods, fruits and flowers, grow in large clumps that are easy to defend. When these are exhausted they switch to seeds, insects, and grasses. The females form long-lasting relationships within their groups, and establish stable dominance hierarchies.

Chimpanzees provide an illustration of how females behave when their food isn't in clumps big enough to feed everybody. Female chimps eat flowers, shoots, leaves, and insects, but their diet is composed largely of fruits that are widely scattered and often not very plentiful. They may occasionally gather at a particularly abundant fruit tree, but when the fruit is gone they disperse to forage individually for other foods. Members of the troop are constantly meeting at fruit trees, splitting up, and gathering again.

These two types of female groups, the "bonded" savanna baboons and "fissioning" chimps, as Wrangham calls them, pose very different mating opportunities for the males of their species. As a consequence, the social behavior of the two species is different. For a male baboon, groups of females represent the perfect opportunity for him to get cops. All he has to do is exclude other males. A baboon troop includes a clan of females accompanied by a number of males, which compete fiercely for access to them. For baboons there are few advantages to fraternal cooperation, and many to competition.

Male chimpanzees fight far less over females than male baboons do, principally because there's little point—the females don't stick together. Instead, the males form strong alliances with their fellows. They roam in gangs looking for females in heat, and patrol their troop's borders against male interlopers.

Wrangham's theory made so much sense, Strier says, that it inspired researchers to go back into the field with a new perspective. She saw the muriqui as an excellent species for evaluating the model, since Wrangham had constructed it before anyone knew the first thing about this monkey. His idea would seem all the more reasonable if it could predict the muriqui's behavior.

It couldn't, at least not entirely. Strier has found that the females fit Wrangham's predictions: they stick together and eat a combination of preferred and subsistence foods, defending the preferred from other troops. But the males don't conform to the theory. "Considering that the females are foraging together, there should be relatively low pressure on the males to cooperate," she says. "It's odd: the males should compete, but they don't."

She thinks that limitations on male competition may explain muriqui behavior. First, the muriquis are too big to fight in trees. "I think these monkeys are at about the limit of size for rapid brachiation," she says. "If they were bigger, they couldn't travel rapidly through the trees. They fall a lot as

it is, and it really shakes them up. I've seen an adult fall about sixty feet, nearly to the ground, before catching hold of a branch. That means that whatever they fight about has got to be worth the risk of falling out of a tree."

Moreover, fighting may require more energy than the muriquis can afford. Milton has estimated the caloric value of the food eaten by a muriqui each day and compared it to the amount of energy she would expect a monkey of that size to need. She concluded that the muriqui had little excess energy to burn on combat.

The restriction that rapid brachiation sets on the muriqui's size discourages competition in more subtle ways, as well. Given that muriquis are polygynous, the male should be bigger than the female, as is almost invariably the case among other polygynous species—but he's not. The link between larger males and polygyny is created by sexual selection, an evolutionary force that Darwin first recognized, and which he distinguished from natural selection by the fact that it acts exclusively on one sex. Sexual selection is responsible for the manes of male lions, for instance, and for the large canines of male baboons.

In a polygynous society, the advantages to being a large male are ob-

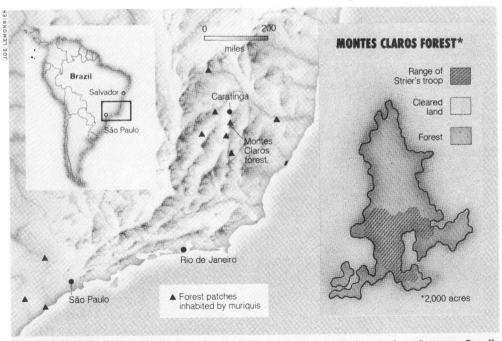

MONTES CLAROS FOREST*

Range of Strier's troop

Cleared land

Forest

*2,000 acres

Brazil
Salvador
São Paulo
Caratinga
Montes Claros forest
Rio de Janeiro
São Paulo

▲ Forest patches inhabited by muriquis

0   200 miles

The 350 to 500 surviving muriquis live in ten patches of the Atlantic forest of southeastern Brazil.

vious: he who's biggest is most likely to win the battles over females—and pass on his genes for size. But sexual selection's push toward large males has been thwarted in the muriqui, says Strier. Any competitive benefits greater size might bring a male would be offset in part by the excessive demands on his energy and the costs of falling out of trees.

She believes that the constraints on the males' size have had a profound effect on the muriquis' social behavior. Most important, says Strier, with males and females being the same size, the females can't be dominated, which means they can pick their mates. Most female primates aren't so fortunate: if they copulate with subordinate males, they risk being attacked by dominant ones. But a female muriqui in heat can easily refuse a suitor, simply by sitting down or by moving away.

The size of the males has a profound effect on muriqui behavior. For one thing, they are simply too big to fight in trees.

Fighting not only doesn't help the male muriqui in his quest for cops; it may even harm his chances, since females can shun an aggressive male. Strier believes that females may also be responsible for the male muriquis' canine teeth not being oversized. As a rule, the male's canines are the same size as the female's only in monogamous primate species, but over the generations female muriquis may have mated more readily with males whose teeth were no bigger than their own. In sum, Strier thinks, for a male muriqui the costs of competing are far outweighted by the benefits of avoiding it.

But he has the means to vie for reproductive success and still come across as Mr. Nice Guy: his sperm. Sperm competition, as it's called, is a hot new idea in sociobiology, originally proposed to explain male bonding

in chimpanzees, and, as Milton was the first to suggest, it may explain why the muriqui has such enormous testicles.

The competition is something like a game of chance. Imagine a bucket with a hole in the bottom just big enough for a marble to pass through. People gather round, each with a handful of marbles. They drop their marbles in the bucket, mix them up, and one comes out the bottom. Whoever owns that marble is the winner.

In the sperm competition among male muriquis, the bucket is a female, the marbles are sperm, and winning means becoming a father. No male can be sure it will be his sperm that impregnates a female, since she mates with a number of his fellows. His chances are further complicated by the fact that the female muriqui, like all New World monkeys, gives no visible indication of ovulation; there may be nothing that signals the male (or the female) when during her heat that occurs. So it's to the male's advantage to continue mating as often as the female will have him.

This may sound like monkey heaven, but it puts the male on the horns of a dilemma. If he copulates as often as possible, he could run low on sperm just when the female is ovulating. On the other hand, if he refrains from copulating to save sperm, he may miss his chance at procreating altogether. Selection may have come to his aid, Strier reasons, by acting on his testicles.

Here's a plausible scenario. Suppose a male came along that could produce more sperm than the average muriqui because his testicles were bigger than average. That male would clean up in the reproductive arena. The ratio of testicle size to body weight has been correlated with high sperm count and repeated copulation over a short period in other mammals, and bigger testicles probably also increase the percentage of viable and motile sperm.

If the muriqui's testicles are anything like those of other species, then a male with extra big ones has a slight reproductive advantage. Like a player with more marbles to put in the bucket, a male that can produce more and

better sperm has a better than average chance of impregnating females and passing on this advantageous trait to his sons. Just as important, the outsized organs probably don't cost him much in metabolic energy. Thus, over generations, the muriqui's testicles have grown larger and larger.

Strier's theory has five years of data behind it, and it's the kind of theory that will stimulate researchers to re-examine their ideas about other species. Yet it isn't her only concern; she concentrates equally on the muriqui's uncertain future. On our last day in the forest we watched the monkeys cross a six-foot gap in the canopy 60 feet above us. One by one they stood poised for a moment on the end of a branch before launching themselves. Strier counted them as they appeared in silhouette against a grey sky. The total was 33, including the twins. "They're up from twenty-two in 1982," she said. "That's a very fast increase."

The muriquis at Montes Claros make up almost one-tenth of the total population of the species, and they're critical to its survival—as are all the other isolated and widely separated troops. Each group's genetic pool is limited, and eventually the troops could suffer inbreeding depression, a decline in fecundity that often appears in populations with little genetic variability.

Strier and Mittermeier predict that one day muriquis will have to be managed, the way game species are in the U.S. They may be transported between patches of forest to provide some gene flow. But that's a dangerous proposition now. There are too few muriquis to risk it, and none has ever bred or survived for long in captivity. "Before my study, conservationists would probably have moved males between forests," Strier says. "That would've been a mistake. I have tentative evidence that in a natural situation the females may be the ones that do the transferring between groups."

For now, though, she thinks the biggest concern isn't managing the monkeys but preventing their habitat from disappearing. Preserving what remains of the Atlantic forest won't be easy, and no one knows this better than Feliciano Miguel Abdala, the man responsible for there being any forest at all at Montes Claros.

Abdala has little formal education, but he's rich; he owns nine plantations besides Montes Claros. His family lives in relative splendor in Caratinga, but he likes to spend the weekdays here. His house is just beyond the edge of the forest, and sunlight filters through the bougainvillea vine entwining the front porch. Chickens can be seen through the cracks in the floorboards, scratching in the dirt under the house. Electric cords are strung crazily from the rafters, and a bare bulb dangles in the center of his office. Abdala removes his straw hat decorously and places it on a chair before sitting at his desk.

Abdala bought the 5,000 acres of Montes Claros in 1944. The region was barely settled then, and smoke still rose from the great burning heaps of slash left from clearing the forest. Abdala's land included one of the last stands of trees. I ask him why he saved it. "I am a conservationist," he says. "For a long time the local people thought I was crazy because I wouldn't cut the forest. I told them not to shoot the monkeys, and they stopped. Now all my workers are crazy, too."

I ask Abdala about his plans for his forest. He rubs his head distractedly and says, vaguely. "I hope it will continue."

Abdala believes the government should buy Montes Claros—plantation and rain forest—to create a nature reserve. He'll probably maintain the forest as long as he lives, but the land is quite valuable, and his heirs might not share his lofty sentiments.

As important as the muriquis have become to understanding social systems, and as much as U.S. conservationists may wish to see these monkeys preserved, Strier thinks that in the end it's up to the Brazilians to save them. She's expecting a three-year grant from the National Science Foundation; part of the money will go toward allowing her to observe the monkeys in other forest patches, watching for variation in their behavior as a test of her ideas. Studies like hers will be critical not only for proving theories but also for ensuring that plans for managing the muriquis will work. The rest of the money will permit her to train seven Brazilian graduate students, because she says, "the future of the muriqui lies with the Brazilians."

Evolution of the Big O

Are orgasms function or fun? Inquiring biologists want to know.

Karen Wright

"The expense of spirit in a waste of shame" is how William Shakespeare described lust, but he was speaking as a poet, not a pragmatist. True, copulation is not cheap—it always exacts a toll, spiritual or otherwise, from its participants. But "a waste"? Hardly. Sex perpetuates the species, and lust—shameful though some human primates choose to make it—is the overnight express to sex.

For men and women alike the objective of lust is orgasm. It's hard to imagine a more powerful inducement to sexual activity. Indeed, orgasm is the kind of experience that could have been invented by gametes (reproductive cells). Imagine being stuck in somebody's gonads, where your goal in life is to form a union with someone else's gamete. The objective? To produce an organism that makes more gametes. What possible incentive could you offer your host to bring about that union? Try a somatic blitzkrieg of ecstasy, courtesy of the limbic system, the pleasure (as well as the pain) center of the brain. That's orgasm.

Today, when orgasm has been divorced almost entirely from reproduction, the "how" of sexual climax has been largely demystified. Masters and Johnson established the physical parameters of orgasm in their landmark 1966 book, *Human Sexual Response.* These include, in men, contraction of the rectal sphincter at .8-second intervals, a reduction of voluntary muscle control, and involuntary muscle spasms throughout the body (one distinctive example being the so-called carpope-

dal spasm, in which the big toe is held straight out while the other toes bend back and the foot arches—a contortion most people couldn't pull off consciously if they were paid to). And of course, there is ejaculation, which is usually, but not always, a telltale sign. In women the telltale signs are similar: along with its chaotic effects on other muscles, orgasm causes contractions of the uterus, vagina, and rectal sphincter, again at .8-second intervals. For both sexes, the pudendal cataclysm typically lasts less than a minute.

Despite such insights on the mechanics of orgasm, the origins of the phenomenon are as mysterious as ever. When did orgasm evolve? Who (or what) had the first orgasm? What selective pressures shaped the redoubtable reflex? Without fossil evidence, scientists interested in those questions must examine in excruciating detail the sexual practices of contemporary human cultures as well as the sex lives of chimpanzees, gorillas, orangutans, and other uninhibited relatives of *Homo sapiens.*

The monumental problem confronting anyone who wants to explore the antiquity of orgasm is the difficulty of ascertaining, even in existing animals, who has orgasms and who does not. Most experts believe that most male mammals do—which would make the experience at least 65 million years old, since that's when modern mammals began to evolve. But the logical pitfalls of such speculation are manifold. While the mechanics of an orgasm may be known, it is still a sensation, and like all sensations it's subjective. As a result, its existence

can't be incontrovertibly demonstrated or disproved by empirical measures. That unhappy truth becomes especially clear when evolutionary biologists turn their attention to the female orgasm—which they do with unseemly fascination. Even human lovers have to take their lady's word for it. How much more ineffable, then, must be the coital consciousness of Madame Marmoset.

To complicate matters, some critics charge that personal experience often shapes a theorist's conclusions. "Sex is one of those subjects that everybody thinks they know about," says Elisabeth Lloyd, a philosopher at the University of California at Berkeley who's writing a book about bias in evolutionary theories about female sexuality. "People just assume that what they know is right, even if they learned it in the locker room." That said, the students of orgasm's evolution know a few things you wouldn't expect to hear at halftime.

Researchers generally use Masters and Johnson's description of human orgasm as evidence of orgasm in other species as well. In every species the apparent symptoms of satiety are more conspicuous among males than females. Ejaculation is of course the least subtle index, but there are others. For example, at the pinnacle of the sex act, a male rat gives a final thrust, straightens his front legs, and abandons his erstwhile desperate grasp on the female; then, with an abstracted gaze one researcher describes as "starry-eyed," the male slowly rises up on his rear legs and relinquishes the mount.

He saw; he conquered; he came. But did he feel the earth move? Does the rat's behavior necessarily correspond to the very particular neural experience we call orgasm? For that matter, does the salmon that spills its seed over a bed of eggs feel a frisson of pleasure? In short, does ejaculation equal orgasm?

There's reason to believe it doesn't. Whereas ejaculation is a somatic phenomenon, orgasm (as Shakespeare implies) is a phenomenon of the spirit, and even in human males a strict correlation between mind and matter hasn't been established. Ejaculation in men is not always coincident with orgasm: paralysis victims bereft of feeling below the waist often get erections and ejaculate without having a climax, and prepubescent boys can achieve orgasm, even multiple ones, without ejaculating. But if ejaculation doesn't equal orgasm, how can you tell whether an erupting male is enjoying himself?

Does the rat's behavior correspond to orgasm? Does the salmon spilling its seed feel a frisson of pleasure? In short, does ejaculation equal orgasm?

Trouble is, you can't. "I observe insects mating all the time," says John Alcock, a zoologist at Arizona State University. "But I see no way of answering the question of whether male carpenter bees experience anything remotely similar to pleasure when they succeed in copulating with a female."

For that very reason, Alcock says, evolutionary biologists have shied away from tracing orgasm's lineage: "People don't see the point of getting worked up about a question they can't answer." Says Donald Symons, an anthropologist at the University of California at Santa Barbara, "I can't remember any serious discussion of male orgasm at all." Yet scientific debate *has* raged for years over an even more elusive phenomenon: the female orgasm. And the issue being debated

isn't who, how, when, or where, but why. Why should women have the capacity for climax when they can make babies perfectly well without it? In Darwinian terms, what is the adaptive value of the female orgasm?

No one questions the Darwinian wisdom of the mammalian male orgasm. The first male to demonstrate such an aptitude would be inclined to indulge it so ferociously that other males' anorgasmic sex drives would pale in comparison. Adaptation can also explain the relative speed with which males achieve their bliss. Since the limiting factor in male reproductive success is usually the availability of receptive females, when said females make themselves available, a guy who can work fast has a distinct advantage over the slow male. He begets more kids, for one, and he is also less likely to fall prey to enemies that might attack while a couple is flagrante delicto. Furthermore, the less time it takes to philander, the more time there is to eat—another essential component of survival.

Female reproductive success, in contrast, is usually limited by the availability of resources to sustain mother and child through pregnancy, labor, and nursing, rather than an availability of mating partners. Because most females must gestate and raise their offspring, repeated bouts of lovemaking yield diminishing returns where conception is concerned and interfere considerably with the duties of motherhood. There is no strong evidence that orgasm in females directly contributes to fertility or fecundity. So why is it there at all?

Some evolutionary theorists, including Desmond Morris, maintain that human female orgasm was adaptive because it helped cement the "pair-bond" between ancestral parents that was necessary to ensure the survival of vulnerable infants. If the woman is rewarded during sex as much as (or more than) the man, goes the theory, then she will remain perpetually eager for intercourse and retain her allure with her mate, who will be less likely to stray. Scientists had also speculated that female orgasm aided conception

by keeping a woman on her back long enough for her to ensure insemination, or by actively sucking sperm up into the uterus (an idea whose time has gone, since the contractions that accompany climax turn out to be expulsive).

Such theories assume that female orgasm is a reliable companion of copulation. But as Alfred Kinsey announced in his landmark 1953 report, it's not. Kinsey's interviews with nearly 6,000 women, as well as subsequent surveys, revealed that the vast majority of women do not climax during sexual intercourse without direct stimulation of the clitoris. Even in today's era of relative enlightenment, the most recent statistics from the Kinsey Institute for Research in Sex, Gender, and Reproduction show that fewer than half the women surveyed achieve orgasm through intercourse. The disparity between the reproductive act and the orgasmic reflex prompted Shere Hite, in her controversial 1976 *Hite Report,* to call sexual intercourse the Rube Goldberg method of female sexual fulfillment.

Such data present a conundrum to anyone who wants to argue that female orgasm is a sexually selected trait. John Alcock suggests that the legerdemain required to bring about the effect may have helped our foremothers distinguish between the sensitive guys who would make good parents and the love-'em-and-leave-'em louts. But the bitter truth, as Margaret Mead pointed out, is that many, many human cultures don't even recognize that women can enjoy sex, let alone climax the way men do. If female orgasm is an adaptive behavior, then there are plenty of women whose genes are headed the way of the dinosaurs.

The tenuous link between orgasm and intercourse in women has led other theorists, including Donald Symons, to conclude that the female climax is more accident than adaptation. "Saying that a trait is adaptive is different from saying a trait has an evolutionary history," says Symons. "Everything has an evolutionary history. To show that something is an adaptation, you have to be able to explain the how and the why, show that it has some kind of special design, a design that solved a specific problem.

"In the case of males, the design argument makes good sense. Male orgasm doesn't occur at just any time—there's this intense burst of pleasure that accompanies ejaculation, which is of extreme reproductive significance," he says. "That's an obvious adaptation."

Symons says that the most parsimonious interpretation of the evidence is that the female orgasm is a by-product, like male nipples, that exists merely because the same trait in the opposite sex confers a selective advantage. In other words, male orgasm by way of the penis is a smashing success, and since the clitoris is made from the same fetal tissue as the penis, it can't help but precipitate orgasms too. That's not to say that female arousal is superfluous, or that it doesn't have a function. Symons believes arousal is an adaptive mechanism in female sexuality, and that female genitals have indeed been "designed" to provide pleasurable stimulation during intercourse. But the particular experience of orgasm, he says, is neither a necessary nor sufficient condition for reproductive fitness in females. "It's simply a by-product of the ability of males to have orgasms."

Such a view, however reasonable, cannot go uncontested, and the contest comes primarily from Sarah Blaffer Hrdy, an anthropologist at the University of California at Davis. Hrdy has marshaled evidence from studies of nonhuman primates to make hypotheses about human sexuality. "There is just no reason to think that orgasm is nonadaptive," she says. Her research suggests that among our closest relatives, promiscuous rather than connubial behavior greatly behooves females who want their progeny to survive.

She points out that in virtually all primates male behavior has an important effect on the survival of infants. A male can lavish a youngster with care and protection or he can kill it, depending on how confident he is that he's sired the youngster in question. A female that can persuade the community's males to be nice to her kids

stands a better chance of passing on her genes. And she can do so, says Hrdy, by pulling a few males into "the web of possible paternity"; that is, by sleeping around.

"For a number of years," Hrdy says, "I've been arguing that for non-human female primates, the goal is not simply to be inseminated by the single best male—that's an old Darwinian and Victorian notion. What really happens is that a female primate tries to mate with a number of males to establish a network that will preclude males from attacking her offspring. It will also increase the amount of resources the males are likely to provide the infants. If a male isn't certain that he's not the father, he cannot afford to kill the infants—it's too big a risk. This margin of error that males must allow is one of the few advantages females have.

"If you look at primate breeding systems the way I do, where the problem that the female faces is how to draw multiple partners into this net, then you see the need for a psycho-physiological phenomenon that keeps her motivated to solicit and mate with a number of male partners"—in short, she needs an incentive for promiscuity. And Hrdy believes the most expedient route to promiscuity is via the clitoral orgasm. "The very fact," she says, "that it is erratic in its relationship with intercourse means it works as a more powerful conditioning mechanism." A female that does not climax during her first coital encounter has the incentive to demand another round—immediately. Chances are her newly sated mate won't be able to gratify her, so she dumps him for a fresh partner. The principle is a familiar one: if at first you don't succeed, try, try again. And again. And again, each time expanding the web of possible paternity.

This is something that B. F. Skinner pointed out years ago, Hrdy says—the principle of intermittent reinforcement. In the behavioral psychologist's scenario, a rat that is rewarded a pellet when it presses a bar in its cage will press the bar only when it's hungry. If, however, the rat gets a pellet every 10 or 20 times it presses a bar, it will spend every waking hour pumping

away at the bar. The rat learns that a great deal of effort is required for any return at all. Hrdy suggests that our female ancestors may have been subject to similar conditioning.

Hrdy's notion that female primates must be ever-ready lovers also jibes with Masters and Johnson's finding that women remain sexually excitable after orgasm. Whereas men's anticlimactic physiology quickly returns to its baseline level, women, before they cool down, retrace their steps, so to speak, to the plateau of arousal that immediately preceded their climax. It's now widely accepted that women can experience more prolonged arousal and more orgasms per unit of time than men—which, without benefit of Hrdy's interpretation, would seem to run counter to what you'd expect in a Darwinian world.

In her 1991 book, *Mystery Dance*, biologist Lynn Margulis of the University of Massachusetts tries to walk the center line of the design argument, claiming that while early on "the clitoris had no evolutionary significance . . . the opportunities for evolutionary invention were so rich that such a useful little mechanism was eventually put to use within the complex framework of human evolution."

Trouble is, according to Symons and other critics, "adaptationists" such as Hrdy have precious little evidence to appeal to. "It's pure imagination about some polygynous past we supposedly had," carps Symons. "You find no evidence that women anywhere are behaving in ways to confuse the issue of paternity."

That's because human males, Hrdy argues, developed institutions such as marriage and clitoridectomy (the amputation of the clitoris) to repress women's indiscriminate sexuality, so that paternity could not be so easily confused. She points to the behavior of female chimpanzees, gorillas, and macaques as an indication of a past in which human females flaunted their desire. She notes too that if the evolution of the clitoris were dependent on the simultaneous development of the penis, you'd expect to see some correspondence between penis size and clitoris size in primates—which you often don't.

"What you do see," she says, "is variation across primate species. If you look at species where you have multiple-mate breeding systems, the clitoris is more developed. So it is not tracking the penis." The chimpanzee penis, for example, is "very small and pencillike" in comparison with the human penis, while the clitoris is among the more pendulous of its class.

Hrdy's argument would be buttressed by observations showing that orgasm among nonhuman female primates is correlated with promiscuous behavior. But again, while a physical reaction that is probably an orgasm can be noted, unequivocal evidence of the sensation of orgasm among species less articulate than our own is impossible to come by. There's the clutching reaction of the rhesus monkey, in which the female generally reaches

back with one hand and grasps the male, sometimes turning and looking over her shoulder at the presumed moment of his climax—which, if it does indicate female eruption as well, would leave people in the dust when it comes to simultaneous orgasms.

Then there's the disturbingly familiar "ejaculation face" of the stumptailed macaque: a round-mouthed expression composed of one part surprise, one part epiphany, and one part catatonia. Males and females alike commonly adopt such expressions in the throes of passion. The unanswerable question is, of course, does the "face" correspond to a seismic tweak of ecstasy?

In fact, there is ample evidence of masturbation among captive animals, and contractions à la Masters and Johnson have been recorded in artificially stimulated female primates of

several species. "It's much more logical to assume that they do have orgasms than that they don't," says Helen Fisher, a research associate of the American Museum of Natural History. "We're not talking about a complicated physiological response here."

But primate researchers say the animals don't have much spare time in the wild for mating, let alone for playing with themselves, and it's in the wild that the evolutionary pressures Hrdy talks about are exerted. So in lieu of sworn testimonials from the animal kingdom, the "proof" of female orgasm's adaptive value still redounds to the person who can tell the most convincing story about its history of selection. "The beauty of this topic is that you, too, can make up a theory," says Fisher. The truth probably lies somewhere between Shakespeare's poetry and Darwin's pragmatism.

"Everything *Else* You Always Wanted to Know About Sex . . . But That We Were Afraid You'd Never Ask"

Jared Diamond

Among the various species of apes and man, which has the biggest penis?

And why?

Why do men have much smaller testes than chimpanzees?

Why are men bigger than women?

Why are humans the only social animals that prefer copulating in private?

Why don't human females, unlike almost all other female mammals, have easily recognized days of fertility, with sexual receptivity confined largely to those intervals?

If your answer to the first question was the gorilla, you're wrong. The correct reply is man. If you gave intelligent answers to the remaining questions, publish them; scientists are still debating rival theories.

The six questions illustrate the difficulty of explaining the most obvious facts of our sexual anatomy and physiology. Part of the problem is our hangups about sex: scientists didn't begin to study it seriously until recently, and they still have trouble being objective. Another difficulty is that they can't do controlled experiments on sexual practices, as they can on our intake of cholesterol or our tooth-brushing habits. Finally, our sex organs didn't just evolve in isolation: they're an outgrowth of our social habits, which in turn stem from the way we once obtained food. Given knowledge of how an animal feeds, a biologist can often predict its mating system and genital anatomy. Hence if we want to understand how human sexuality got to be the way it is, we have to begin by exploring the evolution of our diet and our society.

From the vegetarian preferences of our ape ancestors, we diverged within the last several million years to become social carnivores who eat meat as well as vegetables. Yet our teeth and claws remained relatively harmless, like those of apes, not the jagged instruments of true carnivores like the tiger. Our hunting prowess depended on large brains instead. By acting in coordinated groups, using shrewd tactics and primitive weaponry, our ancestors killed large, dangerous prey and regularly shared food with each other. And while the human child was acquiring the skills to become a hunter-gatherer, it was fed by both parents for years after weaning. In contrast, apes obtain their own food as soon as they are weaned. Gorilla, chimpanzee, and gibbon fathers offer protection only to their young; orangutan fathers provide nothing beyond their sperm.

The social system we've developed to accommodate our un-apelike nurturing habits seems utterly normal to us, but it's bizarre by ape standards and virtually unique among animals. Adult orangutans are essentially solitary. Adult gibbons live in separate, monogamous, male-female pairs, while gorillas live in polygamous harems of several adult females, usually dominated by a single adult male. Our closest kin, the chimpanzees, are fairly promiscuous; they exist in communities of dispersed females, attended by a group of adult males. By contrast, human societies, like human food habits, resemble those of lions and wolves: we live in bands containing many adult males and many adult females. Furthermore—and here we diverge even from the social carnivores and are most like colonies of sea birds—our males and females pair off with each other. The pairing is more or less monogamous in most modern political states, but it's still mildly polygynous among most surviving hunter-gatherer bands, like the !Kung San of the Kalahari desert, which may provide clues to how people lived over the last million years. By mildly polygynous, I mean that most hunter-gatherer men can support only one wife, but a few successful men have several. (I'll discuss the "science" of extramarital sex by and by.)

How does this social organization shape the bodies of men and women? Consider the fact that adult men are slightly bigger than woman of their age (on average, about eight per cent taller and 20 per cent heavier). A zoologist from outer space would take one look at my wife, who's 5′8″, next to me (5′10″), and would instantly conclude, if the evolutionary rules on his planet were the same as ours, that we belonged to a mildly polygynous species. How could he guess mating practices from relative body size? He would know that among mammals, the greater the male's size advantage over the female, the larger the harem size. Male and female gibbons are the same size, and they are monogamous. Male gorillas weigh nearly twice as much as females, and have harems containing three to six females. But the greatest weight advantage belongs to the male southern elephant seal, whose three tons entitle him to as many as 48 wives. In a monogamous species, every male can win a female, so the males don't need overpowering size. But only a few males can get the females in a very polygynous species. Hence, the bigger the harem, the fiercer the competition among males is likely to be and the more important it is for a male to be able to ward off competing males. Size obviously helps. With our bigger males and occasional polygyny, humans fit this pattern: males are just slightly bigger than females. (However, at some point in human evolution male intelligence and personality came to count for more than size: male basketball players and football linemen don't seem to have more wives than male jockeys or coxwains.)

The males and females of polygynous species tend to have more marked differences in secondary sexual characteristics, which also play a role in attracting mates and dominating rivals. For instance, male and female gibbons look alike at a distance, while male gorillas (befitting their polygyny) are easily recognized by their crested heads and silver-haired backs. Humans fall somewhere in between. Here, too, our anatomy reflects our mild polygyny. The external differences between men and women aren't nearly as marked as sex-related differences in gorillas or orangutans, but the zoologist from outer space could probably distinguish men and women by the body and facial hair of men, men's unusually large penises (of which more soon), and the large breasts of women even before their first pregnancy (in this we are unique among primates).

Now to the genitals themselves: the combined weight of the testes in the average man is about an ounce and a half, compared to an ounce and a quarter for a 450-pound male gorilla. But macho human males really have nothing to boast about: their testes are put to shame by the four-ounce testes of a 100-pound male chimpanzee. Why is the chimp so well endowed?

For an answer, we turn to one of the triumphs of modern physical anthropology, the Theory of Testis Size. By weighing the testes of 33 primate species, British scientists were able to identify two trends: males of species that copulate more often need bigger testes, and those of promiscuous species in which several males routinely copulate in quick sequence with one female need especially big testes (reason: the male that injects the most semen has the best chance of fertilizing the egg). What

about the tiny-testicled gorilla? In fact, his modest testes are perfectly adequate for his modest needs. Even for a male with a harem of several females, the sex act is a rare treat; it occurs only a few times a year. That is because a female gorilla doesn't resume sexual activity until three to four years after giving birth, and even then is receptive for only a couple of days a month (until she becomes pregnant again).

The sex life of a male orangutan may be only slightly more demanding. But the male chimp lives in the simian equivalent of sexual nirvana. He has almost daily opportunities to copulate. That, plus his need to outdo other males in semen output if he is to fertilize the profligate female, explains his need for giant testes. Human males make do with medium-sized testes, because the average man copulates more often than a gorilla or an orangutan but less often than a chimp. In addition, the typical human female in an average menstrual cycle doesn't force several males into a sperm competition to fertilize her.

From this triumph of scientific sexual exegesis, we now descend to a glaring failure: the inability of twentieth-century science to formulate an adequate Theory of Penis Length. The erect penis averages one and a quarter inches in a gorilla, an inch and a half in an orangutan, three inches in a chimp, and six inches in a man. Visual conspicuousness similarly varies: a gorilla's penis can hardly be seen even when erect because of its black color, whereas the chimp's erect pink penis stands out boldly against the bare white skin behind it. The flaccid penis isn't even visible in apes. Why does the human male need a penis that is larger and more conspicuous than that of any other primate? Doesn't it represent an evolutionary waste—an expenditure of protoplasm that could be better devoted to, say, expanding the cerebral cortex or improving the fingers?

Biologists usually reply by citing distinctive features of human coitus that they suppose might be served by a long penis: our frequent use of the face-to-face "missionary" position, our acrobatic variety in intercourse, and the supposedly long duration of our coital

bouts. None of these explanations survives close scrutiny. The face-to-face position is also the one preferred by orangutans and pygmy chimps, and is occasionally used by gorillas. Orangs mix face-to-face copulation with dorso-ventral (à la canines) and sideways positions. What's more, they copulate hanging from tree branches, a feat that vies with or even surpasses our ingenious and often exacting gyrations. As for the duration of human intercourse, studies have shown that coitus lasts on average about four minutes in Americans. This is much longer than the performance of gorillas (one minute) or chimps (eight seconds), but is only a fraction that of orangutans (15 minutes).

A popular alternative theory for the long penis is that it evolved as an organ of display, like a peacock's tail or a lion's mane. This explanation really begs the question: What type of display, and to whom? Proud male anthropologists unhesitatingly answer: an attraction display, to women. It's hard to decide whether this answer is correct—or just wishful thinking by men. Many women say that they are "turned on" more by a man's voice, legs, shoulders, and buttocks than by his penis.

Another possible role for a large penis is as a threat or status display vis-à-vis other men. This explanation is supported by the phallic art that men create for men, and the widespread male obsession with penis size. Evolution of the human penis was limited by the length of the vagina: a penis would damage a women if it were significantly larger. However, I can guess what the penis would look like if this practical constraint were removed and if men could design themselves. It would resemble the penis sheaths (phallocarps) used as everyday male attire in some areas of New Guinea where I do field work. Phallocarps vary in length (up to two feet), diameter (up to four inches), shape (curved or straight), the angle made with the wearer's body, and decoration (for example, a tuft of fur at the end). Each man has a wardrobe of several sizes and shapes. Western male anthropologists interpret the phallocarp as something worn for modesty or concealment, to which my wife had a succinct rebuttal: "The most immodest display of modesty I've ever seen!"

If these aspects of human sexual anatomy are a puzzlement, so are our sexual activities, which must be considered freakish by any decent mammalian standards. Most mammals are sexually inactive most of the time, copulating only when the female is in heat, or estrus—that is, when she's ovulating and therefore capable of being fertilized. Female mammals apparently "know" when they're ovulating, for they solicit copulation at those times by presenting their genitals towards the males. Lest a male be particularly dense, many female primates go farther: the area around the vagina, and in some species the buttocks and breast, swells up and turns red, pink, or blue. This visual advertisement of female availability affects male monkeys in the same way that *Playboy* centerfolds affect male humans. In the presence of females with brightly swollen genitals, male monkeys stare much more often at the female's genitals, develop higher testosterone levels, attempt to copulate more often, and penetrate more quickly and after fewer pelvic thrusts than in the presence of females who aren't displaying themselves.

The human sexual cycle is different. A woman's receptivity is more or less constant, year round. Numerous studies have tried to determine whether receptivity varies at all through a woman's monthly cycle, but scientists still don't agree on an answer.

Indeed, the period of human ovulation is so well concealed that we didn't have accurate scientific information on its timing until fairly recently. Until the 1930s, many doctors thought that women could conceive at any point in their cycle, or even that conception was most likely at the time of menstruation. In contast to the male baboon, who has only to scan his surroundings for brightly swollen females, the human male hasn't the foggiest notion of which females around him are ovulating. A woman herself may learn to recognize sensations associated with ovulation, but this "rhythm method" is tricky, even with the help of thermometers and ratings of vaginal mucus quality. Besides, it's based on hard-won, modern book knowledge—not on the innate sense of sexual readiness that drives female mammals of other species.

The human female's concealed ovulation, constant receptivity, and brief fertile period in each menstrual cycle ensure that most copulations take place at the wrong time for conception. Worse still, menstrual cycle length varies more between women, or from cycle to cycle in a given woman, than among most other mammals. As a result, even young newlyweds who make love at maximum frequency and without contraceptives have only a 28 per cent probability of conception per menstrual cycle. Animal breeders would be in despair if a prize cow had such low fertility.

In these days of growing human overpopulation, one of the most paradoxical tragedies, in my view, is the Roman Catholic church's insistence that copulation has conception as its only natural purpose, and that the rhythm method is the only proper means of birth control. These claims would be valid for gorillas and most other mammals, but not for us. In no species besides man has the purpose of copulation become so unrelated to conception, or the rhythm method so unsuited by contraception.

As a way of achieving fertilization, sex for us is a huge waste of time. Had we retained a proper estrous cycle like other mammals, our ancestors could have devoted much more time to butchering mastodons than to the sexual chase. And females could thereby have fed more babies and outcompeted neighboring clans whose females no longer advertised estrus. Thus, the most hotly debated problem in the evolution of human reproduction is why we ended up concealing ovulation, and what good all our mis-timed copulations do us.

A related paradox is that of concealed copulation. Promiscuous or monogamous, all other group-living animals have sex in public. Paired sex gulls mate in the midst of the colony; a female chimpanzee may mate consecutively with five or more males in each other's presence. Why are we unique in our strong preference for privacy?

Biologists are currently arguing over at least six different theories to explain the origin of concealed ovulation and copulation. Interestingly, the theories often turn out to be a reflection of the gender and outlook of their proponents:

1. Theory preferred by many traditional male anthropologists

Concealed ovulation and copulation both evolved to enhance cooperation and reduce aggression among male hunters. How could cavemen have brought off the teamwork needed to spear a mammoth if they'd been fighting for the public favors of a cavewoman in estrus? The implicit message: women's physiology is important chiefly for its effect on bonds between men, the real movers of society. However, one can broaden this theory to make it less blatantly sexist: visible estrus and public sex would disrupt human society by affecting female/female and male/female as well as male/male bonds.

2. Theory preferred by many other traditional male anthropologists

Concealment cements the bonds between a particular man and woman, thereby laying the foundations of the human family. A woman remains sexually attractive and receptive so that she can satisfy a man sexually all the time, bind him to her, and reward him for his help in rearing her baby. The message: women evolved to make men happy. Left unexplained is why pairs of gibbons, whose unwavering devotion to monogamy should make them role models for the Moral Majority, remain constantly together even though they have sex only every few years.

3. Theory of a more modern male anthropologist

Donald Symons, of the University of California at Santa Barbara, notes that a male chimpanzee which kills a small animal is more likely to share the meat with an estrous female than with a nonestrous female. This suggests to him that human females may have evolved the ability to be in a constant state of estrus to ensure a frequent meat supply from male hunters. Another possibility, Symons says, is that women in most hunter-gatherer societies, even though they have little say in choosing a husband, by being constantly attractive could privately seduce a superior male and secure his genes for her children. Symons's theories, while still male-oriented, at least view women as cleverly pursuing their own goals.

4. Theory of a male biologist and a female biologist

If a man could recognize signs of ovulation, say Richard Alexander and Katherine Noonan, he could use that knowledge to fertilize his wife and then safely go off philandering the rest of the time. Hence women evolved concealed ovulation to force men into marriage by exploiting male paranoia about fatherhood. Not knowing the time of ovulation, a man must copulate with his wife often to have a chance of fertilizing her, and that leaves him less time to dally with other women. The wife benefits, but so does the husband. He gains confidence in the paternity of his children, and he needn't worry that his wife will suddenly attract many competing men by turning bright red on a particular day. At last, we have a theory seemingly grounded in sexual equality.

5. Theory of a feminist sociobiologist

Sarah Hrdy, of the University of California at Davis, was impressed by the frequency with which many male primates kill infants not their own. The bereaved mother is thereby induced to come into estrus again, and often mates with the murderer, thus increasing his output of progeny. (Such violence has been common in human history: male conquerors kill the vanquished men and children but spare the women.) As a counter-measure, Hrdy says, women evolved concealed ovulation to manipulate men by confusing the issue of paternity. A woman who distributed her favors widely would thereby enlist many men to help feed (or at least not to kill) her infant, since many men could suppose themselves to be the infant's father. Right or wrong, Hrdy's theory transfers sexual power to women.

6. Theory of a female zoologist

At seven and a half pounds, the average human newborn weighs about twice as much as a newborn gorilla, but the 200-pound gorilla mother is much heavier than the average human mother. Because the human newborn is so much larger in relation to its mother, human birth is exceptionally painful and dangerous. Until the advent of modern medicine, women often died in childbirth, whereas I've never heard of this happening to a female gorilla or chimpanzee. Once humans evolved enough intelligence to associate conception with copulation, estrous women could choose to avoid copulating at the time of ovulation in order to spare themselves the pain and peril of childbirth. But such women would leave fewer descendants than women who couldn't detect their ovulation. Thus, where male anthropologists saw concealed ovulation as something evolved by women for men (Theories 1 and 2), Nancy Burley, of the University of Illinois, sees it as a trick that natural selection evolved to deceive women.

Which, if any, of these six theories is correct? Not only are biologists uncertain; it's only in recent years that concealed ovulation, as well as questions involving human testes and penis size, has begun to receive serious attention. Even more tantalizing is why a subject about which we're so obsessed is the one we understand the least. Many of our explanations have scarcely advanced beyond the level of cocktail-party speculation.

The meagreness of data is nowhere more apparent than in the study of adultery. People have reason to lie when asked whether they've committed adultery, which makes it difficult for serious scholars to get accurate information about this important subject. One of the few available sets of hard facts emerged as a totally unexpected byproduct of a medical study performed nearly half a century ago for a different reason.

I recently learned of the findings, which have never been revealed until now, from the distinguished medical scientist who ran the study. (Since he doesn't want to be identified, I'll call him Dr. X.) In the 1940s Dr. X was studying the genetics of human blood groups, which are molecules acquired only by inheritance. Each of us has dozens of blood group substances on our red blood cells, and each substance must come from either our mother or father. Dr. X's research plan was straightforward: go to an obstetrics ward of a respectable U.S. hospital; collect blood samples from 1,000 newborn babies and their parents; identify the individual blood groups; and then use standard genetic reasoning to deduce the inheritance patterns.

To Dr. X's shock, the blood groups revealed that almost ten per cent of the babies were the products of adultery. Proof of their illegitimacy came from the discovery that they had one or more blood groups that were lacking in both alleged parents. There could be no question of mistaken maternity: the blood samples were drawn from the babies soon after they emerged from their mothers. A blood group present in a baby but absent in its undoubted mother could only have come from its father. Thus, absence of that blood group from the mother's husband as well showed conclusively that the baby had been sired by some other man. The true incidence of adulterous sex was probably considerably higher than ten per cent, since many blood group substances now used in paternity tests were not known in the 1940s, and because intercourse doesn't necessarily result in conception.

Since the 1940s, the myth that marital infidelity is rare in the U.S. has been exploded by a long succession of surveys, beginning with the Kinsey Report. Nevertheless, even liberated Americans of the 1980s are still profoundly ambivalent about adultery. It's thought of as exciting: no soap opera could get high ratings without it. And it has few rivals as a basis of jokes. Yet we often use humor to deal with painful subjects. Certainly, in the course of history, adultery has had few rivals as a cause of murder and human misery.

What makes a married person decide to seek extramarital sex—or shun it when it's available? Because scientists have theories about almost everything else, it isn't surprising that they've also got a theory of extramarital sex (abbreviated EMS, and not to be confused with premarital sex = PMS or premenstrual syndrome = PMS). With many species of animals the problem of EMS never arises, because they don't opt for "marriage" in the first place. A female Barbary ape (a species of macaque monkey) in heat copulates promiscuously with every adult male in her troop, averaging one copulation per 17 minutes. However, some mammals and most bird species prefer marriage. That is, a male and a female form a lasting pair bond to provide care or protection to their offspring. Once there's marriage, there's also the possibility of what sociobiologists euphemistically term the pursuit of a "mixed reproductive strategy"—MRS, or in plain English, both monogamous and extramarital sex.

Married animals vary enormously in the degree to which they mix their reproductive strategies. There appears to be no recorded instance of EMS in gibbons, whereas snow geese indulge in it regularly. Human societies similarly vary. To explain all this variation, sociobiologists have found it useful to apply game theory, whereby life is considered an evolutionary contest whose winners are those players leaving the largest number of offspring.

The problem for the animal is to figure out what strategy is most likely to win: rigid fidelity, pure promiscuity, or MRS. It quickly becomes apparent that the best strategy is not the same for males and females of the same species. This is because of two profound differences in their reproductive biology: the minimum effort that's required and the risk of being cuckolded.

For human males, the minimum effort needed to sire an offspring is the act of copulation, a very small expenditure of time and energy. The man who sires a baby by one woman one day is biologically capable of siring a baby by another woman the next. For women, however, the minimum effort consists of copulation plus pregnancy plus (throughout most of human history) several years of nursing—a vast commitment of time and energy. A man can have far more children than a woman. A nineteenth century visitor to the court of the Nizam of Hyderabad, a polygynous Indian potentate, reported that four of the Nizam's wives gave birth within eight days, and that nine more births were anticipated the following week. The record number of offspring for a man is 888, set by Emperor Moulay Ismail "the Blood-thirsty" of Morocco, in the early eighteenth cen-

tury, while the record for a woman is only 69 (an eighteenth century Muscovite who gave birth only to twins, triplets, and quadruplets). Few women have topped 20 children, a mark easily achieved by men in polygynous societies.

If the sole objective is achieving the greatest number of offspring, a man stands to gain much more from EMS or polygamy than a woman. In the sole polyandrous society for which I could find data, the Tre-ba of Tibet, women with two husbands average fewer children, not more, than women with one husband. In the nineteenth century, Mormon men realized big benefits from polygyny: men with one wife averaged only seven children, but men with two or three wives averaged 16 and 20, respectively. Polygynous Mormon men averaged 2.4 wives and 15 children, while polygynous Mormon church leaders averaged five wives and 25 children. Similarly, among the polygynous Temne people of Sierra Leone, a man's average number of children increases from 1.7 to 7 as his number of wives increases from one to five.

The other sexual asymmetry relevant to reproductive strategy involves confidence that one really is the biological parent of one's putative offspring. A cuckholded animal deceived into rearing offspring not its own has lost the game—its genes aren't passed on—to another player, the real parent, whose genes are. Barring a switch of babies in the hospital nursery, women can't be betrayed in this way: they usually see their babies born. Nor can there be cuckoldry of males in species practicing external fertilization. For instance, some male fish watch the female shed eggs, then immediately deposit sperm on them and scoop them up to care for them, secure in their paternity. But men and other male animals practicing internal fertilization run a greater risk. All the would-be father knows for sure is that his sperm went in, and eventually an offspring came out. Only observation of the female throughout her whole fertile period can exclude the possibility that some other male's sperm also entered and did the fertilizing.

In the past, the Nayar society of southern India had an extreme solution

to this simple asymmetry. The Nayar women freely took many lovers, depriving husbands of any confidence in their paternity. To make the best of a bad situation, a Nayar man didn't live with his wife or care for her children. He lived with his sisters instead, and tended their children. These nieces and nephews were sure to share some of his genes. . . .

[S]urveys show that men are more interested in EMS than women are; that men are more inclined to seek a variety of partners; that women's motives for EMS are more likely to be marital dissatisfaction and/or a desire for a new lasting relationship; and that men are less selective in taking on casual partners than women. Among the New Guinea highlanders with whom I work, the men say they seek EMS because sex with their own wives inevitably becomes boring, even if they have several wives, while the women who seek it do so mainly because their husbands cannot satisfy them (often because of old age). In the debriefing questionnaires that several hundred young Americans filled out for a computer dating service, women expressed stronger partner preferences than men did: they cared more about intelligence, status, dancing ability, or a particular religion or race. The only category in which men were more selective was physical attractiveness. After a date, two and a half times as many men as women expressed a strong romantic attraction to their computer-selected partners, which means the women were choosier than the men.

Our attitudes toward EMS are also revealed in laws and behavior. Some particularly hypocritical and sadistic features of human societies stem from two fundamental difficulties that men face in seeking EMS. First, a man who pursues a MRS is trying to have it both ways: sex with other men's wives, while denying other men sex with his own wife (or wives). Thus, some men inevitably gain at the expense of other men. Second, there's a realistic biological basis for men's widespread paranoia about being cuckolded.

Adultery laws provide a clear example of how men have dealt with these dilemmas. Until recently, such laws have existed essentially to secure a man's confidence in the paternity of his children, not for the benefit of the wife. They define adultery by the woman's marital status; the man's is irrelevant. EMS by a married woman is considered an offense against her husband, who's commonly entitled to damages—often violent revenge, or else divorce with refund of the bride price. EMS by a married man isn't considered an offense against his wife, however. If his partner in adultery is married, the offense is against her husband; if unmarried, against her father or brothers (because her value as a prospective bride is reduced).

No criminal law against male infidelity even existed until a French statute of 1810, and that only forbade a married man to keep a concubine in his conjugal house against his wife's wishes. Even today, courts in the U.S. and England often reduce a homicide charge to manslaughter or else acquit altogether when a husband kills an adulterous wife or her lover caught in the act.

Perhaps the most elaborate system to uphold confidence of paternity was that maintained by Chinese emperors, especially during the T'ang Dynasty (618-907). A team of court ladies kept records of menstruation dates for each of the emperor's hundreds of wives and concubines, so that he could copulate on a day likely to result in fertilization. The dates of intercourse were also recorded, and commemorated by a silver ring on the woman's left leg.

Preoccupation with paternity continues. In some cultures it involves limiting sexual access to wives, or to daughters or sisters who would command a high bride price if delivered as virgins. Women may be closely chaperoned or even held under virtual house arrest. The same objective underlies the code of "honor and shame" widespread in Mediterranean countries (translation: EMS for me but not for you). Stronger measures include the barbaric mutilations euphemistically and misleadingly termed female circumcision. These consist of removal of the clitoris or most of the external female genitals to reduce female interest in sex, marital or otherwise. Men bent on certainty invented mechanical contrivances, called chastity belts, and infibulation—suturing a woman's labia majora nearly shut, so as to make intercourse impossible. An infibulated wife can be de-infibulated for childbirth or for insemination after each child is weaned, and can be re-infibulated when the husband takes a long trip. Female circumcision and infibulation are still practiced in 23 countries today, from Africa through Arabia to Indonesia.

When all else fails, murder is available as a last resort. Sexual jealousy is one of the commonest causes of homicide in many U.S. cities, and in a number of other countries as well. Usually, the murderer is a husband and the victim his adulterous wife or her lover; or else the lover kills the husband. Until the formation of centralized political states provided soldiers with loftier motives for combat, sexual jealousy loomed large in human history as a cause of war. It was Paris's seduction (abduction? rape?) of Helen, Menelaus's wife, that provoked the Trojan War. In the modern New Guinea highlands, only disputes over ownership of pigs rival those over sex in triggering war.

Asymmetric adultery laws, and all the other means of ensuring paternity, serve as ways for males to promote their genes. As studies of apes illustrate, some of the tactics used by human males are shared with many animals, including jealous murder, infanticide, rape, inter-group warfare, and adultery itself. Some male snakes, worms, and insects achieve the same result as human infibulators by plugging up a female's vagina after copulating with her.

Sociobiologists have had considerable success at understanding the markedly different sexual strategies in animal species. It's no longer controversial to contend that natural selection causes animals to evolve behaviorally, as well as anatomically, for the purpose of maximizing the number of their descendants. But no theory has caused bitterer division among contemporary biologists than the suggestion that natural selection has likewise molded our *social* behavior. Many of the practices I've discussed are considered barbaric by modern Western society. Yet some biologists are outraged not only by the practices themselves but also by sociobiological explanations of their evolution.

Like any other science, sociobiology is open to abuse. People have never lacked for pretexts, scientific and otherwise, to justify the subjugation or killing of other people. Even Darwinian evolution has been twisted to this end. Sociobiological explanations of human sexuality are sometimes seen as seeking to justify men's abuse of women, and are analogous to the biological justifications advanced for whites' treatment of blacks or the Nazis' treatment of Jews. In the critiques of sociobiology, two fears recur: that an evolutionary basis for abhorrent behavior would seem to justify it; and that a genetic basis for the behavior would imply the futility of attempts at change.

Neither fear warrants a blanket condemnation of sociobiology. We can seek to understand how something arose, regardless of whether we consider it admirable or abominable. Also, we aren't mere slaves to our evolved characteristics, not even to genetically acquired ones. Modern civilization is fairly successful at thwarting ancient practices like infanticide and murder, and modern medicine sometimes succeeds at thwarting our genes when they cause disease. Our objections to infibulation aren't based on the outcome of evolutionary or genetic debates. We condemn it because the mutilation of one person by another is ethically loathsome.

In short, we've evolved, like other animals, to win at a single game: to leave as many descendants as possible. Much of the legacy of this strategy is still buried in our psyches. But we've also chosen to pursue loftier, ethical goals, which may conflict with our ingrained Darwinian ones. The ability to make a moral choice between them represents our most radical break with other animals.

What's Love Got to Do With It?
Sex Among Our Closest Relatives Is a Rather Open Affair

Meredith F. Small

Maiko and Lana are having sex. Maiko is on top, and Lana's arms and legs are wrapped tightly around his waist. Lina, a friend of Lana's, approaches from the right and taps Maiko on the back, nudging him to finish. As he moves away, Lina enfolds Lana in her arms, and they roll over so that Lana is now on top. The two females rub their genitals together, grinning and screaming in pleasure.

This is no orgy staged for an X-rated movie. It doesn't even involve people—or rather, it involves them only as observers. Lana, Maiko, and Lina are bonobos, a rare species of chimplike ape in which frequent couplings and casual sex play characterize every social relationship—between males and females, members of the same sex, closely related animals, and total strangers. Primatologists are beginning to study the bonobos' unrestrained sexual behavior for tantalizing clues to the origins of our own sexuality.

In reconstructing how early man and woman behaved, researchers have generally looked not to bonobos but to common chimpanzees. Only about 5 million years ago human beings and chimps shared a common ancestor, and we still have much behavior in common: namely, a long period of infant dependency, a reliance on learning what to eat and how to obtain food, social bonds that persist over generations, and the need to deal as a group with many everyday conflicts. The assumption has been that chimp behavior today may be similar to the behavior of human ancestors.

Bonobo behavior, however, offers another window on the past because they, too, shared our 5-million-year-old ancestor, diverging from chimps just 2 million years ago. Bonobos have been less studied than chimps for the simple reason that they are difficult to find. They live only on a small patch of land in Zaire, in central Africa. They were first identified, on the basis of skeletal material, in the 1920s, but it wasn't until the 1970s that their behavior in the wild was studied, and then only sporadically.

Bonobos, also known as pygmy chimpanzees, are not really pygmies but welterweights. The largest males are as big as chimps, and the females of the two species are the same size. But bonobos are more delicate in build, and their arms and legs are long and slender.

On the ground, moving from fruit tree to fruit tree, bonobos often stand and walk on two legs—behavior that makes them seem more like humans than chimps. In some ways their sexual behavior seems more human as well, suggesting that in the sexual arena, at least, bonobos are the more appropriate ancestral model. Males and females frequently copulate face-to-face, which is an uncommon position in animals other than humans. Males usually mount females from behind, but females seem to prefer sex face-to-face. "Sometimes the female will let a male start to mount from behind," says Amy Parish, a graduate student at the University of California at Davis who's been watching female bonobo sexual behavior in several zoo colonies around the world. "And then she'll stop, and of course he's really excited, and then she continues face-to-face." Primatologists assume the female preference is dictated by her anatomy: her enlarged clitoris and sexual swellings are oriented far forward. Females presumably prefer face-to-face contact because it feels better.

Like humans but unlike chimps and most other animals, bonobos separate sex from reproduction. They seem to treat sex as a pleasurable activity, and they rely on it as a sort of social glue,

---

"Sex is fun. Sex makes them feel good and keeps the group together."

---

to make or break all sorts of relationships. "Ancestral humans behaved like this," proposes Frans de Waal, an ethologist at the Yerkes Regional Primate Research Center at Emory University. "Later, when we developed the family system, the use of sex for this sort of purpose became more limited, mainly occurring within families. A lot of the things we see, like pedophilia and homosexuality, may be leftovers that some now consider unacceptable in our particular society."

Depending on your morals, watching bonobo sex play may be like watching humans at their most extreme and perverse. Bonobos seem to have sex more often and in more combinations than the average person in any culture, and most of the time bonobo sex has nothing to do with making babies. Males mount females and females sometimes mount them back; females rub against other females just for fun; males stand rump to rump and press their scrotal areas together. Even juveniles participate by rubbing their genital areas against adults, although ethologists don't think that males actually insert their penises into juvenile females. Very young animals also have sex with each other: little males suck on each other's penises or French-kiss. When two animals initiate sex, others freely join in by poking their fingers and toes into the moving parts.

One thing sex does for bonobos is decrease tensions caused by potential competition, often competition for food. Japanese primatologists observing bonobos in Zaire were the first to notice that when bonobos come across a large fruiting tree or encounter piles of provisioned sugarcane, the sight of food triggers a binge of sex. The atmosphere of this sexual free-for-all is decidedly friendly, and it eventually calms the group down. "What's striking is how rapidly the sex drops off," says Nancy Thompson-Handler of the State University of New York at Stony Brook, who has observed bonobos at a site in Zaire called Lomako. "After ten minutes, sexual behavior decreases by fifty percent." Soon the group turns from sex to feeding.

But it's tension rather than food that causes the sexual excitement. "I'm sure the more food you give them, the more sex you'll get," says De Waal. "But it's not really the food, it's competition that triggers this. You can throw in a cardboard box and you'll get sexual behavior." Sex is just the way bonobos deal with competition over limited resources and with the normal tensions caused by living in a group. Anthropologist Frances White of Duke University, a bonobo observer at Lomako since 1983, puts it simply: "Sex is fun. Sex makes them feel good and therefore keeps the group together."

Sexual behavior also occurs after aggressive encounters, especially among males. After two males fight, one may reconcile with his opponent by presenting his rump and backing up against the other's testicles. He might grab the penis of the other male and stroke it. It's the male bonobo's way of shaking hands and letting everyone know that the conflict has ended amicably.

Researchers also note that female bonobo sexuality, like the sexuality of female humans, isn't locked into a monthly cycle. In most other animals, including chimps, the female's interest in sex is tied to her ovulation cycle.

"Females rule the business. It's a good species for feminists, I think."

Chimp females sport pink swellings on their hind ends for about two weeks, signaling their fertility, and they're only approachable for sex during that time. That's not the case with humans, who show no outward signs that they are ovulating, and can mate at all phases of the cycle. Female bonobos take the reverse tack, but with similar results. Their large swellings are visible for weeks before and after their fertile periods, and there is never any discernibly wrong time to mate. Like humans, they have sex whether or not they are ovulating.

What's fascinating is that female bonobos use this boundless sexuality in all their relationships. "Females rule the business—sex and food," says De Waal. "It's a good species for feminists, I think." For instance, females regularly use sex to cement relationships with other females. A genital-genital rub, better known as GG-rubbing by observers, is the most frequent behavior used by bonobo females to reinforce social ties or relieve tension. GG-rubbing takes a variety of forms. Often one female rolls on her back and extends her arms and legs. The other female mounts her and they rub their swellings right and left for several seconds, massaging their clitorises against

each other. GG-rubbing occurs in the presence of food because food causes tension and excitement, but the intimate contact has the effect of making close friends.

Sometimes females would rather GG-rub with each other than copulate with a male. Parish filmed a 15-minute scene at a bonobo colony at the San Diego Wild Animal Park in which a male, Vernon, repeatedly solicited two females, Lisa and Loretta. Again and again he arched his back and displayed his erect penis—the bonobo request for sex. The females moved away from him, tactfully turning him down until they crept behind a tree and GG-rubbed with each other.

Unlike most primate species, in which males usually take on the dangerous task of leaving home, among bonobos females are the ones who leave the group when they reach sexual maturity, around the age of eight, and work their way into unfamiliar groups. To aid in their assimilation into a new community, the female bonobos make good use of their endless sexual favors. While watching a bonobo group at a feeding tree, White saw a young female systematically have sex with each member before feeding. "An adolescent female, presumably a recent transfer female, came up to the tree, mated with all five males, went into the tree, and solicited GG-rubbing from all the females present," says White.

Once inside the new group, a female bonobo must build a sisterhood from scratch. In groups of humans or chimps, unrelated females construct friendships through the rituals of shopping together or grooming. Bonobos do it sexually. Although pleasure may be the motivation behind a female-female assignation, the function is to form an alliance.

These alliances are serious business, because they determine the pecking order at food sites. Females with powerful friends eat first, and subordinate females may not get any food at all if the resource is small. When times are rough, then, it pays to have close female friends. White describes a scene at Lomako in which an adolescent female, Blanche, benefited from her established friendship with Freda. "I was following Freda and her boyfriend, and they found a tree that they didn't expect to be there. It was a small tree, heavily in fruit with one of their favorites. Freda went straight up the tree and made a food call to Blanche. Blanche came tearing over—she was quite far away—and went tearing up the tree to join Freda, and they GG-rubbed like crazy."

Alliances also give females leverage over larger, stronger males who otherwise would push them around. Females have discovered there is strength in numbers. Unlike other species of primates, such as chimpanzees or baboons (or, all too often, humans), where tensions run high between males and females, bonobo females are not afraid of males, and the sexes mingle peacefully. "What is consistently different from chimps," says Thompson-Handler, "is the composition of parties. The vast majority are mixed, so there are males and females of all different ages."

HIDDEN HEAT

Standing upright is not a position usually—or easily—associated with sex. Among people, at least, anatomy and gravity prove to be forbidding obstacles. Yet our two-legged stance may be the key to a distinctive aspect of human sexuality: the independence of women's sexual desires from a monthly calendar.

Males in the two species most closely related to us, chimpanzees and bonobos, don't spend a lot of time worrying, "Is she interested or not?" The answer is obvious. When ovulatory hormones reach a monthly peak in female chimps and bonobos, and their eggs are primed for fertilization, their genital area swells up, and both sexes appear to have just one thing on their mind. "These animals really turn on when this happens. Everything else is dropped," says primatologist Frederick Szalay of Hunter College in New York.

Women, however, don't go into heat. And this departure from our relatives' sexual behavior has long puzzled researchers. Clear signals of fertility and the willingness to do something about it bring major evolutionary advantages: ripe eggs lead to healthier pregnancies, which leads to more of your genes in succeeding generations, which is what evolution is all about. In addition, male chimps give females that are waving these red flags of fertility first chance at high-protein food such as meat.

So why would our ancestors give this up? Szalay and graduate student Robert Costello have a simple explanation. Women gave heat up, they say, because our ancestors stood up. Fossil footprints indicate that somewhere around 3.5 million years ago hominids—non-ape primates—began walking on two legs. "In hominids, something dictated getting up. We don't know what it was," Szalay says. "But once it did, there was a problem with the signaling system." The problem was that it didn't work. Swollen genital areas that were visible when their owners were down on all fours became hidden between the legs. The mating signal was lost.

"Uprightness meant very tough times for females working with the old ovarian cycle," Szalay says. Males wouldn't notice them, and the swellings themselves, which get quite large, must have made it hard for two-legged creatures to walk around.

Those who found a way out of this quandary, Szalay suggests, were females with small swellings but with a little less hair on their rears and a little extra fat. It would have looked a bit like the time-honored mating signal. They got more attention, and produced more offspring. "You don't start a completely new trend in signaling," Szalay says. "You have a little extra fat, a little nakedness to mimic the ancestors. If there was an ever-so-little advantage because, quite simply, you look good, it would be selected for."

And if a little nakedness and a little fat worked well, Szalay speculates, then a lot of both would work even better. "Once you start a trend in sexual signaling, crazy things happen," he notes. "It's almost like: let's escalate, let's add more. That's what happens in horns with sheep. It's a particular part of the body that brings an advantage." In a few million years human ancestors were more naked than ever, with fleshy rears not found in any other primate. Since these features were permanent, unlike the monthly ups and downs of swellings, sex was free to become a part of daily life.

It's a provocative notion, say Szalay's colleagues, but like any attempt to conjure up the past from the present, there's no real proof of cause and effect. Anthropologist Helen Fisher of the American Museum of Natural History notes that Szalay is merely assuming that fleshy buttocks evolved because they were sex signals. Yet their mass really comes from muscles, which chimps don't have, that are associated with walking. And anthropologist Sarah Blaffer Hrdy of the University of California at Davis points to a more fundamental problem: our ancestors may not have had chimplike swellings that they needed to dispense with. Chimps and bonobos are only two of about 200 primate species, and the vast majority of those species don't have big swellings. Though they are our closest relatives, chimps and bonobos have been evolving during the last 5 million years just as we have, and swollen genitals may be a recent development. The current unswollen human pattern may be the ancestral one.

"Nobody really knows what happened," says Fisher. "Everybody has an idea. You pays your money and you takes your choice."

—Joshua Fischman

Female bonobos cannot be coerced into anything, including sex. Parish recounts an interaction between Lana and a male called Akili at the San Diego Wild Animal Park. "Lana had just been introduced into the group. For a long time she lay on the grass with a huge swelling. Akili would approach her with a big erection and hover over her. It would have been easy for him to do a mount. But he wouldn't. He just kept trying to catch her eye, hovering around her, and she would scoot around the ground, avoiding him. And then he'd try again. She went around full circle." Akili was big enough to force himself on her. Yet he refrained.

In another encounter, a male bonobo was carrying a large clump of branches. He moved up to a female and presented his erect penis by spreading his legs and arching his back. She rolled onto her back and they copulated. In the midst of their joint ecstasy, she reached out and grabbed a branch from the male. When he pulled back, finished and satisfied, she moved away, clutching the branch to her chest. There was no tension between them, and she essentially traded copulation

for food. But the key here is that the male allowed her to move away with the branch—it didn't occur to him to threaten her, because their status was virtually equal.

Although the results of sexual liberation are clear among bonobos, no one is sure why sex has been elevated to such a high position in this species and why it is restricted merely to reproduction among chimpanzees. "The puzzle for me," says De Waal, "is that chimps do all this bonding with kissing and embracing, with body contact. Why do bonobos do it in a sexual manner?" He speculates that the use of sex as a standard way to underscore relationships began between adult males and adult females as an extension of the mating process and later spread to all members of the group. But no one is sure exactly how this happened.

It is also unclear whether bonobo sexuality became exaggerated only after their split from the human lineage or whether the behavior they exhibit today is the modern version of our common ancestor's sex play. Anthropologist Adrienne Zihlman of the University of California at Santa Cruz, who has used the evidence of fossil

bones to argue that our earliest known non-ape ancestors, the australopithecines, had body proportions similar to those of bonobos, says, "The path of human evolution is not a straight line from either species, but what I think is important is that the bonobo information gives us more possibilities for looking at human origins."

Some anthropologists, however, are reluctant to include the details of bonobo life, such as wide-ranging sexuality and a strong sisterhood, into scenarios of human evolution. "The researchers have all these commitments to male dominance [as in chimpanzees], and yet bonobos have egalitarian relationships," says De Waal. "They also want to see humans as unique, yet bonobos fit very nicely into many of the scenarios, making humans appear less unique."

Our divergent, non-ape path has led us away from sex and toward a culture that denies the connection between sex and social cohesion. But bonobos, with their versatile sexuality, are here to remind us that our heritage may very well include a primordial urge to make love, not war.

The Hominid Transition

One of the most intriguing and perplexing gaps in the fossil record for human evolution has to do with the transition from a common link between apes and humans to that which is clearly recognizable as a member of our own kind, the family *Hominidae*.

The issues involving this "black hole" cannot be resolved by simply filling it in with fossil finds. Even if we had the physical remains of the earliest hominids in front of us, which we do not, there is no way such evidence could thoroughly answer the questions that physical anthropologists care most deeply about: How did these creatures move about and get their food? Did they cooperate and share? On what levels did they think and communicate? Did they have a sense of family, let alone a sense of self? In one way or another, all of the previous articles on primates relate to these issues, as do some of the subsequent ones on the fossil evidence. But what sets off this section from the others is that the various authors attempt to deal with these matters head on, even in the absence of direct fossil evidence. For example, Christophe Boesch and Hedwige Boesch-Achermann ("Dim Forest, Bright Chimps") indicate that some aspects of "hominization" (the acquisition of such human-like qualities as cooperative hunting and food-sharing) may have actually begun in the African rain forest rather than in the dry savanna region, as has usually been proposed. They base their suggestions upon some rather remarkable first-hand observations of forest-dwelling chimpanzees.

Even as recent research has shown some striking resemblances between apes and humans, hinting that such qualities might have been characteristic of our common ancestor, there are nevertheless significant differences that need to be acknowledged as well. In this vein, Pete Wheeler ("Human Ancestors Walked Tall, Stayed Cool") and Tony Layng ("What Makes Us So Different From the Apes?") show us just how far we have come since our ancestral line diverged from that of the apes.

Then there is the issue of the differing roles played by males and females in the transition to humanity and all that it implies with regard to bipedalism, toolmaking, and the origin of the family. As the article "Flesh and Bone," by Ellen Ruppel Shell, puts it, the question is whether the primary theme of human evolution should be summed up as "man the hunter" or "woman the gatherer."

The notion of *orthogenesis*—the theory that trends in evolution constitute a driving force and continue under their own momentum—has long been discredited. This is not to deny, however, that progressive changes, in a limited, value-neutral sense, have occurred. A biological view of progress is presented by Richard Dawkins in "The Evolutionary Future of Man."

Taken collectively, the articles in this section show how far anthropologists are willing to go to construct theoretical formulations based upon limited data. Although making so much out of so little may be seen as a fault, and may generate irreconcilable differences among theorists, a readiness to entertain new ideas should be welcomed for what it is: a stimulus for more intensive and meticulous research.

Looking Ahead: Challenge Questions

What are the implications for human evolution of tool use, social hunting, and food-sharing among Ivory Coast chimpanzees?

What did the common ancestor of apes and humans probably look like?

What is the "man the hunter" theory? What is the "woman the gatherer" theory? What evidence is there for each?

What makes humans so different from apes?

Why did our ancestors become bipedal?

Unit 4

Dim Forest, Bright Chimps

In the rain forest of Ivory Coast, chimpanzees meet the challenge of life by hunting cooperatively and using crude tools

Christophe Boesch and Hedwige Boesch-Achermann

Taï National Park, Ivory Coast, December 3, 1985. Drumming, barking, and screaming, chimps rush through the undergrowth, little more than black shadows. Their goal is to join a group of other chimps noisily clustering around Brutus, the dominant male of this seventy-member chimpanzee community. For a few moments, Brutus, proud and self-confident, stands fairly still, holding a shocked, barely moving red colobus monkey in his hand. Then he begins to move through the group, followed closely by his favorite females and most of the adult males. He seems to savor this moment of uncontested superiority, the culmination of a hunt high up in the canopy. But the victory is not his alone. Cooperation is essential to capturing one of these monkeys, and Brutus will break apart and share this highly prized delicacy with most of the main participants of the hunt and with the females. Recipients of large portions will, in turn, share more or less generously with their offspring, relatives, and friends.

In 1979, we began a long-term study of the previously unknown chimpanzees of Taï National Park, 1,600 square miles of tropical rain forest in the Republic of the Ivory Coast (Côte d'Ivoire). Early on, we were most interested in the chimps' use of natural hammers—branches and stones—to crack open the five species of hard-shelled nuts that are abundant here. A

sea otter lying on its back, cracking an abalone shell with a rock, is a familiar picture, but no primate had ever before been observed in the wild using stones as hammers. East Africa's savanna chimps, studied for decades by Jane Goodall in Gombe, Tanzania, use twigs to extract ants and termites from their nests or honey from a bees' nest, but they have never been seen using hammerstones.

As our work progressed, we were surprised by the many ways in which the life of the Taï forest chimpanzees differs from that of their savanna counterparts, and as evidence accumulated, differences in how the two populations hunt proved the most intriguing. Jane Goodall had found that chimpanzees hunt monkeys, antelope, and wild pigs, findings confirmed by Japanese biologist Toshida Nishida, who conducted a long-term study 120 miles south of Gombe, in the Mahale Mountains. So we were not surprised to discover that the Taï chimps eat meat. What intrigued us was the degree to which they hunt cooperatively. In 1953 Raymond Dart proposed that group hunting and cooperation were key ingredients in the evolution of *Homo sapiens.* The argument has been modified considerably since Dart first put it forward, and group hunting has also been observed in some social carnivores (lions and African wild dogs, for instance), and even some birds of prey. Nevertheless, many anthropologists still hold that hunting cooperatively and sharing food played a central role in the drama that enabled early hominids, some 1.8 mil-

lion years ago, to develop the social systems that are so typically human.

We hoped that what we learned about the behavior of forest chimpanzees would shed new light on prevailing theories of human evolution. Before we could even begin, however, we had to habituate a community of chimps to our presence. Five long years passed before we were able to move with them on their daily trips through the forest, of which "our" group appeared to claim some twelve square miles. Chimpanzees are alert and shy animals, and the limited field of view in the rain forest—about sixty-five feet at best—made finding them more difficult. We had to rely on sound, mostly their vocalizations and drumming on trees. Males often drum regularly while moving through the forest: pant-hooting, they draw near a big buttress tree; then, at full speed they fly over the buttress, hitting it repeatedly with their hands and feet. Such drumming may resound more than half a mile in the forest. In the beginning, our ignorance about how they moved and who was drumming led to failure more often than not, but eventually we learned that the dominant males drummed during the day to let other group members know the direction of travel. On some days, however, intermittent drumming about dawn was the only signal for the whole day. If we were out of earshot at the time, we were often reduced to guessing.

During these difficult early days, one feature of the chimps' routine proved to be our salvation: nut cracking is a noisy business. So noisy, in fact, that in the early days of French colonial rule, one officer apparently even proposed the theory that some unknown tribe was forging iron in the impenetrable and dangerous jungle.

Guided by the sounds made by the chimps as they cracked open nuts, which they often did for hours at a time, we were gradually able to get within sixty feet of the animals. We still seldom saw the chimps themselves (they fled if we came too close), but even so, the evidence left after a session of nut cracking taught us a great deal about what types of nuts they were eating, what sorts of hammer and anvil tools they were using, and—thanks to the very distinctive noise a nut makes when it finally splits open—how many hits were needed to crack a nut and how many nuts could be opened per minute.

After some months, we began catching glimpses of the chimpanzees before they fled, and after a little more time, we were able to draw close enough to watch them at work. The chimps gather nuts from the ground. Some nuts are tougher to crack than others. Nuts of the *Panda oleosa* tree are the most demanding, harder than any of the foods processed by present-day hunter-gatherers and breaking open only when a force of 3,500 pounds is applied. The stone hammers used by the Taï chimps range from stones of ten ounces to granite blocks of four to forty-five pounds. Stones of any size, however, are a rarity in the forest and are seldom conveniently placed near a nut-bearing tree. By observing closely, and in some cases imitating the way the chimps handle hammerstones, we learned that they have an impressive ability to find just the right tool for the job at hand. Taï chimps could remember the positions of many of the stones scattered, often out of sight, around a panda tree. Without having to run around rechecking the stones, they would select one of appropriate size that was closest to the tree. These mental abilities in spatial representation compare with some of those of nine-year-old humans.

To extract the four kernels from inside a panda nut, a chimp must use a hammer with extreme precision. Time and time again, we have been impressed to see a chimpanzee raise a twenty-pound stone above its head, strike a nut with ten or more powerful blows, and then, using the same hammer, switch to delicate little taps from a height of only four inches. To finish the job, the chimps often break off a small piece of twig and use it to extract the last tiny fragments of kernel from the shell. Intriguingly, females crack panda nuts more often than males, a gender difference in tool use that seems to be more pronounced in the forest chimps than in their savanna counterparts.

After five years of fieldwork, we were finally able to follow the chimpanzees at close range, and gradually, we gained insights into their way of hunting. One morning, for example, we followed a group of six male chimps on a three-hour patrol that had taken them into foreign territory to the north. (Our study group is one of five chimpanzee groups more or less evenly distributed in the Taï forest.) As always during these approximately monthly incursions, which seem to be for the purpose of territorial defense, the chimps were totally silent, clearly on edge and on the lookout for trouble. Once the patrol was over, however, and they were back within their own borders, the chimps shifted their attention to hunting. They were after monkeys, the most abundant mammals in the forest. Traveling in large, multi-species groups, some of the forest's ten species of monkeys are more apt than others to wind up as a meal for the chimps. The relatively sluggish and large (almost thirty pounds) red colobus monkeys are the chimps' usual fare. (Antelope also live in the forest, but in our ten years at Taï, we have never seen a chimp catch, or even pursue, one. In contrast, Gombe chimps at times do come across fawns, and when they do, they seize the opportunity—and the fawn.)

The six males moved on silently, peering up into the vegetation and stopping from time to time to listen for the sound of monkeys. None fed or groomed; all focused on the hunt. We followed one old male, Falstaff, closely, for he tolerates us completely and is one of the keenest and most experienced hunters. Even from the rear, Falstaff set the pace; whenever he stopped, the others paused to wait for him. After thirty minutes, we heard the unmistakable noises of monkeys jumping from branch to branch. Silently, the chimps turned in the direction of the sounds, scanning the canopy. Just then, a diana monkey spotted them and gave an alarm call. Dianas are very alert and fast; they are also about half the weight of colobus monkeys. The chimps quickly gave up and continued their search for easier, meatier prey.

Shortly after, we heard the characteristic cough of a red colobus monkey. Suddenly Rousseau and Macho, two twenty-year-olds, burst into action, running toward the cough. Falstaff seemed surprised by their precipitousness, but after a moment's hesitation, he also ran. Now the hunting barks of the chimps mixed with the sharp alarm calls of the monkeys. Hurrying behind Falstaff, we saw him climb up a conveniently situated tree. His position, combined with those of Schubert and Ulysse, two mature chimps in their prime, effectively blocked off three of the monkeys' possible escape routes. But in another tree, nowhere near any escape route and thus useless, waited the last of the hunters, Kendo, eighteen years old and the least experienced of the group. The monkeys, taking advantage of Falstaff's delay and Kendo's error, escaped.

The six males moved on and within five minutes picked up the sounds of another group of red colobus. This time, the chimps approached cautiously, nobody hurrying. They screened the canopy intently to locate the monkeys, which were still unaware of the approaching danger. Macho and Schubert chose two adjacent trees, both full of monkeys, and started climbing very quietly, taking care not to move any branches. Meanwhile, the other four chimps blocked off anticipated escape routes. When Schubert was halfway up, the monkeys finally detected the two chimps. As we watched the colobus monkeys take off in literal panic, the appropriateness of the chimpanzees' scientific name—*Pan* came to mind: with a certain stretch of the imagination, the fleeing monkeys could be shepherds and shepherdesses frightened at the sudden appearance of Pan, the wild Greek god of the woods, shepherds, and their flocks.

Taking off in the expected direction, the monkeys were trailed by Macho and Schubert. The chimps let go with loud hunting barks. Trying to escape, two colobus monkeys jumped into smaller trees lower in the canopy. With this, Rousseau and Kendo, who had been watching from the ground, sped up into the trees and tried to grab them. Only a third of the weight of the chimps, however, the monkeys managed to make it to the next tree along branches too small for their pursuers. But Falstaff had anticipated this move and was waiting for them. In the following confusion, Falstaff seized a juvenile and killed it with a bite to the neck. As the chimps met in a rush on the ground, Falstaff began to eat, sharing with Schubert and Rousseau. A juvenile colobus does not provide much meat, however, and this time, not all the chimps got a share. Frustrated individuals soon started off on another hunt, and relative calm returned fairly quickly: this sort of hunt, by a small band of chimps acting on their own at the edge of their territory, does not generate the kind of high excitement that prevails when more members of the community are involved.

So far we have observed some 200 monkey hunts and have concluded that success requires a minimum of three motivated hunters acting cooperatively. Alone or in pairs, chimps succeed less than 15 percent of the time, but when three or four act as a group, more than half the hunts result in a kill. The chimps seem well aware of the odds; 92 percent of all the hunts we observed were group affairs.

Gombe chimps also hunt red colobus monkeys, but the percentage of group hunts is much lower: only 36 percent. In addition, we learned from Jane Goodall that even when Gombe chimps do hunt in groups, their strategies are different. When Taï chimps

arrive under a group of monkeys, the hunters scatter, often silently, usually out of sight of one another but each aware of the others' positions. As the hunt progresses, they gradually close in, encircling the quarry. Such movements require that each chimp coordinate his movements with those of the other hunters, as well as with those of the prey, at all times.

Coordinated hunts account for 63 percent of all those observed at Taï but only 7 percent of those at Gombe. Jane Goodall says that in a Gombe group hunt, the chimpanzees typically travel together until they arrive at a tree with monkeys. Then, as the chimps begin climbing nearby trees, they scatter as each pursues a different target. Goodall gained the impression that Gombe chimps boost their success by hunting independently but simultaneously, thereby disorganizing their prey; our impression is that the Taï chimps owe their success to being organized themselves.

Just why the Gombe and Taï chimps have developed such different hunting strategies is difficult to explain, and we plan to spend some time at Gombe in the hope of finding out. In the meantime, the mere existence of differences is interesting enough and may perhaps force changes in our understanding of human evolution. Most currently accepted theories propose that some three million years ago, a dramatic climate change in Africa east of the Rift Valley turned dense forest into open, drier habitat. Adapting to the difficulties of life under these new conditions, our ancestors supposedly evolved into cooperative hunters and began sharing food they caught. Supporters of this idea point out that plant and animal remains indicative of dry, open environments have been found at all early hominid excavation sites in Tanzania, Kenya, South Africa, and Ethiopia. That the large majority of apes in Africa today live west of the Rift Valley appears to many anthropologists to lend further support to the idea that a change in environment caused the common ancestor of apes and humans to evolve along a different line from those remaining in the forest.

Our observations, however, suggest quite another line of thought. Life in dense, dim forest may require more sophisticated behavior than is commonly assumed: compared with their savanna relatives, Taï chimps show greater complexity in both hunting and tool use. Taï chimps use tools in nineteen different ways and have six different ways of making them, compared with sixteen uses and three methods of manufacture at Gombe.

Anthropologist colleagues of mine have told me that the discovery that some chimpanzees are accomplished users of hammerstones forces them to look with a fresh eye at stone tools turned up at excavation sites. The important role played by female Taï chimps in tool use also raises the possibility that in the course of human evolution, women may have been decisive in the development of many of the sophisticated manipulative skills characteristic of our species. Taï mothers also appear to pass on their skills by actively teaching their offspring. We have observed mothers providing their young with hammers and then stepping in to help when the inexperienced youngsters encounter difficulty. This help may include carefully showing how to position the nut or hold the hammer properly. Such behavior has never been observed at Gombe.

Similarly, food sharing, for a long time said to be unique to humans, seems more general in forest than in savanna chimpanzees. Taï chimp mothers share with their young up to 60 percent of the nuts they open, at least until the latter become sufficiently adept, generally at about six years old. They also share other foods acquired with tools, including honey, ants, and bone marrow. Gombe mothers share such foods much less often, even with their infants. Taï chimps also share meat more frequently than do their Gombe relatives, sometimes dividing a chunk up and giving portions away, sometimes simply allowing beggars to grab pieces.

Any comparison between chimpanzees and our hominid ancestors can only be suggestive, not definitive. But our studies lead us to believe that the process of hominization may have begun independently of the drying of the environment. Savanna life could even have delayed the process; many anthropologists have been struck by how slowly hominid-associated remains, such as the hand ax, changed after their first appearance in the Olduvai age.

Will we have the time to discover more about the hunting strategies or other, perhaps as yet undiscovered abilities of these forest chimpanzees? Africa's tropical rain forests, and their inhabitants, are threatened with extinction by extensive logging, largely to provide the Western world with tropical timber and such products as coffee, cocoa, and rubber. Ivory Coast has lost 90 percent of its original forest, and less than 5 percent of the remainder can be considered pristine. The climate has changed dramatically. The harmattan, a cold, dry wind from the Sahara previously unknown in the forest, has now swept through the Taï forest every year since 1986. Rainfall has diminished; all the rivulets in our study region are now dry for several months of the year.

In addition, the chimpanzee, biologically very close to humans, is in demand for research on AIDS and hepatitis vaccines. Captive-bred chimps are available, but they cost about twenty times more than wild-caught animals. Chimps taken from the wild for these purposes are generally young, their mothers having been shot during capture. For every chimp arriving at its sad destination, nine others may well have died in the forest or on the way. Such priorities—cheap coffee and cocoa and chimpanzees—do not do the economies of Third World countries any good in the long run, and they bring suffering and death to innocent victims in the forest. Our hope is that Brutus, Falstaff, and their families will survive, and that we and others will have the opportunity to learn about them well into the future. But there is no denying that modern times work against them and us.

Flesh & Bone

The story of human evolution has been largely written by male scientists, says Adrienne Zihlman. And they've left women out of the plot.

Ellen Ruppel Shell

Ellen Ruppel Shell is codirector of the program in science journalism at Boston University. This is her first article for DISCOVER.

A tour of Adrienne Zihlman's laboratories at the University of California at Santa Cruz is an exercise in the macabre. There's a hairy arm and ghostly white hand, the last vestiges of a chimp, poking over the rim of what looks like a stainless steel pasta pot. There's a pair of human cadavers laid out neatly under a sky-blue tarpaulin like slabs of bread dough beneath a towel. There's a sealed aquarium swarming with carnivorous beetles polishing off the last bits of flesh from a dog's skull. And then there are the bones.

"I collected most of these from road kills," Zihlman says, pulling drawer after drawer of animal skeletons, zipped neatly in thick plastic bags. "We've got skeletons of possum, lynx, fox, raccoon, and coyote."

The bones are here because Zihlman, a paleoanthropologist, contrives and tests ideas about the origins of humankind by studying the remains of living things. The dog skull, for instance, will be used to highlight differ-

ences between primates like us and other mammals for her anatomy students. And the human cadavers will become part of the university's burgeoning collection of primate skeletons.

Such remnants and fragments of life allow Zihlman to wrestle with some of the most thorny and fundamental issues in human evolution. Not content to tinker at the periphery of her field, she's challenged colleagues to rethink long-standing ideas about how people came to be. One of these cherished notions is that the initiation of hunting by males made us what we are today: it spurred us to stand on two feet and freed up our hands for toolmaking. Most important, it forged the first social contract between males and females.

"—the origin of the human line can be traced to a change in locomotion."

Zihlman has come up with evidence showing this is not necessarily the way things were. She has fashioned a convincing argument that activities pursued by females, such as food gathering and

caring for infants, were just as likely as hunting to be behind two-legged walking and more stable social relationships. The major reason that male hunting has been portrayed as a seminal event in human development, she says, is that men—male anthropologists, in particular—were doing the portraying.

"Science has been characterized as a masculine activity," she says. "I think that is precisely the case."

Zihlman is firm in her belief that the evolutionary picture has been distorted by people who have yet to acknowledge their own biases. Much of this distortion occurs, she says, when researchers attempt to force the archeological and fossil record into the context of modern Western male-dominated culture.

For her views, Zihlman has endured more than a little criticism, ranging from thoughtless dismissals in academic journals to vilification at international meetings. Her ideas have caused her to clash with prominent researchers, such as Donald Johanson, famed as the discoverer of "Lucy," a 3-million-year-old ancestor and a cornerstone of the latest version of the male-hunting hypothesis. Although clearly shaken by these battles, Zihlman, at 50, shows no signs of retreat. "I don't have ulcers," she says, alternating dainty bites of avocado and yogurt in a lunch break wedged between meetings. "I give them to other people."

The daughter of working-class parents who felt that their children should be "exposed to everything," Zihlman has fond memories of trips to the Field Museum in Chicago, where she grew up, and to her grandmother's farm in Iowa. "My grandmother gave me my first lesson in neuroanatomy," she says. "I learned that a chicken really does run around after it gets its head cut off." Zihlman attended Miami University in Ohio, where, after reading Margaret Mead's *Coming of Age in Samoa* for a class, she decided to major in anthropology. When she found that Miami University had no such department, she transferred to the University of Colorado in Boulder, which did. She completed her degree and, in 1962, went on to do graduate work at Berkeley, where she set herself to the task of finding out how our ancestors began to walk.

"In monkeys," she explains, "seventy percent of bones, muscle, and skin are devoted to moving around. And almost everything about what humans are is about being bipeds. I was always interested in the anatomical basis of behavior, and locomotion is the key thing—the origin of the human line can be traced to a change in locomotion. It was the first feature to definitely indicate a hominid."

As part of her doctoral research, Zihlman traveled to the Transvaal Museum in Pretoria, South Africa, to measure, describe, and photograph the fossilized bones of our oldest preserved ancestors, the australopithecines. Her thesis compared chimpanzees with these hominids and detailed the changes in the angle of the hip sockets, the length and thickness of the thigh-bones, and other modifications that made bipedality possible for these creatures. And—ironically, in light of her current views—Zihlman included in her thesis a conjecture about the origins of the two-legged gait: it evolved, she wrote, to allow more efficient movement on long hunting trips through the African savanna. "Later I changed my mind

about the hunting part," she says, smiling.

That Zihlman included hunting at all is a measure of the pervasive influence of the idea at the time. Hunting, in the 1960s, had become the standard by which most prehistoric artifacts were judged, and upon which most theories of early humans were built. The objects that supported the "man the hunter" theory were pieces of sharpened bone found in close proximity to antelope skeletons in some South African caves—caves inhabited by australopithecines 2 million years ago. Zihlman saw these bones herself during her travels; she also met the man who found them, the late anthropologist Raymond Dart. "At the time I met Dart I received my own personal demonstration of how the bones were used to kill animals, a sort of reenactment of the film *2001*," she recalls.

And it was the males—assumed by Dart and most other anthropologists, including Zihlman's adviser, Sherwood Washburn, to be larger, more powerful, and unencumbered by the care of young children—who did the hunting. Anthropologists went on to reconstruct a strictly sex-specific picture of early human social life: males invented and built tools, hunted the food and dragged it home to hungry females, who were tied, helpless, to the hearth by demanding infants. Pair-bonds between males and females formed for the good of the species, monogamy giving a male more reason to defend his home and family.

But after completing her thesis in 1967, Zihlman got to thinking that there was something wrong with this picture of early human life. The reconstruction placed females at the mercy of the all-powerful male and gave them no purpose other than to reproduce and serve. In 1970 she heard a paper delivered by anthropologist Sally Linton entitled "Woman the Gatherer: Male Bias in Anthropology" that seemed to crystallize her thoughts. Linton argued that men's control and dominance of women should be seen as a modern institution, not a natural fact arising from our animal past.

That same year some holes in the man-the-hunter hypothesis started to appear when paleontologist C. K. Brain of the Transvaal Museum examined some bite and gnaw marks on animal bones in australopithecine caves near Dart's celebrated sites. Brain concluded that the bones had been dragged in by leopards, not hunted and killed by hominids. Similar marks on the hominid bones themselves led Brain to suggest that Dart had the food chain going in the wrong direction: australopithecines were more likely to be prey than predators.

"I was teaching a course in biology and the culture of sex roles at Santa Cruz at the time," Zihlman says, "and I had become alerted to the fact that women had essentially been invisible as far as evolutionary theory was concerned. The man-the-hunter theory has the male bringing home food to one female and to their offspring, and this pair-bond was key. But the data anthropologists were getting on the !Kung, a hunter-gatherer society in southern Africa, showed the women were pretty independent. They controlled the resources they collected."

"The whole idea of pair-bonding is completely overrated. It's a typical projection of the ideal American family life back in time."

!Kung women, according to studies by anthropologist Richard Lee, gathered the tubers, roots, and fruits that are the staples of the !Kung diet. No one was suggesting that the !Kung were living australopithecines, but they lived in a similar environment and had only rudimentary technology. So it was possible that early hominid female life resembled the life of !Kung women, who weren't tethered to a home base by child rearing. Instead they carried their young while walking miles across the savanna in search of food. And food gathering, Zihlman realized, was just as likely as hunting to have brought early hominids to their feet.

"A lot of the African vegetation went underground or grew thick coverings to protect itself through the dry season," she says. "Hominids needed tools to dig these fruits out or crack them open." Carrying these tools around, and using them to dig, required free hands. And that left only two feet for walking.

It also seemed less and less likely to Zihlman that the carnivorous, monogamous early hominids presumed by the hunting hypothesis would have evolved out of chimps or other apes who ate little meat and were rather fluid in their sexual relationships.

"I had done my dissertation on chimps," Zihlman says, "and I knew that chimps did not form stable pair-bonds and that the males came and went. Females and their offspring formed the core group within chimp societies. The whole idea of pair-bonding is completely overrated. It's a typical projection of the ideal American family life back in time. Gradually I was developing a view of human origins that took into consideration comparative anatomy, ape and human behavior, and the fossil record. And it firmly put women into the story of human evolution."

Zihlman began publishing a series of papers that drew these lines of evidence together to show gathering was an alternate route for human evolution to travel. "Woman the gatherer," in Zihlman's view, was not the absolute prehistoric truth. But it was a scenario at least as plausible as "man the hunter."

Many of Zihlman's arguments rested on her contention that current primate behavior, particularly that of chimpanzees, provided a rough analogue to early hominid behavior. This reasoning was supported by studies done in the mid-1960s, comparing chimp and human blood proteins. Biochemists Vincent Sarich and the late Allan Wilson of Berkeley had used similarities in these proteins to show that chimps are our closest living primate relatives, probably diverging from a common ancestor 5 million years ago.

Zihlman became particularly intrigued by Sarich's speculation that the common ancestor must have looked something like a small chimpanzee (since animals tend to evolve into larger forms). To Zihlman, this called to mind the pygmy chimp, a species native to the Zaire River basin in equatorial Africa. The notion that pygmy chimps were "living links" to man's earliest ancestor was first put forward by Harvard zoologist Harold J. Coolidge in 1933. But it was never substantiated, partly because not enough was known of this rare and elusive animal to take the theory beyond the realm of speculation.

"There just weren't that many pygmy chimps around to study," Zihlman says. So in 1973, along with Douglas Cramer, a graduate student at the University of Chicago who was studying pygmy chimp cranial features, Zihlman visited the African Museum in Belgium (Zaire was a Belgian colony until 1960) to study the museum's relatively extensive collection of pygmy and common chimp skeletons. Zihlman and Cramer found that pygmy chimps differ from common chimps in a number of ways—their trunks are smaller, their arms are shorter, and their legs are a little longer.

Zihlman then observed pygmy chimps in action at the Yerkes Primate Center in Atlanta. She noticed that they often assumed a two-legged position when climbing, jumping, and standing. In essence, though arboreal by nature, pygmy chimps seemed to her to be poised on the edge of bipedalism. At Yerkes, Zihlman also observed that pygmy chimps seemed more social and less aggressive—more "human"—than common chimps.

"All the differences were in the human direction," Zihlman says. "Here, it seemed to me, was an even better prototype for the ancestral human than the common chimpanzee. The pygmy chimp was a living ape that seemed to represent the 'transition' from quadrupedal to bipedal locomotion."

Zihlman went so far as to compare the pygmy chimpanzee with "Lucy," the hominid fossil skeleton found at Hadar in Ethiopia in 1974 by Donald Johanson, then at the Cleveland Museum of Natural History. The similarities between the two seemed striking. They were almost identical in brain and body size and stature, and the major differences, the hip and knee, could well be the outgrowth of Lucy's adaptation to bipedal walking. In an illustration Zihlman published in 1982 of Lucy's left side abutting the right side of a pygmy chimp, the two creatures looked almost like one image in a slightly cracked mirror.

One consequence of tying Lucy so tightly to pygmy chimp anatomy was that Zihlman theorized that males and females of Lucy's species were about the same size, as are male and female pygmy chimps. This innocuous-sounding conclusion unleashed a storm of controversy that's still raging today. For one of Johanson's cherished assertions about Lucy's kind is that males were much bigger than females.

"The whole idea of pair-bonding is completely overrated. It's a typical projection of the ideal American family life back in time."

Johanson and his colleague Tim White of Berkeley had taken Lucy's skeleton and similar bones from other hominids and put them into one species—the oldest one known, they claim, the ancestor to all other forms—called *Australopithecus afarensis*. Some of these individuals were much bigger than others, and Johanson and White accounted for this by saying that the big ones were males. "It was necessary for the females to be small," says Johanson, who is now president of the Institute of Human Origins in Berkeley. "If they were large, they wouldn't have been able to survive on the low quality food available to them and still nourish their fetus and their young. The males needed to be large in order to compete for the females and to protect the troop." Another of Johanson's colleagues, Owen Lovejoy of Kent State University, has proposed that these large males had begun to come down from the trees to hunt far and wide for food to bring up to their patiently waiting mates. So males invented walking, and man the hunter stalked again.

Zihlman, not surprisingly, doesn't buy this idea at all. No such extreme size difference between sexes has been noted before in other australopithecine species, she says, no such difference exists in chimps, and there is no con-

> *"Studies in anthropology, sociolinguistics, and psychology document that men and women communicate differently."*

vincing evidence that it exists in Johanson's fossils. It's entirely possible, Zihlman argues, that Johanson has taken two or more different species, including a big one and a small one, and lumped them together.

"Johanson is asserting, not demonstrating, that there is this extreme size difference in *Australopithecus afarensis*," Zihlman says. "But he's never published a detailed argument with measurements to back this up. In modern humans, males and females can be distinguished most of the time by the pelvis, but in *Australopithecus afarensis,* with only one pelvis—Lucy's—there can be no comparisons. For all we know, Lucy might just as well have been a male as a female. As far as I'm concerned, it's a toss-up. All we know for sure is that Lucy was small."

Such statements infuriate Johanson and White, who have all but based their careers on the theory that *Australopithecus afarensis* is a single species. "What we are looking at in these samples is one geologic second in time," Johanson says. "And what we have

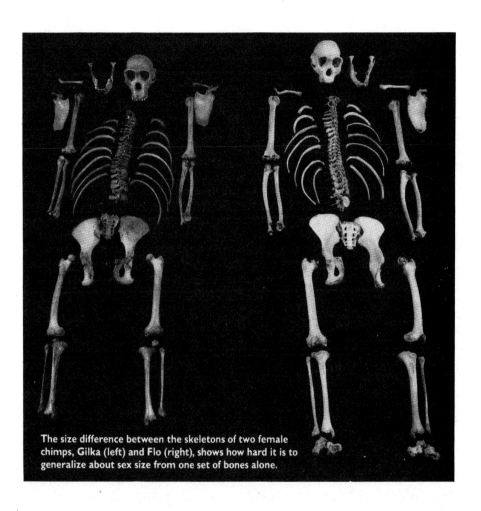

The size difference between the skeletons of two female chimps, Gilka (left) and Flo (right), shows how hard it is to generalize about sex size from one set of bones alone.

found in that slice are some rather large and some rather small specimens of the same species." In the first place, he says scornfully, anatomical comparisons show the pygmy chimp is no more closely related to Lucy than it is to modern humans. He argues that the teeth of pygmy chimps are much smaller than those of early hominids. Turning Zihlman's argument back on itself, he notes that while male and female pygmy chimps differ very little in anatomy, the fossil record shows dramatic differences between male and female hominids.

"I don't put a lot of emphasis on this

notion of a 'living link,' " Johanson scoffs. "But in any case, it is clear to me that the pygmy chimp does not appear to be it."

White goes even further, accusing Zihlman of distorting her science to fit her politics. "The bones that were found at Hadar don't have labels, so you can interpret them any way you want," White says. "You could also go to a cemetery, dig up the bones you find there, and say that each skeleton represents a different species. The question is whether the fossils show so much variation that we need to recognize them as two different species, and they don't. We've grounded our inference in the modern world. If Zihlman must accommodate the data of the real world to some politically correct manifesto, then she should write science fiction, not science."

Zihlman agrees that differences exist

between the early hominids and the pygmy chimp, especially when it comes to their teeth. But the chimp is only a model of the early ancestor, one that probably shared both common and pygmy chimp characteristics. "I never meant to suggest that pygmy chimps were exactly like the apes that gave rise to humans," she says. "But in terms of their body proportions, the early hominids are more like the pygmy chimp than any other ape."

As for the rest of the dispute, Zihlman contends that she is willing to defend her view in an open forum, but that so far she has not been asked to sit on the same podium with Johanson and White to argue her case. Zihlman says she tried to take measurements of the fossils herself, but when she asked Johanson for permission to see the collection when it was under his care at the Cleveland Museum, he said she could do so only if she gave him the right to review any paper she wrote on the fossils before she sent it to a journal. "The implication was that he had to approve it," Zihlman says. She felt that was a form of censorship and refused to work under those conditions. The collection has since been returned to Ethiopia.

Stalemates such as this, marked by displays of territoriality and possessiveness, have frustrated Zihlman to the point where this past year she decided to do something about it. With Mary Ellen Morbeck, an anthropologist at the University of Arizona, she organized a conference on female biology and evolution with the explicit purpose of encouraging free and open speech among the participants. To that end, the organizers invited only women researchers.

The move was immediately denounced as sexist by critics, both in her profession and in the press. However, Zihlman remains staunch in its defense, saying that what distinguished conference participants was not the possession of two X chromosomes but a supportive and cooperative attitude. "Studies in anthropology, sociolinguistics, and psychology document that men and women communicate differently," she says. "Men frequently use

language to dominate. My goal at the meeting was that language be used to communicate. And as it turned out, that is what happened. People didn't compete with one another, they didn't interrupt one another, they actually listened. We got down to the nitty-gritty very fast and could really discuss the issues."

" . . . fossils and bones are not enough—they just don't tell you all that much."

For Zihlman, one of the key issues was the effect females have on the evolution of their species. "Natural selection is operating at all stages of life, not just reproduction," she says. But most studies of the role of the individual in evolution focus on mating, she notes, on getting the genes into the next generation. "But mating is a male-dominated behavior," Zihlman says. "For females, that's just the beginning. They're involved with offspring for their whole lives."

This is particularly true for primates. "A primate lives a long life, with distinct stages of development," she says. "Chimps live twelve to thirteen years before they reproduce, and there are many things that happen during that time that can influence the health of their offspring. They can get sick or lose a parent or be injured. This is experiential, not genetic. To say genes are the be-all and end-all renders everything else—development, life experience, ecology—irrelevant. I don't think getting genes into the next generation is what it's all about. To reduce everything to genes is boring and simplistic, and I don't buy it for a minute. It might work for insects or birds—though I have my doubts—but it certainly does not work for primates." This is what Zihlman calls looking at the whole organism—and that, ulti-

mately, is what she is interested in.

"I knew early on that if I was going to survive in this business, I was going to have to diversify," Zihlman says. "If I had committed myself to studying fossils and only fossils, I would have failed, because when it comes to looking at fossils, access is everything and I knew I wouldn't get it. But fossils and bones are not enough—they just don't tell you all that much. For example, there's nothing in the bones of the goats in the Galápagos Islands that says they should be able to climb trees and eat vegetation. But they do. The whole point is trying to conceptualize what was on the bones and what it allowed individuals to do."

To illustrate the limitations of trying to reconstruct the life of an animal from its fossil remains, Zihlman walks back to one of the tall wooden bone chests in her laboratory and pulls out drawers filled with plastic bags that hold the remains of common chimps brought to her by Jane Goodall from her research center at Gombe National Park in Tanzania. Goodall has followed these chimps for 30 years, sometimes from birth to death, and has kept detailed records on the events that shaped their lives. Zihlman and Morbeck examined and measured the bones and skulls of the Gombe chimps to determine the extent to which these events also shaped their bodies.

For example, the bones of one chimp, "Gilka," are small and asymmetrical. If Gilka were the only female skeleton available, this might lead researchers to speculate that females of her species are much smaller than males. In fact, Gilka was stunted by a bout of polio suffered early in life. She bore four infants, all of whom died. By contrast "Flo," who lived to be 43, had a larger skeleton than many Gombe males and gave birth to five infants, three of whom survived to adulthood.

"The variation among individuals regardless of sex is enormous," Zihlman says. "What the Gombe studies show is the importance of the individual in evolution, that it's reductionist to focus on a few bones. Animals don't go from gene to protein to bone, there's a life that is lived in between. Bone is one of the most mobile of tissues, it is constantly being turned over and re-modeled—the bone you have today is not the same bone you had six years ago."

Zihlman says she and Morbeck plan to use the data they glean from the Gombe bones in concert with Good-all's field notes to provide a basis for reevaluating what has been written about the early hominid fossil record. "Here we have information on the skeleton and information on the whole animal," she says. "From this we have a holistic view, we can learn what bones really tell us, and what they do not. There's a good chance we might overturn a lot of what's been accepted about the fossil record. Right now, it's only a work in progress, but of course, I hope it shakes things up."

It's likely to. Fossil hunters are often strongly wedded to their interpretations of their finds and are unlikely to accept criticism gracefully, particularly from an outsider who has not devoted her life to the dig. While not oblivious to the possibility of backlash, Zihlman is not overly concerned about it.

"In science, being outspoken and being a woman is an unforgivable combination," she says. "I've learned to live with the consequences. For me, there is no choice. I really don't know how to play the game, even if I wanted to."

What Makes Us So Different from the Apes?

Tony Layng

Elmira College

In order to learn more about ourselves, our own species, scholars have long been asking questions about other animals, especially the great apes, since they closely resemble us in so many ways. Gorillas and chimpanzees, and to a lesser extent the gibbons and orangutans, are our closest living relatives; so they have come under much scrutiny in this regard.

Physically, the differences are more apparent than real. The body hair of apes is far more conspicuous than is our own, but we have no fewer hair follicles than they do. Their craniums are proportionately smaller than our own, and their arms are proportionately longer and stronger, but they have the same skeletal structure as we do, bone for bone. Theirs is not as well designed for standing upright, but chimps and gorillas have little difficulty walking in this fashion when they choose to do so.

Of greater significance, most likely, are those differences that have to do with their behavior. For example, they seem capable of surviving only in a certain type of environment, unable to alter their behavior in ways that might enable them to live in other places; and, consequently, they inhabit very few locations. We, on the other hand, thrive in many different kinds of environments. And apes do very little to reshape their habitats, while humans extensively alter the territories they occupy. Such differences are illustrated by the wide range of different human cultures and the contrasting uniformity of behavior throughout each ape species.

These differences are more descriptive than explanatory. Such descriptions often pose as explanations of what makes us fundamentally unlike the apes, but to merely point out that there are dissimilarities does not account for these dissimilarities. Answers to the question: "What makes us so different from the apes?" have been around for a long time, but even modern scholars have not yet fully explained these differences. Why, for example, have humans accomplished so much and apes so little? Common sense explanations have always been available, but they are far too simplistic; and as modern scholarship expands, these answers keep changing.

Western scholars at one time posited that since an ape has no soul, unlike humans, this fact alone was largely responsible for the fundamental differences between the destinies of our two species. Our place in the universe, after all, was supposedly guided by an omnipotent supreme being; how could apes possibly compete with that? Part of this divine plan, according to Christians, was that humans were created to "rule" the apes, and all other animals of course.

Others in the West have supposed that the fundamental difference between apes and people is mostly a matter of different instincts, that humans have "higher" natural predispositions that clearly distinguish us from the baser tendencies of all animals, apes or otherwise.

Another answer to the question, one that is still popular among intellectuals, is that our rationality set us apart from these, the most intelligent nonhuman animals. Apes, so goes this theory, cannot reason, or at least they are not capable of truly abstract thought. Our superior brains, it is surmised, not only make us more intelligent but give us mental capabilities that are wholly lacking in apes.

These and other popular beliefs, which most of us might use to explain what makes us so different from the apes, are all deficient to some degree. Even though such attempts to explain what makes us so different from the apes are likely to be viewed by most as both logical and convincing, all are fallacious or at least unsubstantiated in light of what we know about humans and other primates. For example, the belief that the human soul distinguishes "man" from the apes is both ethnocentric and "speciescentric." It is, of course, a common belief among peoples all over the world that we have souls, some tribal populations believing that each of us has multiple souls; and a few societies, the Eskimos for instance, believe that even animals have souls. Now the Eskimos might not know much about apes, but that they attribute souls to the seals and whales that they hunt illustrates the degree to which such beliefs are a reflection of one's culture.

Similarly, to claim that God has a special role in mind for our species entirely contradicts what we now know objectively about religious beliefs in non-Western societies. For example, a number of traditional tribes lacked any belief in a creator god prior to being influenced by Christian missionaries; so to suggest that "God" has imposed a special destiny on us only illustrates

 Reprinted from *Between the Species*, Winter 1991, pp. 40-43. *Between the Species*, P. O. Box 254, Berkeley, CA 94701.

the degree to which our thinking is shaped by our cultural biases. And how does one test or confirm these essentially theological premises? The answer, of course, is that one does not, for they are entirely a matter of religious faith.

Then what about instincts? Is it our innate predispositions which separate us most clearly from the apes? When we ask about human nature, rather than about human spirituality, are we at least asking a scientific question? Perhaps, if humans have instincts. If we do, are some of them uniquely human? It is clearer that we have inborn drives—a sex drive and a hunger drive for example—but these do not make our species special. Instincts are more complicated than unlearned drives, for they involve not only a need to respond to some stimuli but inborn programmed behavior as well. A bird, for example, will build a distinctive style of nest unique to its species even though it has never previously observed nest building or had any other opportunity to learn how to do this kind of construction.

A maternal instinct is the one most often cited when the subject of human instincts comes up, but those who suggest that women have a natural affinity to protect their young would, presumably, agree that female gorillas are no different in this regard. Do humans have any peculiar instincts, ones that cause them to behave quite differently from the way apes do? It is not at all clear that we do. In fact, it is not certain that humans or apes have any real instincts, at least none that are comparable to those found commonly in animals such as birds.

Western scholars used to attribute quite a bit of human behavior to instincts. We all supposedly had a self-preservation instinct, and males, at least, had an aggression instinct. Women were considered to be instinctually intuitive and emotional. And just as men and women were instinctually different, races were also predisposed to behave in distinctive ways; darker races were naturally "lazy and child-like, and superstitious." Not surprisingly, white men were consistently

presented as having the most desirable instincts, those consistent with the highest values of Western society. Now that social scientists know far more about learning theory, animal behavior, ethnocentrism, racial bigotry, and sexism, we hear far less about human instincts. As our knowledge of human behavior becomes increasingly informed, we refer to less and less of it as being innate.

Well then, what about abstract thought? Sorry. Here too, recent research by primatologists and anthropologists suggests that apes are smarter than we had previously assumed. We have known for years that chimpanzees in captivity were capable of problem solving abstractly; it has been clearly demonstrated that they could conceptually figure out, when sufficiently motivated by hunger, that tools absent from their view were applicable to obtaining a meal otherwise out of reach. This certainly required abstract thought. Now, of course, we know that chimpanzees and gorillas have the capacity to communicate symbolically, to learn and use language. Washoe the chimp and Koko the gorilla have become celebrities of a sort, appearing in numerous television documentaries demonstrating their ability to "speak" American sign language; and more recently, some chimpanzee students have had success in instructing others of their species in how to utilize this highly abstract form of symbolic communication.

So what can we conclude at this point about the basic differences between apes and humans? As far as religious claims are concerned, there is absolutely no objective evidence that humans have any special spiritual advantage, or that apes lack either a soul or divine guidance. Conclusions about such things are entirely a matter of one's faith in things supernatural. Those who suggest that what is special about humans is our peculiar destiny, that we were ordained to have dominion over all other species, inform us only about their own religious tenets.

Instincts? The continued use of this term in reference to human behavior is little more than a confession of igno-

rance, something to call the behavior until we come to understand it more fully. Rationality? Abstract thought? We no longer are justified in believing that these are uniquely human attributes, for we now know that chimpanzees use and even make tools for specific purposes, and they are capable of learning and rationally using abstract symbols in the form of complex communication.

So, again, what accounts for the vast differences between ourselves and the apes? Many anthropology textbooks state that only humans have culture, and that is what makes us so special; but we are discovering more and more instances of cultural behavior (patterned behavior that is learned and shared by members of a social group) among apes and even the less intelligent monkeys. We now know that wild bands of primates can alter their collective, customary learned behavior, and that is what culture is all about.

Just as our uniqueness in the animal world cannot be explained in terms of mysticism or supernaturalism, neither can it be attributed to self-flattering claims to having unique mental abilities, or any other abilities for that matter. Our mental superiority is merely a matter of degree, not a difference of kind. To explain what we have achieved in this world, in contrast to what apes have failed to achieve, we must consider more than our capacity for abstract thought, language, and culture.

Well what is left to consider? If we are to clarify what it is that sets us apart from other animals, I suggest that we concentrate not on presumed or relative differences in capability but, rather, on different needs, for in this regard, the differences may be far more significant. For example, chimpanzees can learn to invent new words and construct original sentences, but they are satisfactorily adapted to their natural environment without doing so. We, on the other hand, must learn to do these things, or we would fail to survive. A human population lacking a language would be unable to sustain itself, for without language we could not adequately share newly derived information and pass it on to subsequent generations. Humans must do this and more; they must discuss past events and plan future activities, they must coordinate their economic behavior and maintain a moral code, and they must reckon their kin and recount their myths. None of these matters are human luxuries; they all are prerequisite to sustaining an orderly society. And human populations which fail to do this are not equipped to survive, especially where they must compete for food with societies that do rely on language.

When the first hominids (primates who walked fully upright) began to develop language and sexual division of labor (lacking among apes), they did so because they *had* to, not simply because they were able to do so. These early steps in the development of culture gave them a clear advantage over other hominids who failed to invent these things. For example, assigning economic activities by sex, teaching males to hunt and females to collect other foods, not only raised the level of skill employed in these tasks but created an interdependence between men and women which formed the basis of

important economic units—families. Through intermarriage between family units, hunting and gathering bands gave structure and cohesion to their composition. And intermarriage between bands enabled practical information gained by one (how to make a new hunting weapon, where to find an additional source of food, etc.) to diffuse to the other. Such information sharing, of course, was much facilitated as language continued to evolve.

Populations which lacked language and a division of labor were at a decided disadvantage. They were far less likely to invent tools or plan cooperative economic activities. Apes in the wild make and use some tools, but they are not *dependent* on those tools, nor is it necessary for them to coordinate their use of tools. Their survival does not necessitate tool use, but humans must invent tools or perish. Our earliest ancestors were rather bright, but, more importantly, because they were neither particularly strong nor swift, they were often short of food and frequently preyed upon by other animals. The best defense against starvation and predation that they were able to come up with was culture (learning

better methods of coping), and culture worked rather well in this regard.

Humans, far more than apes, desperately need to rely on complex learned and shared behavior. All human societies have clear rules of social conduct, all have religious beliefs, all have a political system and an economic system, all have a complex kinship system, and all have a fully evolved language. If our early ancestors had failed to develop language and culture, long ago they most likely would have become just another extinct species.

So the most fundamental difference between us and the apes is not our capacity to invent tools, language, and a sexual division of labor; it is the fact that apes can get along quite well without these things while humans cannot. Without tools, language, and a sexual division of labor, our early ancestors would not have continued to evolve; and today apes and any surviving hominids would be far more similar than they now are. It is not that gorillas and chimpanzees are incapable of language or a division of labor; it is that humans are unable to survive without these. In short, we *need* culture; they do not.

Human Ancestors
Walked Tall, Stayed Cool

Pete Wheeler

Hominids, or humanlike primates, first appeared in Africa five to seven million years ago, when that continent's climate was becoming increasingly arid and large tracts of woodland and savanna were replacing the unbroken canopy of the equatorial rain forest. While the ancestors of chimpanzees and gorillas remained in the moist forests, the hominids started to exploit the more open, drier habitats. The exact nature of the transition remains hidden, because the oldest-known hominid fossils (*Australopithecus afarensis*) are only four million years old. But the intense sunshine in the new environment, combined with a scarcity of drinking water, must have severely challenged the ability of early hominids to regulate their body temperature.

Many savanna mammals do not even attempt to dissipate all the additional heat they absorb during the day, allowing it instead to accumulate within their bodies until nightfall, when they can cool off without expending precious water. But this strategy works only if delicate tissues, such as the central nervous system, are protected from surges in body temperature. Most savanna mammals possess special physiological mechanisms to cool the brain—notably the carotid rete, a network of fine arteries near the base of the brain, coupled with venous circulation through the muzzle.

Humans, apes, and monkeys, however, lack these features. Although humans appear to have eventually evolved an alternative mechanism to help cool the surface of their enlarged brains, the first hominids could have prevented damaging elevations of brain temperature only by keeping their entire body cool. Any adaptations that either reduced the amount of heat absorbed from the environment or facilitated its rapid dissipation would have proved highly advantageous.

Walking on two feet—the unique mode of terrestrial locomotion that is widely recognized as the first key development in hominid evolution—conferred precisely these benefits. Bipedalism dramatically reduces exposure to direct solar radiation during the middle of the equatorial day. I have placed scale models of early australopithecines in quadrupedal and bipedal postures to measure how the sun would hit them. These experiments show that when the sun is high, bombarding the earth's surface with intense radiation (because the rays pass through less atmosphere), far less body surface is exposed on a biped than on a quadruped. When the sun is directly overhead, the heat load on an upright hominid is only about 40 percent of that received by a quadruped of similar size.

Bipedalism also raises most of the body well above the ground, so that the skin contacts cooler and faster-moving air currents. This favors heat dissipation through convection. Allowing for variation in environmental conditions and vegetation, I calculate that hominids would have lost about one-third more heat through convection by adopting a bipedal posture.

Finally, human bipedalism at low speeds uses less energy than does either true quadrupedalism or the knuckle walking used by African apes. This reduces both dietary requirements (and the time and effort spent foraging) and the rate at which heat is generated internally as a byproduct of muscular activity.

Taking these factors into account in calculating the overall energy and water budgets of the early hominids, I conclude that bipedalism significantly decreased early hominids' dependence on shade, allowing them to forage in the open for longer periods and at higher temperatures. Bipedalism also greatly reduced the amount of drinking water they needed for evaporative cooling through sweating. I estimate that a knuckle-walking ape, active throughout the day on the savanna, would typically need to drink about five pints of water. Just by assuming bipedal posture and locomotion, a hominid of similar size would get by with three pints daily.

Bipedalism appears to be an ideal mode of terrestrial locomotion for a mammal foraging in the equatorial savanna, where food and water resources are dispersed and far from abundant. But if so, why do we find bipedalism only in humans? Probably because all other mammals of the African savanna, including monkeys such as baboons, are descended from ancestors that were already true quadrupeds.

4. THE HOMINID TRANSITION

In contrast, humans, along with chimpanzees and gorillas, probably descended from tree-dwelling primates that brachiated, or swung from branches using their arms. These ancestors were not strongly committed to one particular mode of terrestrial locomotion and may have been predisposed to walking upright. As they moved into more open habitats, the overheating problems they encountered may have tipped the balance in favor of bipedalism. (An alternative possibility is that bipedalism was first perfected in the forest habitat for some entirely different reason, and that our ancestors just happened to be preadapted for the problems they would encounter on the expanding savanna.)

Following the acquisition of an upright posture, humans evolved in other ways that enabled them to keep cool. Average body weight rose, slowing dehydration under savanna conditions. Larger hominids would have been able to forage for longer periods, and across greater distances, before needing to drink.

Later hominids—members of our own genus, *Homo*—are also taller for their body weight than their stockier and rather more apelike ancestors, the australopithecines. By at least 1.6 million years ago, *H. erectus* had acquired the tall, linear physique, with relatively narrow shoulders and hips, characteristic of many human populations inhabiting hot, arid regions of the tropics today. A tall, thin body maximizes the skin area available for heat dissipation, while minimizing the exposure of these surfaces to the overhead sun. Longer legs help by raising the body still farther above the hot ground.

Scientists have long reasoned that one of the most obvious and unusual human features, the loss of insulating body hair, is an adaptation to the hot savanna. Although follicles are still densely distributed over most of the human body, the hairs they produce are so short and fine that the underlying skin is exposed directly to the flow of air, promoting the shedding of excess heat by convection and, when necessary, enhancing the effectiveness of sweating.

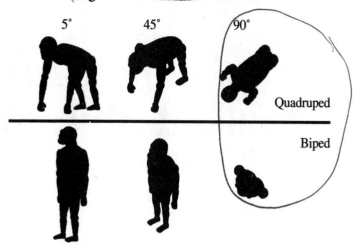

Angle of Sun above the Horizon

5°   45°   90°

Quadruped

Biped

On all fours (top row), a hypothetical human progenitor exposes considerable body surface to direct solar radiation, whether the sun is low on the horizon, intermediate, or directly overhead. In contrast, the same creature in a bipedal posture is far less vulnerable to the intense rays of the midday sun (bottom row, right).
Pete Wheeler

The problem with this hypothesis has always been explaining why humans differ from other savanna mammals, which have retained dense coats of hair. In environments where mammals are exposed to strong solar radiation, the coat acts as a shield, reflecting and reradiating heat before it reaches the skin. For most mammals, the loss of this insulation would create more problems that it would solve: I calculate that on the savanna, naked quadrupeds would actually need to drink additional water to cope with the extra heat load. For a biped, in contrast, a naked skin saves water because so little skin surface is exposed to the sun. Mainly the head and upper shoulders are exposed, and these can be protected by the retention of a relatively small amount of hair cover. Bipedalism and the strategy of cooling the whole body (rather than just the brain) probably explain why humans evolved a naked skin, while other savanna mammals of comparable size did not.

The stability in body temperature provided by bipedalism and a naked skin may have been an essential step in allowing our large, heat-sensitive brains to evolve further. A parallel to this can

be seen in the development of modern computers. Information-processing systems—semiconductor as well as biological—generate substantial heat and are vulnerable to damage from overheating. This presents a major obstacle to electronics engineers attempting to build ever more capable machines. The circuits of the Cray 2 supercomputer, for example, are so densely packed that they must be immersed in a tank of fluorocarbon liquid maintained at about 65° F. As in the case of the evolution of the human brain, the development of such an elaborate cooling system does not inevitably lead to higher-performance machines, but it does make them possible.

As humans spread outward from Africa, they encountered different levels of heat, exposure, and moisture. Many studies suggest that these factors determined, at least in part, the variation we now observe in features as diverse as nose shape, limb proportions, hair structure, skin pigmentation, and eye color. Modern humans inhabiting savanna and desert environments near the equator, such as the Nilotic peoples of Africa and the Australian aborigines, commonly have tall, thin physiques resembling that of early

Homo erectus. Their skin, especially among groups that have traditionally worn little clothing, is generally very dark, owing to the high concentration of melanin pigment that protects underlying tissues from sunburn and the carcinogenic effects of ultraviolet radiation.

As humans migrated north into colder regions, where retaining heat became more vital, they evolved proportionately shorter limbs, a trend seen in many other groups of mammals. In these populations the skin has lost most of its pigmentation, apparently because of the milder impact of ultraviolet radiation at high latitudes. The reduction in pigment may simply reflect the relaxation of the need for it, or it may have been demanded to allow sufficient penetration of ultraviolet radiation (which humans need to synthesize essential vitamin D).

As they colonized—or recolonized—tropical rain forests, humans faced another obstacle. Although the canopy affords shade, the humidity inhibits the evaporation of sweat. The resultant dependence on convective heat loss favors a body form with a large surface area relative to volume. Unfortunately, the tall, linear physique that works so well in open equatorial habitats is not practical when negotiating dense vegetation. A better solution may be a small body, exemplified by the Mbuti Pygmies of the Congo Basin, who benefit from a high surface-to-volume ratio and can move with agility across the forest floor.

The evolutionary future of man

A biological view of progress

Richard Dawkins

Richard Dawkins is reader in zoology at Oxford University

Evolution is widely regarded as a progressive force thrusting inexorably towards racial improvement, which may be seen as offering some tangible hope for our troubled species. Unfortunately this way of thinking is based on two misunderstandings. First, it is by no means clear that evolution is necessarily progressive. Second, even when it is progressive, significant change proceeds on a time-scale many orders of magnitude longer than the scale of tens or hundreds of years with which historians feel at home.

We can define evolutionary progress either in a value-laden or a value-neutral way—ie, either with or without building in notions of what is good or bad. A value-laden definition specifies whether the factor being monitored, be it brain-size, intelligence, artistic ability, physical strength or whatever, is desirable or undesirable. If a desirable factor increases, that is progress. But on a value-neutral definition, any change at all counts as progress, just so long as it continues on its course. Such a definition simply takes three entities in a time sequence—think of them as a series of ancestral fossils and call them Early, Middle and Late—and asks whether the change from Early to Middle is in the same direction as the change from Middle to Late. If the answer is yes, that is a progressive change. This definition is value-neutral

because the factor which we discover to be "progressive" could be something which we regard as bad—say, idleness or stupidity. In this value-neutral sense, a continued trend towards decreased brain size would be progressive, just as much as a trend towards increased brain size would be. The only thing that would not be progressive would be a reversal of the trend.

It was once fashionable for biologists to believe in something called orthogenesis. This was the theory that trends in evolution constitute a driving force and continue under their own momentum. The Irish Elk was thought to have been driven extinct by its huge antlers, which in turn were thought to have grown bigger under the influence of an orthogenetic force. Perhaps initially there was some advantage in larger antlers and this was how the trend started. But, once started, the trend had its own internal unstoppability, and, as the generations went by, the antlers continued inexorably to grow until they drove the species extinct.

We now think that the theory of orthogenesis is wrong. If a trend is seen towards increasing antler size, this is because natural selection favours larger antlers. Individual stags with large antlers have more offspring than stags with average-sized antlers, either because they survive better (unlikely) or attract females (probably irrelevant) or because they are better at intimidating rivals (likely). If the trend appears to persist for a long time in the fossil record, this indicates that natural selection was pushing in that direction

for all that time. Metaphors like "inherent force" and "inexorable momentum" have no validity.

It seems to follow that there is no general reason to expect evolution to be progressive—even in the weak, value-neutral sense. There will be times when increased size of some organ is favoured and other times when decreased size is favoured. Most of the time, average-sized individuals will be favoured in the population and both extremes will be penalised. During these times the population exhibits evolutionary stasis (ie, no change) with respect to the factor being measured. If we had a complete fossil record and looked for trends in some particular dimension, such as leg length, we would expect to see periods of no change alternating with fitful continuations or reversals in direction—like a weathervane in changeable, gusty weather.

It is all the more intriguing to find that sometimes long, progressive trends in one direction do turn up. When an organ is used for intimidation (like a stag's antlers) or for attraction (like the peacock's tail), it may be that the best size to have—from the point of view of intimidation or attraction—is always slightly larger than the average in the population. Even when the average gets bigger, the optimum is always one step ahead. It is possible that such "moving-target selection" did drive the Irish Elk extinct after all: by pushing the "intimidation optimum" too far ahead of what would have been the overall "utilitarian optimum". Peacocks and male birds of paradise also seem to have been pushed, in this case by female-taste selection, far from the utilitarian optimum of an efficient flying and surviving machine (though they have not been driven over the edge into extinction).

Another force driving progressive evolution is the so-called "arms-race". Prey animals evolve faster running speeds because predators do. Consequently predators have to evolve even faster running speeds, and so on, in an escalating spiral. Such arms races probably account for the spectacularly advanced engineering of eyes, ears, brains, bat "radar" and all the other high-tech weaponry that animals display. Arms races are a special case of "co-evolution." Co-evolution occurs whenever the environment in which creatures evolve is itself evolving. From an antelope's point of view, lions are part of the environment like the weather—with the important difference that lions evolve.

VIRTUAL PROGRESS

I want to suggest a new kind of co-evolution which, I believe, may have been responsible for one of the most spectacular examples of progressive evolution: the enlargement of the human brain. At some point in the evolution of brains, they acquired the ability to simulate models of the outside world. In its advanced forms we call this ability "imagination." It may be compared to the virtual-reality software that runs on some computers. Now here is the point I want to make. The internal "virtual world" in which animals live may in effect become a part of the environment, of comparable importance to the climate, vegetation, predators and so on outside. If so, a co-evolutionary spiral may take off, with hardware—especially brain hardware—evolving to meet improvements in the internal "virtual environment." The changes in hardware then stimulate improvements in the virtual environment, and the spiral continues.

The progressive spiral is likely to advance even faster if the virtual environment is put together as a shared enterprise involving many individuals.

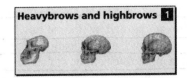

Heavybrows and highbrows **1**

And it is likely to reach breakneck speeds if it can accumulate progressively over generations. Language and other aspects of human culture provide a mechanism whereby such accumulation can occur. It may be that brain hardware has co-evolved with the internal virtual worlds that it creates. This can be called hardware-software co-evolution. Language could be both a vehicle of this co-evolution and its most spectacular software product. We know almost nothing of how language originated, since it started to fossilise only very recently, in the form of writing. Hardware has been fossilising for much longer—at least the brain's bony outer casing has. Its steadily increasing size, indicating a corresponding increase in the size of the brain itself, is what I want to turn to next.

It is almost certain that modern *Homo sapiens* (which dates only from about 100,000 years ago) is descended from a similar species, *H. erectus,* which first appeared a little before 1.6m years ago. It is thought that *H. erectus,* in turn, was descended from some form of *Australopithecus.* A possible candidate which lived about 3m years ago is *Australopithecus afarensis,* represented by the famous "Lucy." These creatures, which are often described as upright-walking apes, had brains about the size of a chimpanzee's. Figure 1 shows pictures of the three skulls, in chronological order. Presumably the change from Australopithecus] to *erectus* was gradual. This is not to say that it took 1½m years to accomplish at a uniform rate. It could easily have occurred in fits and starts. The same goes for the change from *erectus* to *sapiens.* By about 300,000 years ago, we start to find fossils that are called "archaic *H. sapiens*", largish-brained people like ourselves but with heavy brow ridges more like *H. erectus.*

It looks, in a general way, as though there are some progressive changes running through this series. Our braincase is nearly twice the size of *erectus*'s; and *erectus*'s braincase, in turn, is about twice the size of that of *Australopithecus afarensis.* This impression is vividly illustrated in Figure 2, which was prepared using a program called Morph.*

* Written for Apple Mac by Gryphon Software Corporation of San Diego, California, and kindly supplied to me by Softline Distribution in London. The original drawings of skulls and the projection were done by my wife, Lalla Ward.

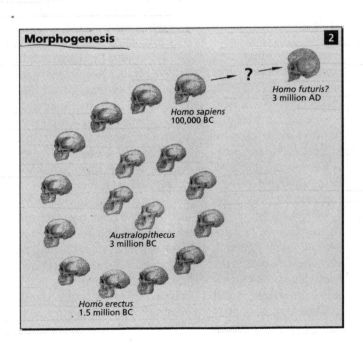

Morphogenesis **2**

Homo futuris?
3 million AD

Homo sapiens
100,000 BC

Australopithecus
3 million BC

Homo erectus
1.5 million BC

4. THE HOMINID TRANSITION

To use Morph, you supply it with a starting picture and an ending picture, and tell it which points on the starting picture correspond to which opposite-number points on the ending picture. Morph then computes a series of mathematical intermediates between the two pictures. The series may be viewed as ciné film on the computer screen, but for printing it is necessary to extract a series of still frames—arranged here in order in spiral (Figure 2). The spiral includes two concatenated sequences: *Australopithecus* to *H. erectus* and *H. erectus* to *H. sapiens.* Conveniently the two time intervals separating these three landmark fossils are approximately the same, about 1.5m years. The three labelled landmark skulls constitute the data supplied to Morph. All the others are the computed intermediates (ignore *H. futuris* for the moment).

Swirl your eye round the spiral looking for trends. It is broadly true that any trends you find before *H. erectus* continue after him. The film version shows this much more dramatically, so much so that it is hard, as you watch the film, to detect any discontinuity as you pass through *H. erectus.* We have made similar films for a number of probable evolutionary transitions in human ancestry. More often than not, trends show reversals of direction. The relatively smooth continuity around *H. erectus* is quite unusual.

We can say that there has been a long, progressive—and by evolutionary standards very rapid—trend over the past 3m years of human skull evolution. I am speaking of progress in the value-neutral sense here. As it happens, anybody who thinks increased brain size has positive value can also claim this trend as value-laden progress too. This is because the dominant trend, flowing both before and after *H. erectus,* is the spectacular ballooning of the brain.

What of the future? Can we extrapolate the trend from *H. erectus* through and beyond *H. sapiens,* and predict the skull shape of *H. futuris* 3m years hence? Only an orthogeneticist would take it seriously; but, for what it is worth, we have made an extrapolation

with the aid of Morph, and it is appended at the end of the spiral diagram. It shows a continuation of the trend to inflate the balloon of the brain-case; the chin continues to move forward and sharpen into a silly little goatee point, while the jaw itself looks too small to chew anything but baby pap. Indeed the whole cranium is quite reminiscent of a baby's skull. It was long ago suggested that human evolution is an example of "paedomorphosis": the retention of juvenile characteristics into adulthood. The adult human skull looks more like a baby chimp's than like an adult chimp's.

DON'T BANK ON *H. FUTURIS*

Is there any likelihood that something like this hypothetical large-brained *H. futuris* will evolve? I'd put very little money on it, one way or the other. Certainly the mere fact that brain inflation has been the dominant trend over the past 3m years says almost nothing about probable trends in the next 3m. Brains will continue to inflate only if natural selection continues to favour large-brained individuals. This means, when you come down to it, if large-brained individuals manage to have, on average, more children than small-brained ones.

It is not unreasonable to assume that large brains go with intelligence, and that intelligence, in our wild ancestors, was associated with ability to survive, ability to attract mates or ability to outwit rivals. Not unreasonable—but both these clauses would find their critics. It is an article of passionate faith among "politically correct" biologists and anthropologists that brain size has no connection with intelligence; that intelligence has nothing to do with genes; and that genes are probably nasty fascist things anyway.

Leaving this to one side, problems with the idea remain. In the days when most individuals died young, the main qualification for reproduction was survival into adulthood. But in our western civilisation few die young, most adults choose to have fewer children than they are physically and economi-

cally capable of, and it is by no means clear that people with the largest families are the most intelligent. Anybody viewing future human evolution from the perspective of advanced western civilisation is unlikely to make confident predictions about brain size continuing to evolve.

In any case, all these ways of viewing the matter are far too short-term. Socially important phenomena such as contraception and education exert their influences over the timescale of human historians, over decades and centuries. Evolutionary trends—at least those that last long enough to deserve the title progressive—are so slow that they are all but totally insensitive to the vagaries of social and historical time. If we could assume that something like our advanced scientific civilisation was going to last for 1m, or even 100,000, years, it might be worth thinking about the undercurrents of natural-selection pressure in these civilised conditions. But the likelihood is that, in 100,000 years time, we shall either have reverted to wild barbarism, or else civilisation will have advanced beyond all recognition—into colonies in outer space, for instance. In either case, evolutionary extrapolations from present conditions are likely to be highly misleading.

Evolutionists are usually pretty coy about predicting the future. Our species is a particularly hard one to predict because human culture, at least for the past few thousand years and speeding up all the time, changes in ways that mimic evolutionary change, only thousands to hundreds of thousands of times faster. This is most clearly seen when we look at technical hardware. It is almost a cliché to point out that the wheeled vehicle, the aeroplane, and the electronic computer, to say nothing of more frivolous examples such as dress fashions, evolve in ways strikingly reminiscent of biological evolution. My formal definitions of value-laden and value-neutral progress, although designed for fossil bones, can be applied, without modification, to cultural and technological trends.

Prevailing skirt and hair lengths in western society are progressive—

value-neutrally, because they are too trivial to be anything else—for short periods if at all. Viewed over the timescale of decades, the average lengths fritter up and down like yo-yos. Weapons improve (at what they are designed to do, which may be of positive or negative value depending on your point of view) consistently and progressively, at least partly to counter improvements in the weaponry of enemies. But mostly, like any other technology, they improve because new inventions build on earlier ones and inventors in any age benefit from the ideas, efforts and experience of their predecessors. This principle is most spectacularly demonstrated by the evolution of the digital computer. The late Christopher Evans, a psychologist and author, calculated that if the motor car had evolved as fast as the computer, and over the same time period, "Today

you would be able to buy a Rolls-Royce for £1.35, it would do three million miles to the gallon, and it would deliver enough power to drive the QE2. And if you were interested in miniaturisation, you could place half a dozen of them on a pinhead."

Science and the technology that it inspires can, of course, be used for backward ends. Continued trends in, say, aeroplane or computer speed, are undoubtedly progressive in a value-neutral sense. It would be easy to see them also as progressive in various value-laden senses. But such progress could also turn out to be laden with deeply negative value if the technologies fall into the hands of, say, religious fundamentalists bent on the destruction of rival sects who face a different point of the compass in order to pray, or some equally insufferable habit. Much may depend on whether the societies

with the scientific know-how and the civilised values necessary to develop the technologies keep control of them; or whether they allow them to spread to educationally and scientifically backward societies which happen to have the money to buy them.

Scientific and technological progress themselves are value-neutral. They are just very good at doing what they do. If you want to do selfish, greedy, intolerant and violent things, scientific technology will provide you with by far the most efficient way of doing so. But if you want to do good, to solve the world's problems, to progress in the best value-laden sense, once again, there is no better means to those ends than the scientific way. For good or ill, I expect scientific knowledge and technical invention to develop progressively over the next 150 years, and at an accelerating rate.

The Fossil Evidence

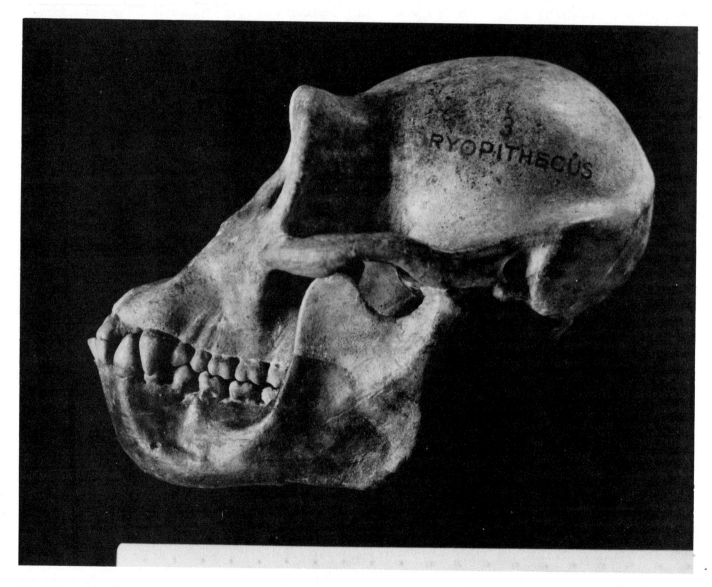

One of the primary focal points of this book, as well as the whole of biological anthropology, is the search for, and interpretation of, the fossil evidence for hominid (meaning human or human-like) evolution. Paleoanthropologists are those who carry out this task by conducting the painstak-

ing excavations and detailed analyses that serve as a basis for understanding our past. Every fragment found is cherished like a ray of light that may help to illuminate the path taken by our ancestors in the process of becoming "us." At least, this is what we would like to believe. In reality, each discovery leads to further mystery, and, for every fossil-hunting paleoanthropologist who thinks his or her find supports a particular theory, there are many others anxious to express their disagreement.

How wonderful it would be, we sometimes think in moments of frustration with inconclusive data, if the fossils would just speak for themselves and every primordial piece of humanity were to carry with it a self-evident explanation for its place in the evolutionary story. Paleoanthropology would then be more of a quantitative problem of amassing enough material to reconstruct our ancestral development rather than the qualitative problem of interpreting what it all means. It would certainly be a simpler process, but would it be as interesting? In "A Skull to Chew On," for example, Donald Johanson shows us how just one fossil find, and not even one in our direct ancestry, can throw the whole field of early hominid evolution into disarray, causing anthropologists to rethink treasured notions and shift away from established positions.

Most scientists tolerate, welcome, or even (dare it be said?) thrive on the resulting controversy, recognizing that a diversity of opinion refreshes the mind, rouses students, and captures the imagination of the general public. After all, where would paleoanthropology be without the gadflies, the near-mythic heroes, and, lest we forget, the research funds they generate?

None of this is to say that all the research and theoretical speculation taking place in the field of paleoanthropology is so highly volatile. Most scientists, in fact, go about their work quietly and methodically, generating hypotheses that are much less explosive and yet have the cumulative effect of enriching our understanding of the details of human evolution. By studying the stratigraphic sequences of fossil remains of other species, for example, Elisabeth Vrba ("The Pulse That Produced Us") is able to show how climatic change in East Africa had a significant impact on hominid evolutionary developments such as the increase in brain size. Then, Stephen Gould shows (in "Sizing Up Human Intelligence") that the significance of the human brain size is not truly revealed without a comparison with body size of a whole range of mammals, particularly primates. Pat Shipman, furthermore, shows us in "Scavenger Hunt" how modern technology, in the form of the scanning electron microscope, combined with meticulous, detailed analysis of cut marks on fossil animal bones, can help us better understand the locomotor and food-getting adaptations of our early hominid ancestors. In one stroke, she is able to challenge the traditional "man the hunter" theme that has pervaded most early hominid research and writing and simultaneously sets forth an alternative hypothesis that will, in turn, inspire further research.

As we mull over the controversies outlined in this section, therefore, we should not take them to reflect upon an inherent weakness of the field of paleoanthropology, but rather accept them as symbolic of its strength: the ability and willingness to scrutinize, question, and reflect (seemingly endlessly) upon every bit of evidence. Even in the case of purposeful deception, as recounted in "Dawson's Dawn Man: The Hoax at Piltdown" by Kenneth Feder, it should be remembered that it was the skepticism of scientists themselves that finally led to the revelation of fraud.

Contrary to the way some would have it, the creationists coming to mind, an admission of doubt is not an expression of ignorance, but is simply a frank recognition of an imperfect state of our knowledge. If we are to improve upon our understanding of ourselves, we must maintain an atmosphere of free inquiry without preconceived notions and an unquestioning commitment to a particular point of view. To paraphrase Ashley-Montagu, whereas creationism seeks certainty without proof, science seeks proof without certainty.

Looking Ahead: Challenge Questions

What effect did the Piltdown hoax have upon paleoanthropology?

In what ways did the "black skull" shake up the family tree?

What has climatic change in East Africa had to do with hominid evolution?

What evidence is there that human brain size is unprecedented in the natural world?

What is the "man the hunter" hypothesis, and how might the "scavenging theory" better suit the early hominid data?

How would you draw the family tree?

Dawson's Dawn Man: The Hoax at Piltdown

Kenneth L. Feder

The Piltdown Man fossil is a literal skeleton in the closet of prehistoric archaeology and human paleontology. This single specimen seemed to turn our understanding of human evolution on its head and certainly did turn the heads of not just a few of the world's most talented scientists. The story of Piltdown has been presented in detail by Ronald Millar in his 1972 book *The Piltdown Men,* by J. S. Weiner in his 1955 work *The Piltdown Forgery,* and most recently in 1986 by Charles Blinderman in *The Piltdown Inquest.* The story is useful in its telling if only to show that even scientific observers can make mistakes. This is particularly the case when trained scientists are faced with that which they are not trained to detect—intellectual criminality. But let us begin before the beginning, before the discovery of the Piltdown fossil.

THE EVOLUTIONARY CONTEXT

We need to turn the clock back to Europe of the late nineteenth and early twentieth centuries. The concept of evolution—the notion that all animal and plant forms seen in the modern world had descended or evolved from earlier, ancestral forms—had been debated by scientists for quite some time (Greene 1959). It was not until Charles Darwin's *On the Origin of Species* was published in 1859, however, that a viable mechanism for evolution was proposed and supported with an enormous body of data. Darwin had meticulously studied his subject, collecting evidence from all over the world for more than thirty years in support of his evolutionary mechanism called *natural selection.* Darwin's arguments were so well reasoned that most scientists soon became convinced of the explanatory power of his theory. Darwin went on to apply his general theory to humanity in *The Descent of Man,* published in 1871. This book was also enormously successful, and more thinkers came to accept the notion of human evolution.

Around the same time that Darwin was theorizing about the biological origin of humanity, discoveries were being made in Europe and Asia that seemed to support the concept of human evolution from ancestral forms. In 1856, workmen building a roadway in the Neander Valley of Germany came across some remarkable bones. The head was large but oddly shaped (Figure 1). The cranium (the skull minus the mandible or jaw) was much flatter than a modern human's, the bones heavier. The face jutted out, the forehead sloped back, and massive bone ridges appeared just above the eye sockets. Around the same time, other skeletons were found in Belgium and Spain that looked very similar. The postcranial bones (all the bones below the skull) of these fossils were quite similar to those of modern humans.

There was some initial confusion about how to label these specimens. Some scientists concluded that they simply represented pathological freaks. Rudolf Virchow, the world's preeminent anatomist, explained the curious bony ridges above the eyes as the result of blows to the foreheads of the creatures (Kennedy 1975). Eventually, however, scientists realized that these creatures, then and now called *Neandertals* after their most famous find-spot, represented a primitive and ancient form of humanity.

The growing acceptance of Darwin's theory of evolution and the discovery of primitive-looking, though humanlike, fossils combined to radically shift people's opinions about human origins. In fact, the initial abhorrence many felt concerning the entire notion of human evolution from lower, more primitive forms was remarkably changed in just a few decades (Greene 1959). By the turn of the twentieth century, not only were many people comfortable with the general concept of human evolution, but there actually was also a feeling of national pride concerning the discovery of a human ancestor within one's borders.

The Germans could point to their Neandertal skeletons and claim that the first primitive human being was a German. The French could counter that their own Cro-Magnon—ancient, though not as old as the German Neandertals—was a more humanlike and advanced ancestor; therefore, the first true human was a Frenchman. Fossils had also been found in Belgium and Spain, so Belgians and Spaniards could claim for themselves a place within the story of human origin and development. Even so small a nation as Holland could lay claim to a place in human evolutionary history since a Dutchman, Eugene Dubois, in 1891 had discovered the fossilized remains of a primitive human ancestor in Java, a Dutch-owned colony in the western Pacific.

However, one great European nation did not and could not participate fully in the debate over the ultimate origins of humanity. That nation was England. Very simply, by the beginning of the second decade of the twentieth century, no fossils of human evolutionary significance had been located in England. This lack of fossils led French scientists to label English human paleontology mere "pebble-collecting" (Blinderman 1986).

The English, justifiably proud of their cultural heritage and cultural evolution, simply could point to no evidence that humanity had initially developed within their borders. The conclusion reached by most was completely unpalatable to the proud English—no one had evolved in England. The English must have originally arrived from somewhere else.

At the same time that the English were feeling like a people with no evolutionary roots of their own, many other Europeans were still uncomfortable with the fossil record as it stood in the first decade of the twentieth century. While most were happy to have human fossils in their countries, they were generally not happy with what those fossils looked like and what their appearance implied about the course of human evolution.

Java Man (now placed in the category *Homo erectus* along with Peking Man), with its small cranium—its volume was about 900 cubic centimeters (cc), compared to a modern human average of about 1,450 cc—and large eyebrow ridges seemed quite apelike (see Figure 1). Neandertal Man, with his sloping forehead and thick, heavy brow ridges appeared to many to be

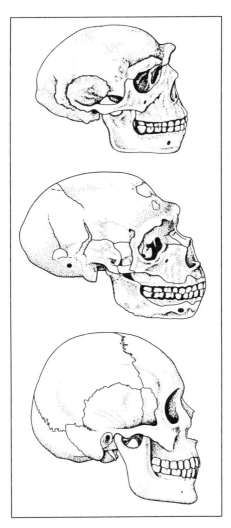

Figure 1 *Drawings showing the general differences in skull size and form between* Homo erectus *(Peking Man—500,000 years ago [top]), Neandertal Man (100,000 years ago [center]), and a modern human being [bottom]. Note the large brow ridges and forward-thrusting faces of* Homo erectus *and Neandertal, the rounded outline of the modern skull, and the absence of a chin in earlier forms. (Carolyn Whyte)*

quite ugly, stupid, and brutish. While the skulls of these fossil types were clearly not those of apes, they were equally clearly not fully human. On the other hand, the femur (thigh bone) of Java Man seemed identical to the modern form. While some emphasized what they perceived to be primitive characteristics of the postcranial skeleton of the Neandertals, this species clearly had walked on two feet; and apes do not.

All this evidence suggested that ancient human ancestors had primitive heads and, by implication, primitive

brains, seated atop rather modern-looking bodies. This further implied that it was the human body that evolved first, followed only later by the development of the brain and associated human intelligence.

Such a picture was precisely the opposite of what many people had expected and hoped for. After all, it was argued, it is intelligence that most clearly and absolutely differentiates humanity from the rest of the animal kingdom. It is in our ability to think, to communicate, and to invent that we are most distant from our animal cousins. This being the case, it was assumed that such abilities must have been evolving the longest; in other words, the human brain and the ability to think must have evolved first. Thus, the argument went, the fossil evidence for evolution should show that the brain had expanded first, followed by the modernization of the body.

Such a view is exemplified in the writings of anatomist Grafton Elliot Smith. Smith said that what most characterized human evolution must have been the "steady and uniform development of the brain along a well-defined course . . ." (as quoted in Blinderman 1986:36). Arthur Smith Woodward, ichthyologist and paleontologist at the British Museum of Natural History, later characterized the human brain as "the most complex mechanism in existence. The growth of the brain preceded the refinement of the features and of the somatic characters in general" (Dawson and Woodward 1913).

Put most simply, many researchers in evolution were looking for fossil evidence of a creature with the body of an ape and the brain of a human being. What was being discovered, however, was the reverse; both Java and Neandertal Man seemed more to represent creatures with apelike, or certainly not humanlike, brains but with humanlike bodies. Many were uncomfortable with such a picture.

A REMARKABLE DISCOVERY IN SUSSEX

Thus was the stage set for the initially rather innocuous announcement that

5. THE FOSSIL EVIDENCE

appeared in the British science journal *Nature* on December 5, 1912, concerning a fossil find in the Piltdown section of Sussex in southern England. The notice read, in part:

Remains of a human skull and mandible, considered to belong to the early Pleistocene period, have been discovered by Mr. Charles Dawson in a gravel-deposit in the basin of the River Ouse, north of Lewes, Sussex. Much interest has been aroused in the specimen owing to the exactitude with which its geological age is said to have been fixed. . . . (p. 390)

In the December 19 issue of *Nature*, further details were provided concerning the important find:

The fossil human skull and mandible to be described by Mr. Charles Dawson and Dr. Arthur Smith Woodward at the Geological Society as we go to press is the most important discovery of its kind hitherto made in England. The specimen was found in circumstances which seem to leave no doubt of its geological age, and the characters it shows are themselves sufficient to denote its extreme antiquity. (p. 438)

According to the story later told by those principally involved, in February 1912 Arthur Smith Woodward at the British Museum received a letter from Charles Dawson—a Sussex lawyer and amateur scientist. Woodward had previously worked with Dawson and knew him to be an extremely intelligent man with a keen interest in natural history. Dawson informed Woodward in the letter that he had come upon several fragments of a fossil human skull. The first piece had been discovered in 1908 by workers near the Barcombe Mills manor in the Piltdown region of Sussex, England. In 1911, a number of other pieces of the skull came to light in the same pit, along with a fossil hippopotamus bone and tooth.

In the letter to Woodward, Dawson expressed some excitement over the discovery and claimed to Woodward that the find was quite important and might even surpass the significance of Heidelberg Man, an important specimen found in Germany just the previous year.

Due to bad weather, Woodward was not immediately able to visit Piltdown. Dawson, undaunted, continued to work

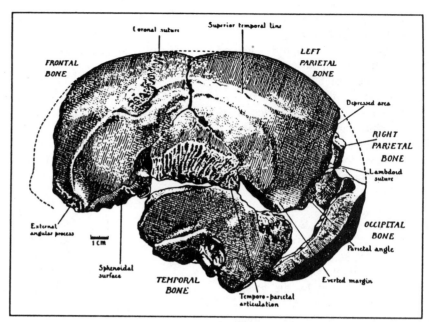

Figure 2 *This drawing with anatomical labels of the fragmentary remains of the Piltdown cranium appeared in a book written by one of the fossil's chief supporters. (From* The Evolution of Man, *by Grafton Elliot Smith, Oxford University Press)*

in the pit, finding fossil hippo and elephant teeth. Finally, in May 1912, he brought the fossil to Woodward at the museum. What Woodward saw was a skull that matched his own expectations and those of many others concerning what a human ancestor should look like. The skull, stained a dark brown from apparent age, seemed to be quite modern in many of its characteristics. The thickness of the bones of the skull, however, argued for a certain primitiveness. The association of the skull fragments with the bones of extinct animals implied that an ancient human ancestor indeed had inhabited England. By itself this was enormous news; at long last, England had a human fossil (Figure 2).

Things were to get even more exciting for English paleontologists. At the end of May 1912 Dawson, Woodward, and Pierre Teilhard de Chardin—a Jesuit priest with a great interest in geology, paleontology, and evolution whom Dawson had met in 1909—began a thorough archaeological excavation at the Piltdown site. . . . More extinct animal remains and flint tools were recovered. The apparent age of the fossils based upon comparisons to other sites indicated not only that Pilt-

down was the earliest human fossil in England, but also that, at an estimated age of 500,000 years, the Piltdown fossil represented potentially the oldest known human ancestor in the world.

Then, to add to the excitement, Dawson discovered one half of the mandible. Though two key areas—the chin, and the condyle where the jaw connects to the skull—were missing, the preserved part did not look anything like a human jaw. The upright portion or *ramus* was too wide, and the bone too thick. In fact, the jaw looked remarkably like that of an ape (Figure 3). Nonetheless, and quite significantly, the molar teeth exhibited humanlike wear. The human jaw, lacking the large canines of apes, is free to move from side to side while chewing. The molars can grind in a sideways motion in a manner impossible in monkeys or apes. The wear on human molars is, therefore, quite distinct from that of other primates. The Piltdown molars exhibited such humanlike wear in a jaw that was otherwise entirely apelike.

That the skull and the jaw had been found close together in the same geologically ancient deposit seemed to argue for the obvious conclusion that

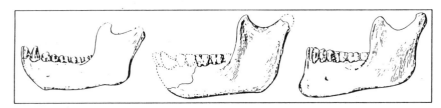

Figure 3 *Comparison of the mandibles (lower jaws) of a young chimpanzee [left], modern human [right], and Piltdown [center]. Note how much more similar the Piltdown mandible is to that of the chimp, particularly in the absence of a chin. The presence of a chin is a uniquely human trait. (From Dawson and Woodward, 1913, The Geological Society of London)*

they belonged to the same ancient creature. But what kind of creature could it have been? There were no large brow ridges like those of Java or Neandertal Man. The face was flat as in modern humans and not snoutlike as in the Neandertals. The profile of the cranium was round as it is in modern humans, not flattened as it appeared to be in the Java and Neandertal specimens (Figure 4). According to Woodward, the size of the skull indicated a cranial capacity or brain size of at least 1,100 cc (Dawson and Woodward 1913), much larger than Java and within the range of modern humanity. Anatomist Arthur Keith (1913) suggested that the capacity of the skull was actually much larger, as much as 1,500 cc, placing it close to the modern mean. But the jaw, as described above, was entirely apelike.

The conclusion drawn first by Dawson, the discoverer, and then by Woodward, the professional scientist, was that the Piltdown fossil—called *Eoanthropus dawsoni,* meaning Dawson's Dawn Man—was the single most important fossil find yet made anywhere in the world. Concerning the Piltdown discovery, the *New York Times* headline of December 19, 1912, proclaimed "Paleolithic Skull Is a Missing Link." Three days later the *Times* headline read "Darwin Theory Is Proved True."

The implications were clear. Piltdown Man, with its modern skull, primitive jaw, and great age, was the evidence many human paleontologists had been searching for: an ancient man with a large brain, a modern-looking head, and primitive characteristics below the important brain. As anatomist G. E. Smith summarized it:

The brain attained what may be termed the human rank when the jaws and face, and no doubt the body also, still retained much of the uncouthness of Man's simian ancestors. In other words, Man at first, so far as his general appearance and "build" are concerned, was merely an Ape with an overgrown brain. The importance of the Piltdown skull lies in the fact that it affords tangible confirmation of these inferences. (Smith 1927:105–6)

If Piltdown were the evolutionary "missing link" between apes and people, then neither Neandertal nor Java Man could be. Since Piltdown and Java Man lived at approximately the same time, Java might have been a more primitive offshoot of humanity that had

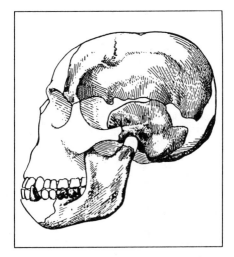

Figure 4 *Drawn reconstruction of the Piltdown skull. The portion of the skull actually recovered is shaded. As reconstructed, the cranium shows hominid (human) traits and the mandible shows pongid (ape) traits. Compare this drawing to those in Figure 1. With its humanlike head and apelike jaw, the overall appearance of the Piltdown fossil is far different from* Homo erectus, *Neandertal, or modern humans. (From* The Evolution of Man, *Grafton Elliot Smith, Oxford University Press)*

become extinct. Since Neandertal was much more recent than Piltdown, yet looked more primitive where it really counted (that is, the head), Neandertal must have represented some sort of primitive throwback, an evolutionary anachronism (Figure 5).

By paleontological standards the implications were breathtaking. In one sweeping blow Piltdown had presented England with its first ancestral human fossil, it had shown that human fossils found elsewhere in the world were either primitive evolutionary offshoots or later throwbacks to a more primitive type, and it had forced the rewriting of the entire story of human evolution. Needless to say, many paleontologists, especially those in England, were enthralled by the discovery in Sussex.

In March 1913, Dawson and Woodward published the first detailed account of the characteristics and evolutionary implications of the Piltdown fossil. Again and again in their discussion, they pointed out the modern characteristics of the skull and the simian appearance of the mandible. Their comments regarding the modernity of the skull and the apelike characteristics of the jaw, as you will see, turned out to be accurate in a way that few suspected at the time.

Additional discoveries were made at Piltdown. In 1913 a right canine tooth apparently belonging to the jaw was discovered by Teilhard de Chardin. It matched almost exactly the canine that had previously been proposed for the Piltdown skull in the reconstruction produced at the British Museum of Natural History. Its apelike form and wear were precisely what had been expected: "If a comparative anatomist were fitting out *Eoanthropus* with a set of canines, he could not ask for anything more suitable than the tooth in question," stated Yale University professor George Grant MacCurdy (1914: 159).

Additional artifacts, including a large bone implement, were found in 1914. Then, in 1915, Dawson wrote Woodward announcing spectacular evidence confirming the first discovery; fragments of another fossil human skull were found (possibly at a site just two miles from the first—Dawson never revealed the location). This skull, dubbed Piltdown II, looked just like the first with a rounded profile and thick cranial bones. Though no jaw was discovered, a molar recovered at the site bore the same pattern of wear as that seen in the first specimen.

Dawson died in 1916 and, for reasons not entirely clear, Woodward held back announcement of the second discovery until the following year. When the existence of a second specimen became known, many of those skeptical after the discovery of the first Piltdown fossil became supporters. One of those converted skeptics, Henry Fairfield Osborn, president of the American Museum of Natural History, suggested:

If there is a Providence hanging over the affairs of prehistoric man, it certainly manifested itself in this case, because the three minute fragments of this second Piltdown man found by Dawson are exactly those which we should have selected to confirm the comparison with the original type. (1921:581)

THE PILTDOWN ENIGMA

There certainly was no unanimity of opinion, however, concerning the significance of the Piltdown discoveries. The cranium was so humanlike and the jaw so apelike that some scientists maintained that they simply were the fossils of two different creatures; the skeptics suggested that the association of the human cranium and ape jaw was entirely coincidental. Gerrit S. Miller, Jr. (1915) of the Smithsonian Institution conducted a detailed analysis of casts of Piltdown I and concluded that the jaw was certainly that of an ape (See Figure 3). Many other scientists in the United States and Europe agreed. Anatomy professor David Waterson (1913) at the University of London, King's College, thought the mandible was that of a chimpanzee. The very well-known German scientist Franz Weidenreich concluded that Piltdown I was " . . . the artificial combination of fragments of a modern-human braincase with an orangutan-like mandible and teeth" (1943:273).

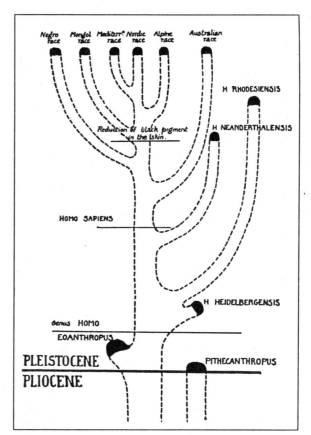

Figure 5 *Among its supporters,* Eoanthropus (Piltdown Man) *was seen as more directly ancestral to modern humanity than either* Homo erectus—*here labeled* Pithecanthropus *and depicted as an entirely separate evolutionary pathway—or Neandertal—shown here as a short-lived diversion off the main branch of human evolution. (From* The Evolution of Man, *Grafton Elliot Smith, Oxford University Press)*

Coincidentally or not, after Dawson's death no further discoveries were made in either the Piltdown I or II localities, though Woodward continued excavating at Piltdown through the 1920s. Elsewhere in the world, however, human paleontology became an increasingly exciting and fruitful endeavor. Beginning in the late 1920s as many as forty individuals of a species now called *Homo erectus* were unearthed at Zhoukoudian, a cave near Beijing in China (see Figure 1). Ironically, Davidson Black, anatomist at the Peking Union Medical College, who was instrumental in obtaining financial support for the excavation, had visited Grafton Elliot Smith's laboratory in 1914 and had become fascinated by the Piltdown find (Shapiro 1974). Further, Teilhard de Chardin participated in the excavation at the cave. The Zhoukoudian fossils were estimated to be one-half million years old. Also on Java,

another large group of fossils (close to twenty) were found at Sangiran; these were similar to those from Zhoukoudian.

Also in the 1920s, in Africa, the discovery was made of a fossil given the name *Australopithecus africanus.* It was initially estimated to be more than one million years old. In the 1930s and 1940s additional finds of this and other varieties of *Australopithecus* were made. In Europe the number of Neandertal specimens kept increasing; and even in England, in 1935, a fossil human ancestor was discovered at a place called Swanscombe.

Unfortunately for *Eoanthropus,* all of these discoveries seemed to contradict its validity. The Chinese and Sangiran *Homo erectus* evidence pointed to a fossil ancestor with a humanlike body and primitive head; these specimens were quite similar to Java Man in appearance (Java Man is also now considered to belong to the species *Homo erectus*), possessing large brow ridges, a flat skull, and a thrust-forward face while being quite modern from the neck down. Even the much older australopithecines showed clear evidence of walking on two feet; their skeletons were remarkably humanlike from the neck down, though their heads were quite apelike. Together, both of these species seemed to confirm the notion that human beings began their evolutionary history as upright apes, not as apelike people. *Eoanthropus* seemed more and more to be the evolutionary "odd man out."

How could Piltdown be explained in light of the new fossil evidence from China, Java, Europe, and Africa? Either Piltdown was a human ancestor, rendering all the manifold other discoveries members of extinct offshoots of the main line of human evolution, or else Piltdown was the remarkable coincidental find of the only known ape fossil in England within a few feet of a rather modern human skull that seemed to date back 500,000 years. Neither explanation sat well with many people.

UNMASKING THE HOAX

This sort of confusion characterized the status of Piltdown until 1949, when a new dating procedure was applied to the fossil. A measurement was made of the amount of the element fluorine in the bones. This was known to be a relative measure of the amount of time bone had been in the ground. Bones pick up fluorine in groundwater; the longer they have been buried, the more fluorine they have. Kenneth Oakley of the British Museum of Natural History conducted the test. While the fossil animal bones from the site showed varying amounts of fluorine, they exhibited as much as ten times more than did either the cranium or jaw of the fossil human. Piltdown Man, Oakley concluded, based on comparison to fluorine concentrations in bones at other sites in England, was no more than 50,000 years old (Oakley and Weiner 1955).

While this certainly cast Piltdown in a new light, the implications were just as mysterious; what was a fossil human doing with an entirely apelike jaw at a date as recent as 50,000 years ago? Then, in 1953 a more precise test was applied to larger samples of the cranium and jaw. The results were quite conclusive; the skull and jaw were of entirely different ages. The cranium possessed .10 percent fluorine, the mandible less than .03 percent (Oakley 1976). The inevitable conclusion was reached that the skull and jaw must have belonged to two different creatures.

As a result of this determination, a detailed reexamination of the fossil was conducted and the sad truth was finally revealed. The entire thing had been a hoax. The skull was that of a modern human being. Its appearance of age was due, at least in part, to its having been artificially chemically stained. The thickness of the bone may have been due to a pathological condition (Spencer 1984) or the result of a chemical treatment that had been applied, perhaps to make it appear older than it was (Montague 1960).

Those scientific supporters of *Eoanthropus* who previously had pointed out the apelike character of the jaw were more right than they could have imagined; it was, indeed, a doctored ape jaw, probably that of an orangutan. When Gerrit Miller of the Smithsonian Institution had commented on the broken condyle of the mandible by saying, "Deliberate malice could hardly have been more successful than the hazards of deposition in so breaking the fossils as to give free scope to individual judgement in fitting the parts together" (1915:1), he was using a literary device and not suggesting that anyone had purposely broken the jaw. But that is likely precisely what happened. An ape's jaw could never articulate with the base of a human skull, and so the area of connection had to be removed to give "free scope" to researchers to hypothesize how the cranium and jaw went together. Otherwise the hoax would never have succeeded. Beyond this, the molars had been filed down to artificially create the humanlike wear pattern. The canine tooth had been

stained with an artist's pigment and filed down to simulate human wear; the pulp cavity had been filled with a substance not unlike chewing gum.

It was further determined that at least one of the fragments of the Piltdown II skull was simply another piece of the first one. Oakley further concluded that all the other paleontological specimens had been planted at the site; some were probably found in England, but others had likely originated as far away as Malta and Tunisia. Some of the ostensible bone artifacts had been carved with a metal knife.

The verdict was clear; as Franz Weidenreich (1943) put it, Piltdown was like the chimera of Greek mythology—a monstrous combination of different creatures. The question of Piltdown's place in human evolution had been answered: it had no place. That left still open two important questions: who did it and why?

WHODUNNIT?

The most succinct answer that can be provided for the question "Whodunnit?" is "No one knows." It seems, however, that every writer on the subject has had a different opinion.

Each of the men who excavated at Piltdown has been accused at one time or another. . . . Charles Dawson is an obvious suspect. He is the only person who was present at every discovery. He certainly gained notoriety; even the species name is *dawsoni*. Blinderman (1986) points out, however, that much of the evidence against Dawson is circumstantial and exaggerated. Dawson did indeed stain the fossil with potassium bichromate and iron ammonium sulfate. These gave the bones a more antique appearance, but such staining was fairly common. It was felt that these chemicals helped preserve fossil bone, and Dawson was quite open about having stained the Piltdown specimens. In an unrelated attack on his character, some have even accused Dawson of plagiarism in a book he wrote on Hastings Castle (Weiner 1955), but this seems to be unfair; as Blinderman points out, the book was explicitly a compilation of previous sources and Dawson did not attempt to take credit for the work of others.

Dawson's motive might have been the fame and notoriety that accrued to this amateur scientist who could command the attention of the world's most famous scholars. But there is no direct evidence concerning Dawson's guilt, and questions remain concerning his ability to fashion the fraud. And where would Dawson have obtained the orangutan jaw?

Arthur Smith Woodward certainly possessed the opportunity and expertise to pull off the fraud. His motive might have been to prove his particular view of human evolution. That makes little sense though, since he could not have expected the kind of confirming evidence he knew his colleagues would demand. Furthermore, his behavior after Dawson's death seems to rule out Woodward as the hoaxer. His fruitlessly working the original Piltdown pit in his retirement renders this scenario nonsensical.

Even the priest Teilhard de Chardin has been accused, most recently by Harvard paleontologist and chronicler of the history of science Stephen Jay Gould (1980). The evidence marshalled against the Jesuit is entirely circumstantial, the argument strained. The mere facts that Teilhard mentioned Piltdown but little in his later writings on evolution and was confused about the precise chronology of discoveries in the pit do not add up to a convincing case.

Others have had fingers pointed at them. W. J. Sollas, a geology professor at Oxford and a strong supporter of Piltdown, has been accused from beyond the grave. In 1978, a tape-recorded statement made before his death by J. A. Douglass, who had worked in Sollas's lab for some thirty years, was made public. The only evidence provided is Douglass's testimony that on one occasion he came across a package containing the fossil-staining agent potassium bichromate in the lab—certainly not the kind of stuff to convince a jury to convict.

Even Sir Arthur Conan Doyle has come under the scrutiny of would-be Piltdown detectives. Doyle lived near Piltdown and is known to have visited the site at least once. He may have held a grudge against professional scientists who belittled his interest in and credulity concerning the paranormal. Doyle, the creator of the most logical, rational mind in literature, Sherlock Holmes, found it quite reasonable that two young English girls could take photographs of real fairies in their garden. But why would Doyle strike out at paleontologists, who had nothing to do with criticizing his acceptance of the occult? Again, there is no direct evidence to implicate Doyle in the hoax.

The most recent name added to the roster of potential Piltdown hoaxers is that of Lewis Abbott, another amateur scientist and artifact collector. Blinderman (1986) argues that Abbott is the most likely perpetrator. He had an enormous ego and felt slighted by professional scientists. He claimed to have been the one who directed Dawson to the pit at Piltdown and may even have been with Dawson when Piltdown II was discovered (Dawson said only that he had been with a friend when the bones were found). Abbott knew how to make stone tools and so was capable of forging those found at Piltdown. Again, however, the evidence, though tantalizing, includes no smoking gun.

A definitive answer to the question "whodunnit" may never be forthcoming. The lesson in Piltdown, though, is clear. Unlike the case for the Cardiff Giant where scientists were not fooled, here many were convinced by what appears to be, in hindsight, an inelegant fake. It shows quite clearly that scientists, though striving to be objective observers and explainers of the world around them, are, in the end, human. Many accepted the Piltdown evidence because they wished to—it supported a more comfortable view of human evolution. Furthermore, perhaps out of naïveté, they could not even conceive that a fellow thinker about human origins would wish to trick them; the possibility that Piltdown was a fraud probably occurred to few, if any, of them.

Nevertheless, the Piltdown story, rather than being a black mark against science, instead shows how well it ultimately works. Even before its unmasking, Piltdown had been consigned by most to a netherworld of doubt. There was simply too much evidence supporting a different human pedigree than that implied by Piltdown. Proving it a hoax was just the final nail in the coffin lid for this fallacious fossil. As a result, though we may never know the hoaxer's name, at least we know this: if the goal was to forever confuse our understanding of the human evolutionary story, the hoax ultimately was a failure.

CURRENT PERSPECTIVES HUMAN EVOLUTION

With little more than a handful of cranial fragments, human paleontologists defined an entire species, *Eoanthropus,* and recast the story of human evolution. Later, in 1922, on the basis of a single fossil tooth found in Nebraska, an ancient species of man, *Hesperopithecus,* was defined. It was presumed to be as old as any hominid species found in the Old World and convinced some that then-current evolutionary models needed to be overhauled. The tooth turned out to belong to an ancient pig. Even in the case of Peking Man, the species was defined and initially named *Sinanthropus pekinensis* on the basis of only two teeth.

Today, the situation in human paleontology is quite different. The tapestry of our human evolutionary history is no longer woven with the filaments of a small handful of gauzy threads. We can now base our evolutionary scenarios (Figure 6) on enormous quantities of data supplied by several fields of science (see Feder and Park 1989 for a detailed summary of current thinking on human evolution).

Australopithecus afarensis, for example, the oldest known hominid, dating to more than 3.5 million years ago, is represented by more than a dozen fossil individuals. The most famous specimen, known as "Lucy," is more than 40 percent complete. Its pelvis is remarkably modern and provides clear evidence of its upright, and therefore

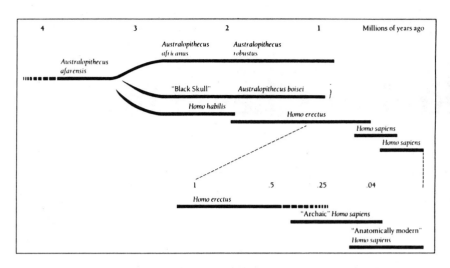

Figure 6 *Current human evolutionary chronologies are based on a large body of paleontological, archaeological, and genetic data. There is no room for—and no need for—a precociously large-brained human ancestor like* Eoanthropus *in the human pedigree. (From* Human Antiquity, *Feder and Park, Mayfield Publishing)*

humanlike, posture. Its skull, on the other hand, is quite apelike and contained a brain the size of a chimpanzee's. We even have a preserved pathway of footprints dating to the time when Lucy and her cohorts walked the earth, showing as dramatically as possible that they did so in a bipedal, humanlike fashion.

Homo erectus is known from dozens of individuals—forty from Zhoukoudian alone, nearly twenty from Java, and more than a dozen from Africa. In Kenya, the 80 percent complete skeleton of a twelve-year-old *Homo erectus* boy has been dated to more than 1.5 million years ago.

Archaic forms of *Homo sapiens,* especially the famous Neandertals, number in the hundreds. The fossil human record is rich and growing. Our evolutionary scenarios are based, not on a handful of fragmentary bones, but on the remains of hundreds of individuals. Grafton Elliot Smith, Arthur Smith Woodward, and the others were quite wrong. The abundant evidence shows very clearly that human evolutionary history is characterized by the precedence of upright posture and the tardy development of the brain. It now appears that while our ancestors developed upright posture and humanlike bodies more than 3.5 million years ago, the modern human brain did not develop until as recently as 100,000 years ago.

Beyond this, human paleontologists are no longer restricted solely to the paleontological record. Exciting techniques of genetic analysis have allowed scientists to develop measures of difference between living species, including humans and our nearest extant relatives, the apes. Genetic "clocks" have been created from the results of such techniques.

For example, through DNA hybridization, scientists can quantify the difference between the genetic codes of people and chimpanzees. Here, an attempt is made to bond human and chimp DNA, much in the way the separate strands of the DNA double helix bond to produce the genetic code for a single organism. It turns out that the DNA of our two species is so similar that we can form a nearly complete bond. The opinion of most is that our two species could have split evolutionarily no more than five or six million years ago.

New dating techniques based on radioactive half-lives, biomechanical analysis of bones, scanning electron microscopy in bone and artifact examination, and many other new forms of analysis all make our evolutionary scenarios more concrete. It is to be expected that ideas will change as new data are collected and new analytical techniques are developed. Certainly our current views will be fine-tuned, and perhaps even drastic changes of opinion will take place. This is the nature of science. It is fair to suggest, however, that no longer could a handful of enigmatic bones that contradicted our mutually supportive paleontological, cultural, and genetic data bases cause us to unravel and reweave our evolutionary tapestry. Today, the discovery of a Piltdown Man likely would fool few.

A Skull to Chew On

A cranium from northern Kenya forces some rethinking of the human family tree

Donald C. Johanson

Paleoanthropologist Donald C. Johanson attained worldwide fame for the discovery of "Lucy," a fossil skeleton from the Afar region of Ethiopia. Founder and president of the Institute of Human Origins in Berkeley, California, Johanson is coauthor, with James Shreeve, of Lucy's Child *(New York: William Morrow and Co., 1989).*

The Black Skull (or KNM-WT 17000, as it is formally called) was recovered in the summer of 1985, in the desolate wastes west of Africa's Lake Turkana, where it was first identified by Alan Walker, of Johns Hopkins University. The skull—more properly a cranium because the mandible is missing—has been stained blue black by manganese-rich minerals. It has cheekbones like stout flying buttresses, a projecting face, and a swept-back braincase with a prominent longitudinal (or sagittal) crest, presenting an overall architecture reminiscent of a Boeing blueprint. The *International Herald Tribune* called it "the 'most exciting' discovery in the evolution of early man in years." Nevertheless, the truth is that it represents a dead end on the tree of human evolution. So why all the fuss about a creature that wasn't even our ancestor?

When I first laid eyes on a cast of the Black Skull, I was immediately impressed by its mixture of advanced and primitive traits. By advanced traits I don't mean more humanlike ones but simply specialized characteristics, indicating that the anatomy has diverged from the ancestral condition. On the one hand, the projecting face, very small cranial capacity, cresting pattern on the rear of the cranium, and a host of other features recall the more ancient species *Australopithecus afarensis,* which includes the well-known skeleton Lucy. On the other hand, the prominent sagittal crest, the dish-shaped (flat, concave) face, and enormous molars and premolars (inferred from the large tooth roots) are typical of later creatures known as robust australopithecines.

With their massive jaws, greatly enlarged chewing muscles, and huge crushing and grinding cheek teeth, the robust australopithecines were once successful members of the hominid family—the group that includes humans and their extinct close relatives. Their distinctive cranial architecture was forged by natural selection to process a tough, fibrous, vegetarian diet. Robert Broom first recognized this adaptation in fossils from South Africa, which he christened *Paranthropus robustus,* meaning a "robust near relative of man." In 1959, Mary Leakey found an East African version at Olduvai Gorge that was first named *Zinjanthropus boisei* by Louis Leakey. (*Zinj* derives from an Arabic word that means "East Africa," and *boisei* honors Charles Boise, who financed the work at Olduvai.) Most anthropologists now lump these two species in the genus *Australopithecus,* but there is an increasing tendency to use Broom's genus, *Paranthropus.*

When Frank Brown, of the University of Utah, a recognized expert on the geology of the Lake Turkana Basin, reported an age of roughly 2.5 million years for the Black Skull, there were lots of raised eyebrows in the anthropological community. Hominid fossils in East Africa from between 2 and 3 million years ago are exceedingly rare, so the Black Skull was a welcome addition to the fossil record. At the same time, it called into question many people's pet theories concerning the timing and manner of change in hominid evolution.

In 1979, Tim White, my colleague at the University of California, Berkeley, and I had proposed a version of the human family tree in which we placed *A. afarensis,* at 3.5 to 3 million years ago, at the base of a simple Y pattern. We considered it to be the primitive, generalized species ancestral to both the robust australopithecines and the genus *Homo* (the line culminating in modern humans). There was a limited choice of fossils to guide us in the interval between late *A. afarensis* and the good samples of fossil hominids a million years later. Perhaps the most controversial aspect of our tree was how we treated *A. africanus,* a "gracile" australopithecine species discovered by Raymond Dart in South Africa and dated between *A. afarensis* and the robust australopithecines. Others considered this fossil species to be, if anything, on the line leading to *Homo,* but we saw it as ancestral exclusively to the robust australopithecines. In my opinion, *A. africanus,* with its heavily buttressed mandible and expanded chewing teeth, forecasts the vegetarian specialization of the robust forms.

At that time we placed all the robust types in a single species, but the East

African vegetarians have a distinctive facial anatomy, as well as larger cheek teeth and stronger cresting patterns than their South African relatives. They are sometimes called hyperrobust. Yoel Rak, of Tel Aviv University, subsequently convinced us we should therefore distinguish two species—*A. robustus* in South Africa and *A. boisei* in East Africa.

This is the way things stood until the Black Skull appeared, forcing anthropologists to go back to the blackboard and draw some new family trees. The first task was to establish the relationship of the Black Skull to the other robust types. To resolve this, Walker and his colleagues looked at the degree of anatomical resemblance of forty features common to the Black Skull and other species of *Australopithecus*. This is standard procedure—the more traits that are shared between any two species, the more trust we have that there is a close evolutionary relationship between them. This exercise led Walker and his colleagues to conclude that "for most of the features the new specimen resembles *A. boisei.*"

Using that list as a guide, Bill Kimbel, of the Institute of Human Origins, Tim White, and I embarked on a similar exercise incorporating thirty-two cranial features (some were also on Walker's list, but we added a few and combined those we felt were redundant). In some respects our conclusions were similar. Since twelve of the traits of the Black Skull were shared with both *boisei* and *robustus* (and not with other hominids), the robust nature of the skull was certain. But we felt it could not be tied exclusively to either species: of the remaining traits, the Black Skull shared only two exclusively with *boisei*. What most surprised us was the close relationship between the Black Skull and *afarensis:* they shared a total of twelve of the remaining traits.

The Black Skull thus seemed to us a potential evolutionary link between *afarensis* and the later *robustus* and *boisei.* The timing was also right—at 2.5 million years, the Black Skull was also intermediate in age. Calling it *afarensis* would obscure the evolutionary importance of the enigmatic cranium as much as calling it *boisei.* This sort of reasoning prompted a number of anthropologists to say, "If you don't give this thing a new name when you publish it, someone else will."

In their paper, Walker and his colleagues had referred to a nearly forgotten robust mandible, found in 1967 in the Omo River deposits in southern Ethiopia, that was identical in geological age to the Black Skull. It had been named *A. aethiopicus* to distinguish it from other robust forms. They suggested that if future finds justified a species distinction for the Black Skull, then the name *A. aethiopicus* would be the appropriate choice. But they believed the Black Skull was an early member of a distinct line leading to *boisei* and thought it unwise to give different names to successive parts of a continuous evolutionary lineage.

This is one of the problems in naming different parts of a continuum. On the scale from black to white, there are innumerable shades of gray, but at the ends of the scale, black and white are very distinct. Walker and his associates saw the Black Skull and *boisei* as two shades of gray. But we saw the differences as black and white, and so went with the designation *A. aethiopicus.* Although any tie between the toothless old mandible from Ethiopia and the new cranium is at best tenuous, most anthropologists appear satisfied with this decision. To be sure, when intermediates are recognized between *aethiopicus* and *boisei,* this distinction will become less clear.

The evolutionary implications of the Black Skull are far more important than the nomenclature debates. KNM-WT 17000 is the oldest robust fossil ever found. This means it could be ancestral to *boisei* or *robustus* or possibly both. Even more important, the South African *A. aficanus* lacks the primitive features shared by *afarensis* and *aethiopicus* and can no longer be considered an ancestor to all the robust forms.

In the process of redrawing the human family tree, we generated a number of plausible hypotheses. The discovery of the Black Skull does not alter the position of *A. afarensis* as the last common ancestor of all the later hominids. Some researchers have argued that another hominid ancestor lived at the same time as *afarensis,* but at the moment there is no convincing evidence. Others have argued that the *afarensis* fossils may themselves represent more than one species, but we remain confident of our original interpretation. But after *afarensis,* what?

I lean toward the view that *A. africanus* is the ancestor of *A. robustus,* and *A. aethiopicus* is the ancestor of *A. boisei.* An interesting implication of this view is that the specialized features that characterize these robust hominids evolved independently in East and South Africa. We call this parallel evolution: descendants of a common ancestor diverge and subsequently evolve similar adaptations independently.

The development of a robust, vegetarian specialization was a viable hominid adaptation. Although we are not certain exactly when our robust relatives died out, the last of their fossils date to about 1.2 million years ago in East Africa, while those in South Africa may be slightly younger than 1 million years old. In terms of our existence, it is humbling to think that they survived for more than 1.5 million years and still went extinct. If, as I believe, the robust adaptation arose twice, then both times it met with extinction.

Most monkeys and apes are plant eaters. The vegetarian specialization of our robust relatives was a continuation of a longstanding dietary adaptation and feeding strategy among hundreds of species of primates. Perhaps the real lesson we can learn from the Black Skull is the reminder that we, *Homo sapiens,* are clinging to a side branch of the primate family tree.

The Pulse That Produced Us

Two major global coolings may have prodded antelopes and humans to evolve

Elisabeth S. Vrba

Elisabeth S. Vrba attended the University of Cape Town, graduating in 1964 with a B.S. in zoology and mathematical statistics. She earned her doctorate in paleontology from the University of Cape Town in 1974 and is now a professor of geology and geophysics at Yale University, as well as an adjunct professor of biology there.

Earth's crust and atmosphere change constantly, and wedged in between them like a sandwich filling, life evolves as well. To what extent are extinction and speciation—the evolution of new species out of ancestral populations—tied to geophysical changes? Did humans originate in response to some identifiable cosmic or climatic event?

Charles Darwin, in an 1838 notebook, noted that "man is a species produced like any other—lawfully." To learn more about our own origins, I have looked for evolutionary patterns in other organisms that lived at the dawn of humanity. Antelopes are good animals to examine for clues because they are reliable indicators of past environments and shared the African savanna with our early ancestors, the australopithecines, or man-apes. Conveniently, antelopes make up 60 to 80 percent of all large mammal fossils found in the same strata as hominids, the family of primates that includes australopithecines and humans.

About twenty years ago, as a South African paleontologist studying the Transvaal's limestone caves, I first noticed that somewhere in the fossil deposits between 2.5 million and 2 million years ago, antelopes and other animals changed strikingly. Anatomical features such as teeth indicated that antelopes living before 2.5 million years ago had occupied moist woodlands. Shortly afterward, however, these forest antelopes disappeared and were replaced by many new species that graze only in dry, open savannas.

About 2.5 million years ago global temperatures may have plummeted by as much as 10° to 20°F, colder than at any time in the past 65 million years.

But because the Transvaal cave strata were jumbles of washed-in bones, the sequence was not reliable and had to be dated by being compared with deposits elsewhere. Some years later, in East Africa, other researchers found similar fossils in deposits that could be dated by radiometric techniques. Several independent studies have since confirmed that the same kind of faunal change that took place in South Africa also occurred in Ethiopia, Kenya, and Tanzania close to 2.5 million years ago.

Such a dramatic change in large fauna, and by inference in vegetation, is one line of evidence that southern Africa became significantly drier about 2.5 million years ago. I wondered if this was a purely local phenomenon and whether the change was slow or rapid. A 1980s study of deep-sea cores near Greenland by Nick Shackleton, of Cambridge University, contributed some answers. Shackleton discovered abundant evidence for an extensive arctic glaciation dated close to 2.5 million years ago.

During that period, global temperatures may have plummeted by as much as 10° to 20°F, and the world became colder than at any time in the past 65 million years. The continents became much more arid, and the steppes advanced toward the equator. The earliest fossils of *Oryx*, the most arid-adapted antelopes of all, appeared along with other grazers of open savannas, such as the giant buffaloes *Pelorovis* and giant hartebeests *Megalotragus*. These species soon extended their ranges from southern and eastern Africa toward the equator, where we find fossil testimony of their presence. Steppe and grassland horses, *Equus*, from Europe moved east into India and Pakistan. They also migrated south into Africa, together with Asian forms like the Indian black buck, *Antilope cervicapra*, but while the horses evolved into several varieties of zebras, the Asian antelopes did not last long in Africa.

A similar, earlier cooling also seemed to affect all of sub-Saharan Africa about 5 million years ago, close to the Miocene-Pliocene boundary. Climatologists John Mercer and James Kennett and paleoanthropologist C. K. Brain have documented marked swings in the global climate at that time, with widespread continental cooling and the lowering and retreat of oceans. We also know that the Mediterranean dried up, leaving massive salt deposits, and that thousands of miles of savannas opened up at the expense of forests on several continents. This earlier cooling also produced waves of extinctions and radiations of species, giving rise to the seven major groups of antelopes that still dominate the African savannas today. Within these groups, however, many species went extinct at the later cooling 2.5 million years ago.

How did our primate ancestors fare during these climatic changes in South Africa? About 5 million years ago, the first proliferation of antelope species coincided with the occurrence of the first australopithecines in East Africa—perhaps their first appearance on the planet. Before that time, large primates were apish forest dwellers that shared their leafy refuges with ancestral antelopes. In between the 5-million-year-old deposits and those 2.5 million years old, the only known hominids are the lightly built australopithecines, five-foot-tall, bipedal primates with ape-sized brains and upright posture. After 2.5 million years ago, however, we see evidence of an explosive radiation among hominids. Apparently several different species appeared; paleoanthropologists are still arguing about how many. Clark Howell, of the University of California at Berkeley, for instance, thinks there were five or six. Among them were the large, vegetarian manape *Paranthropus* and various members of the human genus, Homo—who thrived with the further spread of dry grasslands and the continued shrinking of forest habitats. Other evidence of new kinds of hominids include the first-known robust australopithecine

fossil, the Black Skull, found by Richard Leakey and Alan Walker near Kenya's Lake Turkana and the oldest-known fragment of a *Homo* species, from Lake Beringo, Kenya, dated by Andrew Hill's group at Yale to 2.5 million years ago.

The archeological record of artifacts offers additional corroboration of dramatic change. Stone tools from Ethiopia—the earliest yet discovered—date to between 2.4 and 2.6 million years ago. Using tools to obtain and prepare food was an important innovation for hominids and indicates increased brain size and function.

The British ecologist Evelyn Hutchinson once referred to the "evolutionary theater and the ecological play." Halfway through the hominid play that began 5 million years ago, something happened that pushed most of the old cast members (including the small-bodied australopithecines) off the stage and introduced new ones (such as *Homo* species)—a process I call turnover-pulse. I believe that when we better understand the events at the Miocene-Pliocene boundary, we will find that the appearance of the australopithecines was only one part of a global turnover of species, one of the recurrent pulses in the history of life.

New species of primates, antelopes, birds, and carnivores may all have originated in response to several successive cooling plunges during the later Miocene. Many African lineages survived the climatic changes intact, but those that underwent extinctions and speciations appear to have done so in concert with others: plants, hominoids, antelopes, rodents, and such marine invertebrates as snails and foraminifera. All the evidence, as I see it, indicates that the lineage of upright primates known as australopithecines, the first hominids, was one of the founding groups of the great African savanna biota.

My hypothesis that the same climatic pulses dramatically stimulated both antelope and human evolution has increasingly gained support from specialists studying many disparate creatures. A decade ago, paleontologist

Hank Wesselman discovered a rapid pulse of extinctions and speciations in African rodents at the 2.5-million-year mark. In addition, Raymonde Bonefille, of Marseille, has found that pollens in Ethiopa show that there was a simultaneous "turnover" of many plant species. In each case, the pattern is wholly consistent with global cooling, increased glaciation, a shrinking of wet, forested country, and the rise of vast, dry grasslands. Animal species everywhere either moved, bowed out, or evolved into new groups, as Italian paleontologist Augusto Azzaroli has demonstrated for many lineages of Eurasian mammals, including deer, cattle, various carnivores, and rodents.

During a climatic shift, species may either find some safety as generalists, or they may cling unchanged to the shrinking habitats in which they evolved.

According to the classic Darwinian view, the "engine" that drives the evolution of species is competition between organisms; extinctions occur when species outcompete others for the same resources. If one were to represent each species as a star that lights up in the sky, the Darwinian model would show some stars appearing and others going dark in a fairly random pattern. But the fossil record appears to tell a different tale. Species seem to arise and vanish in pulses of varying intensities, with many appearing and others disappearing at the same time. Some of these pulses would appear to be dim, while others would light up the heavens.

As a rain forest or grassland shifts or disappears, diminishing animal populations can remain unchanged within the shrinking habitats in which they evolved, perhaps expanding again when and if a favorable climate returns. On the other hand, if conditions are right, evolution within the threatened population may produce a new species. According to the scenario first proposed by Harvard biologist Ernst Mayr in the 1940s, an animal species may occupy an extensive geographic range until major changes in rainfall, temperature, or geographical boundaries break the population into smaller, isolated groups. These "island populations" cease to trade genes, and eventually some may diverge sufficiently to form the cores of new species. Without

the impetus of environmental pulses, most species and ecosystems seem to remain in equilibrium most of the time and resist change until they are pushed.

I see the biosphere as a living layer, stretched thinly over the globe, responding rhythmically to the beat of the earth. During a climatic shift, species may either find some safety as generalists, able to tolerate a wide range of foods and conditions, or they may cling unchanged to the shrinking habitats in which they evolved. In the long

run, however, both of these strategies may lead to dead ends. If a lineage's evolutionary success is measured by the production of many diverse species, then the successful gamblers on speciation are the big winners. Our ancestral species, the early australopithecines, entered a narrow genetic corridor about 2.5 million years ago. They disappeared, but as the progenitors of novelty—ultimately including the most ubiquitous large mammal species on earth—they hit the jackpot.

us.

Sizing Up Human Intelligence

Stephen Jay Gould

HUMAN BODIES

"Size," Julian Huxley once remarked, "has a fascination of its own." We stock our zoos with elephants, hippopotamuses, giraffes, and gorillas; who among you was not rooting for King Kong in his various battles atop tall buildings? This focus on the few creatures larger than ourselves has distorted our conception of our own size. Most people think that *Homo sapiens* is a creature of only modest dimensions. In fact, humans are among the largest animals on earth; more than 99 percent of animal species are smaller than we are. Of 190 species in our own order of primate mammals, only the gorilla regularly exceeds us in size.

In our self-appointed role as planetary ruler, we have taken great interest in cataloging the features that permitted us to attain this lofty estate. Our brain, upright posture, development of speech, and group hunting (to name just a few) are often cited, but I have been struck by how rarely our large size has been recognized as a controlling factor of our evolutionary progress.

Despite its low reputation in certain circles, self-conscious intelligence is surely the *sine qua non* of our current status. Could we have evolved it at much smaller body sizes? One day, at the New York World's Fair in 1964, I entered the hall of Free Enterprise to escape the rain. Inside, prominently displayed, was an ant colony bearing the sign: "Twenty million years of evolutionary stagnation. Why? Because the ant colony is a socialist, totalitarian system." The statement scarcely requires serious attention; nonetheless, I should point out that ants are doing very well for themselves, and that it is their size rather than their social structure that precludes high mental capacity.

In this age of the transistor, we can put radios in watchcases and bug telephones with minute electronic packages. Such miniaturization might lead us to the false belief that absolute size is irrelevant to the operation of complex machinery. But nature does not miniaturize neurons (or other cells for that matter). The range of cell size among organisms is incomparably smaller than the range in body size. Small animals simply have far fewer cells than large animals. The human brain contains several billion neurons; an ant is constrained by its small size to have many hundreds of times fewer neurons.

There is, to be sure, no established relationship between brain size and intelligence among humans (the tale of Anatole France with a brain of less than 1,000 cubic centimeters vs. Oliver Cromwell with well above 2,000 is often cited). But this observation cannot be extended to differences between species and certainly not to ranges of sizes separating ants and humans. An efficient computer needs billions of circuits and an ant simply cannot contain enough of them because the relative constancy of cell size requires that small brains contain few neurons. Thus, our large body size served as a prerequisite for self-conscious intelligence.

We can make a stronger argument and claim that humans have to be just about the size they are in order to function as they do. In an amusing and provocative article (*American Scientist*, 1968), F. W. Went explored the impossibility of human life, as we know it, at ant dimensions (assuming for the moment that we could circumvent—which we cannot—the problem of intelligence and small brain size). Since weight increases so much faster than surface area as an object gets larger, small animals have very high ratios of surface to volume: they live in a world dominated by surface forces that affect us scarcely at all. . . .

An ant-sized man might don some clothing, but forces of surface adhesion would preclude its removal. The lower limit of drop size would make showering impossible; each drop would hit with the force of a large boulder. If our homunculus managed to get wet and tried to dry off with a towel, he would be stuck to it for life. He could pour no liquid, light no fire (since a stable flame must be several millimeters in length). He might pound gold leaf thin enough to construct a book for his size, but surface adhesion would prevent the turning of pages.

Our skills and behavior are finely attuned to our size. We could not be twice as tall as we are, for the kinetic energy of a fall would then be 16 to 32 times as great, and our sheer weight (increased eightfold) would be more than our legs could support. Human giants of eight to nine feet have either died young or been crippled early by failure of joints and bones. At half our size, we could not wield a club with sufficient force to hunt large animals (for kinetic energy would decrease 16 to 32-fold); we could not impart sufficient momentum to spears and arrows; we could not cut or split wood with primitive tools or mine minerals with picks and chisels. Since these all were essential activities in our historical development, we must conclude that the path of our evolution could only have been followed by a creature very close to our size. I do not argue that we inhabit the best of all possible worlds, only that our size has limited our activities and, to a great extent, shaped our evolution.

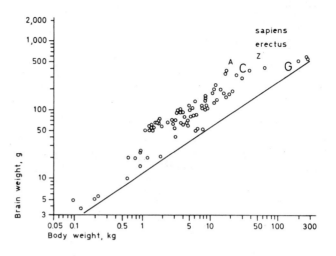

The correct criterion for assessing the superiority in size of our brains. The solid line represents the average relationship between brain weight and body weight for all body weights among mammals in general. Superiority in size is measured by upward deviation from this curve (i.e., "more" brain than an average mammal of the same body weight). Open circles represent primates (all have larger brains than average mammals). C is the chimpanzee, G the gorilla, and A the fossil hominid Australopithecus: erectus *covers the range of* Homo erectus *(Java and Peking Man);* sapiens *covers the field for modern humans. Our brains have the highest positive deviations of any mammal. (F. S. Szalay,* Approaches to Primate Paleobiology, *Contrib. Primat. Vol. 5, 1975, p. 267. Reproduced with the permission of S. Karger AG, Basel)*

HUMAN BRAINS

An average human brain weights about 1,300 grams (45.5 ounces); to accommodate such a large brain, we have bulbous, balloon-shaped heads unlike those of any other large mammal. Can we measure superiority by the size of our brains?

Elephants and whales have larger brains than ours. But this fact does not confer superior mental ability upon the largest mammals. Larger bodies need larger brains to coordinate their actions. We must find a way to remove the confusing influence of body size from our calculation. The computation of a simple ratio between brain weight and body weight will not work. Very small mammals generally have higher ratios than humans; that is, they have more brain per unit of body weight. Brain size does increase with body size, but it increases at a *much slower rate*.

If we plot brain weight against body weight for all species of adult mammals, we find that the brain increases at about two-thirds the rate of the body. Since surface areas also increase about two-thirds as fast as body weight, we

conjecture that brain weight is not regulated by body weight, but primarily by the body surfaces that serve as end points for so many innervations. This means that large animals may have absolutely larger brains than humans (because their bodies are bigger), and that small animals often have relatively larger brains than humans (because body size decreases more rapidly than brain size).

A plot of brain weight vs. body weight for adult mammals points the way out of our paradox. The correct criterion is neither absolute nor relative brain size—it is the difference between actual brain size and expected brain size at that body weight. To judge the size of our brain, we must compare it with the expected brain size for an average mammal of our body weight. On this criterion we are, as we had every right to expect, the brainiest mammal by far. No other species lies as far above the expected brain size for average mammals as we do.

This relationship between body weight and brain size provides important insights into the evolution of our brain. Our African ancestor (or at least close cousin), *Australopithecus afri-*

canus, had an average adult cranial capacity of only 450 cubic centimeters. Gorillas often have larger brains, and many authorities have used this fact to infer a distinctly prehuman mentality for *Australopithecus.* A recent textbook states: "The original bipedal apeman of South Africa had a brain scarcely larger than that of other apes and presumably possessed behavioral capacities to match." But *A. africanus* weighed only 50 to 90 pounds (female and male respectively—as estimated by Yale anthropologist David Pilbeam), while large male gorillas may weigh more than 600 pounds. We may safely state that *Australopithecus* had a much larger brain than other nonhuman primates, using the correct criterion of comparison with expected values for actual body weights.

The human brain is now about three times larger than that of *Australopithecus.* This increase has often been called the most rapid and most important event in the history of evolution. But our bodies have also increased greatly in size. Is this enlargement of the brain a simple consequence of bigger bodies or does it mark new levels of intelligence?

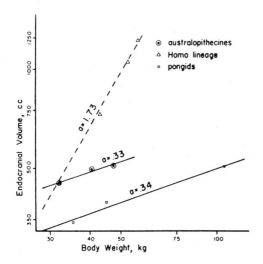

Evolutionary increase in human brain size (dotted line). The four triangles represent a rough evolutionary sequence: Australopithecus africanus, ER-1470 (Richard Leakey's new find with a cranial capacity just slightly less than 800 cc), Homo erectus (Peking Man), and Homo sapiens. The slope is the highest ever calculated for an evolutionary sequence. The two solid lines represent more conventional scaling of brain size in australopithecines (above) and great apes (below). ("Size and Scaling in Human Evolution," Pilbeam, David, and Gould, Stephen Jay, *Science* Vol. 186, pp. 892–901, Fig. 2, 6 December 1974. Copyright 1974 by the American Association for the Advancement of Science)

To answer this question, I have plotted cranial capacity against inferred body weight for the following fossil homids (representing, perhaps, our lineage): *Australopithecus africanus;* Richard Leakey's remarkable find with a cranial capacity of nearly 800 cubic centimeters and an antiquity of more than two million years (weight estimated by David Pillbeam from dimensions of the femur); *Homo erectus* from Choukoutien (Peking Man); and modern *Homo sapiens.* The graph indicates that our brain has increased much more rapidly than any prediction based on compensations for body size would allow.

My conclusion is not unconventional, and it does reinforce an ego that we would do well to deflate. Nonetheless, our brain has undergone a true increase in size not related to the demands of our larger body. We are, indeed, smarter than we were.

Scavenger Hunt

As paleoanthropologists close in on their quarry, it may turn out to be a different beast from what they imagined

Pat Shipman

Pat Shipman is an assistant professor in the Department of Cell Biology and Anatomy at The Johns Hopkins University School of Medicine.

In both textbooks and films, ancestral humans (hominids) have been portrayed as hunters. Small-brained, big-browed, upright, and usually mildly furry, early hominid males gaze with keen eyes across the gold savanna, searching for prey. Skillfully wielding a few crude stone tools, they kill and dismember everything from small gazelles to elephants, while females care for young and gather roots, tubers, and berries. The food is shared by group members at temporary camps. This familiar image of Man the Hunter has been bolstered by the finding of stone tools in association with fossil animal bones. But the role of hunting in early hominid life cannot be determined in the absence of more direct evidence.

I discovered one means of testing the hunting hypothesis almost by accident. In 1978, I began documenting the microscopic damage produced on bones by different events. I hoped to develop a diagnostic key for identifying the post-mortem history of specific fossil bones, useful for understanding how fossil assemblages were formed. Using a scanning electron microscope (SEM) because of its excellent resolution and superb depth of field, I inspected high-fidelity replicas of modern bones that

had been subjected to known events or conditions. (I had to use replicas, rather than real bones, because specimens must fit into the SEM's small vacuum chamber.) I soon established that such common events as weathering, root etching, sedimentary abrasion, and carnivore chewing produced microscopically distinctive features.

In 1980, my SEM study took an unexpected turn. Richard Potts (now of Yale University), Henry Bunn (now of the University of Wisconsin at Madison), and I almost simultaneously found what appeared to be stone-tool cut marks on fossils from Olduvai Gorge, Tanzania, and Koobi Fora, Kenya. We were working almost side by side at the National Museums of Kenya, in Nairobi, where the fossils are stored. The possibility of cut marks was exciting, since both sites preserve some of the oldest known archaeological materials. Potts and I returned to the United States, manufactured some stone tools, and started "butchering" bones and joints begged from our local butchers. Under the SEM, replicas of these cut marks looked very different from replicas of carnivore tooth scratches, regardless of the species of carnivore or the type of tool involved. By comparing the marks on the fossils with our hundreds of modern bones of known history, we were able to demonstrate convincingly that hominids using stone tools had processed carcasses of many different animals nearly two million years ago. For the first time, there was a firm link

between stone tools and at least some of the early fossil animal bones.

This initial discovery persuaded some paleoanthropologists that the hominid hunter scenario was correct. Potts and I were not so sure. Our study had shown that many of the cut-marked fossils also bore carnivore tooth marks and that some of the cut marks were in places we hadn't expected—on bones that bore little meat in life. More work was needed.

In addition to more data about the Olduvai cut marks and tooth marks, I needed specific information about the patterns of cut marks left by known hunters performing typical activities associated with hunting. If similar patterns occurred on the fossils, then the early hominids probably behaved similarly to more modern hunters; if the patterns were different, then the behavior was probably also different. Three activities related to hunting occur often enough in peoples around the world and leave consistent enough traces to be used for such a test.

First, human hunters systematically disarticulate their kills, unless the animals are small enough to be eaten on the spot. Disarticulation leaves cut marks in a predictable pattern on the skeleton. Such marks cluster near the major joints of the limbs: shoulder, elbow, carpal joint (wrist), hip, knee, and hock (ankle). Taking a carcass apart at the joints is much easier than breaking or cutting through bones. Disarticulation enables hunters to carry food back to a central place or camp, so that they can share it with others or cook it or even store it by placing portions in trees, away from the reach of carnivores. If early hominids were hunters who transported and shared their kills, disarticulation marks would occur near joints in frequencies comparable to those produced by modern human hunters.

Second, human hunters often butcher carcasses, in the sense of removing meat from the bones. Butchery marks are usually found on the shafts of bones from the upper part of the front or hind limb, since this is where the big muscle masses lie. Butchery may be carried out at the kill site—especially if the animal is very large and its bones very heavy—or it may take place at the base camp, during the process of sharing food with others. Compared with disarticulation, butchery leaves relatively few marks. It is hard for a hunter to locate an animal's joints without leaving cut marks on the bone. In contrast, it is easier to cut the meat away from the midshaft of the bone without making such marks. If early hominids shared their food, however, there ought to be a number of cut marks located on the midshaft of some fossil bones.

Finally, human hunters often remove skin or tendons from carcasses, to be used for clothing, bags, thongs, and so on. Hide or tendon must be separated from the bones in many areas where there is little flesh, such as the lower limb bones of pigs, giraffes, antelopes, and zebras. In such cases, it is difficult to cut the skin without leaving a cut mark on the bone. Therefore, one expects to find many more cut marks on such bones than on the flesh-covered bones of the upper part of the limbs.

Unfortunately, although accounts of butchery and disarticulation by modern human hunters are remarkably consistent, quantitative studies are rare. Further, virtually all modern hunter-gatherers use metal tools, which leave more cut marks than stone tools. For these reasons I hesitated to compare the fossil evidence with data on modern hunters. Fortunately, Diane Gifford of the University of California,

Santa Cruz, and her colleagues had recently completed a quantitative study of marks and damage on thousands of antelope bones processed by Neolithic (Stone Age) hunters in Kenya some 2,300 years ago. The data from Prolonged Drift, as the site is called, were perfect for comparison with the Olduvai material.

Assisted by my technician, Jennie Rose, I carefully inspected more than 2,500 antelope bones from Bed I at Olduvai Gorge, which is dated to between 1.9 and 1.7 million years ago. We made high-fidelity replicas of every mark that we thought might be either a cut mark or a carnivore tooth mark. Back in the United States, we used the SEM to make positive identifications of the marks. (The replication and SEM inspection was time consuming, but necessary: only about half of the marks were correctly identified by eye or by light microscope.) I then compared the patterns of cut mark and tooth mark distributions on Olduvai fossils with those made by Stone Age hunters at Prolonged Drift.

By their location, I identified marks caused either by disarticulation or meat removal and then compared their frequencies with those from Prolonged Drift. More than 90 percent of the Neolithic marks in these two categories were from disarticulation, but to my surprise, only about 45 percent of the corresponding Olduvai cut marks were from disarticulation. This difference is too great to have occurred by chance; the Olduvai bones did not show the predicted pattern. In fact, the Olduvai cut marks attributable to meat removal and disarticulation showed essentially the same pattern of distribution as the carnivore tooth marks. Apparently, the early hominids were not regularly disarticulating carcasses. This finding casts serious doubt on the idea that early hominids carried their kills back to camp to share with others, since both transport and sharing are difficult unless carcasses are cut up.

When I looked for cut marks attributable to skinning or tendon removal, a more modern pattern emerged. On both the Neolithic and Olduvai bones, nearly 75 percent of all cut marks

occurred on bones that bore little meat; these cut marks probably came from skinning. Carnivore tooth marks were much less common on such bones. Hominids were using carcasses as a source of skin and tendon. This made it seem more surprising that they disarticulated carcasses so rarely.

A third line of evidence provided the most tantalizing clue. Occasionally, sets of overlapping marks occur on the Olduvai fossils. Sometimes, these sets include both cut marks and carnivore tooth marks. Still more rarely, I could see under the SEM which mark had been made first, because its features were overlaid by those of the later mark, in much the same way as old tire tracks on a dirt road are obscured by fresh ones. Although only thirteen such sets of marks were found, in eight cases the hominids made the cut marks *after* the carnivores made their tooth marks. This finding suggested a new hypothesis. Instead of hunting for prey and leaving the remains behind for carnivores to scavenge, perhaps hominids were scavenging from the carnivores. This might explain the hominids' apparently unsystematic use of carcasses: they took what they could get, be it skin, tendon, or meat.

Man the Scavenger is not nearly as attractive an image as Man the Hunter, but it is worth examining. Actually, although hunting and scavenging are different ecological strategies, many mammals do both. The only pure scavengers alive in Africa today are vultures; not one of the modern African mammalian carnivores is a pure scavenger. Even spotted hyenas, which have massive, bone-crushing teeth well adapted for eating the bones left behind by others, only scavenge about 33 percent of their food. Other carnivores that scavenge when there are enough carcasses around include lions, leopards, striped hyenas, and jackals. Long-term behavioral studies suggest that these carnivores scavenge when they can and kill when they must. There are only two nearly pure predators, or hunters—the cheetah and the wild dog—that rarely, if ever, scavenge.

What are the costs and benefits of scavenging compared with those of predation? First of all, the scavenger avoids the task of making sure its meal is dead: a predator has already endured the energetically costly business of chasing or stalking animal after animal until one is killed. But while scavenging may be cheap, it's risky. Predators rarely give up their prey to scavengers without defending it. In such disputes, the larger animal, whether a scavenger or a predator, usually wins, although smaller animals in a pack may defeat a lone, larger animal. Both predators and scavengers suffer the dangers inherent in fighting for possession of a carcass. Smaller scavengers such as jackals or striped hyenas avoid disputes to some extent by specializing in darting in and removing a piece of a carcass without trying to take possession of the whole thing. These two strategies can be characterized as that of the bully or that of the sneak: bullies need to be large to be successful, sneaks need to be small and quick.

Because carcasses are almost always much rarer than live prey, the major cost peculiar to scavenging is that scavengers must survey much larger areas than predators to find food. They can travel slowly, since their "prey" is already dead, but endurance is important. Many predators specialize in speed at the expense of endurance, while scavengers do the opposite.

The more committed predators among the East African carnivores (wild dogs and cheetahs) can achieve great top speeds when running, although not for long. Perhaps as a consequence, these "pure" hunters enjoy a much higher success rate in hunting (about three-fourths of their chases end in kills) than any of the scavenger-hunters do (less than half of their chases are successful). Wild dogs and cheetahs are efficient hunters, but they are neither big enough nor efficient enough in their locomotion to make good scavengers. In fact, the cheetah's teeth are so specialized for meat slicing that they probably cannot withstand the stresses of bone crunching and carcass dismembering carried out by scavengers. Other carnivores are less successful at hunting, but have specializations of size, endurance, or

(in the case of the hyenas) dentition that make successful scavenging possible. The small carnivores seem to have a somewhat higher hunting success rate than the large ones, which balances out their difficulties in asserting possession of carcasses.

In addition to endurance, scavengers need an efficient means of locating carcasses, which, unlike live animals, don't move or make noises. Vultures, for example, solve both problems by flying. The soaring, gliding flight of vultures expends much less energy than walking or cantering as performed by the part-time mammalian scavengers. Flight enables vultures to maintain a foraging radius two to three times larger than that of spotted hyenas, while providing a better vantage point. This explains why vultures can scavenge all of their food in the same habitat in which it is impossible for any mammal to be a pure scavenger. (In fact, many mammals learn where carcasses are located from the presence of vultures.)

Since mammals can't succeed as fulltime scavengers, they must have another source of food to provide the bulk of their diet. The large carnivores rely on hunting large animals to obtain food when scavenging doesn't work. Their size enables them to defend a carcass against others. Since the small carnivores—jackals and striped hyenas—often can't defend carcasses successfully, most of their diet is composed of fruit and insects. When they do hunt, they usually prey on very small animals, such as rats or hares, that can be consumed in their entirety before the larger competitors arrive.

The ancient habitat associated with the fossils of Olduvai and Koobi Fora would have supported many herbivores and carnivores. Among the latter were two species of large saber-toothed cats, whose teeth show extreme adaptations for meat slicing. These were predators with primary access to carcasses. Since their teeth were unsuitable for bone crushing, the saber-toothed cats must have left behind many bones covered with scraps of meat, skin, and tendon. Were early hominids among the scavengers that exploited such carcasses?

All three hominid species that were present in Bed I times (*Homo habilis, Australopithecus africanus, A. robustus*) were adapted for habitual, upright bipedalism. Many anatomists see evidence that these hominids were agile tree climbers as well. Although upright bipedalism is a notoriously peculiar mode of locomotion, the adaptive value of which has been argued for years (see Matt Cartmill's article, "Four Legs Good, Two Legs Bad," *Natural History,* November 1983), there are three general points of agreement.

First, bipedal running is neither fast nor efficient compared to quadrupedal gaits. However, at moderate speeds of 2.5 to 3.5 miles per hour, bipedal *walking* is more energetically efficient than quadrupedal walking. Thus, bipedal walking is an excellent means of covering large areas slowly, making it an unlikely adaptation for a hunter but an appropriate and useful adaptation for a scavenger. Second, bipedalism elevates the head, thus improving the hominid's ability to spot items on the ground—an advantage both to scavengers and to those trying to avoid becoming a carcass. Combining bipedalism with agile tree climbing improves the vantage point still further. Third, bipedalism frees the hands from locomotive duties, making it possible to carry items. What would early hominids have carried? Meat makes a nutritious, easy-to-carry package; the problem is that carrying meat attracts scavengers. Richard Potts suggests that carrying stone tools or unworked stones for toolmaking to caches would be a more efficient and less dangerous activity under many circumstances.

In short, bipedalism is compatible with a scavenging strategy. I am tempted to argue that bipedalism evolved because it provided a substantial advantage to scavenging hominids. But I doubt hominids could scavenge effectively without tools, and bipedalism predates the oldest known stone tools by more than a million years.

Is there evidence that, like modern mammalian scavengers, early hominids had an alternative food source, such as either hunting or eating fruits and insects? My husband, Alan Walker, has shown that the microscopic wear on an animal's teeth reflects its diet. Early hominid teeth wear more like that of chimpanzees and other modern fruit eaters than that of carnivores. Apparently, early hominids ate mostly fruit, as the smaller, modern scavengers do. This accords with the estimated body weight of early hominids, which was only about forty to eighty pounds—less than that of any of the modern carnivores that combine scavenging and hunting but comparable to the striped hyena, which eats fruits and insects as well as meat.

Would early hominids have been able to compete for carcasses with other carnivores? They were too small to use a bully strategy, but if they scavenged in groups, a combined bully-sneak strategy might have been possible. Perhaps they were able to drive off a primary predator long enough to grab some meat, skin, or marrow-filled bone before relinquishing the carcass. The effectiveness of this strategy would have been vastly improved by using tools to remove meat or parts of limbs, a task at which hominid teeth are poor. As agile climbers, early hominids may have retreated into the trees to eat their scavenged trophies, thus avoiding competition from large terrestrial carnivores.

In sum, the evidence on cut marks, tooth wear, and bipedalism, together with our knowledge of scavenger adaptation in general, is consistent with the hypothesis that two million years ago hominids were scavengers rather than accomplished hunters. Animal carcasses, which contributed relatively little to the hominid diet, were not systematically cut up and transported for sharing at base camps. Man the Hunter may not have appeared until 1.5 to 0.7 million years ago, when we do see a shift toward omnivory, with a greater proportion of meat in the diet. This more heroic ancestor may have been *Homo erectus,* equipped with Acheulean-style stone tools and, increasingly, fire. If we wish to look further back, we may have to become accustomed to a less flattering image of our heritage.

Late Hominid Evolution

The most important aspect of human evolution is also the most difficult to decipher from the fossil evidence: our development as sentient, social beings capable of communicating by means of language. Although we may detect hints of incipient humanity in the form of crudely chipped tools, the telltale signs of a home base or the artistic achievements of ornaments and cave art, none of these indicators of a distinctly hominid way of life can provide us with the nuances of the everyday lives of these creatures, their social relations, or their supernatural beliefs, if any. Most of what remains is the rubble of the bones and stones from which we interpret what we can of their lifestyle, thought processes, and communicating ability. Our ability to glean from the fossil record is not completely without hope, however. In fact, informed speculation is what makes possible such articles as "Bamboo and Human Evolution" by Geoffrey Pope, "Hard Times Among the Neanderthals" by Erik Trinkaus, "Old Masters" by Pat Shipman, and "The Dawn of Adornment" by Randall White. Each is a fine example of the kind of careful, systematic, and thought-provoking work that is based upon an increased understanding of hominid fossil sites as well as the more general environmental circumstances in which our predecessors lived.

Beyond the technological and anatomical adaptations, questions have arisen as to how our hominid forebears organized themselves socially and whether or not modern-day human behavior is inherited as a legacy of our evolutionary past or is a learned product of contemporary circumstances. Attempts to address this issue have given rise to the technique referred to as the "ethnographic analogy." This is a method whereby anthropologists use "enthnographies" or field studies of modern-day hunters and gatherers whom we take to be the best approximations we have of what life might have been like for our ancestors. While it is granted that these contemporary foragers have been living under conditions of environ-

mental and social change just as industrial peoples have, it nevertheless seems that, at least in some aspects of their lives, they have not changed as much as we have, and if we are to make any kind of enlightened assessments of prehistoric behavior patterns, we are better off looking at them than looking at ourselves. This technique of interpreting the past by observing contemporary peoples is the basis for the article "Life as a Hunter-Gatherer" by Richard Leakey.

As if to show that controversy over lineages is not limited to the earlier hominid period (see unit 5), in this section we have the raging debate surrounding the "Eve hypothesis," as dealt with in "The Search for Eve" and "A Multiregional Model," both by Michael Brown. In this case, the issue of when and where the family tree of modern humans actually began has pitted the bone experts, on the one hand, against a new type of anthropologist specializing in molecular biology, on the other. Granted, for some scientists, the new evidence fits in quite comfortably with previously held positions; for others it seems that reputations, as well as theories, are at stake.

Looking Ahead: Challenge Questions

Where and why might bamboo have been important to hominid survival?

What evidence is there for hard times among the Neanderthals?

What were Cro-Magnons trying to say or do with their cave art?

What are the social functions of personal adornment?

What are the strengths and weaknesses of the "Eve hypothesis"?

What happened to the Neanderthals?

How would you draw the late hominid family tree?

What can contemporary hunter-gatherers tell us about the lives of our ancestors over the past million years?

Are human beings innately aggressive?

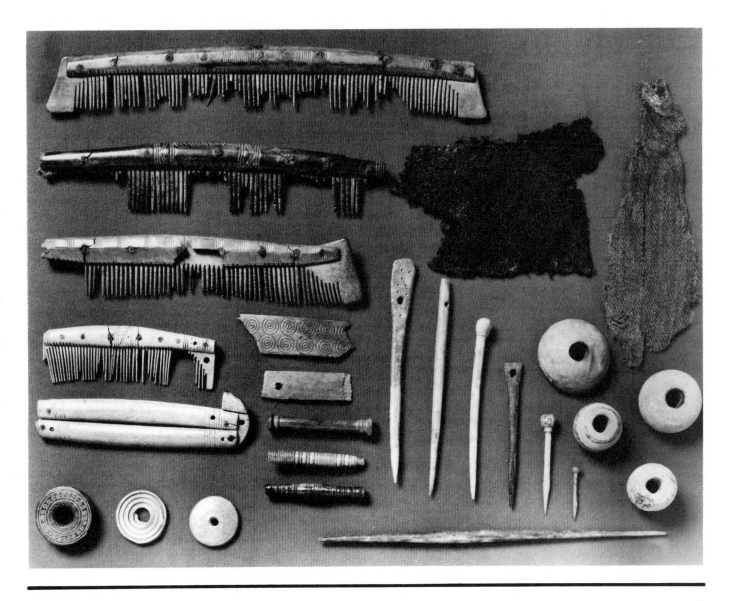

Bamboo and Human Evolution

In Asia, a giant grass may have shaped the course of prehistoric technology for more than one million years.

Geoffrey G. Pope

Today the seven-mile journey from the highway to our field camp in the Wang Valley seems almost too easy. In the ten years since I began paleoanthroplogical work in northern Thailand, roads have replaced bullock paths, and sugar cane fields lie where dense teak stands once towered. Taking only minutes to pass through the local village, our *song-tao,* or "two-bench" pickup truck, is well on the way to Kao Pah Nam (Wild Thorn Hill), a craggy spine of limestone clothed in treacherous thorn scrub. Everybody in the *song-tao* knows enough to lean into the center of the vehicle to avoid the razor-sharp thorns that rake the open sides.

Reaching our destination, we file out, impatient to flex cramped limbs, shake off the layers of cold dust, and rub new bruises. We are standing at the base of a karst ridge. Karst (first named for the Karst region of Yugoslavia) is an irregular terrain that develops when ground water saturated with carbonic acid erodes limestone. In tropical forests the effects are particularly striking because the dense root systems and thick layers of decaying organic matter give off a great deal of carbon dioxide, which in combination with water forms carbonic acid. All around us are imposing pinnacles with intriguing fissures and caves. For the paleoanthropologist, karst is especially inviting since caves attract animals seeking shelter, and early hominids—

human ancestors and their relatives—would have been no exception. The caves trap bones and cement them in a limestone breccia, preserving fossils that would otherwise disintegrate on the tropical forest floor, with its acid soil and its active insect and micro-organic life.

In prehistoric times the karst environment would have provided attractive resources for early humans. Today people still seek out caves during the hot dry season for their shaded, cool, subterranean waters. Bats, birds, snakes, and small mammals that live there are routinely collected for food. Karst towers also provide convenient points from which to survey the surrounding countryside and are important in the rainy season, when most rivers flood and the lowland country becomes inundated for months at a time. The limestone is also mined for phosphates, quicklime, and building stone.

From the forest around us comes the complacent, comforting cooing of "forest chickens." Suddenly, a series of explosions silences the birds. Some of the reports are as loud as dynamite blasts, but local inhabitants take no notice. For them the explosions are as natural as the sounds of the forest animals. They emanate from an unseen grove of bamboo that some villagers have set alight; the crackling sound of a brush fire accompanies them. The air in the sealed bases of the hollowed bamboo trunks expands until they blow apart, felling the giant stalks (the word

bamboo is Malay in origin and thought to be onomatopoeic for these explosions). This is the first step in the harvesting of a versatile raw material. For me, the explosions are fascinating, because I suspect that these same sounds have echoed in this valley for a million years, and that bamboo has shaped the course of human evolution in this part of the world.

Bamboo provides, I believe, the solution to a puzzle first raised in 1943, when the late archeologist Hallam Movius of Harvard began to publish his observations on paleolithic (Old Stone Age) cultures of the Far East. In 1937 and 1938 Movius had investigated a number of archeological localities in India, Southeast Asia, and China. Although most of the archeological "cultures" that he recognized are no longer accepted by modern workers, he made another, more lasting contribution. This was the identification of the "Movius line" (which his colleague Carleton Coon named in his honor): a geographical boundary, extending through northern India, that separates two long-lasting paleolithic cultures. West of the line are found collections of tools with a high percentage of symmetrical and consistently proportioned hand axes (these are called Acheulean tools, after the French site of Saint Acheul). More or less similar tool kits also occur in Mongolia and Siberia, but with few exceptions (which are generally relatively late in time), not in eastern China or Southeast Asia, where more crudely made tools known as choppers and chopping tools prevail.

Although both types of tools are attributed to our hominid ancestor *Homo erectus* and are of similar age (Acheulean tools are from 1.5 million to 200,000 years old; chopper-chopping tools from 1 million to 200,000 years old), Acheulean tools have long been regarded as more advanced than the more crudely made and less standardized tools of the Far East, which some have called a smash-and-grab technology. Movius was among the first to ponder the significance of this geographical division. In 1948 he published his conclusion that the Far East was a region of "cultural retardation," which he believed could never have

played a vital and dynamic role in early human evolution, although very primitive forms of Early Man apparently persisted there long after types at a comparable stage of physical evolution had become extinct elsewhere.

For years this explanation was accepted and even, in the interpretations of Carleton Coon and others, taken as evidence of racial isolation and backwardness.

With the flowering of the civil rights movement in the 1960s, most anthropologists rejected the notion of cultural retardation, especially if it had racial overtones. Now some suggest that *all* early human ancestors (not just the Asian hominids) had minimal capacities for culture, that is, for toolmaking and other types of socially learned behavior. Lewis Binford, of the University of New Mexico, has been influential in this view. He has spent the last few years reexamining evidence from a number of archeological localities and has concluded that many characterizations of past cultural behavior are based on very little solid data. At any rate, Binford and others would attribute the crudeness of the artifacts from China to the general inability of early hominids to manufacture standardized stone tools.

The problem with this is that it doesn't really solve the mystery of the Movius line. Over the years, however, a few archeologists have put forward a very different line of reasoning, which

I have found to be more fruitful. Their idea is that the early Asians may have relied heavily on tools that they made from raw materials other than stone, and since these are seldom preserved at archeological sites, we simply lack a balanced appreciation of their accomplishments. This suggestion has not generally been pursued, primarily because it is hard to confirm—after all, there is not much use in going out to dig for what probably has not been preserved.

One promising method of detecting nonlithic technology is to study the cut marks on fossil bones. Jolee West, a graduate student at the University of Illinois, has been experimenting with using the electron microscope to differentiate between the kinds of damage left by stone and other cutting implements. Continued development of this approach should eventually offer a direct means to test for the prehistoric use of nonlithic tools.

My own research on the Movius line and related questions evolved almost by accident. During the course of my work in Southeast Asia, I excavated many sites, studied a variety of fossil faunal collections, and reviewed the scientific literature dealing with Asia. As part of this research I compared fossil mammals from Asia with those recovered from other parts of the world. In the beginning, my purpose was biostratigraphic—to use the animals to estimate the most likely dates of various sites used by early hominids. On the basis of the associated fauna, for example, I estimate that Kao Pah Nam may be as old as 700,000 years.

After years of looking at fossil collections and faunal lists, I realized that something was very strange about the collections from Southeast Asia: there were no fossil horses of Pleistocene age (1.6 million to 12,000 years ago) or for a considerable time before that. The only exceptions were a few horse fossils from one place in southern China, the Yuanmou Basin, which was and is a special grassland habitat in a low, dry valley within the Shan-Yunnan Massif.

To mammalian biostratigraphers this is unusual, since members of the horse

family are so common in both the Old and New World that they are a primary means of dating various fossil localities. Fossil horses have been reported from western Burma, but the last one probably lived there some twenty million years ago. Not a single fossil horse turns up later than that in Southeast Asia, although they are known from India to the west and China to the north and every other part of Europe and Asia.

I then began to wonder what other normally common animals might be missing. The answer soon became apparent: camels—even though they too were once widespread throughout the world—and members and relatives of the giraffe family. Pleistocene Southeast Asia was shaping up as a kind of "black hole" for certain fossil mammals! These animals—horses, camels, and giraffids—all dwell in open country. Their absence on the Southeast Asian mainland and islands (all once connected, along with the now inundated Sunda Shelf) is indicative of a forested environment. The mammals that are present—orangutans, tapirs, and gibbons—confirm this conclusion.

The significance of this is that most reconstructions of our evolutionary past have emphasized the influence of savanna grassland habitats, so important in Africa, the cradle of hominid evolution. Many anthropologists theorize that shrinking forests and spreading grasslands encouraged our primarily tree-dwelling ancestors to adapt to ground-dwelling conditions, giving rise to the unique bipedal gait that is the hallmark of hominids. Bipedalism, in turn, freed the hands for tool use and ultimately led to the evolution of a large-brained, cultural animal. Tropical Asia, instead, apparently was where early hominids had to readapt to tropical forest.

In studying the record, I noticed that the forested zone—the zone that lacked open-dwelling mammals—coincided generally with the distribution of the chopper-chopping tools. The latter appeared to be the products of a forest adaptation that, for one reason or another, deemphasized the utilization of standardized stone tools. At least this held for Southeast Asia; what at first I could not explain was the existence of similar tools in northern China, where fossil horses, camels, and giraffids were present. Finally, I came upon the arresting fact that the distribution of naturally occurring bamboo coincided almost perfectly with the distribution of chopper-chopping tools. The only exceptions that may possibly be of real antiquity—certain hand ax collections from Kehe and Dingcun, in China, and Chonggok-Ni, in Korea—fall on the northernmost periphery of the distribution of bamboo and probably can be attributed to fluctuation of the boundary.

Today there are, by various estimates some 1,000 to 1,200 species of bamboo. This giant grass is distributed worldwide, but more than 60 percent of the species are from Asia. Only 16 percent occur in Africa, and those on the Indian subcontinent—to an unknown extent the product of human importation and cultivation—are discontinuous in distribution and low in diversity. By far, the greatest diversity occurs in East and Southeast Asia.

Based on these observations, I hypothesized that the early Asians relied on bamboo for much of their technology. At first I envisioned bamboo simply as a kind of icon representing all nonlithic technology. I now think bamboo specifically must have been an extremely important resource. This was not, in my opinion, because appropriate rock was scarce but because bamboo tools would have been efficient, durable, and highly portable.

There are few useful tools that cannot be constructed from bamboo. Cooking and storage containers, knives, spears, heavy and light projectile points, elaborate traps, rope, fasteners, clothing, and even entire villages can be manufactured from bamboo. In addition to the stalks, which are a source of raw material for the manufacture of a variety of artifacts, the seeds and shoots of many species can be eaten. In historical times, bamboo has been to Asian civilization what the olive tree was to the Greeks. In the great cities of the Far East, bamboo is still the preferred choice for the scaffolding used in the construction of skyscrapers. This in-comparable resource is also highly renewable. One can actually hear some varieties growing, at more than one foot per day.

Some may question how bamboo tools would have been sufficient for killing and processing large and medium-size animals. Lethal projectile and stabbing implements can in fact be fashioned from bamboo, but their importance may be exaggerated. Large game accounts for a relatively small proportion of the diet of many modern hunters and gatherers. Furthermore, animals are frequently trapped, collected, killed, and then thrown on a fire and cooked whole prior to using bare hands to dismember the roasted carcass. There are many ethnographic examples among forest peoples of this practice.

The only implements that cannot be manufactured from bamboo are axes or choppers suitable for the working of hard woods. More than a few archeologists have suggested that the stone choppers and resultant "waste" flakes of Asia were created with the objective of using them to manufacture and maintain nonlithic tools. Bamboo can be easily worked with stone flakes resulting from the manufacture of choppers (many choppers may have been a throwaway component in the manufacture of flakes).

In addition to bamboo, other highly versatile resources such as liana, rattan, and various reeds are also found in Asian forests. To really appreciate the wealth of resources one has to visit Southeast Asia today. Even though many forested areas have been disturbed or even destroyed by humans, those that remain offer an accurate picture of the variety of habitats that early hominids encountered when they first reached the Far East. Southeast Asia is dominated by tropical forest, but this is not necessarily rain forest. While evergreen rain forest exists in Indonesia, the monsoon forest in northern Thailand is deciduous. In northern China there is boreal woodland forest.

Most of my work has been in northern Thailand where the forests are burned every year, frequently not for agricultural reasons but to permit the passage of human foot traffic. Despite burning during the dry season (January-April), the forests are once again impenetrable at the end of the wet season (September-December). Many of the hardwood trees, such as the various kinds of teak, are fire resistant and seem little affected by these seasonal conflagrations, indicating that fire played an important role in their evolution. This may be evidence that fire, first used by our ancestors in tropical Africa, aided the colonization of the Asian forests by *Homo erectus.* Fire would also have been instrumental in the working and utilization of nonlithic resources such as bamboo. This relationship between humans, fire, and the forest is probably more than one million years old in Asia.

Our thorn-bedecked site of Kao Pah Nam, where we have been excavating a rock-shelter (shallow cave), itself preserves evidence of fire. Here we have discovered a roughly circular arrangement of fire-cracked basalt cobbles, in association with other artifacts and animal bones. These hearth stones had to have been brought in by early hominids, as very few nonlimestone rocks lie in the rock-shelter. At first I wondered why our early ancestors would have bothered to lug these heavy rocks into their shelter when limestone was abundant at the site.

The answer emerged as the result of a sort of accident in our field camp. For a number of days we had been cooking our meals on a hearth made of local limestone. A few days into the field season we began to notice that people were complaining of itchy and burning skin rashes. The symptoms were very unpleasant. At first we assumed the cause to be some sort of malevolent plant or fungus. By this time camp life had become uncomfortable and there were further complaints of shortness of breath and burning lungs. Finally, one of our Thai workers pointed out that the rocks of our cooking hearth, after numerous heatings and coolings from our fires, had begun to turn to quicklime. The heat, in conjunction with water from numerous spilled pots of soup and boiling kettles of coffee, had caused this caustic sub-

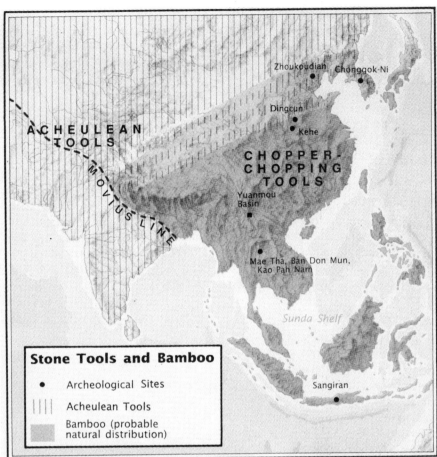

Stone Tools and Bamboo

● Archeological Sites

||| Acheulean Tools

Bamboo (probable natural distribution)

Prehistoric tools made in eastern and southeastern Asia are less standardized than those—such as the Acheulean hand ax—fashioned elsewhere in the Old World during the same period. A distinct boundary between the two types was delineated more than forty years ago by archeologist Hallam Movius. Since then, new finds have begun to fill in our knowledge of toolmaking in northern Asia. The distribution of the Asian tools corresponds closely to the natural range of bamboo.

stance to become distributed throughout the dusty camp. We quickly replaced the limestone rocks with ones made of basalt. Only months later did it dawn on me that the early hominids that lived at Kao Pah Nam also must have known about the dangers of cooking on limestone. This explained why they bothered to bring in non-native rocks.

On the basis of our ongoing excavations we have concluded that Kao Pah Nam was occupied intermittently by both carnivores and hominids. Bones of extinct hyenas, tigers, and other carnivores are confined primarily to

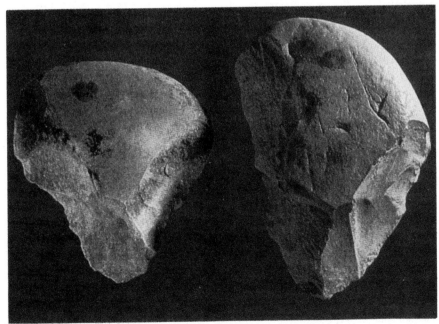

Jia Lanpo, *Early Man in China*

the deeper recesses of the rock-shelter, likely to have been preferred by denning animals. The hearth and other artifacts, on the other hand, are located near what was the entrance. Many of the prey animals that have been recov-

ered are large by modern standards and include hippo and giant forms of ox, deer, bamboo rat, and porcupine. Nothing about the animals suggests anything but a forested environment.

Artificial cut marks (as well as gnaw

marks of large porcupines) are present on the bones associated with the hearth and artifacts. Bones that apparently had been burned have also been recovered. Other evidence that bears on the diet of early hominids consists of extinct freshwater oyster shells piled on top of one another against the rock-shelter wall. This area remains to be fully excavated.

As the result of our work at Kao Pah Nam and other early Pleistocene sites in Thailand, we are beginning to put together a picture of regional artifact types, frequency, and age. There appears to be a simple but systematic pattern of manufacturing choppers and other artifacts by removing a few flakes from one side of a lump of stone.

A similar pattern is turning up in karst caves in southern China. In all these sites, small flakes are absent or rare. One interpretation is that the flakes were carried off into the forest for use in processing raw materials.

Of particular concern to paleoanthropologists is establishing the age of early Asian artifacts. In China, a number of sites are now reliably dated (by paleomagnetic evidence) to approximately one million years ago, and a variety of dating techniques suggest the earliest fossils and artifacts of *Homo erectus* on Java (so-called Java man) are somewhere between 800,000 and 1.3 million years old. In mainland Southeast Asia, however, artifacts demonstrably older than 100,000 years have long been elusive. Paleomagnetic studies have not yet been carried out to check our estimated biostratigraphic age of 700,000 years for Kao Pah Nam, but both radiometric and paleomagnetic studies were conducted at another site, Ban Don Mun. Artifacts beneath a basalt flow at that site can be assigned an early Pleistocene age of at least 700,000 years. For stratigraphic reasons, artifacts from a nearby site, Mae Tha, can also be accorded that antiquity.

One thing that still eludes us in mainland Southeast Asia are the fossils of the hominids that made the artifacts we have found. As we learn more about their environment, technology, and diet, however, we can see how capably they adapted to a land of bamboo and karst.

Hard Times Among the Neanderthals

Although life was difficult, these prehistoric people may not have been as exclusively brutish as usually supposed

Erik Trinkaus

Throughout the century that followed the discovery in 1856 of the first recognized human fossil remains in the Neander Valley (*Neanderthal* in German) near Düsseldorf, Germany, the field of human paleontology has been beset with controversies. This has been especially true of interpretations of the Neanderthals, those frequently maligned people who occupied Europe and the Near East from about 100,000 years ago until the appearance of anatomically modern humans about 35,000 years ago.

During the last two decades, however, a number of fossil discoveries, new analyses of previously known remains, and more sophisticated models for interpreting subtle anatomical differences have led to a reevaluation of the Neanderthals and their place in human evolution.

This recent work has shown that the often quoted reconstruction of the Neanderthals as semierect, lumbering caricatures of humanity is inaccurate. It was based on faulty anatomical interpretations that were reinforced by the intellectual biases of the turn of the century. Detailed comparisons of Neanderthal skeletal remains with those of modern humans have shown that there is nothing in Neanderthal anatomy that conclusively indicates locomotor, manipulative, intellectual, or linguistic abilities inferior to those of modern humans. Neanderthals have therefore been added to the same spe-

cies as ourselves—*Homo sapiens*—although they are usually placed in their own subspecies, *Homo sapiens neanderthalensis*.

Despite these revisions, it is apparent that there are significant anatomical differences between the Neanderthals and present-day humans. If we are to understand the Neanderthals, we must formulate hypotheses as to why they evolved from earlier humans about 100,000 years ago in Europe and the Near East, and why they were suddenly replaced about 35,000 years ago by peoples largely indistinguishable from ourselves. We must determine, therefore, the behavioral significance of the anatomical differences between the Neanderthals and other human groups, since it is patterns of successful behavior that dictate the direction of natural selection for a species.

In the past, behavioral reconstructions of the Neanderthals and other prehistoric humans have been based largely on archeological data. Research has now reached the stage at which behavioral interpretations from the archeological record can be significantly supplemented by analyses of the fossils themselves. These analyses promise to tell us a considerable amount about the ways of the Neanderthals and may eventually help us to determine their evolutionary fate.

One of the most characteristic features of the Neanderthals is the exaggerated massiveness of their trunk and limb bones. All of the preserved bones

suggest a strength seldom attained by modern humans. Furthermore, not only is this robustness present among the adult males, as one might expect, but it is also evident in the adult females, adolescents, and even children. The bones themselves reflect this hardiness in several ways.

First, the muscle and ligament attachment areas are consistently enlarged and strongly marked. This implies large, highly developed muscles and ligaments capable of generating and sustaining great mechanical stress. Secondly, since the skeleton must be capable of supporting these levels of stress, which are frequently several times as great as body weight, the enlarged attachments for muscles and ligaments are associated with arm and leg bone shafts that have been reinforced. The shafts of all of the arm and leg bones are modified tubular structures that have to absorb stress from bending and twisting without fracturing. When the habitual load on a bone increases, the bone responds by laying down more bone in those areas under the greatest stress.

In addition, musculature and body momentum generate large forces across the joints. The cartilage, which covers joint surfaces, can be relatively easily overworked to the point where it degenerates, as is indicated by the prevalence of arthritis in joints subjected to significant wear and tear over the years. When the surface area of a joint is increased, the force per unit

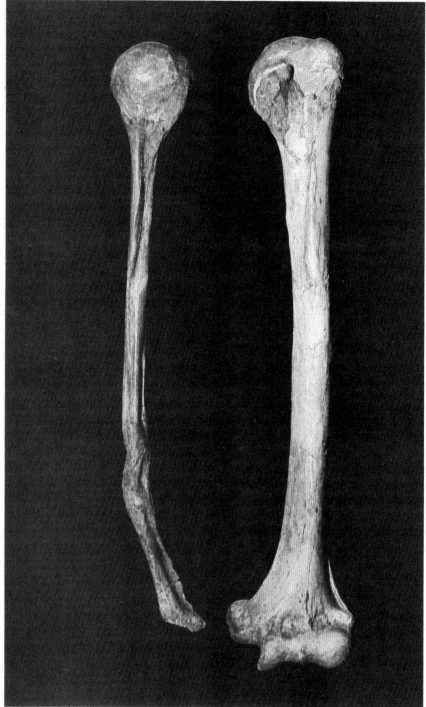

Diagonal lines on these two arm bones from Shanidar 1 are healed fractures. The bone on the right is normal. That on the left is atrophied and has a pathological tip, caused by either amputation or an improperly healed elbow fracture.

area of cartilage is reduced, decreasing the pressure on the cartilage.

Most of the robustness of Neanderthal arm bones is seen in muscle and ligament attachments. All of the muscles that go from the trunk or the shoulder blade to the upper end of the arm show massive development. This applies in particular to the muscles responsible for powerful downward movements of the arm and, to a lesser extent, to muscles that stabilize the shoulder during vigorous movements.

Virtually every major muscle or ligament attachment on the hand bones is clearly marked by a large roughened area or a crest, especially the muscles used in grasping objects. In fact, Neanderthal hand bones frequently have clear bony crests, where on modern human ones it is barely possible to discern the attachment of the muscle on the dried bone.

In addition, the flattened areas on the ends of the fingers, which provide support for the nail and the pulp of the finger tip, are enormous among the Neanderthals. These areas on the thumb and the index and middle fingers are usually two to three times as large as those of similarly sized modern human hands. The overall impression is one of arms to rival those of the mightiest blacksmith.

Neanderthal legs are equally massive; their strength is best illustrated in the development of the shafts of the leg bones. Modern human thigh and shin bones possess characteristic shaft shapes adapted to the habitual levels and directions of the stresses acting upon them. The shaft shapes of the Neanderthals are similar to those in modern humans, but the cross-sectional areas of the shafts are much greater. This implies significantly higher levels of stress.

Further evidence of the massiveness of Neanderthal lower limbs is provided by the dimensions of their knee and ankle joints. All of these are larger than in modern humans, especially with respect to the overall lengths of the bones.

The development of their limb bones suggests that the Neanderthals frequently generated high levels of mechanical stress in their limbs. Since most mechanical stress in the body is produced by body momentum and muscular contraction, it appears that the Neanderthals led extremely active lives. It is hard to conceive of what could have required such exertion, especially since the maintenance of vigorous muscular activity would have required considerable expenditure of energy. That level of energy expenditure would undoubtedly have been maladaptive had it not been necessary for survival.

The available evidence from the archeological material associated with the Neanderthals is equivocal on this matter. Most of the archeological evidence at Middle Paleolithic sites concerns stone tool technology and hunting activities. After relatively little change in technology during the Middle Paleolithic (from about 100,000 years to 35,000 years before the present), the advent of the Upper Paleolithic appears to have brought significant technological advances. This transition about 35,000 years ago is approximately coincident with the replacement of the Neanderthals by the earliest anatomically modern humans. However, the evidence for a significant

change in hunting patterns is not evident in the animal remains left behind. Yet even if a correlation between the robustness of body build and the level of hunting efficiency could be demonstrated, it would only explain the ruggedness of the Neanderthal males. Since hunting is exclusively or at least predominantly a male activity among humans, and since Neanderthal females were in all respects as strongly built as the males, an alternative explanation is required for the females.

Some insight into why the Neanderthals consistently possessed such massiveness is provided by a series of

partial skeletons of Neanderthals from the Shanidar Cave in northern Iraq. These fossils were excavated between 1953 and 1960 by anthropologist Ralph Solecki of Columbia University and have been studied principally by T. Dale Stewart, an anthropologist at the Smithsonian Institution, and myself. The most remarkable aspect of these skeletons is the number of healed injuries they contain. Four of the six reasonably complete adult skeletons show evidence of trauma during life.

The identification of traumatic injury in human fossil remains has plagued paleontologists for years. There has been a tendency to consider any form of damage to a fossil as conclusive evidence of prehistoric violence between humans if it resembles the breakage patterns caused by a direct blow with a heavy object. Hence a jaw with the teeth pushed in or a skull with a depressed fracture of the vault would be construed to indicate blows to the head.

The central problem with these interpretations is that they ignore the possibility of damage after death. Bone is relatively fragile, especially as compared with the rock and other sediment in which it is buried during fossilization. Therefore when several feet of sediment caused compression around fossil remains, the fossils will almost always break. In fact, among the innumerable cases of suggested violence between humans cited over the years, there are only a few exceptional examples that cannot be readily explained as the result of natural geologic forces acting after the death and burial of the individual.

One of these examples is the trauma of the left ninth rib of the skeleton of Shanidar 3, a partially healed wound inflicted by a sharp object. The implement cut obliquely across the top of the ninth rib and probably pierced the underlying lung. Shanidar 3 almost certainly suffered a collapsed left lung and died several days or weeks later, probably as a result of secondary complications. This is deduced from the presence of bony spurs and increased density of the bone around the cut.

The position of the wound on the

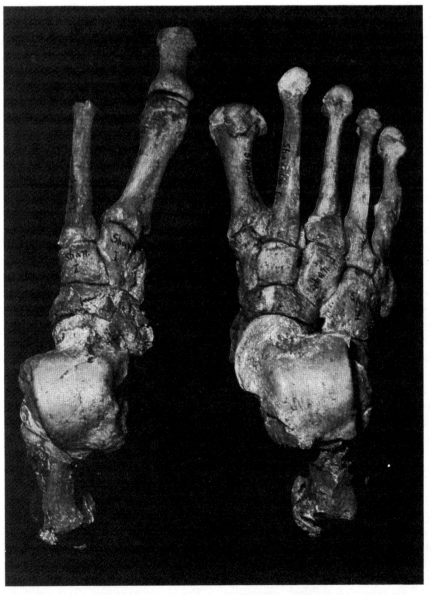

The ankle and big toe of Shanidar 1's right foot show evidence of arthritis, which suggests an injury to those parts. The left foot is normal although incomplete.

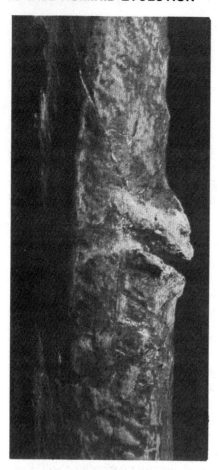

The scar on the left ninth rib of Shanidar 3 is a partially healed wound inflicted by a sharp object. This wound is one of the few examples of trauma caused by violence.

rib, the angle of the incision, and the cleanness of the cut make it highly unlikely that the injury was accidentally inflicted. In fact, the incision is almost exactly what would have resulted if Shanidar 3 had been stabbed in the side by a right-handed adversary in face-to-face conflict. This would therefore provide conclusive evidence of violence between humans, the *only* evidence so far found of such violence among the Neanderthals.

In most cases, however, it is impossible to determine from fossilized remains the cause of an individual's death. The instances that can be positively identified as prehistoric traumatic injury are those in which the injury was inflicted prior to death and some healing took place. Shortly after an injury to bone, whether a cut or a fracture, the damaged bone tissue is resorbed by the body and new bone

tissue is laid down around the injured area. As long as irritation persists, new bone is deposited, creating a bulge or spurs of irregular bone extending into the soft tissue. If the irritation ceases, the bone will slowly re-form so as to approximate its previous, normal condition. However, except for superficial injuries or those sustained during early childhood, some trace of damage persists for the life of the individual.

In terms of trauma, the most impressive of the Shanidar Neanderthals is the first adult discovered, known as Shanidar 1. This individual suffered a number of injuries, some of which may be related. On the right forehead there are scars from minor surface injuries, probably superficial scalp cuts. The outside of the left eye socket sustained a major blow that partially collapsed that part of the bony cavity, giving it a flat rather than a rounded contour. This injury possibly caused loss of sight in the left eye and pathological alterations of the right side of the body.

Shanidar 1's left arm is largely preserved and fully normal. The right arm, however, consists of a highly atrophied but otherwise normal collarbone and shoulder blade and a highly abnormal upper arm bone shaft. That shaft is atrophied to a fraction of the diameter of the left one but retains most of its original length. Furthermore, the lower end of the right arm bone has a healed fracture of the atrophied shaft and an irregular, pathological tip. The arm was apparently either intentionally amputated just above the elbow or fractured at the elbow and never healed.

This abnormal condition of the right arm does not appear to be a congenital malformation, since the length of the bone is close to the estimated length of the normal left upper arm bone. If, however, the injury to the left eye socket also affected the left side of the brain, directly or indirectly, by disrupting the blood supply to part of the brain, the result could have been partial paralysis of the right side. Motor and sensory control areas for the right side are located on the left side of the brain, slightly behind the left eye socket. This would explain the atrophy

of the whole right arm since loss of nervous stimulation will rapidly lead to atrophy of the affected muscles and bone.

The abnormality of the right arm of Shanidar 1 is paralleled to a lesser extent in the right foot. The right ankle joint shows extensive arthritic degeneration, and one of the major joints of the inner arch of the right foot has been completely reworked by arthritis. The left foot, however, is totally free of pathology. Arthritis from normal stress usually affects both lower limbs equally; this degeneration therefore suggests that the arthritis in the right foot is a secondary result of an injury, perhaps a sprain, that would not otherwise be evident on skeletal remains. This conclusion is supported by a healed fracture of the right fifth instep bone, which makes up a major portion of the outer arch of the foot. These foot pathologies may be tied into the damage to the left side of the skull; partial paralysis of the right side would certainly weaken the leg and make it more susceptible to injury.

The trauma evident on the other Shanidar Neanderthals is relatively minor by comparison. Shanidar 3, the individual who died of the rib wound, suffered debilitating arthritis of the right ankle and neighboring foot joints, but lacks any evidence of pathology on the left foot; this suggests a superficial injury similar to the one sustained by Shanidar 1. Shanidar 4 had a healed broken rib. Shanidar 5 received a transverse blow across the left forehead that left a large scar on the bone but does not appear to have affected the brain.

None of these injuries necessarily provides evidence of deliberate violence among the Neanderthals; all of them could have been accidentally self-inflicted or accidentally caused by another individual. In either case, the impression gained of the Shanidar Neanderthals is of a group of invalids. The crucial variable, however, appears to be age. All four of these individuals died at relatively advanced ages, probably between 40 and 60 years (estimating the age at death for Neanderthals beyond the age of 25 is extremely difficult); they therefore had considerable time to accumulate the scars of past injuries. Shanidar 2 and 6, the other reasonably complete Shanidar adults, lack evidence of trauma, but they both died young, probably before reaching 30.

Other Neanderthal remains, all from Europe, exhibit the same pattern. Every fairly complete skeleton of an elderly adult shows evidence of traumatic injuries. The original male skeleton from the Neander Valley had a fracture just below the elbow of the left arm, which probably limited movement of that arm for life. The "old man" from La Chapelle-aux-Saints, France, on whom most traditional reconstructions of the Neanderthals have been based, suffered a broken rib. La Ferrassi 1, the old adult male from La Ferrassie, France, sustained a severe injury to the right hip, which may have impaired his mobility.

In addition, several younger specimens and ones of uncertain age show traces of trauma. La Quina 5, the young adult female from La Quina, France, was wounded on her right upper arm. A young adult from Sala, Czechoslovakia, was superficially wounded on the right forehead just above the brow. And an individual of unknown age and sex from the site of Krapina, Yugoslavia, suffered a broken forearm, in which the bones never reunited after the fracture.

This evidence suggests several things. First, life for the Neanderthals was rigorous. If they lived through childhood and early adulthood, they did so bearing the scars of a harsh and dangerous life. Furthermore, this incidence of trauma correlates with the massiveness of the Neanderthals; a life style that so consistently involved injury would have required considerable strength and fortitude for survival.

There is, however, another, more optimistic side to this. The presence of so many injuries in a prehistoric human group, many of which were debilitating and sustained years before death, shows that individuals were taken care of long after their economic usefulness to the social group had ceased. It is perhaps no accident that among the Neanderthals, for the first time in human history, people lived to a comparatively old age. We also find among the Neanderthals the first intentional burials of the dead, some of which involved offerings. Despite the hardships of their life style, the Neanderthals apparently had a deep-seated respect and concern for each other.

Taken together, these different pieces of information paint a picture of life among the Neanderthals that, while harsh and dangerous, was not without personal security. Certainly the hardships the Neanderthals endured were beyond those commonly experienced in the prehistoric record of human caring and respect as well as of violence between individuals. Perhaps for these reasons, despite their physical appearance, the Neanderthals should be considered the first modern humans.

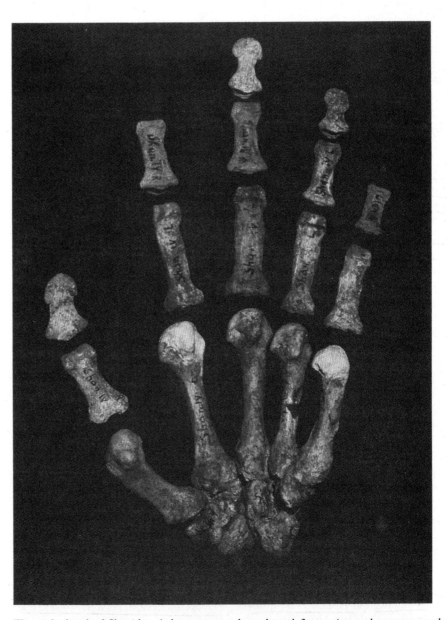

The right hand of Shanidar 4 demonstrates the enlarged finger tips and strong muscle markings characteristic of Neanderthal hands.

OLD MASTERS

Brilliant paintings brightened the caves of our early ancestors. But were the artists picturing their mythic beliefs or simply showing what they ate for dinner?

Pat Shipman

Pat Shipman wrote about killer bamboo in February.

Fifty years ago, in a green valley of the Dordogne region of southwest France, a group of teenage boys made the first claustrophobic descent into the labyrinthine caverns of Lascaux. When they reached the main chamber and held their lamps aloft, the sight that flickered into view astonished them. There were animals everywhere. A frieze of wild horses, with chunky bodies and fuzzy, crew-cut manes, galloped across the domed walls and ceiling past the massive figure of a white bull-like creature (the extinct aurochs). Running helter-skelter in the opposing direction were three little stags with delicately drawn antlers. They were followed by more bulls, cows, and calves rounding the corner of the chamber.

Thousands have since admired these paintings in Lascaux's Hall of the Bulls, probably the most magnificent example of Ice Age art known to us today. In fact, by 1963 so many tourists wanted to view the cave that officials were forced to close Lascaux to the general public; the paintings were being threatened as the huge influx of visitors warmed the air in the cave and brought in corrosive algae and pollen. (Fortunately, a nearby exhibit called Lascaux II faithfully reproduces the paintings.) After I first saw these powerful images, they haunted me for several months. I had looked at photographs of Lascaux in books, of course, so I knew that the paintings were beautiful; but what I didn't know was that they would reach across 17,000 years to grab my soul.

The image of Paleolithic humans moving by flickering lamps, singing, chanting, and drawing their knowledge of their world is hard to resist.

Lascaux is not an Ice Age anomaly. Other animal paintings, many exquisitely crafted, adorn hundreds of caves throughout the Dordogne and the French Pyrenees and the region known as Cantabria on the northern coast of Spain. All these images were created by the people we commonly call Cro-Magnons, who lived during the Upper Paleolithic Period, between 10,000 and 30,000 years ago, when Europe lay in the harsh grip of the Ice Age.

What did this wonderful art mean, and what does it tell us about the prehistoric humans who created it?

These questions have been asked since the turn of the century, when cave paintings in Spain were first definitively attributed to Paleolithic humans. Until recently the dominant answers were based on rather sweeping symbolic interpretations—attempts, as it were, to read the Paleolithic psyche.

These days some anthropologists are adopting a more literal-minded approach. They are not trying to empathize with the artists' collective soul—a perilous exercise in imagination, considering how remote Cro-Magnon life must have been from ours. Rather, armed with the tools of the late twentieth century—statistics, maps, computer analyses of the art's distribution patterns—the researchers are trying to make sense of the paintings by piecing together their cultural context.

This is a far cry from earlier attempts at interpretation. At the beginning of the century, with little more to go on than his intuition, the French amateur archeologist Abbé Henri Breuil suggested that the pictures were a form of hunting magic. Painting animals, in other words, was a magical way of capturing them, in the hope that it would make the beasts vulnerable to hunters. Abstract symbols painted on the walls were interpreted as hunting paraphernalia. Straight lines drawn to the animals' sides represented spears, and V and O shapes on their hides were seen as wounds. Rectangular grids, some observers thought, might have been fences or animal traps.

In the 1960s this view was brushed aside for a much more complex, somewhat Freudian approach that was brought into fashion by anthropologist André Leroi-Gourhan. He saw the cave paintings as a series of mythograms, or symbolic depictions, of how Paleolithic people viewed their world—a world split between things male and female. Femaleness was represented by animals such as the bison and aurochs (which were sometimes juxtaposed with human female figures in the paintings), and maleness was embodied by such animals as the horse and ibex (which, when accompanied by human figures, were shown only with males). Female images, Leroi-Gourhan suggested, were clustered in the central parts of the dark, womblike caves, while male images either consorted with the female ones or encircled them in the more peripheral areas.

Leroi-Gourhan also ascribed sex to the geometric designs on the cave walls. Thin shapes such as straight lines, which often make up barbed, arrowlike structures, were seen as male (phallic) signs. Full shapes such as ovals, V shapes, triangles, and rectangles were female (vulval) symbols. Thus, an arrow stuck into a V-shaped wound on an animal's hide was a male symbol entering a complementary female one.

. . . animals may have been depicted more or less frequently depending on how aggressive they were to humans.

Leroi-Gourhan was the first to look for structure in the paintings systematically, and his work reinforced the notion that these cave paintings had underlying designs and were not simply idle graffiti or random doodles. Still, some scholars considered his *"perspective sexomaniaque"* rather farfetched; eventually even he played down some of the sexual interpretations. However, a far bigger problem with both his theory and Breuil's was their sheer monolithic scope: a single explanation was assumed to account for 20,000 years of paintings produced by quite widely scattered groups of people.

Yet it is at least as likely that the paintings carried a number of different messages. The images' meaning may have varied depending on who painted them and where. Increasingly, therefore, researchers have tried to relate the content of the paintings to their context—their distribution within a particular cave, the cave's location within a particular region, and the presence of other nearby dwelling sites, tools, and animal bones in the area.

Anthropologist Patricia Rice and sociologist Ann Paterson, both from West Virginia University, made good use of this principle in their study of a single river valley in the Dordogne region, an area that yielded 90 different caves containing 1,955 animal portrayals and 151 dwelling sites with animal bone deposits. They wanted to find out whether the number of times an animal was painted simply reflected how common it was or whether it revealed further information about the animals or the human artists.

By comparing the bone counts of the various animals—horses, reindeer, red deer, ibex, mammoths, bison, and aurochs—Rice and Paterson were able to score the animals according to their abundance. When they related this number to the number of times a species turned up in the art, they found an interesting relationship: Pictures of the smaller animals, such as deer, were proportionate to their bone counts. But the bigger species, such as horses and bison, were portrayed more often than you'd expect from the faunal remains. In fact, it turned out that to predict how often an animal would appear, you had to factor in not just its relative abundance but its weight as well.

A commonsense explanation of this finding was that an animal was depicted according to its usefulness as food, with the larger, meatier animals shown more often. This "grocery store" explanation of the art worked well, except for the ibex, which was portrayed as often as the red deer yet was only half its size and, according to the bone counts, not as numerous. The discrepancy led Rice and Paterson to explore the hypothesis that animals may have also been depicted more or less frequently depending on how aggressive they were to humans.

To test this idea, the researchers asked wildlife-management specialists to score the animals according to a "danger index." The feisty ibex, like the big animals, was rated as highly aggressive; and like these other dangerous animals, it was painted more often than just the numbers of its remains would suggest. Milder-tempered red deer and reindeer, on the other hand, were painted only about as often as you'd expect from their bones. Rice and Paterson concluded that the local artists may have portrayed the animals for both "grocery store" and "danger index" reasons. Maybe such art was used to impress important information on the minds of young hunters—drawing attention to the animals that were the most worthwhile to kill, yet balancing the rewards of dinner with the risks of attacking a fearsome animal.

One thing is certain: Paleolithic artists knew their animals well. Subtle physical details, characteristic poses, even seasonal changes in coat color or texture, were deftly observed. At Lascaux bison are pictured shedding their dark winter pelts. Five stags are shown swimming across a river, heads held high above the swirling tide. A stallion is depicted with its lip curled back, responding to a mare in heat. The reddish coats, stiff black manes, short legs, and potbellies of the Lascaux horses are so well recorded that they look unmistakably like the modern Przhevalsky's horses from Mongolia.

New findings at Solutré, in east-central France, the most famous horse-hunting site from the Upper Paleolithic, show how intimate knowledge of the animal's habits was used to the early hunter's advantage. The study, by archeologist Sandra Olsen of the Virginia Museum of Natural History, set out to reexamine how vast numbers of horses—from tens to hundreds of thousands, according to fossil records—came to be killed in the same, isolated spot. The archeological deposits at Solutré are 27 feet thick, span 20,000 years, and provide a record of stone tools and artifacts as well as faunal remains.

The traditional interpretation of this site was lots of fun but unlikely. The Roche de Solutré is one of several high limestone ridges running east-west from the Saône River to the Massif Central plateau; narrow valleys run between the ridges. When the piles of bones were discovered, in 1866, it was proposed that the site was a "horse jump" similar to the buffalo jumps in the American West, where whole herds of bison were driven off cliffs to their death. Several nineteenth-century paintings depict Cro-Magnon hunters driving a massive herd of wild horses up and off the steep rock of Solutré. But Olsen's bone analysis has shown that the horse jump scenario is almost certainly wrong.

For one thing, the horse bones are not at the foot of the steep western end of Solutré, but in a natural cul-de-sac along the southern face of the ridge. For the horse jump hypothesis to work, one of two fairly incredible events had to occur. Either the hunters drove the horses off the western end and then dragged all the carcasses around to the southern face to butcher them or the hunters herded the animals up the steep slope and then forced them to veer off the southern side of the ridge. But behavioral studies show that, unlike bison, wild horses travel not in herds but in small, independent bands. So it would have been extremely difficult for our Cro-Magnons on foot to force lots of horses together and persuade them to jump en masse.

Instead the horse behavior studies suggested to Olsen a new hypothesis. Wild horses commonly winter in the lowlands and summer in the highlands. This migration pattern preserves their forage and lets them avoid the lowland's biting flies and heat in summer

and the highland's cold and snow in winter. The Solutré horses, then, would likely have wintered in the Saône's floodplain to the east and summered in the mountains to the west, migrating through the valleys between the ridges. The kill site at Solutré, Olsen notes, lies in the widest of these valleys, the one offering the easiest passage to the horses. What's more, from the hunters' point of view, the valley has a convenient cul-de-sac running off to one side. The hunters, she proposes, used a drive lane of brush, twigs, and rocks to divert the horses from their migratory path into the cul-de-sac and then speared the animals to death. In deed, spear points found at the site support this scenario.

For all the finely observed animal pictures, we catch only the sketchiest glimpses of humans, in the form of stick figures or stylized line drawings.

The bottom line in all this is that Olsen's detailed studies of this prehistoric hunting site confirm what the cave art implies: these early humans used their understanding of animals' habits, mating, and migration patterns to come up with extremely successful hunting strategies. Obviously this knowledge must have been vital to the survival of the group and essential to hand down to successive generations. Perhaps the animal friezes in the cave were used as a mnemonic device or as a visual teaching aid in rites of initiation—a means for people to recall or rehearse epic hunts, preserve information, and school their young. The emotional power of the art certainly suggests that this information was crucial to their lives and could not be forgotten.

The transmission of this knowledge may well have been assisted by more

than illustration. French researchers Iégor Reznikoff and Michel Dauvois have recently shown that cave art may well have been used in rituals accompanied by songs or chants. The two studied the acoustic resonances of three caves in the French Pyrenees by singing and whistling through almost five octaves as they walked slowly through each cave. At certain points the caves resonated in response to a particular note, and these points were carefully mapped.

When Reznikoff and Dauvois compared their acoustic map with a map of the cave paintings, they found an astonishing relationship. The best resonance points were all well marked with images, while those with poor acoustics had very few pictures. Even if a resonance point offered little room for a full painting, it was marked in some way—by a set of red dots, for example. It remains to be seen if this intriguing correlation holds true for other caves. In the meantime, the image of Paleolithic humans moving by flickering lamps, singing, chanting, and drawing their knowledge of their world indelibly into their memories is so appealing that I find it hard to resist.

Yet the humans in this mental image of mine are shadowy, strangely elusive people. For all the finely observed animal pictures, we catch only the sketchiest glimpses of humans, in the form of stick figures or stylized line drawings. Still, when Rice and Paterson turned to study these human images in French and Spanish caves, a few striking patterns did emerge. Of the 67 images studied, 52 were male and a mere 15 were female. Only men were depicted as engaged in active behavior, a category that included walking, running, carrying spears, being speared, or falling. Females were a picture of passivity; they stood, sat, or lay prone. Most women were shown in close proximity to another human figure or group of figures, which were always other women. Seldom were men featured in social groups; they were much more likely to be shown facing off with an animal.

These images offer tantalizing clues to Paleolithic life. They suggest a society where males and females led very separate lives. (Male-female couples do not figure at all in Paleolithic art, for all the sexual obsessions of earlier researchers.) Males carried out the only physical activities—or at least the only ones deemed worthy of recording. Their chief preoccupation was hunting, and from all appearances, what counted most was the moment of truth between man and his prey. What women did in Paleolithic society (other than bear children and gather food)

remains more obscure. But whatever they did, they mostly did it in the company of other women, which would seem to imply that social interaction, cooperation, and oral communication played an important role in female lives.

If we could learn the sex of the artists, perhaps interpreting the social significance of the art would be easier. Were women's lives so mysterious because the artists were male and chauvinistically showed only men's activities in

their paintings? Or perhaps the artists were all female. Is their passive group activity the recording and encoding of the information vital to the group's survival in paintings and carvings? Did they spend their time with other women, learning the songs and chants and the artistic techniques that transmitted and preserved their knowledge? The art that brightened the caves of the Ice Age endures. But the artists who might shed light on its meaning remain as enigmatic as ever.

The Dawn of Adornment

Forty thousand years ago, humans began to fashion ornaments and images. Why?

Randall White

Randall White, an associate professor of anthropology at New York University, served from 1986 to 1987 as the guest curator of the American Museum of Natural History's exhibition "Dark Caves, Bright Visions."

Some 2.5 million years after our ancestors began hammering out stone tools, early members of our own subspecies, *Homo sapiens sapiens,* started sculpting animal and human figurines from ivory, engraving and painting images on limestone blocks, and carefully crafting personal adornments of ivory, shell, soapstone, and animal teeth. In Europe, these creations, as well as innovative stone tools and weapons, first appeared about 40,000 years ago, well before the famous 17,500-year-old cave paintings at Lascaux. They were the work of the Cro-Magnons, successors to the Neanderthals (*H. sapiens neanderthalensis*). Although they had successfully occupied Europe and western Asia from about 200,000 years ago, the Neanderthals had shown only glimmerings of symbolic representation, doing little more than collecting fossils, minerals, and other objects that held some attraction for them. They vanished from Europe several thousand years after the Cro-Magnons appeared.

The rapid emergence of personal ornamentation in particular may have marked, not a difference in mental capabilities between Cro-Magnons and Neanderthals, but rather the emergence of new forms of social organization that facilitated and demanded the communication and recording of complex ideas. As anthropologist Andrew Strathern has observed,

What people wear, and what they do to and with their bodies in general, forms an important part of the flow of information—establishing, modifying, and commenting on major social categories, such as age, sex and status, which are also defined in speech and in actions. Whatever the precise origins of clothing, then, they can be sought only within the general context of the development of social communication and of society itself.

A clue that social factors played a key role in this cultural watershed is that significant innovations in technology seem to have been developed not so much to improve hunting or gathering efficiency as to achieve aesthetic goals. For example, during the Aurignacian cultural period (about 40,000 to 28,000 years ago), the Cro-Magnons devised various techniques for working ivory, including the preparation and use of metallic abrasives (notably powdered hematite) for polishing. They used ivory in the creation of beads, pendants, and figurines, but almost never for manufacturing utilitarian weapons and tools.

In addition to ivory, the Cro-Magnons made representational objects from mammal bones and teeth, antlers, fossil and contemporary species of marine and freshwater shells, fossil coral, limestone, schist, talc-schist, steatite, jet, lignite, hematite, and pyrite. They did not choose these raw materials at random. Some came from sources hundreds of miles away, possibly obtained by trade. Only a dozen or so of the thousands of shell species available on the Atlantic and Mediterranean shores were transformed into personal ornaments. Only the teeth of certain animals were chosen. In some cases, the Cro-Magnons crafted ivory and soapstone facsimiles of these same marine shells and animal teeth.

Techniques for producing Aurignacian ivory and stone beads varied from one European region to the next. In France, the most common beads, represented by more than 1,000 specimens dated to between 33,000 and 32,000 years ago, were created in several steps. The Cro-Magnons first fashioned pencil-like rods of ivory or soapstone, inscribed them circumferentially at intervals of one-half to three-quarters of an inch, and then snapped off cylindrical blanks. These they thinned and perforated by gouging from each side, rather than by drilling (the technique of choice elsewhere). The roughed-out beads were then ground and polished into their final form, using hematite as an abrasive.

At the 36,000-year-old site of Kostenki 17 in the Don Valley of Russia, archeologists have discovered ornaments made from fossil coral and from belemnites, the fossilized, cigar-shaped shells of a kind of extinct squid. Beads made from belemnites are a translucent gold or brown and are easily mistaken for amber. The bead maker began with the naturally cylindrical belemnites, cut them into segments, split each segment to make semicylindrical blanks, perforated them by drilling from each side, and polished them into final form. Similar techniques were used to make ivory beads at contemporaneous sites in central and western Europe.

The inhabitants of the Russian site of Sungir, an open-air camp, wore elaborate personal ornaments of ivory and schist and carved geometric and animal forms out of ivory. At 28,000 years, the site is one of the oldest in which archeologists have discovered ornaments on human skeletons. The remains include the skeleton of a sixty-year-old man, buried in one trench, and the skeletons of two children (one aged seven to nine, the other about thirteen) buried head to head in another. Based primarily on differences in the grave goods, Russian physical anthropologists believe the younger child was a girl and the older one was a boy.

These three burials were decorated with thousands of painstakingly prepared ivory beads arranged in dozens of strands, perhaps originally basted to clothing. Although the three who died apparently were members of the same social group, the burials differed in the details of body decoration and grave offerings. For example, the man's forearms and biceps bore a total of twenty-five polished mammoth-ivory bracelets, some showing traces of black paint. Around his neck, he wore a small, flat schist pendant, painted red with a small black dot on one side.

As was common elsewhere, the beads were mass produced in a methodical, step-by-step fashion. They were scored across each face so that when strung they would fall into an interlocking, criss-cross pattern. Careful analysis shows that the scoring was done on each blank bead before the hole was drilled, indicating that the creator had the desired aesthetic effect in mind at even the earliest stages of production. Experiments reveal that each bead took more than an hour to make.

The adult male burial contained about 3,000 beads, while each child's burial contained 5,000. Thus the man's beadwork required more than 3,000 hours of labor, while that of each child took more than 5,000 hours. The other objects placed on and alongside the children's corpses also represented a

greater investment of labor. The extra attention lavished on the children may simply show that those who buried them felt a very deep loss. But it could mean the children had inherited a high social rank. If so, hierarchical societies arose—contrary to what some have assumed—well before economic systems based on agricultural production.

In creating representational images, the Cro-Magnons applied many of the techniques employed in the production of personal ornaments. They shaped three-dimensional ivory and steatite sculptures by gouging, grinding, and polishing. Such sculptures were often perforated for suspension. An experimental reconstruction of an ivory horse from the south German cave site of Vogelherd took archeologist Joachim Hahn nearly forty hours. The Cro-Magnons also marked limestone slabs. Frequently they first smoothed the surface by abrasion. Then they used diverse techniques—engraving, pecking, chiseling, gouging, and occasionally painting—to make desired lines.

The several dozen Aurignacian engraved blocks that have been discovered are difficult to interpret. Their arrays of punctuations, cup marks, incisions, and notches form few recognizable images. The dominant engraved sign—an oval or triangle partly bisected by a line—has been commonly identified as a representation of the vulva. An alternative interpretation is that such signs, as well as other arrangements of cuplike marks, represent hoof prints. Such symbolism could have arisen from a very natural association between animals and their tracks.

Perhaps the most unexpected object that has survived from Aurignacian times is a flute from the site of Isturitz in southwestern France. Made of bird bone, which is naturally hollow, it had at least three finger holes. This flute indicates that in addition to other forms of expression, the Aurignacians also had music. At least a dozen more such flutes are known from the succeeding cultural period, the Gravettian (roughly 28,000 to 22,000 years ago).

The Gravettian period also witnessed the emergence of the first fired

ceramics, which appeared in central and eastern Europe about 26,000 years ago. Many thousands of fragments of animal and human figurines, as well as kilns for their production, have been recovered from sites in Moravia, in what is now the Czech Republic, and Russia. The figurines were shaped from moistened loess, a fine sediment underlying the campsites where they have been found, and fired at high temperatures. This invention preceded by at least 10,000 years the first known ceramic vessels. Because the figurines are often fragmented, some archeologists suggest that the kilns were purposely designed to explode them.

By far the most famous Gravettian representations are the female statuettes and bas-reliefs popularly (but inappropriately) called Venuses. Some are ceramic, but others are sculpted from a variety of materials—ivory, limestone, steatite, and calcite. Varying regionally in form and manufacturing technique, they are found throughout Europe. At the 26,000-year-old site of Avdeevo, in Russia, Maria Gvozdover and her colleague Gennadi Grigoriev have excavated more than a dozen such figurines, nearly as many as have been found at all of the other sites of this age in western Europe combined. Most were sculpted from the tusks of woolly mammoths and depict women in the late stages of pregnancy, frequently in birthing postures. Many were buried in pits, sometimes more than one to a pit. In some cases, different fragments of a broken statuette were buried in pits dug several yards apart. This careful placement must have reflected some ritual concern.

Gravettian sites have also yielded numerous animal engravings, often done in a rather stiff, flat style, with the lower limbs left unfinished. Finally, the Gravettian is famous for its numerous hand stencils, found at habitation sites beneath rock overhangs and in shallow to medium-depth caves. One French cave, Gargas, has more than 150 hands stenciled on its walls. In Grotte Cosquer, the underwater cave recently discovered near Marseille, the charcoal-based paint used to spray the numerous hand stencils has now been radiocarbon dated to about 27,000 years ago *(see* "Neptune's Ice Age Gallery," *Natural History,* April 1993).

This great commitment of labor, technological innovation, and creativity implies that ornamentation and representation served practical, adaptive functions for early Cro-Magnon people. Neanderthals and their contemporaries outside of Europe may have had the mental capacity to use lines and materials to represent natural objects—some apparently did so when exposed to Aurignacian cultures—but on their own they do not seem to have appreciated the advantages of such exercises. Cro-Magnons used two- and three-dimensional forms of representation systematically—to render concepts tangible, to communicate, and to explore social relations and technological possibilities. This powerfully enhanced their evolutionary fitness. As University of Miami archeologist Heidi Knecht has argued, the ability to simulate visually things that do not yet exist is essential to any degree of innovation.

Around the world today, images and icons—from tattoos to national flags—are frequently brandished to assert social and political authority. Personal ornaments, constructed of rare, sacred, or exotic materials or requiring great labor, knowledge, or skill, serve universally to distinguish people and groups. Modern culture in any of its diverse forms is unimaginable without the kind of material symbols that humans first devised 40,000 years ago.

The Search For Eve

Michael H. Brown

It was on New Year's Day that the geneticists staked their claim. On page 31 in the January 1, 1987, issue of *Nature,* two scientists from the University of California at Berkeley and another from the University of Hawaii presented a highly technical paper entitled "Mitochondrial DNA and human evolution." Under the heading was a summary (known as the "abstract") that made all of paleoanthropology take note. It was even startling: "Mitochondrial DNAs from 147 people, drawn from five geographic populations, have been analyzed by restriction mapping. All these mitochondrial DNAs stem from one woman who is postulated to have lived about 200,000 years ago. . . ."

While most of the rest of the world was unfamiliar with the article (and was recovering from the night before), the diverse worlds of anthropology and genetics were immediately seized by the significance of the piece. *Nature* was not quick to accept new claims, and the journal had the first and final say in many matters of science. Though the average person had never seen the magazine (with an international circulation of just 40,000, it wasn't to be found at the corner store), *Nature* was a bible of new biological, astronomical, chemical, and anthropological assertions—the most prestigious science publication in all the world. It was where the first identification of the AIDS virus was announced, where the discovery of lasers was originally explained, and where James Watson and Francis Crick had first propounded the very structure of DNA itself. One could go back decades, at least to the announcement of the Taung child, and

note its lofty paleoanthropological role. It was where debate over the status of man-apes—the australopithecines—still took place. It was where the Leakeys announced many of their great fossils. Intense commotion could be caused by technical reports that were hardly more than a page in length. Crucial intellectual debates were spawned by mere letters to the editor. Scientists chewed every morsel like cud.

This report ran for five full pages, tucked between a cover story on light emission from the hydroid *Obelia* and a report on optical computers. That was fairly good play. But, as with many of its articles, *Nature* had waited a good while before publishing it. Almost ten months of agonizing debate went on, ten months of struggle to reach a consensus on whether or not the article, with its loud and hypothetical claims, should be published by such an august journal. It was sure to generate some newspaper articles—location of a woman who inevitably would be referred to as "Eve"—and though it was hardly able to compete with the top stories of the week (the Iran-Contra affair was coming into bloom, and in the science world all the talk was of superconductivity), the report, crammed with lab results and the spectacular claim of finally locating man's one common ancestor, was nonetheless destined to spark years of argument. Such was always assured in the small, aloof, and extraordinarily contentious world of paleoanthropology.

If the average *Homo sapien* was oblivious to the report (it didn't exactly make a news bulletin during the football games), that didn't detract from the fact that science was suddenly taking a wholly new approach to the

history of its own species. What the article explained was that, in analyzing DNA from the energy-producing compartments of the human cell known as the mitochondria, the authors, Rebecca L. Cann, Mark Stoneking, and Allan C. Wilson, had discovered that this genetic material, inherited through the ages, provided "new perspectives on how, where, and when the human gene pool arose and grew."

From samples of placenta, they had extracted and purified enough hereditary material to compare the intricate variations between and among peoples of Asian, European, African, Australian, and New Guinean descent. The mitochondrial DNA—or "mtDNA," as they insisted upon calling it—offered a wholly unique attribute that couldn't be found elsewhere: it was inherited only maternally, from the mother. Except for occasional minor mutations, this type of DNA was passed intact from great-grandmother to grandmother to daughter with virtually no input from males and thus no mixing—no blending of father's and mother's genes—that would jumble, complicate, and thus obscure its history. It survived the generations—the millennia—without being fudged by recombination. And for that reason, explained the paper, mitochondrial DNA—as opposed to nuclear DNA, where such blending does occur—was a powerful new tool "for relating individuals to one another."

In sum, mitochondrial DNA was a convenient tool because it was much smaller and simpler than the DNA in a cell's nucleus. While the nuclear DNA, composed of perhaps 100,000 genes, had not yet been mapped to spell out the entire message hidden in its chemical codes (and is currently the subject of a $3 billion federal effort, expected to take fifteen years, aimed at just that), the DNA in a cell's mitochondria had already been fully mapped and found to contain but thirty-seven genes, all of them inherited solely from our mothers (instead of the complicating mix from both parents that, again, occurs in the nucleus). "So you're connected by an unbroken chain of mothers—whether you're a son or a daughter—back into the past," explains one of the authors, Allan Wilson. "And what we're interested in doing is building up a genealogical tree that connects those maternal chains."

Although the metaphor is anything but perfect, for our uncomplicated purposes we can visualize DNA—or deoxyribonucleic acid—as the biological equivalent of computer punchtape. The "holes" in the punchtape are codes which direct the cell to form the proteins that serve as the foundation for our bodies. Certain portions and sequences of the computer tape are what we call the genes. Besides directing the daily activities that keep the body humming, DNA determines our heredity: height, skin pigmentation, and eye color down the generations, the transmissions of traits that keep the race or species going for thousands or millions of years. DNA is, in fact, literally a blueprint for life itself.

Where DNA in the nucleus, as Cann said, may determine everything from whether we have curly hair to whether we can curl our tongues, the role of DNA in the *mitochondria* is much more limited but nonetheless extremely vital: it codes for key components of our energy-production system. Put another way, it is a piece of coded information in the mitochondria, and the mitochondria are bean-shaped structures that, in their turn, are the power plants of the cell. It is the task of these microscopic components to extract energy from food molecules floating in the sappy cytoplasm outside the nucleus.

While it is the nuclear DNA that determines what the next generation will look and perhaps even act like, the DNA in the mitochondria—circular-shaped and densely packed with its own brand of genes—has several characteristics that make it more valuable

in studying evolution. In addition to the fact that it's simpler and maternally inherited, allowing a geneticist to look straight into the female past, it grants a magnified view of genetic diversity because mutations—changes in the tiny biochemical configurations that happen as a matter of course—accumulate much faster in mitochondrial DNA than in the nucleus. They give each individual a "signature" that can be compared with others. (Most evolutionary change, it is believed, starts with mutations in genetic molecules.)

But many mutations have little or no effect on the functioning of our organisms. They are "neutral." They seem to occur randomly. And they accumulate over time, changing ever so slightly the configuration of certain of those "holes" in the "punchtape." By zeroing in on the patterns, geneticists, after relating one person's DNA to another's, can supposedly determine how close people are, and can then represent them as twigs on a genealogical tree. "If you're good enough a molecular biologist," says Wilson, who clearly thought he was, "you can reconstruct that branching diagram leading back to that one mother by taking a count of the number of mutational differences among the twigs. We build genealogical trees by comparing mitochondrial DNA from the terminal twigs connecting through unbroken chains of mothers back to the mother of us all."

The geneticists felt, in effect, that they had come upon a means of studying the origins of modern man without resorting to chips of flint and scraps of fossil. They could even date backward (far backward, without studying paleontology or geology), for the mutational differences (or "divergences") between people that occurred, they calculated, at a set rate of 2 to 4 percent every million years. In other words, small but regular changes in the DNA through the ages functioned as sort of a molecular clock. The ticks were mutations, the minutes were many centuries.

It seemed, in mitochondrial DNA, that a new window—really a looking glass—had opened onto previously impenetrable history.

As Wilson goes on to explain, the key findings were "that these mutations, the neutral ones, accumulate at much the same rate in all organisms ranging from bacteria to plants to animals, that the same basic rate of ticking, the same rate per year, is observed in all of these creatures, so in this vast array of organisms, we have a timepiece ticking away in a statistical fashion (not like a metronome), and allowing us the possibility of being able to put a time scale onto all of evolution, regardless of whether the species have a fossil record."

So powerful was the new technique that it was "entirely possible," said another of the geneticists, Rebecca Cann, "that we could identify Cleopatra's mitochondrial genes in modern people, and, at least theoretically, also specify her entire mitochondrial genotype."

More to the point, they could look for the genes of cavemen in a future Yuppie.

And whatever population had accumulated the most mutations—was the most divergent among each other—could be assumed to have been the oldest. The longer a population had been around, the more mutations.

Such a possibility was enough to cause paleoanthropological angina. It was one thing to be hit with a process that seemed frighteningly complex, but then for these geneticists to take a new, nearly unknown technique—a technique the vast majority of anthropologists were totally unfamiliar with—and swiftly pronounce a major evolutionary find based upon that technique, well . . . There is nothing more controversial to a paleoanthropologist than a claim that someone can precisely describe when and where and how man arose from a primordial, ape-filled past.

As frequently as not, paleoanthropologists can't even agree on the most basic things. Often they see different traits, different species, and far different implications—sometimes even a different genus—in the very same cranium.

Each major anthropologist has a highly opinionated way of interpreting fossils and a highly individualistic way of presenting evolutionary trees. When two or three of them agree on an issue (or *part* of an issue), this becomes a theory or "school" of thought. That's all it takes. And the ground is constantly shifting. "You can't really tell who thinks what this week or last month," comments one such eminent paleoanthropologist, Clark Howell. "The consensus is who shouts the loudest."

In short, it's bad enough when paleoanthropologists squabble among themselves, but now outsiders—geneticists—were in effect proclaiming—shouting—that they could solve what fossil hunters and anatomists had never been able to resolve themselves: the period of time during which primitive or "archaic" humans transformed into fully modern beings.

With equal audacity, the geneticists were going to say *where* modern man arose, with an air of unprecedented authority. It is difficult to describe the emotions such an assertion can provoke. While paleoanthropologists had pretty much reached a consensus that Africa was the place of birth for the oldest of the man-apes and ape-men, the place of origin for the next major stage in human development, anatomically modern men, was still very much up in the air. Since the old caveman *erectus* and his nearly equally beetle-browed descendants had spread pretty much around the Old World—Africa, China, Indonesia, Europe, Israel—the transition into modern human form could have occurred in any of those places. From the raw ingredients of *Homo erectus* (which, miraculously enough, nearly everyone seemed to agree was the major precursor of the sapient strain), evolution appeared to have reached sort of a critical mass, erupting here and there first from *erectus* into the slightly less primitive "archaic" *Homo sapiens* (which included Neandertals) and then into the nearly browless, smooth-headed, small-faced *Homo sapiens sapiens*.

All Eurasia and Africa were therefore the stage. Though best symbolized by Eugène Dubois's finds in Java, *Homo erectus* or archaic descendants were now even known to have existed in India and the Soviet Union. Up until

400,000 years or so ago, *erectus* was the dominant caveman—hunter, maker of fire, uttering perhaps a few rudimentary but decipherable sounds. He was the caveman's caveman, granddad of Neandertals and us as well! And the very "type" specimens for *erectus*—the fossils looked upon as those which defined the species—were the ones composing Peking Man and Dubois's monumental finds in Java.

So for many years an overshadowing dispute had been the basic one of modern origins, and debate was intensifying. There were those who believed anatomically modern man evolved over a broad geographical front. That is, that Chinese *erectus* gave birth to modern Chinese, that African *erectus* fathered modern Africans, and that the old cavemen of Europe led to modern Europeans. They were all connected to each other by occasional sexual intermingling.

An *erectus* from China, in other words, might have a fling with an *erectus* carrying African genes.

This was the "multi-regional" model.

And there was no single Garden of Eden.

The opposing school of thought conceded readily that *erectus* was our precursor, but did not accept that a wide range of these primitive men evolved *simultaneously* into fully modern beings. Instead, adherents to this school believed a select population of the *erectus* assumed modern characteristics in one region, and then simply replaced the more primitive types in other regions. This school of thought is known, because of the idea that a small group served as the founding population, as "Garden of Eden." Although the nickname is an obvious one, it manages nicely to convey the idea that we rose from a single, rather confined, even isolated population of *erectus* that then fanned out from its original locale. Those who adhere to this proposition tend to believe Neandertals were an extinct and meaningless side branch of humanity, disappearing with nary a trace, overflooded by Eve's offspring.

No one had been able to settle the issue once and for all. The biggest problem for the Garden of Eden

school, proposing as it did a single point of origin, was proving where that single point was. There was that void in the fossil record. Or, as always, the bones told conflicting tales. While Africa had been a contender for the seat of humanity ever since the Taung finding, that continent was considered by many to figure most prominently only in the far past—and it was a long way from bipedal apes to Java Man. "The idea of an African origin for anatomically modern man was still not quite there," says Howell, an especially influential paleoanthropologist who teaches at Berkeley. "There was the conceivable possibility, but the evidence was still so scrappy, the dating was so equivocal or unconvincing or inadequate, that people were probably unwilling to hang their hats on that stance. Eurasia was still a consideration. India was a possibility talked about."

The candidates even included Arabia.

Europe, where cave art hinted at the transition to modern man in the form of Cro-Magnon, and Asia, where *erectus* had been found to be at the very least half a million years old, were, meanwhile, still in the running as places where *erectus* had evolved into precious *Homo sapiens sapiens*. Because no one seemed to doubt the pivotal role *erectus* played in the human lineage, and because its most famous representations were in Asia—once again, the Java *erectus* and also the *erectus* known as Peking Man—there was a strong tendency (despite growing leanings toward Africa) to keep Asia as a bona fide candidate for the cradle of modern mankind. There seemed to be a continuity in Asia from half a million years ago to the present populations. Even the Garden-of-Edeners conceded some gene mixture.

The Aborigines of Australia, who must have gotten down there from Asia, actually *looked,* to some scholars, like conceptions of old Asian *erectus.* Thick brows. Strong at the jaw. Africa was fine as the rootstock of man-apes and ape-men, but the delicate evolution to *Homo sapiens*—millions of years after the first australopithecines had been spawned—seemed better placed in areas where civilization was most advanced.

Europe was also still in the running, favored by a few scholars who resided in England, Germany, and France, but the real debate was Asia versus Africa. The most famous and best-loved fossils of *erectus*—the very skulls that had defined the *erectus* species, for many years the most ancient human fossils anywhere, or at least the ones known for the longest time to the general public as most ancient—came not from Africa but Asia. Franz Weidenreich, a German who was perhaps the most meticulous describer of fossils ever known, believed that development into modern form was the destiny of a number of major lineages over that broad geographical front I mentioned. Those who followed Weidenreich figured each region had its own distinct rootstock which had evolved to form the various races and ethnic groups that exist today, and though there was some mixture and migration between the rootstocks, remnants of the original, primitive people could be spotted in modern populations. Besides the European genes derived from Neandertal, Weidenreich's disciples, especially the American anthropologist Carleton Coon, envisioned Peking Man leading to modern Mongoloids (an idea enshrined in the *World Book* encyclopedia), while Java Man led to those Australian Aborigines. The Aborigines, thought Coon, were so thick of brow it looked like they were still sloughing off *erectus* traits. Coon went so far as to conceive that evolution into modern man developed in each major part of the world nearly independently.

While no one could prove that Asia was our first homeland, neither could anyone *disprove* it. "Paucity of fossils and infirmity of dates," repeated another noted authority of the day, William W. Howells, "remains a central problem." No one could even discard Europe once and for all—no one until now. Though, in true scientific form, they were going to be ponderous enough to appear a little bit conservative, the geneticists, writing this New Year's Day in *Nature,* did not mince

too many words in venturing their key claim: that modern man arose, alas, in sub-Saharan Africa.

Forget the nonsense about Aborigines looking like primitive Indonesians. Australia was colonized by Africans. *China* was conquered by Africans. Europe had been taken over by Africans. The Neandertals? They weren't direct ancestors. Their genes had not even been incorporated into those of the advancing Africans. They weren't the precursors of modern Europeans or anyone else, despite what many paleoanthropologists continued to believe. They had been swept into complete extinction, warranting little more than a footnote, irrelevant in the grand scheme of things.

Instead, every existing human could be traced back to a very special colony of humans from the deep, dark continent of Africa, said the genticists. They had found, it seemed, the oldest maternal lineage leading to modern-day humans! Everyone had recent African roots, whether the leather-faced Indians who first crossed the Bering Strait or the milk-white Swedes.

The geneticists set the age of "Eve" (their predictable nickname for the one African woman whose mitochondrial DNA they had tracked all the way down the ages) at between 140,000 and 290,000 years. They rounded her median age to 200,000. She was almost surely a highly evolved descendant of an African *erectus*—as opposed to the more famous Asian variety of *erectus* like Peking Man. And her offspring, in turn, helped found a population that was growing increasingly sapient and increasingly migratory, sloughing off old *erectus* traits and spreading out of Africa perhaps 90,000 to 180,000 years ago to take over the world, although it was warned that the migration may have been as "recent" as 21,000 B.C. In other words, a population of *erectus* in a single and isolated spot had made the momentous change into modern humans, displacing the other citizens of our planet like a fast and colorful and aggressive fish—a beta—assuming complete control of an aquarium.

There was little evidence, said the geneticists, that this advanced African

population interbred with existing and more primitive populations in Asia and Europe. Instead, they simply outbred and conquered them. They must have possessed some vast superiority, and perhaps a streak of real nastiness. "Thus we propose," said Cann, Stoneking, and Wilson, "that *Homo erectus* in Asia was replaced without much mixing with the invading *Homo sapiens* from Africa."

Invading! The very word sent the imagination into a frenzy: gnashing teeth, clubs against thick skulls, hurled dolomite stones, the new, "invading" *Homo sapiens* versus the old beetle-brows. It was breathtaking to envision sweeping hordes moving from deepest Africa up through the Mediterranean, trampling mud huts, raiding stocks of food, stealing caves, conquering and killing populations of unevolved *erectus* and Neandertals.

Although the geneticists, gentle in their lab coats, weren't trying to project any such violent scenario, the words meant to some paleoanthropologists that at one time in the past a population of Africans had taken over the world by raising something on the order of a Pleistocene holocaust. The most "rational, commonsense interpretation" of the DNA hypothesis is that the fanning out of modern humans and their replacement of those older and more primitive populations entrenched in Europe, Asia, and elsewhere in Africa involved "turmoil and bloodshed," says Harvard's Ernst Mayr, one of the century's great evolutionary biologists and the man who engineered the reclassification of Java and Peking men as *Homo erectus*. Mayr, who has been described as a final court of opinion in paleoanthropology, found aspects of the *Nature* piece "staggering."

Guaranteed to raise paleoanthropology's collective blood pressure was the assertion that there had been little or no intermixing between the African "invaders" and the Asian populations. Even the other Garden-of-Edeners accepted *some* reproductive exchange. The geneticists took the extreme view that there was perhaps *none*. That was what caused talk of a holocaust: how could there have been no sexual intermixing unless there had been outright warfare and annihilation of the Asian *erectus*-like people? But that was just a side issue. The real poignancy of what Cann, Stoneking, and Wilson were implying was that they were ready to dismiss a thick branch—or better put, part of the very trunk—of certain time-honored human trees. They were saying that populations in Asia were not only overwhelmed but contributed virtually no genes to modern humanity.

"We see no indication of any deep lineage in Asia," was how Wilson later put it.

The European Neandertals were implicitly disposed of, but that wasn't totally surprising. Now the geneticists were getting their turn to look back at the crucial Asian specimens, however, and what they had to say, in the *Nature* report, must have caused Weidenreich's own bones to turn in the grave. The geneticists themselves emphasized the original, founding role of *erectus* in human evolution, but they were referring, as I said, to an African *erectus*—not Java or Peking Man. Theirs was a beetle-brow south of the Sahara who turned into modern form before the Asian *erectus* could do the same, and then overtook all the Java and Peking descendants, who left not a trace.

"The greatest divergences within clusters specific to non-African parts of the World correspond to times of only 90,000–180,000 years," the geneticists said. "This might imply that the early Asian *Homo* (such as Java man and Peking man) contributed no surviving mtDNA lineages to the gene pool of our species. Consistent with this implication are features, found recently in the skeletons of the ancient Asian forms, that make it unlikely that Asian *erectus* was ancestral to *Homo sapiens*."

They were trying to get rid of Dubois's *erectus*! They were saying that Peking Man too was pretty meaningless, despite fifty years of uninterrupted hype. They were knocking from the human lineage a specimen so revered by Chinese as a sacred ancestor that even Mao and Henry Kissinger were peripherally involved in trying to

locate the Zhoukoudian fossils when they were lost during the last world war. They were screwing up the dioramas in a hundred museums!

It was one thing to discard the klutzing, lame-brain Neandertals of Europe, who never had been totally accepted as direct human ancestors and who, Cann said, showed no evidence of contributing maternal lineages to modern Europeans, but the geneticists were also strongly implying that all those furry cavemen who had operated with cunning about the caves of Asia—for millennia—had no direct bearing on human evolution either. Those precious fossils from the limestone near Trinil and Beijing, the most ancient form of true man known to science for much of this century—the skilled hunters and firemakers and cannibals, prototype, along with Neandertals, for a thousand cartoons and the unilinear charts of human development—had sown no permanent oats. Their heyday was now meaningless history.

It was Maalox time for textbook editors, not to mention the encyclopedias. In place of the simple line charts—Java Man → Peking → Neandertal → *Homo sapiens*—was now a genealogical tree that resembled a huge, encrypted horseshoe. There were 134 little twigs to represent the genetic sampling, with two major branches connecting to the trunk, which represented the mitochondrial mother. It was a maze. Ancestral lines like a diagram for an electric plant. Next to it was a long and undecipherable block of code numbers listing what they called "polymorphic restriction sites." It looked like something only a computer could read.

While one branch of the tree led back solely to Africans, the second branch also included Africans, along with Asians, Australians, New Guineans, and Europeans. That was a fairly strong suggestion that Africa was the origin. "This inference comes from the observation that one of the two primary branches leads exclusively to African mtDNAs while the second primary branch also leads to African mtDNA," was the way Cann, Stoneking, and Wilson put it. Moreover,

they said, the Africans displayed the most diverse DNA types. (Again, the longer time a lineage is around, the more mutations it collects, and thus the more diversity within such a population.) It was a fairly compelling indication that Africans were the originals, the oldest. Their divergence was 0.47 percent. Asia was a distant second, with 0.35. Those two were followed by Australian Aborigines, New Guineans, and finally Caucasians, who weighed in at only 0.23 percent.

This was what Ernst Mayr found staggering: the Aborigines of Australia appeared genetically closer to Europeans, in some cases, than they did to Africans!

But then, the geneticists were also saying that there had been no distinct races until after much of the world was settled, so back then, who knew what a European or Australian looked like? They hadn't settled down to form races yet. And we shouldn't get away from the more immediate issue of intermixing. "If there was hybridization between the resident archaic forms in Asia and anatomically modern forms emerging from Africa, we should expect to find extremely divergent types of mtDNA in present-day Asians, more divergent than any mtDNA found in Africa," said the geneticists. "There is no evidence for these types of mtDNA among the Asians studied."

Africa, it was stressed again and again, "is a likely source of the human mitochondrial gene pool."

Archeological evidence, they said, was also pointing to an African origin for mankind's shared grandmother.

After all, blades were in common use there long before they replaced the flake tools in Asia and Europe.

For the paleoanthropologist, it was not going to be a relaxed day of ham and football. To recap where we were now: The man-apes known as *Australopithecus* still stood as the supposed ancestors the farthest distance back (best remembered as the Taung child but best visualized as an erect chimpanzee), and of course there was still *Homo erectus* in our more immediate lineage, though minus the Java and Peking specimens that once stood as the very symbols of fossilized ape-men. It was still true that *erectus* had spread around the world about a million years ago, but only a small, isolated portion of those primitive humans—presumably a type developed in Africa alone—had evolved into the *Homo sapiens* who then took over the globe, replacing the *erectus* from everywhere else. Woe to those who thought modern man had started 40,000 years ago, as a Cro-Magnon in France. Woe too to the religious fundamentalists, like the followers of Rev. Jerry Falwell, who believed man was created in 4004 B.C.

One of the geneticists, Rebecca Cann, could barely contain her disdain for popular genealogy. "Dioramas in a natural history museum can be counted on," noted Cann, "to show some primitive ape-human (*Australopithecus*) emerging into some early species of our own genus *Homo*. Then *Homo erectus* evolves into *Homo sapiens,* along with mortgages, star wars, and ice cream. Such schemes imply a genetic continuity in space and time that contains more fantasy than Spiderman's best escapades."

The geneticists weren't mincing many words. It was a preemptive strike. They knew they were in for heat. Already a paleoanthropologist from Michigan had been grumbling very loudly and was mounting a major attack. Cann and Allan Wilson, who had fought long and hard with old-school paleoanthropologists, had the opportunity now to get their digs in. Both were calling for increased interaction between paleoanthropologists and geneticists—peace—at the same time they were firing off subtle and sometimes not-so-subtle salvos. The geneticists were in effect pronouncing themselves as the best hope for settling age-old disputes and finding the real answers.

Fossils would have to take a back seat.

"Besides the likelihood that the most sought after bones never will materialize," wrote Cann, "there is the problem of properly identifying the fossils that *are* found. It is hard to know, by bone shape alone, whether a fossil represents a species already identified or whether it is different enough to represent a species of its own. Then there is the difficulty of knowing whether the fossil was left by a human ancestor or by a related primate that became extinct. All in all, it is too much to hope that the trickle of bones from the fossil beds of eastern Africa will, in itself, provide a clear picture of human evolution any time soon."

Elsewhere she added pointedly: "As molecular biologists, we at least knew that the genes available from present-day specimens came from some ancestor. In contrast, paleontologists can never be certain that a given fossil has left descendants."

Wilson was blunter still. "Some people don't like our conclusions, but I expect they will be proved wrong again." The old-school paleoanthropologists, relying as they did on analyzing fossil fragments and physical features (the practice known as "morphology"), would probably have to be dragged by their own noses, but they would come around to his view. He'd seen it before, and he wasn't happy at all with paleoanthropology. Back when he was studying man's relationship with primates, the paleoanthropologists had badly shunned him. He wasn't the sort to forgive and forget. He had once said his group had developed "a set of data that's much larger than I think has ever existed. The morphologists can't come close to us." Now there was more data still. And more sophistication. The paleoanthropologists had been left in the dust.

It certainly sounded like war was developing between the fossils and genes. It was a war that had been a long time in the making. Of all the nerve: upstarts from Berkeley and Hawaii deciding they will provide the final answers not with an ossified skull but with genetic mutations. The big paleoanthropological news of the year was not made by a suntanned, dust-laden paleontologist in the outback of the Fayum Desert, not by the unearthing of a skeleton caked in breccia or kept preserved in a prehistoric bog, but rather by those stiff and haughty lab coats.

A new age was clearly dawning. While street sweepers were piling kazoos and party hats in the gutters of Times Square, the geneticists had completed the big play, opening the new year with a discovery that—though not yet garnering the same level of publicity—rivaled the most celebrated of fossil discoveries.

Could it be true that the geneticists did hold the key to the past? Was Eve alive and well in the whir of a centrifuge?

A Multiregional Model

Michael H. Brown

Milford H. Wolpoff was often described as the man who had examined more fossils than anyone alive. He didn't actually dig for artifacts. Rather, his expertise was measuring, interpreting, and comparing what fossil hunters already had at hand. He had seen it all, from modern populations in Australia to the oldest *Australopithecus*. He knew the European archaics well enough to write whole papers on them, and he was one of the world's foremost experts on the *erectus* from Asia. When it came to analyzing fossils, his name was as frequent in some journals as the Leakeys were for the discoveries themselves. Whether or not anyone could lay claim to examining the most fossils, Wolpoff was the walking personification of paleoanthropology, and he *detested* DNA.

That is, he strongly disliked how Berkeley was using the stuff, and he hated what he saw as overblown claims. He did not believe there was any such thing as a molecular "clock," arguing against it since the old blood protein days. His was also that first voice of opposition in the *Chronicle* article on an "African Eve" back in 1986.

Wolpoff was a natural enemy of molecules, and when Cann, et al., referred to paleoanthropologists in the negative, as they had in those preemptive strikes early on, it was people like Wolpoff they had in mind. That had rankled him, things like Cann saying "it is too much to hope" that "the

trickle of bones from fossil beds" would "provide a clear picture of human evolution any time soon." He might even agree to a certain extent (and by the way, he had never been a supporter of *Ramapithecus*), but it was still irritating when she kept twisting in the fact that "the traditional portrayal of fossil evidence" had left the impression that "scientists have reliably mapped the evolution of humans" when it was obvious, said Cann, that they hadn't. She, Stoneking, and Wilson had made it clear that they didn't think their critics understood the new technology.

They seemed awfully condescending. They were also bewildering. Cann would throw down the gauntlet and in the same breath extend an olive branch. "This could be the start of a wonderful working relationship," she had concluded in one paper—after declaring that *her* genes were superior to *their* fossils and making the provocative remark that museum dioramas contained "more fantasy than Spiderman's best escapades."

While paleoanthropologists could never be sure a certain fossil actually left descendants, she emphasized, there was "100 percent certainty that genes in modern populations have a history that can be examined and will trace back in absolute time to *real ancestors*" (author's emphasis). Through genes, Cann pointed out, they had found a female who was probably the

only common link in our species, "and through those genes, we are uncovering areas of the past that have been hidden from us by history, culture, and our own eyes." That was rapping them over the head with the olive branch.

Wilson referred to Wolpoff and his colleagues as "certain loud voices raised in Michigan." He was still obsessed with their initial rejection of his albumin results. Now he was sure they'd be eating crow just as other anthropologists who'd dared to criticize him before had eaten crow over *Ramapithecus*. "The anthropologists said the first hominid evolved at least 15 million years ago, and we said it was more like 5 million," he reiterated to the journal *Science*. "It took a decade and a half before the anthropologists realized they were wrong." And now, in the wake of the new DNA "clock," to repeat what Wilson thought, "Some people don't like our conclusions but I expect they will be proved wrong again."

At the same time all those feelings were starting to run so high, Cann, et al., had not been able to avoid citing Wolpoff's work in their own *Nature* paper. Everywhere you went, there, in citation parentheses, or at the top as a co-author, or in the bibliography, was that name: Wolpoff. He had started out as an expert on australopithecines and now he was an expert on Neandertals and *erectus* and European archaics. He could argue obscure points of interpretation in hominids and humanoids scattered across three continents and 4 million years. He also had a working knowledge of genetics. And he had one word to describe what was coming out of Berkeley:

"Wacko!"

That was Milford Wolpoff, a character as well as a scholar, looking a bit like Ernest Borgnine, street smart, son of a Chicago taxi driver. For kicks he played the clarinet in the Ann Arbor Symphony Band. At conferences he held debates in the pubs. That was where some of the best discussions with fellow anthropologists occurred, sudsing it up after a long dry day of seminars. He was a very serious scholar, and a very thorough one. Everywhere you went: (Wolpoff). And though, like many of his colleagues, his ego was large enough to consume the western end of Olduvai Gorge (and many of his associates complained that a conversation with Wolpoff was usually a Wolpoff monologue), he could be a teddy bear of a man, very witty, generous with his knowledge, and his ego somehow didn't translate into off-putting haughtiness.

Unless you were his opponent. Then his ego was just fierce and abrasive. Cann was clearly daunted by his experience with fossils. She had fairly shrunk from him one time when they met. "There was some worry on her part about whether I was going to chew her head off," says Wolpoff with a twinkle in his eyes. "But I didn't."

She thought him "real bombastic," and accused him of quoting her work out of context. At one convocation he had attacked her rather personally, and her allies like Chris Stringer at the British Museum had also borne Milford's wrath. "Historically the British Museum has been responsible for many important advances in paleoanthropology," said Wolpoff during another conference in Europe. Then he flashed a slide of the fraudulent Piltdown skull.

A teddy bear or a grizzly one? Call this chapter "Cann and the Cave Bear": Wolpoff was going to go full force and claws bared after Berkeley, leaving no rock unturned, fighting

even on genetic grounds, while off to the side, once everyone had begun to understand what Cann, et al., were up to, there were any number of other skirmishes breaking out.

Wolpoff thought the use of American blacks as a sample for Africans, to start off with, was "bizarre, ludicrous." The entire DNA hypothesis was untenable, in his opinion. For the DNA "clock" to function, he figured, the mutations had to be both constant and random, implying that this type of DNA was not distorted by forces of natural selection (whereby certain mutations are eliminated and thus would not be there to be counted centuries later by geneticists). In other words, the changes in mitochondrial DNA would virtually all have to be "neutral," which he didn't believe was the case. He also didn't believe for a minute that Africans could take over whole continents without interbreeding with the resident populations like *erectus* and Neandertals.

"I don't think Rebecca thought the consequences through, I think she just got carried away by believing she was right," he says. "It's like preaching a new religion. If fossils don't fit her model, she feels it's our problem. I had an adviser who was a geneticist, I took population genetics, I think I understand this stuff. And what I want to see is the model where one species of humans replaces another through only subtle competition without directly interacting with each other. And if they're not different species, wouldn't one assume that the women would be incorporated? Do they envision that the archaics and *Homo sapiens sapiens* lived next to each other or waved at each other as they walked by, but never mixed?"

If the Berkeley group was right, thought Wolpoff, then someone should be able to find African-like fossils in Asia from around the time of the hypothetical invasion. Yet no one had. "We've never found the combination of small browridges, high foreheads, and jutting faces of the Africans in Asia," he argues.

Instead of bearing African features, says Wolpoff, Chinese and other Asians

today bear resemblances to those old *erectus* populations that Cann and her colleagues say went extinct. They did not go extinct, argued Wolpoff. Peking and Java Man instead contributed substantially to modern gene pools. He had the fossils to show it. And what they showed, those fossils, was a facial and forehead form that is still detectable in modern Chinese. In regions where the fossils had flat faces, one could find flat faces today. That didn't speak well for the concept of an African "invasion."

"It's a neat story, the out-of-Africa hypothesis, and if I was a graduate student I'd be sucked right into this," he said. "But there are problems. The problem is that as Eves left Africa, they left as Africans, but when they arrived in Asia, they arrived as Asians! When they arrived in Europe, they arrived as Europeans!"

In presentations at places such as the University of Pennsylvania, Wolpoff used more slides and more sarcasm to get across his point. One was a photograph taken from the rear of Africans walking down a path with baskets on their heads. That represented the migration from the sub-Sahara. In the next slide he showed a Chinese family smiling as they approached on bikes. *That* was Eve's clan arriving to Asia.

"Wacko!" repeated Wolpoff, determined to show just how ridiculous the Berkeley hypothesis was. It came down to this: if he could demonstrate genetic continuity somewhere outside of Africa—if just one place in Europe or Asia had connections between old cavemen and modern humans—he felt that would be enough to disprove the idea of a common recent origin and an African takeover. Evolution into anatomically modern humans had taken place across the board, he believed, with archaic populations in Asia, Africa, and Europe all turning modern as genes and cultural ideas flowed between them. This was called "multiregional continuity." *Erectus* in Africa served as the founding population for current-day Africans, *erectus* descendants in Europe for current Europeans, and *erectus* in Asia for any number of populations ranging from Australians and Eskimos to Chinese and American Indians. There was no single and magical "Garden of Eden."

Although Wolpoff had modified it, the theory of continuity went back to Franz Weidenreich and Carleton Coon, two of the science's most historical figures. Like Wolpoff, who had assumed his mantle, Weidenreich was an indefatigable morphologist and an unambiguous man. He made clear his position that "there was certainly not one Adam and one Eve who could be claimed as a progenitor by every living man today." While Wolpoff disagreed with certain of their precepts and thought some of Coon's ideas had been rightly rejected as racist, he did not want to "throw the baby out with the bathwater," and the baby was that concept of regional continuity.

Both Weidenreich and Coon had written in detail of similarities between *erectus* populations in Asia and modern man—exactly the type of stuff that contradicted the Berkeley replacement theory. Weidenreich in fact was the first to see the supposedly unbroken chain of links from the Java *erectus* through the archaics of Ngandong and on to living Australian Aborigines. This in turn resurrected the memory of how Dubois himself had described the Ngandong archaics as "proto-Australians." There were also those resemblances between the fossils at Zhoukoudian, where Peking Man had been found, and modern Chinese. Take flat faces: they were present in both the fossils and current Asians. The inescapable implication was that whatever the role of Africa back in the days of man-apes, the origin of modern Asians was Asia.

Coon, a Harvard man who retired in 1963 as curator of ethnology and professor of anthropology at the University of Pennsylvania, had taken it upon himself to interpret much of Weidenreich's work and had listed a whole slew of features which he said were shared between the *erectus* from China and living Mongoloids. These common traits included a ridge down the middle of the skull found in North Chinese, bony growths of the mandible that were noticeable in 2 to 5 percent of Japanese, Lapps, and natives of Siberia,

a general thickening of the tympanic (outer ear opening) plate found mainly in Eskimos, American Indians, and Icelanders, a special growth on the tympanic plate found in 20 percent of Polynesians, broad nasal bones, and incisor teeth that were oddly shovel-shaped in both living Asians and Peking Man. As for the caveman from Java, he'd had a skull ridge (or sagittal keeling) that appeared to have been handed down to modern Australians and Tasmanians.

This argued powerfully for regional continuity in Asia from ancient times to today and certainly suggested that the Asian *erectus* had not been rendered totally obsolete. The problem was that aside from tossing in certain half-baked notions with his morphological evaluations, Coon was astonishingly indifferent to racial sensitivities.

"My thesis is, in essence, that at the beginning of our record, over half a million years ago, man was a single species, *Homo erectus,* perhaps already divided into five geographic races or subspecies," Coon wrote in his classic book *The Origin of Races* (1973). "*Homo erectus* then gradually evolved into *Homo sapiens* at different times, as each subspecies, living in its own territory, passed a critical threshold from a more brutal to a more *sapient* state, by one genetic process or another."

That wasn't so horrible, but then Coon went on to make that statement about how Australian Aborigines were still in the process of "sloughing off" *erectus* characteristics (their brow-ridges, as I said, were unusually pronounced) and included the photograph in a previous book of an Ituri Pygmy that was obviously intended to show how much the Pygmy's jutting jaw resembled a caveman's. Coon believed that after a certain point in evolution, major African populations had stagnated, lagging behind the other races.

If that wasn't enough to get the baby thrown out with the bathwater, Coon wrote this gem in a third book:

Anthropologists might opt for the preservation and wit-sharpening of elderly Australians aborigines and Bushmen, to serve as permanent informants to future generations of students. . . . The negroes, mean-

while, have another innovation to look forward to. Research on the actions of two hormones secreted by the pineal body make it possible that before long people will be able to change their skin color whenever they like, by simple injections. A colored woman could thus turn white with less effort than it takes to have her hair straightened, waved, and set. This would be particularly effective for those with narrow features and dark skins.

That was strong stuff even for a Klansman in the Louisiana legislature. No wonder Wolpoff denounced Coon for "silly" and "racist" ideas. But there was the tradition of regional continuity buried in all that gunk, and despite everything else, Coon had been a brilliant morphologist. Many of his observations remained relevant. Wolpoff felt it his task to scrape Coon's crud off Weidenreich's old work and excavate veins of truth that had been buried along with Coon's various outrages.

In 1978, Wolpoff had gone to Indonesia and had reconstructed an *erectus* found on the island where Java Man had been discovered during the last century. The previously unreconstructed fossil, "Sangiran 17," retained a very vital feature missing in most such fossils: its facial skeleton. Wolpoff reassembled it himself, holding it on his lap and gluing the various pieces together. When it was dry enough to move he had looked at the skull from various angles, and to his astonishment the 500,000-year-old fossil looked like an Australian Aborigine. "I just never believed in continuity until I saw that skull from the side," he says with lingering amazement.

That characteristics of the skull and face could persist in one region over the course of half a million years did not bode well for Garden of Eden theories of population replacement with little or no interbreeding. More than anything, it was the impact of the entire suite of features that impressed the Michigan paleoanthropologist. When Wolpoff, trying to quantify this overwhelming impression, measured the skull and compared it to some Aborigines who had been exhumed from a series of graves at Kow Swamp in northern Victoria, Australia, he found that both the aboriginal specimens (which were at least 9,000 years old but good samples of anatomically modern men) and this *erectus* from Java shared a distinct flatness of the skull frontal, a rounding of the lower border near the eyes, similar facial height, and teeth that fell within the same dimensional range. Though a characteristic so general that it might have also been found in any number of populations elsewhere, the nasal breadths of the *erectus* and Aborigines served as a metaphor for the striking closeness of certain traits: 26.4 millimeters in Sangiran 17 and 26.8 in the Aborigines.

Nor was that the whole of it. There were also the Ngandong specimens, which seemed like intermediates between *erectus* and *Homo sapiens,* and there was another "intermediate" from a place called Sambungmachan, and there were what are now called the Wajak skulls, an example of the earliest Java *Homo sapiens.* The picture forming in Wolpoff's mind was that of continuity in Indonesia from Java Man to Sambungmachan to Ngandong to Wajak to modern Aborigines. The Australians, who were thought to have originated in Indonesia, shared a number of features with archaics such as Ngandong Man, including long, flat, receding foreheads and indeed browridge similarities. Meanwhile, in Wolpoff's opinion, a 28,000-year-old skull found at Lake Garnpung in Australia (known as "WLH 50" for the Willandra Lakes region) was also like the far more ancient Ngandong Man, especially in its thick cranial vault, general robustness, and the shape of the frontal just above its eyes. "The Australian skull shares twelve character states uniquely with the Indonesians," wrote Wolpoff, while not one character state, he said, was uniquely shared with a similarly archaic African.

As for China, Wolpoff, like Coon and Weidenreich before him, saw, in the famous Zhoukoudian caves, a veritable time capsule of continuity, from Peking Man to modern *Homo sapiens* dated at 15,000 years in the Upper Cave. Anything dated so recently as 15,000 would have come long after Berkeley's alleged replacement of Asian *erectus* by those sub-Saharan Africans,

and so should not have resembled an Asian *erectus* whatsoever. Certainly, if *erectus* had left no genes, none of its unique characteristics should show up in present-day populations; and yet, in addition to the flat faces and shovel-shaped incisors that Chinese ape-men possessed long before Eve's time and which are still prevalent in Mongoloid populations today, there was a Chinese mandible of more than half a million years that showed the absence of third molars, a condition not uncommon in modern Chinese. The archaic from Dali, meanwhile, possessed a naso-malar angle of 145 degrees, approximating the flat facial angle of Eskimos, who are descendants of Asians. In the Philippines yet another cave yielded browridges reminiscent of Zhoukoudian, bringing still more of Asia into play.

Working assiduously with Alan G. Thorne, a prehistorian from Australian National University in Canberra, and Wu Xin Zhi, a paleoanthropologist in Beijing, Wolpoff had set about propounding a new view of regional continuity, and in 1984, just three years before the Eve hypothesis, they coauthored a 61-page treatise on fossil evidence from East Asia, replete with both extensive personal analyses of fossils and 274 source citations. In it, Wolpoff envisioned the human race as remaining ethnically distinguishable because populations had existed in certain regions long enough to acquire distinctive local traits, all the while maintaining an evolutionary course in the same general direction—remaining all one species worldwide—because there had been genetic contact (or "gene flow") between the various populations.

That gave much more a sense of brotherhood, equality, and one human kind. But it had no room whatsoever for a single point of recent modern origin, as Berkeley was claiming. "I can go on forever," said Wolpoff, when I paid a visit to his home in rural Michigan. "The fact is that there are features like this that show continuity in China, and what they seem to show is that there are no invading African populations, no place where different

African morphology is intrusive. Each region of that part of the world has different features of what is primitive. There are faces that look Chinese even though they're found on vaults that look like *Homo erectus.* Dali is an example. It happens in every region of the world. I call this 'multi-regional continuity' and emphasize gene flow more than anyone has before. I didn't think gene flow as so important earlier in my career but now I believe it's fundamental to all change. Changes don't happen in local isolated populations, but rather they happen in populations connected to each other."

Wolpoff agreed in part with Richard Leakey, who in his book *Origins* (1982) saw the transition to modern humanity as like taking a handful of pebbles and flinging them into a pool of water: "Each pebble generates outward-spreading ripples that sooner or later meet the oncoming ripples set in motion by other pebbles. The pool represents the Old World with its basic *sapiens* population; the place where each pebble lands is a point of transition to *Homo sapiens sapiens.* . . ."

Beck Cann responded that the idea of continuity was an "outdated" one. Referring to the conception that "large-bodied, big-brained, long-lived animals spread out over three continents suddenly converge on the same genetic basis of whatever kind of morphology and intelligence and become one big species," she noted bluntly that "speciation doesn't work that way. It occurs in small, isolated populations and moves them divergently. So I think it's unlikely that the model of continuous evolution is correct for humans."

As for the incisor argument and other similarities between the Asian *erectus* and Asians of today, Cann implied that such seemingly unique traits could have evolved two different times in two separate populations because of similar environmental factors that spurred a peculiar adaptation. In other words, while the Chinese *erectus* had shoveled incisors, maybe some of the invading Africans had or later developed that trait too. Anyway it was quite clear from the DNA results, she wrote, that "the roots of Asian mitochondrial

DNA diversity are simply not as ancient as those in Africa. Significant genetic contributions of people from this ancient Asian line of descent should have produced modern Asian maternal lineages which at least match the age of the African ones. Since they did not, we conclude that even though fossils of considerable antiquity are known from Asia, they were replaced by lines of African origin."

Wolpoff liked Cann but resented how the geneticists had an "arrogance that they're trained in a 'harder' science than we are, and that there's something more scientific about work done in a laboratory and on a computer than work done over bones in a museum. It's a combination of arrogance and that geneticists are not familiar with the fossil record. When you say the word 'arrogance,' Allan Wilson comes to mind. I sometimes get the feeling that what the geneticists do is read through our literature until they find something they want to hear, and then quote it, all the while sneering at paleoanthropology!"

But where were the geneticists going to turn once they admitted that their date was wrong? "Maybe to the fossil record!" says Wolpoff with glee.

And his voice was becoming more than just distant thunder. He was gathering his troops. It was clearly an urgent effort. He had to halt any more defections to the Garden of Eden school. Already the followers of Weidenreich, according to Howells, were probably a minority.

Wilson tried to ignore Wolpoff, showing his usual disdain. He closeted himself in his office out of reach of critics, disliking conversation with people who didn't have a biochemistry degree. When I asked him about Wolpoff, Wilson replied simply: "I persist in trying to distinguish between fact and opinion and treat the data in a statistical framework."

Like Cann, Wilson had less than high regard for fossil interpretations. "I know from previous experience that they can feel quite confident that they're right about something when in fact they're wrong." While it was true that paleoanthropology was more often than not in utter disarray (Wolpoff himself freely acknowledged that paleoanthropologists often tried "to pull something out of what isn't there"), and while it was also true at least initially that mitochondrial DNA was difficult for an outsider to comprehend—complex, its language an inbred foreign language, heavy on logarithms, unclear charts, and computer jargon—Wilson reacted with what had the appearance of simple intolerance. When questions came that didn't reflect wholesale acceptance of his results, his immediate reaction was that the skeptical questioner didn't have a "feel" for the subject, and he was too busy to explain it.

"Wilson at times was much less arrogant than now," says Sarich, no shrinking violet himself. (After all, Sarich was known to describe his own thinking as "brilliant.") But Wilson didn't have the charm Sarich did, and

he seemed to believe that the nickname for his MacArthur grant was an accurate way of putting things. That nickname of course was the "genius award."

Big egos here, all trying to tell everyone who their grandmother was. But with Wilson behind the barracks, and Sarich only indirectly involved with the mitochondrial DNA, the task of fending off Wolpoff, and bearing the brunt of his quickly materializing offensive, had fallen upon Cann. She stood at the front line as Wolpoff began churning out prodigiously detailed arguments on how the fossil record proved Berkeley wrong. They had to be wrong. This "wacko" Eve hypothesis was in irreconcilable opposition to his cherished theories of evolutionary continuity and regionalism. Did they think he'd spent all that time in Jogjakarta for nothing?

And how was it that all the *erectus*, archaics, and Neandertals from Eurasia simply disappeared? No one from Berkeley had convincingly answered that yet. To a number of paleoanthropologists, there was only one way for the Eve hypothesis to have happened, and that was by means of some kind of holocaust or warfare. "This rendering of modern populational dispersals is a story of 'making war and not love,' and if true its implications are not pleasant," wrote Wolpoff.

It was a concept that Wolpoff used to irritate the Berkeley group, and it was a concept that made Cann want to scream.

Life as a

Hunter-gatherer

Richard E. Leakey

For at least two million years our ancestors followed a technologically simple but highly successful way of life. The initial strategy of the opportunistic scavenging of carrion combined with the organized collection of plant foods gradually evolved into a hunting-and-gathering way of life, the transition probably taking place somewhere between one million and half-a-million years ago. Not until relatively recently, between 20,000 and 10,000 years go, did that long-established lifestyle begin to be replaced by systematic food production in the form of pastoralism or agriculture. The change came late in our history, but it developed with astonishing speed and is now virtually total. Only a handful of people, living in isolated parts of the globe, still subsist by the ancient hunter-gatherer way of life.

Hunting-and-gathering was a permanent and stable feature of our biological evolution through *Homo*

erectus to early *Homo sapiens* and finally to modern man. Given the importance of hunting-and-gathering through the many thousands of generations of our forebears, it may well be that this way of life is an indelible part of what makes us human. Prehistorians like Glynn Isaac try to piece together scraps of evidence from the fossil record to discover what they can about early human behaviour. . . . This kind of work has revealed a great deal, but, inevitably, it is limited in what it can expose of complex social behaviour. We know that until the advent of agriculture, humans made a living by gathering plant foods and hunting or scavenging meat, activities that centered on some form of home base. We can assume from this that there must have been some social organization, but the fossil record remains silent about what it was like to be a member of such a hunter-gatherer group. It indicates nothing of what was impor-

tant to individuals in the group or what moral codes they adhered to, and it only hints at the skills required in order to survive. Of course, one can never know for certain the answers to these questions. But one can obtain some clues through the careful study of contemporary hunter-gatherers.

THE IMAGE OF HUNTER-GATHERER SOCIETIES

Nineteenth-century anthropologists viewed hunter-gatherers as fossilized societies, primitive savages who had somehow slipped unnoticed and unnoticing into the modern world. This is, of course, nonsense. The hunter-gatherers were as modern in biological terms as the explorers who 'discovered' them; they just happened to be sustaining themselves by an ancient method. Misconceptions about non-agricultural people abounded, often inspired by Thomas Hobbes's seventeenth-century notion of life in a state of nature: 'No arts; no letters; no society; and which is worst of all, continual fear and danger of violent death; and the life of man, solitary, poor, nasty, brutish, and short.'

During the past couple of decades, and particularly in the last ten years, the image of hunter-gatherers has undergone a transformation. Writing in his classic book *Stone Age Economics,* anthropologist Marshall Sahlins argued that in studying hunter-gatherers, Western anthropologists must not impose Western, that is, materialistic, ethics on their subjects. This goes farther than just overcoming the revulsion of nineteenth-century explorers at certain food items. (The consumption of large, juicy insect larvae, for example, was often assumed to be the desperate act of starving people, whereas the hunter-gatherers considered them to be great delicacies.) Marshall Sahlins refers to the different goals of the different societies: the pursuit of wealth, property and prestige in the one, and something totally different in the other. He even goes as far as to suggest that the hunting-and-gathering way of life is 'the original affluent society . . . in which all the people's wants are easily satisfied.' As it happens, the hunting-and-gathering economy is not an incessant search for food, as many anthropologists have supposed, but a system that allows a good deal more leisure than is possible in either agricultural or industrial society.

Marshall Sahlins's conclusion rests in part on an important study carried out on the !Kung San (formerly called Bushmen, a derogatory term coined by Dutch colonialists in southern Africa), who live close to the border between Botswana and Namibia, on the northern fringe of the Kalahari Desert. Since 1963 a number of researchers, principally based at Harvard University, have been analysing many aspects of the !Kung's hunter-gather way of life. Since the project began the inevitable march of 'progress' has impinged on the region and only a very small number of people in the area still hunt-and-gather for a living, the rest having been persuaded to settle down as agri-

culturalists. Some of the !Kung have even been recruited by the South African government as anti-terrorist trackers along the Botswana—Namibia border. The transition from a nomadic to a settled existence has in fact been highly instructive about the social components of each way of life. . . .

Richard Lee, one of the principal investigators, recalls his motives for embarking on the study: 'I wanted to get away from the earlier misconceptions about hunter-gatherers. I wanted to find out what were the important elements of their way of life, without romanticizing them either in the Hobbesian "nasty, brutish, and short" manner or by putting them in a Garden of Eden.' Richard Lee is confident that his work is a legitimate way of gaining a glimpse of the past. 'The !Kung are a good model,' he claims, 'because, compared with prehistoric hunters and gatherers, they are living in a very marginal environment. Hunters of the past would have had the pick of rich resources and would undoubtedly have had an easier time of it than do the modern San.' The strength of the conclusions based on the study of the !Kung is that they are largely corroborated by other observations—some anecdotal, some scientific—on hunter-gatherers in many parts of the world. Through such peoples one can gain a valuable impression of the social and technical implications of the hunter-gatherer existence. One does not see exact replicas of our ancestors, but one can understand the principles that governed their lives.

LIFE ON THE EDGE OF THE KALAHARI

To many people, the name Kalahari conjures images of a desert of unrelenting aridity. To the !Kung, however, it is home and has been for at least 10,000 years. It is a place where they make a very reasonable living in a manner that, until recently, had remained unchanged for millennia. Richard Lee describes the area in the following manner: 'The first impression of a traveller to this region is of an im-

mense flatness where the sky dominates the landscape. The Aha Hills rise only a hundred metres above the surrounding plain, and from their top one sees what seem to be endless vistas of brush and savannah stretching to the horizon in every direction. . . . At several points in the landscape the sandy plain is broken by dry river courses. . . . They rarely hold water, perhaps twice in a decade, but when they do the flow can be considerable. . . . At night the stars overhead have an unbearable beauty, with the crystal clear high desert air and the central spine of the Milky Way galaxy arching overhead. It is with good reason that the !Kung name the Milky Way *!ku !ko !kumi,* the backbone of the sky.'

The desert winds have sculpted the sands into long, low red-topped dunes which run from east to west. Groves of mongongo nut trees cover many of the dune ridges, a feature of Kalahari life that is vital to the !Kung both for food and water. Gigantic baobab trees stand here and there, often the largest physical object within view. Everywhere is 'unbroken, unhumanized bush.'

Richard Lee chose an isolated group of !Kung to study, in an area he called the Dobe, which has nine water holes and inhabited by about 450 people. He tackled and overcame the immense challenge of learning the !Kung language: 'The !Kung word can be described as an explosion of sound surrounded by a vowel. The bundle of clicks, fricatives and glottal stops that begins most words makes !Kung a difficult language to record, let alone to speak.' (The use of !,/, and other such marks in written !Kung represents the various clicks and explosive sounds.)

Once settled with his chosen group of !Kung, Richard Lee inevitably was exposed to the predominant feature of hunter-gatherer life: its mobility. During the wet summer season, from October to May, the small foraging bands erect modest temporary camps among the mongongo nut groves, moving on to new camps every few weeks. The band moves, not in a constant and desperate search for food, but because the longer people stay in one place the further they must walk each day in order to collect food. It is a question of convenience, not a flight from starvation.

The foraging bands at this time of year are small, having about six families in them. At least some of the families are likely to be related to each other, either by blood or by marriage. In any case, the !Kung create an extensive network of informal affiliations throughout their neighbouring bands. Giving gifts and receiving them (not trading) are essential elements in weaving together the social fabric of !Kung life, and relationships within and between bands are complex and close.

The numerical composition of a foraging band, roughly thirty people, has been called one of the 'magic numbers' of hunter-gatherer life. Throughout the world hunting-and-gathering people have as the core of their social and economic life a band of about this size. It appears to be the optimum combination of adults and children for exploiting the widespread plant and animal foods that hunter-gatherers live on: fewer than this and the social structure is weakened; more, and the work effort has to be increased in order to collect enough food for everyone. . . . Only when the mode of production changes from the basic hunting-and-gathering system to more settled agriculture do groups larger than thirty become viable over long periods.

When the dry winter months come, the !Kung congregate around permanent water holes in concentrations of a hundred or more people. This 'public' phase of their life is very important. It is the time of intense socializing, large-scale trance-dancing and curing, initiations, story-telling, exchange of gifts and marriage-brokering. If one sees the dispersed summer camps as being connected by an invisible network of kinship, friendship and material obligation, then the winter is the time when the net is pulled together, bonds are strengthened and new alliances made.

This highly valued public phase of !Kung life is not without its drawbacks, however. The unusual concentrations of people inevitably means that people

have to do more work: they have to travel farther to collect plant food and to find animals to hunt. And with the high-density living there often comes personal conflict. As soon as the rains begin, people once again disperse in small bands to the mongongo groves. The bands are, however, not necessarily of the same composition as those of the previous summer: the public phase is an opportunity for people to join with others with whom they would prefer to live and for tensions and conflicts to be resolved by the splitting up of some bands.

Public-phase camps and the fission and fusion of bands are very common among foraging people. For instance, the G/wi San of the much more arid Central Kalahari live in small bands for about 300 days of the year without any standing water. They survive for most of the time on moisture obtained from melons and tubers. During the summer rains, however, they congregate around the few meagre and ephemeral water holes. The ostensible reason for the coming together is to take advantage of the standing water, which is briefly available. But the opportunity for intense socializing is not lost, and one suspects that the prospect of mixing with relatively large numbers of people is anticipated with even more relish than is the chance of drinking from a pool.

Hunter-gatherer peoples frequently give elaborate reasons why they come together in large groups and then break up again, but the real motive seems to be a strong need for formal and informal socializing within a large number of relatives, friends and affiliates. While non-human primates frequently live in social groups of about thirty individuals, they do not usually come together in the larger groups that are such a feature of the human hunter-gatherer way of life.

Hobbes's view that non-agricultural people have 'no society' and are 'solitary' could hardly be more wrong. To be a hunter-gatherer is to experience a life that is intensely social. As for having 'no arts' and 'no letters,' it is true that foraging people possess very little in the form of material culture,

but this is simply a consequence of the need for mobility. When the !Kung move from camp to camp they, like other hunter-gatherers, take all their worldly goods with them: this usually amounts to a total of 12 kilograms (26 pounds) per person, just over half the normal baggage allowance on most airlines. There is an inescapable conflict between mobility and material culture, so the !Kung carry their culture in their heads, not only their backs. Their songs, dances and stories form a culture as rich as that of any people.

In spite of the apparently inhospitable aspect of the northern Kalahari, it does in fact support a large number of wild animals. Richard Lee explains: 'To give some idea of abundance, fresh warthog, steenbok and duiker tracks can be seen every day of the year. Kudu, wildebeest and gemsbok tracks might be seen several times a week. Tracks of giraffe, eland, hartebeest and roan antelope would be seen perhaps once a month or once in two months; buffalo have been sighted only about a dozen times in ten years, zebra perhaps three times and impala only once in the same period.' The natural array of plant foods is impressive too. 'The !Kung are superb botanists and naturalists with an intimate knowledge of their environment,' Richard Lee says. 'Over 200 species of plant are known and named by them, and of these a surprisingly high proportion is considered by the !Kung to be edible.'

THE ROLE OF WOMEN

Referring specifically to the !Kung, Richard Lee gave a paper at a symposium in 1966 entitled *What hunters do for a living*. This revealed that, contrary to popular conception, meat constitutes only thirty to forty percent of the diet. Moreover, in studies of other hunter-gatherers in similar latitudes, the same sort of figure cropped up again and again. The conclusion was inescapable: plant foods are the staple of hunter-gatherer life. Only in the higher latitudes, where the changing seasons make plant foods an unreliable resource, do hunter-gatherers turn to fish or meat for the bulk of their diet.

In virtually all foraging people, as with the !Kung, it is the women who do most of the gathering of plant foods while the men do most of the hunting. There are exceptions, of course, such as the Agta people of the Philippines where the women share the hunting with the men. But in the vast majority of cases, there is a sexual division of labour. The most obvious reason for this arrangement is the incompatibility between the demands of the hunt—the long distances travelled while tracking prey and the quiet and stealth that is critical during the final stalk—and the problems involved in carrying weighty and noisy infants.

!Kung women give birth once every three to four years. Once again, the birth interval of roughly four years is a worldwide phenomenon among hunter-gatherer peoples, and it appears to be a biological response to the physical demands of mobility. Very young children must be carried while gathering and on migrations from an old camp to a new location. Transporting two children *and* gathering food would be extremely arduous. Richard Lee has calculated the amount of work which would be involved in carrying infant- and food-loads if the birth intervals were one year, two years, three years and so on. At the shorter intervals the work load is enormous and decreases rapidly when the birth interval is about four years, but does not drop significantly as the birth interval gets longer than four years. The world's hunter-gatherers therefore appear to have hit upon the optimum spacing entirely independently of each other. Only with a sedentary existence, such as in an agricultural economy, can women have babies more frequently without imposing on themselves an enormous carrying burden.

Why some kind of crèche system is not more common among foraging people is a mystery, but it may be because the mother's presence is necessary for suckling, which, with !Kung mothers, goes on for three or four years, often long after milk has ceased to flow. This extended suckling may be a physiological mechanism for preventing ovulation and therefore reducing the chances of another pregnancy. On the other hand, a crèche would make long birth spacing less necessary and eliminate the need for prolonged suckling.

The consequence of the sexual division of labour and the long birth interval is that food gathering is a highly social activity involving several mothers and their young, whereas hunting is a much more solitary affair, usually undertaken by a pair of men, possibly with an 'apprentice' adolescent. The economic differences between hunting and gathering are also profound. A woman can gather in one day enough food for her family for three days, and she seldom fails. A man may bring down a large animal that will feed the band for several weeks, or he may come home with only a small spring hare. Often he returns empty-handed.

According to Lee's calculations, !Kung men work just over twenty-one hours a week in contributing meat to the camp whereas women spend slightly more than twelve hours a week supplying plant foods which constitute about seventy percent of the diet. When all other forms of work—including making tools and housework, but excluding child care—are added together, a man's week is over forty-four hours and a woman's forty hours. But as women do most of the child care, their total work load is greater than the men's. Richard Lee considers that the women do not feel themselves exploited: they have economic prestige and political power, a situation denied to many women in the 'civilized' world.

THE ETHICS OF HUNTER-GATHERERS

Anyone going into a !Kung camp and expecting to find a cache of food is in for a surprise. Hunter-gatherers simply do not lay up stocks against future shortages. Such an 'extraordinary' attitude provoked nineteenth-century anthropologists into commenting that hunter-gatherers behaved 'as if the game were locked up in a stable,' and that they had 'not the slightest thought of, or care for, what the morrow may bring forth.' Rodney Needham, writing in 1954, said that foraging people have 'a confidence in the capacity of the environment to support them, and in their own ability to extract their livelihood from it.'

Food storage would run counter to the !Kung's habit of sharing food, particularly meat. Perhaps because it is a relatively rare commodity, meat is highly prized by the !Kung, as it is among most hunter-gatherers. When an animal is killed, the hunter (or rather the person whose arrow struck the prey—and that is not always the same person as he who shot the arrow) initiates an elaborate process of sharing the raw meat. The sharing runs along the lines of kinship, alliances and obligations. Lorna Marshall, a pioneer in !Kung studies, once witnessed the butchering of an eland, the largest of the African antelopes, and she counted sixty acts of meat distribution within a short time of the initial sharing. The network of sharing and obligation is very important among the !Kung. Richard Lee emphasizes the point strongly: 'Sharing deeply pervades the behaviour and values of !Kung foragers, within the family and between families, and it is extended to the boundaries of the social universe. Just as the principle of profit and rationality is central to the capitalist ethic, so is sharing central to the conduct of social life in foraging societies.'

This ethic is not confined to the !Kung: it is a feature of hunter-gatherers in general. Such behaviour, however, is not automatic; like most of human behavior, it has to be taught from childhood. 'Every human infant is born with the capacity to share and the capacity to be selfish,' Richard Lee says. That which is nurtured and developed is that which each individual society regards as most valuable.

In the same vein as the sharing ethic comes a surprising degree of egalitarianism. The !Kung have no chiefs and no leaders. Problems in their society are mostly solved long before they mature into anything that threatens social harmony. Although the !Kung are very thinly distributed overall—occupying on average about 4 square kilometres (1.5 square miles) per person—their camps, by contrast, are an intense compression of humanity. People's conversations are common property, and disputes are readily defused through communal bantering. No one gives orders or takes them. Richard Lee once asked /Twi!gum whether the !Kung have headmen. 'Of course we have headmen,' he replied, much to Richard Lee's surprise. 'In fact, we are all headmen; each one of us is a headman over himself!' /Twi!gum considered the question and his witty answer to be a great joke.

The stress on equality demands that certain rituals are observed when a successful hunter returns to camp. The object of these rituals is to play down the event so as to discourage arrogance and conceit. 'The correct demeanour for the successful hunter,' explains Richard Lee, 'is modesty and understatement.' A !Kung man, /Gaugo, described it this way: 'Say that a man has been hunting. He must not come home and announce like a braggart, "I have killed a big one in the bush!" He must first sit down in silence until I or someone else comes up to his fire and asks, "What did you see today?" He replies quietly, "Ah, I'm no good for hunting. I saw nothing at all . . . maybe just a tiny one." Then I smile to myself because I now know he has killed something big.' The bigger the kill, the more it is played down.

'The theme of modesty is continued when the butchering and carrying party goes to fetch the kill the following day,' Richard Lee explains. The helpers joke, complaining that surely the hunter did not need so many people to carry such a puny kill. And the hunter will agree, suggesting that they just cut out the liver and go and look for something more worthwhile. The jesting and understatement is strictly followed, again not just by the !Kung but by many foraging people, and the result is that although some men are undoubtedly more proficient hunters than others, no one accrues unusual prestige or status because of his talents.

When one examines the technology of the hunter, and that of the other aspects of !Kung life, one is very impressed not by its complexity or sophistication but rather by its simplicity. A club and bows-and-arrows, the arrows tipped with insect-larvae poison, are the hunter's prime equipment, though they also use hooks for retrieving spring hares from their burrows, snares for entrapping small animals, and net-bags made from animal sinews for carrying various items. For plant-food gathering, the technical array is even more modest: a digging stick and some kind of container. The !Kung women use a kaross, which is made from antelope hide, in which they can transport the nuts, fruits, roots and berries, together with their infant. Back at camp, crude stones are sufficient for the initial cracking open of the plentiful and valued mongongo nut. A wooden mortar and pestle are all that is required for pounding the inner nut meat, so as to render it digestible to the young and the old, or to mix it with other foods. And as water, or rather lack of it, dominates !Kung life, containers, such as ostrich eggshells or bags made from animal stomachs, are also important.

By contrast with the simple equipment used in hunting-and-gathering, the *skill* demanded is prodigious. Hunters must be able to identify an animal from its tracks, know how old it is, how long ago it passed by, whether it was running or idling, and whether it is injured or healthy. Once within striking distance of the prey, considerable cunning is needed to approach close enough for a telling shot with the diminutive arrows. Only the smallest antelope is knocked down by such a shot and most prey has to be tracked for several hours, sometimes days, before the poison kills it.

The !Kung are finely tuned to their environment, reading it closely and more thoroughly than people from a non-foraging society could ever comprehend. Two ethologists, Nicholas Blurton-Jones and Melvin Konner, once talked with the !Kung hunters to see how much of the animal world they

understood. They were astonished at the !Kung knowledge: 'Some !Kung observations which we refused to believe were later proved correct when checked with ethologists who have worked in Africa,' they admitted.

Gathering also requires a great deal of skill. Patricia Draper, who has made a special study of women in !Kung society, puts it this way: 'The !Kung economy looks simple in comparison with other more diversified economies with greater division of labour, but from the point of view of the individual actor, subsistence is quite complex. For example, although it is simple enough to pick up nuts or melons once one is standing where they are found, it requires enough strength to walk 16 kilometres [10 miles] or more per day carrying a full day's harvest and perhaps a child. A woman needs to know where various foodstuffs are to be found, in what season they are edible, and how to keep oriented in the bush. !Kung women, like their men, pay close attention to animal tracks as they pass through the bush; and they tell the men about recent game movements when they return home in the evening.'

It is clear when looking at a wide range of hunter-gatherers that there are significant similarities in the way they run their lives. These similarities seem to be imposed by their way of life, and they are therefore important in forming an impression of the general character of our ancestors' lives. We can make the following general statements about hunter-gatherers:

The main social and economic focus of the hunter-gatherer existence is the home base, probably occupied by about six families. The main social consequence of the dual pursuit of meat and plant foods is a sexual division of labour, with the males doing most of the hunting and the females most of the gathering. The quest for meat is surprisingly unrewarding, and unless plant foods are too seasonal to act as a staple they will provide the largest proportion of the diet. The practice of bringing plant and animal foods back to a home base where they are shared with all members of the band demands a highly developed sense of co-operation and equality. The system also allows for an unusually large amount of spare time which people divide between visiting relatives and friends in nearby bands and entertaining visitors at their own camp. Indeed, the degree of socialization is intense and reaches a pitch when, for a short while, bands coalesce into larger groups. Above all, foraging people deploy tremendous skill and only minimal technology in exploiting their environment.

As Richard Lee says, 'We mustn't imagine that this is the exact way in which our ancestors lived. But I believe that what we see in the !Kung and other foraging people are patterns of behaviour that were crucial to early human development.' Of the several types of hominid that were living two to three million years ago, one of them—the line that eventually led to us—broadened its economic base by sharing food and including more meat in its diet. The development of a hunting-and-gathering economy was a potent force in what made us human.

Living With the Past

Anthropology continues to evolve as a discipline, both in terms of the tools and techniques of the trade as well as in terms of the application of whatever knowledge we stand to gain about ourselves. It is in this context that Phillip Tobias ("On the Scientific, Medical, Dental, and Educational Value of Collections of Human Skeletons") reviews the medical and educational benefits derived from collecting human skeletons. Patrick Huyghe, in "Profile of an Anthropologist: No Bone Unturned," extends this line of reasoning in describing "forensic anthropology," a whole new field involving the use of physical similarities and differences between people in order to identify human remains. Finally, in the same practical vein, Edward Humes, in "The DNA Wars," discusses the legal ramifications of the use of DNA in criminal law. If there is one theme that ties the articles of this section together, then, it is that they have as much to do with the present as they have to do with the past.

There is an axiom in evolutionary theory called the "law of irrevocability" that holds that no species completely revokes or sheds the vestiges of even its distant ancestors. Given the fact that each of us is a product of that which went before, we carry with us a certain amount of "evolutionary baggage." Some of this "baggage" may present problems that will not go away—any more than the baboons described by Jim Bell (in "Farmers and Baboons in the Taita Hills: Inter-Species Warfare in Southeastern Kenya") that have been a part of the human evolutionary scene since time immemorial. We can make adjustments, however. How we attempt to live with our past is very much the point of Lee Cronk's article, "Old Dog, Old Tricks," where he shows that certain aspects of our contemporary social and physical environments may be very much at odds with our legacy of previously established biological needs. Marcia Thompson and David Harsha provide a specific example of this in "Our Rhythms Still Follow the African Sun," as they point out how our tropically derived biorhythms must be acknowledged in organizing people's work schedules, if for no other reason than for the sake of human safety and efficiency.

Sometimes an awareness of our biological and behavioral past may even make the difference between life and death, as Meredith Small writes in "A Reasonable Sleep." Recent research indicates that the sleeping arrangement of mothers and their young, that is, whether or not they conform to the traditional pattern of bedding down together, has a contributing effect upon the incidence of Sudden Infant Death Syndrome. Meanwhile, at the other end of the human life cycle, Jared Diamond argues in "The Saltshaker's Curse" that a physiological adaptation that once helped African Americans survive slavery may now be predisposing their descendants to an early death from hypertension.

If most of the above-mentioned articles emphasize the dysfunctional aspects of our genetic heritage, Randolph Nesse ("What Good Is Feeling Bad?") makes the case that seemingly negative, destructive emotions such as anxiety and pain may actually represent positive, adaptive responses, not just in the past but also in today's rapidly changing world as well.

As we reflect upon where we have been and how we came to be as we are in the evolutionary sense, the inevitable question arises as to what will happen next. This is the most difficult issue of all, since our biological future depends so much upon long-range ecological trends that no one seems to be able to predict. Some will wonder if we will even survive long enough as a species to experience any significant biological changes. Perhaps our capacity for knowledge is outstripping the wisdom to use it wisely, and the consequent destruction of our earthly environments and wildlife is placing us in ever-greater danger of creating the circumstances of our own extinction.

Counterbalancing this pessimism is the view that, since it has been our conscious decision-making (and not the genetically predetermined behavior that characterizes some species) that has gotten us into this mess, then it will be the conscious will of our generation and future generations that will get us out. But can we wait much longer for humanity to collectively come to its senses? Or is it already too late?

Looking Ahead: Challenge Questions

What are the educational and medical benefits of collecting human skeletons?

What can a physical anthropologist do for the Federal Aviation Administration?

What is "forensic anthropology"?

How reliable is DNA matching in criminal cases?

Why has the conflict between humans and baboons intensified over time?

In what ways are we humans building a strange and novel environment for ourselves?

To what extent do our daily routines depend upon biorhythms inherited from the past?

How might sleeping patterns in the United States be contributing to the incidence of Sudden Infant Death Syndrome?

What is the "saltshaker's curse" and why are some people more affected by it than others?

What are the survival benefits of psychic pain?

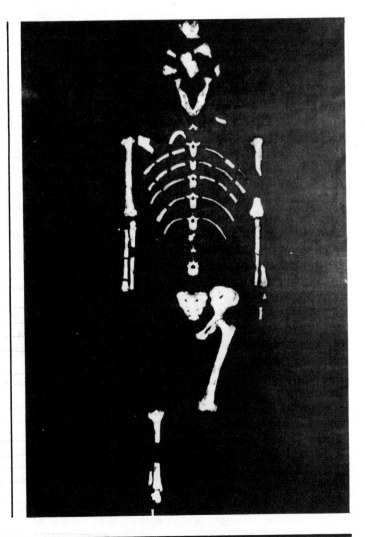

On The Scientific, Medical, Dental and Educational Value of Collections of Human Skeletons

Phillip V. Tobias

University of the Witwatersrand, Medical School, 7 York Road, Parktown, Johannesburg 2193, South Africa

Having been approached from time to time by various museum, university and governmental authorities in Australia, California and Scotland, I have set down some brief notes on the scientific, medical, dental and educational importance and value of collections of recent human skeletons drawn from populations in all parts of the world.

This article does not pretend to completeness. It has been set down in the hope that it may be of assistance to those officers in charge of such collections and who may be pondering upon the worthwhileness of such collections being retained and maintained.

INTRODUCTORY AND HISTORICAL

Collections of modern human skeletons are to be found in every continent. They exist mainly in three categories of institution: (a) Museums; (b) University Departments of (Physical or Biological) Anthropology; and (c) Departments of (Human) Anatomy in Medical Schools. It is a common misconception that such collections are mainly those of formerly subject peoples, whose remains were collected by the conquerors during earlier colonial days. While there can be little denying the fact that some of the skeletons in the great collections of the world were amassed under less than ethically desirable conditions, it would be inaccurate to regard this as the major basis of collections. *All* of the populations of mankind, and not just formerly subject peoples, are represented in these collections. For example, in Great Britain, there are several large collections of British skeletons, dating from the historical and recent periods, often derived from old churchyards, from which the remains were exhumed.

The practice of building up collections of, and studying, the skeletons of recent and present day mankind goes back at least for several centuries. The diversity of living human beings became an object of study especially from the 18th Century onwards and a number of collections of skeletons were obtained from the exhumation of old churchyards, from remote parts of the world and from other sources.

In the English speaking world a key role was played by Sir William Turner (1823–1916) at Edinburgh University. Turner had been the leading British anatomist of his day. He was an early pioneer in the broking of the marriage between anatomy and physical anthropology in the United Kingdom and he built up a collection of human skeletons at Edinburgh University. After his realisation of the value of such a collection of comparative human skeletons of modern mankind, the idea was transplanted to the New World.

Carl August Hamann (1868–1930), in the Anatomy Department at Western Reserve University, Cleveland, Ohio, started building up a similar collection of human skeletons, before the end of the 19th Century. His successor, Thomas Wingate Todd (1885–1938), after 1912, added appreciably to the materials which later came to be called the Hamann-Todd Collection. One of Turner's students was Robert James Terry (1871–1966) and he obtained his medical degree in 1895 at what was then the Missouri Medical College. He then studied under Sir William Turner at Edinburgh in 1898. Soon after Terry's return to Missouri, he was appointed Head of the Anatomy department at Washington University in 1900. He started to build up a collection of human skeletons derived from cadavers and hence of known sex, age and race. He had been inspired to do so by the example of Turner.

In due course, Raymond Arthur Dart (1893–1988) worked under Terry in 1921, as one of the first two Foreign Fellows of the Rockefeller Foundation. When Dart was appointed to the Chair of Anatomy at the University of the Witwatersrand in Johannesburg in 1923, he transplanted there the idea of

From *International Journal of Anthropology,* Vol. 6, No. 3, 1991, pp. 277-280. Reprinted by permission.

such a collection. Much later, P. V. Tobias, Dart's successor, named it the Raymond Dart Collection of Human Skeletons and doubled its previous size. Thus, in the English-speaking world, at least, one can trace the genesis of this type of collection from the Old World to the New and then back to the Old World again. Further offshoots of the concept went from Johannesburg to several other parts of Africa and to Australia (Perth).

Studies on such collections of human skeletons have been made in all parts of the world and continue to receive attention. Thus, researches on human skeletal collections have yielded, and continue to yield, results of value in human and primate anatomy, human biology and physical anthropology, human population biology, growth and development, odontology and dentistry, orthodontics, pathology, forensic medicine, epidemiology, orthopaedics, obstetrics, neurosurgery, paediatrics, and other clinical disciplines.

The value of such collections

1) The anthropological value of such collections is immense. They have permitted comparative studies to be made of different human populations, in regard to anatomical variability, the metrical and non-metrical characteristics of the skeletons of different populations as a pointer to the interrelationships of the populations sampled.

2) The world-wide diversification of the species, *Homo sapiens,* and the skeletons representing human beings in every continent, have provided invaluable data on the biological processes exemplified by such diversity—for here we have an example of one of the few living species which has adapted itself to ecological niches in every part of the globe and in diverse climatic zones, without transcending the biological boundaries of its monospecific status.

3) Where collections include skeletons of immature and of mature subjects, studies of growth changes in the human skeleton are made possible: these are valuable in paediatrics, growth and development, and biological anthropology.

4) Collections permit the study of sex differences in adult skeletal features, both metrical and non-metrical, the study of sexual dimorphism having become a major focus of interest in studies of present-day primates, including human beings.

5) An important objective which the study of a variety of modern human skeletons has made possible is the establishment of a secure baseline for the metrical and nonmetrical variability of recent humankind: with an increasing interest in hominid evolutionary studies and the discovery, especially in eastern and south-eastern Asia, east Africa and southern Africa, of great numbers of early members of the family of man, it has become obvious that the determination of the affinities of these early hominids, or putative hominids, is absolutely dependent upon the availability of modern human skeletal standards. In an earlier period, European colleagues were inclined to use only European skeletons as a standard of comparison, but this is manifestly unsuitable in the study of a highly diversified species such as *Homo sapiens*. For standards, there are needed collections representative of all, or at least a good array, of the population's of present-day humankind.

6) Obstetrically important studies on pelvic form and size and their variability are another important objective, which the existence of human skeletal collections permits us to pursue. Moreover, the study of pelvic variations in populations of varied socioeconomic background permits a study of the relationships of pelvic variables to the nutritional status of the communities sampled.

7) The external form, overall dimensions, internal structure and mechanical strength of the bones of the human skeleton are vital, not only to anatomists and physical anthropologists, but to orthopaedists. Numerous studies have been made by orthopaedic surgeons on the variability of the skeletal structures in human collections.

8) Important for the orthopaedic specialist and also for the functional anatomist is the range of variability in the structure of the bony joints, especially the hip-, knee-, and ankle-joints, upper limb joints, vertebral column joints, angles and ranges of movement. All of these may be studied on human skeletal collections. Notable in this regard is the vertebral-sacral-pelvic complex and its diversity in males and females, in light and heavy individuals (irrespective of sex) and in different human populations.

9) A most useful object of study is provided by the absolute dimensions of limb-bones and their relationships to one another. Thus, numerous studies are made on the metrical relationships of fore-arm to arm, leg to thigh, upper limb to lower limb; and, where data are available, the regression of limb-bone lengths on total body height. Hence, from such studies, one is able to make a fair estimate of the total height of an individual's body, given the length of one or more isolated limb-bones: this is of high importance to physical anthropologists, palaeo-anthropologists and medicolegal or forensic specialists.

10) In the field of population biology and pathology, studies are made on osseous variants, anomalies and pathology. For example, both the incidence of lines of retarded growth in the human tibia and that of dental hypoplasia are related to environmental inadequacy and disadvantage. In other conditions the causation is less obvious, such as perforations in the roof of the eye-sockets (cribra orbitalia), vermiculate texture of bone surfaces, florid crenulations of molar tooth crown surfaces. Also evident in human skeletal collections may be bone tumours, and signs of syphilis, leprosy and other infections of bones of great relevance to the epidemiologist and the bone pathologist.

11) Neurosurgically significant studies have been made, in human skeletal collections, on the base of the cranium and the relations of the posterior cranial fossa to the form, size, position and orientation of the foramen magnum. Such studies not only are of interest in the study of basicranial morphology, but are relevant to a number of congenital and acquired malformations in modern man, e.g. platybasia.

12) Valuable data may be obtained on the size and form of the spinal

canal. These are germane in relation to spinal cord volume and levels and also to the clinical condition of spinal stenosis.

13) Dental studies: the existence of modern human skeletal collections permits a large number of studies of importance in odontology and dentistry. These include the comparative human odontology of large-toothed, medium-toothed and small-toothed populations, to make possible studies on such odontological problems as tooth size and its heritability, secular and evolutionary trends in tooth—and cusp—size, sexual dimorphism, variability within and between tooth groups, field theory, epigenetic canalisation, compensatory interactions in the size of adjacent teeth, fluctuating odontometric asymmetry and allometric relationships.

14) The existence of skeletal collections permits the study of tooth-jaw interrelationships, as regards spacing, crowding, presence of gaps (diastemata), evidence of displacement, mesial drift, occlusal relations and patterns, masticatory stress patterns and gnathofacial architecture, and other aspects of importance not only to craniofacial morphologists but also to orthodontists.

15) The existence of human skeletons in such collections is crucial for the teaching of human anatomy, including dental anatomy, to students of medicine, dentistry, physiotherapy, occupational therapy, nursing and pharmacy; as well as students of comparative anatomy, primatology and general morphology.

The above list of topics and areas of relevance is incomplete. It is based on the personal knowledge of the undersigned, of theses, dissertations and project reports which have been made on such human skeletal collections and which are still the subject of intensive research. Clearly the continued existence of human skeletal collections is of critical importance for purposes of education and research in a wide variety of medical, dental and pure scientific disciplines.

ACKNOWLEDGEMENTS—I am grateful to Dr Frank Spencer for some useful items of information and to Mrs Heather White for typing the manuscript. Received: 6 August 1990. Accepted: 3 November 1990.

Profile of an Anthropologist
No Bone Unturned

Patrick Huyghe

The research of some physical anthropologists and archaeologists involves the discovery and analysis of old bones (as well as artifacts and other remains). Most often these bones represent only part of a skeleton or maybe the mixture of parts of several skeletons. Often these remains are smashed, burned, or partially destroyed. Over the years, physical anthropologists have developed a remarkable repertoire of skills and techniques for teasing the greatest possible amount of information out of sparse material remains.

Although originally developed for basic research, the methods of physical anthropology can be directly applied to contemporary human problems. . . . In this profile, we look briefly at the career of Clyde C. Snow, a physical anthropologist who has put these skills to work in a number of different settings. . . .

As you read this selection, ask yourself the following questions:

- *Given what you know of physical anthropology, what sort of work would a physical anthropologist do for the Federal Aviation Administration?*
- *What is* anthropometry*? How might anthropometric surveys of pilots and passengers help in the design of aircraft equipment?*
- *What is* forensic anthropology*? How can a biological anthropologist be an expert witness in legal proceedings?*

Clyde Snow is never in a hurry. He knows he's late. He's always late. For Snow, being late is part of the job. In fact, he doesn't usually begin to work until death has stripped some poor individual to the bone, and no one—neither the local homicide detectives nor the pathologists—can figure out who once gave identity to the skeletonized remains. No one, that is, except a shrewd, laconic, 60-year-old forensic anthropologist.

Snow strolls into the Cook County Medical Examiner's Office in Chicago on this brisk October morning wearing a pair of Lucchese cowboy boots and a three-piece pin-striped suit. Waiting for him in autopsy room 160 are a bunch of naked skeletons found in Illinois, Wisconsin, and Minnesota since his last visit. Snow, a native Texan who now lives in rural Oklahoma, makes the trip up to Chicago some six times a year. The first case on his agenda is a pale brown skull found in the garbage of an abandoned building once occupied by a Chicago cosmetics company.

Snow turns the skull over slowly in his hands, a cigarette dangling from his fingers. One often does. Snow does not seem overly concerned about mortality, though its tragedy surrounds him daily.

"There's some trauma here," he says, examining a rough edge at the lower back of the skull. He points out the area to Jim Elliott, a homicide detective with the Chicago police. "This looks like a chopping blow by a heavy bladed instrument. Almost like a decapitation." In a place where the whining of bone saws drifts through hallways and the sweet-sour smell of death hangs in the air, the word surprises no one.

Snow begins thinking aloud. "I think what we're looking at here is a female, or maybe a small male, about thirty to forty years old. Probably Asian." He turns the skull upside down, pointing out the degree of wear on the teeth. "This was somebody who lived on a really rough diet. We don't normally find this kind of dental wear in a modern Western population."

"How long has it been around?" Elliott asks.

Snow raises the skull up to his nose. "It doesn't have any decompositional odors," he says. He pokes a finger in the skull's nooks and crannies. "There's no soft tissue left. It's good and dry. And it doesn't show signs of having been buried. I would say that this has been lying around in an attic or a box for years. It feels like a souvenir skull," says Snow.

Souvenir skulls, usually those of Japanese soldiers, were popular with U.S. troops serving in the Pacific during World War II; there was also a trade in skulls during the Vietnam War years. On closer inspection, though, Snow begins to wonder about the skull's Asian origins—the broad nasal aperture and the jutting forth of the upper-tooth-bearing part of the face suggest Melanesian features. Sifting through the objects found in the abandoned building with the skull, he finds several loose-leaf albums of 35-millimeter transparencies documenting life among the highland tribes of New Guinea. The slides, shot by an anthropologist, include graphic scenes of ritual warfare. The skull, Snow concludes, is more likely to be a trophy from one of these tribal battles than the result of a local Chicago homicide.

"So you'd treat it like found property?" Elliott asks finally. "Like somebody's garage-sale property?"

"Exactly," says Snow.

Clyde Snow is perhaps the world's most sought-after forensic anthropologist. People have been calling upon him to identify skeletons for more than a quarter of a century. Every year he's involved in some 75 cases of identification, most of them without fanfare. "He's an old scudder who doesn't have to blow his own whistle," says Walter Birkby, a forensic anthropologist at the University of Arizona. "He know's he's good."

Yet over the years Snow's work has turned him into something of an unlikely celebrity. He has been called upon to identify the remains of the Nazi war criminal Josef Mengele, reconstruct the face of the Egyptian boy-king Tutankhamen, confirm the authenticity of the body autopsied as that of President John F. Kennedy, and examine the skeletal remains of General Custer's men at the battlefield of the Little Bighorn. He has also been involved in the grim task of identifying the bodies in some of the United States' worst airline accidents.

Such is his legend that cases are sometimes attributed to him in which he played no part. He did not, as the *New York Times* reported, identify the remains of the crew of the *Challenger* disaster. But the man is often the equal of his myth. For the past four years, setting his personal safety aside, Snow has spent much of his time in Argentina, searching for the graves and identities of some of the thousands who "disappeared" between 1976 and 1983, during Argentina's military regime.

Snow did not set out to rescue the dead from oblivion. For almost two decades, until 1979, he was a physical anthropologist at the Civil Aeromedical Institute, part of the Federal Aviation Administration in Oklahoma City. Snow's job was to help engineers improve aircraft design and safety features by providing them with data on the human frame.

One study, he recalls, was initiated in response to complaints from a flight attendants' organization. An analysis of accident patterns had revealed that inadequate restraints on flight attendants' jump seats were leading to deaths and injuries and that aircraft doors weighing several hundred pounds were impeding evacuation efforts. Snow points out that ensuring the survival of passengers in emergencies is largely the flight attendants' responsibility. "If they are injured or killed in a crash, you're going to find a lot of dead passengers."

Reasoning that equipment might be improved if engineers had more data on the size and strength of those who use it, Snow undertook a study that required meticulous measurement. When his report was issued in 1975, Senator William Proxmire was outraged that $57,800 of the taxpayers' money had been spent to caliper 423 airline stewardesses from head to toe. Yet the study, which received one of the senator's dubious Golden Fleece Awards, was firmly supported by both the FAA and the Association of Flight Attendants. "I can't imagine," says Snow with obvious delight, "how much coffee Proxmire got spilled on him in the next few months."

It was during his tenure at the FAA that he developed an interest in forensic work. Over the years the Oklahoma police frequently consulted the physical anthropologist for help in identifying crime victims. "The FAA figured it was a kind of community service to let me work on these cases," he says.

The experience also helped to prepare him for the grim task of identifying the victims of air disasters. In December 1972, when a United Airlines plane crashed outside Chicago, killing 43 of the 61 people aboard (including the wife of Watergate conspirator Howard Hunt, who was found with $10,000 in her purse), Snow was brought in to help examine the bodies. That same year, with Snow's help, forensic anthropology was recognized as a specialty by the American Academy of Forensic Sciences. "It got a lot of anthropologists interested in forensics," he says, "and it made a lot of

pathologists out there aware that there were anthropologists who could help them."

Each nameless skeleton poses a unique mystery for Snow. But some, like the second case awaiting him back in the autopsy room at the Cook County morgue, are more challenging than others. This one is a real chiller. In a large cardboard box lies a jumble of bones along with a tattered leg from a pair of blue jeans, a sock shrunk tightly around the bones of a foot, a pair of Nike running shoes without shoelaces, and, inside the hood of a blue windbreaker, a mass of stringy, blood-caked hair. The remains were discovered frozen in ice about 20 miles outside Milwaukee. A rusted bicycle was found lying close by. Paul Hibbard, chief deputy medical examiner for Waukesha County, who brought the skeleton to Chicago, says no one has been reported missing.

Snow lifts the bones out of the box and begins reconstructing the skeleton on an autopsy table. "There are two hundred six bones and thirty-two teeth in the human body," he says, "and each has a story to tell." Because bone is dynamic, living tissue, many of life's significant events—injuries, illness, childbearing—leave their mark on the body's internal framework. Put together the stories told by these bones, he says, and what you have is a person's "osteobiography."

Snow begins by determining the sex of the skeleton, which is not always obvious. He tells the story of a skeleton that was brought to his FAA office in the late 1970s. It had been found along with some women's clothes and a purse in a local back lot, and the police had assumed that it was female. But when Snow examined the bones, he realized that "at six foot three, she would have probably have been the tallest female in Oklahoma."

Then Snow recalled that six months earlier the custodian in his building had suddenly not shown up for work. The man's supervisor later mentioned to Snow, "You know, one of these days when they find Ronnie, he's going to be dressed as a woman." Ronnie, it turned out, was a weekend transvestite. A copy of his dental records later confirmed that the skeleton in women's clothing was indeed Snow's janitor.

The Wisconsin bike rider is also male. Snow picks out two large bones that look something like twisted oysters—the innominates, or hipbones, which along with the sacrum, or lower backbone, form the pelvis. This pelvis is narrow and steep-walled like a male's, not broad and shallow like a female's. And the sciatic notch (the V-shaped space where the sciatic nerve passes through the hipbone) is narrow, as is normal in a male. Snow can also determine a skeleton's sex by checking the size of the mastoid processes (the bony knobs at the base of the skull) and the prominence of the brow ridge, or by measuring the head of an available limb bone, which is typically broader in males.

From an examination of the skull he concludes that the bike rider is "predominantly Caucasoid." A score of bony traits help the forensic anthropologist assign a skeleton to one of the three major racial groups: Negroid, Caucasoid, or Mongoloid. Snow notes that the ridge of the boy's nose is high and salient, as it is in whites. In Negroids and Mongoloids (which include American Indians as well as most Asians) the nose tends to be broad in relation to its height. However, the boy's nasal margins are somewhat smoothed down, usually a Mongoloid feature. "Possibly a bit of American Indian admixture," says Snow. "Do you have Indians in your area?" Hibbard nods.

Age is next. Snow takes the skull and turns it upside down, pointing out the basilar joint, the junction between the two major bones that form the underside of the skull. In a child the joint would still be open to allow room for growth, but here the joint has fused—something that usually happens in the late teen years. On the other hand, he says, pointing to the zigzagging lines on the dome of the skull, the cranial sutures are open. The cranial sutures, which join the bones of the braincase, begin to fuse and disappear in the mid-twenties.

Next Snow picks up a femur and looks for signs of growth at the point where the shaft meets the knobbed end. The thin plates of cartilage—areas of incomplete calcification—that are visible at this point suggest that the boy hadn't yet attained his full height. Snow double-checks with an examination of the pubic symphysis, the joint where the two hipbones meet. The ridges in this area, which fill in and smooth over in adulthood, are still clearly marked. He concludes that the skeleton is that of a boy between 15 and 20 years old.

"One of the things you learn is to be pretty conservative," says Snow. "It's very impressive when you tell the police, 'This person is eighteen years old,' and he turns out to be eighteen. The problem is, if the person is fifteen you've blown it—you probably won't find him. Looking for a missing person is like trying to catch fish. Better get a big net and do your own sorting."

Snow then picks up a leg bone, measures it with a set of calipers, and enters the data into a portable computer. Using the known correlation between the height and length of the long limb bones, he quickly estimates the boy's height. "He's five foot six and a half to five foot eleven," says Snow. "Medium build, not excessively muscular, judging from the muscle attachments that we see." He points to the grainy ridges that appear where muscle attaches itself to the bone. The most prominent attachments show up on the teenager's right arm bone, indicating right-handedness.

Then Snow examines the ribs one by one for signs of injury. He finds no stab wounds, cuts, or bullet holes, here or elsewhere on the skeleton. He picks up the hyoid bone from the boy's throat and looks for the tell-tale fracture signs that would suggest the boy was strangled. But, to Snow's frustration, he can find no obvious cause of death. In hopes of identifying the missing teenager, he suggests sending the skull, hair, and boy's description to Betty Pat Gatliff, a medical illustrator and sculptor in Oklahoma who does facial reconstructions.

Six weeks later photographs of the boy's likeness appear in the *Milwaukee Sentinel.* "If you persist long enough," says Snow, "eighty-five to ninety percent of the cases eventually get positively identified, but it can take anywhere from a few weeks to a few years."

Snow and Gatliff have collaborated many times, but never with more glitz than in 1983, when Snow was commissioned by Patrick Barry, a Miami orthopedic surgeon and amateur Egyptologist, to reconstruct the face of the Egyptian boy-king Tutankhamen. Normally a facial reconstruction begins with a skull, but since Tutankhamen's 3,000-year-old remains were in Egypt, Snow had to make do with the skull measurements from a 1925 postmortem and X-rays taken in 1975. A plaster model of the skull was made, and on the basis of Snow's report—"his skull is Caucasoid with some Negroid admixtures"—Gatliff put a face on it. What did Tutankhamen look like? Very much like the gold mask on his sarcophagus, says Snow, confirming that it was, indeed, his portrait.

Many cite Snow's use of facial reconstructions as one of his most important contributions to the field. Snow, typically self-effacing, says that Gatliff "does all the work." The identification of skeletal remains, he stresses, is often a collaboration between pathologists, odontologists, radiologists, and medical artists using a variety of forensic techniques.

One of Snow's last tasks at the FAA was to help identify the dead from the worst airline accident in U.S. history. On May 25, 1979, a DC-10 crashed shortly after takeoff from Chicago's O'Hare Airport, killing 273 people. The task facing Snow and more than a dozen forensic specialists was horrific. "No one ever sat down and counted," says Snow, "but we estimated ten thousand to twelve thousand pieces or parts of bodies." Nearly 80 percent of the victims were identified on the basis of dental evidence and fingerprints. Snow and forensic radiologist John Fitzpatrick later managed to identify two dozen others by comparing postmortem X-rays with X-rays taken during the victim's lifetime.

Next to dental records, such X-ray comparisons are the most common way of obtaining positive identifications. In 1978, when a congressional committee reviewed the evidence on John F. Kennedy's assassination, Snow used X-rays to show that the body autopsied at Bethesda Naval Hospital was indeed that of the late president and had not—as some conspiracy theorists believed—been switched.

The issue was resolved on the evidence of Kennedy's "sinus print," the scalloplike pattern on the upper margins of the sinuses that is visible in X-rays of the forehead. So characteristic is a person's sinus print that courts throughout the world accept the matching of antemortem and postmortem X-rays of the sinuses as positive identification.

Yet another technique in the forensic specialist's repertoire is photo superposition. Snow used it in 1977 to help identify the mummy of a famous Oklahoma outlaw named Elmer J. McCurdy, who was killed by a posse after holding up a train in 1911. For years the mummy had been exhibited as a "dummy" in a California funhouse—until it was found to have a real human skeleton inside it. Ownership of the mummy was eventually traced back to a funeral parlor in Oklahoma, where McCurdy had been embalmed and exhibited as "the bandit who wouldn't give up."

Using two video cameras and an image processor, Snow superposed the mummy's profile on a photograph of McCurdy that was taken shortly after his death. When displayed on a single monitor, the two coincided to a remarkable degree. Convinced by the evidence, Thomas Noguchi, then Los Angeles County coroner, signed McCurdy's death certificate ("Last known occupation: Train robber") and allowed the outlaw's bones to be returned to Oklahoma for a decent burial.

It was this technique that also allowed forensic scientists to identify the remains of the Nazi "Angel of Death," Josef Mengele, in the summer of 1985. A team of investigators, including Snow and West German forensic anthropologist Richard Helmer, flew to Brazil after an Austrian couple claimed that Mengele lay buried in a grave on a São Paulo hillside. Tests revealed that the stature, age, and hair color of the unearthed skeleton were consistent with information in Mengele's SS files; yet without X-rays or dental records, the scientists still lacked conclusive evidence. When an image of the reconstructed skull was superposed on 1930s photographs of Mengele, however, the match was eerily compelling. All doubts were removed a few months later when Mengele's dental X-rays were tracked down.

In 1979 Snow retired from the FAA to the rolling hills of Norman, Oklahoma, where he and his wife, Jerry, live in a sprawling, early-1960s ranch house. Unlike his 50 or so fellow forensic anthropologists, most of whom are tied to academic positions, Snow is free to pursue his consultancy work full-time. Judging from the number of miles that he logs in the average month, Snow is clearly not ready to retire for good.

His recent projects include a reexamination of the skeletal remains found at the site of the Battle of the Little Bighorn, where more than a century ago Custer and his 210 men were killed by Sioux and Cheyenne warriors. Although most of the enlisted men's remains were moved to a mass grave in 1881, an excavation of the battlefield in the past few years uncovered an additional 375 bones and 36 teeth. Snow, teaming up again with Fitzpatrick, determined that these remains belonged to 34 individuals.

The historical accounts of Custer's desperate last stand are vividly confirmed by their findings. Snow identified one skeleton as that of a soldier between the ages of 19 and 23 who weighed around 150 pounds and stood about five foot eight. He'd sustained gunshot wounds to his chest and left forearm. Heavy blows to his head had fractured his skull and sheared off his teeth. Gashed thigh bones indicated that his body was later dismembered with an ax or hatchet.

Given the condition and number of the bodies, Snow seriously questions the accuracy of the identifications made by the original nineteenth-century burial crews. He doubts, for example, that the skeleton buried at West Point is General Custer's.

For the last four years Snow has devoted much of his time to helping two countries come to terms with the horrors of a much more recent past. As part of a group sponsored by the American Association for the Advancement of Science, he has been helping the Argentinian National Commission on Disappeared Persons to determine the fate of some of those who vanished during their country's harsh military rule: between 1976 and 1983 at least 10,000 people were systematically swept off the streets by roving death squads to be tortured, killed, and buried in unmarked graves. In December 1986, at the invitation of the Aquino government's Human Rights Commission, Snow also spent several weeks training Philippine scientists to investigate the disappearances that occurred under the Marcos regime.

But it is in Argentina where Snow has done the bulk of his human-rights work. He has spent more than 27 months in and around Buenos Aires, first training a small group of local medical and anthropology students in the techniques of forensic investigation, and later helping them carefully exhume and examine scores of the *desaparecidos,* or disappeared ones.

Only 25 victims have so far been positively identified. But the evidence has helped convict seven junta members and other high-ranking military and police officers. The idea is not necessarily to identify all 10,000 of the missing, says Snow. "If you have a colonel who ran a detention center where maybe five hundred people were killed, you don't have to nail him with five hundred deaths. Just one or two should be sufficient to get him convicted." Forensic evidence from Snow's team may be used to prosecute several other military officers, including General Suarez Mason. Mason is the former commander of the I Army Corps in Buenos Aires and is believed to be responsible for thousands of disappearances. He was recently extradited from San Francisco back to Argentina, where he is expected to stand trial this winter [1988].

The investigations have been hampered by a frustrating lack of antemortem information. In 1984, when commission lawyers took depositions from relatives and friends of the disappeared, they often failed to obtain such basic information as the victim's height, weight, or hair color. Nor did they ask for the missing person's X-rays (which in Argentina are given to the patient) or the address of the victim's dentist. The problem was compounded by the inexperience of those who carried out the first mass exhumations prior to Snow's arrival. Many of the skeletons were inadvertently destroyed by bulldozers as they were brought up.

Every unearthed skeleton that shows signs of gunfire, however, helps to erode the claim once made by many in the Argentinian military that most of the *desaparecidos* are alive and well

and living in Mexico City, Madrid, or Paris. Snow recalls the case of a 17-year-old boy named Gabriel Dunayavich, who disappeared in the summer of 1976. He was walking home from a movie with his girlfriend when a Ford Falcon with no license plates snatched him off the street. The police later found his body and that of another boy and girl dumped by the roadside on the outskirts of Buenos Aires. The police went through the motions of an investigation, taking photographs and doing an autopsy, then buried the three teenagers in an unmarked grave.

A decade later Snow, with the help of the boy's family, traced the autopsy reports, the police photographs, and the grave of the three youngsters. Each of them had four or five closely spaced bullet wounds in the upper chest—the signature, says Snow, of an automatic weapon. Two also had wounds on their arms from bullets that had entered behind the elbow and exited from the forearm.

"That means they were conscious

when they were shot," says Snow. "When a gun was pointed at them, they naturally raised their arm." It's details like these that help to authenticate the last moments of the victims and bring a dimension of reality to the judges and jury.

Each time Snow returns from Argentina he says that this will be the last time. A few months later he is back in Buenos Aires. "There's always more work to do," he says. It is, he admits quietly, "terrible work."

"These were such brutal, cold-blooded crimes," he says. "The people who committed them not only murdered; they had a system to eliminate all trace that their victims even existed."

Snow will not let them obliterate their crimes so conveniently. "There are human-rights violations going on all around the world," he says. "But to me murder is murder, regardless of the motive. I hope that we are sending a message to governments who murder in the name of politics that they can be held to account."

The DNA Wars

Touted as an infallible method of identifying criminals, DNA matching has mired courts in a vicious battle of expert witnesses.

Edward Humes

Edward Humes is the author of "Murderer With a Badge," published by Dutton. He won a 1989 Pulitzer Prize for specialized reporting while at the Orange County Register.

The ambush was waiting for Prof. Laurence Mueller long before he arrived at the courthouse with his bar charts and slides and other hieroglyphs of science. You could see it in the deputy D.A.'s bear-trap smile, in the pile of dog-eared files he had amassed on Mueller's past courtroom performances, in the patiently highlighted inconsistencies ferreted out of those transcripts. The prosecutor and his experts were even making book—inaccurately, it turned out—that the good professor would wear his trademark tweed blazer, a coat that announces academe faster than any resume.

Mueller, a professor of evolutionary biology at UC Irvine, had been hired on behalf of an accused rapist to testify on the potentially eye-glazing subject of population genetics as it applies to that *Wunderkind* police technology, DNA "fingerprinting." With such a topic, his main concern should have been keeping the jury awake.

He needn't have worried. By the time Mueller left that courtroom in Santa Ana last spring, science, the presumptive subject of the day, had taken a back seat to more personal, and far more heated, topics. In short order, Mueller was branded a hired gun devoid of principles because he has

earned more as an expert witness in DNA cases than as a university professor. As for his opinions, Mueller wasn't just proclaimed mistaken, he was accused of attempting to "lie with statistics" and of making deliberately erroneous conclusions with false data, a cardinal sin in the scientific world. (Mueller and his colleagues say his only sin was disagreeing with the government's experts.) Finally, Mueller was mocked for daring to apply lessons from his experiments with fruit flies to human genetics, even though the lowly fruit fly, with its prodigious birth rate, has been a staple of genetic science for most of this century.

LAURENCE MUELLER: The professor's opposition to DNA evidence has prompted vitriolic personal attacks.

The two-fisted, in-your-face cross-examination had jurors on the edges of their chairs and the defense lawyer itching to fling a similar attack at the prosecution's three experts. Which he did, with the same sort of biting accusations Mueller had withstood, charging the experts with ignoring data to reach false conclusions.

Funny thing was, Mueller declared the experience one of his milder courtroom bouts to date. More often than not, the verbal body blows get a lot nastier. "It was heated, yes, but not as bad as some," Mueller said. Later he

added, "And I've taken a few other jackets out of mothballs."

Genetic printing, a once seemingly unassailable technology for identifying criminals through their DNA, has been stripped of its luster by a series of furious academic debates, vicious legal battles and highly personal attacks on scientists nationwide. Mueller's experience has become the rule, not the exception, and people on either side of the equation say that both justice and science are the ultimate casualties of this war.

DNA printing, it turns out, though an undeniably powerful tool for the police, is not the nearly infallible magic bullet for solving crimes its proponents once claimed. Bottom line: Much of the time this method of comparing a suspect's DNA to blood, semen or hair found at crime scenes works, sometimes it doesn't. And the close calls—when the spotty, ink-blot-like patterns of deoxyribonucleaic acid are blurred or faint—become so subjective that their utility is questionable. Matching a suspect's DNA to evidence from a crime scene becomes an art, not a science, with lives and liberty hanging in the balance.

This simple realization has created chaos in the courts. Judges and juries with no scientific training are being asked to decide which scientists are right: those who believe DNA printing works well, or those who believe it is fatally flawed. Each side is sincere. Each cites reams of data. Each boasts

From *Los Angeles Times Magazine*, November 29, 1992, pp. 20-22, 24, 26, 54-57. © 1992 by Edward Humes. Reprinted by permission.

impeccable resumes, and equally impeccable reasons for slamming those who disagree. So how do jurors know whether a complex technology is being used to convict the guilty, or to railroad the innocent? They can listen to hours of testimony and still not know. Innocents might be sent to Death Row, while killers are set free. It all depends on which side has the cleverest lawyers and the most persuasive scientists. Across the country, the confusion is so great that one judge can allow DNA printing as evidence while another, in the same state or even the same courthouse, could rule that the technology is still too unreliable.

And so, perhaps inevitably, a strange thing has happened as lawyers jockey for the sympathies of juries and jurists. Instead of the science, the scientists themselves are being challenged with unprecedented venom. Reputations have been tarnished, accusations of government conspiracies and defense lawyers' cabals have been thrown onto the fire and bitter rifts among researchers have arisen, making it increasingly difficult for them to work together to resolve the very debate causing the courtroom combat.

The reason for this lies in a longstanding legal principle that judges may admit new scientific evidence in the courtroom only when there is no significant debate within the scientific community over its validity. That means government prosecutors and experts who want to use DNA to convict people cannot simply disagree with scientists who question the reliability of genetic printing. They must discredit and denounce the critics, questioning their motives, ethics and abilities to show that there really is no legitimate debate. Defense lawyers have responded in kind, attacking with equal zest.

Scientists accustomed to the sterility of the laboratory and the decorum of university conferences have been left blinking in anger, and sometimes fear, at the withering attacks. Allegations of perjury and hidden conflicts of interest, smirking remarks about sexual orientation, insinuations about tax audits and immigration status—nothing is off-limits. Many researchers now simply refuse to testify rather than face being shredded on the stand.

"It's not about science," says a rueful Mueller. "They are interested in dirty laundry."

ROCKNE HARMON: The deputy D.A. is noted for his use of DNA matching—and for discrediting its opponents.

"I'm not ashamed," counters Alameda County Deputy Dist. Atty. Rockne Harmon, a nationally prominent expert at using DNA evidence in court who has been equally prominent in efforts to discredit Mueller and other scientists critical of the technology. During charitable moments, he calls Mueller a "knucklehead." "A dangerous criminal," he says, "could be set free to rape, rob or kill people."

In short, the battle over DNA fingerprinting has become the most entertaining and bewildering legal spectacle around. With jurors and judges unsure just whom to believe, resolution is nowhere in sight.

By the end of last year, the FBI had performed 4,000 DNA comparisons in criminal cases, with private, state and county labs adding thousands more. In about a third of those cases, the tests cleared the suspect. But hundreds of people were prosecuted using DNA evidence in more than 40 states.

Most of these defendants were convicted, a testament to the power of this new scientific evidence. But even when DNA tests were ruled inadmissible, the suspects usually were still found guilty. In part, that is because prosecutors chose slam-dunk cases for their first DNA trials, under the theory that obviously guilty individuals were less likely to pursue appeals of the DNA portion of their cases. Only now are numbers of cases beginning to appear in which DNA is the key piece of evidence, the only link between a suspect and a crime.

In the earlier mold, one case stands out. In New York, a handyman by the name of Joseph Castro was accused of fatally stabbing a pregnant South Bronx woman and her 2-year-old daughter in February, 1987. Lifecodes Corp. of Valhalla, N.Y., one of three private labs in the United States that does forensic genetics testing, was hired by prosecutors to do a DNA analysis. Lifecodes' tests said the DNA from a tiny bloodstain on Castro's wristwatch matched the woman's genes, and that the odds against the blood belonging to someone else were 1 in 100 million.

But the Castro case represented the first full-blown challenge to DNA evidence. Castro's lawyers amassed a team of prestigious scientists, who examined Lifecodes' test results and found numerous errors. Even one of the prosecution experts, after conferring with the defense scientists, reversed himself and said that the vaunted 1 in 100 million match was wrong. The judge hearing Castro's case kicked the DNA evidence out.

Yet prosecutors also proclaimed a victory: Castro later pleaded guilty, admitting that the blood on his watch really had come from the victim. Prosecutors say the Castro case, in which the tests were accurate but ruled inadmissible, raises the specter of criminals' going free. Had there not been other, damning evidence in the case, they say, a double murderer would have walked. (In fact, although no national statistics are kept, experts on both sides of the DNA issue could recall only three or four defendants who won acquittals after DNA evidence was excluded.) Defense attorneys counter that bogus DNA evidence could just as easily convict an innocent person.

The prosecution of David Hicks, meanwhile, demonstrates another extreme—a case where DNA was the pivotal evidence despite problems with the test results. A young, unskilled laborer now on Death Row for the murder-rape of his grandmother in rural Freestone County, Tex., Hicks lacked the expert witnesses and skilled attorneys Castro had. The blurry DNA prints obtained in his case, and the 96 million to 1 probability of guilt announced by prosecution experts, again from Lifecodes, were barely challenged. The one expert hired for Hicks' defense, former UC Irvine geneticist Simon Ford, said he got such limited and late access to lab data that he was unprepared when he testified. Yet the defense attorney appointed to represent Hicks declined to ask for more time.

After Hicks was convicted in early 1989 and sentenced to death, Ford and other scientists, Laurence Mueller among them, reviewed the Lifecodes lab work and concluded that the DNA match was improperly done and vastly overstated. An accurate analysis, Ford estimates, would show not a 96 million to 1 probability that Hicks was the killer, but something on the order of hundreds to 1. Furthermore, in Furney-Richardson, Tex., population 300, where Hicks was born and lived, many residents are genetically related. Families have lived there, married their neighbors and passed around the same genetic patterns, the same DNA, for generations. Therefore, people in the community are far more likely to share DNA prints with Hicks—and the killer. Indeed, relatives of Hicks were suspects early in the case, raising an even greater possibility that the killer's DNA pattern could appear to match Hicks', yet not be his.

Hicks' jury never heard any of this because Ford never had a chance to do his analysis before the trial. Had they known, Hicks might easily have been acquitted, since there was little more than circumstantial evidence against him and no eyewitnesses, says William C. Thompson, the attorney and UC Irvine professor now helping Hicks to find legal representation for his appeal. Because of the certainty the 96 million to 1 finding implied, "the jurors were told that there was no way anyone other than Hicks could have been the killer," Thompson says. "That simply is not true."

Hicks' prosecutor, Robert W. Gage, said in a letter to The Sciences magazine that he was convinced Hicks received a fair trial. Gage also asserted that Ford and Thompson, who together have written articles on DNA printing,

have less than altruistic motives behind their criticism. They "profit by traveling around the country and testifying for desperate defendants about the pitfalls of DNA identification," Gage claimed, noting that Ford and Thompson, thanks to their DNA work for defendants, are known to prosecutors nationwide as the "Combine from Irvine."

Both Ford and Thompson say such remarks are examples of widespread harassment against DNA critics. Thompson, who is married and lives with his wife and children near the UC Irvine campus, says opponents are spreading false rumors among the DNA litigation set that he and Ford are lovers using their DNA legal fees to build a home in Laguna Beach. He has also endured bar complaints filed by prosecutors in New Mexico and California, accusing him of conflict of interest for publishing academic articles on cases in which he had been a lawyer. The complaints were ruled groundless, he says.

Ford also complains of prosecutorial harassment and, though still active as a consultant in DNA cases, now avoids testifying in court. A British national, Ford was on the witness stand in an Arizona murder case two years ago when an FBI lawyer abruptly asked about his visa status. Ford was then trying to obtain a permanent resident "green card." Though the judge quickly silenced the attorney for straying into irrelevant areas, Ford saw it as a veiled threat from a federal official.

"It definitely was chilling," Ford recalls. The judge in the Arizona case eventually dealt a stinging blow to the FBI, by finding that its DNA methods were not generally accepted by the scientific community and so could not be used in court. A state appeals court is currently considering whether to ban DNA evidence throughout Arizona.

In Texas, however, David Hicks remains on Death Row, convicted on similar evidence, insisting he is innocent, but garnering few sympathetic ears. Thompson believes Hicks might well be an innocent man convicted wrongly by his own DNA. But given the current conservative climate in ap-

pellate courts, Thompson concedes, stopping Hicks' date with lethal injection will be an uphill battle. Yet the question his case poses is a haunting one: How can evidence be too unreliable in Arizona, yet be used to put a man to death in Texas?

To keep defense experts at bay, an informal network of prosecutors and scientists who wholeheartedly support DNA printing has sprung up across the country. Rockne Harmon, the Alameda County deputy district attorney, is its unofficial clearinghouse. To help discredit defense experts, network members regularly fax articles, transcripts and other tidbits to one another, including, at times, unpublished papers that DNA experts have tried to keep confidential.

Researchers critical of the technology say they have been pressured to alter or withdraw scientific papers from publication. When pressure on individual scientists has failed, government officials and the experts they employ have lobbied publications, including the prestigious journal Science, to reject articles that challenge DNA fingerprinting. In one highly publicized case last December, Science—after pressure from DNA proponents—published an unprecedented, simultaneous rebuttal to an article criticizing the government's theories on DNA printing.

"I never expected that the government would attempt to interfere in my scholarly activities or publications," wrote Daniel L. Hartl, a co-author of the Science article and a professor of genetics at Washington University School of Medicine in St. Louis, in a sworn affidavit. James Wooley, a federal prosecutor from an organized crime strike force in Ohio, obtained the article before it was published, then telephoned Hartl, who had been a defense witness in a case Wooley prosecuted. According to the professor, Wooley "proceeded to badger me for almost an hour asserting that the article would do incalculable harm to government prosecutions and the criminal justice system. . . . I was particularly disturbed when Mr. Wooley . . . asked me whether I was afraid of having my taxes audited."

Wooley denies any attempt to stifle Hartl's, or anyone else's, academic freedom, saying he may have made some sarcastic remarks toward the end of his telephone conversation with Hartl, but that the scientist was being paranoid.

Perhaps more than anyone, Laurence Mueller has been a favorite whipping boy in the DNA debate. Deputy Dist. Atty. Harmon has written harsh letters questioning the quality and accuracy of his testimony, not only to various scientific journals to which Mueller has submitted articles, but to his department chairman and the UC Irvine chancellor. Editors at Science even informed Harmon by mail that they had rejected an article by Mueller before they told the scientist of their decision. "It sounds like they respect me more than they do him," Harmon says.

The government is not the only side getting down and dirty: Defense lawyers active in DNA cases also have their own network of litigators and scientists, and the government's "pro-DNA" experts have begun to complain that they, too, are being harassed by harsh attacks on their integrity.

In U.S. vs. Yee, an Ohio murder case, both sides of the DNA war pulled out all stops. Last spring, New York defense lawyers Barry Scheck and Peter Neufeld filed a motion for a new trial, charging the government with conducting a national campaign to harass and stifle DNA critics. At the same time, the two attorneys launched an attack of their own: The motion accuses two prominent Texas genetics researchers of warping their scientific opinions in favor of DNA printing in order to garner $500,000 in Justice Department grants.

Scheck and Neufeld's broadside also accuses the FBI's chief expert in DNA printing, Bruce Budowle, of citing a nonexistent study to support convictions in the Yee case. The lawyers have demanded an investigation of this alleged perjury by the FBI, the nation's preeminent purveyor of DNA printing. Budowle did not return repeated phone messages, but his boss, FBI Assistant

Director John W. Hicks, defended the DNA expert, saying that Budowle knows that teams of defense lawyers and experts will scrutinize every word he says on the witness stand. "He knows not to say something dumb."

Not even Hicks is immune from attack: Yee lawyers say he tried to destroy evidence that could aid defendants in DNA cases—allegations that Hicks hotly denies, although government memos do show that he wanted to destroy certain files that might have contained information on FBI lab errors. They also criticized Hicks for attempting to influence a recent report by a committee of the prestigious National Academy of Sciences, which in April issued a qualified endorsement of the use of DNA fingerprinting in court, but rejected certain crucial techniques used by the FBI. Hicks calls the allegations raised in the Yee case "a witch hunt."

Finding common ground between the opposing sides has been nearly impossible, in part because of the way DNA evidence was first presented to the courts and the public: as a magic bullet.

The technique first was used in 1985 in Great Britain, when blood was taken from more than 4,000 men to identify a rapist-murderer who had killed two 15-year-old girls in two neighboring villages. The DNA fragments extracted from these blood samples were then compared to DNA from semen found in the victims; police found their man when he tried to get someone else to contribute a blood sample for him.

Proponents of the technique claimed that the genetic comparison was so exact that the odds of a false match were 1 in hundreds of millions. In other words, they said, the odds of a mistake were so minuscule that DNA was as good as a fingerprint.

By 1987, the technology had crossed the Atlantic, with three private laboratories offering DNA analyses in criminal cases. The FBI soon followed with labs in Washington and Quantico, Va., and various state and local government

DNA laboratories came on line in the next two years. DNA printing became a growth industry.

Its appeal was enormous, especially in rape and murder cases. Previously, forensic scientists charged with finding evidence at crime scenes could only compare blood types, or a somewhat more refined analysis of blood enzymes. Semen or blood found in the victims or at the crime scenes was collected and compared to blood from suspects. If there was a different blood type, a suspect was exonerated. If there was a match, however, it often proved little; millions of people share the same blood type or enzyme.

"Before DNA, if we got a figure of 1 in 4, maybe 1 in 10, we were lucky. One in 100, we were ecstatic," says John Hartmann of the Orange County sheriff-coroner's DNA lab, one of the most respected in the nation. "It was not very discriminating."

Then, suddenly, a quantum advance occurred. Compare DNA, proponents of the new technology announced, and you could be sure you had the right culprit. To men like Hartmann, who genuinely agonized at the thought of criminals' going free because their lab work was too inexact, DNA printing represented a law-enforcement "home run." Now rapists who might have gone free because of the vagaries of eyewitness testimony or the lack of hard proof could be prosecuted. Serial murderers who left no living witnesses would no longer prey on society with impunity. Their DNA, with the help of the knowing, dispassionate men in white lab coats who analyzed it, would answer the questions of guilt and innocence. And the odds that they might be wrong would be 1 in millions, maybe billions. It almost seemed too good to be true.

It was.

Even the term genetic "fingerprint" turned out to be a misnomer, granting an unwarranted aura of infallibility to the technique. Now many jurisdictions prohibit the term's use in court out of concern that it misleads juries, using instead DNA "profiling" or "typing."

Jurors can look at a projection of conventional fingerprint comparisons and say, yeah, they really do look alike. Furthermore, it is uncontrovertible that no two people possess the same fingerprints, not even twins.

Neither is true with DNA prints.

Unlike fingerprints, a person's entire DNA is not examined in the technique—current technology is too primitive. Instead, scientists analyze only a few areas of the long, complex chains of deoxyribonucleic acid that contain the genetic blueprint for all organisms, bacteria to Homo sapiens. The regions of the DNA molecule that are studied, fragments called VNTRs, serve no known purpose other than linking other portions of DNA, like empty boxcars in the middle of a freight train.

When semen, blood or hair is left by a rapist or killer at a crime scene, the DNA can be chemically removed and broken up into fragments in a solution of organic solvents and enzymes. The purified DNA that results is poured into an electrified gel, which spreads out the fragments according to their length. After several more steps, another chemical solution called a "probe" is added, which mates with a specific group of VNTRs, highlighting it with a radioactive tag. The final step uses radiation-sensitive film to record the VNTR pattern. The resulting "autoradiograph" bears a passing resemblance to a very sloppy bar code like that on most grocery labels. The crime-scene autorad can then be compared to a suspect's autorad. Theoretically, different patterns mean innocence; a match means guilt.

Sounds a lot like fingerprinting. And proponents and critics agree that the technique is theoretically sound. But in practice, the autorads are occasionally hazy and incomplete, due in part to the decomposition that typically occurs before forensic evidence is gathered. The blurry images that can result may lead one expert to see a match where another sees none. Many matches are clear-cut; others are so subjective that the certainty DNA printing is supposed to convey simply vanishes. Worse, jurors and judges at times don't know what they're really looking at when the scientists start passing out the auto-

rads. So one focus of the debate is whether a match can be declared reliably in each and every case.

The hottest battle, though, revolves around what it means when DNA prints do clearly match. Does a match really mean that only one person matches the criminal's DNA print, or are there other people walking around with the same patterns? Proponents of the technology say the odds of more than one person bearing the same VNTR patterns are extremely small. Critics say prosecutors and their witnesses are vastly overstating this certainty level.

To understand this aspect of the debate, you have to understand how the chemical "probes" work. There are several kinds, and each probe examines a different grouping of genetic "boxcars"—the VNTRs. According to FBI population studies of several thousand people who gave blood samples, one VNTR grouping may occur in 1 out of 100 people. Another grouping may occur in 1 out of 17 individuals, another, 1 in 2,000. By using three, four or more such probes, then multiplying the odds together, incredibly small probabilities are generated, anywhere from 1 in 100,000 to 1 in billions. Thus, the image of DNA printing as magic bullet was born.

In the Hicks case in Texas, for example, Lifecodes declared a six-probe match in calculating the 96 million to 1 probability that he raped and murdered his grandmother. In theory, this should be irrefutable evidence. But defense witness Ford's analysis showed that four of the six VNTR patterns contained in a vaginal swab of the victim could have come from the grandmother's cells, not the killer's—there was no way of telling them apart in this case. As relatives, Hicks and his grandmother had identical VNTR groupings in four places. Using only the two VNTR groupings that must have come from the killer and that do match Hicks, the odds of Hicks' being the guilty party, Ford says, are a few hundred to 1, nothing close to the level of certainty represented to the jury that convicted Hicks. By Ford's estimate, millions of others could have commit-

ted the crime, including many people in Hicks' insular hometown.

The possibility that such communities might contain people with common VNTR patterns is another hot point of contention in the DNA wars. Defense attorneys recently sought to embarrass one of the government's most prominent DNA experts, Kenneth Kidd, a professor of genetics, psychiatry and biology at Yale University for claiming that a four-probe match between two different people was virtually impossible. This claim was refuted—with Kidd's own research on an isolated Amazonian Indian tribe called the Karitiana, in which about a third of the 54 people tested had identical DNA patterns for four different probes. (Hicks was sent to Death Row on the basis of two distinct probes.) Once confronted with his own data, Kidd and prosecutors dismissed the inbred Karitiana community as an aberration that does not apply to the much larger gene pool of U.S. populations.

"That's what they say now," Thompson argues. "But before, they said it couldn't happen at all, anywhere."

The DNA critics say such findings dictate that more conservative probabilities should be used to explain to juries what a DNA match means. Prosecutors resist this, saying the FBI and other labs already build in error factors that give defendants the benefit of the doubt. Obviously, they also oppose change because less dramatic odds leave too much room for doubt about a suspect's guilt. The magic bullet turns into a blank.

The recent National Academy of Sciences report, however, urges somewhat more conservative numbers than the FBI and other labs generate—striking a rare compromise between the two DNA factions. It remains to be seen if either side adopts the report's recommendations. So far, the FBI is resisting change, while defense lawyers lobby for probabilities more in their favor. A series of recent appellate court decisions against DNA evidence, including one in Massachusetts and two in California, cite the academy report and side with the critics.

"Really, when you get down to it, there's not much difference between a million to 1 and 100 million to 1, or a million to 1 and a 100,000 to 1, which is really what they're arguing about," Orange County's John Hartmann says. "Either way, we've hit a home run."

If such arguments were all there was to it, the viciousness that marks DNA court battles probably wouldn't have erupted. Each side merely would amass its experts, let them testify, and the judge and jury would decide. But the battle also revolves around a legal precedent set by a federal appeals court in 1923, the Frye Rule, which governs the admissibility of new scientific evidence in many, though not all, jurisdictions. The legal rule was first established to examine (and ultimately bar from court) lie-detector tests, but 70 years later, it provides an uneasy fit with the state-of-the-art technology of DNA printing. In DNA cases, Frye's peculiarities make the intense attacks on scientists' integrity all but inevitable.

According to the Frye decision, scientific discoveries should be admitted only when there is no substantial debate about them within the relevant scientific communities—in this case, geneticists, molecular biologists and statisticians. Under Frye, judges aren't supposed to decide who is right in a scientific debate—they aren't qualified—but merely whether a legitimate debate exists.

That explains the vicious attacks on the scientists, and why so many complaints of harassment have been generated. If government officials can halt articles and paint DNA critics as unethical charlatans, judges may decide there is no legitimate debate.

Naturally, defense lawyers respond in kind, attempting to prove the government experts are the real charlatans whenever they testify that there is no debate about DNA printing. "It's trench warfare, no doubt about that," Hartmann says.

Until recently, prosecutors have won most of the skirmishes: DNA evidence has been admitted in most cases, with decisive results. Only one state's Supreme Court has ruled DNA inadmissible—Massachusetts—while one other, Minnesota, severely limits the way it can be used. Numerous other states, including California, are reconsidering its admissibility. The U.S. Supreme Court has yet to specifically rule on the issue.

At the trial court level, the results are more contradictory. In the same courthouse, one judge may admit a DNA test while another finds a legitimate scientific dispute exists, rendering the DNA evidence inadmissible. Justice, when it comes to DNA evidence, is unequal, varying from state to state and judge to judge. The U.S. 2nd Circuit Court of Appeals (with jurisdiction over New York, Vermont and Connecticut), for instance, recently approved the use of DNA evidence without lengthy admissibility hearings; at the same time, a District of Columbia judge barred prosecutors from using DNA printing in court.

Another example: last year, one division of the California Court of Appeal upheld DNA evidence in a Ventura murder case, which could have set a precedent for all of California. But a month before that ruling, Los Angeles County Superior Court Judge C. Robert Simpson Jr. ruled in a different murder case that DNA evidence was too questionable to be admitted. "There is a profound, significant and honestly held disagreement among these men of science," Simpson wrote. Because that case developed after the Ventura prosecution, Simpson's decision was not undone by the appellate court's embrace of DNA evidence. The two at-odds rulings stand, their illogic intact.

In August, a different division of the state Court of Appeal, citing the national academy report, ruled that DNA evidence was not admissible. Now the state Supreme Court has been asked to rule definitively.

An Orange County rape trial earlier this year, in which Mueller and Kidd were lambasted, shows the kind of balancing act juries must perform to deal with the attacks, disputes and contradictions. Frank Lee Soto was charged with raping his neighbor, an elderly woman in Westminster. The only hard evidence against him was a DNA test of his blood—he provided it voluntarily—that showed a clear match with the rapist's semen. (The victim, too ill to testify, told police Soto didn't do it.)

Soto's attorney, Paul Stark, fought bitterly with Deputy Dist. Atty. Dennis Bauer over what the DNA match meant. Bauer, with Yale's Kidd and several other of the most prominent pro-DNA printing experts in the country, said the odds were 189 million to 1 that Soto was the right man. Equally prominent experts suggested the numbers should be more favorable to Soto; in particular, biology professor William Shields of the State University of New York at Syracuse said the correct number was between 65,000 to 1 and 23,000 to 1. Given Orange County's population, that meant 17 other potential suspects were running around, five times that in all of Southern California.

Both sides sounded certain and sincere. Both had the charts and the numbers and other paraphernalia to support their positions. Both sides impugned the abilities and motives of the opposing experts in typical vitriolic fashion. There was literally no way for the jurors (or the judge, for that matter) to know whom to believe.

Doing what the scientists refused to do, the jurors sought compromises. Their statements after the trial showed that they accepted the smaller defense numbers put forward by Shields, and so convicted Soto of the lesser charge of attempted rape. Had Soto not been a neighbor, they said, they would have acquitted him. But 65,000 to 1, coupled with the fact that he lived next door, was enough to cinch the case. Soto received a three-year prison sentence, but, because of the uncertainties revolving around the DNA issue, he is free on bail while he appeals.

Hartmann, whose Orange County lab performed the tests on Soto's blood, applauded the jury's decision that DNA evidence alone is insufficient to convict. His attitude is among the most reasonable of any expert in the field and though he is ardent in his support for DNA printing, he does not believe that it should on its own determine anyone's fate: "If I was on that jury, I would have had a real problem with it, too. . . . No one should be convicted solely on the basis of DNA evidence, not even a billion to 1. If there was no other evidence, I would vote not guilty, too."

But for most of the combatants, the DNA debate has assumed the aspect of a religious argument, each side certain it is right, each incapable of seeing the other's point of view. Voices of compromise are drowned out.

There is one unique case in Virginia that calls into question the sincerity of these head-butting positions. Joseph R. O'Dell III was convicted of a vicious and sensational murder in Virginia Beach in 1985. O'Dell was seen at the bar where the murder victim had been on the night of her death, though no one saw them arrive or leave together. Later, police seized bloody men's clothes in O'Dell's garage after they received an angry call from his girlfriend. O'Dell, who had a robbery conviction and other legal run-ins behind him, told police his shirt and jacket got bloody from a bar fight that night, but detectives figured they had found their man. Lab results seemed to confirm their opinion. The case predates DNA printing, but less sophisticated blood enzyme tests showed that the blood on O'Dell's clothes was consistent with the victim's blood. O'Dell was convicted and sentenced to death.

Since then, with the advent of DNA testing, his appellate lawyers petitioned the court for new tests. The result: the more refined DNA technology shows the blood on O'Dell's clothing cannot be matched to the victim's, according to briefs filed in his appeal. Key evidence against O'Dell apparently has been invalidated, a case where DNA printing seemingly exonerates rather than convicts.

But O'Dell remains on Death Row. He has been unable to win a new trial. Prosecutors, who in other courtrooms have championed the use of DNA evidence against defendants, are so convinced of O'Dell's guilt that they have opposed its use in his case, even as defense attorneys want the test results admitted.

The prosecution is winning so far, keeping the Virginia appellate courts from considering the DNA evidence in O'Dell's case by focusing on a technicality. O'Dell's out-of-state lawyers filed an appeal petition that lacked a table of contents and a memorandum of facts summarizing the case (a formulaic introduction to the appeal). The prosecution seized on this procedural gaffe as a means of throwing out the entire appeal. By the time the defense lawyers noticed the oversight, a filing deadline had passed by three days, and the Virginia Supreme Court refused to consider the case.

Recently, three justices of the U.S. Supreme Court suggested that the Virginia courts ought to think again. Although the full court declined to hear O'Dell's direct appeal, Harry A. Blackmun, John Paul Stevens and Sandra Day O'Connor decided that putting a man to death because his lawyers forgot a table of contents was going to far, especially if he might be innocent. In an unusual letter handed down in the case, they instructed lower federal courts in Virginia to give careful consideration to O'Dell's next appeal, a habeas corpus petition to be filed this year, "because of the gross injustice that would result if an innocent man were sentenced to death." And there it stands.

O'Dell remains on Death Row, waiting for his case to be heard, even as prosecutors across the country continue to use DNA evidence to send him companions.

Old Dog, Old Tricks

Lee Cronk

Lee Cronk is an assistant professor of anthropology at Texas A&M University in College Station.

HELP WANTED: "Healthy males wanted as semen donors. Help infertile couples." The advertisement runs in the classified section of *The Battalion,* the student newspaper at Texas A&M University. "Confidentiality ensured. Ages 18 to 35, excellent compensation." But in spite of the blandishments, donors are scarce. Meanwhile, on highways in the surrounding Texas countryside, armadillos routinely kill themselves by springing into the air in front of oncoming cars, in misguided attempts to foil their perceived attackers.

What could two such disparate phenomena possibly have in common? Each of them sheds light on the environment in which a species evolved. In each case some aspect of the original environment has changed, and an old behavior that might once have been adaptive is no longer so. The problem for the armadillos is cars: for most of armadillo evolution there were none, and the armadillo's habit of springing into the air when it is threatened worked well enough to confuse snakes and other predators. Leap two feet high in front of a Buick, though, and you're buzzard bait.

The Texas A&M undergraduates also are disadvantaged—somewhat less drastically, to be sure—by their evolutionary heritage. In a Darwinian sense, an adaptive behavior is one that increases the individual organism's chance of passing on its genes. The

adaptive response to the sperm bank's advertisement (which represents a chance to reproduce, free of any cost beyond a few minutes' effort) would be to visit the bank as often as possible. But throughout most of human evolution, reproductive opportunities have involved human females, not test tubes. Focusing on females was adaptive in the past, but here, in the novel environment of a sperm bank, it is a diversion and a handicap. For the few men who do make deposits, the incentive is usually financial, not sexual; an acceptable donor can make more than $100 a week for just a few minutes' work.

The English psychologist John Bowlby, in his treatise *Attachment and Loss,* was the first to point out the importance of understanding the environment in which an adaptation arose— what he called the environment of evolutionary adaptedness. Behavioral and physical adaptations that seem to make no sense in an organism's current environment can be traced to the legacy of an earlier, different environment in which those traits were favored. Human beings, now the major source of environmental change on earth, have altered the environments of many other animals besides the armadillo, and the results have been incongruous and often poignant.

Rabbits dart back and forth in the paths of oncoming cars, attempting to confuse what they perceive as predators intensely bearing down on them at great speed. Toads are undone by their feeding behavior. They snap reflexively at almost any small, moving object—behavior that serves them well in

their normal surroundings, where such an object is likely to be a tasty insect. But when cane toads were introduced on the Hawaiian islands in 1932, their environment included a novel element: trees that produce strychnine and deposit the poison in their flowers for protection against insects. As the blossoms fall from the trees and blow along the ground, toads searching for food sometimes snatch them up, with predictable results. In Korea toads faced another novel environment when they were captured by bored American GIs, who amused themselves by rolling shotgun pellets past the toads. The animals would fill up with lead like little amphibious beanbags until they were unable even to hop.

In addition to changing the environments of other species, we humans are building a strange and in many ways novel environment for ourselves. The ability to do so sets us apart from other species. Fortunately, so does the ability to respond flexibly to new conditions of our own making. Any animal is likely to be confused between a new stimulus and a familiar one. Rabbits and armadillos react to moving cars as if they were predators; toads react to blossoms and shotgun pellets as if they were insects. Most people react to sperm banks as if they had nothing to do with reproduction; after all, sperm donation certainly lay outside the behavioral repertoire of our ancestors. But people also have fewer simple behavioral programs, and our intelligence makes it possible for us to shape our behavior to new circumstances. The sperm bank near Texas A&M may not be as popular as the

This article is reprinted by permission of *The Sciences* and is from the January/February 1992 issue, pp. 13-15. Individual subscriptions are $18.00 per year. Write to *The Sciences*, 2 East 63rd Street, New York, NY 10021 or call 1-800-THE-NYAS.

local ice-cream parlor, but the bank still attracts enough donors to stay in business.

Yet there are limits to our flexibility. In some features of our physiology or psychology we seem to be rather like the armadillo and the toad: we carry on in ways that were once adaptive but have become a handicap in our new, artificial environment. Many of those legacies remain obscure. But by conceptually reconstructing the environment of our own evolutionary upbringing and comparing it with our present surroundings, we may be able to locate the roots of certain contemporary medical, behavioral and social problems. We may even find clues about how best to deal with them.

To begin we need a picture of our ancestors' world. That phrase usually conjures images of the African savanna or the caves of Ice Age Europe—in other words, the physical environments in which the human species evolved. Changes in the physical environment surely lie at the root of some of the current difficulties. Certain diseases of advanced age, for example—high blood pressure, heart disease, some cancers—seem to emerge from the clash between a Stone Age physiology and one aspect of the new physical environment: diet. Salt was once scarce, and early humans evolved both a taste for it and some mechanisms for conserving it. Those adaptations no longer serve now that salt is plentiful. By the same token, the human body became adapted, over tens of thousands of years, to a diet low in fat and high in fiber, and the recent departure from that pattern is blamed for many health problems.

But emphasizing the physical aspects of our species' past may be a mistake. Investigators are beginning to explore the possibility that the social environment may have been a source of selective pressure at least as strong as the physical environment during the evolution of humans and other primates. The psychologist Nicholas Humphrey of Kings College at the University of Cambridge draws an analogy between human evolution and the story of Robinson Crusoe. Crusoe certainly faced physical challenges when he was alone on the island—getting enough to eat and drink, avoiding danger and so on—but, as Humphrey puts it, "it was the arrival of man Friday [that] really made things difficult for Crusoe. If Monday, Tuesday, Wednesday and Thursday had turned up as well then Crusoe would have had every need to keep his wits about him."

Indeed, the anthropologist Sue Taylor Parker of Sonoma State University in Rohnert Park, California, has argued that one defining human characteristic, the capacity for abstract reasoning, evolved in response to the demands of the social world, as well as to the demands of toolmaking and tool use. The traditional human societies in our time all impose on their members an exceedingly complicated social environment, no matter how simple their technology. The Australian aborigines, for example, never developed the bow and arrow, but their social systems are well known among anthropologists for their intricacy. The Tiwi of northern Australia maintain an elaborate system of political bargaining, favors and intrigue, all centered on the rights of men to bestow women on one another. Other aboriginal groups regulate marriage and kinship according to systems of Byzantine complexity. Such social systems, assuming they existed earlier in human evolution, would have strongly favored an ability to generalize rules from experience and apply the rules in new situations.

If the social environment of our ancestors played a major role in shaping human physiology and behavior, current social, economic and political arrangements might be a good hunting ground for conditions that strain our evolutionary heritage. One main difference between the present environment and that of our ancestors is in the nature of work. Traditional societies have simple divisions of labor, based only on age and sex, and consequently their members are generalists. In foraging societies men usually do most of the hunting for meat and women do most of the gathering of plant foods. All grown men take part in such activities as toolmaking, stalking and butchering, and the women likewise share a broad range of activities. Many herding societies go even further in sharing tasks: all members—men, women and children—tend the livestock.

Modern societies, in contrast, subdivide labor in infinite and subtle ways. Some people specialize in deboning chickens or soldering circuit boards; others spend their days taking telephone orders or running office copiers. An office, a hospital or a construction site is a hive of finely divided responsibilities. Although such division of labor has brought enormous increases in productivity and wealth, it has led also to specific physical problems.

Through most of evolution everyone performed a wide range of physical activities. Today specialization has gone so far that some jobs have been reduced to a single pattern of motion, repeated over and over again, day after day. The result, for some workers, is a cumulative trauma disorder. Carpal tunnel syndrome is one of the most common of those ailments: the tissues of the wrist and hand become inflamed and press on the nerves that run through the carpal tunnel, causing pain, numbness and weakness. Butchers, meat packers and assembly line workers have long been subject to carpal tunnel syndrome, but as computer keyboards have proliferated, the ailment has spread to white-collar workers as well. Indeed, carpal tunnel syndrome has now become so common among the new groups that it is sometimes called computeritis or journalist's disease. According to Linda H. Morse, medical director of the Repetitive Motion Institute in San Jose, California, the growth of cumulative trauma disorders is a sign that "the electronic revolution has outstripped our human muscular and skeletal evolution."

Economic changes have not only led to physical activities unanticipated by evolution; they have also disrupted traditional patterns of childbearing and child rearing. Again specialization is to blame, at least in part. Many jobs now require long periods of schooling and apprenticeship. Women are finding increased opportunities in such specialized fields, and as a result they are delaying childbearing, often into their thirties. In response to career pressures, many limit the size of their families and return to work quickly after giving birth. Breast-feeding is also curtailed, since it is rarely accommodated in the workplace. In all, fewer than 10 percent of married American women between the ages of eighteen and thirty-four expect to have more than three babies, and fewer than 20 percent of American women nurse their babies for six months or more.

A strikingly different pattern prevailed for most of human evolution, and it is still evident in traditional societies. There, women usually become pregnant not long after they begin to ovulate, between the ages of fifteen and nineteen. They continue to bear children until menopause, nursing each one for as long as three years. Although both the rights of women and population control make such a pattern unacceptable in modern industrial societies, it may be what human physiology is best equipped for. Consider that tens of thousands of years has settled the body into the strategy of early and abundant childbirth. Only in the past few decades has that pattern changed.

There is increasing evidence that the change may not sit well with our Stone Age reproductive physiology. For example, the change in reproductive behavior may be contributing to the high incidence of breast cancer in industrial society. An epidemiological study by Peter M. Layde and others at the Centers for Disease Control in Atlanta found that getting pregnant early in life, having several children and breast-feeding them for long periods—in other words, following the reproductive regimen of early humans—all reduced the risk of breast cancer. In some cases the reductions were dramatic. Women who had breast-fed for a total of more than twenty-five months were 33 percent less likely to develop breast cancer than were women who

had children but had never breast-fed. And women who had had only one child had more than twice the cancer risk of women with seven or more children.

People have carried a Stone Age physiology into an age of fast food and commuter marriages, but they may also be carrying some aspects of Stone Age psychology—traits evolved over tens of thousands of years of foraging. Are there any signs of an emotional legacy from the past? No one knows how much human behavior comes from the genes and how much is learned; any argument that people are hobbled by a Stone Age psychology is necessarily speculative. But it may prove useful to look at certain modern social problems from the perspective of the early human environment, where aspects of the psyche may have been forged.

Just as the division of labor has fragmented the economy, so it has atomized social life. We move from city to city; we work with colleagues and bosses rather than with kinfolk; we often gain recognition and rewards for our own efforts rather than through family influence. The clans, lineages and extended-family networks that structured life for our ancestors (and for the members of traditional societies today) have disintegrated, and in the West most people now live in nuclear families. The loss of such kin networks may be another factor that has led parents to have fewer children, later in life: many people can no longer call on relatives to share the work of child rearing.

It may also have had disturbing psychological effects. The feelings of alienation so often ascribed to modern urban life may reflect the evolutionary novelty of that environment, in which families and small, often short-lived webs of friendship take the place of widespread kin networks. David P. Barash, a professor of psychology and zoology at the University of Washington in Seattle, has argued that social pathologies such as drug use and crimes against strangers may reflect

this uneasy fit between aspects of our psyche, evolved long ago, and the strange social world we now inhabit.

Although traditional societies have drugs, the drugs rarely become the center of a person's life. And crime is less of a problem, because it is difficult to accomplish anonymously. Crimes of passion and impulse concerning adultery, unpaid debts and unreturned favors predominate, whereas premeditated robberies and burglaries barely exist. "A small-town resident doesn't rob the corner grocer; everyone knows nice old Mr. McPherson," Barash writes in his 1986 book *The Hare and the Tortoise.* "But if McPherson is a nameless, familyless, disembodied, and anonymous spirit in a big city, he can be attacked with relative ease."

Even if the novel human environment is perilous to creatures that evolved to meet the demands of the Pleistocene, what can be done about it? After all, the adaptive advantages of the artificial environment far outweigh its drawbacks, as the health and prosperity of many people in the industrial world make clear. Quite apart from its benefits in a Darwinian sense, the modern world created by human effort offers freedoms and pleasures unknown in traditional societies. Alienating as they may be, cities are also exciting and fun. Kinship networks offer psychological support during child rearing, but the obligation to support is reciprocal, and many people prefer the family ties loosely knotted. Delayed reproduction may have medical risks, but careers can bring rewards that breast-feeding cannot.

What is more, it may be possible to relieve some of the problems of the novel contemporary environment without returning to the Stone Age, by mimicking some of its key features. Cumulative trauma disorders such as carpal tunnel syndrome are currently treated with drugs and surgery. But they also improve when the sufferer's job is redesigned to allow a greater range of motion—making it perhaps more like the ancestral activities of root grubbing and spear throwing. The risk of breast cancer may one day be reduced by hormone treatments that mimic the cancer-reducing effects of the traditional reproductive pattern, without its career-reducing effects as well.

Alienation is a more subtle problem, calling for a more imaginative solution. The novelist Kurt Vonnegut offered one in *Slapstick, or Lonesome No More!* The second part of the title is the campaign slogan of Wilbur Daffo-dil-11 Swain, the last president of the U.S. His sole issue is the loneliness of his compatriots, and his solution is to engage the computers of the federal government in recreating kinship networks like the ones of prehistory.

In Vonnegut's fantasy everyone gets a new middle name, corresponding to something in nature—Chipmunk, Hollyhock, Raspberry, Uranium—and a number. By name and number everyone is instantly linked to 10,000 brothers and sisters and 190,000 cousins, all obligated to help out fellow clan members. That's a lot of kinfolk, but individually the obligations are mild. And, as Swain explains, "We need all the help we can get in a country as big and clumsy as ours."

People may never shed the need for kinship networks, but perhaps some day in the distant future adaptations to the modern environment will begin to appear. As sperm banks account for more and more babies, for instance, men may eventually evolve a propensity to find test tubes downright arousing. By the same token, it is not inconceivable that the division of labor could lead to the development or the atrophy of certain physical characteristics in human beings. But, surely, it will be a long time before laboratory supply catalogs are sold at convenience stores and armadillos stop littering the Texas highways.

Farmers and Baboons in the Taita Hills: Inter-Species Warfare in Southeastern Kenya

Jim Bell

ABSTRACT: *In a mountainous region of southeastern Kenya, horticulturists and troops of wandering baboons have engaged in inter-species warfare for countless generations. Such warfare has been over food and territory. Often, the battles are not just confined to elements of protecting, or stealing food from garden plots, or capturing territories, but they are psychological contests involving a show of will and "clever" strategies in which mankind does not necessarily prevail. This paper is a humorous view of a confrontation between one set of men and a single baboon troop in the East African bush, an insight into conflict resolution between man and monkey in modern times.*

INTRODUCTION

East Africa, ancestral origin of humankind, has long served as a battleground between animal species in their quest for survival. This region's river valleys, plateau plains, rift valley, seemingly endless savannahs, and deep upland forests have all witnessed the daily aggression and mortal combat between those animals that are hunted and those that hunt. Among the most successful animal populations to survive such aggression through the millennia in East Africa have been various primate species.

Paleontologists suggest that primate species may have a long history of violent competition between one another for the nutritional resources of a local area. And, as their territories become smaller in contemporary times, zoologists and primatologists discuss food competition between modern primate species. Of course, topping the list of successful primate competitors at the moment is *Homo sapiens*.

One can easily observe that human beings have overwhelming control of the earth's food resources, especially those resources in East Africa, where other primate species live. There is, however, at least one of these other species who seems not in total agreement with this observation: the common, or savannah, baboon. Baboons usually view all food stuffs within the troop's range as theirs. This simple, yet irritating, fact was made clear to me while investigating the affects of local socialization practices on the academic performance of primary school children in southeastern Kenya.

On several occasions during my research, I had an opportunity to observe first-hand the foraging methods of baboons as they went into local garden plots and stole crops intended for humans. On one such occasion, I had the misfortune of being part of this inter-species warfare; a confrontation as old as the domestication of plants in the region and, perhaps, as old as the two species themselves.

The following is offered as a sometimes humorous view of a rather serious aspect of life in the bush-lands of East Africa. Such conflict between these particular anthropoids does provide some indication as to mankind's rise above the lower primates and, at the same time, serves to illustrate how the alleged domination of our species over these other animals may owe more to dumb luck than to brain size or superior intellect and fighting skills.

THE SETTING

The Taita Hills are a cluster of mountain groups located in the southern portion of Kenya, slightly less than 192 miles (309 kilometers) southeast of the nation's capital of Nairobi and

From *California Anthropologist*, Vol. 19, No. 1, 1992, pp. 1-6. *California Anthropologist*, Department of Anthropology, California State University, Los Angeles, CA.

where the eastern-most fingers of the Serengeti extend into the western edge of the coastal plateau. Here, too, lies Kenya's famous Tsavo National Game Park. Free-roaming baboon troops constantly wander away from the game park and raid *shambas* (garden plots) of the people living in, and around, the Taita Hills. The residents of these isolated inselbergs in the midst of the plateau plains refer to themselves as *Wataita, Taita,* or "The People." Their native language, Kitaita, is one of several Bantu tongues common to this part of East Africa. Owing to their colonial past, many Wataita are proficient in English, and all are fluent in Kiswahili as well.

Wataita live in scattered nuclear and/or extended family units which are located within easy access to one or two of the many compact village communities.

Cultivation of cash crops, such as vegetables and coffee, and wage labor, both in their homeland and in far off urban centers like Mombasa and Nairobi, are the major sources of income for the Wataita. Small herds of cattle, goats, and sheep serve as a source of income, but cash crops and wage labor are the primary means of acquiring wealth.

Taita men are the principle landowners, and they are most often in control of those agricultural duties connected with the production of cash crops. One of these duties includes protecting the *shambas* from raids by others. Women usually concentrate on cultivating the grains, varieties of peas and beans, and the root crops used in the local diet. In general, the Wataita live in scattered nuclear and/or extended family units which are located within easy access to one or two of the

many compact village communities found throughout the Taita Hills.

Descent among the Wataita is patrilineal, with many living in extended family groups consisting of brothers and their wives and children. At a higher level of social organization, the Wataita also possess a fictive kin-group they refer to as *Kichuku*. Many Wataita also use the English term "clan" when referring to *Kichuku*. Members of a *Kichuku* usually live in close proximity to each other so that they can assist one another in times of trouble.

It is in this setting, and among these people, that I experienced one of this century's most hard-fought, yet fruitless, battles. A *shamba* belonging to my friend and key informant became the ground for hostilities between man and monkey.

THE RAID ON SIKUKU'S *SHAMBA*

I had been living in the Taita Hills slightly over a month when I was initiated *(blooded)* into one of the most sacred male rituals associated with farming in this part of the world. I and a young Wataita, Sikuku, who was my key informant and friend, sat just inside of the open door of his small two-room home. We were planning our next day's research problem, drinking beer, and watching the sun accentuate the various hues of green in the valley below. His younger female cousin, Mwakio, ran past the door delivering a panicky message in a high-pitched Kitaita no one could initially understand. She was told to calm down and repeat herself. The girl managed, in a squealing voice, to relay her bulletin. I did not understand the meaning; the presentation was much too fast for my limited Kitaita at the time, but the tone indicated serious trouble.

"Quickly!," Sikuku snapped. So away we went, bolting through the door and down a narrow path toward the valley. "We must remove those ones from the *shamba!,*" he shouted to me. I ran head-long down the path, trying to keep up with this younger man who had travelled this trail a

thousand times in a single year. He knew it well. I, on the other hand, was moving on unfamiliar terrain.

"Remove who? What? How?," I yelled while traversing the steep path.

Sikuku said nothing. He just seemed to increase his speed as I tried to coordinate the rate of my descent with the movement of my feet. I had to keep my feet under my body, or I would fall on my face. Whatever we had to remove from the *shamba*, I wanted to arrive in one piece.

Mwakio was far above us squealing out more alarms, calling on members of Sikuku's *Kichuku* to assist at the *shamba*. A man from a nearby household joined us. He too was moving with great speed and he, like Sikuku, made it look easy. My feet, the path, and my body were still at odds with one another. We continued down and down, turning and twisting, jumping over felled trees, trying to avoid toppling head-over-heels toward God-only-knew what. I tried to maintain some dignity in my demeanor. I did not want anyone to say I did not have a "handle" on the situation.

"How many of these notorious creatures are there?," a calm voice behind me asked.

"I do not know," I replied, huffing and puffing like an old steam engine. Three of Sikuku's male cousins passed me on the right and another two men shot by on my left. "Whose *shamba* is it?," I questioned, but no one answered. Everyone was busy trying to maintain his balance as the incline steepened.

"My *shamba* is under attack," Sikuku finally answered.

Immediately I began to gear down, trying to slow my descent, but to no avail. "Under attack?" Noticing that none of the men carried weapons of any kind, no bows and arrows, not even the all-purpose *ponga* (machete), I simply asked, "By what?"

"By nasty baboons," one of the men explained.

After descending approximately three-quarters of a mile, we reached a small hillock overlooking Sikuku's larger *shamba*. He was growing maize and beans on a little less than half an acre of prime bottom land. Scattered throughout the *shamba* was a troop of baboons. There were seven of us on the hillock. We picked up rocks, sticks, bits and pieces of decaying palm-leaves, or anything we thought suitable as a weapon. I still wondered why the men did not bring *pongas* or bows and arrows, but I thought it best not to ask. I had already made a fool of myself coming down the path. This was war time. Quickly devised estimates of the enemy's number came forth. Some of the men calculated perhaps 25 to 30 baboons in the *shamba,* with 6 or 7 on the outskirts of the plot. Others guessed the creatures were at least 30 to 40 strong, including some 20 adult males, because they believed this troop had raided the *shamba* in the past. I figured there were in the neighborhood of several hundred, probably because I had never been so close to baboons before, and they were larger than I had thought they would be.

Of course, as with most military campaigns, no one was really sure of the enemy's numbers. The confusion, coupled with fear and panic, caused an inflation in the estimates of enemy strength. If we had taken the time to count their correct numbers, we would have found only 19 of the "nasty creatures," as my Taita mates called them. Most of the enemy, it later turned out, were females and their offspring. There were four alpha males and five or six adolescent beta-sized males trying to stay out of everyone else's way. These little details were not available to us until after the battle. But, knowing how war-stories have a tendency to grow with the passage of time, my original guess of several hundred baboons on the field of honor that bygone day seems nearer the correct number as the years pass. Their strengths increase at each retelling of the event.

Sikuku's older cousin and a man from his *Kichuku* came up behind us. "What do we do?," I wished to know. I was hoping for some definite answer steeped in the wisdom of traditionally proven strategies, an answer that came from Wataita ancestors, an answer that was handed down from the ancient

gods of the Old Ones. I wanted something that would allow us to best these animals and evict them from the *shamba*. My knees were hurting from the rapid descent, and I missed the comfort of Sikuku's house. I was not ready for any major exertion.

Instead, I got puzzled looks and the most wonderful of East African rationales for an answer: "Of course, we must remove these rascals from the *shamba.*" I was now sure this man, Sikuku's cousin, thought me a fool. The logic was masterful. If only I could say as much for the question.

The nine of us were simply going to attack. We moved toward the *shamba* secure in the knowledge of our ten thousand years or so of experience expelling unwanted pests from cultivated lands and millions of years of evolution. We advanced with determination and a sense of quick victory.

"Charge them, but do not go directly at them or chase one for any long time," Sikuku advised me over the shouts and yells of the other men.

As we stormed the *shamba,* I shouted back to him, "Why not?"

"They will bite you," Sikuku warned just before disappearing into a row of maize plants.

My pace immediately slowed to a cautious walk. I suddenly realized that the baboons had also been evolving for millions of years, and they also had thousands of years of experience to count upon. I crept slowly into the maize row. An adolescent male faked an attack; I yelled. There we were, two horrified combatants trying to decide what came next. I continued yelling, threw one of the small rocks I had brought from the hillock, and he retreated out of sight. Round one was mine, and my confidence was building. Deeper in the maize field, I encountered two small females and another adolescent male. They retreated without any challenge from me. As I continued to the next row, a large alpha male shot past me like a bullet.

"Baboons," I thought aloud, "are not suppose to move that fast." I froze in fear, unable to retreat or go forward. Fortunately, one of the fellows came up

behind me and, with a proper shove, got me moving again.

We were nine representatives of the earth's most dominant primate species, running back and forth, in and out of maize rows, chasing baboons that barked, displayed their canines, flashed their eye-lids, engaged in mock attacks, or simply sat on their haunches yawning. In short, they were handling us better than we were controlling them. Some of the braver animals actually retrieved the smaller stones thrown at them to see if they were edible.

We had been stumbling around for five or ten minutes, a lifetime it seemed, in an effort to wrest Sikuku's fields and crops from these primates, who should have, in my estimation, run at our first appearance. Since they did not, we continued to score direct hits, only on each other, with our rocks and sticks. One of our party had been beaten over the head by another member with a dead palm-branch by mistake. The victim refused to speak to his attacker for several days. After being struck twice with missiles myself, I developed a quick appreciation for the absence of bows and arrows, *pongas,* and spears in this endeavor.

We pulled back to the hillock for a bit of rest and regrouping. It was, "Really not a retreat," I was informed by one of the men. I suppose one could say it was a strategic withdrawal to assess the damage and to reevaluate the course of action. At the time, I believed it to be a retreat not fully completed. I felt that we should have returned to the village, and not stopped at the hillock. I knew that safety and rest were further up the mountain-side.

Most of the baboons collected in the open area of the *shamba,* where the beans grew, and where they could see us more clearly. Still, many of them continued to eat some of the crops. They were, however, very agitated and began snapping at one another as they watched us. The largest of the alpha males, and the one who was clearly the leader, was exerting his dominance over the others within a five yard radius. We humans seemed as agitated as the baboons. Two of the men, exhibiting a paroxysmal fear, blamed the rest of us for not adhering to their verbal commands during the first phase of the battle. It became our collective fault that the baboons remained in the *shamba*. We, like the enemy, were short tempered and confused about the next tactic to be employed. Each time failures were cited, my name was mentioned and my maneuvers were metaphorically likened to cow dung.

Sikuku and his cousin, Mwandawa, devised a plan whereby we would form a semi-circle of sorts and progress into the *shamba* in three teams of three men each. This plan called for three men to flank the baboons on the right, three men on the left, and three men to come at them straight-on. This would force the animals out of the *shamba* and push them further down into the valley. Loading up with more ammunition, we set out to drive the enemy from "our" land.

The more the enemy scampered about, criss-crossing in front and behind us, the less able we were to secure clear targets.

The baboons became more agitated as we drew near their position in the *shamba*. We divided ourselves into our three-man teams and proceeded with our flanking movement. As we came closer, the females with infants clustered around the leader. Three alpha males spread out so that one was confronting each of our teams. They could keep our separate units under intense scrutiny. As we approached, adolescent males moved toward us in mock attacks. Then, the second phase of the campaign was underway. Again, two primate species were in full combat.

The men, yelling and screaming, inched forward. Rocks and sticks were thrown in every direction. The baboons barked, bared their teeth, and bounced on all fours with furor. Both sides meant serious business. I sensed

that saving the crops was no longer the point of our spirited charge. Demonstrating our dominance over the arrogant little "beasties" was the rationale of the contest. How dare they refuse to run before their superiors!

Within a matter of minutes, our superior strategy and tactics gave way to confusion and panic. Baboons, except for three females and their infants, bolted in alarm and scattered throughout the *shamba*. This sudden movement was so unexpected that we too scattered in fright. Again, we humans pelted one another with stones. All five of the adolescent males had broken through our lines and threatened our retreat to the hillock. We were out-maneuvered and, seemingly, out-smarted. The more the enemy scampered about, criss-crossing in front and behind us, the less able we were to secure clear targets. Fortunately, the adolescent males at our rear were not confident enough, or large and mature enough, to charge us. The alpha males in front of us, however, were getting closer with each of their mock attacks. It was time for another strategic withdrawal. We had to fight our way past the adolescent males, while holding the three alpha males at a safe distance, and keeping an eye on the few females who had tried to join the engagement. At a time like this, one's senses increase ten-fold. Colors became more vivid, sounds increased in clarity, and the air seemed alive with differing odors that were concentrated just in the *shamba*. It was one of those moments when time is motionless, when one is at once part of, and apart from, the action that is taking place. One is a participant and, yet, one can view one's performance from a distance at the same time.

On Sikuku's cousin's command, we ran for home base (the hillock). My heart was pumping, my mouth was dry, and my legs worked only half as well as they should have. But, I managed to reach the hillock and collapse with the other men. My wind was lost somewhere back in the *shamba*. My head throbbed, my throat was raw, and my body felt like it had been crushed by an eighteen-wheeler. We lay on the hillock for what seemed forever.

Finally, after about 15 or 20 minutes, an additional four men from Sikuku's *Kichuku* arrived to help. We prepared for another attack. One of the new arrivals noticed the baboons departing down the slope toward the deeper reaches of the valley floor. "Let us give chase!," exclaimed another of the new men.

"No brother," Sikuku replied, "let them go."

Another of the newly arrived warriors looked us over carefully, saw our dusty appearance, noticed our fatigue, lack of fighting spirit, and said, "Ahy! You have let those ones defeat you!" Not one of us contradicted him.

. . . each species views the world as theirs to control. Conflict mounts when the one cannot maintain control over the other.

Almost one-third of Sikuku's crops were eaten or destroyed. Nine of us had formed an alliance, a partnership with each other, and a covenant with the ancestors to battle another species to save our food resources. We had pledged to defend "our" land from the enemy, and to maintain dominance over so-called "lesser creatures." All had not gone quite the way we had envisioned. We had not really wrested the *shamba* from the baboons. They left in their own good time. However, two-thirds of Sikuku's crops were saved from destruction and damage, which counted for something. That alone keeps us humans ahead on overall points, and maybe that is how it has been for millennia in this region.

CONCLUSION

The events in Sikuku's *shamba* are a continuation of a centuries-old struggle in this part of the world between those that have and those that have not. Man and beast alike are the offended and offender in this ritual of life and survival. The very nature of farming in East Africa, during the past ten thousand years or so, would have been marked by such encounters. Human primates toil in the sun, turn the land, plant and weed the fields, and wait for the earth to bring forth food. These crops are a means of securing the survival of the species *Homo sapiens* and, in some instances, the excess food produced is employed to maintain economic and political ties to other human populations. Once in a while mankind's more distant relatives claim some of the fruits of this difficult labor.

In the past, the farmers of the Taita Hills lost portions of their production efforts to nomadic herders like the Maasai and some Galla groups. The baboon, perhaps the most persistent of the local animal population to raid their *shambas,* added to these losses as well. Today, an occasional human family may steal from a lowland garden, or one midway up into the foothills, but the baboon continues to pillage *shambas* throughout large areas of the Taita Hills. Baboons, like their human counterparts, have the right to exploit the environment. After all, each species views the world as theirs to control. Conflict mounts when the one cannot maintain control over the other. Humans have infringed on baboon territory in the Taita region for ten or more millennia, and it only seems fair that baboons exploit the labors of their human invaders in return.

Our Rhythms Still Follow the African Sun

In icy Antarctica, or sunny Miami, our daily tempos reveal their tropical roots.

Marcia J. Thompson and David W. Harsha

Marcia J. Thompson is a social anthropologist. She has done field work in Yucatán and is currently doing housing-market research in New Orleans.

David W. Harsha, a physical anthropologist, is engaged in heart disease research at the School of Public Health, Tulane University.

By early afternoon, the hunt is over. A pride of lions, having eaten their fill, gathers in the shade of a thorn tree. Other animals drowse, play or groom each other quietly. They have behaved this way in the early afternoon for millions of years, in a land where the heat of the sun rules all.

Far from the tropics, Scandinavian factory workers make more mistakes on the job, German schoolchildren stumble over their arithmetic exercises and Greek merchants close their shops. In offices everywhere, people have returned from lunch, but alertness flags and daydreams intrude. Some people tell themselves they must have eaten too heavily, while others begin to doubt that the hasty sandwich was enough and listen for the bell of the coffee cart. In truth, the post-lunch dip has little to do with food and much to do with our tropical heritage.

We have all experienced this fading sensation an hour or two after the traditional noon meal. Yet by late afternoon, whether we've napped, drunk coffee or just plugged along, alertness returns. We rally in time to wrap our tasks, clear our desks and head home.

There is an obvious temptation to attribute the phenomenon to biochemical effects of eating, hence the "post-lunch" tag often attributed to circadian researcher M. J. F. Blake. But why is there no similar reaction after breakfast or supper, which in many cases are much heavier meals? In an unpublished study, Blake tested three groups of 12 subjects for efficiency in a range of tasks—vigilance, card-sorting, time estimation and others—five times during the day. There were no significant differences between the group that ate lunch at 10 a.m., the one that ate at noon and the one that ate at 2 p.m. Yet all three groups experienced a mid-afternoon drop in efficiency. Many other, more recent studies have documented the same pattern among people in varied cultures and occupations all over the world.

For years, another popular explanation for fluctuations in efficiency was body temperature: As our temperature rises and falls, it was said, so does our efficiency. But in fact, body temperature rises steadily through the morning, reaching its high point in early or middle afternoon, just when our ability to do all but the simplest tasks declines markedly. And efficiency rises again later in the afternoon, as body temperature declines toward its low point at night when we sleep.

If food isn't the answer, nor temperature, what does explain the post-lunch dip and the other variations we experience daily? Nearly every process in our bodies, from glandular secretions to our ability to memorize telephone numbers, fluctuates in a predictable 24-hour cycle. Researchers have plotted daily peaks and troughs of more than 100 physiological and performance variables, each with its own "natural" period, which may be longer or shorter than 24 hours. The periods are coaxed into synchrony by *zeitgebers,* or time cues, that mesh them with our patterns of sleeping and waking.

We believe that the explanation lies in the tropical environment in which our species evolved. We have lived in temperate climates for less than a million years, and only in the last hundred thousand years or so have we wandered into the sub-arctic latitudes. In evolutionary time, this was last week. Man is still fundamentally a tropical creature. Warm-blooded tropical animals exhibit a bigeminous, or two-peaked, daily rhythm of activity, with the late-morning peak more marked than the late-afternoon one. This rhythm, we suggest, stayed with us after we left the African plains and continues to thwart our efforts to live and work as if the hours of the day were as identical as spark plugs off an assembly line.

Our primate relatives all observe a midday lull in activity. Generally, monkeys and apes spend their mornings in active, noise communal feeding. During the hottest part of the day, roughly from one to three hours after noon, activity subsides. This is not a mere rest period, but time for a different sort of activity. Older primates groom each other and their young, picking patiently through each other's fur rather than dozing; some use the time to build sleeping nests for the night to come. Jane Goodall's chimpanzees follow a similar pattern, sleeping for half an hour and spending the rest of the lull sprawling idly or grooming. Later in the afternoon, the animals resume active feeding until sunset.

The periods of high collective activity can be considered the primates' working times, when they fulfill the most basic function of feeding themselves. By contrast, relaxed grooming and play may seem much less vital pursuits. But these are highly social species. During grooming and play, they reinforce the dominance and bonding relationships that establish social structure. Primates seem to seize the time when lions or elephants drowse as an opportunity to carry out activities which require less alertness but are just as necessary as eating.

Among humans, we find a rich and varied array of daily activity. The most striking difference from other animals, of course, is that fire and electricity have stretched our day beyond the limits set by the sun, enabling us to add a new set of nighttime activities. These, too, show intriguing common threads.

Let us sketch a simplified, worldwide human day. In the morning, a woman of the household arises and rekindles the fire, putting water on to boil. This occurs, with technological variations, among the Mbuti pygmies, the Irish, the Monguors and the Americans. Men and children often awaken a little later. Morning ablutions and other preparations for the day accompany breakfast.

After the morning meal, adults engage in the most important work of the day, work connected with the group's

The end of the work day is a social time; some variant of the cocktail hour occurs in many cultures.

subsistence. The Shilluk and the Navajo herd their livestock. The Mixtecs, the Rajputs, the Maltese, the Yucatec Maya and the Koreans work their fields. Samoyed men hunt wild reindeer and Arctic geese. Women may participate in this labor or do their own work, often in cooperation with other females.

The midday meal may occur any time between 11 a.m. and 2 p.m. In most societies, it is a family meal with the breadwinner returning from work. Less often, the women and children eat at home while the men eat at work.

Then comes the afternoon lull. In nonindustrial cultures, this break is nearly universal. People retreat from the heat of the sun in warm climates, often choosing sedentary individual or small-group pursuits such as repairing tools or weaving mats, rather than those requiring large-group cooperation. Adults may visit and chat, while

children play. Despite a common tendency to speak disparagingly of the "siesta," naps are not the usual activity, even in the tropics.

In late afternoon, people resume animated activity, at a pace slower than the morning's. They continue until sunset, depending on the time of year and how long it takes to travel between work and home.

The end of the work day is a social time; some variant of the cocktail hour occurs in many cultures. In Indian Latin America, women gather inside each other's homes for novenas, while husbands outside discuss politics and business. In Spain, older students crowd into bars to drink with their cronies before going home. In rural Okinawa, people invite their neighbors in for tea and sweets. Strong drink is often part of the ceremonial transition from work to the dinner hour.

After dinner, early-rising groups usually end the day in sleep by 10 or 11 p.m. But the young, the strong, the enthusiastic (and even the early risers on ceremonial occasions) may enter a late-night, optional phase reserved for especially intense activities. Contacts are less likely to be business or political, more likely to have emotional, erotic and sometimes hostile overtones.

Risky Shifts

In our industrial society, the requirement that many workers change from one shift to another creates problems by disrupting the body's natural rhythms. Charles F. Ehret, a biologist at the Department of Energy's Argonne National Laboratory, points out that "when your body rhythms are upset, you are more likely to become ill. You are less alert, and you are more likely to make mistakes."

Based on his experience—35 years of studying natural rhythms in humans, laboratory animals and protozoa—Ehret has found that the problems caused by shift changes can be lessened by proper diet and careful planning of meal and sleep times. He advises workers going from Friday's day shift (8 a.m. to 4 p.m.) to Monday's afternoon shift (4 p.m. to midnight) to:

Sleep late on Saturday and eat sparingly all day: soups, salads, fruits. Avoid carbohydrates.

Sleep late Sunday. Eat a big, high-protein meal about 3 p.m. (breakfast time on Monday) and have a high-protein lunch about 8 p.m. (Monday's lunch time).

Eat a big, high-carbohydrate supper about 2 a.m. Monday. Go to bed about 7 a.m.

In American college fraternities and dormitories, this is the time when revellers hear the call to "rally." On Broadway, composers of musicals insert what they call an "11 o'clock song," a boisterous number designed to rouse a fading audience and hold its attention through the last act. In modern Spain, the 10 p.m.-to-11 p.m. dinner hour marks the distinction between the early-evening round of theater and club activity (after which well-brought-up young people should be home) and more intense social functions. A popular song of the 1960s, "Poco antes de que den las diez" ("A little before 10"), told of a young girl who rushes from her lover's bed to get home in time for supper. The song mocked the traditional belief that early evening is sexually safe while later hours are dangerous . . . but it is the belief that counts.

We have found such daily transitions in societies from equatorial to polar latitudes, among nomadic hunter-gatherers and workers in modern industrial nations. No culture institutionalizes every phase, but when it doesn't, vestiges can often be found in casual behavior. This near-universality suggests that the transitions have a biological base. We believe they do, but the basis is complex, as the levels of hundreds of hormones, neurotransmitters and other body chemicals rise and fall with their own circadian rhythms. Until we know much more about the interactions of such substances, we may learn more by looking carefully at cross-cultural patterns in daily activity.

Whether the human organism is examined from the cell out or from the society in, it remains faithful to the rhythm of the tropical day that shaped its activities until very recently. Our ancestors learned to avoid heat stress on their uniquely complex nervous systems. While both prey and predators slept, they did things they alone needed to do: manufacturing and caring for the tools, making the fabrics that came to

Primates seize the time when lions and elephants drowse to carry out social activities that require less alertness and exertion but that are just as necessary as eating.

replace other primates' fur, refining the symbolic connections that made them fully human.

In America today, most of us go through daily routines that are less predictable than those of a peasant farmer, a fisherman or even a factory worker. Tasks are often distributed haphazardly, on an as-needed basis throughout the work day, which we divide symmetrically with three to four hours before lunch and about four hours afterward. We assume that these hours are functionally identical.

But if we keep the traditional lunch hour starting about noon, we cut out the most productive part of the day, when our mental and motor aptitudes are at their peak. It would be better to schedule lunch an hour or two later. In keeping with the bigeminous patterns of cultures all over the world, as well as those of nonhuman primates. This would place lunch at the beginning of the dip in alertness, a time best suited for conversations, such as business lunches, and still leave a concentrated work period at the end of the day.

A business day restructured in this way would have important meetings and other activities requiring cooperation scheduled for mid- to late-morning. Mid-afternoon would be reserved for less demanding mental tasks; time for visits rather than meetings, for communication to strengthen ties rather than to exchange vital information. The mid-afternoon is not a period during which people deal well with the unexpected or the demanding task.

Later, when efficiency and energy were on the upswing, we would return to vigorous activity, perhaps taking up a limited project that requires full concentration. These valuable hours should not be wasted in simply cleaning up work begun earlier.

The content of our workdays has changed, but our tropical origins are still with us. Though we drill for oil beneath the ice caps and walk on the moon, though we shuffle our work routines to accommodate new production quotas and overseas conference calls, we remain subject to the dictates of the African sun.

A Reasonable Sleep

Meredith F. Small

Three-month-old Jenny lies in the crook of her mother's arm. As the infant twitches in her sleep, ten thin wires taped to her face and bald head wiggle in all directions, giving her a baby Medusa look. Jenny's mother opens her sleepy eyes in the dimly lit room and stares blankly into the tiny face only inches away. The matching wires on the mother's head nod toward her baby as she unconsciously reaches out and pats Jenny reassuringly a few times. She adjusts the baby's blanket, and they both drift back into a deeper level of sleep.

One room away James McKenna watches the needles on a 12-channel polygraph jump in tandem as Jenny and her mother experience this mutual arousal. An elfin grin spreads across his face. He's recorded so many of these unconscious stirrings that they seem to him to map out a nightlong dance.

McKenna, an anthropologist at Pomona College, has come to the nearby Sleep Disorders Laboratory at the University of California at Irvine to test a hypothesis: he believes that the Western practice of placing babies in their own beds at night is at odds with human nature—so odd that sudden infant death syndrome (SIDS), the mysterious killer of babies, can more easily come stalking. But he is just as interested in the vast majority of babies who don't succumb to SIDS. Sleeping in isolation affects them too, he suspects, though more subtly than in the rare cases of SIDS. Jenny and her mother are providing the numbers to support what McKenna has been advocating for the past eight years: "If you have a baby, sleep with it."

His idea developed from years of watching infant monkeys cling to their mothers day and night. He also knew that babies sleep with their parents in the vast majority of human cultures. Both facts suggested to McKenna that it's inconsistent with our evolutionary roots to put babies in their own beds at

Evolution suggests that if we sleep with our babies, we might help some of them escape sudden infant death syndrome.

night. What's more, he points out, the current Western practice is only a century or two old, "just a wink" in human history. As an anthropologist with no formal medical training, however, McKenna hesitated to push for co-sleeping. Most pediatricians, after all, thought babies should sleep alone. Yet as he began to talk about his ideas, he found a receptive audience. His words, some parents told him, finally gave them "permission" to do what seemed to come naturally—sleep with their babies.

Many parents have fears about the safety of co-sleeping. They've been told that bed-sharing puts a squirming baby at risk of being suffocated by well-meaning but exhausted parents. This is probably no more than an old wives' tale. As McKenna points out, most babies worldwide sleep with an adult without ill effects. Other parents feel that they need a break from the baby's constant demands, or they crave time for intimacy. And current advice books uniformly reinforce the idea that sleep practices should accommodate parents, not babies.

Parenting advice in the 1990s, post–Dr. Spock, tends to be permissive. But in one area discipline survives: when, where, and how much babies should sleep. In *The Well Baby Book*, a popular guide, Mike and Nancy Samuels give parents hints to aid their quest to get tiny infants to sleep through the night. "Don't bring the baby into the parents' bed and let it sleep there till morning," they say. "It is more likely to be disturbed." Penelope Leach, in *Babyhood*, admits that babies sleep better when snuggled between adults. But Leach also writes that parents are often disturbed by the baby's fidgeting, and many are uncomfortable with an infant in the "marital bed." What's worse, she and other authorities claim, co-sleeping establishes a dependency that will be difficult to break, making it hard for the older child to fall asleep when alone, although there is no evidence to support this.

McKenna believes the notion that solitary sleep is healthier for babies in the long run is based not on biology but on a recent adoption of urban-industrial values. Modern society requires "good" citizens—independent people not making too many demands on others. In this scenario, autonomy must be fostered as soon as possible. We begin early, McKenna claims, by placing babies alone at night so that busy parents can get on with their lives. "In our modern day," he says, "the biological interests of the infants might not coincide with the best interests of the parents. But evolution never promised us a rose garden."

McKenna's observation of mothers and infants began decades ago, with his training in primate behavior. "As a junior at U.C. Berkeley in 1969, I took

---

In the natural state, monkey and ape babies always sleep with their mother, clinging to her belly until the infant *initiates independence.*

---

a course in primatology," he says. "I learned that monkeys and apes need so much physical attention and contact. I remember thinking, when I have a baby, ['m going to give it as much affection as it can take. You cannot understand primates without coming to appreciate that very early physical contact is everything. It's what we're all about."

Now, at 43, he realizes that his later diversion to sleep research has even earlier origins. "I grew up in a large family of six children. There weren't enough beds in my house and we all shared beds. I slept at my brother Tommy's feet for over a year!" But it wasn't until the birth of his son Jeffrey, in 1978, that McKenna put those research interests together.

"I noticed that one way to get Jeff to sleep was to nap with him. I'd lie down with him and breathe as if I was asleep." He breathes in and out, in and out, pumping his chest up and down as if baby Jeff were still bundled on top of him. "I became really skilled at getting him to sleep. I also found it totally amusing." But the scholar in McKenna was intrigued. "I noticed he was so responsive to these breathing cues. And then I wondered why I was surprised. Here was a primate baby, undeveloped at birth, selected to be responsive to parental contact and care. The fact that he *was* responsive to my sounds and breathing patterns was

everything the last ten years of anthropological research had told me he would be."

McKenna soon realized the implications of what he'd observed. In the United States one in every 500 babies is found dead during the first year of life, most often between two and four months of age. These babies usually show no previous signs of illness, and no known cause of death can be determined at autopsy—although recent research suggests that abnormalities in fetal development may predispose some infants to an early death. But it now occurred to McKenna that the absence of cues from co-sleeping parents might also play a role.

Since the medical community concentrates on physiological causes for SIDS, McKenna knew that any suggestion of a cultural influence would be considered radical. He knew he would need to explain how co-sleeping had evolved—how it contributed to a baby's physical well-being. "The difficulty is explaining to medically trained specialists what it means to apply evolutionary theory in the context of infancy and parenthood. That's where I thought I could fill a role—making evolution alive and meaningful in the context of clinical research."

There were experiments McKenna could cite. As several psychologists showed in the 1960s, the infant's physical dependence on its mother is a primate universal, and it involves more than simple providing. When infant macaque monkeys were separated from their mothers, even for a few hours, they experienced physiological effects such as changes in heart rate and body temperature, sleep disturbances, increases in cardiac arrhythmias, and signs of clinical depression. In short the animals' immature nervous systems just didn't function as well. In the natural state, McKenna adds, monkey and ape babies always sleep with their mother, clinging to her belly until the *infant* initiates independence.

Human babies are even more dependent on adults. No other animal needs

so much nurturing and takes so long to mature. The advantage to being so unformed at birth is the great capacity for learning and social interaction.

As with other primates, McKenna speculates, in humans the strong mother-infant bond was selected for because it helped babies get through their long formative period. But human babies are so helpless they can't even cling to their mothers like monkeys. Instead, they are carried. In humans, McKenna says, "infant sleep evolved against a background of being jerked up and down in the back of a sling." Even today you can see babies carried this way throughout Africa and Asia: mothers out hoeing in the garden, baby sleeping on their back. "There is a physicality in the relationship," he says. "We can't go on assuming that there are no physiological consequences to sleeping alone."

McKenna suggests that all human babies benefit from hearing their parents breathe, feeling their parents' touches, and just being close to adults. Although the long-term effects of solitary versus co-sleeping are unknown, McKenna suspects there's a connection between nocturnal closeness and mental health later on, even into adulthood. "A feeling of social-psychological connectedness allows infants to later become more independent from parents. It may also result in higher self-esteem

---

"Mothers usually say the time in the lab is the first reasonable night's sleep they've had since the baby was born."

---

and a good sense of empathy for others. These infants might also be able to better monitor nonverbal cues given by others."

More dramatically, McKenna believes, co-sleeping may be important in avoiding the particularly human problem of SIDS. Humans, he notes, are different from other primates in a way that makes us vulnerable: we rely so heavily on speech that we use "voluntary," or controlled, breathing far more than any other mammal. We have to learn how to modulate our breathing to talk, though we never lose the ability to return to automatic pilot—the involuntary, reflexive breathing we use during sleep or reading.

Human babies begin switching back and forth from automatic to controlled breathing between two and four months of age. At this developmental stage, the infant neocortex, the higher brain, becomes functionally connected to the primitive brain stem. Behavior becomes less a series of reflex actions and more voluntary. Babies start to smile because they want to, and their vocalizations are no longer mere reactions to hunger or wet diapers. They begin to manipulate their breathing by changing airflow rates, air pressure, and lung volume. A cry will suddenly carry specific information to a carefully listening parent; it's a form of speech-breathing that will later become talking. This is also a susceptible time for infants. Most do fine, but McKenna thinks some can't manage the flip-flop between the two types of breathing. They stop, and succumb to SIDS.

To support his claims about the importance of co-sleeping, McKenna knew he would first need to show that babies are physically affected when they spend the night in contact with an adult. His co-sleeping hypothesis works only if infants sleep differently—presumably better—when tucked in with Mom.

One day in 1984 McKenna walked into the first open door in the pediatrics department at the University of California at Irvine and bent the ear of pediatrician Claibourne Dungy. Dungy quickly assembled what McKenna recalls as "four people in white lab coats staring at me skeptically." One of them was Sarah Mosko, a clinical psychologist, a sleep expert, and most important for McKenna, a trained polysomnographer—a person who knows how to wire sleepers and interpret the squiggles on the polygraph. McKenna asked if she'd like to collaborate with him on his research. "It didn't take much for

me to say yes," recalls Mosko, who now works as a sleep-disorders consultant in addition to her research with McKenna.

Together McKenna and Mosko have collected sleep data on eight mother and infant pairs at the Sleep Disorders Lab. In the first study, conducted from 1986 to 1987, five mother-infant pairs were tracked for one night. In the second study, finished last year, three mothers and infants spent the first two nights sleeping alone but in adjacent rooms, so that the mothers could get up and feed the babies. The third night each mother and baby slept in the same bed—an unusual event for two of the pairs.

Mothers and their infants report to the lab at 8:00 p.m. The sleep room, with a hospital bed and blackout curtains, seems to them an inviting haven. "These are sleep-deprived new mothers," says Mosko. "They usually say the time in the lab is the first reasonable night's sleep they've had since the baby was born."

Before mother and baby settle down for the night, each has four wires taped to the head to record electroencephalographic, or brain wave, signals. Another two wires, placed close to each eye orbit, monitor eye movements, and three more wires on the chin measure muscle relaxation. Heartbeats are picked up by two wires on the chest. A thin wire placed beneath the nose monitors breathing by sensing the temperature of the passing air; exhaled air is warmer than inhaled air. (Breathing is also recorded as chest-wall movement.)

The data from all these sources help differentiate the five levels of sleep a person traverses during the night. Rapid eye movement, or REM, sleep is the most active—the eyes flicker, the face and limbs twitch as muscles tense and relax, brain waves come faster but with lower voltage, and breathing and heart rate become less regular. This is a dreaming state, although dreams sometimes occur in other stages. There are four non-REM levels; deep sleep occurs in levels three and four. Individuals vary in the amount of time they spend at each stage, and infants have

fewer distinct levels—at three months they typically have three. In any case, several cycles through the various levels seem to be important for a satisfying snooze.

As McKenna and Mosko's subjects sleep, impulses from the wires travel to the recording room, where inked needles leave tracks on long sheets of paper. Later Mosko gathers the pages and marks out sleep levels in 30-second intervals. She determines if each subject is sleeping at a certain level, awake, or experiencing transient arousal—moving into lighter levels of sleep but not to full wakefulness. McKenna, with his animal-behavior background, scores the videotape—baby lifts head, mother opens eyes, and so on. The two researchers eventually compare mothers and babies sleeping alone and together, interval by interval.

These data choreograph the nocturnal dance of mothers and babies—the dance McKenna had predicted—but with mutual promptings and responses. It's not that mothers regulate their babies' breathing. The sleepers are, instead, physiologically entwined; the movements and breathing of each partner affect the other. When one arouses, the other often wakes up a bit, too.

McKenna proposes that transient arousals are especially important because they give babies practice in waking up. All babies experience apneas, or pauses in breathing, several times a night. If a pause becomes prolonged, a healthy baby will wake up to breathe. Many researchers believe that SIDS babies have some deficiency that inhibits their arousal. When they stop breathing, they're less apt to wake up—and thus more likely to die. But if aroused more often by a parent, McKenna reasons, they may learn better how to do it on their own, and wake up one night when it really matters.

McKenna also suggests that co-sleeping helps a baby master breathing techniques. During sleep, just as during wakefulness, adults shift through periods of controlled or automatic breathing, switching between neocorti-

Medical Research on SIDS

Each year hundreds of papers are published on SIDS, pointing the finger at a host of possible culprits. Mothers who smoke during pregnancy, for example, have been told they're upping their baby's risk of SIDS about threefold. Babies may also be at higher risk if they are born prematurely or of low birth weight, as a sibling rather than a first born, or to a young mother. Babies who lie on their stomach have a higher risk; more babies die of SIDS in winter; elevated body temperature from a stuffy room or overdressing may be a factor.

Still, none of this explains the actual cause of sudden death. "Risk factors are simply things that may make a baby more vulnerable," explains Marian Willinger, who directs SIDS research for the National Institute of Child Health and Human Development. "Just because cigarette smoking is linked with an increased risk doesn't mean that cigarette smoking causes SIDS. A lot of SIDS babies' mothers don't smoke. There's something about the baby itself that predisposes it to SIDS."

Pinning down that something, however, has so far proved impossible. "At this point," explains Willinger, "SIDS is a diagnosis of exclusion. If you can't find any other cause of death after a full postmortem, then it's called SIDS—so by definition we're starting without much to help us."

Nevertheless, some strides have been made. The most popular theory is that something is wrong with the way vulnerable babies arouse themselves from sleep—they're supposed to wake up when they stop breathing for an unusual length of time, but they don't. To investigate this idea, neurophysiologist Ron Harper and his colleagues at UCLA checked the records of nearly 7,000 babies whose heartbeats and breathing were recorded in a British study. Sixteen of those babies later died of SIDS; Harper found that they had gone through far fewer short respiratory pauses while sleeping than the ones who were still alive. Although the reason for this difference is not yet known, it is a true disparity.

Other researchers are looking at where respiration is controlled—in the brain. The brains of all newborns are still developing; for instance, the neurons are not all covered by their protective sheaths of myelin. Early last year Hannah Kinney of Children's Hospital in Boston and her colleagues showed that myelination in the brains of 61 infants who died of SIDS lagged significantly behind myelination in 89 children who died of other causes—though again this is so far just a clue.

Of course, a disease with such a nebulcus definition can easily fool you. Researchers are fairly certain that 3 to 10 percent of SIDS cases are actually the result of inborn metabolic defects. And a study published last summer showed that a few babies diagnosed as succumbing to SIDS —fewer than 1 percent—might have suffocated on soft bedding such as beanbag cushions.

Yet researchers do feel that SIDS is a discrete entity with its own physiological mechanism, not just a conglomeration of other syndromes that simply need to be teased apart. "The scientists really believe that after all is said and done there will be a core of babies with a certain characteristic abnormality that makes them vulnerable to sudden death," says Willinger. "We won't keep peeling away layers of onion until there is nothing left."

—*Lori Oliwenstein*

cal-driven breaths and brain stem-operated breaths. Babies undergo that flip-flop each time they wake up. When sleeping with Mom, a baby reacts to her movements and wakes up more times during the night—an average of 24 percent more, McKenna finds, than when sleeping alone—thus getting more practice in the repeated hop from one kind of breathing to the other. "Sleep has evolved against these interruptions," says McKenna, "and they may serve as practice for the baby when it has more serious, internally based interruptions in breathing."

Such fitful sleep may, in fact, be the norm for adults as well. The mothers in McKenna's experiments passed through transient arousals 60 percent more frequently when sleeping with their babies then when sleeping alone.

"We Westerners have the 'die' theory of sleep," McKenna says, laughing. "You close your eyes, fall asleep, and basically die—you become totally unconscious until you wake up in the morning—and you hope for the best. If there's anything in between, there's something wrong with you. Other people in the world don't sleep like that. The !Kung bushmen, for example, get up, tend the fire, talk, then go back to sleep. Western culture has streamlined what we think is normal. And if people can't conform, there's disease out there for them—it's called insomnia. A small group of sleep researchers have also admitted that humans are not monophasic sleepers—they are biphasic. The afternoon nap is biologically based."

His point is that cultures dictate norms unrelated to what might or might not be evolutionarily natural—that is, bred into human physiology. He feels that the extreme American emphasis on individualism, and the view that husband and wife have a relationship apart from the children, have reinforced notions that infants are born too dependent and should sleep by themselves as soon as possible. In contrast, Japanese infants normally sleep with their parents. This, too, is a culturally bound notion, but instead of opting for independence, the Japanese foster interdependence. Interestingly enough, the rate of SIDS is significantly lower in Japan than in the United States: less than one per 1,000 births.

Data for immigrant populations in the United States suggest that such cultural differences may indeed play a role. For example, Chinese immigrants in California have an incidence of SIDS 38 times higher than nonimmigrant Chinese in Hong Kong. Among other Asian-American populations the SIDS rates vary, but the rate increases the longer a group has lived in the United States. The Vietnamese, for example, arrived later than the Japanese, and their SIDS rate is lower. McKenna feels that the pattern may be explained by immigrants' adopting the American style of placing babies in their own beds. His speculation cannot be confirmed, of course, until other possible influences—such as changes in feeding practices—are ruled out.

McKenna began giving talks about his ideas in the early eighties. Then, in 1986, he published a massive paper on his work, which attracted a lot of attention. So far the response from the medical community has not been as critical as McKenna first feared. Marian Willinger, who directs SIDS research at the National Institute of Child Health and Human Development, says, "In general this is a new area for infant and child health—tying parenting styles with physiology—and therefore McKenna and Mosko's basic research is important for *all* babies."

One medical researcher was deeply impressed. "I think their work is terrific," says Jeffrey Laitman, an anatomist at New York's Mount Sinai School of Medicine. His own research on the development of the throat and voice box in infants supports McKenna's hunch that SIDS is linked to the evolution of speech making. "In newborns, as in many animals, the larynx locks into the back of the nasal cavity," Laitman explains. "This enables them to breathe and swallow at roughly the

"We Westerners have the 'die' theory of sleep. You close your eyes, fall asleep, and basically die—you become unconscious and hope for the best."

same time. But in humans the larynx begins to drop down into the throat in the first few months of life. No other mammal goes through such a tremendous metamorphosis, and there's a great possibility of miscues"—as well as a far greater ability to make the wide range of sounds used in talking.

But McKenna's not just out to prevent SIDS; his approach has always been more anthropological than medical. His larger goal is to show that early sleeping practices are important to everyone's health. This past January he and Mosko brought the first of 30 mother-baby pairs, including 15 co-sleepers, into the lab to investigate whether the sleep and breathing patterns of the co-sleeping babies are different from those of the babies who habitually sleep alone. McKenna expects to finish this study by the end of the year, but even then he'll be a long way from proving that co-sleeping is best for everyone in the long run. His argument that it seems to work well in traditional cultures cuts two ways. After all, most American babies, with their background of solitary sleeping, also grow up apparently healthy.

For now, McKenna aims to prove that co-sleeping is natural and normal for the average baby, a reasonable option rather than a dangerous, misguided practice that should be discouraged, as stated in current advice books. "Should a parent or parents feel good about co-sleeping, elect it as a favored strategy, and it is done responsibly," he writes, "nothing could be better for their infant or child."

He is also philosophical about his potential role as a revolutionary in American parenting styles. "There is nothing profound about what I am trying to document or argue for—it's based on evolutionary history. It doesn't take any genius to know there may be some naturalistic interactions between co-sleeping babies and mothers, or babies and caretakers. Like those who have discovered in the twentieth century that breast-feeding is good for babies, I spend all my time documenting the obvious."

The Saltshaker's Curse

Physiological adaptations that helped American blacks survive slavery may now be predisposing their descendants to hypertension

Jared Diamond

Jared Diamond is a professor of physiology at UCLA Medical School.

On the walls of the main corridor at UCLA Medical School hang thirty-seven photographs that tell a moving story. They are the portraits of each graduating class, from the year that the school opened (Class of 1955) to the latest crop (Class of 1991). Throughout the 1950s and early 1960s the portraits are overwhelmingly of young white men, diluted by only a few white women and Asian men. The first black student graduated in 1961, an event not repeated for several more years. When I came to UCLA in 1966, I found myself lecturing to seventy-six students, of whom seventy-four were white. Thereafter the numbers of blacks, Hispanics, and Asians exploded, until the most recent photos show the number of white medical students declining toward a minority.

In these changes of racial composition, there is of course nothing unique about UCLA Medical School. While the shifts in its student body mirror those taking place, at varying rates, in other professional groups throughout American society, we still have a long way to go before professional groups truly mirror society itself. But ethnic diversity among physicians is especially important because of the dangers inherent in a profession composed of white practitioners for whom white biology is the norm.

Different ethnic groups face different health problems, for reasons of genes as well as of life style. Familiar examples include the prevalence of skin cancer and cystic fibrosis in whites, stomach cancer and stroke in Japanese, and diabetes in Hispanics and Pacific islanders. Each year, when I teach a seminar course in ethnically varying disease patterns, these by-now-familiar textbook facts assume a gripping reality, as my various students choose to discuss some disease that affects themselves or their relatives. To read about the molecular biology of sickle-cell anemia is one thing. It's quite another thing when one of my students, a black man homozygous for the sickle-cell gene, describes the pain of his own sickling attacks and how they have affected his life.

Sickle-cell anemia is a case in which the evolutionary origins of medically important genetic differences among peoples are well understood. (It evolved only in malarial regions because it confers resistance against malaria.) But in many other cases the evolutionary origins are not nearly so transparent. Why is it, for example, that only some human populations have a high frequency of the Tay-Sachs gene or of diabetes? . . .

Compared with American whites of the same age and sex, American blacks have, on the average, higher blood pressure, double the risk of developing hypertension, and nearly ten times the risk of dying of it. By age fifty, nearly half of U.S. black men are hypertensive. For a given age and blood pressure, hypertension more often causes heart disease and especially kidney failure and strokes in U.S. blacks than whites. Because the frequency of kidney disease in U.S. blacks is eighteen times that in whites, blacks account for about two-thirds of U.S. patients with hypertensive kidney failure, even though they make up only about one-tenth of the population. Around the world, only Japanese exceed U.S. blacks in their risk of dying from stroke. Yet it was not until 1932 that the average difference in blood pressure between U.S. blacks and whites was clearly demonstrated, thereby exposing a major health problem outside the norms of white medicine.

What is it about American blacks that makes them disproportionately likely to develop hypertension and then to die of its consequences? While this question is of course especially "interesting" to black readers, it also concerns all Americans, because other ethnic groups in the United States are not so far behind blacks in their risk of hypertension. If *Natural History* readers are a cross section of the United States, then about one-quarter of you now have high blood pressure, and more than half of you will die of a heart attack or stroke to which high blood pressure predisposes. Thus, we all have valid reasons for being interested in hypertension.

First, some background on what those numbers mean when your doctor inflates a rubber cuff about your arm, listens, deflates the cuff, and finally pronounces, "Your blood pressure is 120 over 80." The cuff device is called a sphygmomanometer, and it measures the pressure in your artery in units of millimeters of mercury (that's the height to which your blood pressure would force up a column of mercury in case, God forbid, your artery were suddenly connected to a vertical mercury column). Naturally, your blood pressure varies with each stroke of your heart, so the first and second numbers refer, respectively, to the peak pressure at each heartbeat (systolic pressure) and to the minimum pressure between beats (diastolic pressure). Blood pressure varies somewhat with position, activity, and anxiety level, so the measurement is usually made while you are resting flat on your back. Under those conditions, 120 over 80 is an average reading for Americans.

There is no magic cutoff between normal blood pressure and high blood pressure. Instead, the higher your blood pressure, the more likely you are to die of a heart attack, stroke, kidney failure, or ruptured aorta. Usually, a pressure reading higher than 140 over 90 is arbitrarily defined as constituting hypertension, but some people with lower readings will die of a stroke at age fifty, while others with higher readings will die in a car accident in good health at age ninety.

Why do some of us have much higher blood pressure than others? In about 5 percent of hypertensive patients there is an identifiable single cause, such as hormonal imbalance or use of oral contraceptives. In 95 percent of such cases, though, there is no such obvious cause. The clinical euphemism for our ignorance in such cases is "essential hypertension."

Nowadays, we know that there is a big genetic component in essential hypertension, although the particular genes involved have not yet been identified. Among people living in the same household, the correlation coefficient for blood pressure is 0.63 between identical twins, who share all of their genes. (A correlation coefficient of 1.00 would mean that the twins share identical blood pressures as well and would suggest that pressure is determined entirely by genes and not at all by environment.) Fraternal twins or ordinary siblings or a parent and child,

who share half their genes and whose blood pressure would therefore show a correlation coefficient of 0.5 if purely determined genetically, actually have a coefficient of about 0.25. Finally, adopted siblings or a parent and adopted child, who have no direct genetic connection, have a correlation coefficient of only 0.05. Despite the shared household environment, their blood pressures are barely more similar than those of two people pulled randomly off the street. In agreement with this evidence for genetic factors underlying blood pressure itself, your risk of actually developing hypertensive disease increases from 4 percent to 20 percent to 35 percent if, respectively, none or one or both of your parents were hypertensive.

But these same facts suggest that environmental factors also contribute to high blood pressure, since identical twins have similar but not identical blood pressures. Many environmental or life style factors contributing to the risk of hypertension have been identified by epidemiological studies that compare hypertension's frequency in groups of people living under different conditions. Such contributing factors include obesity, high intake of salt or alcohol or saturated fats, and low calcium intake. The proof of this approach is that hypertensive patients who modify their life styles so as to minimize these putative factors often succeed in reducing their blood pressure. Patients are especially advised to reduce salt intake and stress, reduce intake of cholesterol and saturated fats and alcohol, lose weight, cut out smoking, and exercise regularly.

Here are some examples of the epidemiological studies pointing to these risk factors. Around the world, comparisons within and between populations show that both blood pressure and the frequency of hypertension increase hand in hand with salt intake. At the one extreme, Brazil's Yanomamö Indians have the world's lowest-known salt consumption (somewhat above 10 milligrams per day!), lowest average blood pressure (95 over 61!), and lowest incidence of hypertension (no cases!). At the opposite extreme, doc-

tors regard Japan as the "land of apoplexy" because of the high frequency of fatal strokes (Japan's leading cause of death, five times more frequent than in the United States), linked with high blood pressure and notoriously salty food. Within Japan itself these factors reach their extremes in Akita Prefecture, famous for its tasty rice, which Akita farmers flavor with salt, wash down with salty miso soup, and alternate with salt pickles between meals. Of 300 Akita adults studied, not one consumed less than five grams of salt daily, the average consumption was twenty-seven grams, and the most salt-loving individual consumed an incredible sixty-one grams—enough to devour the contents of the usual twenty-six-ounce supermarket salt container in a mere twelve days. The *average* blood pressure in Akita by age fifty is 151 over 93, making hypertension (pressure higher than 140 over 90) the norm. Not surprisingly, Akita's frequency of death by stroke is more than double even the Japanese average, and in some Akita villages 99 percent of the population dies before age seventy.

Why salt intake often (in about 60 percent of hypertensive patients) leads to high blood pressure is not fully understood. One possible interpretation is that salt intake triggers thirst, leading to an increase in blood volume. In response, the heart increases its output and blood pressure rises, causing the kidneys to filter more salt and water under that increased pressure. The result is a new steady state, in which salt and water excretion again equals intake, but more salt and water are stored in the body and blood pressure is raised.

At this point, let's contrast hypertension with a simple genetic disease like Tay-Sachs disease. Tay-Sachs is due to a defect in a single gene; every Tay-Sachs patient has a defect in that same gene. Everybody in whom that gene is defective is certain to die of Tay-Sachs, regardless of their life style or environment. In contrast, hypertension involves several different genes whose molecular products remain to be identified. Because there are many causes of raised blood pressure, different hypertensive patients may owe their condition to different gene combinations. Furthermore, whether someone genetically predisposed to hypertension actually develops symptoms depends a lot on life style. Thus, hypertension is not one of those uncommon, homogeneous, and intellectually elegant diseases that geneticists prefer to study. Instead, like diabetes and ulcers, hypertension is a shared set of symptoms produced by heterogeneous causes, all involving an interaction between environmental agents and a susceptible genetic background.

Since U.S. blacks and whites differ on the average in the conditions under which they live, could those differences account for excess hypertension in U.S. blacks? Salt intake, the dietary factor that one thinks of first, turns out on the average not to differ between U.S. blacks and whites. Blacks do consume less potassium and calcium, do experience more stress associated with more difficult socioeconomic conditions, have much less access to medical care, and are therefore much less likely to be diagnosed or treated until it is too late. Those factors surely contribute to the frequency and severity of hypertension in blacks.

However, those factors don't seem to be the whole explanation: hypertensive blacks aren't merely like severely hypertensive whites. Instead, physiological differences seem to contribute as well. On consuming salt, blacks retain it on average far longer before excreting it into the urine, and they experience a greater rise in blood pressure on a high-salt diet. Hypertension is more likely to be "salt-sensitive" in blacks than in whites, meaning that blood pressure is more likely to rise and fall with rises and falls in dietary salt intake. By the same token, black hypertension is more likely to be treated successfully by drugs that cause the kidneys to excrete salt (the so-called thiazide diuretics) and less likely to respond to those drugs that reduce heart rate and cardiac output (so-called beta blockers, such as propanolol). These facts suggest that there are some qualitative differences between the causes of black and white hyperten-

sion, with black hypertension more likely to involve how the kidneys handle salt.

Physicians often refer to this postulated feature as a "defect": for example, "kidneys of blacks have a genetic defect in excreting sodium." As an evolutionary biologist, though, I hear warning bells going off inside me whenever a seemingly harmful trait that occurs frequently in an old and large human population is dismissed as a "defect." Given enough generations, genes that greatly impede survival are extremely unlikely to spread, unless their net effect is to increase survival and reproductive success. Human medicine has furnished the best examples of seemingly defective genes being propelled to high frequency by counterbalancing benefits. For example, sickle-cell hemoglobin protects far more people against malaria than it kills of anemia, while the Tay-Sachs gene may have protected far more Jews against tuberculosis than it killed of neurological disease. Thus, to understand why U.S. blacks now are prone to die as a result of their kidneys' retaining salt, we need to ask under what conditions people might have benefited from kidneys good at retaining salt.

That question is hard to understand from the perspective of modern Western society, where saltshakers are on every dining table, salt (sodium chloride) is cheap, and our bodies' main problem is getting rid of it. But imagine what the world used to be like before saltshakers became ubiquitous. Most plants contain very little sodium, yet animals require sodium at high concentrations in all their extracellular fluids. As a result, carnivores readily obtain their needed sodium by eating herbivores, but herbivores themselves face big problems in acquiring that sodium. That's why the animals that one sees coming to salt licks are deer and antelope, not lions and tigers. Similarly, some human hunter-gatherers obtained enough salt from the meat that they ate. But when we began to take up farming ten thousand years ago, we either had to evolve kidneys superefficient at conserving salt or learn to

extract salt at great effort or trade for it at great expense.

Examples of these various solutions abound. I already mentioned Brazil's Yanomamö Indians, whose staple food is low-sodium bananas and who excrete on the average only 10 milligrams of salt daily—barely one-thousandth the salt excretion of the typical American. A single Big Mac hamburger analyzed by *Consumer Reports* contained 1.5 grams (1,500 milligrams) of salt, representing many weeks of intake for a Yanomamö. The New Guinea highlanders with whom I work, and whose diet consists up to 90 percent of low-sodium sweet potatoes, told me of the efforts to which they went to make salt a few decades ago, before Europeans brought it as trade goods. They gathered leaves of certain plant species, burned them, scraped up the ash, percolated water through it to dissolve the solids, and finally evaporated the water to obtain small amounts of bitter salt.

Thus, salt has been in very short supply for much of recent human evolutionary history. Those of us with efficient kidneys able to retain salt even on a low-sodium diet were better able to survive our inevitable episodes of sodium loss (of which more in a moment). Those kidneys proved to be a detriment only when salt became routinely available, leading to excessive salt retention and hypertension with its fatal consequences. That's why blood pressure and the frequency of hypertension have shot up recently in so many populations around the world as they have made the transition from being self-sufficient subsistence farmers to members of the cash economy and patrons of supermarkets.

This evolutionary argument has been advanced by historian-epidemiologist Thomas Wilson and others to explain the current prevalence of hypertension in American blacks in particular. Many West African blacks, from whom most American blacks originated via the slave trade, must have faced the chronic problem of losing salt through sweating in their hot environment. Yet in West Africa, except on the coast and certain inland areas, salt was traditionally as scarce for African farmers as it has been for Yanomamö and New Guinea farmers. (Ironically, those Africans who sold other Africans as slaves often took payment in salt traded from the Sahara.) By this argument, the genetic basis for hypertension in U.S. blacks was already widespread in many of their West African ancestors. It required only the ubiquity of saltshakers in twentieth-century America for that genetic basis to express itself as hypertension. This argument also predicts that as Africa's life style becomes increasingly Westernized, hypertension could become as prevalent in West Africa as it now is among U.S. blacks. In this view, American blacks would be no different from the many Polynesian, Melanesian, Kenyan, Zulu, and other populations that have recently developed high blood pressure under a Westernized life style.

But there's an intriguing extension to this hypothesis, proposed by Wilson and physician Clarence Grim, collaborators at the Hypertension Research Center of Drew University in Los Angeles. They suggest a scenario in which New World blacks may now be at more risk for hypertension than their African ancestors. That scenario involves very recent selection for superefficient kidneys, driven by massive mortality of black slaves from salt loss.

Grim and Wilson's argument goes as follows. Black slavery in the Americas began about 1517, with the first imports of slaves from West Africa, and did not end until Brazil freed its slaves barely a century ago in 1888. In the course of the slave trade an estimated 12 million Africans were brought to the Americas. But those imports were winnowed by deaths at many stages, from an even larger number of captives and exports.

First, slaves captured by raids in the interior of West Africa were chained together, loaded with heavy burdens, and marched for one or two months, with little food and water, to the coast. About 25 percent of the captives died en route. While awaiting purchase by slave traders, the survivors were held on the coast in hot, crowded buildings called barracoons, where about 12 percent of them died. The traders went up

and down the coast buying and loading slaves for a few weeks or months until a ship's cargo was full (5 percent more died). The dreaded Middle Passage across the Atlantic killed 10 percent of the slaves, chained together in a hot, crowded, unventilated hold without sanitation. (Picture to yourself the result of those toilet "arrangements.") Of those who lived to land in the New World, 5 percent died while awaiting sale, and 12 percent died while being marched or shipped from the sale yard to the plantation. Finally, of those who survived, between 10 and 40 percent died during the first three years of plantation life, in a process euphemistically called seasoning. At that stage, about 70 percent of the slaves initially captured were dead, leaving 30 percent as seasoned survivors.

Even the end of seasoning, however, was not the end of excessive mortality. About half of slave infants died within a year of birth because of the poor nutrition and heavy workload of their mothers. In plantation terminology, slave women were viewed as either "breeding units" or "work units," with a built-in conflict between those uses: "These Negroes breed the best, whose labour is least," as an eighteenth-century observer put it. As a result, many New World slave populations depended on continuing slave imports and couldn't maintain their own numbers because death rates exceeded birth rates. Since buying new slaves cost less than rearing slave children for twenty years until they were adults, slave owners lacked economic incentive to change this state of affairs.

Recall that Darwin discussed natural selection and survival of the fittest with respect to animals. Since many more animals die than survive to produce offspring, each generation becomes enriched in the genes of those of the preceding generation that were among the survivors. It should now be clear that slavery represented a tragedy of unnatural selection in humans on a gigantic scale. From examining accounts of slave mortality, Grim and Wilson argue that death was indeed selective: much of it was related to unbalanced salt loss, which quickly

brings on collapse. We think immediately of salt loss by sweating under hot conditions: while slaves were working, marching, or confined in unventilated barracoons or ships' holds. More body salt may have been spilled with vomiting from seasickness. But the biggest salt loss at every stage was from diarrhea due to crowding and lack of sanitation—ideal conditions for the spread of gastrointestinal infections. Cholera and other bacterial diarrheas kill us by causing sudden massive loss of salt and water. (Picture your most recent bout of *turista*, multiplied to a diarrheal fluid output of twenty quarts in one day, and you'll understand why.) All contemporary accounts of slave ships and plantation life emphasized diarrhea, or "fluxes" in eighteenth-century terminology, as one of the leading killers of slaves.

Grim and Wilson reason, then, that slavery suddenly selected for superefficient kidneys surpassing the efficient kidneys already selected by thousands of years of West African history. Only those slaves who were best able to retain salt could survive the periodic risk of high salt loss to which they were exposed. Salt supersavers would have had the further advantage of building up, under normal conditions, more of a salt reserve in their body fluids and bones, thereby enabling them to survive longer or more frequent bouts of diarrhea. Those superkidneys became a disadvantage only when modern medicine began to reduce diarrhea's lethal impact, thereby transforming a blessing into a curse.

Thus, we have two possible evolutionary explanations for salt retention by New World blacks. One involves slow selection by conditions operating in Africa for millennia; the other, rapid recent selection by slave conditions within the past few centuries. The result in either case would make New World blacks more susceptible than whites to hypertension, but the second explanation would, in addition, make them more susceptible than African blacks. At present, we don't know the relative importance of these two explanations. Grim and Wilson's provocative hypothesis is likely to stimulate medical and physiological comparisons of American blacks with African blacks and thereby to help resolve the question.

While this piece has focused on one medical problem in one human population, it has several larger morals. One, of course, is that our differing genetic heritages predispose us to different diseases, depending on the part of the world where our ancestors lived. Another is that our genetic differences reflect not only ancient conditions in different parts of the world but also recent episodes of migration and mortality. A well-established example is the decrease in the frequency of the sickle-cell hemoglobin gene in U.S. blacks compared with African blacks,

because selection for resistance to malaria is now unimportant in the United States. The example of black hypertension that Grim and Wilson discuss opens the door to considering other possible selective effects of the slave experience. They note that occasional periods of starvation might have selected slaves for superefficient sugar metabolism, leading under modern conditions to a propensity for diabetes.

Finally, consider a still more universal moral. Almost all people alive today exist under very different conditions from those under which every human lived 10,000 years ago. It's remarkable that our old genetic heritage now permits us to survive at all under such different circumstances.

But our heritage still catches up with most of us, who will die of life style related diseases such as cancer, heart attack, stroke, and diabetes. The risk factors for these diseases are the strange new conditions prevailing in modern Western society. One of the hardest challenges for modern medicine will be to identify for us which among all those strange new features of diet, life style, and environment are the ones getting us into trouble. For each of us, the answers will depend on our particular genes, hence on our ancestry. Only with such individually tailored advice can we hope to reap the benefits of modern living while still housed in bodies designed for life before saltshakers.

What Good Is Feeling Bad?

The Evolutionary Benefits of Psychic Pain

Randolph M. Nesse

Randolph M. Nesse is an associate professor of psychiatry at the University of Michigan in Ann Arbor, where he directs the adult ambulatory care division and the evolutionary psychiatry project. He is also associate director of the anxiety disorder program there.

Most people come to me for the treatment of anxiety, but recently a new patient came in with only a simple request. "All I really need is a refill," she said, handing me a nearly empty bottle of an antidepressant medication. She had just moved from another city, and for the previous year she had been taking fluoxetine for weight loss, one of the side effects of the drug. "I lost a few pounds," she said, "but I want to keep taking it mainly because it makes me feel better." She denied feeling unusually depressed before, but she insisted that the drug made her more confident and energetic. "I used to be uncomfortable with strangers at parties, but now I can go up to anyone and say anything I want to," she said. "I don't feel nervous or worried about what people think of me. Also, I am more decisive, and people say I am more attractive. I'm usually even eager to get out of bed in the morning. Everything is just—well, better. I hardly ever feel bad anymore."

A routine psychiatric examination uncovered no history of clinical depression. In fact, even before taking fluoxetine she had had relatively few days of feeling down. She reported no family history of mood disorders, no unusual personal or family conflicts. She had sometimes felt uncomfortable

in social situations, but she had not avoided giving speeches or going to parties. She denied abusing drugs or alcohol. As far as I could determine, she was a normal person whose normal feelings of distress were blocked by the drug.

Fluoxetine, commonly known as Prozac, has been on the market for slightly more than a year. In that short time it has become the most prescribed antidepressant, because it does not cause dependency and its side effects are, for most patients, few and mild. My patient had only minor insomnia and occasional nausea—and she lost those few pounds. For others, some 15 percent of patients, the side effects are intolerable, and in a few extreme cases patients reportedly became suicidal or began behaving uncontrollably after starting treatment with the drug; studies have not verified the extreme reactions in large, controlled samples of people who use the drug.

Whatever may eventually be discovered about fluoxetine, it is clear that psychopharmacology is entering a new era. In the old days—three or four years ago—all antidepressants had side effects so annoying that normal people would not take them. Fluoxetine is one of the first effective agents with only minor side effects in a class of drugs the psychiatrist Peter D. Kramer of Brown University has called mood brighteners. Several more will be introduced within the next few years, some from whole new classes of drugs that promise even more specific actions than fluoxetine with still fewer side effects.

"So what do you think, doctor?" my patient asked. "All I really want is another prescription—unless there's

some danger. Do you think it's safe for me to keep taking this?" I wrestled with the question. If the drug makes her feel better, why not give it to her? Maybe it is relieving a subclinical depression. Then again, it might have unknown side effects, despite its approval by the Food and Drug Administration and a year of clinical experience. But a separate possibility gave me pause: Are bad feelings somehow useful? If they are, is blocking them wise?

Consider pain and anxiety. Much as people want to avoid those feelings, each is essential in a dangerous world. Pain motivates people to avoid actions that might cause injury or death. Anxiety induces changes that make it easier to protect oneself from physical or social threats. The capacity for such feelings must have conferred an advantage in the course of human evolution. Do other bad feelings, such as jealousy and sadness, also serve worthwhile, possibly crucial purposes? If emotions did indeed come about through natural selection—whereby nature selects characteristics if they help organisms survive longer or reproduce more—then bad, as well as good, feelings are probably useful. And though specific experiences or environmental influences may modulate feelings differently in each individual, the basic capacity for the various emotions must somehow have assisted human survival. The task of understanding the evolutionary functions of emotions is a scientific frontier, one that urgently needs exploration, especially if psychotropic drugs are to be used wisely.

One day in the sixth grade, when I was on the playground, a friend pointed out a boy who could not feel pain. This bit of information was not a mere curiosity but a valuable warning: if the boy wanted to give someone a good drubbing, he would be undeterred by counterpunches, no matter how solidly planted. Getting up my nerve, I asked the fellow about his unusual condition. Obviously embarrassed, he said he had no concept of pain, just as someone who is color-blind cannot fathom color. Yet he seemed to feel guilt and social rejection like everyone else. Later it came to light that his mother had to check over his entire body inch by inch every night to make sure he had not been injured. My playground group made fun of him for that, but always behind his back.

Today he is almost certainly dead. People who cannot feel pain are extremely rare and usually die in early adulthood. Their joints fail from excess strain, caused in part by the lack of the normal discomfort that makes most people shift position from time to time. The effects of multiple injuries accumulate rapidly, infections and appendicitis go unnoticed, and death from one cause or another comes prematurely. The disease syringomyelia also illustrates the utility of pain. A degeneration of the center of the spinal cord, the condition selectively eliminates pain in various parts of the body, especially the hands. Smokers with syringomyelia repeatedly let cigarettes burn down to nubbins, unaware that their fingers are being charred.

Physical pain is essential to the body's defense against future, as well as immediate, tissue injury. Years ago, a hook impaled my brother's ear while he was fishing. The acute pain moved him to extract the hook immediately (even though the fish had just started biting). And the memory of the pain arouses enough anxiety to ensure that, while fishing, he always wears a hat.

Why is pain painful? If a person simply noticed when tissue was being damaged, would the same purpose not be served? Why must suffering be involved? Surprisingly enough, there is an answer. Pain must be aversive in order to arouse the motivating mechanisms of the mind. Those mechanisms

ensure that eliminating the source of pain gets the highest priority in the body's regulation of behavior, for rarely is anything more important to an individual's Darwinian fitness than stopping tissue damage. Patients with chronic pain, who are at the opposite end of the pain-arousal spectrum from my school-yard mate, know only too well the near futility of trying to ignore pain. Its urgent call for attention is crucial to its evolutionary function.

To gain a broader perspective on the defensive systems of the body, consider some of the other, more elaborate mechanisms that have evolved. Many of them are triggered by disease; they include nausea, vomiting, cough, diarrhea, fever, fatigue and anxiety. Each is called forth when specialized detectors in the body warn of a threat. Nausea, vomiting and diarrhea eliminate toxins detected in the gastrointestinal tract, and coughing expels harmful matter in the respiratory tract. Fever counters infection, and fatigue prevents damage from overexertion. Anxiety protects the organism from a wide range of dangers.

Such defenses are analogous to the low-oil pressure light on an automobile dashboard. In that case it is clear the glowing light itself is not the problem; instead, the light is a protective response to the problem of low oil pressure. The dashboard indicator is one component of a system carefully designed to warn of dangerous conditions: an oil-pressure sensor set to respond at an appropriate threshold, wires for transmitting the signal, and a light bulb, positioned for visibility on the dash. If the driver has sense enough to stop, the defense system works. If instead the driver responds, say, by cutting the wire to the light, the engine is likely to be irreparably damaged.

It is important to note, however, that not all manifestations of disease are defenses; many are a result of a defect in the body's machinery. Paralysis, seizures, tumors and jaundice, for example, serve no function; they merely reflect a breakdown in the workings of the body. They are analogous to a clank

in the transmission, a plume of steam from an overheated radiator or the silence one gets when turning the ignition key of a car with a dead battery.

The distinction between defenses and defects calls attention to the usefulness of defenses—and the dangers of blocking them. Physicians well know that suppressing a cough can turn a routine pneumonia into a life-threatening illness. It is also true—though not so commonly known—that blocking diarrhea can aggravate certain infections and increase complications. And forcing a fever down can prolong an illness. Even low iron levels in the blood, which often accompany chronic infections, counteract bacteria by depriving them of a crucial mineral. Physicians unaware of that defensive role may unwittingly aid a pathogen by prescribing iron supplements.

Defects, in contrast, are useless. Physicians need have no trepidation about trying to stop seizures, paralysis or jaundice. Furthermore, defects in themselves are not painful, except when they disrupt normal function. Most tumors come to medical attention only after they form noticeable lumps or when they interfere with a bodily function. Kidney failure can be quite advanced before a person notices anything wrong. And a person may be alerted to a weak leg muscle only by scuffs on the toe of one shoe. The capacity for pain is present only where, in an evolutionary sense, it has been able to help. As the evolutionist George C. Williams of the State University of New York at Stony Brook pointed out in his 1966 book *Adaptation and Natural Selection,* damage to the heart or the brain was so often fatal in the natural environment that the capacity for pain or even repair in those tissues would have been irrelevant to survival.

Thus the presence of bad feelings is most reliably associated with defenses, not defects. Nausea, diarrhea, cough, fatigue and anxiety all are distressing; they must be to carry out their protective functions. Indeed, one can argue that all bad feelings are components of defenses. Natural selection has molded each kind of bad feeling to help protect against a specific threat. A person who does not experience nausea as aversive is liable to eat the same toxic food again and again; a person who does not get fatigued will suffer damage to muscles and joints.

Emotional suffering can be just as useful as physical discomfort. Emotions adjust a person's response to the task at hand. In that sense they are similar to computer programs, which adjust the setup of the computer to carry out a certain kind of task. The program may change what appears on the screen, the functions of certain keys, how memory is allocated, or the way information is processed. Like computers, living organisms are faced with a variety of challenges. The behavioral, physiological and cognitive responses that help a person elude a tiger are different from those that help woo a lover or attack a competitor. Thus fear, love and anger are highly distinct psychological subroutines gradually shaped by natural selection to improve the person's ability to cope with each challenge.

All emotions can help in certain situations but hinder in others. Anxiety is welcome when it aids escape from a pack of wild dogs, but it can become a clumsy intruder at delicate moments in courtship. Conversely, though romantic fantasizing may enhance courtship, it can fatally distract a person fleeing wild dogs. Emotions are excellent examples of the "Darwinian algorithms" described by Leda Cosmides and John Tooby, psychologists at the University of California at Santa Barbara, in the 1987 book *The Latest on the Best: Essays on Evolution and Optimality*:

When a tiger bounds toward you, what should your response be? Should you file your toenails? Do a cartwheel? Sing a song? Is this the moment to run an uncountable number of randomly generated response possibilities through the decision rule? . . . How could you compute which possibility would result in more grandchildren? The alternative: Darwinian algorithms specialized for predator avoidance, that err on the side of false positives in predator detection, and, upon detecting a potential predator, constrain your responses to flight, fight or hiding.

Why are emotions always positive or negative, never neutral? As the biologists Randy and Nancy Thornhill of the University of New Mexico have pointed out, circumstances that pose neither opportunity nor threat arouse no emotion. Why should they if they are unrelated to Darwinian fitness? A falling leaf rarely stirs any feeling, unless perhaps it is seen as a symbol of mortality. A tree leaning precariously over one's bedroom, however, arouses anxious apprehension that is quite unpleasant. If anxiety were pleasant, would people not seek out bedrooms under large, dead, leaning trees, instead of avoiding them?

There are more negative emotions than positive ones—twice as many, by one count. The imbalance arises because people encounter only a few kinds of opportunity, and so—in the Darwinian sense, again—they need only a small number of positive emotions. Happiness, excitement, joy and desire motivate people to take full advantage of each opportunity. Threats, however, come in many forms—predators, poisonous small animals, disease, exposure, starvation, exclusion from a group, loss of allies, loss of stored food, loss of territory, loss of a mate and on and on. Consequently, many distinct patterns of response have been developed to contend with those threats.

Of all the negative emotions, anxiety is the most obviously useful. Although there are many kinds of anxiety, the well-known fight-or-flight response, first described by the American psychologist Walter B. Cannon in 1915, best exemplifies the value of anxiety. In the dangerous environment of early humans the response was highly beneficial for the frequent occasions when life was in danger. The strong, rapid heartbeat that accompanies panic anxiety brings extra nutrition and oxygen to muscles and speeds the removal of wastes. Muscle tension prepares for flight or physical defense. Shortness of breath induces rapid breathing, hyperoxygenating the blood. Sweating cools the body in anticipation of flight. Greater production of blood glucose

also helps bring more nutrition to the muscles. Secretion of adrenaline into the blood makes it clot faster, should injury occur. Blood circulation shifts from the digestive system to the muscles, leaving a cold, empty feeling in the pit of the stomach and a tense readiness in the muscles.

Accompanying all those physiological changes are psychological and behavioral ones. A person having a panic attack puts aside concerns about paying debts and fantasies about having sex to focus all mental energy on assessing the danger and determining the best means of escape. Often, even before finding out what the danger is, the person makes behavioral adjustments, standing ready to take headlong flight at the slightest provocation.

Social dangers pose equally severe threats. Many of my patients tell me they are too sensitive to social pressures; they are deathly afraid of being left out of a group, and they feel they must always please people. Typically, they have tried hard, sometimes with the help of a therapist, to overcome those "insecurities." They often think they should have high self-esteem regardless of social opinion. But imagine what would happen to a relentlessly self-confident person in the natural environment. Such a person would have no qualms about challenging the leader or doing other things that would cause exclusion from the group. Then the outcast might well walk off confidently onto the savanna, a response that would almost certainly end in death.

The political scientist Robert Axelrod of the University of Michigan has described some of the many ways individual human relationships depend on the exchange of favors and the adherence to certain rules. Within any network of social obligations one has many chances to violate the rules to gain a short-term advantage over one's fellows. In my view, it is the conscience that advocates following the rules and accepting the short-term costs of rule compliance for a chance at greater long-term benefits. But primitive unconscious drives lobby for violating the rules to exploit the immediate opportunity. People usually forgo ephemeral gains to avoid risking the relationship, thanks in large part to anxiety that arises out of guilt or fear of punishment. According to one of the more widely accepted findings of psychoanalysis, anxiety is aroused by socially unacceptable unconscious wishes. It thus inhibits actions that would give immediate pleasure but cause the loss of long-term rewards. Anxiety, even the vague kind that seems to have no specific source, is often useful.

Of course there are circumstances in which anxiety is excessive and serves no purpose. Although the capacity for the state came about through natural selection, environmental variables—early childhood experiences, for instance—and genetic differences affect the individual's susceptibility to anxiety. Those influences are widely recognized. But psychiatry has yet to fully acknowledge the value and evolutionary origins of anxiety and other bad feelings, though the psychiatrists Isaac M. Marks of the University of London and Brant Wenegrat of Stanford University have begun leading the field in that direction.

Another emotion that often seems useless and damaging is jealousy. In a cross-cultural study of sexual jealousy the psychologists Martin Daly and Margo Wilson of McMaster University found such jealousy present in every culture they investigated. Moreover, it was consistently more intense for males than females. Male sexual jealousy is simpler than anxiety in that it defends against a fairly circumscribed threat—sexual infidelity; hence it need not arise in a variety of forms. In another sense, though, it is more complex, because it is a swirl of diverse, conflicting emotions—anger, loneliness, sadness and unworthiness, among others. For all the research on it, jealousy is still widely misunderstood.

Several years ago a patient came to me because he felt he was excessively jealous. "I am constantly jealous of my wife," he told me. "I even follow her to find out what she is doing. I know it is wrecking the relationship, but I can't

help it." When I asked him whether he had any reason to be jealous, he said, "Well, she goes out a few nights a week with another man, but she says they are just friends, and that she will leave me unless I can be less jealous and give her more freedom."

He felt jealousy was abnormal and had never considered that it might be valuable. As the anthropologist Donald Symons of the University of California at Santa Barbara has pointed out, in the course of human evolution a man who did not experience jealousy would risk his wife's becoming impregnated by other men and thus having fewer children of his own. Without jealously guarding his mate, he could never be certain about who was the father of her babies. He would then run the further risk of investing effort in the parenting of other men's children, diverting effort from his own. In present times, as women achieve more power, male jealousy is becoming less beneficial to fitness, since fewer women will tolerate an intensely jealous spouse. Furthermore, there is no doubt that jealousy in the extreme has provoked men to behave destructively and abuse their mates. Nevertheless, in the long run and on average, the moderately jealous man has had more children. Jealousy in women has different cues and other motivations, which would require a separate, lengthy discussion; suffice it to say, it is directed primarily toward ensuring survival of her offspring by keeping a male provider from deserting her for another woman.

Elucidating the evolutionary origin of sadness poses a special challenge. It is easy to see how happiness can be beneficial; it motivates people to seek out and meet new people, attempt difficult tasks and persist in the face of adversity. But sadness is another story. Not only does it seem maladaptive; it also is increasingly viewed as a socially unacceptable result of wrong thinking or of bad genes. When I lecture on the utility of emotions, the question invariably arises: What benefit could sadness possibly confer?

The hypothesis I favor is that mood regulates the allocation of resources.

High mood allocates energy, time and social resources to the enterprises most likely to pay off. Low mood withdraws investments from wasted enterprises. According to the principles of resource allocation developed by workers in behavioral ecology, every animal must decide at every moment what to do next—sleep, forage, find a mate, dig a den. All those activities are important, but each must be done at the right time and in proper proportion. Even a single activity such as foraging requires complex decisions about which foods to pursue and how to divide the effort among the accessible patches of land. Any animal, whether wolf or wasp, that pursues less than optimal prey or does not choose the best time to pursue it will lose out in the long run.

People also must make decisions about where, when and how to invest their resources. Shall I write a paper, paint the living room, read a book or clean the basement? At every moment people are deciding. Life's important decisions are usually questions about whether to maintain the status quo or to change patterns of resource allocation.

Making changes is not easy. The life circumstances people fashion for themselves generally require substantial investments in education, physical skills, social skills, relationships and reputation. Changing long-term strategies—gaining, leaving or changing a mate; switching careers; setting new life goals—is risky business. It requires, at the least, giving up on major life investments and starting anew, usually at a lower level, in some new arena. Such a change also usually entails a period of uncertainty, as one experiments with new possibilities. Because of the risks, it is wise not to undertake such changes lightly; it is often better to persist in an enterprise that is, for the moment, not paying off. A mechanism that induces people to stay with their current life strategies despite fallow periods might be quite useful.

Evidence of such a mechanism appears in recent research showing that most people are consistently overly optimistic. Shelley Taylor, a psychologist at the University of California at Los Angeles, has reviewed extensive work showing that, on average, normal people believe that they are more highly skilled than they really are and that they have more control over their environment than they actually do. Furthermore, other work shows that people generally think fewer bad things will happen to themselves than to others. Many depressives, in contrast, seem to be brutally accurate in their assessments of themselves—not pessimistic, merely accurate. Normally, people see the world through rose-colored glasses. That optimism is just what is needed to get people to persist in temporarily unprofitable enterprises and to stay with good relationships that are not going well at the moment.

When efforts fail repeatedly, however, the rose tint fades, and people become harshly realistic about the future and their friends, abilities and problems. When things are bad enough long enough, illusions must be abandoned to make major changes possible. If a farmer plants a field three years in a row and it washes out every year, it is time to stop. If a man is turned down by every beautiful woman he asks for a date, it is time he consider other types. If a person is repeatedly passed over for a promotion, it may be time to change goals or look for another position. As the Swedish psychiatrist Emmy Gut has pointed out, depression often arises when a primary life strategy is failing and no alternatives seem available. She argues that the withdrawal and rumination characteristic of depression help motivate a deep reassessment of life goals and strategies.

The loss of a relationship through death or separation brings on a special form of sadness: grief. Although it can motivate people to prevent such losses, grief is an unusually harsh teacher. An adequate explanation of its function does not yet exist; the links between behavior and psychodynamics must first be more clearly defined and the complexities of attachment taken into account.

Another school of thought argues that mood helps people adapt to their social position. In the 1960s the English psychiatrist John Price proposed that primates exhibit low-mood characteristics when their continued membership in a group demands that they submit to others. The idea has been supported in experiments by the psychiatrists Michael T. McGuire and Michael J. Raleigh of the University of California at Los Angeles, who showed that the dominant males in the social hierarchy of vervet monkeys have high levels of blood serotonin, a chemical that acts as a messenger between neurons in the brain. When the dominant male is removed from the colony, however, and can no longer rule the others, his serotonin level plummets. He stops eating, huddles and appears to be deeply depressed. Intriguingly, many antidepressants, including Prozac, work by increasing serotonin in the brain. In another experiment the UCLA investigators removed the dominant monkey from each of twelve groups, and gave one of the two remaining males in each group a drug that increases serotonin. In each case the drugged monkey became dominant. The next experiment, it seems to me, is to give the drug to a submissive male while the dominant male remains in the group: I suspect the normally submissive monkey, spurred by raised serotonin levels, would foolishly challenge the leader and get beaten back into his usual place in the hierarchy. One can only wonder whether widespread use of antidepressants might similarly be tampering with the mechanisms that regulate human social hierarchies.

Several alternative explanations for sadness have been proposed. For example, perhaps it serves as a cry for help. Just like an infant's wail, sadness can elicit aid from relatives. Indeed, communication is an important function of sadness; after all, it is often marked by distinctive facial features and tears. But if the only purpose of sadness were communication, it should take place almost exclusively in public. That is evidently not the case; people often feel saddest when they are home alone at night. Some investigators think sadness may aid creativity by somehow giving people access to unconscious thoughts and feelings, but few conclusions can yet be drawn because of a lack of data and uncertainty about how creativity influences fitness. To get to the heart of sadness, the next step is to find people without the capacity for mood and to look for any disadvantages they share. If the resource-allocation hypothesis is correct, for instance, such people ought to waste substantial effort in useless enterprises and yet be unable to take full advantage of brief windows of opportunity.

An understanding of the functions of negative feelings would give psychiatry the tools it needs to treat patients more effectively. Currently the field often tacitly assumes that bad feelings are caused by some defect in the brain, and many investigators are preoccupied with finding the neurochemical mechanisms that mediate anxiety and depression. People do inherit susceptibilities to depression and anxiety. In some cases, the susceptibilities certainly come from brain defects. Such conditions are true diseases arising from faulty regulation and are comparable to an excessive immune response. But if sadness is useful, a tendency to depression might better be compared with a propensity to vomit readily or to get high fevers than with diseases such as epilepsy or tuberculosis. Some people may simply have their baseline level of mood set too low, a condition called dysthymia. For others the gain of the system is excessive, causing moods to fluctuate wildly in response to ordinary events. In the clinic that condition is described as cyclothymia or, if it is severe, manic-depressive disorder.

Rather than assuming that negative feelings are symptoms of a physical abnormality or a dysfunctional personality, family or society, the therapist can consider the possibility that some suffering is part of a vital mechanism shaped by natural selection to help people survive in their environment. For many of my patients it is a wonderful revelation to realize that there are benefits to the capacities for various kinds of unhappiness—that there is some sense to their suffering. The new perspective allows them to quit blaming themselves and others and to concentrate instead on making their lives better.

If the mechanisms that regulate the emotions are products of evolution, it might seem to follow that interfering with them will usually be unwise. After all, natural selection has had millions of years to shape the mechanisms, and so by now their thresholds should be set to near-optimum levels. But everyday medical practice contradicts that conclusion. People routinely take aspirin for pain and fever with few untoward consequences; antinausea and antidiarrhea medications relieve much suffering with only occasional complications; ten million Americans each year take anxiety medications, yet there is no epidemic of risky behavior. Nature may seem overly protective, in part because the earliest human environments presented many more dangers than modern industrial society does. People today face few tigers in the street. The readiness to panic may have been a great boon at the oasis, but it is a bane at the grocery store. Exclusion from a social group may have

been fatal back then, but today it is not.

A changed environment may not be the only reason defenses seem overresponsive. Be it vomiting, fever or a panic attack, a defense is usually cheap in terms of calories lost and time taken from other activities. But if the defense is not expressed when it is needed, the cost can be enormous. The absorption of bacterial toxins into the stomach, a mauling by a tiger or rejection by a mate can exact huge costs. If the defense is to protect from every instance of danger, the threshold for response must be set low, so low that many false alarms will occur—thus the illusion that the defenses are overresponsive. Patients with agoraphobia, a fear of open places, say they feel silly avoiding a place where they once had a panic attack. But if they are asked what the best response would be if years ago they had been attacked by a tiger at that spot, most quickly realize that a hundred false alarms would be worth a single escape from an attack.

Emotions are set to maximize Darwinian fitness, not happiness. In that dismal conclusion is a kernel of optimism. If

much suffering is unnecessary, there should be many occasions on which it can be safely blocked—throughout much of the lives of chronic depressives, for instance. Given the growing power of drugs to influence feelings, top priority should go to gathering the knowledge needed to distinguish the safe occasions from others, in which bad feelings are vital. If we continue to let only side effects or dependency dictate the use of psychotropic drugs, people will take new agents to change their feelings at will, with little idea of the purposes those feelings serve. It is time to make a vigorous study of the evolutionary functions of emotions.

Until that takes place, psychiatry is increasingly going to find itself in a quandary. Indeed, with little knowledge about when bad feelings are useful, I felt quite lost with my new patient, trying to decide whether to refill her prescription. I finally agreed to let her have a few more pills, but I also asked to see her again to explore her life in more detail. And I vowed to do whatever possible to further the understanding of the evolutionary functions of emotions.

Credits/ Acknowledgments

Cover design by Charles Vitelli

1. Natural Selection
Facing overview—New York Public Library.

2. Primates
Facing overview—United Nations photo by George Love.

3. Sex and Society
Facing overview—WHO photo.

4. The Hominid Transition
Facing overview—Courtesy of the American Museum of Natural History. 125—Andy Freeberg.

5. The Fossil Evidence
Facing overview—Courtesy of the American Museum of Natural History.

6. Late Hominid Evolution
Facing overview—Courtesy of York Archaelogical Trust. 165—(top, left) American Museum of Natural History. 168-171—Erik Trinkaus.

7. Living With the Past
Facing overview—Cleveland Museum of Natural History.

ANNUAL EDITIONS ARTICLE REVIEW FORM

■ NAME: _____ DATE: _____

■ TITLE AND NUMBER OF ARTICLE: _____

■ BRIEFLY STATE THE MAIN IDEA OF THIS ARTICLE: _____

_____

_____

_____

_____

■ LIST THREE IMPORTANT FACTS THAT THE AUTHOR USES TO SUPPORT THE MAIN IDEA:

_____

_____

_____

_____

_____

_____

■ WHAT INFORMATION OR IDEAS DISCUSSED IN THIS ARTICLE ARE ALSO DISCUSSED IN YOUR TEXTBOOK OR OTHER READING YOU HAVE DONE? LIST THE TEXTBOOK CHAPTERS AND PAGE NUMBERS:

_____

_____

_____

_____

_____

_____

■ LIST ANY EXAMPLES OF BIAS OR FAULTY REASONING THAT YOU FOUND IN THE ARTICLE:

_____

_____

_____

_____

■ LIST ANY NEW TERMS/CONCEPTS THAT WERE DISCUSSED IN THE ARTICLE AND WRITE A SHORT DEFINITION:

_____

_____

_____

_____

_____

ANNUAL EDITIONS:
PHYSICAL ANTHROPOLOGY 94/95
Article Rating Form

Here is an opportunity for you to have direct input into the next revision of this volume. We would like you to rate each of the 43 articles listed below, using the following scale:

1. **Excellent: should definitely be retained**
2. **Above average: should probably be retained**
3. **Below average: should probably be deleted**
4. **Poor: should definitely be deleted**

Your ratings will play a vital part in the next revision. So please mail this prepaid form to us just as soon as you complete it.
Thanks for your help!

Rating	Article	Rating	Article
	1. The Growth of Evolutionary Science		24. A Skull to Chew On
	2. A Pox Upon Our Genes		25. The Pulse That Produced Us
	3. Curse and Blessing of the Ghetto		26. Sizing Up Human Intelligence
	4. The Arrow of Disease		27. Scavenger Hunt
	5. The Future of AIDS		28. Bamboo and Human Evolution
	6. Racial Odyssey		29. Hard Times Among the Neanderthals
	7. Machiavellian Monkeys		30. Old Masters
	8. What Are Friends For?		31. The Dawn of Adornment
	9. Leading Ladies		32. The Search for Eve
	10. The Young and the Reckless		33. A Multiregional Model
	11. "Science With a Capital S"		34. Life as a Hunter-Gatherer
	12. Dian Fossey and Digit		35. On the Scientific, Medical, Dental, and Educational Value of Collections of Human Skeletons
	13. Biruté Galdikas		36. Profile of an Anthropologist: No Bone Unturned
	14. These Are Real Swinging Primates		37. The DNA Wars
	15. Evolution of the Big O		38. Old Dog, Old Tricks
	16. "Everything *Else* You Always Wanted to Know About Sex . . . But That We Were Afraid You'd Never Ask"		39. Farmers and Baboons in the Taita Hills: Inter-Species Warfare in Southeastern Kenya
	17. What's Love Got to Do With It?		40. Our Rhythms Still Follow the African Sun
	18. Dim Forest, Bright Chimps		41. A Reasonable Sleep
	19. Flesh and Bone		42. The Saltshaker's Curse
	20. What Makes Us So Different From the Apes?		43. What Good Is Feeling Bad?
	21. Human Ancestors Walked Tall, Stayed Cool		
	22. The Evolutionary Future of Man		
	23. Dawson's Dawn Man: The Hoax at Piltdown		

(Continued on next page)

ABOUT YOU

Name_____ Date_____

Are you a teacher? ☐   Or student? ☐

Your School Name _____

Department _____

Address _____

City _____ State _____ Zip _____

School Telephone # _____

YOUR COMMENTS ARE IMPORTANT TO US!

Please fill in the following information:

For which course did you use this book? _____

Did you use a text with this Annual Edition?   ☐ yes   ☐ no

The title of the text? _____

What are your general reactions to the Annual Editions concept?

Have you read any particular articles recently that you think should be included in the next edition?

Are there any articles you feel should be replaced in the next edition? Why?

Are there other areas that you feel would utilize an Annual Edition?

May we contact you for editorial input?

May we quote you from above?